Current Issues in Public Administration

FIFTH EDITION

Current Issues in Public Administration

FIFTH EDITION

Edited by
Frederick S. Lane

St. Martin's Press

New York

Senior editor: Don Reisman
Manager, publishing services: Emily Berleth
Project management: Beckwith-Clark, Inc.

Acknowledgments

It is a violation of the law to reproduce these selections by any means whatsoever without the written permission of the copyright holder.

"Why Study Bureaucracy?" by Peter M. Blau and Marshall W. Meyer. From Peter M. Blau and Marshall W. Meyer, *Bureaucracy in Modern Society*, Third Edition, pp. 3–14, 18–25. Copyright © 1987 by Random House. Used by permission of McGraw-Hill, Inc.

"Public and Private Management: Are They Fundamentally Alike in All Unimportant Respects?" by Graham T. Allison, Jr. This article was presented as part of the Public Management Research Conference, Brookings Institution, Washington, D. C., November 1979. Used by permission of the author.

"The Rise of the Bureaucratic State" by James Q. Wilson. From *The Public Interest*, No. 41 (Fall 1975). Used by permission of the author.

"American Bureaucracy in a Changing Political Setting" by Francis E. Rourke. From *Journal of Public Administration Research and Theory*, I, No. 2 (April 1991), pp. 111–129. Reprinted by permission.

"The Evolution of American Federalism" from *Reviving the American Dream* by Alice M. Rivlin. Copyright © 1992. Reprinted by permission of the Brookings Institution.

"Challenges to State Governments: Policy and Administrative Leadership in the 1990's" by F. Ted Herbert, Deil S. Wright, and Jeffrey I. Brudney. From *Public Productivity & Management Review*, M. Holzer, ed., Vol. XVI, No. 1, pp. 1–21. Copyright 1992 by Jossey-Bass Inc., Publishers.

"Policy Making in a Democracy" from *The Power of Public Ideas* edited by Robert B. Reich. Copyright © by Robert B. Reich. Reprinted by permission of HarperCollins Publishers, Inc.

Acknowledgments and copyrights are continued at the back of the book on pages 469–470, which constitute an extension of the copyright page.

This book is dedicated to the "reunion group":

Cary,

Josh,

J.Peter, and

Rand.

PREFACE

ABOUT THE BOOK

There are 19 million civilian public employees in some 80,000 units of government in the United States today. Governmental expenditures add up to about one-third of the nation's total of goods and services. It is hard to imagine any aspect of contemporary life in which government and especially its administrative agencies are not involved. Public bureaucracies deliver most of our educational and health care services, fight fires and crime, protect the air and water, and regulate business practices—just to list a few public functions. No matter what the contemporary challenge—AIDS, drugs, homelessness, political change in Eastern Europe—public administration is central to the response.

As important as public bureaucracies are, Americans have shown concern about the bureaucratization of modern society. Many claim that government is too big and tries to do too much, that bureaucracy only means red tape and inefficiency, and that public administrators are too powerful in American life. Yet there are others who claim that government needs to provide even more services, especially for the poor and disadvantaged; these Americans often view public organizations more favorably, although they are still interested in making government work better. These concerns are as current as today's newspaper headlines or TV news stories. And the background for much of this discussion can be found in this volume, *Current Issues in Public Administration*.

This fifth edition of *Current Issues* has five main objectives:

1. To *introduce and survey* the workings of public organizations and public administrators for students without any previous coursework in this field.
2. To present articles that are *interesting, readable,* and *thought-provoking,* involving and challenging the student to learn how these bureaucracies actually work.
3. To provide a *comprehensive* set of readings, blending material about the political environment in which public agencies operate, the organizational and managerial aspects of work inside bureaucracies, and analytical approaches to improving public administration.

4. To focus on *state, local,* and *intergovernmental aspects* of modern public administration in addition to the *national* scene, even when it is the federal government that sets the tone for much public administrative activity in our country.
5. In all this, to emphasize the *current dimensions* of the many important issues facing governmental administrative agencies in the 1990s.

All of these have been carefully placed into the thirty articles in this volume. In terms of student reading, this means two or three articles a week during a typical academic term.

NEW TO THE FIFTH EDITION

Looking forward to the decade of the 1990s, twenty-four of the thirty articles included in the following pages are new to *Current Issues in Public Administration.* The emphasis in this edition has shifted toward a somewhat more managerial approach—to an examination of how public agencies manage today and how they might manage better in the future. Four topics are new in this edition: total quality management (TQM), sexual harassment in the workplace, public infrastructure problems, and the relationships between public administration and nonprofit organizations. Additionally, far more state and local issues are treated in the fifth edition than in earlier editions. Finally, although the subject is touched on in earlier selections, the last chapter, Chapter 10, raises the question of reform in American public administration as we approach the twenty-first century. It asks whether public agencies and public executives can be more entrepreneurial? Can they be less "bureaucratic"? More responsive to citizens and clients?

ACKNOWLEDGMENTS

In preparing the fifth edition, we have sought the advice of sixteen faculty members throughout the nation who regularly teach the introductory graduate and undergraduate courses in public administration. Their advice was most helpful, and their contributions are hereby acknowledged: Robert Agranoff, Indiana University at Bloomington; Deborah Auger, University of Delaware; Dean S. Caldwell, Northern Michigan University; William L. Chappell, Jr., Columbus College; Ruth H. DeHoog, University of North Carolina at Greensboro; Dean F. Eitel, Roosevelt University; Gil Fairholm, Virginia Commonwealth University; William Gansi, St. John's University; George M. Guess, Georgia State University; Leda McIntyre Hall, Indiana University at South Bend; Tom Konda, State University of New York, College at Plattsburgh; Harry W. Reynolds, Jr., University of Nebraska at Omaha; Dolph Santello, University of New Haven; Harold E. Sweeney, Jr., Shippensburg University of Pennsylvania; Louis F. Weschler, Arizona State University, Tempe; and Gwen Wood, Georgia Southern University.

The observations of Helmut Hohmann and George V. Wing are also gratefully acknowledged.

In this revision, several academic libraries provided valuable assistance: the College Library at Bernard M. Baruch College, City University of New York; the Francis Harvey Green Library at West Chester University, West Chester, Pennsylvania; and the Lloyd George Sealy Library at John Jay College of Criminal Justice, City University of New York. Furthermore, largely in connection with library research, I would like to express my appreciation to my graduate assistant, Nikhil Naik. Erin Link assisted with duplication.

For their continuing professionalism and interest in the field of Public Administration, the work of Don Reisman, Frances Jones, and the staff at St. Martin's Press is greatly appreciated.

For her caring and support, and for her help with this volume, I am deeply indebted to my wife, Madeleine Wing Adler, who is also an exceptional public executive.

In this and so many other things, I often chat with four very special young men: Cary Lane, Randall Lane, J.Peter Adler, and Josh Lane. They are the "reunion group" at the annual Lane family reunion, and this book is dedicated, with love, to them.

CONTENTS

Introduction   **xv**

PART ONE   Introduction to Public Administration   **1**

1 What Is Public Administration?   **3**

PETER M. BLAU AND MARSHALL W. MEYER
Why Study Bureaucracy?   5

GRAHAM T. ALLISON, JR.
Public and Private Management: Are They Fundamentally Alike
in All Unimportant Respects?   16

PART TWO   Bureaucracy, Politics, and Public Policy   **33**

2 The Political Setting of Public Administration   **35**

JAMES Q. WILSON
The Rise of the Bureaucratic State   36

FRANCIS E. ROURKE
American Bureaucracy in a Changing Political Setting   56

3 Public Policy and Administration in a Federal System   **72**

ALICE M. RIVLIN
The Evolution of American Federalism   73

F. TED HEBERT, DEIL S. WRIGHT, AND JEFFREY I. BRUDNEY
Challenges to State Governments: Policy and Administrative
Leadership in the 1990s   93

4 Public Administration in a Democratic Society 111

ROBERT B. REICH
Policy Making in a Democracy 113

WILLIAM T. GORMLEY, JR.
Accountability Battles in State Administration 140

BARBARA S. ROMZEK AND MELVIN J. DUBNICK
Accountability in the Public Sector: Lessons from the
Challenger Tragedy 158

DWIGHT WALDO
Public Administration and Ethics 176

PART THREE The Management of Government Agencies 191

5 Organization Theory and Public Administration 193

HAROLD F. GORTNER, JULIANNE MAHLER, AND JEANNE BELL
NICHOLSON
Organization Theory: The Pivotal Controversies 194

LEE G. BOLMAN AND TERRENCE E. DEAL
Reframing Organizational Leadership 214

GERALD E. CAIDEN
What Really Is Public Maladministration? 226

6 Public Personnel Management and Labor Relations 238

PATRICIA W. INGRAHAM AND DAVID H. ROSENBLOOM
The State of Merit in the Federal Government 242

JOEL M. DOUGLAS
Public Sector Collective Bargaining in the 1990s 261

WALTER D. BROADNAX
Managing Diversity: From Civil Rights to Valuing Differences 274

RITA MAE KELLY AND PHOEBE MORGAN STAMBAUGH
Sexual Harassment in the States 282

7 Public Budgeting and Financial Management 295

DENNIS S. IPPOLITO
The Budget Process and Budget Policy: Resolving the
Mismatch 297

IRENE S. RUBIN
Budget Reform and Political Reform: Conclusions from
Six Cities 306

ALAN S. BLINDER
The Public's Capital   327

8 Policy Analysis, Planning, and Strategic Management   334

LAURENCE E. LYNN, JR.
Policy Analysis   336

BARTON WECHSLER AND ROBERT W. BACKOFF
Policy-Making and Administration in State Agencies:
Strategic Management Approaches   345

SANDRA J. HALE
Reinventing Government the Minnesota Way   356

JOSEPH SENSENBRENNER
Quality Comes to City Hall   364

PART FOUR Public Administration and Change   375

9 Working Together: Relations among the Public, Business, and Nonprofit Sectors   377

NORMAN R. AUGUSTINE
Public Employees and the Global Landscape   380

MURRAY WEIDENBAUM
Regulation as a Consumer Issue   386

E. S. SAVAS
On Privatization   404

MICHAEL LIPSKY AND STEVEN RATHGEB SMITH
Nonprofit Organizations, Government, and the Welfare State   414

10 Reforming Public Administration?   437

DAVID OSBORNE AND TED GAEBLER
Reinventing Government   438

MICHAEL BARZELAY
The Post-Bureaucratic Paradigm in Historical Perspective   449

About the Authors   471

INTRODUCTION

Public administration is an ancient activity common to just about all countries and all levels of government.[1] But public administrative traditions, structures, and processes vary widely from one country to another. This volume concerns public administration in the United States.

The term *public administration* combines two words. *Administration* is easier to define: organizing and maintaining human and fiscal resources to attain a group's goals. The group might be a small social club or a large automobile manufacturer. It might also be your local police department or the U.S. Department of Health and Human Services.

Public is harder to define. Public has to do with people, a community, or a society. Most of us went to public schools. We play in public parks. Your state's governor and others hold public office.

Public has another meaning. It also suggests that public administration is open to general knowledge, scrutiny, and review.

A variety of other terms are closely associated with the field of public administration. Higher education for public administration takes place in a wide range of settings: political science departments; schools and programs called public affairs, public policy, public service, government, or public administration; and schools of business and public administration, where public administration is sometimes called public management. Closely related courses can also be found in programs dealing with criminal justice, health care, social work, education, and recreation administration. All of these terms and activities are closely related. The traditional, most widely accepted, and most meaningful label, however, remains *public administration*.

THE PUBLIC POLICY SYSTEM

For the introductory student, it is particularly important to understand the relationships between government, politics, public policy, and public administration. To begin with, government is the mechanism that a human community employs to protect its members from internal and external threats and to establish the policies that will provide the most favorable conditions for pursuing individuals' lives.[2] Government then, is the formal mechanism created and used to guide a society. Democratic government is influenced and, in the end, controlled by the participants in the political system through the process of politics.

As indicated in the foregoing definition, public policies are the results of government. The nation's political system is also its policy system. Social and economic factors are important to policy-making but influence public policies only as they affect the political system.

Figure 1 depicts the national policy system, or policy "octagon." There are eight principal participants in the national policy system:

1. citizens
2. Congress
3. the president
4. the U.S. Supreme Court and federal court system
5. the federal bureaucracy
6. interest groups
7. political parties
8. the media

The lines in Figure 1 represent the relationships and interactions among the actors in the policy system. Depending on the issues at any particular time and the specific actors involved, these relations range from direct and continuous and intense to indirect and intermittent.

In the United States, state and local levels of government have their own policy systems, which are connected through our federal form of government. Federalism and intergovernmental relations raise some of the most important current issues regarding the formulation of public policy and its implementation.

Governmental administrative agencies make up the overwhelming majority of the apparatus of government. These public agencies are often called

Figure 1. The National Policy System

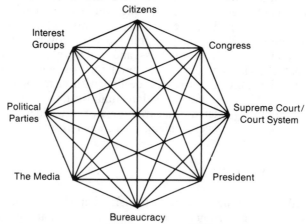

Adapted from a pictorial scheme developed by the late Professor Roscoe C. Martin.

bureaucracies. The field of public administration is the study of the activities and impact of governmental bureaucracies.

THE STAGES OF THE PUBLIC POLICY MAKING PROCESS

We think of public policy as occurring in five stages:

1. policy initiation
2. policy formulation, articulation, and consideration
3. policy legitimation (formal approval)
4. policy implementation
5. policy evaluation

These stages are shown in Figure 2.

Public bureaucracies are most often associated with policy implementation. This has a long tradition in the public administration literature. A century ago, in 1887, a then young scholar, Woodrow Wilson, published an essay titled "The Study of Administration."[3] In this article, Wilson advocated a distinction between the first three stages of the policy-making process—initiation, formulation, and legitimation—and the fourth stage, implementation. This is sometimes referred to as the policy-administration dichotomy.

Wilson's essay came out of a legally oriented tradition in political science, where elected legislators, "lawmakers," were expected to make public policy, and administrators were expected to carry out these policies. Wilson's essay also appeared after a century of the "spoils" approach to governmental employment, and Wilson sought to increase the competence and ethics expected of public employees.

From the beginning, Wilson's dichotomy greatly oversimplified reality. And if it was ever true, the policy-administration dichotomy is certainly not valid today. As shown in Figure 2, public administrative agencies are engaged in all stages of public policy-making, in addition to implementation. Some examples: Public executives often initiate ideas for new or improved public policies. Public administrators regularly interact with their agency's clients and other

Figure 2. Public Administration in Terms of the Public Policy Making Process

Stages in the Policy Making Process	Relative Contribution of Public Administrative Agencies
Policy initiation	
Policy formulation/articulation/ consideration	
Policy legitimation	
Policy implementation	
Policy evaluation	

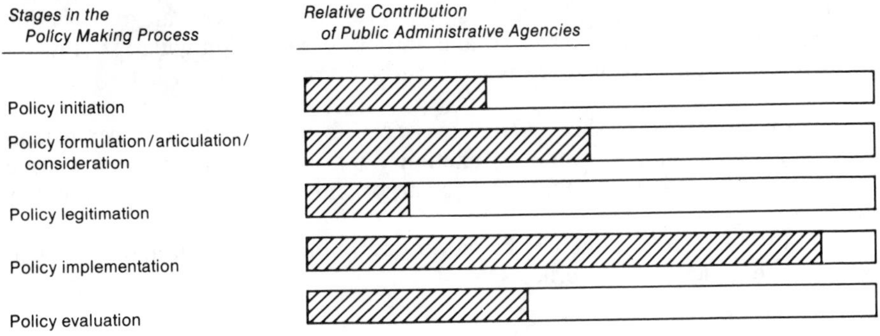

interested groups as well as with legislative committees, their members, and their staffs in the formulation of new public policies. Public executives testify regularly at legislative hearings considering proposals for different public policies. And administrative agencies increasingly evaluate the effectiveness and impact of public policies by surveying citizens and otherwise employing systematic research methods.

PUBLIC ADMINISTRATION AND POWER

Much is said these days about the power of public bureaucracies. It is a topic we will begin to address in the first chapter and continue to consider throughout this book. The basic reason public administrative agencies have power is because of their expertise—to build dams, fight fires, even just process the paperwork so that an elderly relative receives a social security check on time. But power and public administration are far more complicated than that.

How can we understand why bureaucracies have power within the policy system and even why some bureaucracies are more powerful than others? To begin with, the power of public agencies derives from two main sources: the influence of the agency's clients and constituents and the character and priority of the agency's activities.[4] If an agency's clients are organized and powerful—business groups, for example—the agency has relatively greater authority and influence. In addition, if a public agency is concerned with broad-based matters of importance—like national defense or economic development—it is more powerful. The relative importance of an agency can change over time, as in the example of public policy toward the energy issue and the federal Department of Energy.

There are other sources of agency power as well. The technical nature of the organization's work (if its activities are hard for the average person to understand, much less perform) and the agency's record of accomplishment also influence an agency's power.

The quality of organizational leadership may also be important. The skill, style, experience, personality, and ability to communicate of the top agency executives are naturally related to the power of an agency.

Similarly, organizational morale and commitment by employees can influence an agency's power. There is a big difference between an organization where everyone leaves at 5:00 P.M. and another organization where staff members remain after 5:00 if there is work to be completed, even if they are not paid to do so.

Finally, an agency's sheer size also affects its power. The number of employees, size of budget, scope of functions, and even geographic distribution of an agency's activities often influence an organization's power in the policy system.

All of these factors influence the power of a public agency—the power available in the policy-making process.

ORGANIZATION OF THIS BOOK

This volume has been divided into four parts, generally parallel to many of the textbooks in this field. Part One provides reasons for the study of public administration and distinguishes administration in government from administration in business.

Parts Two and Three are the core of this book. Part Two focuses on the political environment in which public bureaucracies operate. It treats the interaction of administrative agencies with the other policy-making participants. At the end of Part Two, special attention is given to the fit between bureaucracy and democracy in modern America.

If Part Two stresses the external relations of public agencies, Part Three turns attention to the internal, organizational dynamics basic to understanding bureaucracies and making them work. Part of this emphasis is on the use of resources—people, money, and technology—in improving the management of the public's business at all levels of American government.

Part Four examines two key topics in the future of public administration. The first focuses on the relations between business and government, including the relative size of the public and for-profit sectors as well as government regulation of business practices. The second topic treats in depth the need for reforming public bureaucracies in the 1990s and beyond.

In the last decade, the United States celebrated two important landmarks in the development of public administration. In 1987 the nation commemorated the centennial of the publication of Woodrow Wilson's article, from which most scholars in this field date the formal study of public administration in this country. In 1989 we celebrated the bicentennial of the U.S. Constitution, the charter for our form of government. This fifth edition of *Current Issues in Public Administration* is designed to provide a solid background for understanding American public administration as we enter the second century of its systematic study and our third century as a nation. It is a time of dynamic change in both theory and practice.

Notes

1. See Frederick C. Mosher, "Public Administration," *Encyclopaedia Britannica*, 15th ed. (1974).
2. Adapted from Max J. Skidmore and Marshall Carter Tripp, *American Government: A Brief Introduction*, 4th ed. (New York: St. Martin's Press, 1985), p. 1.
3. Woodrow Wilson, "The Study of Administration," *Political Science Quarterly* 2 (June 1887), pp. 197–222.
4. This section is drawn from Francis E. Rourke, *Bureaucracy, Politics, and Public Policy* (Boston: Little, Brown, 1969).

Current Issues in Public Administration

FIFTH EDITION

PART ONE

Introduction to Public Administration

1

WHAT IS PUBLIC ADMINISTRATION?

Most of us were born in public hospitals, graduated from public schools, and brush our teeth with water from a public water supply system. We ride public transportation or drive on public roads in automobiles whose safety features are regulated by another public agency.

Public bureaucracy is a key characteristic of modern society. Public organizations, large and small, are needed to provide these types of services or implement these kinds of regulations to promote the well-being of citizens.

The term *bureaucracy* has a negative connotation these days. As a result, some authors prefer the terms *public organizations* or *administrative agencies*. These try to get around the negative tone often encountered in everyday language or in the media when "bureaucracy"—governmental or business—is mentioned.

There is another reason why the term *bureaucracy* is misleading. It suggests that there actually is a single, large, monolithic organizational entity somewhere, like in Washington, D.C. or Sacramento. Such an entity does not exist. Studies of public agencies indicate that, in actuality, there are many administrative agencies rather than a single government bureaucracy, and these organizations often have difficulty coordinating activities and sometimes even compete with each other.

At the federal level, there are three different kinds of administrative agencies: cabinet-level departments, independent agencies, and boards and commissions. These are shown, with examples, in Table 1-1.

In the first article in this chapter, sociologists Peter M. Blau and Marshall W. Meyer introduce us to the study of bureaucracy in society, what the term means, and why bureaucracy is so important. Blau and Meyer also explain the classic formulation of bureaucracy by the great German sociologist Max Weber.

Written by Graham T. Allison, Jr., the second article helps the reader to understand the differences between business administration and public administration. Allison makes clear that the most important difference is in the context in which administration takes place: public management occurs pri-

Table 1-1
Three Types of Federal Agencies

Departments	Agriculture
	Commerce
	Defense
	Education
	Energy
	Health and Human Services
	Housing and Urban Development
	Interior
	Justice
	Labor
	State
	Transportation
	Treasury
	Veterans Affairs
Independent agencies (examples only)	Environmental Protection Agency
	General Services Administration
	National Aeronautics and Space Administration
	National Science Foundation
	Small Business Administration
Boards and Commissions (examples only)	Consumer Product Safety Commission
	Equal Employment Opportunity Commission
	Federal Communications Commission
	Federal Reserve Board
	Interstate Commerce Commission
	Nuclear Regulatory Commission
	Securities and Exchange Commission

Based on "Major Organizational Units of the Executive Branch," in Lawrence C. Dodd and Richard L. Schott, *Congress and the Administrative State* (New York: John Wiley & Sons, Inc., 1979).

marily in a political environment, while business takes place primarily in a market situation. As it turns out, this key difference in the environment for administration also has a great deal to do with internal organizational activities.

The key questions in this chapter for the student of public administration are:

- What does "bureaucracy" mean?
- Why is it important to study public bureaucracy in today's society?
- Is there something inherently bad about bureaucracy?
- How is public administration different from business administration? Is this significant to public executives? To citizens?

Why Study Bureaucracy?

PETER M. BLAU
MARSHALL W. MEYER

"That stupid bureaucrat!" "That dumb bureaucracy!" Who has not felt this way at one time or another? When we are sent from one office to the next without getting the information we want; when forms are returned to us because of some inconsequential omission; when rules are of such complexity that no two people understand them alike—these are the times when we think of bureaucracy. "Bureaucracy" is often used as an epithet connoting inefficiency and confusion in government or elsewhere, such as in universities. But this is not its only meaning, and it is not the way the word will be used in this article.

If you alone had the job of collecting the dues in a small fraternity, you could proceed at your own discretion. However, if five persons had this job in a large club, they would find it necessary to organize their work, lest some members were asked for dues repeatedly and others never. If hundreds of persons had the assignment of collecting taxes from the citizens of a city or state, their work would have to be organized systematically to prevent chaos. A hundred years ago, there was little coordination of tax collecting in most U.S. municipalities. Tax "farmers" had license to collect from whomever they could persuade to pay. Chaos and corruption resulted. Through the efforts of reformers, modern bureaus responsible for collecting taxes systematically and fairly from everyone were put in place. The type of organization designed to accomplish large-scale administrative tasks by coordinating the work of many people systematically is called a bureaucracy. *The concept of bureaucracy, then, applies to organizing principles that are intended to achieve control and coordination of work in large organizations.* Since control and coordination are required in most large organizations nowadays, bureaucracy is not confined to government but is found in businesses, voluntary organizations, and wherever administrative tasks are undertaken.

Control and coordination are not, of course, ends in themselves. They are means toward the end of administrative efficiency, of completing successfully large and complicated tasks that no individual person could accomplish alone. The organizing principles of bureaucracy thus have the purpose of creating efficient organizations, not inefficient ones. But simply because bureaucracy is intended as an efficient form of organization does not mean that it always achieves efficiency. Critics of bureaucracy claim that its principles are inherently inefficient, and many citizens who are irritated by unresponsive and sometimes inept government agencies tend to agree.

Interestingly, while the term "bureaucratic" is often used as a synonym for "inefficient," at other times it is used to imply ruthless efficiency. The German sociologist Max Weber, whose analysis of bureaucratic structures will be discussed presently, held bureaucracy to be so efficient that its power was "overtowering." Weber's American contemporaries, such as Woodrow Wilson, also worried considerably that the power of a large civil service organized according to bureaucratic principles would be inconsistent with democratic governance. Contemporary critics of both the political left and right also fear the power of bureaucracy. The left blames bureaucratic institutions for many of the evils of the world—the domination of weak nations by imperialist powers, the oppression of poor people, the uncertainties facing today's youth. The right blames bureaucracy for inflation, high taxes, and the sapping of individual initiative by excessive regulation. There is some truth to all these allegations, but there is also much exaggeration.

The criticisms of bureaucracy leveled by the political right and left can be understood as a result of its ethical neutrality. Bureaucratic administration can be used as an instrument of economic domination, or it can be used to curb inequities that would arise were economic forces permitted to operate without restraint. Bureaucratic administration is necessarily employed to administer health and social service programs, whether governmental or private, whose purpose is to sustain the ill and needy. Bureaucracies have also been responsible for evils unimaginable in the prebureaucratic era. Hannah Arendt's *Eichmann in Jerusalem* portrays Adolph Eichmann as the consummate bureaucrat meticulously carrying out Hitler's orders to implement the "final solution" by exterminating all the Jews of Europe. The abolition of bureaucracies, to be sure, would limit the possibility of evils such as the Holocaust. But it would also eliminate their positive accomplishments. The challenge for democratic societies is to gain and maintain control over their bureaucracies so that they function for the benefit of the commonweal rather than for that of bureaucrats themselves or of special interests. . . .

THE RATIONALIZATION OF MODERN LIFE

Much of the magic and mystery that used to pervade human life and lend it enchantment has disappeared from the modern world.[1] This is largely the price of rationalization. In olden times, nature was full of mysteries, and humanity's most serious intellectual endeavors were directed toward discovering the ultimate meaning of existence. Today, nature holds fewer secrets for us. Scientific advances, however, have not only made it possible to explain many natural phenomena but have also channeled human thinking. In modern times, people are less concerned than they were, say, in the medieval era with ultimate values and symbolic meanings, with those aspects of mental life that are not subject to scientific inquiry, such as religious truth and artistic creation. This remains an age of science, not of philosophy or of religion, even though there is now greater interest in philosophy and religious belief than there was twenty years ago.

The secularization of the world that spells its disenchantment is indicated by the large amount of time we spend in making a living and getting ahead and the little time we spend in contemplation and religious activities. Compare the low prestige of moneylenders—lending at interest was once considered sinful—and the high prestige of priests in former eras with the very different position of bankers and preachers today. Preoccupied with perfecting efficient means for achieving objectives, we tend to forget why we want to reach these goals. Since we neglect to clarify the basic values that determine why some objectives are preferable to others, objectives lose their significance, and their pursuit becomes an end in itself. This tendency is portrayed in Budd Shulberg's novel *What Makes Sammy Run?* The answer to the question in the title is that only running makes him run, because he is so busy trying to get ahead that he has no time to find out where he is going. Continuous striving for success is not Sammy's means for the attainment of certain ends but the very goal of his life.

These consequences of rationalization have often been deplored, and some observers have even suggested that it is not worth the price.[2] There is no conclusive evidence, however, that alienation from profound values is the inevitable and permanent by-product of rationalization; it may be merely an expression of its growing pains. The beneficial results of rationalization—notably the higher standard of living and greater amount of leisure it makes possible, and the raising of the level of popular education it makes necessary—permit an increased proportion of the population, not just a privileged elite, to participate actively in the cultural life of a society.

Our high standard of living is usually attributed to the spectacular technological developments that have occurred since the Industrial Revolution, but this explanation ignores two related facts. First, the living conditions of most people during the early stages of industrialization, after they had moved from the land into the cities with their sweatshops, were probably much worse than they had been before. Dickens depicts these terrible conditions in certain novels, and Marx describes them in his biting critique of the capitalistic economy.[3] Second, major improvements in the standard of living did not take place until administrative procedures as well as material technology had been revolutionized. Modern machines could not be utilized without the complex administrative machinery needed for running industries employing thousands of people. For example, it was not so much the invention of railroad technology as the invention of management that permitted railroads to traverse long distances. Early railroads had no managers supervising operations and no printed timetables. At fixed times—say 9 A.M., noon, and 4 P.M.—trains would start at both ends of the line. The first to reach the midpoint, where there was a passing siding, would simply wait for the other. And each train had to reach the end of the line before another could begin its journey in the opposite direction. This system worked well so long as rail lines were short: thirty to forty miles. Once railroads were extended beyond this distance, however, trains could no longer wait for one another at the midpoint of a line. Many accidents resulted; to guarantee safety, therefore, the management of railroads was bureaucratized. Managers responsible for coordinating train movements were hired and timetables printed.[4] Rationalization of railroad administration, in other words, was necessary to take advantage of technological changes.

Let us examine some of the administrative principles on which the productive efficiency of modern organizations—whether railroads, factories, or government offices—depends. If a person were responsible for all the different tasks at a given place of work, he or she would have to have many years of education and would still not be able to perform the job well. Imagine, for example, an automobile factory where every car was planned and assembled by a single worker. That worker would have to be at once a designer, a mechanical engineer, and a skilled craftsman. Not only would there be a shortage of people with these qualifications, but those workers who had the necessary skills would probably produce cars of low quality, since none of them would have the time or experience to perfect the manufacture or assembly of any particular part. Specialization, whereby only a small number of tasks are assigned to each worker, permits the hiring of less qualified employees, and, moreover, workers with superior qualifications for the most difficult jobs; it also permits workers to become experienced at their jobs.

What has been taken apart through specialization must be put back together again. A high degree of specialization creates a need for a complex system of coordination. Formal coordination is not needed in a small workplace where tasks are less specialized, all workers have direct contact with one another, and the boss can supervise everyone's performance directly. But the president of a large company cannot possibly discharge his responsibilities through direct supervision of each of several thousand workers. Managerial responsibility is therefore exercised through a hierarchy of authority, which furnishes lines of communication between top management and every employee for obtaining information on operations and transmitting operating directives. (Sometimes, these lines of communication become blocked, and this is a major source of inefficiency in administration.)

Effective coordination requires disciplined performance, which cannot be achieved by supervision alone but must pervade the work process. This is a function of rules and regulations that govern operations, whether they specify the dimensions of nuts and bolts or the criteria to be used in promoting subordinates. Even in the ideal case, where every employee is a highly intelligent and skilled expert, there is a need for disciplined adherence to regulations. Imagine that one worker had discovered that he could produce bolts of superior quality by making them $\frac{1}{8}$ inch larger and another worker had found that she could increase her efficiency by making nuts $\frac{1}{8}$ inch smaller. Although each made the most rational decision in terms of the given task, the nuts and bolts would be useless because they would not match. How one's work fits with that of others is usually far less obvious than in this illustration. If the operations of hundreds of employees are to be coordinated, each must conform to prescribed standards even in situations where a different course of action appears to the individual to be most reasonable. This is a requirement of all teamwork, although in genuine teamwork the rules are based on common agreement rather than being imposed from above.

Efficiency also suffers when emotions or personal considerations influence administrative decisions. If the owner of a small grocery expands her business and opens a second store, she may put her son in charge even though another employee is more qualified for the job. She acts on the basis of her personal attachment rather than in the interest of business efficiency. Similarly, an official in a large company might not promote the best qualified worker to supervisor if one of the candidates were his brother. Indeed, his personal feelings could prevent him from recognizing that his brother's qualifications were inferior. Since the subtle effects of strong emotions cannot easily be suppressed, the best way to check their interference with efficiency is to exclude from the administrative hierarchy those interpersonal relationships that are characterized by emotional attachments. While relatives sometimes work for the same company, they are generally not put in charge of one another. Impersonal relationships assure the detachment necessary if efficiency alone is to govern administrative decisions. However, relationships between employees who have frequent social contacts do not remain impersonal, as we shall see.

These four factors—specialization, a hierarchy of authority, a system of rules, and impersonality—are the basic characteristics of bureaucratic organization. Factories are bureaucratically organized, as are government offices; if this were not the case, they could not operate on a large scale. . . .

THE VALUE OF STUDYING BUREAUCRACY

Learning to understand bureaucracies is more important today than it ever was. It has, moreover, special significance in a democracy. In addition, the study of bureaucratic organization makes a particular contribution to the advancement of sociological knowledge.

Today

Bureaucracy is not a new phenomenon. It existed in relatively simple forms thousands of years ago in Egypt and Rome. But the trend toward bureaucratization has greatly accelerated since the beginning of this century. In contemporary society, bureaucracy has become a dominant institution—indeed, the institution that epitomizes modernity. Unless we understand this form, we cannot understand the social life of today.

The enormous size of modern nations and the organizations within them is one reason for the spread of bureaucracy. In earlier periods, most countries were small, even large ones had only a loose central administration, and there were few formal organizations except the government.[5] Modern nations have many millions of citizens, vast armies, giant corporations, huge unions, and numerous voluntary associations.[6] To be sure, large size does not necessarily compel bureaucratic organization. However, the problems posed by administration on a large scale tend to lead to bureaucratization. Put somewhat differently, in the absence of bureaucratization, large-scale centralized administration has been very difficult to maintain.

In the United States, employment statistics illustrate the trend toward large, bureaucratized organizations. The federal government employed some eight thousand civilian personnel in 1820, a quarter million at the beginning of this century, and almost 3 million now. The largest private firms, such as General Motors and Exxon, have upward of half a million employees apiece. Self-employment, which was once the norm, has become rare. In 1800, 57 percent of the U.S. working population were self-employed; in 1970, however, only 10 percent were.[7] Moreover, within organizations of all kinds, the proportion of employees with supervisory or administrative duties has increased dramatically, especially in recent years. In 1900, the ratio of administrative to production employees in U.S. manufacturing industry was about 1:10; it was approximately 2:10 in 1950.[8] This A/P ratio, as it is known to sociologists, now exceeds 4½:10 in manufacturing. Perhaps of greater importance, supervisory or administrative ratios have increased in other industries—for example, mining, finance and insurance, retailing, service—just as rapidly as in manufacturing.[9]

A large and increasing proportion of the American people, then, spend their working lives in large organizations, and these organizations are increasingly bureaucratized in the sense that a greater proportion of work is of a supervisory or administrative character. To be sure, the average size of workplaces (or what the U.S. Census calls establishments) has decreased slightly since World War II,[10] but individual workplaces are increasingly linked together in bureaucratic hierarchies.[11] Outside of work, the organizations we deal with are themselves becoming more bureaucratic. The corner hamburger stand has been largely displaced by the franchised outlet that is part of a national chain. The independent physician is increasingly rare as medical care becomes organized into group practices and health maintenance organizations, the latter often owned by giant corporations.[12] Bureaucratization of our institutions has become so ubiquitous that it is now difficult to imagine alternatives to the bureaucratic form. But alternatives to bureaucracy are essential, as we shall point out below, to preserve individual autonomy and innovativeness in organizations.

In a Democracy

Bureaucracy, as [German sociologist] Max Weber pointed out, "is a power instrument of the first order—for the one who controls the bureaucratic apparatus."[13]

> Under normal conditions, the power position of the fully developed bureaucracy is always overtowering. The "political master" finds himself in the position of the "dilettante" who stands opposite the "expert," facing the trained official who stands within the management of administration. This holds whether the "master" whom the bureaucracy serves is a "people," equipped with the weapons of "legislative initiative," the "referendum," and the right to remove officials, or a parliament, elected on a . . . "democratic" basis and equipped with the right to vote a lack of confidence, or with the actual authority to vote it.[14]

Totalitarianism is the polar case of such concentration of bureaucratic power that destroys democratic processes, but it is not the only example. The same antidemocratic tendencies can be observed in political machines that allow political bosses to assume power legally belonging to voters, in business corporations that enable managers to take power rightfully belonging to stockholders, and in unions that let union leaders exercise the power rightfully belonging to rank-and-file members. The use of bureaucratic administration by totalitarian regimes has led some writers to contend that the present trend toward bureaucratization spells the doom of democratic institutions.[15] This may well be too pessimistic a viewpoint, but there can be little doubt that this problem constitutes a challenge. To protect ourselves against the threat of bureaucratic domination while continuing to take advantage of the efficiencies of bureaucracy, we must first learn fully to understand how bureaucracies function. Knowledge alone is not power, but ignorance surely facilitates subjugation. This is one reason why the study of bureaucratic organization has such great significance in a democracy.

Another and perhaps more subtle threat posed by bureaucratization is erosion of public confidence in democratic institutions. The taxpayers' revolt evident in California's Proposition 13 is but one expression of the discontent with government that has become widespread in recent years. Discontent with large organizations is also exemplified by the dramatic increase in both antigovernment and antibusiness sentiments found in opinion surveys of the American public. From the late 1950s through the present, increasing numbers of people have expressed doubts about government and business, although negative sentiments about government have risen much more rapidly than negative attitudes toward business.[16] Antigovernment attitudes may be attributed partly to the Watergate scandal and the failure of U.S. policy in Vietnam. But there is evidence also that the large size of government and business organizations has contributed to declining confidence in them. Large institutions, the federal government and large corporations particularly, are suspect.[17] Whether aversion to large size is due to the perception of "fat" or inefficiency in big government and big business, the perception that power is misused by both, or the substantial rewards that accrue to executives, cannot be determined from opinion data. It is clear, however, that considerable distrust of large, bureaucratized organizations has accumulated. An understanding of the sources of perceived inefficiency and misuse of power in both public and private bureaucracies could possibly suggest correctives that would help rebuild confidence in our institutions. . . .

THE CONCEPT OF BUREAUCRACY

The main characteristics of a bureaucratic structure (in the "ideal-typical" case,[18] according to Weber) are the following:

1. "The regular activities required for the purposes of the organization are distributed in a fixed way as official duties."[19] The clear-cut division of labor makes it possible to employ only specialized experts in each particular position and to make every one of them responsible for the effective performance of his duties. This high degree of specialization has become so much part of our life that we tend to forget that it did not prevail in former eras but is a relatively recent bureaucratic invention.

2. "The organization of offices follows the principle of hierarchy; that is, each lower office is under the control and supervision of a higher one."[20] Every official in this administrative hierarchy is accountable to her superior for her subordinates' decisions and actions as well as her own. To be able to discharge the responsibility for the work of subordinates, the superior has authority over them, which means that she has the right to issue directives and they have the duty to obey them. This authority is strictly circumscribed and confined to those directives that are relevant to official operations. The use of status prerogatives to extend the power of control over subordinates beyond these limits does not constitute the legitimate exercise of bureaucratic authority.

3. Operations are governed "by a consistent system of abstract rules . . . [and] consist of the application of these rules to particular cases."[21] This system of standards is designed to assure uniformity in the performance of every task, regardless of the number of persons engaged in it, and the coordination of different tasks. Explicit rules and regulations define the responsibility of each member of the organization and relationships among them. This does not imply that bureaucratic duties are necessarily simple or routine. It must be remembered that strict adherence to general standards in deciding specific cases characterizes not only the job of the file clerk but also that of the Supreme Court justice. For the former, it may involve merely filing alphabetically; for the latter, it involves interpreting the law of the land in order to settle the most complicated legal issues. Bureaucratic duties range in complexity from one of these extremes to the other.

4. "The ideal official conducts his office . . . [in] a spirit of formalistic impersonality, 'Sine ira ac studio,' without hatred or passion, and hence without affection or enthusiasm."[22] For rational standards to govern operations without interference from personal considerations, a detached approach must prevail within the organization and especially toward clients. If an official develops strong feelings about subordinates or clients, she can hardly keep letting those feelings influence her official decisions. As a result, and often without being aware of it herself, she might be particularly lenient in evaluating the work of one of her subordinates or might discriminate against some clients and in favor of others. The exclusion of personal considerations from official business is a prerequisite for impartiality as well as for efficiency. The very factors that make a government bureaucrat unpopular with his clients, an aloof attitude and lack of genuine concern with them as human beings, usually benefits these clients. Disinterestedness and lack of personal interest go together. The official who does not maintain social distance and becomes personally interested in the cases of his clients tends to be partial in his treatment of them, favoring those he likes over others. Impersonal detachment engenders equitable treatment of all persons and thus equal justice in administration.

5. Employment in the bureaucratic organization is based on technical qualifications and is protected against arbitrary dismissal. "It constitutes a career. There is a system of 'promotions' according to seniority or to achievement, or both."[23] These personnel policies, which are found not only in civil service but also in many private companies, encourage the development of loyalty to the organization and esprit de corps among its members. The consequent identification of employees with the organization motivates them to exert greater efforts in advancing its interest. It may also give rise to a tendency among civil servants or employees to think of themselves as a class apart from and superior to the rest of society. This tendency has been especially pronounced among European civil servants, but it may be found in the United States too.

6. "Experience tends universally to show that the purely bureaucratic type of administrative organization . . . is, from a purely technical point of view, capable of attaining the highest degree of efficiency. . . ."[24]

The fully developed bureaucratic mechanism compares with other organizations exactly as does the machine with nonmechanical modes of production. Precision, speed, unambiguity, knowledge of the files, continuity, discretion, unity, strict subordination, reduction of friction and of material and personal costs—these are raised to the optimum point in the strictly bureaucratic administration, and especially in its monocratic form. As compared with all collegiate, honorific, and avocational forms of administration, trained bureaucracy is superior on all these points. And as far as complicated tasks are concerned, paid bureaucratic work is not only more precise but, in the last analysis, it is often cheaper than formally unremunerated honorific service.[25]

Bureaucracy, then, solves the distinctive organizational problem of maximizing coordination and control and thereby organizational efficiency, not only the productive efficiency of individual employees.

The superior effectiveness of bureaucracy—its capacity to coordinate large-scale administrative tasks—and superior efficiency are the expected results of its various characteristics as outlined by Weber. An individual who is to work effectively must have the necessary skills and apply them rationally and energetically; but more is required of an organization that is to operate effectively and efficiently. Every one of its members must have the expert skills needed for the performance of her tasks. This is the purpose of specialization and employment on the basis of technical qualifications, often ascertained by objective tests. Even experts, however, may be prevented by personal bias from making rational decisions. The emphasis on impersonal detachment is needed to eliminate this source of nonrational action. But individual rationality is not enough. As noted above, if members of the organization were to make rational decisions independently, their work would not be coordinated and the efficiency of the organization would suffer. Hence there is need for discipline to limit the scope of rational discretion, which is met by the system of rules and regulations and the hierarchy of supervision. Moreover, there are personnel policies that permit employees to feel secure in their jobs and to anticipate advancements for faithful performance of duties, and these policies discourage attempts to impress superiors by inducing clever innovations, which may endanger coordination. Lest this stress on disciplined obedience to rules and regulations undermine the employee's motivation to devote his energies to his job, incentives for exerting effort must be furnished. Personnel policies that cultivate organizational loyalties and that provide for promotion on the basis of merit serve this function. In other words, bureaucracy's characteristics are intended to create social conditions constraining each member of the organization to act in ways that, whether they appear rational or otherwise from the individual's standpoint, further the rational pursuit of organizational objectives.

So far, Weber's analysis of bureaucratic structures emphasizes mainly their positive functions. The division of labor and specialization promotes expertise, but the work of specialists must be coordinated through organizational hierarchies. Rules and the norm of impersonality contribute further to coordination by removing individual biases from decisions. And career incentives motivate employees to perform their duties diligently. But Weber also identified some potentially negative consequences of bureaucracy. Among these are the following:

1. Bureaucracies tend to monopolize information, rendering outsiders unable to determine the basis on which decisions are made. "Every bureaucracy seeks to increase the superiority of the professionally informed by keeping their knowledge and intentions secret. . . . The concept of the 'official secret' is the specific invention of bureaucracy, and nothing is defended so fanatically by the bureaucracy as this attitude."[26]

2. "Once it is fully established, bureaucracy is among those social structures which are the hardest to destroy. . . . The idea of eliminating these organizations becomes more and more utopian."[27] The very specialization and expertise of bureaucracies makes it almost impossible to administer large nation-states or private enterprises without them. To be sure, individual officials can be replaced should they leave, voluntarily or otherwise. But the overall pattern of administration consistent with the bureaucratic model is not easily changed. This occurs not simply because people are reluctant to change but especially because they rightly fear that the elimination of existing procedures may well lead to disorganization or return to the "spoils system" dominated by favoritism and corrupt practices.

3. Established bureaucracies are, at best, ambivalent toward democracy. On the one hand, bureaucratization tends to accompany mass democracy. "This results from the characteristic principle of bureaucracy: the abstract regularity of the execution of authority, which is a result of the demand for 'equality before the law' in the personal and functional sense—hence of the horror of 'privilege,' and of the principled rejection of doing business 'from case to case.'"[28] On the other hand, bureaucracies tend not to be responsive to public opinion.

Democracy inevitably comes into conflict with the bureaucratic tendencies which, by its fight against notable rule, democracy has produced. . . . The most decisive thing there—indeed it is rather exclusively so—is the *leveling of the governed* in opposition to the ruling and bureaucratically articulated group, which in its turn may occupy a quite autocratic position. . . .[29]

Weber's analysis of bureaucracy leads thereby to paradoxical conclusions. Due to the effectiveness and efficiency it imparts to large-scale administration, bureaucracy has many positive functions. But its tendencies toward monopolizing information, resisting change, and acting autocratically (even if in compliance with rules) are usually not viewed positively; they were not so regarded at the time Weber wrote, nor are they today. Both the positive and negative effects of bureaucracy can be understood as outcomes of organizing principles intended to achieve coordination and control. Effectiveness and efficiency are attained because bureaucracy concentrates technical expertise and acts predictably. But the same predictable action based on expertise makes bureaucracies extremely powerful institutions, which have the capacity to resist external forces pressing for change. In the language of sociological theory, Weber's analysis suggests both positive *functions* as well as negative *dysfunctions* of the bureaucratic form.[30] The fact that bureaucratic organizations (as well as most other social institutions) have both functions that contribute to and dysfunctions that detract from adaptation and adjustment is not always understood, but it is important to a complete and scientific understanding of bureaucracy. Weber's penetrating analysis has become the prototype of bureaucracy—it is the basic concept we use in comparing organizations. . . .

Notes

1. The disenchantment of the world is one of the main themes running through the work of Max Weber.
2. See Pitirim Sorokin, *Cultural and Social Dynamics* (New York: American Book Company, 1937–1941). The author traces fluctuations in cultural emphasis on science and rationality, on the one hand, and faith and supernatural phenomena, on the other, from the earliest times to the present trend toward rationalization.
3. Karl Marx, *Capital* (New York: International Publishers, 1967), vol. I, chaps. 26–31.
4. The bureaucratization of railroads is described fully by Alfred D. Chandler, Jr., in *The Visible Hand* (Cambridge, Mass.: Harvard University Press, 1977), chaps. 3–6.
5. See Robert LaPolombara, *Bureaucracy and Political Development* (Princeton, N.J.: Princeton University Press, 1963).
6. See Kenneth Boulding, *The Organizational Revolution* (New York: Harper & Row, 1953).
7. Lynne G. Zucker, "Organizations as Institutions," *Research in the Sociology of Organizations* 2(1983):14–17.
8. Reinhard Bendix, *Work and Authority in Industry* (Berkeley, Calif.: University of California Press, 1956), chap. 5.
9. Marshall W. Meyer, William Stevenson, and Stephen Webster, *Limits to Bureaucratic Growth* (New York: de Gruyter, 1985), chap. 2.
10. Mark Granovetter, "Small is Beautiful: Labor Markets and Establishment Size," *American Sociological Review* 49(1984):323–334.
11. Meyer, Stevenson, and Webster, loc. cit.
12. See Paul Starr, *The Social Transformation of American Medicine* (New York: Basic Books, 1982).
13. H. H. Gerth and C. W. Mills, eds., *From Max Weber: Essays in Sociology* (New York: Oxford University Press, 1946), p. 228.
14. Ibid., p. 232.
15. See Ludwig von Mises, *Bureaucracy* (New Haven, Conn.: Yale University Press, 1944), and Karl Mannheim, *Man and Society in an Age of Reconstruction* (London: Routledge & Kegan Paul, 1951).
16. Seymour Martin Lipset and William Schneider, *The Confidence Gap* (New York: Free Press, 1983), chap. 1.
17. Ibid., pp. 81–83.
18. The "ideal type" is discussed in Peter M. Blau and Marshall W. Meyer, *Bureaucracy in Modern Society,* 3rd ed. (New York: Random House, 1987), pp. 25–44.
19. Gerth and Mills, op. cit., p. 196.
20. Max Weber, *The Theory of Social and Economic Organization,* trans. A. M. Henderson and Talcott Parsons (New York: Oxford University Press, 1947), p. 331.
21. Ibid., p. 330.
22. Ibid., p. 340.
23. Ibid., p. 334.
24. Ibid., p. 337.
25. Gerth and Mills, op. cit., p. 214.
26. Ibid., p. 233.

27. Ibid., pp. 228–229.
28. Ibid., p. 224.
29. Ibid., p. 226
30. See Robert K. Merton's discussion of functional analysis in *Social Theory and Social Structure*, 3rd ed. (New York: Free Press, 1968), pp. 73–138.

Public and Private Management: Are They Fundamentally Alike in All Unimportant Respects?

GRAHAM T. ALLISON, JR.

My subtitle puts Wallace Sayre's oft quoted "law" as a question. Sayre had spent some years in Ithaca helping plan Cornell's new School of Business and Public Administration. He left for Columbia with this aphorism: public and private management are fundamentally alike in all unimportant respects.

Sayre based his conclusion on years of personal observation of governments, a keen ear for what his colleagues at Cornell (and earlier at OPA) said about business, and a careful review of the literature and data comparing public and private management. Of the latter there was virtually none. Hence, Sayre's provocative "law" was actually an open invitation to research.

Unfortunately, in the 50 years since Sayre's pronouncement, the data base for systematic comparison of public and private management has improved little. . . . I would, in effect, like to take up Sayre's invitation to *speculate* about similarities and differences among public and private management in ways that suggest significant opportunities for systematic investigation. . . .[1]

FRAMING THE ISSUE: WHAT IS PUBLIC MANAGEMENT?

What is the meaning of the term *management* as it appears in *Office of Management and Budget* or *Office of Personnel Management?* Is "management" different from, broader, or narrower than "administration"? Should we distinguish between management, leadership, entrepreneurship, administration, policy-making, and implementation?

Who are "public managers"? Mayors, governors, and presidents? City managers, secretaries, and commissioners? Bureau chiefs? Office directors? Legislators? Judges?

Recent studies of OPM and OMB shed some light on these questions. OPM's major study of the "current status of public management research" completed in May 1978 by Selma Mushkin and colleagues of Georgetown's Public Service Laboratory starts with this question. The Mushkin report notes the definition of *public administration* employed by the Interagency Study Committee on Policy Management Assistance in its 1975 report to OMB. That study identified the following core elements:

1. *Policy Management.* The identification of needs, analysis of options, selection of programs, and allocation of resources on a jurisdiction-wide basis.
2. *Resource Management.* The establishment of basic administrative support systems, such as budgeting, financial management, procurement and supply, and personnel management.
3. *Program Management.* The implementation of policy or daily operation of agencies carrying out policy along functional lines (education, law enforcement, etc.).[2]

The Mushkin report rejects this definition in favor of an "alternative list of public management elements." These elements are:

- Personnel management (other than work force planning and collective bargaining and labor-management relations)
- Work force planning
- Collective bargaining and labor-management relations
- Productivity and performance measurement
- Organization/reorganization
- Financial management (including the management of intergovernmental relations)
- Evaluation research, and program and management audit[3]

Such terminological tangles seriously hamper the development of public management as a field of knowledge. In our efforts to discuss the public management curriculum at Harvard, I have been struck by how differently people use these terms, how strongly many individuals feel about some distinction they believe is marked by a difference between one word and another, and consequently, how large a barrier terminology is to convergent discussion. These verbal obstacles virtually prohibit conversation that is both brief and constructive among individuals who have not developed a common language or a mutual understanding of each other's use of terms.

This terminological thicket reflects a more fundamental conceptual confusion. There exists no overarching framework that orders the domain. In an effort to get a grip on the phenomena—the buzzing, blooming confusion of people in jobs performing tasks that produce results—both practitioners and observers have strained to find distinctions that facilitate their work. The attempts in the early decades of this century to draw a sharp line between "policy" and "administration," like more recent efforts to mark a similar divide between "policy-making" and "implementation," reflect a common search for a simplification that allows one to put the value-laden issues of politics to one side (who gets what, when, and how), and focus on the more limited issue of how to perform tasks more efficiently.[4] But can anyone really deny that the "how" substantially affects the "who," the "what," and the "when"? The basic categories now prevalent in discussions of public management—strategy, personnel management, financial management, and control—are mostly derived from a business context in which executives manage hierarchies. The fit of these concepts to the problems that confront public managers is not clear.

Finally, there exist no ready data on what public managers do. Instead, the academic literature, such as it is, mostly consists of speculation tied to bits and pieces of evidence about the tail or the trunk or other manifestion of the proverbial elephant.[5] In contrast to the literally thousands of cases describing problems faced by private managers and their practice in solving these problems, case research from the perspective of a public manager is just beginning. . . .[6] The paucity of data on the phenomena inhibits systematic empirical research on similarities and differences between public and private management, leaving the field to a mixture of reflection on personal experience and speculation.

For the purpose of this presentation, I will follow Webster and use the term *management* to mean the organization and direction of resources to achieve a desired result. I will focus on *general managers*, that is, individuals charged with managing a whole organization or multifunctional subunit. I will be interested in the general manager's full responsibilities, both *inside* his organization in integrating the diverse contributions of specialized subunits of the organization to achieve results, and *outside* his organization in relating his organization and its product to external constituencies. I will begin with the simplifying assumption that managers of traditional government organizations are public managers, and managers of traditional private businesses [are] private managers. Lest the discussion fall victim to the fallacy of misplaced abstraction, I will take the Director of EPA and the Chief Executive Officer of American Motors as, respectively, public and private managers. Thus, our central question can be put concretely: in what ways are the jobs and responsibilities of Doug Costle as Director of EPA similar to and different from those of Roy Chapin as Chief Executive Officer of American Motors?

SIMILARITIES: HOW ARE PUBLIC AND PRIVATE MANAGEMENT ALIKE?

At one level of abstraction, it is possible to identify a set of general management functions. The most famous such list appeared in Gulick and Urwick's classic *Papers in the Science of Administration*.[7] [They] summarized the work of the chief executive in the acronym POSDCORB. The letters stand for:

- Planning
- Organizing

- Staffing
- Directing
- Coordinating
- Reporting
- Budgeting

With various additions, amendments, and refinements, similar lists of general management functions can be found through the management literature from Barnard to Drucker.[8]

I shall resist here my natural academic instinct to join the intramural debate among proponents of various lists and distinctions. Instead, I simply offer one composite list (see Table 1-2) that attempts to incorporate the major functions that have been identified for general managers, whether public or private.

Table 1-2
Functions of General Management

Strategy

1. *Establishing objectives and priorities* for the organization (on the basis of forecasts of the external environment and the organization's capacities).
2. *Devising operational plans* to achieve these objectives.

Managing Internal Components

3. *Organizing and staffing.* In organizing the manager establishes structure (units and positions with assigned authority and responsibilities) and procedures for coordinating activity and taking action. In staffing he tries to fit the right persons in the key jobs.*
4. *Directing personnel and the personnel management system.* The capacity of the organization is embodied primarily in its members and their skills and knowledge, the personnel management system recruits, selects, socializes, trains, rewards, punishes, and exits the organization's human capital, which constitutes the organization's capacity to act to achieve its goals and to respond to specific directions from management.
5. *Controlling performance.* Various management information systems—including operating and capital budgets, accounts, reports, and statistical systems, performance appraisals, and product evaluation—assist management in making decisions and in measuring progress towards objectives.

Managing External Constituencies

6. *Dealing with "external" units* of the organization subject to some common authority: Most general managers must deal with general managers of other units within the larger organization—above, laterally, and below—to achieve their unit's objectives.
7. *Dealing with independent organizations.* Agencies from other branches or levels of government, interest groups, and private enterprises that can importantly affect the organization's ability to achieve its objectives.
8. *Dealing with the press and the public* whose action or approval or acquiescence is required.

---

*Organization and staffing are frequently separated in such lists, but because of the interaction between the two, they are combined here. See Graham Allison and Peter Szanton, *Remaking Foreign Policy* (New York: Basic Books, 1976), p. 14.

These common functions of management are not isolated and discrete, but rather integral components separated here for purposes of analysis. The character and relative significance of the various functions differ from one time to another in the history of any organization, and between one organization and another. But whether in a public or private setting, the challenge for the general manager is to integrate all these elements so as to achieve results.

DIFFERENCES: HOW ARE PUBLIC AND PRIVATE MANAGEMENT DIFFERENT?

While there is a level of generality at which management is management, whether public or private, functions that bear identical labels take on rather different meanings in public and private settings. As Larry Lynn has pointed out, one powerful piece of evidence in the debate between those who emphasize "similarities" and those who underline "differences" is the nearly unanimous conclusion of individuals who have been general managers in both business and government. Consider the reflections of George Shultz (Secretary of State; former Director of OMB, Secretary of Labor, Secretary of the Treasury, President of Bechtel), Donald Rumsfeld (former congressman, Director of OEO, Director of the Cost of Living Council, White House Chief of Staff, and Secretary of Defense; now President of G. D. Searle and Company), Michael Blumenthal (former Chairman and Chief Executive Officer of Bendix, Secretary of the Treasury, and now Vice Chairman of Burroughs), Roy Ash (former President of Litton Industries, Director of OMB; later President of Addressograph), Lyman Hamilton (former Budget Officer in BOB, High Commissioner of Okinawa, Division Chief in the World Bank and President of ITT), and George Romney (former President of American Motors, Governor of Michigan, and Secretary of Housing and Urban Development).[9] All judge public management different from private management—and harder!

Orthogonal Lists of Differences

My review of these recollections, as well as the thoughts of academics, has identified [two] interesting, orthogonal lists that summarize the current state of the field: one by John Dunlop . . . and one by Richard E. Neustadt, prepared for the National Academy of Public Administration's Panel on Presidential Management.

John T. Dunlop's "impressionistic comparison of government management and private business" yields the following contrasts.[10]

1. *Time Perspective.* Government managers tend to have relatively short time horizons dictated by political necessities and the political calendar, while private managers appear to take a longer time perspective oriented toward market developments, technological innovation and investment, and organization building.
2. *Duration.* The length of service of politically appointed top government managers is relatively short, averaging no more than 18 months recently for assistant secretaries, while private managers have a longer tenure

both in the same position and in the same enterprise. A recognized element of private business management is the responsibility to train a successor or several possible candidates, [whereas] the concept is largely alien to public management, since fostering a successor is perceived to be dangerous.

3. *Measurement of Performance.* There is little if any agreement on the standards and measurement of performance to appraise a government manager, while various tests of performance—financial return, market share, performance measures for executive compensation—are well established in private business and often made explicit for a particular managerial position during a specific period ahead.

4. *Personnel Constraints.* In government there are two layers of managerial officials that are at times hostile to one another: the civil service (or now the executive system) and the political appointees. Unionization of government employees exists among relatively high-level personnel in the hierarchy and includes a number of supervisory personnel. Civil service, union contract provisions, and other regulations complicate the recruitment, hiring, transfer, and layoff or discharge of personnel to achieve managerial objectives or preferences. By comparison, private business managements have considerably greater latitude, even under collective bargaining, in the management of subordinates. They have much more authority to direct the employees of their organization. Government personnel policy and administration are more under the control of staff (including civil service staff outside an agency) compared to the private sector in which personnel are much more subject to line responsibility.

5. *Equity and Efficiency.* In governmental management great emphasis tends to be placed on providing equity among different constituencies, while in private business management relatively greater stress is placed upon efficiency and competitive performance.

6. *Public Processes Versus Private Processes.* Governmental management tends to be exposed to public scrutiny and to be more open, while private business management is more private and its processes more internal and less exposed to public review.

7. *Role of Press and Media.* Governmental management must contend regularly with the press and media; its decisions are often anticipated by the press. Private decisions are less often reported in the press, and the press has a much smaller impact on the substance and timing of decisions.

8. *Persuasion and Direction.* In government, managers often seek to mediate decisions in response to a wide variety of pressures and must often put together a coalition of inside and outside groups to survive. By contrast, private management proceeds much more by direction or the issuance of orders to subordinates by superior managers with little risk of contradiction. Governmental managers tend to regard themselves as responsive to many superiors, while private managers look more to one higher authority.

9. *Legislative and Judicial Impact.* Governmental managers are often subject to close scrutiny by legislative oversight groups or even judicial

orders in ways that are quite uncommon in private business management. Such scrutiny often materially constrains executive and administrative freedom to act.

10. *Bottom Line.* Governmental managers rarely have a clear bottom line, while that of a private business manager is profit, market performance, and survival. . . .

. . . Richard E. Neustadt, in a fashion close to Dunlop's, notes six major differences between presidents of the United States and chief executive officers of major corporations.[11]

1. *Time Horizon.* The private chief begins by looking forward a decade, or thereabouts, his likely span barring extraordinary troubles. The first-term president looks forward four years at most, with the fourth (and now even the third) year dominated by campaigning for reelection (what second-termers look toward we scarcely know, having seen but one such term completed in the past quarter century).

2. *Authority over the Enterprise.* Subject to concurrence from the Board of Directors which appointed and can fire him, the private executive sets organization goals, shifts structures, procedure, and personnel to suit, monitors results, reviews key operational decisions, deals with key outsiders, and brings along his Board. Save for the deep but narrow sphere of military movements, a president's authority in these respects is shared with well-placed members of Congress (or their staffs): case by case, they may have more explicit authority than he does (contrast authorizations and appropriations with the "take-care" clause). As for "bringing along the Board," neither the congressmen with whom he shares power nor the primary and general electorates which "hired" him have either a Board's duties or a broad view of the enterprise precisely matching his.

3. *Career System.* The model corporation is a true career system, something like the Forest Service after initial entry. In normal times the chief himself is chosen from within, or he is chosen from another firm in the same industry. He draws department heads [and other key employees] from among those with whom he's worked or whom he knows in comparable companies. He and his principal associates will be familiar with each other's roles—indeed, he probably has had a number of them—and also usually with one another's operating styles, personalities, idiosyncracies. Contrast the president who rarely has had much experience "downtown," probably knows little of most roles there (much of what he knows will turn out wrong), and less of most associates whom he appoints there, willy nilly, to fill places by Inauguration Day. Nor are they likely to know one another well, coming as they do from "everywhere" and headed as most are toward oblivion.

4. *Media Relations.* The private executive represents his firm and speaks for it publicly in exceptional circumstances; he and his associates judge the exceptions. Those aside, he neither sees the press nor gives its members access to internal operations, least of all in his own office, save to make a point deliberately for public-relations purposes. The

president, by contrast, is routinely on display, continuously dealing with the White House press and with the wider circle of political reporters, commentators, columnists. He needs them in his [day-to-day] business, . . . and they need him in theirs: the TV network news programs lead off with him some nights each week. They and the president are as mutually dependent as he and congressmen (or more so). Comparatively speaking, these relations overshadow most administrative ones much of the time for him.

5. *Performance Measurement.* The private executive expects to be judged, and in turn to judge subordinates, by profitability, however the firm measures it (a major strategic choice). In practice, his Board may use more subjective measures; so may he, but at risk to morale and good order. The relative virtue of profit, of "the bottom line," is its legitimacy, its general acceptance in the business world by all concerned. Never mind its technical utility in given cases; its apparent "objectivity," hence "fairness," has enormous social usefulness: a myth that all can live by. For a president there is no counterpart (except, *in extremis,* the "smoking gun" to justify impeachment). The general public seems to judge a president, at least in part, by what its members think is happening to them, in their own lives: congressmen, officials, interest groups appear to judge by what they guess, at given times, he can do for or to their causes. Members of the press interpret both of these and spread a simplified criterion affecting both, the legislative box score, a standard of the press's own devising. The White House denigrates them all except when it does well.

6. *Implementation.* The corporate chief, supposedly, does more than choose a strategy and set a course of policy; he also is supposed to oversee what happens after, how in fact intentions turn into results, or if they don't to take corrective action, monitoring through his information system, and acting, if need be, through his personnel system. A president, by contrast, while himself responsible for budgetary proposals, too, in many spheres of policy appears ill-placed and ill-equipped to monitor what agencies of states, of cities, corporations, unions, foreign governments are up to or to change personnel in charge. Yet these are very often the executants of "his" programs. Apart from defense and diplomacy the federal government does two things in the main: it issues and applies regulations and it awards grants in aid. Where these are discretionary, choice usually is vested by statute in a Senate-confirmed official well outside the White House. Monitoring is his function, not the president's except at second hand. And final action is the function of the subjects of the rules and funds; they mostly are not federal personnel at all. In defense, the arsenals and shipyards are gone; weaponry comes from the private sector. In foreign affairs it is the *other* governments whose actions we would influence. From implementors like these a president is far removed most of the time. He intervenes, if at all, on a crash basis, not through organizational incentives.

Underlying these lists' sharpest distinctions between public and private management is a fundamental *constitutional difference.* In business, the functions of general management are centralized in a single individual: the chief executive officer. The goal is authority commensurate with responsibility. In contrast, in the U.S. government, the functions of general management are constitutionally spread among competing institutions: the executive, two houses of Congress, and the courts. The constitutional goal was "not to promote efficiency but to preclude the exercise of arbitrary power," as Justice Brandeis observed. Indeed, as *The Federalist Papers* makes starkly clear, the aim was to create incentives to compete: "the great security against a gradual concentration of the several powers in the same branch, consists in giving those who administer each branch the constitutional means and personal motives to resist encroachment of the others. Ambition must be made to counteract ambition." [12] Thus, the general management functions concentrated in the CEO of a private business are, by constitutional design, spread in the public sector among a number of competing institutions and thus shared by a number of individuals whose ambitions are set against one another. For most areas of public policy today, these individuals include at the federal level the chief elected official, the chief appointed executive, the chief career official, and several congressional chieftains. Since most public services are actually delivered by state and local governments, with independent sources of authority, this means a further array of individuals at these levels.

AN OPERATIONAL PERSPECTIVE: HOW ARE THE JOBS AND RESPONSIBILITIES OF DOUG COSTLE, DIRECTOR OF EPA, AND ROY CHAPIN, CEO OF AMERICAN MOTORS, SIMILAR AND DIFFERENT?

If organizations could be separated neatly into two homogeneous piles, one public and one private, the task of identifying similarities and differences between managers of these enterprises would be relatively easy. In fact, as Dunlop has pointed out, "the real world of management is composed of distributions, rather than single undifferentiated forms, and there is an increasing variety of hybrids." Thus for each major attribute of organizations, specific entities can be located on a spectrum. On most dimensions, organizations classified as "predominantly public" and those "predominantly private" overlap. [13] Private business organizations vary enormously among themselves in size, in management structure and philosophy, and in the constraints under which they operate. For example, forms of ownership and types of managerial control may be somewhat unrelated. Compare a family-held enterprise, for instance, with a public utility and a decentralized conglomerate, a Bechtel with ATT and Textron. Similarly, there are vast differences in management of governmental organizations. Compare the Government Printing Office or TVA or the police department of a small town with the Department of Energy or the Department of Health and Human Services. These distributions and varieties should encourage penetrating comparisons within both business and governmental organizations, as well as contrasts and comparisons across these broad categories, a point to which we shall return in considering directions for research.

Absent a major research effort, it may nonetheless be worthwhile to examine the jobs and responsibilities of two specific managers, neither polar extremes, but one clearly public, the other private. For this purpose, and primarily because of the availability of cases that describe the problems and opportunities each confronted, consider Doug Costle, Administrator of EPA, and Roy Chapin, CEO of American Motors.[14]

Doug Costle, Administrator of EPA, January 1977

The mission of EPA is prescribed by laws creating the agency and authorizing its major programs. That mission is "to control and abate pollution in the areas of air, water, solid wastes, noise, radiation, and toxic substances. EPA's mandate is to mount an integrated, coordinated attack on environmental pollution in cooperation with state and local governments."[15]

EPA's organizational structure follows from its legislative mandates to control particular pollutants in specific environments: air and water, solid wastes, noise, radiation, pesticides, and chemicals. As the new administrator, Costle inherited the Ford administration's proposed budget for EPA of $802 million for federal 1978 with a ceiling of 9,698 agency positions.

The setting into which Costle stepped is difficult to summarize briefly. As Costle characterized it:

"Outside there is a confusion on the part of the public in terms of what this agency is all about; what it is doing, where it is going."

"The most serious constraint on EPA is the inherent complexity in the state of our knowledge, which is constantly changing."

"Too often, acting under extreme deadlines mandated by Congress, EPA has announced regulations, only to find out that they knew very little about the problem. The central problem is the inherent complexity of the job that the agency has been asked to do and the fact that what it is asked to do changes from day to day."

"There are very difficult internal management issues not amenable to a quick solution: the skills mix problem within the agency; a research program with laboratory facilities scattered all over the country and cemented in place, largely by political alliances on the Hill that would frustrate efforts to pull together a coherent research program."

"In terms of EPA's original mandate in the bulk pollutants we may be hitting the asymptotic part of the curve in terms of incremental clean-up costs. You have clearly conflicting national goals: energy and environment, for example."

Costle judged his six major tasks at the outset to be:

- Assembling a top management team (six assistant administrators and some 25 office heads).

- Addressing EPA's legislative agenda (EPA's basic legislative charter—the Clean Air Act and the Clean Water Act—was being rewritten as he took office; the pesticides program was up for reauthorization also in 1977).

- Establishing EPA's role in the Carter Administration (aware that the Administration would face hard tradeoffs between the environment and energy, energy regulations and the economy, EPA regulations of toxic substances and the regulations of FDA, CSPS, and OSHA. Costle identified the need to build relations with the other key players and to enhance EPA's standing).

- Building ties to constituent groups (both because of their role in legislating the agency's mandate and in successful implementation of EPA's programs).

- Making specific policy decisions (for example, whether to grant or deny a permit for the Seabrook Nuclear Generating Plant cooling system. Or how the Toxic Substance Control Act, enacted in October 1976, would be implemented; this act gave EPA new responsibilities for regulating the manufacture, distribution, and use of chemical substances so as to prevent unreasonable risks to health and the environment. Whether EPA would require chemical manufacturers to provide some minimum information on various substances, or require much stricter reporting requirements for the 1,000 chemical substances already known to be hazardous, or require companies to report all chemicals, and on what timetable, had to be decided and the regulations issued).

- Rationalizing the internal organization of the agency (EPA's extreme decentralization to the regions and its limited technical expertise).

No easy job.

Roy Chapin and American Motors, January 1967

In January 1967, in an atmosphere of crisis, Roy Chapin was appointed Chairman and Chief Executive Officer of American Motors (and William Luneburg, President and Chief Operating Officer). In the four previous years, AMC unit sales had fallen 37 percent and market share from over 6 percent to under 3 percent. Dollar volume in 1967 was off 42 percent from the all-time high of 1963 and earnings showed a net loss of $76 million on sales of $656 million. Columnists began writing obituaries for AMC. *Newsweek* characterized AMC as "a flabby dispirited company, a product solid enough but styled with about as much flair as corrective shoes, and a public image that melted down to one unshakeable label: loser." Said Chapin, "We were driving with one foot on the accelerator and one foot on the brake. We didn't know where the hell we were."

Chapin announced to his stockholders at the outset that "we plan to direct ourselves most specifically to those areas of the market where we can be fully effective. We are not going to attempt to be all things to all people, but to concentrate on those areas of consumer needs we can meet better than anyone else." As he recalled, "There were problems early in 1967 which demanded immediate attention, and which accounted for much of our time for several months. Nevertheless, we began planning beyond them, establishing objectives, programs and timetables through 1972. Whatever happened in the short run, we had to prove ourselves in the marketplace in the long run."

Chapin's immediate problems were five:

- The company was virtually out of cash and an immediate supplemental bank loan of $20 million was essential.

- Car inventories—company owned and dealer owned—had reached unprecedented levels. The solution to this glut took five months and could be accomplished only by a series of plant shutdowns in January 1967.

- Sales of the Rambler American series had stagnated and inventories were accumulating: a dramatic merchandising move was concocted and implemented in February, dropping the price tag on the American to a position midway between the VW and competitive smaller U.S. compacts, by both cutting the price to dealers and trimming dealer discounts from 21 percent to 17 percent.

- Administrative and commercial expenses were judged too high and thus a vigorous cost reduction program was initiated that trimmed $15 million during the first year. Manufacturing and purchasing costs were also trimmed significantly to approach the most effective levels in the industry.

- The company's public image had deteriorated: the press was pessimistic and much of the financial community had written it off. To counteract this, numerous formal and informal meetings were held with bankers, investment firms, government officials, and the press.

As Chapin recalls, "With the immediate fires put out, we could put in place the pieces of a corporate growth plan—a definition of a way of life in the auto industry for American Motors. We felt that our reason for being, which would enable us not just to survive but to grow, lay in bringing a different approach to the auto market—in picking our spots and then being innovative and aggressive." The new corporate growth plan included a dramatic change in the approach to the market to establish a "youthful image" for the company (by bringing out new sporty models like the Javelin and by entering the racing field), "changing the product line from one end to the other" by 1972, [and] acquiring Kaiser Jeep (selling the company's non-transportation assets and concentrating on specialized transportation, including Jeep, a company that had lost money in each of the preceding five years but that Chapin believed could be turned around by substantial cost reductions and economies of scale in manufacturing, purchasing, and administration).

Chapin succeeded for the year ending September 30, 1971. AMC earned $10.2 million on sales of $1.2 billion.

Recalling the list of general management functions in Table 1-2, which similarities and differences appear salient and important?

Strategy

Both Chapin and Costle had to establish objectives and priorities and to devise operational plans. In business, "corporate strategy is the pattern of major objectives, purposes, or goals and essential policies and plans for achieving these goals, stated in such a way as to define what business the company is in or is to be in and the kind of company it is or is to be." [16] In reshaping the strategy of AMC and concentrating on particular segments of the transportation market, Chapin had to consult his board and had to arrange financing. But the control was substantially his.

How much choice did Costle have at EPA as to the "business it is or is to be in" or the kind of agency "it is or is to be"? These major strategic choices emerged from the legislative process which mandated whether he should be in the business of controlling pesticides or toxic substances and if so on what timetable, and occasionally, even what level of particulate per million units he was required to control. The relative role of the president, other members of the administration (including White House staff, congressional relations, and other agency heads), the EPA Administrator, congressional committee chairmen, and external groups in establishing the broad strategy of the agency constitutes an interesting question.

Managing Internal Components

For both Costle and Chapin, staffing was key. As Donald Rumsfeld has observed, "the single most important task of the chief executive is to select the right people. I've seen terrible organization charts in both government and business that were made to work well by good people. I've seen beautifully charted organizations that didn't work very well because they had the wrong people." [17]

The leeway of the two executives in organizing and staffing were considerably different, however. Chapin closed down plants, moved key managers, hired and fired, virtually at will. As Michael Blumenthal has written about Treasury, "If you wish to make substantive changes, policy changes, and the Department's employees don't like what you're doing, they have ways of frustrating you or stopping you that do not exist in private industry. The main method they have is Congress. If I say I want to shut down a particular unit or transfer the function of one area to another, there are ways of going to Congress and in fact using friends in the Congress to block the move. They can also use the press to try to stop you. If I at Bendix wished to transfer a division from Ann Arbor to Detroit because I figured out that we could save money that way, as long as I could do it decently and carefully, it's of no lasting interest to the press. The press can't stop me. They may write about it in the local paper, but that's about it." [18]

For Costle, the basic structure of the agency was set by law. The labs, their location, and most of their personnel were fixed. Though he could recruit his key subordinates, again restrictions like the conflict of interest laws and the prospect of a Senate confirmation fight led him to drop his first choice for the Assistant Administrator for Research and Development, since he had worked for a major chemical company. While Costle could resort to changes in the process for developing policy or regulations in order to circumvent key office directors whose views he did not share, for example, Eric Stork, the Deputy Assistant Administrator in charge of Mobile Source Air Program, such maneuvers took considerable time, provoked extensive infighting, and delayed significantly the development of Costle's program.

In the direction of personnel and management of the personnel system, Chapin exercised considerable authority. While the United Auto Workers limited his authority over workers, at the management level he assigned people and reassigned responsibility consistent with his general plan. While others may have felt that his decisions to close down particular plants or to drop a particular product were mistaken, they complied. As George Shultz has observed: "One of the first lessons I learned in moving from government to business is that in business you must be very careful when you tell someone who is working for you to do something because the probability is high that he or she will do it."[19]

Costle faced a civil service system designed to prevent spoils as much as to promote productivity. The Civil Service Commission exercised much of the responsibility for the personnel function in his agency. Civil service rules severely restricted his discretion, took long periods to exhaust, and often required complex maneuvering in a specific case to achieve any results. Equal opportunity rules and their administration provided yet another network of procedural and substantive inhibitions. In retrospect, Costle found the civil service system a much larger constraint on his actions and demand on his time than he had anticipated.

In controlling performance, Chapin was able to use measures like profit and market share, to decompose those objectives to subobjectives for lower levels of the organization and to measure the performance of managers of particular models, areas, divisions. Cost accounting rules permitted him to compare plants within AMC and to compare AMC's purchases, production, and even administration with the best practice in the industry.

Managing External Constitutencies

As chief executive officer, Chapin had to deal only with the Board. For Costle, within the executive branch but beyond his agency lay many actors critical to the achievement of his agency objectives: the president and the White House, Energy, Interior, the Council on Environmental Quality, OMB. Actions each could take, either independently or after a process of consultation in which they disagreed with him, could frustrate his agency's achievement of its assigned mission. Consequently, he spent considerable time building his agency's reputation and capital for interagency disputes.

Dealing with independent external organizations was a necessary and even larger part of Costle's job. Since his agency, mission, strategy, authorizations, and appropriations emerged from the process of legislation, attention to congressional committees, congressmen, congressmen's staff, and people who affect congressmen and congressional staffers rose to the top of Costle's agenda. In the first year, top-level EPA officials appeared over 140 times before some 60 different committees and subcommittees.

Chapin's ability to achieve AMC's objectives could also be affected by independent external organizations: competitors, government (the Clean Air Act that was passed in 1970), consumer groups (recall Ralph Nader), and even suppliers of oil. More than most private managers, Chapin had to deal with the press in attempting to change the image of AMC. Such occasions were primarily at Chapin's initiative and around events that Chapin's public affairs office orchestrated, for example, the announcement of a new racing car. Chapin also managed a marketing effort to persuade consumers that their tastes could best be satisfied by AMC products.

Costle's work was suffused by the press: in the daily working of the organization, in the perception by key publics of the agency and thus the agency's influence with relevant parties, and even in the setting of the agenda of issues to which the agency had to respond.

For Chapin, the bottom line was profit, market share, and the long-term competitive position of AMC. For Costle, what are the equivalent performance measures? Blumenthal answers by exaggerating the difference between appearance and reality: "At Bendix, it was the reality of the situation that in the end determined whether we succeeded or not. In the crudest sense, this meant the bottom line. You can dress up profits only for so long—if you're not successful, it's going to be clear. In government there is no bottom line, and that is why you can be successful if you appear to be successful—though, of course, appearance is not the only ingredient of success."[20] Rumsfeld says, "In business, you're pretty much judged by results. I don't think the American people judge government officials this way . . . In government, too often you're measured by how much you seem to care, how hard you seem to try— things that do not necessarily improve the human condition . . . It's a lot easier for a President to get into something and end up with a few days of good public reaction than it is to follow through, to pursue policies to a point where they have a beneficial effect on human lives."[21] As George Shultz says, "In government and politics, recognition and therefore incentives go to those who formulate policy and maneuver legislative compromise. By sharp contrast, the kudos and incentives in business go to the persons who can get something done. It is execution that counts. Who can get the plant built, who can bring home the sales contract, who can carry out the financing, and so on."[22]

This casual comparison of one public and one private manager suggests what could be done if the issue of comparisons were pursued systematically, horizontally across organizations and at various levels within organizations. While much can be learned by examining the chief executive officers of organizations, still more promising should be comparisons among the much larger numbers of middle managers. If one compared, for example, a regional administrator of EPA and an AMC division chief, or two comptrollers, or equivalent plant managers, some functions would appear more similar, and other differences would stand out. The major barrier to such comparisons is the lack of cases describing problems and practices of middle-level managers.[23] This should be a high priority in further research. . . .[24]

Notes

1. To reiterate: this is not a report of a major research project or systematic study. Rather, it is a response to a request for a brief summary of reflections of a dean of a school of government who now spends his time doing a form of public management—managing what Jim March has labeled an "organized anarchy"—rather than thinking, much less writing. Moreover, the speculation here will appear to reflect a characteristic Harvard presumption that Cambridge either is the world or is an adequate sample of the world. I say "appear" since as a North Carolinian, I am self-conscious about this parochialism. Nevertheless, I have concluded that the purposes of this conference may be better served by providing a deliberately parochial perspective on these issues—and thereby presenting a clear target for others to shoot at. Finally, I must acknowledge that this article plagiarizes freely from a continuing discussion among my colleagues at Harvard about the develop-

ment of the field of public management, especially from Joe Bower, Hale Champion, Gordon Chase, Charles Christenson, Richard Darman, John Dunlop, Phil Heymann, Larry Lynn, Mark Moore, Dick Neustadt, Roger Porter, and Don Price. Since my colleagues have not had the benefit of commenting on this presentation, I suspect I have some points wrong, or out of context, or without appropriate subtlety or amendment. Thus I assume full liability for the words that follow.

2. Selma J. Mushkin, Frank H. Sandifer, and Sally Familton, *Current Status of Public Management Research Conducted by or Supported by Federal Agencies* (Washington, D.C.: Public Services Laboratory, Georgetown University, 1978), p. 10.

3. Ibid., p. 11.

4. Though frequently identified as the author who established the complete separation between "policy" and "administration," Woodrow Wilson has in fact been unjustly accused. "It is the object of administrative study to discover, first, what government can properly and successfully do, and, secondly, how it can do these proper things with the utmost possible efficiency . . ." (Wilson, "The Study of Public Administration," published as an essay in 1888 and reprinted in *Political Science Quarterly*, December 1941, p. 481). For another statement of the same point, see Brooks Adams, *The Theory of Social Revolutions* (Macmillan, 1913), pp. 207–208.

5. See Dwight Waldo, "Organization Theory: Revisiting the Elephant," *PAR* (November-December 1978). Reviewing the growing volume of books and articles on organization theory, Waldo notes that "growth in the volume of the literature is not to be equated with growth in knowledge."

6. See *Cases in Public Policy and Management,* Spring 1979, of the Intercollegiate Case Clearing House for a bibliography containing descriptions of 577 cases by 366 individuals from 79 institutions. Current casework builds on and expands earlier efforts on the Inter-University Case Program. See, for example, Harold Stein, ed., *Public Administration and Policy Development: A Case Book* (Orlando, Fla.: Harcourt Brace Jovanovich, 1952), and Edwin A. Bock and Alan K. Campbell, eds., *Case Studies in American Government* (Englewood Cliffs, N.J.: Prentice-Hall, 1962).

7. Luther Gulick and Al Urwick, eds., *Papers in the Science of Public Administration* Washington, D.C.: Institute of Public Administration, 1937).

8. See, for example, Chester I. Barnard, *The Functions of the Executive* (Cambridge, Mass.: Harvard University Press, 1938), and Peter F. Drucker, *Management Tasks, Responsibilities, Practices* (New York: Harper & Row, 1974). Barnard's recognition of human relations added an important dimension neglected in earlier lists.

9. See, for example, "A Businessman in a Political Jungle," *Fortune* (April 1964); "Candid Reflections of a Businessman in Washington," *Fortune* (January 29, 1979); "A Politician Turned Executive," *Fortune* (September 10, 1979); and "The Abrasive Interface," *Harvard Business Review* (November-December 1979) for the views of Romney, Blumenthal, Rumsfeld, and Shultz, respectively.

10. John T. Dunlop, "Public Management," draft of an unpublished paper and proposal, Summer 1979.

11. Richard E. Neustadt, "American Presidents and Corporate Executives," paper prepared for a meeting of the National Academy of Public Administration's Panel on Presidential Management, October 7–8, 1979.

12. Clinton Rossiter, ed., *The Federalist Papers* (New York: New American Library, 1961), No. 51. The word *department* has been replaced by *branch,* which was its meaning in the original papers.

13. Failure to recognize the fact of distributions has led some observers to leap from one instance of similarity between public and private to general propositions about similarities between public and private institutions or management. See, for

example, Michael Murray, "Comparing Public and Private Management: An Exploratory Essay," *Public Administration Review* (July-August, 1975).

14. These examples are taken from Bruce Scott, "American Motors Corporation" (Intercollegiate Case Clearing House #9-364-001); Charles B. Weigle with the collaboration of C. Roland Christensen, "American Motors Corporation II" (Intercollegiate Case Clearing House #6-372-359); Thomas R. Hitchner and Jacob Lew under the supervision of Philip B. Heymann and Stephen B. Hitchner, "Douglas Costle and the EPA (A)" (Kennedy School of Government Case #C94-78-216), and Jacob Lew and Stephen B. Hitchner, "Douglas Costle and the EPA (B)" (Kennedy School of Government Case #C96-78-217). For an earlier exploration of a similar comparison, see Joseph Bower, "Effective Public Management," *Harvard Business Review* (March-April, 1977).

15. U.S. Government Manual, 1978/1979, p. 507.

16. Kenneth R. Andrews, *The Concept of Corporate Strategy* (New York: Dow-Jones-Irwin, 1971), p. 28.

17. "A Politician-Turned-Executive," *Fortune* (September 10, 1979), p. 92.

18. "Candid Reflections of a Businessman in Washington," *Fortune* (January 29, 1979), p. 39.

19. "The Abrasive Interface," *Harvard Business Review* (November-December 1979), p. 95.

20. *Fortune* (January 29, 1979), p. 36.

21. *Fortune* (September 10, 1979), p. 90.

22. *Harvard Business Review* (November-December 1979), p. 95.

23. The cases developed by Boston University's Public Management Program offer a promising start in this direction.

24. The differences noted in this comparison, for example, in the personnel area, have already changed with the Civil Service Reform Act of 1978 and the creation of the Senior Executive Service. Significant changes have also occurred in the automobile industry: Under current circumstances, the CEO of Chrysler may seem much more like the Administrator of EPA. More precise comparison of different levels of management in both organizations, for example, accounting procedures used by Chapin to cut costs significantly as compared to equivalent procedures for judging the costs of EPA-mandated pollution control devices, would be instructive.

PART TWO

Bureaucracy, Politics, and Public Policy

2

THE POLITICAL SETTING OF PUBLIC ADMINISTRATION

In the Introduction to this collection, we learned that politics is a process and that public policies are the results. We referred to the political system as the policy system in order to make explicit the important stakes in politics. This is not a game without consequences—to all of us, almost every day.

In Chapter 1, Allison stressed how important the political environment was in public administration. In this chapter, we examine carefully the relationship between administrative agencies and politics. Here we have two articles that use both historical and political analysis to illuminate the complexity of this relationship.

In the first article, James Q. Wilson seeks to explain how "Big Government" and especially "Big Bureaucracy" came about. He focuses on the interactions of administrative agencies with their clients, a phenomenon often called *clientelism*. Wilson uses clientelism to explain the growth of governmental activities and especially the increased power of bureaucratic agencies in the policy-making process. Much of his attention is on regulatory agencies.

The federal policy-makers we see most often are the president, Congress, the courts (especially the Supreme Court), and administrative agencies. In this sense, administrative agencies are best understood as *the fourth branch of government*, as depicted in Figure 2-1. At least as described here, there is no

Figure 2-1. The Four Branches of the Federal Government

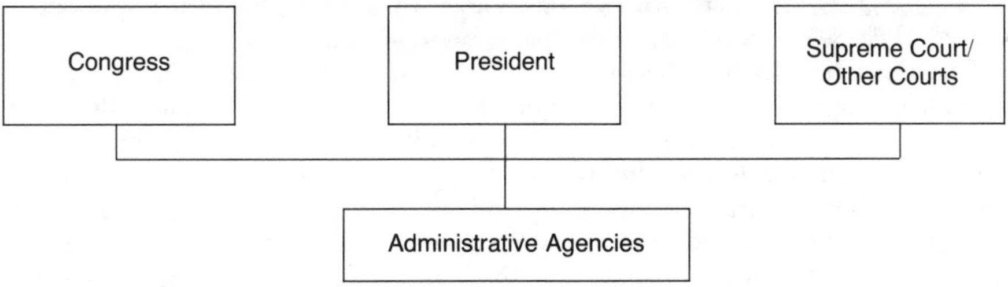

| Congress | President | Supreme Court/ Other Courts |

Administrative Agencies

"executive branch." Rather, there is the presidency—an institution as well as an individual—and many administrative agencies (the bureaucracy).

In the second article in this chapter, Francis E. Rourke carefully examines three recent political developments affecting administrative agencies: divided government, where one political party controls the presidency while another political party has a majority in the legislative branch; the rise of political movements and public interest lobbying groups; and increased policy volatility, where public dissatisfaction and changes in public policies can sometimes be very rapid. If some readers think that "divided government" is less important because of Bill Clinton's election as President, they have only to turn their attention to numerous states—from Massachusetts to California.

These two articles raise many questions:

- How are politics and bureaucracy related?

- What does Wilson mean by "clientelism"? How has it affected administrative agencies?

- How do the three recent trends described by Rourke change the political setting for public administration?

The Rise of the Bureaucratic State

JAMES Q. WILSON

During its first 150 years, the American republic was not thought to have a "bureaucracy," and thus it would have been meaningless to refer to the "problems" of a "bureaucratic state." There were, of course, appointed civilian officials: Though only about 3,000 at the end of the Federalist period, there were about 95,000 by the time Grover Cleveland assumed office in 1881, and nearly half a million by 1925. Some aspects of these numerous officials were regarded as problems—notably, the standards by which they were appointed and the political loyalties to which they were held—but these were thought to be matters of proper character and good management. The great political and constitutional struggles were not over the power of the administrative apparatus, but over the power of the President, of Congress, and of the states.

The Founding Fathers had little to say about the nature or function of the executive branch of the new government. The Constitution is virtually silent on the subject and the debates in the Constitutional Convention are almost devoid of reference to an administrative apparatus. This reflected no lack of concern about the matter, however. Indeed, it was in part because of the Founders' depressing experience with chaotic and inefficient management under the Continental Congress and the Articles of Confederation that they had assembled in Philadelphia. Management by committees composed of part-time amateurs had cost the colonies dearly in the War of Independence and few, if any, of the Founders wished to return to that system. The argument was only over how the heads of the necessary departments of government were to be selected, and whether these heads should be wholly subordinate to the President or whether instead they should form some sort of council that would advise the President and perhaps share in his authority. In the end, the Founders left it up to Congress to decide the matter.

There was no dispute in Congress that there should be executive departments, headed by single appointed officials, and, of course, the Constitution specified that these would be appointed by the President with the advice and consent of the Senate. The only issue was how such officials might be removed. After prolonged debate and by the narrowest of majorities, Congress agreed that the President should have the sole right of removal, thus confirming that the infant administrative system would be wholly subordinate—in law at least—to the President. Had not Vice President John Adams, presiding over a Senate equally divided on the issue, cast the deciding vote in favor of presidential removal, the administrative departments might conceivably have become legal dependencies of the legislature, with incalculable consequences for the development of the embryonic government.

THE "BUREAUCRACY PROBLEM"

The original departments were small and had limited duties. The State Department, the first to be created, had but nine employees in addition to the Secretary. The War Department did not reach 80 civilian employees until 1801; it commanded only a few thousand soldiers. Only the Treasury Department had substantial powers—it collected taxes, managed the public debt, ran the national bank, conducted land surveys, and purchased military supplies. Because of this, Congress gave the closest scrutiny to its structure and its activities.

The number of administrative agencies and employees grew slowly but steadily during the 19th and early 20th centuries and then increased explosively on the occasion of World War I, the Depression, and World War II. It is difficult to say at what point in this process the administrative system became a distinct locus of power or an independent source of political initiatives and problems. What is clear is that the emphasis on the sheer *size* of the administrative establishment—conventional in many treatments of the subject—is misleading.

The government can spend vast sums of money—wisely or unwisely—without creating that set of conditions we ordinarily associate with the bureaucratic state. For example, there could be massive transfer payments made under government auspices from person to person or from state to state, all managed by a comparatively small staff of officials and a few large computers. In 1971, the federal government paid out $54 billion under various social insurance programs, yet the Social Security Administration employs only 73,000 persons, many of whom perform purely routine tasks.

And though it may be harder to believe, the government could in principle employ an army of civilian personnel without giving rise to those organizational patterns that we call bureaucratic. Suppose, for instance, that we as a nation should decide to have in the public schools at least one teacher for every two students. This would require a vast increase in the number of teachers and school rooms, but almost all of the persons added would be performing more or less identical tasks, and they could be organized into very small units (e.g., neighborhood schools). Though there would be significant overhead costs, most citizens would not be aware of any increase in the "bureaucratic" aspects of education—indeed, owing to the much greater time each teacher would have to devote to each pupil and his or her parents, the citizenry might well conclude that there actually had been a substantial reduction in the amount of "bureaucracy."

To the reader predisposed to believe that we have a "bureaucracy problem," these hypothetical cases may seem farfetched. Max Weber, after all, warned us that in capitalist and socialist societies alike, bureaucracy was likely to acquire an "overtowering" power position. Conservatives have always feared bureaucracy, save perhaps the police. Humane socialists have frequently been embarrassed by their inability to reconcile a desire for public control of the economy with the suspicion that a public bureaucracy may be as immune to democratic control as a private one. Liberals have equivocated, either dismissing any concern for bureaucracy as reactionary quibbling about social progress, or embracing that concern when obviously nonreactionary persons (welfare recipients, for example) express a view toward the Department of Health, Education, and Welfare indistinguishable from the view businessmen take of the Internal Revenue Service.

POLITICAL AUTHORITY

There are at least three ways in which political power may be gathered undesirably into bureaucratic hands: by the growth of an administrative apparatus so large as to be immune from popular control, by placing power over a governmental bureaucracy of any size in private rather than public hands, or by vesting discretionary authority in the hands of a public agency so that the exercise of that power is not responsive to the public good. These are not the only problems that arise because of bureaucratic organization. From the point of view of their members, bureaucracies are sometimes uncaring, ponderous, or unfair; from the point of view of their political superiors, they are sometimes unimaginative or inefficient; from the point of view of their clients, they are sometimes slow or unjust. No single account can possibly treat all that is problematic in bureaucracy; even the part I discuss here—the extent to which political authority has been transferred undesirably to an unaccountable administrative realm—is itself too large for a single essay. But it is, if not the most important problem, then surely the one that would most have troubled our Revolutionary leaders, especially those that went on to produce the Constitution. It was, after all, the question of power that chiefly concerned them, both in redefining our relationship with England and in finding a new basis for political authority in the Colonies.

To some, following in the tradition of Weber, bureaucracy is the inevitable consequence and perhaps necessary concomitant of modernity. A money economy, the division of labor, and the evolution of legal-rational norms to justify organizational authority require the efficient adaptation of means to ends and a high degree of predictability in the behavior of rulers. To this, Georg Simmel added the view that organizations tend to acquire the characteristics of those institutions with which they are in conflict, so that as government becomes more bureaucratic, private organizations—political parties, trade unions, voluntary associations—will have an additional reason to become bureaucratic as well.

By viewing bureaucracy as an inevitable (or, as some would put it, "functional") aspect of society, we find ourselves attracted to theories that explain the growth of bureaucracy in terms of some inner dynamic to which all agencies respond and which makes all barely governable and scarcely tolerable. Bureaucracies grow, we are told, because of Parkinson's Law: Work and personnel expand to consume the available resources. Bureaucracies behave, we believe, in accord with various other maxims, such as the Peter Principle: In hierarchical organizations, personnel are promoted up to that point at which their incompetence becomes manifest—hence, all important positions are held by incompetents. More elegant, if not essentially different, theories have been propounded by scholars. The tendency of all bureaus to expand is explained by William A. Niskanen by the assumption, derived from the theory of the firm, that "bureaucrats maximize the total budget of their bureau during their tenure"—hence, "all bureaus are too large." What keeps them from being not merely too large but all-consuming is the fact that a bureau must deliver to some degree on its promised output, and if it consistently underdelivers, its budget will be cut by unhappy legislators. But since measuring the output of a bureau is often difficult—indeed, even *conceptualizing* the output of the State Department is mind-boggling—the bureau has a great deal of freedom within which to seek the largest possible budget.

Such theories, both the popular and the scholarly, assign little importance to the nature of the tasks an agency performs, the constitutional framework in which it is embedded, or the preferences and attitudes of citizens and legislators. Our approach will be quite different: Different agencies will be examined in historical perspective to discover the kinds of problems, if any, to which their operation gave rise, and how those problems were affected—perhaps determined—by the tasks which they were assigned, the political system in which they operated, and the preferences they were required to consult. What follows will be far from a systematic treatment of such matters, and even farther from a rigorous testing of any theory of bureaucratization: Our knowledge of agency history and behavior is too sketchy to permit that.

BUREAUCRACY AND SIZE

During the first half of the 19th century, the growth in the size of the federal bureaucracy can be explained, not by the assumption of new tasks by the government or by the imperialistic designs of the managers of existing tasks, but by the addition to existing bureaus of personnel performing essentially routine, repetitive tasks for which the public demand was great and unavoidable. The principal problem facing a bureaucracy thus enlarged was how best to coordinate its activities toward given and noncontroversial ends.

The increase in the size of the executive branch of the federal government at this time was almost entirely the result of the increase in the size of the

Post Office. From 1816 to 1861, federal civilian employment in the executive branch increased nearly eightfold (from 4,837 to 36,672), but 86 percent of this growth was the result of additions to the postal service. The Post Office Department was expanding as population and commerce expanded. By 1869 there were 27,000 post offices scattered around the nation; by 1901, nearly 77,000. In New York alone, by 1894 there were nearly 3,000 postal employees, the same number required to run the entire federal government at the beginning of that century.

The organizational shape of the Post Office was more or less fixed in the administration of Andrew Jackson. The Postmaster General, almost always appointed because of his partisan position, was aided by three (later four) assistant postmaster generals dealing with appointments, mail-carrying contracts, operations, and finance. There is no reason in theory why such an organization could not deliver the mails efficiently and honestly: The task is routine, its performance is measurable, and its value is monitored by millions of customers. Yet the Post Office, from the earliest years of the 19th century, was an organization marred by inefficiency and corruption. The reason is often thought to be found in the making of political appointments to the Post Office. "Political hacks," so the theory goes, would inevitably combine dishonesty and incompetence to the disservice of the nation; thus, by cleansing the department of such persons these difficulties could be avoided. Indeed, some have argued that it was the advent of the "spoils system" under Jackson that contributed to the later inefficiencies of the public bureaucracy.

The opposite is more nearly the case. The Jacksonians did not seek to make the administrative apparatus a mere tool of the Democratic party advantage, but to purify that apparatus not only of what they took to be Federalist subversion but also of personal decadence. The government was becoming not just large, but lax. Integrity and diligence were absent, not merely from government, but from social institutions generally. The Jacksonians were in many cases concerned about the decline in what the Founders had called "republican virtue," but what their successors were more likely to call simplicity and decency. As Matthew Crenson has recently observed in his book *The Federal Machine*, Jacksonian administrators wanted to "guarantee the good behavior of civil servants" as well as to cope with bigness, and to do this they sought both to place their own followers in office and—what is more important—to create a system of depersonalized, specialized bureaucratic rule. Far from being the enemies of bureaucracy, the Jacksonians were among its principal architects.

Impersonal administrative systems, like the spoils system, were "devices for strengthening the government's authority over its own civil servants"; these bureaucratic methods were, in turn, intended to "compensate for a decline in the disciplinary power of social institutions" such as the community, the professions, and business. If public servants, like men generally in a rapidly growing and diversifying society, could no longer be relied upon "to have a delicate regard for their reputations," accurate bookkeeping, close inspections, and regularized procedures would accomplish what character could not.

Amos Kendall, Postmaster General under President Jackson, set about to achieve this goal with a remarkable series of administrative innovations. To prevent corruption, Kendall embarked on two contradictory courses of action:

He sought to bring every detail of the department's affairs under his personal scrutiny and he began to reduce and divide the authority on which that scrutiny depended. Virtually every important document and many unimportant ones had to be signed by Kendall himself. At the same time, he gave to the Treasury Department the power to audit his accounts and obtained from Congress a law requiring that the revenues of the department be paid into the Treasury rather than retained by the Post Office. The duties of his subordinates were carefully defined and arranged so that the authority of one assistant would tend to check that of another. What was installed was not simply a specialized management system, but a concept of the administrative separation of powers.

Few subsequent postmasters were of Kendall's ability. The result was predictable. Endless details flowed to Washington for decision but no one in Washington other than the Postmaster General had the authority to decide. Meanwhile, the size of the postal establishment grew by leaps and bounds. Quickly the department began to operate on the basis of habit and local custom: Since everybody reported to Washington, in effect no one did. As Leonard D. White was later to remark, "the system could work only because it was a vast, repetitive, fixed, and generally routine operation." John Wanamaker, an able businessman who became Postmaster General under President Cleveland, proposed decentralizing the department under 26 regional supervisors. But Wanamaker's own assistants in Washington were unenthusiastic about such a diminution in their authority and, in any event, Congress steadfastly refused to endorse decentralization.

Civil service reform was not strongly resisted in the Post Office; from 1883 on, the number of its employees covered by the merit system expanded. Big-city postmasters were often delighted to be relieved of the burden of dealing with hundreds of place-seekers. Employees welcomed the job protection that civil service provided. In time, the merit system came to govern Post Office personnel almost completely, yet the problems of the department became, if anything, worse. By the mid-20th century, slow and inadequate service, an inability technologically to cope with the mounting flood of mail, and the inequities of its pricing system became all too evident. The problem with the Post Office, however, was not omnipotence but impotence. It was a government monopoly. Being a monopoly, it had little incentive to find the most efficient means to manage its services; being a government monopoly, it was not free to adopt such means even when found—communities, Congressmen, and special-interest groups saw to that.

THE MILITARY ESTABLISHMENT

Not all large bureaucracies grow in response to demands for service. The Department of Defense, since 1941 the largest employer of federal civilian officials, has become, as the governmental keystone of the "military-industrial complex," the very archetype of an administrative entity that is thought to be so vast and so well-entrenched that it can virtually ignore the political branches of government, growing and even acting on the basis of its own inner imperatives. In fact, until recently the military services were a major economic and political force only during wartime. In the late 18th and early 19th centuries, America was a neutral nation with only a tiny standing army. During the Civil War, over two million men served on the Union side alone and the War Department expanded enormously, but demobilization after the war was virtually complete, except for a small Indian-fighting force. Its peacetime authorized strength was only 25,000 enlisted men and 2,161 officers, and its actual strength for the rest of the century was often less. Congress authorized the purchase and installation of over 2,000 coastal defense guns, but barely six percent of these were put in place.

When war with Spain broke out, the army was almost totally unprepared. Over 300,000 men eventually served in that brief conflict, and though almost all were again demobilized, the War Department under Elihu Root was reorganized and put on a more professionalized basis with a greater capacity for unified central control. Since the United States had become an imperial power with important possessions in the Caribbean and the Far East, the need for a larger military establishment was clear; even so, the average size of the army until World War I was only about 250,000.

The First World War again witnessed a vast mobilization—nearly five million men in all—and again an almost complete demobilization after the war. The Second World War involved over 16 million military personnel. The demobilization that followed was less complete than after previous engagements, owing to the development of the Cold War, but it was substantial nonetheless—the Army fell in size from over eight million men to only half a million. Military spending declined from $91 billion in the first quarter of 1945 to only slightly more than $10 billion in the second quarter of 1947. For the next three years it remained relatively flat. It began to rise rapidly in 1950, partly to finance our involvement in the Korean conflict and partly to begin the construction of a military force that could counterbalance the Soviet Union, especially in Europe.

In sum, from the Revolutionary War to 1950, a period of over 170 years, the size and deployment of the military establishment in this country was governed entirely by decisions made by political leaders on political grounds. The military did not expand autonomously, a large standing army did not find wars to fight, and its officers did not play a significant potential role except in wartime and occasionally as presidential candidates. No bureaucracy proved easier to control, at least insofar as its size and purposes were concerned.

A "MILITARY-INDUSTRIAL COMPLEX"?

The argument for the existence of an autonomous, bureaucratically led military-industrial complex is supported primarily by events since 1950. Not only has the United States assumed during this period worldwide commitments that necessitate a larger military establishment, but the advent of new, high-technology weapons has created a vast industrial machine with an interest in sustaining a high level of military expenditures, especially on weapons research, development, and acquisition. This machine, so the argument goes, is allied with the Pentagon in ways that dominate the political officials nominally in charge of the armed forces. There is some truth in all this. We have become a world military force, though that decision was made by elected officials in 1949–1950 and not dictated by a (then nonexistent) military-industrial complex. High cost, high-technology weapons have become important and a number of industrial concerns will prosper or perish depending on how contracts for those weapons are let. The development and purchase of weapons is sometimes made in a wasteful, even irrational, manner. And the allocation of funds among the several armed services is often dictated as much by interservice rivalry as by strategic or political decisions.

But despite all this, the military has not been able to sustain itself at its preferred size, to keep its strength constant or growing, or to retain for its use a fixed or growing portion of the Gross National Product. Even during the last two decades, the period of greatest military prominence, the size of the Army has varied enormously—from over 200 maneuver battalions in 1955, to 174 in 1965, rising to 217 at the peak of the Vietnam action in 1969, and then declining rapidly to 138 in 1972. Even military hardware, presumably of greater interest to the industrial side of the military-industrial complex, has often declined in quantity, even though per unit price has risen. The Navy had over 1,000 ships in 1955; it has only 700 today. The Air Force had nearly 24,000 aircraft in 1955; it has fewer than 14,000 today. This is not to say the combat strength of the military is substantially less than it once was, and there is greater firepower now at the disposal of each military unit, and there are various missile systems now in place, for which no earlier counterparts existed. But the total budget, and thus the total force level, of the military has been decided primarily by the President and not in any serious sense forced upon him by subordinates. (For example, President Truman decided to allocate one third of the federal budget to defense, President Eisenhower chose to spend no more than 10 percent of the Gross National Product on it, and President Kennedy strongly supported Robert McNamara's radical and controversial budget revisions.) Even a matter of as great significance as the size of the total military budget for research and development has proved remarkably resistant to inflationary trends: In constant dollars, since 1964 that appropriation has been relatively steady (in 1972 dollars, about $30 billion a year).

The principal source of growth in the military budget in recent years has arisen from congressionally determined pay provisions. The legislature has voted for more or less automatic pay increases for military personnel with the result that the military budget has gone up even when the number of personnel in the military establishment has gone down.

The bureaucratic problems associated with the military establishment arise mostly from its internal management and are functions of its complexity, the uncertainty surrounding its future deployment, conflicts among its constituent services over mission and role, and the need to purchase expensive equipment without the benefit of a market economy that can control costs. Complexity, uncertainty, rivalry, and monopsony are inherent (and frustrating) aspects of the military as a bureaucracy, but they are very different problems from those typically associated with the phrase "the military-industrial complex." The size and budget of the military are matters wholly within the power of civilian authorities to decide—indeed, the military budget contains the largest discretionary items in the entire federal budget.

If the Founding Fathers were to return to review their handiwork, they would no doubt be staggered by the size of both the Post Office and the Defense Department, and in the case of the latter, be worried about the implications of our commitments to various foreign powers. They surely would be amazed at the technological accomplishments but depressed by the cost and inefficiency of both departments; but they would not, I suspect, think that our Constitutional arrangements for managing these enterprises have proved defective or that there had occurred, as a result of the creation of these vast bureaus, an important shift in the locus of political authority.

They would observe that there have continued to operate strong localistic pressures in both systems—offices are operated, often uneconomically, in some small communities because small communities have influential congressmen; military bases are maintained in many states because states have powerful senators. But a national government with localistic biases is precisely the system they believed they had designed in 1787, and though they surely could not have then imagined the costs of it, they just as surely would have said (Hamilton possibly excepted) that these costs were the defects of the system's virtues.

BUREAUCRACY AND CLIENTELISM

After 1861, the growth in the federal administrative system could no longer be explained primarily by an expansion of the postal service and other traditional bureaus. Though these continued to expand, new departments were added that reflected a new (or at least greater) emphasis on the enlargement of the scope of government. Between 1861 and 1901, over 200,000 civilian employees were added to the federal service, only 52 percent of whom were postal workers. Some of these, of course, staffed a larger military and naval establishment stimulated by the Civil War and the Spanish-American War. By 1901 there were over 44,000 civilian defense employees, mostly workers in government-owned arsenals and shipyards. But even these could account for less than one fourth of the increase in employment during the preceding 40 years.

What was striking about the period after 1861 was that the government began to give formal, bureaucratic recognition to the emergence of distinctive interests in a diversifying economy. As Richard L. Schott has written, "whereas earlier federal departments had been formed around specialized governmental functions (foreign affairs, war, finance, and the like), the new departments of this period—Agriculture, Labor, and Commerce—were devoted to the interests and aspirations of particular economic groups."

The original purpose behind these clientele-oriented departments was neither to subsidize nor to regulate, but to promote, chiefly by gathering and publishing statistics and (especially in the case of agriculture) by research. The formation of the Department of Agriculture in 1862 was to become a model, for better or worse, for later political campaigns for government recognition. A private association representing an interest—in this case the United States Agricultural Society—was formed. It made every President from Fillmore to

Lincoln an honorary member, it enrolled key congressmen, and it began to lobby for a new department. The precedent was followed by labor groups, especially the Knights of Labor, to secure creation in 1888 of a Department of Labor. It was broadened in 1903 to be a Department of Commerce and Labor, but 10 years later, at the insistence of the American Federation of Labor, the parts were separated and the two departments we now know were formed.

There was an early 19th-century precedent for the creation of these client-serving departments: the Pension Office, then in the Department of the Interior. Begun in 1833 and regularized in 1849, the Office became one of the largest bureaus of the government in the aftermath of the Civil War, as hundreds of thousands of Union Army veterans were made eligible for pensions if they had incurred a permanent disability or injury while on military duty; dependent widows were also eligible if their husbands had died in service or of service-connected injuries. The Grand Army of the Republic (GAR), the leading veterans' organization, was quick to exert pressure for more generous pension laws and for more liberal administration of such laws as already existed. In 1879 congressmen, noting the number of ex-servicemen living (and voting) in their states, made veterans eligible for pensions retroactively to the date of their discharge from the service, thus enabling thousands who had been late in filing applications to be rewarded for their dilatoriness. In 1890 the law was changed again to make it unnecessary to have been injured in the service—all that was necessary was to have served and then to have acquired a permanent disability by any means other than through "their own vicious habits." And whenever cases not qualifying under existing law came to the attention of Congress, it promptly passed a special act making those persons eligible by name.

So far as is known, the Pension Office was remarkably free of corruption in the administration of this windfall—and why not, since anything an administrator might deny, a legislator was only too pleased to grant. By 1891 the Commissioner of Pensions observed that his was "the largest executive bureau in the world." There were over 6,000 officials supplemented by thousands of local physicians paid on a fee basis. In 1900 alone, the Office had to process 477,000 cases. Fraud was rampant as thousands of persons brought false or exaggerated claims; as Leonard D. White was later to write, "pensioners and their attorneys seemed to have been engaged in a gigantic conspiracy to defraud their own government." Though the Office struggled to be honest, Congress was indifferent—or more accurately, complaisant: The GAR was a powerful electoral force and it was ably and lucratively assisted by thousands of private pension attorneys. The pattern of bureaucratic clientelism was set in a way later to become a familiar feature of the governmental landscape—a subsidy was initially provided, because it was either popular or unnoticed, to a group that was powerfully benefited and had few or disorganized opponents; the beneficiaries were organized to supervise the administration and ensure the funding of the program; the law authorizing the program, first passed because it seemed the right thing to do, was left intact or even expanded because politically it became the only thing to do. A benefit once bestowed cannot easily be withdrawn.

PUBLIC POWER AND PRIVATE INTERESTS

It was at the state level, however, that client-oriented bureaucracies proliferated in the 19th century. Chief among these were the occupational licensing agencies. At the time of Independence, professions and occupations either could be freely entered (in which case the consumer had to judge the quality of service for himself) or entry was informally controlled by the existing members of the profession or occupation by personal tutelage and the management of reputations. The latter part of the 19th century, however, witnessed the increased use of law and bureaucracy to control entry into a line of work. The state courts generally allowed this on the grounds that it was a proper exercise of the "police power" of the state, but as Morton Keller has observed, "when state courts approved the licensing of barbers and blacksmiths, but not of horseshoers, it was evident that the principles governing certification were—to put it charitably—elusive ones." By 1952, there were more than 75 different occupations in the United States for which one needed a license to practice, and the awarding of these licenses was typically in the hands of persons already in the occupation, who could act under color of law. These licensing boards—for plumbers, dry cleaners, beauticians, attorneys, undertakers, and the like—frequently have been criticized as particularly flagrant examples of the excesses of a bureaucratic state. But the problems they create—of restricted entry, higher prices, and lengthy and complex initiation procedures—are not primarily the result of some bureaucratic pathology but of the possession of public power by persons who use it for private purposes. Or more accurately, they are the result of using public power in ways that benefited those in the profession in the sincere but unsubstantiated conviction that doing so would benefit the public generally.

The New Deal was perhaps the high water mark of at least the theory of bureaucratic clientelism. Not only did various sectors of society, notably agriculture, begin receiving massive subsidies, but the government proposed, through the National Industrial Recovery Act (NRA), to cloak with public power a vast number of industrial groupings and trade associations so that they might control production and prices in ways that would end the depression. The NRA's Blue Eagle fell before the Supreme Court—the wholesale delegation of public power to private interests was declared unconstitutional. But the piecemeal delegation was not, as the continued growth of specialized promotional agencies attests. The Civil Aeronautics Board, for example, erroneously thought to be exclusively a regulatory agency, was formed in 1938 "to promote" as well as to regulate civil aviation and it has done so by restricting entry and maintaining above-market-rate fares.

Agriculture, of course, provides the leading case of clientelism. Theodore J. Lowi finds "at least 10 separate, autonomous, local self-governing systems" located in or closely associated with the Department of Agriculture that control to some significant degree the flow of billions of dollars in expenditures and loans. Local committees of farmers, private farm organizations, agency heads, and committee chairmen in Congress dominate policy-making in this area—not, perhaps, to the exclusion of the concerns of other publics, but certainly in ways not powerfully constrained by them.

"COOPERATIVE FEDERALISM"

The growing edge of client-oriented bureaucracy can be found, however, not in governmental relations with private groups, but in the relations among governmental units. In dollar volume, the chief clients of federal domestic expenditures are state and local government agencies. To some degree, federal involvement in local affairs by the cooperative funding or management of local enterprises has always existed. The Northwest Ordinance of 1784 made public land available to finance local schools and the Morrill Act of 1862 gave land to support state colleges, but what Morton Grodzins and Daniel Elazar have called "cooperative federalism," though it always existed, did not begin in earnest until the passage in 1913 of the 16th Amendment to the Constitution allowed the federal government to levy an income tax on citizens and thereby to acquire access to vast sources of revenue. Between 1914 and 1917, federal aid to states and localities increased a thousandfold. By 1948 it amounted to over one tenth of all state and local spending; by 1970, to over one sixth.

The degree to which such grants, and the federal agencies that administer them, constrain or even direct state and local bureaucracies is a matter of dispute. No general answer can be given—federal support of welfare programs has left considerable discretion in the hands of the states over the size of benefits and some discretion over eligibility rules, whereas federal support of highway construction carries with it specific requirements as to design, safety, and (since 1968) environmental and social impact.

A few generalizations are possible, however. The first is that the states and not the cities have been from the first, and remain today, the principal client group for grants-in-aid. It was not until the Housing Act of 1937 that money was given in any substantial amount directly to local governments, and though many additional programs of this kind were later added, as late as 1970 less than 12 percent of all federal aid went directly to cities and towns. The second general observation is that the 1960s mark a major watershed in the way in which the purposes of federal aid are determined. Before that time, most grants were for purposes initially defined by the states—to build highways and airports, to fund unemployment insurance programs, and the like. Beginning in the 1960s, the federal government, at the initiative of the President and his advisors, increasingly came to define the purposes of these grants—not necessarily over the objection of the states, but often without any initiative from them. Federal money was to be spent on poverty, ecology, planning, and other "national" goals for which, until the laws were passed, there were few, if any, well-organized and influential constituencies. Whereas federal money was once spent in response to the claims of distinct and organized clients, public or private, in the contemporary period federal money has increasingly been spent in ways that have *created* such clients.

And once rewarded or created, they are rarely penalized or abolished. What David Stockman has called the "social pork barrel" grows more or less steadily. Between 1950 and 1970, the number of farms declined from about 5.6 million to fewer than three million, but government payments to farmers rose from $283 million to $3.2 billion. In the public sector, even controversial programs have grown. Urban renewal programs have been sharply criticized, but federal support for the program rose from $281 million in 1965 to about $1 billion in 1972. Public housing has been enmeshed in controversy, but federal support for it rose from $206 million in 1965 to $845 million in 1972. Federal financial support for local poverty programs under the Office of Economic Opportunity has actually declined in recent years, but this cut is almost unique and it required the steadfast and deliberate attention of a determined President who was bitterly assailed both in the Congress and in the courts.

SELF-PERPETUATING AGENCIES

If the Founding Fathers were to return to examine bureaucratic clientelism, they would, I suspect, be deeply discouraged. James Madison clearly foresaw that American society would be "broken into many parts, interests and classes of citizens" and that this "multiplicity of interests" would help ensure against "the tyranny of the majority," especially in a federal regime with separate branches of government. Positive action would require a "coalition of a majority"; in the process of forming this coalition, the rights of all would be protected, not merely by self-interested bargains, but because in a free society such a coalition "could seldom take place on any other principles than those of justice and the general good." To those who wrongly believed that Madison thought of men as acting only out of base motives, the phrase is instructive: Persuading men who disagree to compromise their differences can rarely be achieved solely by the parceling out of relative advantage; the belief is also required that what is being agreed to is right, proper, and defensible before public opinion.

Most of the major new social programs of the United States, whether for the good of the few or the many, were initially adopted by broad coalitions appealing to general standards of justice or to conceptions of the public weal. This is certainly the case with most of the New Deal legislation—notably such programs as Social Security—and with most Great Society legislation—notably Medicare and aid to education; it was also conspicuously the case with respect to post–Great Society legislation pertaining to consumer and environmental concerns. State occupational licensing laws were supported by majorities interested in, among other things, the contribution of these statutes to public safety and health.

But when a program supplies particular benefits to an existing or newly created interest, public or private, it creates a set of political relationships that make exceptionally difficult further alteration of that program by coalitions of the majority. What was created in the name of the common good is sustained in the name of the particular interest. Bureaucratic clientelism becomes self-perpetuating, in the absence of some crisis or scandal, because a single interest group to which the program matters greatly is highly motivated and well-situated to ward off the criticisms of other groups that have a broad but weak interest in the policy.

In short, a regime of separated powers makes it difficult to overcome objections and contrary interests sufficiently to permit the enactment of a new program or the creation of a new agency. Unless the legislation can be made to pass either with little notice or at a time of crisis or extraordinary majorities—

and sometimes even then—the initiation of new programs requires public interest arguments. But the same regime works to protect agencies, once created, from unwelcome change because a major change is, in effect, new legislation that must overcome the same hurdles as the original law, but this time with one of the hurdles—the wishes of the agency and its client—raised much higher. As a result, the Madisonian system makes it relatively easy for the delegation of public power to private groups to go unchallenged and, therefore, for factional interests that have acquired a supportive public bureaucracy to rule without submitting their interests to the effective scrutiny and modification of other interests.

BUREAUCRACY AND DISCRETION

For many decades, the Supreme Court denied to the federal government any general "police power" over occupations and businesses, and thus most such regulation occurred at the state level and even there under the constraint that it must not violate the notion of "substantive due process"—that is, the view that there were sharp limits to the power of any government to take (and therefore to regulate) property. What clearly was within the regulatory province of the federal government was interstate commerce, and thus it is not surprising that the first major federal regulatory body should be the Interstate Commerce Commission (ICC), created in 1887.

What does cause, if not surprise, then at least dispute, is the view that the Commerce Act actually was intended to regulate railroads in the public interest. It has become fashionable of late to see this law as a device sought by the railroads to protect themselves from competition. The argument has been given its best-known formulation by Gabriel Kolko. Long-haul railroads, facing ruinous price wars and powerless to resist the demands of big shippers for rebates, tried to create voluntary cartels or "pools" that would keep rates high. These pools always collapsed, however, when one railroad or another would cut rates in order to get more business. To prevent this, the railroads turned to the federal government seeking a law to compel what persuasion could not induce. But the genesis of the act was in fact more complex: Shippers wanted protection from high prices charged by railroads that operated monopolistic services in certain communities; many other shippers served by competing lines wanted no legal barriers to prevent competition from driving prices down as far as possible; some railroads wanted regulation to ease competition, while others feared regulation. And the law as finally passed in fact made "pooling" (or cartels to keep prices up) illegal.

The true significance of the Commerce Act is not that it allowed public power to be used to make secure private wealth but that it created a federal commission with broadly delegated powers that would have to reconcile conflicting goals (the desire for higher or lower prices) in a political environment characterized by a struggle among organized interests and rapidly changing technology. In short, the Commerce Act brought forth a new dimension to the problem of bureaucracy: not those problems, as with the Post Office, that resulted from size and political constraints, but those that were caused by the need to make binding choices without any clear standards for choice.

The ICC was not, of course, the first federal agency with substantial discretionary powers over important matters. The Office of Indian Affairs, for a while in the War Department but after 1849 in the Interior Department, coped for the better part of a century with the Indian problem equipped with no clear policy, beset on all sides by passionate and opposing arguments, and infected with a level of fraud and corruption that seemed impossible to eliminate. There were many causes of the problem, but at root was the fact that the government was determined to control the Indians but could not decide toward what end that control should be exercised (extermination, relocation, and assimilation all had their advocates) and, to the extent the goal was assimilation, could find no method by which to achieve it. By the end of the century, a policy of relocation had been adopted *de facto* and the worst abuses of the Indian service had been eliminated—if not by administrative skill, then by the exhaustion of things in Indian possession worth stealing. By the turn of the century, the management of the Indian question had become the more or less routine administration of Indian schools and the allocation of reservation land among Indian claimants.

REGULATION VERSUS PROMOTION

It was the ICC and agencies and commissions for which it was the precedent that became the principal example of federal discretionary authority. It is important, however, to be clear about just what this precedent was. Not everything we now call a regulatory agency was in fact intended to be one. The ICC, the Antitrust Division of the Justice Department, the Federal Trade Commission (FTC), the Food and Drug Administration (FDA), the National Labor Relations Board (NLRB)—all these *were* intended to be genuinely regulatory bodies created to handle under public auspices matters once left to private arrangements. The techniques they were to employ varied: approving rates (ICC), issuing cease-and-desist orders (FTC), bringing civil or criminal actions in the courts (the Antitrust Division), defining after a hearing an appropriate standard of conduct (NLRB), or testing a product for safety (FDA). In each case, however, Congress clearly intended that the agency either define its own standards (a safe drug, a conspiracy in restraint of trade, a fair labor practice) or choose among competing claims (a higher or lower rate for shipping grain).

Other agencies often grouped with these regulatory bodies—the Civil Aeronautics Board, the Federal Communications Commission, the Maritime Commission—were designed, however, not primarily to regulate, but to *promote* the development of various infant or threatened industries. However, unlike fostering agriculture or commerce, fostering civil aviation or radio broadcasting was thought to require limiting entry (to prevent "unsafe" aviation or broadcast interference); but at the time these laws were passed few believed that the restrictions on entry would be many, or that the choices would be made on any but technical or otherwise noncontroversial criteria. We smile now at their naïveté, but we continue to share it—today we sometimes suppose that choosing an approved exhaust emission control system or a water pollution control system can be done on the basis of technical criteria and without affecting production and employment.

MAJORITARIAN POLITICS

The creation of regulatory bureaucracies has occurred, as is often remarked, in waves. The first was the period between 1887 and 1890 (the Commerce Act and the Antitrust Act), the second between 1906 and 1915 (the Pure Food and Drug Act, the Meat Inspection Act, the Federal Trade Commission Act, the Clayton Act), the third during the 1930s (the Food, Drug, and Cosmetic Act, the Public Utility Holding Company Act, the Securities Exchange Act, the Natural Gas Act, the National Labor Relations Act), and the fourth during the latter part of the 1960s (the Water Quality Act, the Truth in Lending Act, the National Traffic and Motor Vehicle Safety Act, various amendments to the drug laws, the Motor Vehicle Pollution Control Act, and many others).

Each of these periods was characterized by progressive or liberal Presidents in office (Cleveland, T. R. Roosevelt, Wilson, F. D. Roosevelt, Johnson); one was a period of national crisis (the 1930s); three were periods when the President enjoyed extraordinary majorities of his own party in both houses of Congress (1914–1916, 1932–1940, and 1964–1968); and only the first period preceded the emergence of the national mass media of communication. These facts are important because of the special difficulty of passing any genuinely regulatory legislation: A single interest, the regulated party, sees itself seriously threatened by a law proposed by a policy entrepreneur who must appeal to an unorganized majority, the members of which may not expect to be substantially or directly benefited by the law. Without special political circumstances—a crisis, a scandal, extraordinary majorities, an especially vigorous President, the support of media—the normal barriers to legislative innovation (i.e., to the formation of a "coalition of the majority") may prove insuperable.

Stated another way, the initiation of regulatory programs tends to take the form of majoritarian rather than coalitional politics. The Madisonian system is placed in temporary suspense: Exceptional majorities propelled by a public mood and led by a skillful policy entrepreneur take action that might not be possible under ordinary circumstances (closely divided parties, legislative-executive checks and balances, popular indifference). The consequence of majoritarian politics for the administration of regulatory bureaucracies is great. To initiate and sustain the necessary legislative mood, strong, moralistic, and sometimes ideological appeals are necessary—leading, in turn, to the granting of broad mandates of power to the new agency (a modest delegation of authority would obviously be inadequate if the problem to be resolved is of crisis proportions), or to the specifying of exacting standards to be enforced (e.g., *no* carcinogenic products may be sold, 95 percent of the pollutants must be eliminated), or to both.

Either in applying a vague but broad rule ("the public interest, convenience, and necessity") or in enforcing a clear and strict standard, the regulatory agency will tend to broaden the range and domain of its authority, to lag behind technological and economic change, to resist deregulation, to stimulate corruption, and to contribute to the bureaucratization of private institutions.

It will broaden its regulatory reach out of a variety of motives: to satisfy the demand of the regulated enterprise that it be protected from competition, to make effective the initial regulatory action by attending to the unanticipated side effects of that action, to discover or stretch the meaning of vague statutory language, or to respond to new constituencies induced by the existence of the agency to convert what were once private demands into public pressures. For example, the Civil Aeronautics Board, out of a desire both to promote aviation and to protect the regulated price structure of the industry, will resist the entry into the industry of new carriers. If a Public Utilities Commission sets rates too low for a certain class of customers, the utility will allow service to those customers to decline in quality, leading in turn to a demand that the Commission also regulate the quality of service. If the Federal Communications Commission cannot decide who should receive a broadcast license by applying the "public interest" standard, it will be powerfully tempted to invest that phrase with whatever preferences the majority of the Commission then entertains, leading in turn to the exercise of control over many more aspects of broadcasting than merely signal interference—all in the name of deciding what the standard for entry shall be. If the Antitrust Division can prosecute conspiracies in restraint of trade, it will attract to itself the complaints of various firms about business practices that are neither conspiratorial nor restraining but merely competitive, and a "vigorous" antitrust lawyer may conclude that these practices warrant prosecution.

BUREAUCRATIC INERTIA

Regulatory agencies are slow to respond to change for the same reason all organizations with an assured existence are slow: There is no incentive to respond. Furthermore, the requirements of due process and of political conciliation will make any response time-consuming. For example, owing to the complexity of the matter and the money at stake, any comprehensive review of the long-distance rates of the telephone company will take years, and possibly may take decades.

Deregulation, when warranted by changed economic circumstances or undesired regulatory results, will be resisted. Any organization, and *a fortiori* any public organization, develops a genuine belief in the rightness of its mission that is expressed as a commitment to regulation as a process. This happened to the ICC in the early decades of this century as it steadily sought both enlarged powers (setting minimum as well as maximum rates) and a broader jurisdiction (over trucks, barges, and pipelines as well as railroads). It even urged incorporation into the Transportion Act of 1920 language directing it to prepare a comprehensive transportation plan for the nation. Furthermore, any regulatory agency will confer benefits on some group or interest, whether intended or not; those beneficiaries will stoutly resist deregulation. (But in happy proof of the fact that there are no iron laws, even about bureaucracies, we note the recent proposals emanating from the Federal Power Commission that the price of natural gas be substantially deregulated.)

The operation of regulatory bureaus may tend to bureaucratize the private sector. The costs of conforming to many regulations can be met most easily— often, *only*—by large firms and institutions with specialized bureaucracies of their own. Smaller firms and groups often must choose between unacceptably high overhead costs, violating the law, or going out of business. A small bakery producing limited runs of a high-quality product literally may not be able to meet the safety and health standards for equipment, or to keep track of and administer fairly its obligations to its two employees; but unless the bakery is willing to break the law, it must sell out to a big bakery that can afford to do these things, but may not be inclined to make and sell good bread. I am not aware of any data that measure private bureaucratization or industrial concentration as a function of the economies of scale produced by the need to cope with the regulatory environment, but I see no reason why such data could not be found.

Finally, regulatory agencies that control entry, fix prices, or substantially affect the profitability of an industry create a powerful stimulus for direct or indirect forms of corruption. The revelations about campaign finance in the 1972 presidential election show dramatically that there will be a response to that stimulus. Many corporations, disproportionately those in regulated industries (airlines, milk producers, oil companies), made illegal or hard-to-justify campaign contributions involving very large sums.

THE ERA OF CONTRACT

It is far from clear what the Founding Fathers would have thought of all this. They were not doctrinaire exponents of laissez-faire, nor were 18th-century governments timid about asserting their powers over the economy. Every imaginable device of fiscal policy was employed by the states after the Revolutionary War. Mother England had, during the mercantilist era, fixed prices and wages, licensed merchants, and granted monopolies and subsidies. (What were the royal grants of American land to immigrant settlers but the greatest of subsidies, sometimes—as in Pennsylvania—almost monopolistically given?) European nations regularly operated state enterprises, controlled trade, and protected industry. But as William D. Grampp has noted, at the Constitutional Convention the Founders considered authorizing only four kinds of economic controls, and they rejected two of them. They agreed to allow the Congress to regulate international and interstate commerce and to give monopoly protection in the form of copyrights and patents. Even Madison's proposal to allow the federal government to charter corporations was rejected. Not one of the 85 *Federalist* papers dealt with economic regulation; indeed, the only reference to commerce was the value to it of a unified nation and a strong navy.

G. Warren Nutter has speculated as to why our Founders were so restrained in equipping the new government with explicit regulatory powers. One reason may have been the impact of Adam Smith's *Wealth of Nations*, published the same year as the Declaration of Independence, and certainly soon familiar to many rebel leaders, notably Hamilton. Smith himself sought to explain the American prosperity before the Revolution by the fact that Britain, through "salutary neglect," had not imposed mercantilist rules on the colonial economy. "Plenty of good land, and liberty to manage their own affairs in their own way" were the "two great causes" of colonial prosperity. As Nutter observes, there was a spirit of individualistic venture among the colonies that found economic expression in the belief that voluntary contracts were the proper organization principle of enterprise.

One consequence of this view was that the courts in many states were heavily burdened with cases testing the provisions of contracts and settling debts under them. In one rural county in Massachusetts the judges heard over 800 civil cases during 1785. As James Willard Hurst has written, the years before 1875 were "above all else, the years of contract in our law."

The era of contract came to an end with the rise of economic organizations so large or with consequences so great that contracts were no longer adequate, in the public's view, to adjust corporate behavior to the legitimate expectations of other parties. The courts were slower to accede to this change than were many legislatures, but in time they acceded completely, and the era of administrative regulation was upon us. The Founders, were they to return, would understand the change in the scale and social significance of enterprise, would approve of many of the purposes of regulation, perhaps would approve of the behavior of some of the regulatory bureaus seeking to realize those purposes, but surely would be dismayed at the political cost resulting from having vested vast discretionary authority in the hands of officials whose very existence—to say nothing of whose function—was not anticipated by the Constitutional Convention, and whose effective control is beyond the capacity of the governing institutions which that Convention had designed.

THE BUREAUCRATIC STATE AND THE REVOLUTION

The American Revolution was not only a struggle for independence but a fundamental rethinking of the nature of political authority. Indeed, until that reformulation was completed the Revolution was not finished. What made political authority problematic for the colonists was the extent to which they believed Mother England had subverted their liberties despite the protection of the British constitution, until then widely regarded in America as the most perfect set of governing arrangements yet devised. The evidence of usurpation is now familiar: unjust taxation, the weakening of the independence of the judiciary, the stationing of standing armies, and the extensive use of royal patronage to reward office-seekers at colonial expense. Except for the issue of taxation, which raised for the colonists major questions of representation, almost all of their complaints involved the abuse of *administrative* powers.

The first solution proposed by Americans to remedy this abuse was the vesting of most (or, in the case of Pennsylvania and a few other states, virtually all) powers in the legislature. But the events after 1776 in many colonies, notably Pennsylvania, convinced the most thoughtful citizens that legislative abuses were as likely as administrative ones: In the extreme case, citizens would suffer from the "tyranny of the majority." Their solution to this problem was, of course, the theory of the separation of powers by which, as brilliantly argued in *The Federalist* papers, each branch of government would check the likely usurpations of the other.

This formulation went essentially unchallenged in theory and unmodified by practice for over a century. Though a sizeable administrative apparatus had come into being by the end of the 19th century, it constituted no serious threat to the existing distribution of political power because it either performed routine tasks (the Post Office) or dealt with temporary crises (the military). Some agencies wielding discretionary authority existed, but they either dealt with groups whose liberties were not of much concern (the Indian Office) or their exercise of discretion was minutely scrutinized by Congress (the Land Office, the Pension Office, the Customs Office). The major discretionary agencies of the 19th century flourished at the very period of greatest congressional domination of the political process—the decades after the Civil War—and thus, though their supervision was typically inefficient and sometimes corrupt, these agencies were for most practical purposes direct dependencies of Congress. In short, their existence did not call into question the theory of the separation of powers.

But with the growth of client-serving and regulatory agencies, grave questions began to be raised—usually implicitly—about that theory. A client-serving bureau, because of its relations with some source of private power, could become partially independent of both the executive and legislative branches—or in the case of the latter, dependent upon certain committees and independent of others and of the views of the Congress as a whole. A regulatory agency (that is to say, a truly regulatory one and not a clientelist or promotional agency hiding behind a regulatory fig leaf) was, in the typical case, placed formally outside the existing branches of government. Indeed, they were called "independent" or "quasi-judicial" agencies (they might as well have been called "quasi-executive" or "quasi-legislative") and thus the special status that clientelist bureaus achieved *de facto,* the regulatory ones achieved *de jure.*

It is, of course, inadequate and misleading to criticize these agencies, as has often been done, merely because they raise questions about the problem of sovereignty. The crucial test of their value is their behavior, and that can be judged only by applying economic and welfare criteria to the policies they produce. But if such judgments should prove damning, as increasingly has been the case, then the problem of finding the authority with which to alter or abolish such organizations becomes acute. In this regard the theory of the separation of powers has proved unhelpful.

The separation of powers makes difficult, in ordinary times, the extension of public power over private conduct—as a nation, we came more slowly to the welfare state than almost any European nation, and we still engage in less central planning and operate fewer nationalized industries than other democratic regimes. But we have extended the regulatory sway of our national government as far or farther than that of most other liberal regimes (our environmental and safety codes are now models for much of Europe), and the bureaus wielding these discretionary powers are, once created, harder to change or redirect than would be the case if authority were more centralized.

The shift of power toward the bureaucracy was not inevitable. It did not result simply from increased specialization, the growth of industry, or the imperialistic designs of the bureaus themselves. Before the second decade of this century, there was no federal bureaucracy wielding substantial discretionary powers. That we have one now is the result of political decisions made by elected representatives. Fifty years ago, the people often wanted more of government than it was willing to provide—it was, in that sense, a republican government in which representatives moderated popular demands. Today, not only does political action follow quickly upon the stimulus of public interest, but government itself creates that stimulus and sometimes acts in advance of it.

All democratic regimes tend to shift resources from the private to the public sector and to enlarge the size of the administrative component of government. The particularistic and localistic nature of American democracy has created a particularistic and client-serving administration. If our bureaucracy often serves special interests and is subject to no central direction, it is because our legislature often serves special interests and is subject to no central leadership. For Congress to complain of what it has created and it maintains is, to be charitable, misleading. Congress could change what it has devised, but there is little reason to suppose it will.

American Bureaucracy in a Changing Political Setting

FRANCIS E. ROURKE

Marked changes in the American political culture in recent years have made life considerably more difficult for national administrative agencies and greatly complicated the task of executive officials charged with managing their affairs. These governmental agencies have had to respond to a continuing public demand both for government services and for a wide range of controls over social and economic activities in American society. This two-fold public demand has persisted even in the face of the deeply antigovernment politics of recent decades.

The fact that government agencies are having trouble doing their work has never been of serious concern in American democracy. After all, constitutional arrangements in the United States were not designed to smooth the way for the exercise of power by the instrumentalities of the state. No amount of anti-bureaucratic rhetoric, however, can obscure the fact that effective national policymaking in the United States, as in other democracies, requires that the elected officials responsible for making policy decisions receive as much help as possible from the permanent organizations of government. The principal question examined here is how changes in American political culture have affected the ability of career civil servants to provide such assistance.

This discussion focuses on three of the changes in modern American politics that have had the most significant effect on the bureaucratic role in the policy process in the United States. The first change is the system of "divided government" that now prevails at the national level—the habit Americans have lately fallen into of putting one political party, the Republicans, in charge of the presidency, while electing a majority of Democrats to a dominant position in either or both houses of the Congress. This unusual form of coalition government has often operated in a surprisingly harmonious way, as each party has gladly seized the opportunity both to have power and to avoid responsibility for its exercise. (A persuasive argument to this effect can be found in Mayhew 1989.) It is, however, an arrangement that has greatly affected the part that career civil servants can play in the development of national policy.

The second important change is the ascent of political movements and public-interest lobbies in American politics. These groups now provide the chief impetus behind policy development in a great variety of government programs in the United States, especially in areas of social policy such as civil rights, environmental protection, and consumer health and safety. The emergence of these new forces on the political scene has disrupted traditional relationships betwen administrative agencies and the groups they serve, presenting these agencies with the difficult task of defining and carrying out policies that will satisfy conflicting demands from an increasingly variegated political support system. Many of the clientele groups within this system are both less supportive and considerably less deferential toward their administrative patrons than was once the case.

The third change is that, along with much of the world, the United States has moved into an era of policy volatility. Dramatic shifts in the direction of government programs have become so commonplace that the old models predicting that public policy would change only at an incremental or gradualist pace look increasingly obsolete.[1] This decline in the incremental style of policy change has had a very visible impact on the role of administrators in the evolution of national policy. Policy volatility is a world that bureaucrats never made, and it is one in which their influence has steadily diminished. The bureaucrats' forte has always been the gradual alteration of existing policy to cope with emerging demands or sudden disturbances in their agencies' environments. They cope with change by adhering to routines that are carefully scripted to deal with similar situations encountered in the past. These routines are often poorly suited to a political culture in which the present radically and frequently departs from the past.

Given these three changes, the question to be confronted here is how they have affected the ability of administrative agencies to contribute to the discourse through which free societies decide on the policies that their governments should follow. Have these changes led to a significant erosion in the opportunities open to career officials to make their voice heard in shaping national policy in the United States? If so, does this erosion of bureaucratic participation in policymaking have a negative impact on the achievement of policy goals? Modern presidents have certainly seemed to believe that it does not. The White House has often operated in recent years on the alternative assumption that national policymaking will most prosper if it is entirely dominated by presidential appointees.

DIVIDED GOVERNMENT

Reformers tend to look at the separation of powers as a source of policy stalemate in American political life. For much of this century, they proposed the development of cohesive political parties that—in the pursuit of common policy goals—would bind the president and the Congress together after an election.[2] In the past three decades, this longstanding aspiration of reformers has finally been realized, and American political parties have indeed achieved such ideological cohesion: Democrats have now become more reliably liberal and Republicans are certainly more consistently conservative.

Irony of ironies, however: this development has served not to bring the two branches of government together but to drive them even further apart. The voters confounded the calculations of reformers by putting a more unified Democratic party in charge of one or both branches of the Congress, even as they were electing Republicans to the presidency.

Observers disagree as to why this odd political coupling has come about.[3] Some suggest the unlikely possibility that it reflects a devious Machiavellian design on the part of the American electorate. In this view, voters—in conformity with the American political tradition—are fearful of putting too much power in the hands of elected officials. They have thus been unwilling to trust either political party with full control over the reins of government. So they have added a political dimension to the institutional separation between the president and the Congress that the Constitution initially prescribed as the most reliable check on the abuse of power by public officials.

Others argue that the emergence of divided government reflects a natural inclination on the part of voters to have their cake and eat it too. The customarily generous Democrats in the Congress give citizens the services and subsidies that they want from government, while a more frugal Republican president provides assurance that the financial burdens necessary to sustain such programs are kept as light (or at least as invisible) as possible for the taxpaying public.

Whatever the validity of these and other explanations for its advent, divided government has had a significant effect on the operation of American political institutions. Not least in importance is the way in which divided government has diminished the ability of civil servants to influence the character of national policy in the United States. It has done so by restricting the discretion allowed to administrative agencies in making day-to-day decisions as they pursue the policy goals entrusted to their care.

Two political developments generated by divided government have played a major role in this respect. The first is the rise of an administrative presidency through which the White House has sought in a variety of ways to centralize executive power in the hands of presidents and their political appointees. The second is the growing tendency of the Congress and congressional committees to subject the decisions of administrative agencies to much closer outside scrutiny, or what its critics describe as legislative "micromanagement."

The Administrative Presidency

When presidents have found themselves confronted with a Congress under the control of the opposition party, as has been the situation normally facing Republican presidents since the 1960s, they have inevitably been tempted to go it alone. They have tried to bring about major policy changes through unilateral executive action rather than by drafting legislation and submitting it to the Congress, where it might easily be derailed. During the Nixon administration, the White House very often saw its strategic alternatives in just such stark terms: the prospect of failure if it sought approval from a Democratic Congress for its policy initiatives; the prospect of success if it was somehow able to finesse the legislative role in policy development altogether.[4]

What the administrative presidency requires more than anything else is the advantageous use of the discretion ordinarily vested in the hands of executive officials. This discretion may come either from the president's constitutional authority, as the White House staff is wont to claim, or from statutes enacted by the Congress that allow executive organizations to enjoy wide latitude in their pursuit of national policy objectives. President Nixon made extensive use of such executive discretion in his efforts to achieve his administration's policy goals. This was particularly visible in his handling of congressional appropriations, where he undertook to impound funds that the Congress had appropriated for programs to which he was opposed. While the courts eventually disallowed this presidential strategy, Nixon's impoundment decisions did impede the implementation of social and economic programs that would have been high on the president's "enemies" list, if the Nixon White House had kept such a list for policies as well as for persons.

The appointment process also presents abundant opportunities to a president determined to follow an administrative strategy of "going it alone"—a strategy under which not only the Congress but much of the executive branch outside the White House is viewed as hostile territory. Both Nixon and subsequently President Reagan appointed executives to run administrative agencies who were openly opposed to many of the goals these agencies were legally mandated to attain. Reagan used this technique in the case of the agency set up to provide legal services for the poor. Alternatively, the White House may deliberately delay appointing an executive to run an agency whose programs it dislikes, so as to weaken the agency's ability to speak with a strong voice in behalf of its programmatic goals or fiscal needs.

While the administrative presidency is mainly designed to increase presidential power at the expense of the Congress, it also serves to reduce the influence of senior career officials in policy discussions within the executive branch. As the system has recently operated, political appointees and sometimes military officers (as in the case of Colonel Oliver North and Admiral John Poindexter in the Iran-Contra affair during the Reagan administration) are the only executive officials whom the White House trusts to use their discretion to advance its policy objectives: political appointees because they are expected to share the president's policy outlook, and military officers because they are thought to be more inclined to defer to their commander-in-chief.

During recent administrations, the number of presidential appointees within the executive branch has multiplied in all directions, and the role of career officials in policy development has correspondingly diminished. This is, as one executive official described it, the equivalent of giving "the federal bureaucracy a lobotomy" (quoted in Heclo 1987, 209). The result is that fewer and fewer career officials are called upon to play important roles in shaping major policy decisions, a development that threatens to make the public service less and less attractive to talented young persons looking for meaningful and challenging job opportunities in government.

Growing Congressional Oversight

In part at least because of its conviction that presidents were ignoring or usurping legislative authority by governing in a unilateral way through the administrative presidency, the Congress has reacted against this presidential strategy. In recent years, the Congress has both strengthened its own surveillance of the executive branch and sought to subject the decisions and actions of executive officials to closer scrutiny by outside forces. Ironically for career officials, this congressional backlash has reinforced the effect of the administrative presidency on the bureaucracy by placing new curbs on the ability of administrators to use their own judgment in exercising their discretionary authority. Under the administrative presidency, both the president and the Congress tend to see bureaucracy as being in the camp of the enemy. Therefore, each institution has a powerful incentive to limit the influence of bureaucrats in the policy process.

The congressional reaction against the administrative presidency has both partisan and ideological roots. The liberal Democrats in the Congress commonly face a Republican regime in the White House that controls and, in their view, often puts a conservative "spin" on the discretion that the Democratic majority in the Congress has intended administrators to use for the pursuit of liberal policy objectives. Congressional Democrats have responded to this threat by strengthening their own ability to oversee and, if necessary, reverse administrative rulings that tilt in a conservative direction. The Congress has also created opportunities for other instruments of oversight—such as public-interest groups and the courts—to challenge or, in the case of the judiciary, to overrule such decisions.

In its various efforts to improve its own oversight capabilities, the Congress has gone a long way toward closing the "expertise gap" that once prevailed in the relationship between the legislature and the executive in this country. In the process of doing so, it has become, as Lawrence Dodd (1989) describes it, almost as "technocratic" as the bureaucracy itself. The Congress has hired an increasingly professionalized staff, created or strengthened its expert advisory institutions (CBO, OTA, CRS, and GAO), and through the poliferation and specialization of its own subcommittees, is now able to conduct a much more sophisticated review of administrative activities. According to Dodd, the principal effect of recent reforms in congressional organization and procedure has been to "put in place a new technocratic government in the Congress, with power passing increasingly to technical experts, including both elected members and nonelected staffers" (pp. 106–7).

Equally important, however, are the efforts that the Congress has made to enhance the ability of groups and organizations outside of government to challenge the way in which administrative agencies use their discretionary authority. The growing influence of public-interest groups in American society is due in no small measure to the fact that liberal Democrats in the Congress have recognized these groups as useful allies in preventing a Republican White House from exploiting administrative discretion to achieve its own conservative policy goals. As one observer notes:

> Republican control of the presidency made liberal Democrats even more wary of placing discretion in the hands of administrators. Encouraging greater participation by "public interest" groups and by "average citizens" was an inviting solution to the problem of administrative discretion. (Melnick 1989, 197)

Environmental statutes, for example, were written by the Congress so as to facilitate challenges in court by public-interest groups opposed to decisions made by the Environmental Protection Agency or other agencies whose decisions had an important environmental impact. They were also designed to strengthen the ability of these groups to prod government agencies to take action to protect the environment whenever the latter seemed reluctant to do so.

The same statutes that eased the ability of private groups to challenge agency action or inaction by taking the executive organization to court also provided an avenue through which the judiciary could become more deeply involved in the task of administrative oversight. This congressional effort to encourage outside challenges to agency decisions can be seen as another example of the risk avoidance at which the national legislature has long been so skilled. Better that tenured judges should make tough policy calls than that members of the Congress who have to run for reelection should do so.

Whatever its motives, the invitation that the legislature handed to the courts to review, and where necessary to reverse, the decisions of administrators was quickly accepted. Even more striking, perhaps, is that the courts began to enjoin administrative agencies to be more energetic in the exercise of their power. The deference to administrative expertise that judges had been practicing since the latter days of the New Deal is now, so to speak, history.

As noted earlier, a strong case can be made that divided government has had much less impact on relations between the president and the Congress than might be expected. There is evidence aplenty that the White House can be just as frustrated by a national legislature dominated by its own party as it is when the Congress is controlled by the political opposition.[5] Moreover, Timothy Conlan (1990) presents convincing evidence that there are situations, like the conflict surrounding enactment of the Tax Reform Act in 1986, where "party competition under divided government can actually propel the enactment of legislation rather than hinder it."[6]

But while its impact on relations between the president and the Congress may have been minimal, the political divergence between the two major governmental institutions in the United States has clearly had pronounced effects on the role of bureaucracy in the American political system. By bringing about the rise of the administrative presidency, divided government has disrupted the alliance that used to exist between presidents and the bureaucracy. Another of its effects, the emergence of a high-powered congressional staff, has eroded the advantage in expertise that executive bureaucrats once enjoyed in dealing with the legislature. Last but not least, divided government has opened a door through which the courts, an old adversary of bureaucracy, have been able to renew and strengthen their influence over agency decision-making.

THE TRANSFORMATION IN AGENCY CONSTITUENCIES

In the past, administrative agencies were able to maintain a highly stable relationship with the outside groups that benefitted from their activities, and these groups could usually be counted on to be highly supportive of the work that an agency did. The durability of the relationship in these earlier days is underlined by the fact that it was conventional to describe it as being one leg in an "iron triangle" system, in which executive agencies drew enduring support not only from their outside clientele but also from the congressional committees that had immediate jurisdiction over their programs.

As it was used in the past, the metaphor of the iron triangle always suggested two of the most salient characteristics of an administrative agency's traditional relationship with its political support system—the strong bonds that held the separate participants together and the power of these participants to prevent outsiders from influencing policy decisions made within the triangular system, or "triocracy," as Louis Galambos has aptly described it (1982, esp. 51–68). Thus, the iron triangle was a highly exclusionary if not actually a closed policymaking system. It maintained the agency's programs as a privileged policy enclave, where an agency might confine itself for many years to cohabiting with groups that had been "present at the creation"—involved, that is, with the organization's birth and early development.

For most administrative agencies today, this closed system is long gone, a casualty of the "glastnost" that swept over American government beginning in the 1960s—long before Soviet President Mikhail S. Gorbachev introduced the Russian term for "openness" into the American vocabulary. In the American case, glastnost was chiefly driven by two developments. The first was the opening up of the internal affairs of public bureaucracies to much greater outside scrutiny—a process that began with the congressional investigations of government secrecy by the so-called "Moss subcommittee" in the late 1950s and that led inexorably to the enactment of freedom of information or "sunshine" legislation in the decades that followed.[7]

Secondly, the American glastnost drew a great deal of impetus from the extraordinary increase in grassroots political activism that began in the 1960s with the civil-rights movement and then spread in a variety of other directions in support of varied causes, such as consumer protection, environmentalism, and worker health and safety. Iron triangles, or "subgovernments" as they were often called, suddenly found themselves beset on all sides by new groups clamoring for a piece of the policy action, or by congressional investigations sparked by charges from such groups that the agency was lax in administering the protective statutes it had been created to enforce.[8]

The enhanced openness of administrative agencies and the ever-increasing intrusion of outside groups into their internal affairs both reflected and have since fostered the growing power of the media in national policymaking. It was pressure from the news organizations that led to the Moss subcommittee investigations into government secrecy in the 1950s and to the eventual triumph of the freedom of information movement. Since that time the media have provided public-interest groups with a platform from which they can draw the country's attention to issues like toxic waste that have now become priority items on the national policy agenda. Moreover, through their own investigative reporting, news organizations have sometimes blazed trails for such public-interest groups to follow.[9]

In the wake of these developments, the political environment in which the average administrative agency now operates has become considerably less supportive and increasingly more adversarial. The number of groups interested in what an agency does has multiplied, and their attitudes toward it, even when the agency is pursuing objectives to which the groups are deeply attached, are often quite hostile. No one has been more critical of the efforts of the National Highway Traffic Safety Administration to promote safety in automobile travel than Ralph Nader, the consumer advocate who has long crusaded in behalf of this cause. As Jeffrey Berry notes, "For many administrators . . . the quiet bargaining of the subgovernment has been replaced by a much more complex and conflictual environment" (1989, 251).

In this new political context, the task of maintaining a favorable balance in their political accounts becomes considerably more difficult for agency executives, who are already operating in a political culture that is highly suspicious of government and all its works. The difficulties that agency officials confront in this new setting are compounded by the fact that many groups within their organization's increasingly diverse constituency are not only inclined to take a more negative view of the agency's performance than was true in the past but also tend to be much better informed than was once the case. Where such constituents relied in the past on agency personnel as their chief source of expertise on the problems with which they were concerned, they are now able to look elsewhere for such professional advice, or even to bring inhouse expertise of their own to bear on policy issues in dispute.

The proliferation of expertise on subjects that bureaucrats may once have monopolized is thus a fact of life for every agency today. As noted earlier in the discussion of increased congressional oversight, expertise has begun to multiply within governmental institutions, as the legislature has begun to catch up with the executive in the quality of its professional staff. Even more important, perhaps, the private sector now abounds with think tanks, consulting firms, and watchdog groups that are widely regarded as more reliable sources of information and advice than the government itself. The specialized knowledge that Max Weber once saw as the comparative advantage that bureaucrats would always enjoy in debates on national policy is now much more widely distributed throughout American society.

In a very influential article, Hugh Heclo (1978) has argued that many agency constituencies today can be more appropriately described as "issue networks" than as "iron triangles." As Heclo describes these networks, they differ from traditional triangles in that their qualification for membership is based not on having some economic or other tangible stake in the decisions that an agency makes, but on being highly knowledgeable about the policy issues that the organization confronts. Heclo's paradigm seems to fit very well for areas of policymaking that are quite technical in character—monetary policy in the economic arena, for example, or the evaluation and application of strategic doctrines in the area of national defense. Whether there is an equally suitable fit in other areas of policy is still being argued.[10]

In any case, if it is true that issue networks are beginning to replace iron triangles as the prime movers in many policy arenas, then further weight is added to the argument that administrative constituencies are increasingly becoming better informed as well as more diversified. It should be noted, however, that this development does not automatically open up the policy dialogue to broader public participation. The issue network's requirement of expertise as a prerequisite for legitimate participation in the policy debate is no less exclusionary than the iron triangle's old precondition that a participant have an economic or other tangible stake in the issues being contested.

But, of course, debates among experts do attract an audience, and as Schattschneider (1960) once noted, this is one of the principal avenues through which a conflict among "insiders" is transformed into a struggle in which outsiders can also participate and make their weight felt in decisions on national policy. Expertise regarding the dangers posed by the depletion of the "ozone layer" or the impact of the "greenhouse effect" on the environment is not widely shared in American society, but the disagreements and debates among scientists who are knowledgeable about such atmospheric phenomena may allow the views of the audience to play a pivotal role in determining which side of the argument carries the day, or as Schattschneider writes, "the audience determines the outcome of the fight" (p. 22).

These twin developments—the increased diversity of constituency groups and the diffusion of expertise on policy issues—have conspired to make the policy views of government organizations less authoritative and consequently more vulnerable to outside criticism in modern American politics. The issue networks on the contemporary scene are much less consensual than were the old-fashioned iron triangles; as Heclo puts it, issue networks provide "a way of processing dissension" (1978, 120). Public administration is thus carried on today in a highly unstable political setting where major segments of its constituency are frequently dissatisfied with an agency's efforts on their behalf and where outside experts constantly question whether the agency is doing the right thing.

For an example of the highly complicated kind of political setting in which an agency might find itself today, witness the case of wetlands management, where the Congress placed policy development under the dual control of the Corps of Engineers and Environmental Protection Agency (EPA). This dual jurisdiction brought environmental policymaking under simultaneous pressure from (a) the economic-development interests traditionally prominent in the Corps' iron-triangle system and (b) the cluster of ecological experts who have always played a leading role in the EPA issue network. Rather than being alternative policymaking systems to which individual agencies may be linked, iron triangles and issue networks may sometimes reinforce one another as sources of potential opposition to agency decisions.[11]

POLICYMAKING VOLATILITY

No area of public policy better exemplifies the changing pattern of policy-making, the shifting role of bureaucracy in the policy process, and especially the volatility of policymaking than does the Social Security system. Originally designed in the 1930s as a retirement program for American wage earners, this system was for decades a model of incremental change, a model in which career officials exercised substantial influence over the direction and pace at which the program developed. A leading student of the program, Carolyn Weaver, goes so far as to claim that the Social Security bureaucracy was the principal force in charting the agency's policies throughout much of its early history. As she writes:

> My reexamination of the history of social security suggests that the bureaucracy, working with and fueling the demands of politicians, played a decisive role in the evolution of the program in the postwar years. The interests of the citizenry, or even the long-term interest of the elderly, cannot be said to have been govern-ing. . . . A complex program, the details of which could be mastered only by experts, removed social security from direct voter as well as legislator control. (Weaver 1987, 54–55)

Weaver's view of the role of bureaucracy in the growth of the Social Security system rests not only on her reading of its history, but also on a theoretical framework she devised for explaining the development of its policies. This model centers attention on the role played by supply-side forces, especially the bureaucracy, in shaping the course of policy change in the United States. Her perspective differs markedly from the conventional view that the evolu-tion of public policy in a democratic society is primarily driven by the shifting demands of citizen groups for public goods. She argues instead that this "de-mand side" view of the policy process ignores the extent to which self-interested parties supplying government services, such as executive agency officials, are active participants in the process through which policy decisions are made.

But, as Weaver herself concedes, her supply-side model is no longer as handy as it once was in explaining Social Security policymaking. During the 1980s, the landmark reforms in this retirement program were initiated by out-side groups like the Greenspan Commission, whose report in 1983 led to broad changes in the Social Security financing system,[12] or by policy entrepre-neurs in the executive and legislative branches of government, such as Dr. Otis Bowen, Secretary of Health and Human Services during the Reagan administration, who was the driving force behind the Medicare Catastrophic Care Act of 1988.[13]

In this new setting in the 1980s, there have been abrupt and stunning rever-sals of Social Security policy. Witness Bowen's Catastrophic Care Act itself, which was both enacted and repealed within the short space of twelve months. The same pattern of policy volatility characterized the agency's administration of its disability program during the 1980s, when, under conflicting pressures from the Reagan White House and the courts, the agency went back and forth on the standards it sought to apply in approving or rejecting disability claims.

In the end, the Congress had to step in to untie the policy knots into which the agency had tied itself; see Mezey (1988).

The recent history of the Social Security system has thus been dominated by two interacting changes: the increasing volatility of policymaking in the field and the diminishing ability of the agency's administrative apparatus to shape the course of its own development. In the early days of the program, when the bureaucracy controlled the evolution of policy, innovations were gradual, centering on an incremental expansion in the number of wage earners included within the system.[14] As outsiders have begun to play a more decisive role in policymaking, the pattern has greatly changed. Shifts in policy have more often been a "great leap forward," or in some cases a sharp break with past practice.

The volatility characteristic of these changes in the Social Security system has been visible in other areas of national policymaking as well. Since the 1960s, for example, there has been an explosive growth in political activism coming from both the left and the right in American politics in support of radical shifts in regulatory policy. Liberals and conservatives have joined in support of far-reaching measures aimed at deregulating key sectors of the economy. Traditional conservative opponents of economic regulation pushed for this deregulation as a means of freeing business organizations from restraints damaging to their effectiveness, while liberals supported it in the belief that it would provide consumers with easier access to goods and services such as airline travel.[15]

But even as the American economy was being deregulated, intense pressure mounted for highly innovative forms of government control in such areas as women's rights, cleaning up the environment, and consumer protection. Regulatory policymaking has thus come under pressure for radical change from opposite directions. One set of reformers has assiduously sought to deregulate the economy, while another has been attempting with equal fervor to break new ground in what is loosely called "social regulation," where noneconomic objectives are of paramount concern.

Even more volatility looms on the horizon in the regulatory field today, in the wake of recent experience in sectors of the economy, such as the financial and telecommunications fields, where deregulation has had some disappointing results, and where pressure is building for some measure of reregulation.

Whatever its other implications, the volatility that has been so common in the recent history of American policymaking both reflects and contributes to a diminishing role for career civil servants in the policy process. The growing use of presidential task forces, commissions, and other kinds of "adhocracies" in major sectors of policymaking in recent years has commonly been interpreted as a no-confidence vote in the ability of the career bureaucracy to generate the policy initiatives required to deal with major problems confronting the country.[16] The working habits of bureaucratic organizations are better adapted to handling the continuing and inescapable tasks of government than they are to implementing the "brave new worlds" in both foreign and domestic policy that liberal and conservative activists have been zealously trying to fashion in recent American politics. As postmortems on Lyndon Johnson's pathbreaking Great Society programs and the counterrevolution led by Ronald Reagan both testify: innovations in policy are much easier for political activists to design than they are for government officials to carry out.

In their pioneering study of how the policy agenda emerges in the United States, Cobb and Elder make the point that policy changes can be driven by both institutional and systemic forces. The primary role in identifying the problems that public officials need to confront may be played by either governmental institutions or by political forces outside of government (1983, 14–16, 85–87). One way of describing what has happened to the role of bureaucracy in this new era of American policymaking is to suggest that administrative institutions have become much less influential in defining the issues with which elected officials should deal, and that systemic forces within the outside political community have become much more important in shaping the policy agenda in the United States, especially in the domestic arena.

BUREAUCRACY AND THE POLICY DISCOURSE

The general tendency of the political changes examined here has been toward diminishing the influence that career civil servants exert over the design and execution of national policy. As this analysis has tried to show, both the president and the Congress have looked elsewhere for advice on policy issues and restricted the discretion allowed to bureaucrats in making the everyday decisions necessary to put policies into effect. In each of these ways the influence of bureaucrats in the policymaking process has been scaled back.

Moreover, the outside groups on which executive agencies could once rely for support are much less likely today to endorse agencies' policy positions. And the movement from incremental to nonincremental styles of decision-making in American politics has given other organizational forms, such as the adhocracies represented by either the commission or the task force, an increasingly prominent role at the cutting edge of policy development.

How, if at all, can these changes be said to have affected the success of national policymaking? What, if anything, does the policy process lose when bureaucrats play a less-important role in policy development than they once did? In the literature on policymaking the contribution that career civil servants can make to the national policy discourse is generally downgraded. Bureaucrats are alledged to be excessively cautious in the advice they give on major policy issues—a timidity rooted in their fear of being held responsible for mistakes.

Their critics also contend that when immediate action is called for, career administrators tend to counsel delay. Or that they shun the possibility of taking bold or unconventional steps—preferring instead the safer path of traditional procedures. In the dramaturgy of American politics, bureaucrats are generally seen as obstructing the pursuit of innovative and imaginative policy options—much to the detriment of the public they serve.[17]

As always, there is an element of truth in such a caricature. In a variety of policy domains, large public organizations and the people who work in them are the chief custodians of whatever wisdom experience has generated in those domains. What these people do best is to apply the knowledge gained from the past to resolve the issues currently facing them. The problems that give them the greatest difficulty are those for which there is no precedent in their organization's previous history. This is why American presidents have so often sought to create new organizations to deal with novel issues confronting the White House. And this is not the least of the reasons for the bureaucratic proliferation in the rapidly changing environment of twentieth-century American politics.

But if there is something in the culture of executive organizations that the standard caricature of bureaucracy captures, there is also much that it misses. In the development of national policy, there are always strong and conflicting pressures between doing something quickly and doing it right. The political sphere commonly generates highly intense pressures for the "quick fix." By way of contrast, bureaucracies are typically focused on the necessity of "getting it right," since these organizations usually have painful memories of mistakes that were made in the past in launching or carrying out policy initiatives that departed widely from past practice.[18]

To be sure, no policymaking system can be effective if it is paralyzed by memories of past mistakes or chooses to focus primarily on the avoidance of error rather than the achievement of results; yet, an abundance of forces in the American political system today are pushing toward radical changes in the direction of national policy. In this volatile political context, there is surely an important role in the policy process for a set of institutions that is primarily committed to the avoidance of error in a political setting otherwise tilted in the direction of achieving short-term results.

Bureaucracies also play an important if not indispensable role in American politics by serving as the chief habitat of professional norms within the policymaking culture. The negative stereotype of bureaucracy commonly emphasizes the close identification of bureaucrats with their own organization and their penchant for promoting its status and power, even when the merits of continued public support for some of its activities may seem highly questionable. What this portrait of administrative behavior chiefly emphasizes is the strong interest that bureaucrats sometimes take in feathering their own nests. What this perspective fails to recognize, however, is that bureaucracies also serve today as the natural habitat of highly trained and very skilled professionals who bring to policy deliberations a critical capacity for both defining the sources of the problem that policymakers confront and identifying the weaknesses of remedies that may be proposed. Moreover, it is common for these experts in scientific and other fields to put adherence to the norms of their craft well ahead of any loyalty they may feel for the government organization by which they happen to be employed.

So if bureaucracies tend to stifle dissent, as is often alleged, it is also true that they provide a haven for very independent or even maverick professionals who are always ready to go public with their disagreement on policy issues—more often than not by "leaking" their critical views to a friendly outside audience.

The promotion of widespread discussion and debate preceding the execution of national policy decisions has always been looked upon as a major practical advantage as well as a moral virtue of policymaking in a democratic society. Bureaucrats, like the other interested parties normally involved in the policy process, have a contribution to make to such a free-wheeling discourse on national policy, even when this contribution is no more than a cautionary tale about the possibility of failure.

Consider, for example, the lesson taught by a recent examination of American involvement in the Vietnam war. The authors point out that a war-game simulation was conducted in 1965 by "a cross section of the best informed and most expert middle-level officials of government" on the eve of a massive expansion in this country's military commitment to the war. The study was "eerily prophetic" of the stalemate to which American intervention eventually led—but its findings never made their way "through the Johnson policy process to the Oval Office." [19]

To be sure this lesson would not find ready acceptance in the arena of American politics. In this political setting it is always easy to find an audience for the unassailable proposition that a policy debate completely dominated by bureaucrats is a violation of the public's right to rule. It is a much greater challenge to elicit support for the alternative possibility that major public policies may sometimes suffer because there has been too little bureaucratic involvement in their design, even though the evidence suggests that administrative agencies can provide the president and the Congress with a very valuable early warning system against costly mistakes in launching new policy ventures.

Notes

1. The classic study of incrementalism is, of course, Braybrooke and Lindblom (1963). For an interesting analysis of incrementalism in recent American policy-making, see Jones (1984, 238–46).
2. James L. Sundquist (1988–89) provides an excellent critique of this reformist orientation.
3. James P. Pfiffner (1989) reviews the varied efforts that have been made to explain the advent of divided government.
4. For a recent discussion of the concept of the administrative presidency by its inventor, see Richard P. Nathan (1986); however, Richard W. Waterman (1989) presents a less sanguine view of the way in which this White House strategy has operated.
5. See Mayhew (1989). Note, however, that Mayhew's argument is not that divided government makes "no difference," but rather that it makes "very little difference" (p. 87).
6. Conlan cites the Clean Air Act of 1970 as another example of legislation that drew much of its force and inspiration from rivalry for political credit between the White House and Congress.
7. For a discussion of the pioneering efforts of the Moss subcommittee to promote openness in government, see Rourke (1961), esp. pp. 107–10, 218–20.
8. "Creedal passion" is the phrase Samuel P. Huntington (1981) uses to describe the primal force that lies behind much of the political action by reform movements today. See especially pp. 85–166.
9. There is a very revealing analysis of the alliance between the media and public interest groups in contemporary American politics by Benjamin Ginsberg and Martin Shefter (1985, esp. pp. 7–8).
10. For a review of some of these arguments, see Berry (1989).
11. I am indebted here to a study of wetlands management policy prepared by Andrew Pavord, a graduate student at Johns Hopkins University.
12. For an analysis of the Greenspan Commission's work, see Light (1985).

13. Bowen's success in overcoming opposition within the Reagan administration to this catastrophic insurance plan is decribed in Thompson (1990).
14. The classic study of the way in which policy changes in the Social Security program evolved over the years is by Martha Derthick (1979).
15. Compare the discussion of the crosspressures to which regulatory agencies are now subject in Harris and Milkis (1989).
16. The role of these temporary organizations in the policymaking process is examined in Rourke and Schulman (1989).
17. For a spirited challenge to these stereotyped images of bureaucracy see Charles T. Goodsell (1983).
18. Two recent studies of policymaking in domestic and foreign affairs provide interesting illustrations of conflicts between the rival imperatives of "getting it right" and "getting it done." David J. Kling (1990) examines this problem in a study of an asbestos cleanup operation managed by EPA. William Bacchus (1990) looks at it from the perspective of the State Department's efforts to develop a better method of handling the flow of refugees from the Soviet Union.
19. See Fred I. Greenstein and John P. Burke (1989–90, 576). Garry Wills (1982) suggests that there was a similar failure to consult knowledgeable bureaucrats before the Kennedy White House launched its ill-fated Bay of Pigs invasion of Cuba in 1961. What the policy process needed in this case, Wills argues, was "more procedure and bureaucratic checking" (p. 230).

Bibliography

Bacchus, William (1990). "U.S. Refugee and Diplomatic Programs in a Rapidly Evolving Foreign Policy Climate: Measuring Program Success." Paper presented at the annual meeting of the American Political Science Association, San Francisco.

Berry, Jeffrey M. (1989). "Subgovernments, Issue Networks, and Political Conflict." In Richard A. Harris and Sidney M. Milkis, eds. *Remaking American Politics.* Boulder, Col.: Westview Press, pp. 239–60.

Braybrooke, David L., and Lindblom, Charles E. (1963). *A Strategy of Decision.* New York: The Free Press.

Cobb, Roger W., and Elder, Charles D. (1983). *Participation in American Politics: The Dynamics of Agenda-Building,* 2nd ed. Baltimore: Johns Hopkins University Press.

Conlan, Timothy J. (1990). "Competitive Government: Policy Escalation and Divided Party Control." Paper presented at the annual meeting of the American Political Science Association, San Francisco.

Derthick, Martha (1979). *Policymaking for Social Security.* Washington, D.C.: Brookings Institution.

Dodd, Lawrence C. (1989). "The Rise of the Technocratic Congress: Congressional Reform in the 1970s." In Richard A. Harris and Sidney M. Milkis, eds. *Remaking American Politics.* Boulder, Col.: Westview Press, pp. 89–111.

Galambos, Louis (1982). *America at Middle Age: A New History of the United States in the Twentieth Century.* New York: McGraw-Hill.

Ginsberg, Benjamin, and Shefter, Martin (1985). "A Critical Realignment? The New Politics, the Reconstituted Right, and the Election of 1984." In Michael Nelson, ed. *The Elections of 1984.* Washington, D.C.: The Congressional Quarterly.

Goodsell, Charles T. (1983). *The Case for Bureaucracy: A Public Administration Polemic.* Chatham, N.J.: Chatham House.

Greenstein, Fred I., and Burke, John P. (1989–90). "The Dynamics of Presidential Reality Testing: Evidence from Two Vietnam Decisions." *Political Science Quarterly* 104 (Winter):557–81.

Harris, Richard A., and Milkis, Sidney M. (1989). *The Politics of Regulatory Change: A Tale of Two Agencies.* New York: Oxford University Press.

Heclo, Hugh (1978). "Issue Networks and the Executive Establishment." In Anthony King, ed. *The New American Political System.* Washington, D.C.; American Enterprise Institute, pp. 87–124.

——— (1987). "The In-and-Outer System: A Critical Assessment." In G. Calvin Mackenzie, ed. *The In-and-Outers: Presidential Appointees and Transient Government in Washington.* Baltimore: Johns Hopkins University Press.

Huntington, Samuel P. (1981). *American Politics: The Promise of Disharmony.* Cambridge, Mass.: Harvard University Press.

Jones, Charles O. (1984). *An Introduction to the Study of Public Policy.* Monterey, Calif.: Brooks/Cole Publishing.

Kling, David J. (1990). "Federal Asbestos Funding for Schools: Public Administration in a Pinch." Paper presented at the annual meeting of the American Political Science Association, San Francisco.

Light, Paul (1985). *Artful Work: The Politics of Social Security Reform.* New York: Random House.

Mayhew, David R. (1989). "Does It Make a Difference Whether Party Control of the American National Government Is Unified or Divided?" Paper presented at the annual meeting of the American Political Science Association, Atlanta.

Melnick, R. Shep (1989). "The Courts, Congress, and Programmatic Rights." In Richard A. Harris and Sidney M. Milkis, eds. *Remaking American Politics.* Boulder, Col.: Westview Press, pp. 188–212.

Mezey, Susan Gluck (1988). *No Longer Disabled: The Federal Courts and the Politics of Social Security Disability.* New York: Greenwood Press.

Nathan, Richard P. (1986). "Institutional Change under Reagan." In John L. Palmer, ed. *Perspectives on the Reagan Years.* Washington, D.C.: Urban Institute Press, pp. 121–45.

Pfiffner, James P. (1989). "Divided Government and the Problem of Governance." Working Paper of the Center for Congressional and Presidential Studies (89-4). Washington, D.C.: The American University, November 8.

Rourke, Francis E. (1961). *Secrecy and Publicity: Dilemmas of Democracy.* Baltimore: Johns Hopkins University Press.

Rourke, Francis E., and Schulman, Paul R. (1989). "Adhocracy in Policy Development." *The Social Science Journal* 26:131–42.

Schattschneider, E. E. (1960). *The Semi-Sovereign People.* Holt, Rinehart and Winston.

Sundquist, James L. (1988–89). "The New Era of Coalition Government in the United States." *Political Science Quarterly* 103 (Winter):613–35.

Thompson, Carolyn R. (1990). "The Political Evolution of the Medicare Catastrophic Health Care Act of 1988." Ph.D. diss. Johns Hopkins University.

Waterman, Richard W. (1989). *Presidential Influence and the Administrative State.* Knoxville, Tenn.: University of Tennessee Press.

Weaver, Carolyn L. (1987). "The Social Security Bureaucracy in Triumph and in Crisis." In Louis Gallambos, ed. *The New American State: Bureaucracies and Policies Since World War II.* Baltimore: Johns Hopkins University Press, pp. 54–84.

Wills, Garry. (1982). *The Kennedy Imprisonment: A Meditation on Power.* Boston: Little, Brown.

3

PUBLIC POLICY AND ADMINISTRATION IN A FEDERAL SYSTEM

Policy-making in America does not occur only at the national level. We are in a federal system, which consists of national, state, and local levels. Interactions among these levels of policy-making are critical in understanding the process and the results; in our federal system, policy-making roles are shared, and the relationships among the levels are constantly changing. In the end, federalism is a contradiction: it tries to marry diversity and central direction.

A number of trends in intergovernmental relations (IGR) should be recognized:

- The emergence of local government, especially cities, as a full partner in the federal system
- The demand for a national urban policy since the late 1960s, but the failure of several administrations to come to grips with these issues
- The historic default of the states in policy leadership, although this is changing
- Increased competition for federal funding among the regions of the country, especially the "Frost Belt" and the "Sun Belt"
- Attempts at simplification to make federal grant programs work better because of fewer restrictions and regulations
- Calls for a "new federalism" by President Reagan to shift greater governmental responsibility to states and localities

Federalism has three principal dimensions: political, economic (or fiscal), and administrative. The political aspect is the most visible, as when President Clinton meets with a group of mayors about the nation's drug problem. Administrative federalism often seems nearly invisible, as when specialists in criminal justice discuss state and local implementation of a federal program.

Economist and public executive Alice Rivlin has recently published a book suggesting that the federal government has taken on too much responsibility and should return some of its functions to the states. She also seeks a clearer division of responsibilities between the states and the federal government so, she says, both levels could operate more effectively. Yet her own historical analysis of federalism and intergovernmental relations indicates that this has not been the case. In the first article here, Rivlin provides a short, analytical history of the way federalism has worked in this century.

The second article in this chapter, by three well known public administration scholars, looks at recent changes in the states that might indicate that they are ready for a greater leadership role in our federal system. They focus on such issues as the expanding scope of state responsibilities, proliferation of state administrative agencies, and increased professionalism and representativeness among state-level managers.

Some discussion questions for Chapter 3 are:

- What are the principal patterns of federalism—political, fiscal, and administrative—that have developed in the United States?

- Could the public policy roles between the states and the federal government be rearranged in a more rational way? What are the obstacles?

- Are the states really doing better? Are they ready for a new position of leadership in making our federal system work?

- Look at your state. Where does it stand in the changes Hebert, Wright, and Brudney describe?

The Evolution of American Federalism

ALICE M. RIVLIN

. . . For much of the twentieth century, power has flowed toward Washington and the functions of federal and state government have become increasingly intertwined. Why did this happen? Are the reasons for the blurring of distinctions between federal and state government still valid today?

CHANGING VIEWS OF FEDERALISM

To the Founding Fathers, the division of responsibility between the states and the federal government was a crucial issue with high emotional and intellectual content. Most of them believed that the states should retain a large measure of autonomy. Their experience with the English crown made them nervous about lodging too much power in any central government. Life under the Articles of Confederation, however, demonstrated that the national government could not function effectively if its powers were too narrow or if it depended on state contributions for revenue. Hence the drafters of the Constitution gave the federal government limited but quite specific powers, including the power to levy and collect taxes. To reduce misunderstanding, they later added a Tenth Amendment stating explicitly that "the powers not delegated to the United States by the Constitution, nor prohibited by it to the States, are reserved to the States respectively, or to the people."

The Tenth Amendment seems clear enough, but the Constitution itself was a document drafted by a committee. It contained some language suggesting more comprehensive powers for the national government, such as the statement that Congress should provide for "the general welfare." Hence the Constitution did not permanently settle the controversies about which level of government should have which functions. It did, however, create a framework for debating and resolving conflicts between the federal government and the states that has stood the test of more than two centuries.

From 1789 to about 1933, all levels of government were small by modern standards, but the states were clearly more important than the federal government, except possibly in time of war. Moreover, the two levels of government usually ran on separate tracks, each in control of its own set of activities. Scholars called the arrangement "dual federalism."

From the Great Depression through the 1970s, all levels of government expanded their activities, but power shifted to Washington. The federal government took on new responsibilities, and the distinction between federal and state roles faded. Scholars talked about "cooperative federalism."

By the beginning of the 1980s, the drive for centralization had peaked, and power began shifting back to state capitals. No new concept emerged, however, of how responsibilities should be divided. The current era has been called a period of "competitive federalism," meaning the federal government and the states are competing with each other for leadership in domestic policy.[1]

SMALL GOVERNMENT AND DUAL FEDERALISM

The national government created by the Constitution was charged with defending the new country and dealing with the rest of the world. It sent diplomats to foreign capitals, dealt with the Tripoli pirates, fought the invading British, invaded Mexico, and warred with Spain. Above all, it kept the nation together despite the disaster of the Civil War and the tensions of reuniting North and South.

In the nineteenth century, much of the national government's attention was devoted to acquiring territory and encouraging its settlement and development. Washington granted land to settlers and developers and encouraged the entry of new states. It fostered trade and interstate commerce and subsidized canals and railroads. It arranged the delivery of mail, managed the national currency—often with conspicuous lack of success—and encouraged the growth of banks.

Sometimes economic development shaded into what is now called "social policy." For example, new states were given land grants for public schools. In 1862 the national government endowed land grant colleges to teach agriculture and the "mechanical arts" and later (in 1890) granted these institutions a modest annual subsidy. The federal government also engaged in a few public health activities early in its history, such as maintaining hospitals for merchant seamen. In general, however, social policy matters such as education, health, and aid to the poor were the concern of state and local governments or private charity.

By the end of the nineteenth century, the excesses of big business and the human cost of unfettered profit seeking were arousing public anger and creating pressure for federal intervention. Antitrust laws reined in monopolies. In the early years of the twentieth century, the "muckrakers" pointed to scandalous health, safety, and labor practices, and the Progressive movement fought for corrective action. The federal government moved to regulate food adulteration, child labor, and other abuses. Progressives had more success in some states, however, than they did in Washington, in part because the courts took a narrow view of the role of the federal government.

Dual federalism was never absolute. Even in the nineteenth century, there were instances of federal-state cooperation on law enforcement or public works and modest overlaps of functions.[2] Scope for intertwining of functions was minimal, however. The national government was remote from most citizens and its activities were few.

Until the early years of the twentieth century, the modest scope of the federal government did not require a broad-based tax system. Revenues from customs duties and the sale of public lands amply covered peacetime spending. Indeed, there was often a surplus of funds. A federal income tax, although used briefly to help finance the Civil War, was thought to be unconstitutional.

In 1913 the Constitution was amended to permit the federal government to levy an income tax, and the Federal Reserve System was created to put banking and credit on a more solid basis. The Federal Reserve was eventually to give Washington a powerful set of tools for influencing the economy by controlling money, credit, and interest rates. The federal income tax was ultimately to finance a huge expansion in federal activities. Both developments, however, lay in the future. In the 1920s, conservatives dominated Washington and the federal role remained limited. In 1929 total federal spending was under 3 percent of GNP. States and localities spent almost three times as much as the federal government.[3]

TWO REASONS FOR FEDERAL GROWTH

In the great Depression of the 1930s, the federal government took on new responsibilities, and its budget grew rapidly. Federal domestic functions continued to expand after World War II, even as America's worldwide responsibilities were growing (Figure 3-1). By the late 1950s federal domestic outlays

Figure 3-1.   Domestic Government Expenditures, Selected Periods, 1947–90

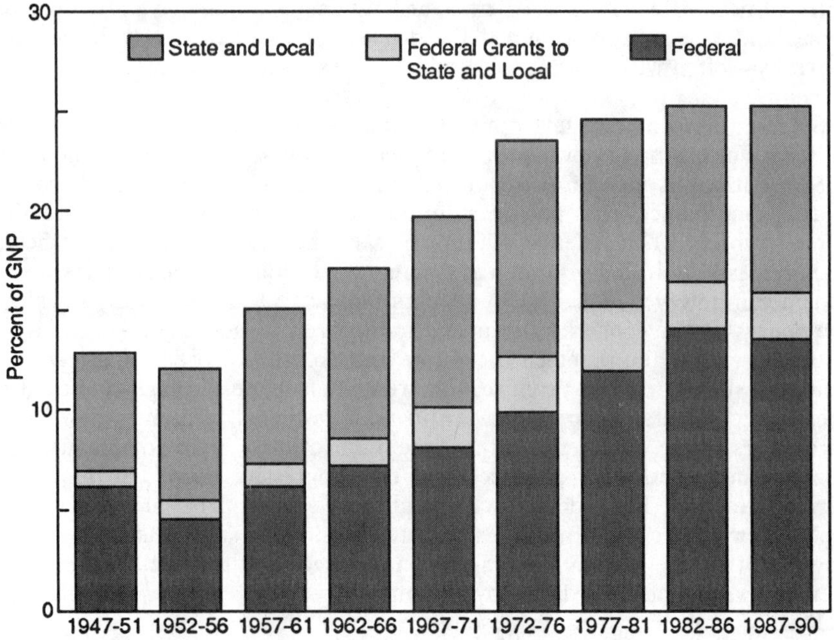

Source: *Budget of the United States Government, Fiscal Year 1992*, tables 1.2, 3.1, 15.2.

exceeded amounts spent by state and local governments from their own sources.

This escalation of Washington's role is often seen as a single juggernaut of centralization, sweeping power toward Washington. Two sources of growth, however, should be distinguished. One was the evolving conviction, dramatically reinforced by the Great Depression, that new national institutions were needed to strengthen the economy and perform functions that states could not be expected to perform on their own. This conviction prompted a wave of institution building that included both purely federal activities and joint federal-state efforts.

A second source was the escalating perception, reinforced by the civil rights movement, that states were performing badly even in areas that almost everyone regarded as properly assigned to them. Frustrated with the states, reformers urged the federal government to augment state spending and redirect state and local priorities. The result was a rapid proliferation of grants to states—and directly to their localities—designed to strengthen their capacities and influence their decisions.

BUILDING NATIONAL INSTITUTIONS

The Great Depression brought the economy close to collapse and radically altered the role of the federal government. The stock market crash of October 1929 presaged an economic freefall. Factories and businesses closed, millions of workers lost their jobs, the banking system tottered, and citizens were frightened and insecure. President Herbert Hoover, unable to stem the tide of economic disintegration, lost the 1932 election in a landslide to Franklin D. Roosevelt, who proclaimed a "New Deal."

The Roosevelt government took over in mid-crisis. Its first task was to get the economy functioning again. To stop a disastrous run on the banks, the new administration briefly closed all banks and then reopened them under new rules. Over a quarter of the labor force was unemployed. The federal government handed out emergency relief. It put people to work on a vast array of projects from building dams and schools to painting murals and recording folk music. The federal government created institutions to buy home and farm mortgages from hard-pressed banks and reschedule them so families could retain their homes and farms. It lent money to businesses on favorable terms and prodded industry to produce and hire. These efforts helped to revive the economy, but unemployment was still high at the end of the 1930s. Only World War II got the economy booming again.

The Great Depression revealed weaknesses of a highly unregulated and decentralized economic system. It changed the public's view of the desirable role of the federal government and impelled the president and the Congress, despite initial resistance from the Supreme Court, to create federal institutions and programs to reduce the chances of economic disaster striking again.

Since the weakness of the banks had nearly brought the economy to a halt, the architects of reform were eager to strengthen banking, credit, and financial systems. Deposit insurance, bank and thrift regulation, and housing and farm credit institutions greatly increased the stability of the banking system and made it easier for business, homeowners, and farmers to obtain credit.

Agricultural distress and rural poverty, aggravated by the worldwide collapse of commodity prices, bad weather, and poor farming practices, dramatized the need for regional development and agricultural assistance. The federal government brought electricity to rural areas, built dams to supply power and control floods, supported agricultural prices, and aided large and small farmers.

A strong national commitment to a freer world trading system also began in the Depression. The U.S. Smoot-Hawley Tariff Act of 1930 had set off a tariff war that was widely blamed for precipitating the worldwide depression. The United States took the lead in reversing course and working with other nations for reciprocal lowering of trade barriers.

The human suffering of the Great Depression, brought on by massive unemployment and falling wages, created public pressure for permanent institutions to protect individuals from the impact of economic catastrophes beyond their control. The institution builders responded with two different approaches: social insurance and welfare programs.

Social Insurance

Social insurance enables the population to pool certain risks, such as losing income because of unemployment, disability, retirement, or death of the family breadwinner. Workers pay a portion of their wages (usually matched by their employer) into a government fund while they are working and are entitled to benefits when they retire or when specified disasters strike. Social insurance taxes are analogous to insurance premiums or private pension contributions. Those who have contributed long enough do not have to prove that they are destitute to get benefits—just that they are disabled or unemployed or retired. Unlike welfare, there is no means test and no shame in accepting benefit checks.

The Social Security System   The biggest social insurance program, social security, evolved from small beginnings in 1935 into a strong and extremely popular national institution. Workers covered by social security pay a tax on their earnings, matched by their employer. In return, when they retire they receive a pension whose level is related to their past earnings. Benefits are paid to disabled workers and to survivors if the worker dies. The social security system gradually expanded to include virtually all workers; benefits increased over several decades. In 1965 medical benefits for the elderly (the medicare program) were added to the social security system.

Unemployment Insurance   Unlike social security, the unemployment insurance system, set up in response to the massive unemployment of the Great Depression, was a joint state and federal effort. The federal government assisted the states in setting up unemployment insurance funds and established many of the rules, but left the level of contributions and benefits up to the states themselves.

Social insurance proved a popular, successful, and enduring concept. Part of its popularity relates to the contributory feature and the specificity of the benefits. People feel they are paying for identifiable benefits that will be there if they need them. They object less to social insurance taxes than to the general taxes that support government services whose benefits are widely dispersed and hard to identify.

Welfare Programs

Social insurance was a response to the economic hardships of the 1930s, but could not be an immediate solution. Workers had to build up eligibility for future benefits. Meanwhile, people were destitute. State welfare programs were totally swamped. To meet part of the need, the federal government put in place a set of means-tested welfare programs to provide income to some poor families and individuals. The elderly, blind, and disabled and women supporting children were entitled to payments if they could prove that they had inadequate means. Like the social insurance programs, these welfare programs were "entitlements": people who met the requirements specified in the law were entitled to benefits. However, the benefits were paid out of general government revenues, not out of a fund to which beneficiaries contributed.

The welfare programs were expected to become less necessary as social insurance coverage widened and gave people who were unemployed, retired, or disabled a means of support. The hope was that widows with children would increasingly be covered by survivors' benefits under social security; the subsequent growth of the number of divorced and single women with children was not anticipated.

Social insurance did reduce poverty, but the means-tested programs did not disappear. Indeed, rising concern about low-income families (especially women with children) prompted not only the expansion of aid to families with dependent children (AFDC), but the addition of other federal means-tested programs in the 1960s and 1970s, including food stamps, expanded housing assistance, and medicaid (the joint federal-state program that finances medical care for low-income people).

Funding and responsibility for welfare programs were shared by federal and state governments (and in some states, by local governments as well) in complex and interlocking ways. In general, the federal government made the rules about who would be eligible for benefits on what conditions, but states set the actual benefit levels and administered the funds. The federal government matched the money paid out by the state according to a formula that gave more federal money (per dollar of state money) to poorer states. Benefit levels varied substantially, with poor states generally providing low benefits despite proportionately higher assistance from the federal government.[4]

Stabilizers for the Economy

Social insurance and welfare programs not only provided income to individuals and families facing economic disaster, they also made economic disaster less likely. If economic activity dropped off sharply, the downward spiral would be cushioned, since individuals drawing social insurance benefits and welfare would be able to buy necessities and pay their rent or mortgages. This increased purchasing power would bolster the income of producers and prevent layoffs of workers and forced sales of homes. Thus both welfare programs and social insurance would act as automatic stabilizers for the economy.

Other National Initiatives

Growing federal activities cost money, but Washington was not short of funds. Federal income tax rates were raised to high levels to finance World War II, and withholding was introduced in 1943. Both personal and corporate taxpayers got used to paying a significant portion of their income to the federal government. Moreover, in the good news period . . . , personal incomes and business profits rose rapidly. Even after taxes, almost everyone was doing well. The federal tax system was generating so much revenue that new programs could be funded while tax rates were reduced. Moreover, the share of GNP devoted to defense declined gradually after the Korean War buildup in the early 1950s. Domestic spending growth could be accomplished without commensurate increases in the overall federal share of GNP.

By 1960 the federal government's budget for domestic programs alone had grown to 8.1 percent of GNP.[5] Between 1933 and 1960, the role of the federal government had changed from that of a minor player on the domestic government scene to a major one.

INFLUENCING AND REFORMING THE STATES

Despite the growth in some types of federal programs, many types of public services were still considered very much the business of the states until the early 1960s. Elementary and secondary education, health services, police and fire protection, sanitation, social services, and most other direct services to citizens were still viewed as overwhelmingly state and local matters.

Only occasionally did Washington intervene in these areas to further an objective deemed worthy of national attention. For example, the federal government began giving the states grants for vocational education programs in high schools as early as 1917. In the late 1950s, when the Soviet Union's Sputnik launch focused attention on technical education, Washington set up grant programs designed to improve science, mathematics, and language teaching in the schools (the National Defense Education Act). These "categorical" grant programs accumulated slowly over the years and then exploded in the 1960s and 1970s.

In the 1960s, President Lyndon B. Johnson's Great Society programs reflected mounting dismay that the states were not performing effectively and were shortchanging the poor, urban dwellers, and minorities. States and their local governments were seen as lacking the means and the capability to provide services in a modern society. Federal programs were designed explicitly to change the way states performed their own functions.

The Sad State of the States

Dissatisfaction with the states had been building for several decades, starting with the Great Depression. State governments were unable to cope with the nation's economic crisis. Reformers turned to the federal government, which responded with a blizzard of new activity. Some began to regard the states as anachronisms that might eventually fade from the American governmental scene. Political scientist Luther Gulick declared in the depths of the Great Depression, "It is a matter of brutal record. The American State is finished. I do not predict that the states will go, but affirm that they have gone."[6]

The challenges of World War II further augmented the powers of the federal government, and activists continued to turn to Washington to deal with perceived needs of the postwar economy for housing, hospitals, and an interstate highway system. Bashing the states was a popular sport. Writing in 1949, Robert S. Allen characterized state government as "the tawdriest, most incompetent and most stultifying unit of the nation's political structure."[7]

By the early 1960s, when national concern about minorities and the poor was rising, states were seen as perpetrators of discrimination. The southern states were overtly racist, defiant of federal efforts to desegregate schools and other public facilities and to ensure the participation of all races in the political process. Moreover, the indictment of states went far beyond the South and beyond issues of race and poverty. As Frank Trippett put it: "One glaring truth of the times is that most of the perplexing domestic problems confronting the country today would not exist if the states had acted."[8] Terry Sanford, a former governor of North Carolina, concurred: "Because many groups and people have encountered evasion of duty by the state, they have felt that they had no choice but to try the road to Washington. The trek to Washington could have been expected, for government is not static." Sanford, a strong believer in the necessity and feasibility of state reform, conceded, "If nothing much can be done, then indeed the states will soon be finished."[9]

The weakness of state government involved both the executive and legislative branches. In many states, governors had relatively few powers and short terms of office. They had small staffs composed of political appointees with limited professional qualifications. They presided over executive branch departments that were often fragmented, poorly organized, and staffed with bureaucrats who had limited training and education and few of the tools and skills of modern government. The office of governor itself often attracted "good-time Charlies" at the end of careers in the private sector. Abler politicians gravitated toward the federal government, where there was more scope for their talents.

State legislatures, before the reforms that began in the 1960s, were far from models of strong democratic institutions. Legislatures often met for only a few weeks every other year. Members served part time, were paid little, and were dependent on their primary jobs. They had hardly any staff, usually not even clerical support.

Rural areas typically dominated the legislature. Cities and their growing suburbs were underrepresented, as were minorities and lower-income people. Rural overrepresentation was often built into state constitutions that required equal representation of sparsely populated rural counties and densely populated urban ones. In many states, entrenched rural interests had simply prevented reapportionment of the legislature for years or even decades. In 1962 Tennessee had not reapportioned its legislature since 1901. Eight states had not redistricted in more than fifty years, and twenty-seven states had not redistricted in more than twenty-five years.[10] "Some of the resulting inequalities were spectacular. In 1960 the five largest counties in Florida had half the population and 5 of 38 Senate seats; the Senate districts ranged in population from 10,000 to 935,000. Los Angeles County had 40 percent of California's population and only 1 of 40 seats."[11]

Although larger, richer states, such as New York and California, tended to have more capable governments, states in general did not inspire confidence. They were seen as "errand boys" of the federal government, helping to carry out policy formulated at the national level. Even this role diminished as the federal government increasingly bypassed states and dealt directly with local governments.

The Civil Rights Revolution

The civil rights movement, which gathered steam in the 1950s and reached a climax in the 1960s, profoundly altered the relationship of the federal government to states and localities. The Civil War, nearly a century earlier, had freed the slaves and amended the Constitution in an attempt to guarantee equal rights for all races. In fact, however, blacks, especially but not exclusively in the South, were denied basic political rights (including the right to vote), excluded from public facilities and services, discriminated against in employment, educated in separate and inferior schools, denied access to higher education, and otherwise relegated to second-class citizenship and economic deprivation.

After World War II, growing outrage on the part of blacks and a rising proportion of the whole population swelled into a national movement. State segregation laws were challenged in the federal courts under the U.S. Constitution, and the federal government passed legislation spelling out equal rights in greater detail. In 1954, in *Brown* v. *Board of Education*, the Supreme Court rejected the idea that separate schools could be regarded as equal. Gradually, schools, universities, and other public facilities were desegregated, but not without dramatic confrontations between state and federal officials.

Enforcing civil rights laws involved the assertion of federal authority in schools, parks, hospitals, restaurants, hotels, and other facilities that had not heretofore been seen as areas of federal concern. Efforts to right past wrongs involved increasingly complex intrusion on state and local autonomy. Even after legal segregation of school systems was abrogated, for example, de facto racial segregation remained because blacks and whites lived in different neighborhoods. As a result, the courts searched for ways of achieving racial desegregation of the schools by redrawing school boundaries and busing children out of their neighborhoods.

The War on Poverty

The civil rights movement, by focusing attention on economic as well as political deprivation of minorities, aroused concern about the general prevalence of poverty. Americans rediscovered that even in their prosperous country a large population, in both rural and urban areas, lived at the margin of subsistence. The poor included low-wage workers in agriculture, manufacturing, and service industries, dwellers in depressed areas such as Appalachia and the Mississippi Delta, native Americans, and Hispanics. Blacks were only about a quarter of the poor.

In 1964 President Johnson called for a war on poverty. He sent an avalanche of proposals to Congress designed to change the lives of the poor in a variety of ways. Most were enacted in a frenzy of legislative activity that rivaled the early days of the New Deal.

The Investment Strategy   The strategists in the war on poverty saw the poor as mired in a cycle of poverty from which they were ill equipped to escape because of bad health, lack of skills, and lack of experience, both in the workplace and in the political process. They emphasized an investment strategy of providing the poor not with money, but with services that would help adults and children break out of the poverty cycle. Providing these services to the poor involved federal intervention in a whole range of government functions previously regarded as state and local prerogatives.

A prime example of the investment strategy was the Head Start program, whose premise was that because poor children came to school less ready to learn than middle-class children, they fell behind and were never able to catch up. Head Start provided intensive preschool education to improve the skills, health, and nutrition of low-income children and enhance their chances of succeeding in school. Other federal programs provided special services for low-income youngsters to help them progress through school, get jobs, or go to college. (Principal programs included follow through, teacher corps, title I of the Elementary and Secondary Education Act, job corps, neighborhood youth corps, and upward bound.) In addition, neighborhood health centers offered health resources in areas with few doctors and medical facilities. Legal services helped poor people obtain redress of grievances and claim benefits to which they were entitled under the law. Community action programs, perhaps the most controversial of all, tried to mobilize the poor to be more effective politically in their own behalf.

Some programs were intended to demonstrate that a broad range of coordinated services could turn a deteriorating area into an improving one. Riots in Los Angeles, Detroit, Washington, and other big cities in the late 1960s directed attention to blighted urban areas. Urban renewal, model cities, and other programs channeled federal funds directly to city governments.

The investment strategy of the war on poverty involved a great many programs and projects. Most were relatively small, however. They reached only a minority of the population in poverty and did so in ways that were usually too fleeting to make a life-changing difference.

Income Strategy Proposals Many people concerned about the poor thought the investment strategy was too slow and indirect. Better education, beginning in preschool, might eventually enable poor children to earn more, but four-year-olds would not be in the labor force for about fourteen years. Meanwhile, they were growing up amid deprivation and blight. What the poor needed most urgently was money—a means of paying for necessities such as food, housing, and medical care.

Some scholars and politicians were attracted to the idea of a guaranteed income, sometimes known as a negative income tax (NIT). They believed that existing welfare programs were demeaning and undermined incentives to work because family earnings were deducted from the welfare grant. A poor family was effectively subject to a 100 percent tax on earnings. Under an NIT, a family with no income would be guaranteed a minimum income and would be encouraged to work because the grant would be reduced (or "taxed") by less than their earnings.[12] Thus an NIT would both provide income for families who could not work and encourage those who could work to do so. Some thought that such a system could be administered by the Internal Revenue Service (IRS). Families with adequate incomes would pay positive taxes, those with low incomes would get checks (or negative taxes), and only the IRS would know the difference.

The NIT was an intriguing idea, although it would have been more expensive and difficult to administer than its initial proponents imagined. Efforts to convert President Johnson to the idea failed. He was committed to the investment strategy, especially to opening educational opportunities for poor children, and had little interest in reforming welfare. In any case, by the end of Johnson's presidency in 1968, escalating defense spending was squeezing domestic programs. The NIT was ruled out by cost as well as philosophy.

To the surprise of most liberals, President Richard M. Nixon endorsed a welfare reform proposal in 1969 that bore striking resemblance to an NIT.

Nixon proposed guaranteeing a minimum income to all families and encouraging work by reducing the guarantee less than the amount of earnings. The proposed guarantee level was below the welfare benefits paid to AFDC families in urban states, but above the benefits in the South. The proposal would have put a national floor under income for the first time and substantially benefited low-wage workers.

President Nixon's family assistance plan, as it was called, passed the House of Representatives twice, but was defeated in the Senate by a coalition of conservatives, who thought it too generous to the poor, and liberals, who thought it not generous enough. The idea survived in the supplementary security income program, which was essentially an NIT for people who were elderly, blind, or disabled.

Despite the absence of an income strategy in the war on poverty and the failure of Nixon's reform, welfare programs grew rapidly in the 1960s and even faster in the 1970s. Collectively, these programs had a much bigger impact on federal budgets than the investment strategy programs. AFDC increased as larger proportions of the poor applied for aid and benefit levels rose. Medicaid, passed at the same time as medicare, provided health benefits for many low-income families, especially those eligible for AFDC. The food stamp program, which went to a broader group of low-income people than AFDC, grew rapidly. Public housing and other housing subsidies for low-income families increased.

The Proliferation of Grants

Federal activism in the 1960s and 1970s spread from poverty and civil rights into many other areas. Turning to Washington for help became routine. Pollution, transportation, recreation, economic development, law enforcement, even rat control, evoked the same response from politicians: create a federal grant. National concern shifted from one problem to another, but existing grants were never terminated. The result was an accumulation of more than 500 categorical programs, each with detailed rules, formulas for matching and distributing the money, bureaucracies charged with carrying out and overseeing the program, and beneficiaries and professional groups with an interest in perpetuating and enlarging the grant.

Some critics worried that the pervasiveness of federal grants reduced state and local autonomy. Others were more concerned that the proliferation of grants allowed state and local authorities to do whatever they wanted and send the bill to the federal government.

States and cities learned to tailor their budgets to maximize federal funding. Unfortunately, they sometimes neglected more routine activities. According to New York City Mayor Edward I. Koch:

> Left unnoticed in the cities' rush to reallocate their budgets so as to draw down maximum categorical aid were the basic service-delivery programs. . . . New roads, bridges, and subway routes were an exciting commitment to the future, but they were launched at the expense of routine maintenance to the unglamorous, but essential, infrastructure of the existing systems.[13]

Another problem was that less affluent jurisdictions often lacked the savvy or the staff to take full advantage of the federal largesse, especially when it took the form of project grants for which they had to compete. Wealthier states and cities were able to put together more sophisticated or better-documented project proposals.

Revenue Sharing

In 1964, Walter Heller, chairman of the Council of Economic Advisers in the Johnson administration, proposed "revenue sharing" to channel federal money to the states without the detailed specifications of categorical grants. Revenue sharing responded to several problems besides the growing concern about categorical grants. Needs for public services at the state and local level were rising more rapidly than revenues; state and local revenues grew more slowly and fell more heavily on low-income people than the federal income tax; federal income tax revenues tended to rise faster than the need for federal spending; and poor states could not be expected to bring services up to acceptable national levels without help. Revenue sharing would address all these concerns by channeling a portion of federal income tax receipts to the states—no strings attached—with low-income states receiving disproportionate shares.[14]

President Johnson rejected the revenue sharing proposal. He favored social programs managed directly by Washington or categorical grants with tight federal controls. During his administration, the number of categorical grants exploded, and the revenue sharing idea remained buried deep in the White House files.

President Nixon, however, was attracted to revenue sharing, which fit well with his "New Federalism" philosophy of increasing state autonomy. . . . His proposal, known as general revenue sharing, was enacted in 1972 with the enthusiastic support of state and local politicians.

General revenue sharing funds were specified in the law, not tied to the federal income tax. The money was disbursed under a formula that benefited poor states disproportionately. The money was divided into two parts, one to be spent at the state level and one to be "passed through" to local governments. The earmarking of a local share reflected the fears of mayors that they would not get enough money if they had to lobby for it in their state capitals. Rules were also introduced to try to prevent the recipients from substituting federal money for existing funding.

That revenue sharing was popular with state and local officials is hardly surprising. It provided financial support and made no onerous demands. It was not, however, equally popular with members of Congress, who preferred more control over how federal funds were used. Hence categorical grant programs continued to grow in the 1970s, while revenue sharing did not.

The Reagan Revolution

President Ronald Reagan was a conservative former governor of California with strong views about the role of government, at both the federal and state levels. He won a landslide victory over President Jimmy Carter in 1980 after vociferously attacking federal domestic spending in his campaign and advocating deep cuts in federal income taxes, more defense spending, and a balanced budget. Within weeks of taking office, Reagan confronted Congress with a drastic budget proposal involving major increases in defense spending, deep cuts in domestic programs, and reductions in federal income taxes over a three-year period. Congress, awed by the electorate's evident desire for change and skillfully manipulated by Reagan's energetic director of the Office of Management and Budget, David Stockman, passed both the tax and budget proposals with astonishing rapidity.

Reagan administration budget policy profoundly influenced the future of relations among federal, state, and local governments. As Richard Nathan and Fred Doolittle put it:

> The cuts made in grants-in-aid in Reagan's first year in office were historic. This was the first time in over thirty years that there had been an actual-dollar decline in federal aid to state and local governments. The cuts produced a 7 percent reduction for fiscal year 1982 in overall federal grants-in-aid to state and local governments. . . . This amounted to a 12 percent decline in real terms.[15]

Federal grants were both reduced and restructured. Categorical programs were grouped into block grants that gave state and local governments more latitude in spending the funds. The Reagan cuts fell heavily on the poor, especially the working poor, and hit cities more dramatically than states.

Most of the reductions in domestic spending came during Reagan's first year in office. Subsequent requests for additional cutbacks met increasing opposition from Congress and the public. Some of the funds cut in the initial reductions were later restored, and modest increases in grants occurred late in the 1980s. Huge federal deficits, however, kept downward pressure on federal spending, especially discretionary spending, which is easier to control than entitlements. Very few new federal grant programs were created in the 1980s. Federal aid to state and local governments (as a percentage of GNP, the federal budget, or state and local spending) stayed well below the level of the late 1970s. The pattern of increasing state and local dependence on federal grants had been broken.

One of the casualties of the Reagan revolution was general revenue sharing. Opponents pointed out that huge deficits left no federal revenue to share. Congressional support for revenue sharing was weaker than support for the categorical programs that affected identifiable clients and professional groups. First the state and then the local components of revenue sharing were eliminated.

Unexpectedly, the Reagan cuts energized state and local governments. The cuts created what Richard Nathan has called "the paradox of devolution." With less federal help, states, and to some extent localities, were forced to strengthen their own capacities and resources to meet the rising social problems of the 1980s. The federal pullback came at a fortunate moment—after two decades that had greatly enhanced states' ability to move into the breach.

THE STATES RISE TO THE CHALLENGE

The dissatisfaction with state government that reached a crescendo in the 1960s not only prompted an explosion of federal activity, it also brought a wave of reform in the states themselves. Goaded partly by the federal government and partly by pressure from their own citizens, states took steps to turn themselves into more modern, responsive, competent governments. By the time the Reagan revolution of the 1980s thrust new responsibilities on them, state governments were far more ready to rise to the challenge than they would have been two decades earlier.

Executive Branch Reforms

One theme of the state reform movement was strengthening the capacity of governors to provide state leadership. Colonial antagonism toward a strong executive had left a legacy of state constitutions with strict separation of powers between the executive and legislative branches and carefully circumscribed gubernatorial powers. As a result, governors frequently lacked the tools and resources needed to lead a modern state.

Presidents, of course, faced the same problem for the same reason, but in the first half of the twentieth century there were major improvements in the organization and staffing of the White House. For example, the Bureau of the Budget (later called the Office of Management and Budget) was created in 1921 and the Council of Economic Advisers was established in 1946.

Efforts to improve the capacity of governors came later. In the early 1960s, many governors served only two years, not long enough to articulate and carry out a strategy for state action. Many were lame ducks, prohibited from succeeding themselves. Many governors had limited powers of appointment; other state officials were directly elected and had their own power bases. Many appointments were made by boards or commissions whose members were elected, controlled by the legislature, or served fixed terms from which they could not be removed. Governors often had neither the authority nor the staff to prepare an executive budget for the legislature. Indeed, states' chief executive officers frequently lacked powers that CEOs of corporations would regard as absolutely essential to leadership and effectiveness.

A common reform was shifting to longer terms, as well as lifting restrictions on succession. In 1955 governros had four-year terms in only twenty-nine states. By 1988 the number had risen to forty-seven. In the same period, the number of states in which governors were barred from a second sucessive term dropped from seventeen to three.[16]

Other reforms shortened the ballot and reduced the number of independently elected state officials. A widely quoted report by the Committee for Economic Development in 1967 urged that only two state executives, the governor and the lieutenant governor, be elected and that they run as a team from the same party, like the president and vice president. More states now elect the governor and lieutenant governor as a team, but the effort to reduce the number of elected officials has met with only modest success. Over the period 1960–80, the number of states electing four or fewer executives rose only from three to nine.[17] Between 1956 and 1988, the number of separately elected officials besides the governor dropped from 709 to 514, still an astonishingly high average of more than 10 per state.[18] Some governors obtained more formal powers of appointment and removal. Longer terms also tended to increase the governors' control of boards and commissions whose members are appointed for fixed terms.

During this era there were also substantial increases in the size and professional qualification of staffs, with the average size of the staff rising from eleven in 1956 to forty-eight in 1988.[19] Governors also created budget and planning offices charged with developing an executive budget reflecting the governor's priorities, formulating longer-term plans for the state and its government, and monitoring the effectiveness of state programs. Almost all governors now prepare an executive budget and submit it to the legislature with extensive backup analysis.[20]

In this period, state agency officials, like the staffs they supervised, became visibly more professional. They had more degrees and were more likely to be career civil servants. State officials became more diverse, although women and minorities are still underrepresented at the top of state governments.

Governors themselves have been described as a "new breed"—younger, better educated, less likely to be lawyers, more likely to seek careers in public service. Many of them have been state legislators or agency executives. Many go on to the U.S. Senate or to other federal positions.[21]

None of these changes, of course, guarantees that governors will be successful or effective. Leadership qualities are in short supply at the state, as at the federal, level. Judgment and luck, as well as formal qualification and power of office, play an enormous role in determining a governor's effectiveness. Nevertheless, an able governor now has far more opportunity in most states to formulate and carry out policy than he (and now occasionally, she) would have had in the early 1960s.

Reforming the Legislative Branch

Reform of state legislatures in the 1960s came partly in reaction to stronger governorships. The American system of separation of powers invites such swings of reformist zeal from one branch to the other. The creation of the Congressional Budget Office in 1974 was in part the result of the strengthening of the presidential budgetmaking capacity in the 1960s and creation of policy analysis staffs in cabinet agencies. Congress needed professional help in responding to the increasingly sophisticated budget presentations of the president's staff. State legislatures, after the strengthening of governors' offices, found themselves in a similar position.

A more urgent impetus, however, came from the Supreme Court. In *Baker* v. *Carr* (1962), the Court indicated its willingness to hear cases in which voters in a state claimed that malapportionment of their legislature denied them equal protection of the laws under the Fourteenth Amendment to the U.S. Constitution. Then in *Reynolds* v. *Sims* (1964) the Court took the startling position that equal protection required *both* houses of the state legislature to be apportioned on a population basis, despite the fact that the U.S. Constitution specifies equal representation for all states in the U.S. Senate regardless of population. States rapidly reapportioned their legislatures to conform to the court's principle of "one person, one vote." This redrawing of the lines, now repeated after every census, brought a new and far more diverse group of legislators to state capitols and added pressure for other kinds of reform.[22]

In general, reapportionment favored metropolitan areas, especially growing suburban communities. It put urban problems on state agendas and eventually led to increased state aid to cities. Political fallout varied. Democrats gained more seats in the Northeast and Midwest, but Republicans benefited in the South.[23]

At the same time, the work load of legislatures was increasing. Short sessions every other year were no longer adequate. More and more states found that part-time citizen-legislators were unable to cope with the demands of modern state activity. Legislative sessions were lengthening, and pay had to be raised to compensate legislators who were now spending a substantial part of their working hours on state business. Legislatures also began to demand better working conditions and more professional and clerical assistance. Members needed staff both to service constituent requests and to work on increasingly technical legislative matters. Committees became more active and utilized more professional staff.

Strengthening State Revenue Systems

In recent years, states have strengthened and diversified their revenue systems. States and localities generally have become much less dependent on property taxes, which used to be almost the sole source of local revenue and an important one for states as well. Sales taxes, whose bases have been significantly broadened, now bring in more total revenue than property taxes. More important, many states and some cities have begun to rely more heavily on income taxes. States and localities have also turned for revenue to a broad range of fees and charges designed to make the actual users of state and local services pay a larger share of the costs. Between 1960 and 1990, property taxes dropped from 37.7 percent to 21.8 percent of the revenue state and local governments raised from their own sources, while individual income taxes grew from 5.7 to 14.8 percent and fees and charges grew from 16.8 to 28.9 percent.[24]

The trend to broader-based state and local revenue systems in this period has been called "one of the most dramatic turnarounds in the annals of American public finance."[25] Although states and localities are still hard-pressed to raise enough revenue to pay for the services demanded by their citizens, their revenue systems are stronger, more responsive to economic growth, and less regressive than they were a few decades ago.

Moreover, states and localities have raised more revenue, despite frequent protests from taxpayers. State and local revenue, exclusive of federal grants, has gone up from 7.6 percent of GNP in 1960 to 10.3 percent in 1990.[26]

Meanwhile, the federal government's fiscal strength has declined. There was a time when revenues from the highly progressive federal income tax tended to grow faster than the economy as a whole. Rising incomes moved taxpayers into higher brackets, where they paid a higher proportion of their income in tax. Even if people's real income had not increased, inflation tended to increase the government's revenue by pushing taxpayers into higher brackets. This phenomenon was known as "bracket creep."

In 1981, however, the federal income tax was made less progressive by reducing rates on high incomes. Moreover, beginning in 1985 the tax brackets were adjusted for inflation to remove bracket creep. Hence federal revenues no longer grow faster than the economy. Moreover, except for social security payroll taxes, federal revenues as a share of GNP have been declining. Federal revenues (excluding social security taxes) fell from 15.4 percent of GNP in 1960 to 12.0 percent in 1990. . . .

MANDATES

The federal government's own fiscal weakness has not made it any less eager to tell states and localities what to do. Indeed, when its ability to make grants declined, the federal government turned increasingly to mandates as a means of controlling state and local activity without having to pay the bill.

Mandates take several forms. Some are direct orders to states and localities to comply with certain rules (such as waste-water treatment standards) or face civil or criminal penalties. Some of them are cross-cutting requirements routinely attached to federal programs (compliance with antidiscrimination rules or minimum wages). Others impose conditions on a whole system (access for disabled people to mass transit or schools) as a condition of receipt of federal grants for any part of the system.

In the 1960s and early 1970s, when federal money was flowing to states and localities in increasing amounts, the recipients expressed little concern about the conditions attached to grants. As money tightened, however, and mandates became more pervasive and expensive, state and local officials became increasingly strident in criticizing federal mandates. David R. Beam noted that the character of the dialogue went from "cooperative" to "other 'c' words—like compulsory, coercive, and conflictual."[27] Complaints from the state and local level were hardly ever about the purposes of federal mandates, which were acknowledged to be laudable. Rather, they were about the federal government's asserting the authority to write complex and costly regulations that then had to be implemented by states and localities. "Cities and states feared that they were becoming the 'field hands of federalism'—simply, tools for implementing national policy directives in environmental protection, race, sex and age nondiscrimination, handicapped access and education, bilingual education, health planning, and other areas."[28]

Mayor Koch expressed the views of many state and local officials on the receiving end of multiple federal mandates in a satirical list of rules that appeared to be followed by the "mandate mandarins" in Washington: (1) "Mandates solve problems, particularly those in which you are not involved"; (2) "Mandates need not be tempered by the lessons of local experience"; (3) "Mandates will spontaneously generate the technology required to achieve them"; (4) "The price tag of the lofty aspiration to be served by a mandate should never deter its imposition on others."[29]

Although state and local governments have challenged federal mandates in the courts in recent years, they have generally lost. New mandates continue to be added. Among the most costly, although the cost has been shared by the federal government, are mandates for additional services to low-income families under medicaid.

Mandates add to citizen confusion about who is in charge. When the federal government makes rules for state and local officials to carry out, it is not clear to voters who should be blamed, either when the regulations are laxly enforced or when the cost of compliance is high.

WHITHER FEDERALISM?

In the last decade, the tide of centralization has turned and the balance of power has generally shifted from the federal government toward the states. The states have strengthened their capacity for governance and their revenue systems, while the federal government has found itself overstretched and short of funds. The intertwining of roles, however, has not diminished. Federal grant programs have received less funding, but their number remains huge—a recent publication lists more than 600 federal grant programs for state and local government.[30] Mandates have been used to enforce federal policy when funds were limited. No new concept of federal and state roles has yet emerged. . . .

Notes

1. John Shannon and James Edwin Kee, "The Rise of Competitive Federalism," *Public Budgeting and Finance*, vol. 9 (Winter 1989), pp. 5–20.
2. Daniel J. Elazar, *The American Partnership: Intergovernmental Cooperation in the Nineteenth-Century United States* (University of Chicago Press, 1962).
3. *Economic Report of the President, February 1991*, pp. 310, 379.
4. The food stamp program is an exception. The funds are federal and the benefit formula is the same in all states.
5. *Budget of the United States Government, Fiscal Year 1992*, p. 182.
6. Quoted in Ann O'M. Bowman and Richard C. Kearney, *The Resurgence of the States* (Prentice Hall, 1986), p. 4.
7. Quoted in Morton Keller, "State Government Needn't Be Resurrected Because It Never Died," in Thad L. Beyle, ed., *State Government: CQ's Guide to Current Issues and Activities, 1989–90* (Washington: Congressional Quarterly, 1989), p. 174.
8. Frank Trippett, *The States: United They Fell* (New York: World Publishing, 1967), p. 2.
9. Terry Sanford, *Storm Over the States* (McGraw-Hill, 1967), pp. 36, 1.
10. Sanford, *Storm Over the States*, p. 35.
11. Malcolm E. Jewell, "What Hath *Baker v. Carr* Wrought?" in Beyle, ed., *State Government*, pp. 85–95, quotation on p. 86.
12. Suppose the guarantee were $8,000 a year for a family of four. If the tax rate were 50 percent and the family earned $4,000, the grant would be reduced by $2,000 and the family would end up with a total income of $10,000.
13. Edward I. Koch, "The Mandate Millstone," *The Public Interest*, no. 61 (Fall 1980), p. 43.
14. Specifically, the federal government would annually deposit funds equal to 2 percent of the federal income tax base in a trust fund for the states. The money would be divided among the states on the basis of population and could be used for any purpose except highways (a trust fund for highways already existed). Each state would work out its own way of sharing the money with its local governments. Task Force on Intergovernmental Fiscal Cooperation, "Strengthening State and Local Government: A Report to the President of the United States," November 11, 1964 (unpublished). The task force was chaired by Joseph A. Pechman. Presi-

dent Johnson, allegedly angry because Heller had leaked the proposal to the *New York Times*, refused to release the report.
15. Richard P. Nathan, Fred C. Doolittle, and Associates, *Reagan and the States* (Princeton University Press, 1987), p. 4.
16. Thad L. Beyle, "From Governor to Governors," in Carl E. Van Horn, ed., *The State of the States* (Washington: Congressional Quarterly, 1989), pp. 35–36. The holdouts for two-year terms are all small New England states: Rhode Island, New Hampshire, and Vermont. Kentucky, Virginia, and New Mexico still bar succession.
17. Bowman and Kearney, *Resurgence of the States*, chap. 2.
18. Beyle, "From Governor to Governors," p. 36.
19. Beyle, "From Governor to Governors," p. 36.
20. By 1983, the governor shared the power to put together an initial budget with the legislature in only three states (South Carolina, Texas, and Mississippi). Bowman and Kearney, *Resurgence of the States*, p. 61.
21. Larry Sabato, *Goodbye to Good-Time Charlie: The American Governorship Transformed*, 2d ed. (Washington: Congressional Quarterly Press, 1983).
22. Alan Rosenthal, "The Legislative Institution: Transformed and at Risk," in Van Horn, ed., *State of the States*, pp. 69–102.
23. Jewell, "What Hath *Baker v. Carr* Wrought?"
24. Advisory Commission on Intergovernmental Relations, *Significant Features of Fiscal Federalism*, vol. 2: *Revenues and Expenditures* (Washington, 1991), p. 132.
25. Shannon and Kee, "Rise of Competitive Federalism," p. 14.
26. *Budget of the United States Government, Fiscal Year 1992*, table 15.1.
27. David R. Beam, "On the Origins of the Mandate Issue," in Michael Fix and Daphne A. Kenyon, eds., *Coping with Mandates: What Are the Alternatives?* (Washington: Urban Institute Press, 1990), p. 23.
28. Beam, "Origins of the Mandate Issue," p. 23.
29. Koch, "The Mandate Millstone," pp. 43–44.
30. U.S. General Accounting Office, *Federal Aid: Programs Available to State and Local Governments*, HRD-91-93FS (May 1991).

Challenges to State Governments: Policy and Administrative Leadership in the 1990s

F. TED HEBERT
DEIL S. WRIGHT
JEFFREY I. BRUDNEY

State governments, collectively and individually, have faced and will continue to confront an array of challenges in their efforts to remain viable and effective governing entities. This is neither the time nor the place to offer historical reflections on the political-economic roller coaster rides the states have experienced over the past half century. Rather, our aim is to sketch prominent features of a portion of the terrain that the American states must traverse en route to the twenty-first century, focusing especially on their need to ensure a well-prepared corps of administrative leaders.

State governments face numerous challenges in the decade of the 1990s. There are economic ones that emerge from the shifting character of the global and U.S. economies. There are natural resource, environmental, and ecological realities, such as water supply, hazardous and solid wastes and air quality. There are social challenges that emerge from changing demographics, the continuing decline of many major cities, and the aging of the population. These economic, resource, and social challenges converge and blend into a complex mix of political and policy issues that seem destined to challenge the wills and skills of every leadership component in all the states. The states respond by assigning expanded responsibilities to their administrative agencies and by creating new agencies. As noted by Dresang and Gosling (1989, p. 86), "State agencies reflect what state governments do." It is critical, then, that we examine the cadre of senior state policy managers and administrators. This top-level group of executives is the focus of our attention, a policy leadership component of state government operationally defined as the heads of state administrative agencies.

Numerous recent articles and statements have highlighted the need to rebuild the public's trust in the public service at the *national* level. The national-level malaise and the ubiquitous anomie within the public service have been noted and commented upon in articles and in official and public documents, most particularly the Volcker Commission report (National Commission on the Public Service, 1990; Wildavsky, 1988; Denhardt and Jennings, 1989; Golembiewski, 1989). Do similar or identical conditions prevail at the state level? It is difficult to offer a well-considered and fully developed response. Comparatively little is known about the public service and administrative management issues across the fifty states. One purpose of this article and this issue's Featured Topic is to share and compare information and to clarify some issues concerning top-level administrative leaders in state government.

With these introductory and orienting comments in mind, we turn to the general theme of change in state governments. After exploring the states' expanded (and expanding) responsibilities, we then focus on the states' responses to these growing demands. In these core sections, we look at organization structure configurations as well as at resources available to the states and the leadership roles of agency heads. The latter topic centers specifically on the changing character and composition of administrative elites over the past three decades. The reported findings are derived from six successive mail questionnaire surveys that began in the 1960s. We then assess the policy management capacities of the states and identify some of the critical administrative issues that need to be addressed by the states in the decade ahead.

CHANGING STATE ROLES

Two themes provide a framework for discussing the reemergent and enlarged roles of the states in the American political system. The first centers on the expanded responsibilities of the states. A significant part of this theme revolves around the intergovernmental positions of the state as a player in national-state and state-local relationships.

A second peg on which changes in the states hang is one of expanded resources. States have found it possible and advisable to elaborate their organizational structures as one means of responding to increased demands. Their access to growing own-source revenues undergirds another element of the resource supply side of the public services ledger. Finally, the ability of state governments to compete in the demand arena by acquiring (purchasing) a growing contingent of public employees is a closely related dimension of expanded resources. We examine all three indicators of expanded resources in this section.

Expanding State Responsibilities

In the mid-1980s, departing Virginia governor Charles Robb (1986, p. 1) offered the following projection concerning national-state relationships: "The shift in responsibilities from Washington to the states will continue regardless of which party is in power. . . . It is not farfetched to project that by the end of the century, if not before, the federal government will be responsible for national defense, the national debt, Social Security, and income maintenance programs and little else.

Robb's speculation was couched chiefly in fiscal and program responsibility terms. He extrapolated, based on so-called shift-and-shaft strategies of the Reagan New Federalism, that significant national program responsibilities would either be dropped entirely or be formally assigned to the states. Robb did not rule out the possibility that programs might informally and slowly gravitate toward the states. There is ample evidence in fiscal and programmatic terms to confirm that the states have moved into a fend-for-oneself federalism mode (or mood) (Shannon, 1989).

There is also a significant body of recent congressional statutes, national administrative regulations, and Supreme Court decisions that document the extent to which Washington-originated mandates have moved major, if not massive, obligations from the national to the state levels. Health, welfare, environmental, and other laws have converged on the states with combined fiscal and legal effects. On the legal point, several phrases have been employed to characterize and emphasize the state-focused impacts: "Juridical federalism" and "regulatory federalism" are two examples.

While national-state interactions have gravitated down toward a state-centered focus for major domestic tasks, the dynamics of state-local relationships have tilted up from the local level. While it is beyond our need to elaborate the shifting character of state-local relations, Table 3-1 shows the movement toward a state-dominated pattern of fiscal-functional-personnel links with local governments in highly aggregated terms.

The centralization index score (Stephens, 1974, 1985) constitutes a composite metric that results from measuring the degree of dominance that individual state governments exert in relation to their respective local governments in three areas: employment of personnel, responsibility for various functional activities or programs, and collection and expenditure of funds. The forty-eight-state mean was 47 in 1957. A quarter-century later, the index stood at 57, marking a distinct shift toward state dominance. In 1957, only four states recorded a score of 60 or higher, which Stephens called *centralized*. By 1982, the number in the centralized category above 60 was sixteen, or nearly one-third of all the states.

Expanding Structural and Institutional Resources

The states have responded to the demands brought by their increased responsibilities in many ways: by adopting new and sharply revised constitutions (Bowman and Kearney, 1986; Council of State Governments, 1990); by improving structures of administrative organization (Garnett, 1980; Conant, 1988); by strengthening principal policy institutions, including governors (Sabato, 1983; Beyle, 1989; Weissert, 1983), legislatures (Rosenthal, 1989; Bowman and Kearney, 1986), and courts (Fino, 1987; Baum, 1989); and by expanding the number and variety of administrative agencies responsible for addressing policy issues at the state level.

Table 3-1.
Changes in State Centralization, Select Years 1957–1982

	Average State Centralization Index	*Number of States in Centralized Category*[a]
1957	47	4
1972	53	8
1982	57	16

Sources: Stephens, 1974, 1985.
[a] The centralized category consists of states with index scores of 60 or higher.

Table 3-2 shows clearly the number of agencies that states have added over the last three decades and the particular agency types coming into wide use.[1] The 1960s saw a modest number of agencies achieve the threshold of use in three-fourths of the states, including several that addressed natural resource and environmental issues. Social service agencies are especially prominent among those reaching wide usage in the 1970s. This period also saw rapid administrative development across a wide variety of fields. Proliferation slowed in the 1980s. If any single field characterizes this period, it is environmental regulation, especially hazardous waste.

In addition to the many and significant structural developments over the last three decades, the states also have found ways to expand the financial and human resources available to carry out their growing responsibilities, and they have taken steps to improve their management and policy-making capacities significantly.

Expanding Financial Resources

The sharp growth in governmental responsibilities over the last three decades can be measured in several ways. If we focus on spending changes, the United States has seen expansion across all governmental levels between 1962 and 1988. States have had to respond with decisions that are revealed both in the generation of financial resources and in the allocation of those resources to particular programs. It is noteworthy that, of the three governmental levels, the states have shown the greatest capacity to generate the needed resources.

During the period between 1962 and 1988, direct state general expenditures increased from $20.4 billion to $280.5 billion.[2] How does this trend compare to the growth of local and federal governments? Figure 3-2 shows that the states have expanded faster than either of the other levels. The slopes on this ratio chart show the rate of change from one year to the next. That the three lines are roughly parallel indicates that the rates of growth do not differ dramatically from each other, but the vertical distances between state and local and between state and federal levels are less in 1988 than they were in 1962. State direct general spending has grown somewhat faster than either local or federal spending.

Another way to capture this change (at least for the two years 1962 and 1988) is to measure percentages of total direct general expenditures by governments that were made by each level in 1962 and 1988. Table 3-3 has this comparison. State spending remains less than federal or local, but it has grown to almost one-fifth of the total, showing the most growth. How can we account for this increase?

One possibility is that states have benefited from available federal aid. The year 1962 predates the period of dramatically expanded federal aid to state and local governments that accompanied the Great Society programs of the 1960s and the general revenue sharing of the 1970s. Federal aid as a percentage of total state and local outlays increased from 14.1 percent in 1962 to a high of 26.5 percent in 1978. Since then, the pattern has been one of decline relative to state and local outlays. In 1988, federal aid constituted only 18.2 percent of the total (Advisory Commission on Intergovernmental Relations, 1990, p. 42). To assess the possible effect of these changes, we must note that

Table 3-2
Proliferation of State Agencies, 1959–1989

Traditional Agencies: Present in Thirty-Eight or More States since 1959

Adjutant General	Geology	Post Audit
Aeronautics	Health	Public Utility Regulation
Aging	Higher Education	Purchasing
Agriculture	Highways	Revenue
Alcoholic Beverage Control	Insurance	Secretary of State
Attorney General	Labor	Securities (regulation)
Banking	Labor Arbitration and	Soil Conservation
Budgeting	Mediation	Solid Waste (Sanitation)
Child Welfare	Law Enforcement	Tourism (Advertising)
Corrections	Library	Treasurer
Education	Mental Health	Unemployment Insurance
Emergency Management	Mining	Veterans Affairs
(Civil Defense)	Motor Vehicles	Vocational Education
Employment Services	Oil and Gas	Water Quality
Fire Marshal	Parks and Recreation	Water Resources
Fish and Game	Parole	Welfare
Food (inspection/purity)	Personnel	Workman's Compensation
Forestry	Planning	

Second-Generation Agencies: Present in Thirty-Eight or More States since 1969[a]

Administration	Comptroller	Federal-State Relations
Air Quality	Court Administration	Highway Safety
Commerce	Criminal Justice Planning	Juvenile Rehabilitation
Community Affairs	Economic Development	Natural Resources

Third-Generation Agencies: Present in Thirty-Eight or More States since 1979[a]

Alcohol and Drug Abuse	Finance	Public Lands
Archives	Historic Preservation	Railroad
Arts Council(s)	Housing Finance	Savings and Loan
Child Abuse	Human Resources	Social Services
Civil Rights	(Human Service)	State-Local Relations
Consumer Affairs	Intrrnational Trade	Telecommunication
(Protection)	Manpower	Transportation
Energy	Mass Transit	Veterinarian
Environment	Medicaid	Vocational Rehabilitation
Ethics	Occupational Health	Women's Commission
Exceptional Children	and Safety	

Fourth-Generation Agencies: Present in Thirty-Eight or More States in 1989[a]

Emergency Medical	Ground Water Management	Training and
Services	Hazardous Waste	Development
Equal Employment	Small and Minority	Underground Storage
Opportunity	Business	Tanks

Emergent Agencies: Present in Twenty-Five or More States in 1989[a]

Coastal Zone Management	Mining Reclamation	Public Defender
Horse Racing	Ombudsman	Victim Compensation
Licensing (occupations)	Public Broadcasting	
Lotteries	System	

Sources: Council of State Governments, 1959, 1969, 1979, 1989.

[a] Agencies listed in these sections are in addition to those in previous sections, which continued to be present in thirty-eight or more states.

Table 3-3

Percentages of Direct General Expenditures by Government Levels, 1962 versus 1988

	1962	1988
Federal	59.0	52.0
State	14.4	19.2
Local	26.6	28.8

Sources: U.S. Department of Commerce, 1962, 1987–1988.

Figure 3-2 and the percentage change figures given earlier concern direct general expenditures. All intergovernmental aid (federal to state and local and state to local as well as the very small amounts flowing in the opposite direction) is treated as expenditures of the recipient units only. Therefore, one possible explanation for the accelerated increase in state and local spending is the availability of intergovernmental aid. Perhaps state and local governments have simply added federal aid to their otherwise available revenues and thereby expanded their activities.

This possibility can be assessed by examining changes in the generation of revenues by each level of government. Have federal revenue sources grown faster than state and local, enabling the federal government to transfer funds to the states and allowing states and localities to expand their own spending? Figure 3-3 shows the pattern of general revenue growth.[3] Here the trend is even clearer than it was with regard to expenditures: State own-source general revenues have grown considerably faster than have the own-source revenues of either federal or local governments. Despite receiving increased federal aid during the three decades, states have found it necessary to increase sharply their own revenues from taxes, fees, and other sources. State own-source revenues have grown from 16.7 percent of total general revenues generated by the three levels to 26.0 percent of the total.

Figure 3-2. Direct General Expenditure, 1962–1988 (in Billions of Dollars)

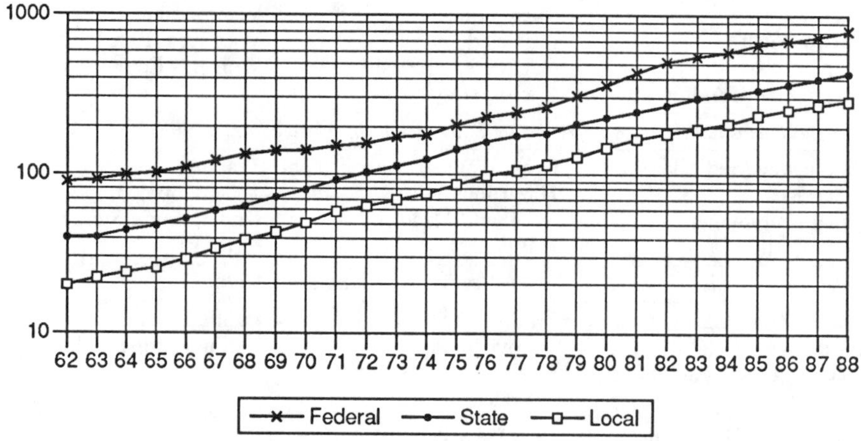

Sources: U.S. Department of Commerce, 1962, 1987–1988.

Figure 3-3. Federal, State, and Local Own-Source General Revenue, 1962–88 (in Billions of Dollars)

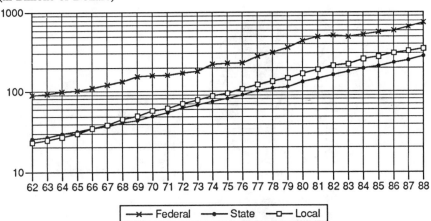

Sources: U.S. Department of Commerce, *Government Finances*, various annual issues.

Over the years, states have provided critical support to local governments. Throughout the three decades, they have given more aid to local governments than they themselves have received from the federal government. Local governments, of course, have benefited from expansion of both federal and state intergovernmental expenditures during most of the period. Even so, they, like the states, have expanded their own-source revenues faster than the federal government.

In attempting to understand the expansion of state governments during the last three decades, we may find it useful to identify the functions on which the states spend money. The Bureau of the Census classifies spending into a number of functional categories, indeed into more categories today than it did in 1962. For comparison, we are limited to the categories used in the earlier year. The two pie charts in Figure 3-4 depict several dramatic shifts in state spending.

In 1988, highway spending was far less prominent than it was in 1962, when the interstate program was rolling ahead. Spending for highways dropped from 32.6 percent to just over 12 percent of the total. Moving in the opposite direction, the portion for public welfare almost doubled, from 12.3 percent to 23.7, and the percentage for interest on general debt grew from 3.1 percent to 6.9. Most of the other categories are not dramatically different, except that the "other and unallocable" category has expanded from 9.9 percent to 14.4. It is instructive to identify some of the newer and expanded functions that are classified here. (These are specified in the 1988 census materials, but they are not set out separately in those of 1962, even though many of them no doubt were represented in the "other" category then.) The only two that exceeded 1 percent of total direct general spending in 1988 are judicial and legal services (2.2 percent) and protective, inspection, and regulative activities (1.1 percent), emphasizing the states' responses in the form of regulatory and law enforcement actions.

Figure 3-4. **Percentage Distribution of State Spending by Functions, 1962 versus 1988**

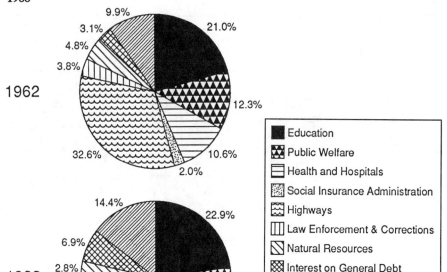

Sources: U.S. Department of Commerce, 1962, 1987–1988.

Regardless of the type of data examined, dramatic changes have taken place in the states over the last three decades. Undoubtedly the states were experiencing many of the pressures felt by federal and local governments, and they responded by generating more financial resources.

Expanding Human Resources

To meet growing service demands, state-level decision makers have been under pressure to expand the number of state employees. During the 1960s, attention was given to the effect of the baby boom, principally on local school systems. Over the whole period, though, public employment has grown much more rapidly at the state than at the local level. This trend, combined with the relative stability of federal civilian employment, has charged the management corps of states with responsibility for supervising a growing portion of total government employees. Figure 3-5 displays the percentage of civilian government employees working for each of the three levels. For the first and last years, Table 3-4 depicts the percentage employment distribution across the three levels. As with spending, the states show the greatest expansion, growing from less than 18 percent of the total to almost one-fourth. Local

Figure 3-5. Percentage Distribution of Total Federal, State, and Local Civilian Employees, 1962–1988

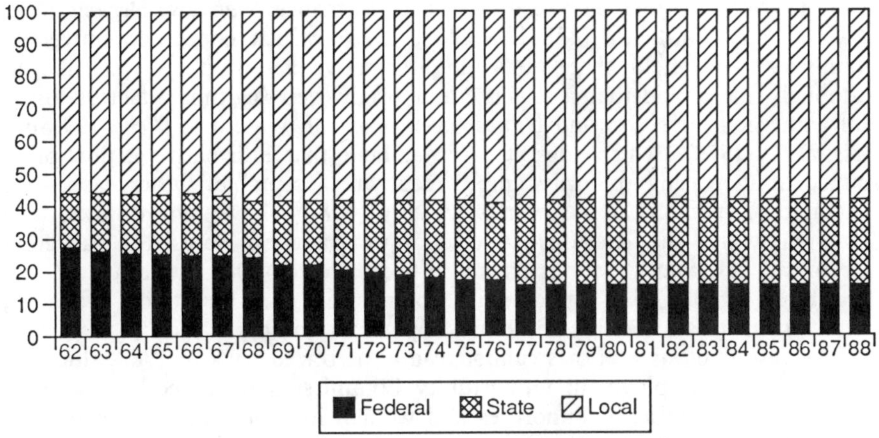

Sources: U.S. Department of Commerce, 1990, pp. 1, 3; 1991, p. 1.

employment (including schools) has risen, too, while the proportion in federal employment has declined sharply.

DEVELOPING LEADERSHIP

Representation: Increasing Diversity

Diversity has been a major theme in state agency staffing for the last three decades, from passage of the Civil Rights Act of 1964, the Age Discrimination in Employment Act of 1967, the Equal Employment Opportunity Act of 1972 (amending the Civil Rights Act to include government personnel practices), and the Vocational Rehabilitation Act of 1973 to the Americans with Disabilities Act of 1990. The Equal Employment Opportunity Act (1972) was especially critical to states, with its direct application to their practices and its breadth in attempting to eliminate discrimination on the basis of race, color, religion, sex, or national origin. The states have been affected as well by critical court decisions, most notably *Griggs* v. *Duke Power Company* (401 U.S.

Table 3-4
Percentage Distribution of Total Civilian Government Employees at Three Levels, 1962 versus 1988

	1962	*1988*
Federal	27.0	17.7
State	17.9	24.1
Local	55.1	58.2

Sources: U.S. Department of Commerce, 1990, p. 1; 1991, p. 1.

424, FEP 175, 1971), which imposed on them and other employers requirements that the tests or criteria used for selecting or promoting employees be valid in the sense that they relate to job performance; *Bakke* v. *Regents of the University of California* (438 U.S. 265, 1978), which concerned university admissions and held that quotas in affirmative action plans were illegal, although it also held that race and ethnic origin were legitimate factors to use for admission purposes; and *United Steelworkers of America* v. *Weber* (99 Sup. Ct. 2721, 1979), which, despite *Bakke*, held that affirmative action plans aimed at increasing minority employment are acceptable. Other cases—for example, *Johnson* v. *Transportation Agency* (1987)—have moved toward an emerging consensus that affirmative action programs can be used in particular circumstances. States' actions have also been affected by activities of the federal Equal Employment Opportunity Commission, the Department of Labor, and state affirmative action and equal opportunity offices.

The results of state efforts cannot readily be traced back to 1962, since the federal Equal Employment Opportunity Commission began collecting information on the status of minorities and women in state employment only in the early 1970s. Nevertheless, from that point forward, it is possible to see some progress, as Table 3-5 demonstrates.

All of the groups show expansion in terms of percentage representation. It is helpful to ask, though, just how these categories might be reflected among various income levels in state government. (Later we look in some detail at their representation among agency heads.) Across all employees, 24.2 percent are minorities, with minorities exceeding this percentage in categories below $20,000. All of the higher classes are heavily dominated by whites. The highest ($43,000 and above) has only 14.6 percent minorities. Blacks are especially underrepresented here with only 6.7 percent (compared to 17.5 percent of employees across all income categories). Comparisons for the other minorities are Hispanic, 2.9 percent compared to 4.4; Asian, 4.7 percent compared to 1.7; and Indians, 0.3 percent compared to 0.6.

Much the same pattern holds for women. Although they now represent 48.7 percent of all full-time state employees, women constitute only 21 percent of employees in the $43,000-and-above group (U.S. Equal Employment Opportunity Commission, 1990)

A major step both to increase diversity and to expand the visibility of a diverse work force, and hence the perception that opportunities are available

Table 3-5
Percentage Distribution of State Full-Time Employees by Ethnic Category and Gender, 1973 versus 1989

Group	1973	1989
Black	10.4	17.5
Hispanic	2.2	4.4
Asian	0.6	1.7
Indian	0.3	0.6
Women	42.9	48.7

Source: U.S. Equal Employment Opportunity Commission, 1990, p. 12.

in state government, is to attract members of previously underrepresented groups to the states' highest positions, that is, agency heads. In this regard, the states have made some limited progress. Most notably, the number of women holding these leadership positions has increased from just under 2 percent in 1964 to 18 percent in 1988 in the twenty-seven agencies included in all six American State Administrators Project (ASAP) surveys (see Figure 3-6).[4] (In 1988, the larger survey of sixty-three agencies found 17 percent headed by women.) There is a tendency for women to cluster in certain agencies, most notably in state and law libraries, Medicaid agencies, and public assistance units.

With regard to ethnic diversity, the pattern is much the same, but progress is slower. In 1964, minorities were at the same place as women, holding 2 percent of agency head positions. That percentage rose to 10 percent in 1988 (as contrasted with 18 percent for the women) for the twenty-seven agencies surveyed across the three decades. The survey of sixty-three agencies in 1988 found that 8 percent were headed by minorities.

Administrative Capacity: Increasing Professionalism

In the 1960s, the American states diverged widely in the degree to which their administrative establishments could be deemed professional in any reasonable use of the word. Almost one-half (twenty-three) did not have general merit system laws covering their employees, having included only those covered by federal grant-in-aid programs (Stahl, 1962, p. 44). Even where general laws did exist, merit system requirements may have been winked at in practice. Although Congress had, since passage of the Social Security Act Amendments of 1939, imposed merit system requirements on a number of federally funded state programs, it took an additional major step in 1970 to strengthen this effort. In that year, Congress passed the Intergovernmental

Figure 3-6. Percentage Distribution of All Agency Heads by Gender, Select Years 1964–1988

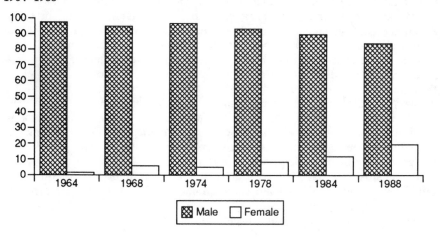

Personnel Act, under which the federal government began providing financial and technical assistance to the states for improving their merit systems. The act set specific standards the states were required to meet to receive the assistance. The criteria were designed to move the states in the direction of professionalizing their work forces.

The question whether public administration should strive to become a "profession" and its practitioners seek to be a professional cadre has been widely debated during the last three decades. Some argue that professionals, by the nature of their training and because they seek to form an in group, tend to isolate themselves from both the public and the elected officials to whom they are accountable. Others argue that the training required for, and norms established by, a profession help to ensure neutral competence and commitment to high-quality and equitable public service.

Beyond the mere establishment and expansion of merit systems, the states have taken other important steps over the last three decades to further professionalism in their administrative corps. One such step is to place a growing emphasis on training. A prime example is the Certified Public Manager (CPM) program, which originated in Georgia during the 1970s and is now operating in seventeen states. Under this program, agreements are reached between a state's human resource management office and a state university to provide supervisory and managerial training for state administrators. Managers who complete the 300 hours of training receive the CPM designation, which is becoming widely recognized among both state and local governments. While CPM programs principally serve managers below the executive level, they demonstrate state commitment to training; no doubt, some portion of CPM designees will rise to executive positions. In some states, carefully designed executive development activities have been introduced. These range from short-term programs introducing an incoming governor's cabinet to state executive responsibilities to more extended training programs for agency heads and other senior administrators.

In most states, though, training reaches far beyond the management level served by CPM or executive programs. In part driven by a growing number of tort liability suits, the states now take more seriously the responsibility to ensure that their administrators are familiar with human resource management policies and procedures (matters ranging from sexual harassment to corrective action and performance evaluation). But expanded training extends as well to more technical topics, from laboratory procedures to equipment operation.

Most of the department heads in the ASAP surveys gain their positions outside the state merit systems (only 27 percent are so appointed). Nevertheless, they are a professional cadre, which is indicated by several measures. Figure 3-7 displays some rather significant changes in educational levels over the last three decades. Most noticeable are the sharp increases in the percentage of all administrators who have completed graduate degrees (approaching or exceeding 60 percent in the last three survey years) and the sharp decline in the percentage having a high school education or less (dropping to 2 percent in recent survey years). Not only does this reflect a high level of education, but the prominence of graduate degree holders is likely to indicate administrators' growing professionalism.

Such professionalism is also reflected dramatically in the changes that have

Figure 3-7. Percentage Distribution of All Agency Heads by Formal Education, Select Years 1964–1988

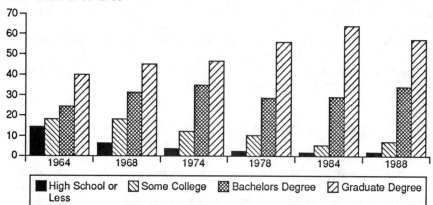

occurred in the reported previous experiences of department heads. Most notably, the proportion who had served in locally elected positions has dropped sharply, while the percentage with experience in one or more other states generally has climbed (see Figure 3-8). This is what one would expect as appointees become more "professional." To a greater extent than in the past, agency heads are following career tracks as state administrators rather than as elected officials (even on the part-time basis usually found at the local level). Further, Figure 3-8 shows that in 1988 (and even slightly more so in 1978), agency heads were likely to assume their positions directly from an agency within the same state. While variation exists from one survey to the next, the trend here is clearly upward, again reflecting growing professionalism.

Two other indicators support the conclusion that agency heads are becoming more professional. One is membership in professional associations.

Figure 3-8. Percentage Distribution of All Agency Heads by Previous and Immediately Prior Experience, Select Years 1964–1988

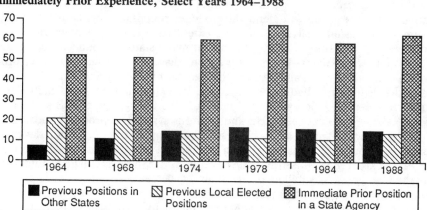

More than 90 percent of agency heads in recent survey years have reported belonging to a professional association, and many were members of several. These links reach across state boundaries, indicating that agency heads get some of their support and their ideas from counterparts in other states.

Finally, agency heads are entering state government at a younger age. This change may signify that they regard state administration as a professional career track. Respondents to the 1984 survey were the first to report entering state government at a median age below thirty.

IMPROVING MANAGEMENT AND POLICY-MAKING CAPACITY

Since the 1960s, there have been several major trends in state government that bear mentioning, both because they represent responses to pressures to act on developing problems and because they set the stage for coming developments. We note three in particular: continuing attempts to improve state budget processes; development of increasingly sophisticated information management systems; and expanded interest in, and increasing energy devoted to, productivity improvement. All three demand technical and management skills from senior executives.

Budgeting Process Improvement

The period under consideration began with the Planning, Programming, Budgeting (PPB) movement, which reached some states in full force. It was felt by all as it affected the federal budget process, but it had little impact on many. By the end of the 1960s, Kenneth Howard (1972, p. 50) could refer to the 1969 meeting of the National Association of State Budget Officers (NASBO) as a point at which "budget officers from all over the country expressed rampant skepticism about PPB," and he mentioned one observer's comment that "it is not going to be as much fun seeing what PPB does to the political system as seeing what the political system does to PPB."

Despite its rapid demise in many states as a formal system of budgeting, PPB left a legacy of improved analytic capability and, at a minimum, a desire for improved capability. Agencies, central executive budget offices, and legislative staffs attempted to defend their budget proposals with better data and more sophisticated analyses. To some extent, this development carried over to the Zero-Base Budget (ZBB) effort that many states introduced during the 1970s (following Georgia's example) and to the analyses used to protect programs and agencies against the automatic termination provisions of sunset laws that legislatures had begun to adopt. In 1976, the Council of State Governments identified eleven states that were using Georgia-type ZBB and noted a successful fusion between ZBB and previous systems of program budgeting.

Beyond these changes in the process of budget preparation, several developments are notable. One is the general decline in the use of dedicated revenues or earmarked funds. Rosenthal (1990) reports that the percentage of total earmarked revenues has fallen from 50 to 21 percent. Another development, whose direction currently seems uncertain, is the shifting responsibility for budget preparation. Even in states that nominally have an executive budget system, the role of the legislature in the preparation process is often substantial (Hebert, 1991; Rosenthal, 1990). As legislatures continue to strengthen their staffs, their roles in the budget process are likely to expand, and they will not be confined merely to reviewing the budgets that governors submit. Even when restricted to review, greater analytic capability will give legislatures an independent source of information for evaluating agencies and their programs.

Information Management System Improvement

The states have neither led the way nor been the last to take advantage of computer hardware and software for improving the flow and use of organizational innovation. A survey with responses from forty-five states in 1976–1977 by the National Association for State Information Systems found that all of the states were using data processing technology for financial and accounting purposes, thirty-three for budgeting, thirty-four for procurement, and forty-one for personnel functions (Vorlander, 1978). In addition, the legislatures have employed new technology for the tracking of bills and increasingly for the drafting of legislation.

The challenge of recent years has been to integrate the variety of individual computer and information technologies acquired over the last three decades or to replace them. This movement has led to a higher level of central control over information resource management, including the creation of telecommunications offices to manage the networks that states have assembled.

Advances in technology make the reduction, and even the elimination of paper possible for many activities, reaching far beyond the routines of accounting and payroll to include such diverse areas as procurement, libraries, and education. From a management perspective, the potential for use of information technology remains far larger than its present use.

Productivity Improvement

California's adoption of Proposition 13 in 1978 and the passage of similar measures in other states may have helped stimulate interest in productivity measurement. Among the responses have been the introduction and expansion of program evaluation efforts. To some extent, these are, no doubt, carryovers from program budgeting efforts, since the techniques employed are closely related. They also have been stimulated by provisions of federal grants that require evaluations.

Jones (1988) reports that legislatures in more than forty states have established their own offices or procedures for evaluating agencies' performance, building on early efforts in Hawaii and New York in the 1960s. In some instances, this has been accomplished by adding performance auditing to the more traditional financial audit function. Eleven legislatures have created separate staff units to focus entirely on program evaluation.

The ASAP surveys of agency heads in 1978 and 1984 inquired whether administrators' own agencies had a separate program evaluation unit. In both years, about two-fifths of the administrators (41.2 percent and 38.2 percent) responded in the affirmative. The directors were quite satisfied with the performance of their units, with 73.9 percent and 82.3 percent, respectively, reporting that, considering the resources devoted to the unit, its performance was good or excellent. In both years, though, more than 60 percent of the administrators of agencies with performance evaluation units indicated that they needed more resources.

The states have also taken important steps to improve their systems for the performance appraisal of employees. In part, this development has been stimulated by court mandates that states validate any tools affecting promotion opportunities. Steps have been taken to move appraisal from person-based criteria toward performance-based criteria. This makes it easier to use the appraisal process as an opportunity to communicate management goals and objectives to employees. At the same time, it increases both the validity and the reliability of the appraisal tools. Adopting systems that focus on job-related behaviors has required that the states devote resources to the development and implementation of appropriate systems and to the training of their supervisors in appraisal procedures. This movement is well established and is attracting a great deal of attention from human resources management personnel at all government levels.

CONCLUSION

In the last three decades, the states have faced dramatic changes in the system of intergovernmental relationships, in economic conditions, in the public's expectations of services from government, and in their awareness of environmental and other major problems. The states have responded. They have not been relegated to insignificant roles, and they have not become minor administrative units in a system dominated by federal and local governments. They have modified their political and administrative structures and processes to meet current and emerging demands, and they have devoted increasing financial and human resources to these tasks.

What do the 1990s and the early years of the next century portend for the states? If the recent past provides any indication, they hold the promise of an expanding role for all their institutions: legislatures, governors, courts, and administrators. This vision brings the states to center stage. Their executives will carry greater and more complex responsibilities than ever before. The states will be a focus of attention for interest groups and others who seek to affect public policy. Attention will not be limited to elected officials but will focus on senior administrators as well. State executives are in positions to exercise leadership, individually and collectively. The next decade will be an exciting time to hold executive positions in state government.

Notes

1. Personnel of the Council of State Governments indicate that the lists of agencies have been developed across the three decades by an interactive process under which staff take the initiative to identify agencies that have come into wide usage and also respond to requests by representatives of emergent agencies who wish to assemble mailing lists of their counterparts in other states. The states are then contacted to

determine whether the agencies identified exist in each state and to solicit names of heads of these agencies.

2. State direct general expenditures are all state expenditures except those that are in the form of aid to local governments or payments to the federal government and those that are for the operation of state-owned utilities and liquor stores or from insurance trust funds.

3. General revenue includes all revenues except those from liquor stores, insurance trusts (notably social security), and utilities.

4. Data presented here on department heads are from the American State Administrators Project. We have conducted a mailed survey of heads of state agencies in the years 1964, 1968, 1974, 1978, 1984, and 1988. All fifty states are represented each time, and the number of respondents has generally grown over the years, as the states have expanded their numbers of agencies. Respondents range from just under 1,000 in the 1960s to approximately 1,500 in the 1970s and 1980s.

Bibliography

Advisory Commission on Intergovernmental Relations. *Significant Features of Fiscal Federalism: Revenues and Expenditures*. Washington, D.C.: Advisory Commission on Intergovernmental Relations, 1990.

Baum, L. "State Supreme Courts: Activism and Accountability." In C. E. Van Horn (ed.), *The State of the States*. Washington, D.C.: CQ Press, 1989.

Beyle, T. L. "From Governor to Governors." In C. E. Van Horn (ed.), *The State of the States*. Washington, D.C.: CQ Press, 1989.

Bowman, A. O., and Kearney, R. C. *The Resurgence of the States*. Englewood Cliffs, N.J.: Prentice Hall, 1986.

Conant, J. K. "In the Shadow of Wilson and Brownlow: Executive Branch Reorganization in the States, 1965–1987." *Public Administration Review*, 1988, *48*, 892–910.

Council of State Governments. *The Book of the States*. Supplement II: *State Administrative Officials Classified by Function*. Lexington, Ky.: Council of State Governments, 1959, 1969, 1979, 1989.

Council of State Governments. *Zero-Base Budgeting in the States*. Lexington, Ky.: Council of State Governments, 1976.

Council of State Governments. *The Book of the States, 1990–91*. Lexington, Ky.: Council of State Governments, 1990.

Denhardt, R. B., and Jennings, E. T. "Image and Integrity in the Public Service." *Public Administration Review*, 1989, *49*, 75–77.

Dresang, D. L., and Gosling, J. J. *Politics, Policy, and Management in the American States*. White Plains, N.Y.: Longman, 1989.

Fino, S. P. *The Role of State Supreme Courts in the New Judicial Federalism*. New York: Greenwood Press, 1987.

Garnett, J. L.: *Reorganizing State Government: The Executive Branch*. Boulder, Colo.: Westview Press, 1980.

Golembiewski, R. T. "Anomie, Resurgence, and Opportunity: Reflections on the Current State of the Public Service." *Public Administration Review*, 1989, *49*, 287–290.

Hebert, F. T. "Legislative Budgeting in an Executive Budget State." In E. Clynch and T. Lauth (eds.), *State Budgeting: Executive and Legislative Decision Making*. New York: Greenwood Press, 1991.

Howard, S. K. "Changing Concepts of State Budgeting." In S. K. Howard and G. Grizzle (eds.), *Whatever Happened to State Budgeting?* Lexington, Ky.: Council of State Governments, 1972.

Jones, R. "Keeping an Eye on State Agencies." In T. L. Beyle (ed.), *State Government: CQ's Guide to Current Issues and Activities, 1988–89*. Washington, D.C.: Congressional Quarterly, 1988.

National Commission on the Public Service. *Leadership for America: Rebuilding the Public Service*. Lexington, Mass.: Lexington Books, 1990.

Robb, C. S. "The State of the States." In Council of State Governments, *The Book of the States, 1986–87*. Lexington, Ky.: Council of State Governments, 1986.

Rosenthal, A. "The Legislative Institution: Transformed and at Risk." In C. E. Van Horn (ed.), *The State of the States*. Washington, D.C.: CQ Press, 1989.

Rosenthal, A. *Governors and Legislatures: Contending Powers*. Washington, D.C.: CQ Press, 1990.

Sabato, L. *Goodbye to Good-Time Charlie*. (2nd ed.). Washington, D.C.: CQ Press, 1983.

Shannon, J. "Competitive Federalism: Three Driving Forces." *Intergovernmental Perspective*, 1989, *15*, 17–18.

Stahl, O. G. *Public Personnel Administration*. (5th ed.). New York: HarperCollins, 1962.

Stephens, G. R. "State Centralization and the Erosion of Local Autonomy." *Journal of Politics*, 1974, *36*, 44–76.

Stephens, G. R. "State Centralization Revisited." Paper presented at the annual meeting of the American Political Science Association, New Orleans, 29 August–1 September, 1985.

U.S. Department of Commerce. Bureau of the Census. *Census of Governments, 1987*. Vol. 3, No. 2: *Public Employment: Compendium of Public Employment*. Washington, D.C.: Government Printing Office, 1991.

U.S. Department of Commerce. Bureau of the Census. *Government Finances*. Washington, D.C.: Government Printing Office, 1962.

U.S. Department of Commerce. Bureau of the Census. *Government Finances*. Washington, D.C.: Government Printing Office, 1987–1988.

U.S. Department of Commerce. Bureau of the Census. *Public Employment*. Washington, D.C.: Government Printing Office, 1990.

U.S. Equal Employment Opportunity Commission. *Job Patterns for Minorities and Women in State and Local Government*. Washington, D.C.: U.S. Equal Employment Opportunity Commission, 1990.

Vorlander, C. "State Information Systems." In Council of State Governments, *The Book of the States 1978–79*. Lexington, Ky.: Council of State Governments, 1978.

Weissert, C. "The National Governors' Association: 1908–1983." *State Government*, 1983, *56*, 44–52.

Wildavsky, A. "Ubiquitous Anomie: Public Service in an Era of Ideological Dissensus." *Public Administration Review*, 1988, *48*, 753–755.

4

PUBLIC ADMINISTRATION IN A DEMOCRATIC SOCIETY

Hostility toward administrative authority is nothing new in this country. It started with colonists revolting against a distant king and his local administrators and continued through the Articles of Confederation and the Constitutional Convention right into the twentieth century. However, the fear that government bureaucracy is too powerful, almost out of control, has probably never been as strong as it is today. This chapter treats the place of bureaucracy in modern society, especially the clash between bureaucracy and democracy.

In the first article, author and U.S. Secretary of Labor Robert Reich examines the role of discretion on the part of administrative agencies in a democratic society. He has a particular interest in the importance of public discussion and public influence on these agencies. He also provides three interesting examples of these issues.

There are inherent contradictions between the concepts of bureaucracy and democracy. One question is whether public bureaucracies can be controlled at all.

Students of public administration have long realized that a *system* of restraints in effect controls the power of public bureaucracies. Always undergoing change, these restraints may be divided into two basic types: intragovernmental and extragovernmental.

Regarding *intragovernmental vehicles* for control, most notable in the American context is the separation of powers. Through hearings and investigations, review of the budget, audits, confirmation of appointments, staff assistance, and individual monitoring of constituency complaints, legislative control of bureaucratic power has been especially important. The courts are increasingly active, and judicial review is also significant.

Hierarchical administration, sometimes referred to as "overhead democracy," is also an important vehicle. Chief political executives are usually elected in our republican form of government, and citizens expect them to hold the bureaucracy accountable.

Chief executives at all levels of American government have increased the size of their staffs to assist them in this function. Consolidation and centralization of agency structures is one common device. Increasingly, chief executives also use modern management techniques and information systems to supervise public agencies under their control.

The final intragovernmental factor that merits attention, but is often neglected in the literature, is internal control within the bureaucracy. Included here is administrative self-restraint, because—as many believe—total outside control is probably impossible. Increasing the sense of personal responsibility among public employees at all levels of government is one of the critical issues of our time.

Extragovernmental forces are represented primarily by a variety of competing interest groups, political parties, public opinion, and direct citizen participation. Scholarly research can also be included here.

Some observers place particular emphasis on the role of the press with its First Amendment privileges. They want to help the media and citizens obtain better access to government: through "sunshine" laws that require governmental meetings to be open, and through freedom of information (FOI) legislation facilitating access to government records. They feel that less secrecy in government means greater control over the power of officeholders.

Trends in the political control of bureaucratic power and the effectiveness of this system are the principal topics of discussion in this chapter. With revelations about the activities of the CIA, FBI, and IRS—not to mention Abscam and President Nixon's "enemies list"—controlling the bureaucracy is a topic of permanent importance as well as contemporary controversy.

There are other related issues. Many Americans believe that government does too much, whereas others contend that government does too little. Businesspeople complain about too much regulation, and citizens of all kinds complain about the red tape and paperwork they encounter in dealing with government.

American society appears to be in the midst of a fundamental rethinking about the scope of government activity. Much of this discussion centers on the role and functions of large public bureaucracies. We will give additional attention to this in Chapters 9 and 10.

The 1980s were a decade of decentralization and deregulation. Previous to President Clinton, the last five presidents—Nixon, Ford, Carter, Reagan, and Bush; four Republicans and a Democrat—were all against Big Government and especially Big Bureaucracy. Public opinion seems to be moving toward a reconsideration of the government's ability to solve societal problems, which has not been seriously challenged since the presidency of Franklin D. Roosevelt.

In the second article here, William Gormley attempts to assess the state of administrative accountability, focusing on the states. Gormley reminds us of the variety of devices available as well as current developments.

In the third article, Barbara Romzek and Mel Dubnick continue the discussion of accountability, but from the point of view of the individual public administrator. Using the Challenger tragedy as a case study, they point out that every executive in government faces four sets of expectations: legal, hierarchical (or bureaucratic), professional, and political. They also point out that conflicting expectations are common in public administration.

In the final selection, Dwight Waldo, this country's leading theorist in public administration, tries to untangle the issue of ethics and public morality. First, Waldo attempts to sort out exactly to whom or to what are public employees obligated. Then he speculates about putting ethics into practice.

This chapter raises some of the most important issues surrounding the practice of public administration today. Some questions to think about in connection with this chapter include:

- Is there a fundamental clash between bureaucracy and democracy?

- How much discretion is available to an administrative leader in our democratic system? When administrators "listen" to the public, is discretion decreased or increased?

- What is new in administrative accountability, at least as it affects state agencies and their administrators? Is accountability increasing in the states?

- Describe the four types of accountability, or sets of expectations, described by Romzek and Dubnick. Which is the most effective? How about all four taken together? How does NASA, in connection with the Challenger disaster, illustrate these?

- Are administrative ethics possible? Why would you think otherwise?

- Looking back at the last three chapters, do you think that administrative agencies at all levels of government are too powerful today? Are they sufficiently controlled? By whom? How?

Policy Making in a Democracy

ROBERT B. REICH

. . . It has been argued that citizens are motivated to act according to ideas about what is good for society; that such ideas determine how public problems are defined and understood; that government depends on such ideas for mobilizing public action; that, in consequence, policy makers find themselves espousing substantive conceptions of the public good (although the expression is often implicit); and that this role, in turn, raises questions about the place of policy making in a democratic society. If conceptions about what is good for society are different from mere aggregations of selfish wants, where should policy makers look for guidance about what they should do? What is the relationship between policy making and democracy? In this [article] I offer tentative responses to these questions, grounded in the idea of public deliberation.

For the typical public manager who heads a bureaucracy charged with implementing the law, public debate is not something to be invited. It is difficult enough to divine what the legislature had in mind when it enacted the law, how the governor or president wants it to be interpreted and administered, and what course is consistent with sound public policy. It is harder still to commandeer the resources necessary to implement the program, to overcome bureaucratic inertia and institutional rigidity, and to ensure that a system for producing the desired result is actually in place and working. In the midst of these challenges, public controversy is not particularly welcome. The tacit operating rule holds that the best public is a quiescent one; the manager should work quietly, get the job done without disturbing the peace, and reassure everyone "out there" that there is no reason to be concerned or involved.

But sometimes, I believe, higher-level public managers have an obligation to stimulate public debate about what they do. Public deliberation can help the manager clarify ambiguous mandates. More importantly, it can help the public discover latent contradictions and commonalities in what it wants to achieve. Thus the public manager's job is not only, or simply, to make policy choices and implement them. It is also to participate in a system of democratic governance in which public values are continuously rearticulated and recreated.

The first part of this [article] considers the problem of administrative discretion in its historical context. The next section examines the two techniques of constraining administrative discretion that have come to dominate our thinking about responsive government. In the third section I will show why these two dominant forms have failed to solve the problem of administrative discretion in a democracy. The fourth section suggests why public deliberation may, at least on occasion, offer a desirable alternative to the dominant forms. The final sections will examine some applications of this errant concept and the lessons they reveal about the possibilities and limits of public deliberation.

THE PROBLEM OF ADMINISTRATIVE DISCRETION

Nonelected public managers at the higher reaches of administration—commissioners, secretaries, agency heads, division chiefs, bureau directors—rarely can rely on unambiguous legislative mandates. The statutes that authorize them to take action are often written in vague language, unhelpful for difficult cases of a sort the legislative drafters never contemplated or did not wish to highlight for fear that explication might jeopardize a delicate compromise. The legislators may have had conflicting ideas about how the law should be implemented and decided to leave the task to those who would be closer to the facts and circumstances of particular applications. Or they may simply have wanted an administrator to take the political heat for doing something too unpopular to be codified explicitly in legislation. Or the legislators may have felt that the issue was not sufficiently important to merit their time and resources.

As a result, higher-level public managers are likely to have significant discretion over many of the problems they pursue, solutions they devise, and strategies they choose for implementing such solutions. To be sure, they will need to keep in touch with key legislators and elected officials within the executive branch who have an interest in the policy area—periodically informing them of plans, seeking their approval of broad purposes and strategies, and reporting on important problems and accomplishments. But despite these informal ties, public managers will have considerable running room. There are typically too many decisions to be made, over too wide a range of issues, for even informal ties to bind. Administrative discretion is endemic.

Given this range of discretion, it may seem curious that so little thought has been given to the relationship between administrative performance and democratic values. It is particularly curious in light of the extraordinary attention devoted to the parallel problem facing the judiciary—the other domain of nonelected discretion in government. A seemingly endless stream of critical commentary has sought to reconcile judge-made law with democratic values. Although the *Federalist* described the judiciary as the "least dangerous branch" of government, having no direct influence over "the sword or the purse,"[1] generations of scholars and commentators have fretted over where judges should find their substantive conception of the public interest— whether from some transcendant notion of natural law, principles deducible from the common law, historical inquiries into what the framers of the Constitution (or the drafters of various statutes) "really" had in mind, or some set of "neutral principles" that reconcile and give consistent meaning to various constitutional and common law provisions.[2]

At the very least, the public has come to expect that judges will justify their decisions by reference to general principles lying beyond the particular situation confronting them, reflecting some intelligible and coherent normative ideas—or that they will refrain from deciding at all. Judges are in the business of articulating public values, within a form of argumentation and logic fundamentally concerned with how such values can and should be found. Judicial opinions are attempts at stating public ideas—trying them out first on other judges, who are either persuaded by them or compelled to say why they are not. This ongoing conversation among judges, as they grapple with public ideas in differing contexts, is a form of public deliberation. Judicial opinions are arguments for public legitimacy. The ultimate test of such an articulation is how persuasive the public finds the argument.

History may explain the different treatments accorded judges and administrators. Judicial discretion has been long understood as a potential threat to democratic values. Not so administrative discretion. In the half-century before World War II, the standard American attitude toward administrative discretion vacillated between efforts to improve its exercise and to deny its existence. Initially, the two coexisted quite peacefully. Administrative action was seen less as an act of discretion than as an application of expertise—the discovery of the best means of executing preordained public goals. No less a Progressive reformer than Woodrow Wilson saw public administration as a "detailed and systematic execution of public law" in which discretion was confined to the expert choice of means for carrying out policies decided on by elected officials.[3] Fellow political scientists Frank Goodnow and Charles Beard called for a science of administration through which public administrators could use their knowledge of administration and the tools of social science to serve the public interest.[4] By 1914 several American universities were offering one-year master's degrees in public administration, and by 1924 the first semi-independent school for training public officials was founded at Syracuse University.

As these Progressive era ideals found expression in independent administrative agencies, some members of the legal community grew concerned about the extraordinary delegation of legislative-like responsibilities these schemes implied. Legal scholars like Ernst Freund warned that broad grants of administrative discretion to set rates and standards would reduce public accountability and cause democratic institutions to atrophy.[5] With increasing enthusiasm—culminating in the Supreme Court's determination that Title I of the National Recovery Act of 1933 represented an unconstitutional delegation of congressional authority—the federal courts struck down statutes that contained broad delegations of administrative responsibility.[6]

This conceptual tension between the benefits of administrative expertise and the evils of administrative discretion continued into the 1930s. New Dealers like Felix Frankfurter and James Landis, among others, saw in the development of administrative agencies a capacity to solve social and economic problems quickly and efficiently, applying systematic knowledge to public issues. These New Deal theorists of public administration perceived no conflict between their vision and democratic ideas: elected representatives would define the broad goals and problems to be addressed; the agencies would solve them. Others, however, particularly those sitting on the federal courts, took a dimmer view.

By the middle of the decade, under pressure from Franklin D. Roosevelt, the courts relented. Most broad delegations of authority would thereafter be declared constitutional. But it was not just Roosevelt's threat to pack the Supreme Court that tipped the scales at the time. Public opinion was solidly behind the ideal of administrative expertise. From the depths of the Depression the public goals seemed self-evident—to get the economy moving again and ameliorate some of the worst suffering. The challenge was to discover and implement solutions. And this was manifestly a job for expert judgment. If not delegated to expert agencies, that job could only be handled by the courts, through case-by-case adjudication of specific applications of broad statutes. But the courts lacked the expertise, they could not be counted on to act quickly, and they had no capacity to solve the inevitable problems of implementation.[7] The logic of the reformers seemed irrefutable.

In reality, of course, no sharp line could be drawn between ends and means, between making policy and implementing it. During the Depression decade of the 1930s and the subsequent war years, there was a broad consensus about the problems that needed to be solved. This left considerable room for administrative discretion that *looked* like implementation. After peace and prosperity had been substantially attained, the next set of goals—having more to do with the quality of the life Americans would lead thereafter—was less clear-cut. Accordingly, administrative discretion began looking more like policy making. This shift in public perceptions, in turn, brought into sharper focus the problem of reconciling discretion with democratic values.

There was another reason why the American public became more sensitive to administrative discretion after 1945. The fresh experience of fascism, Soviet totalitarianism, and then McCarthyism at home caused many to view with alarm any scheme of governance that permitted moral absolutism or smacked of social engineering. To Americans who had emerged from the shadow of demagoguery, the virtue of American democracy appeared to lie in political pluralism and ethical relativism.[8] Political scientists of the era slipped gingerly from description to prescription: American politics was pluralist, composed of shifting and overlapping groups whose leaders bargained with one another; the vast majority of Americans were members of one or more of these groups, even if they remained mostly uninvolved. These features helped to explain why democracy had survived so well in the United States, by contrast to many other nations; these features were thus desirable prerequisites for democracy.[9] Economists began to entertain a similar vision of democracy as a contest among leaders to represent the interests of competing groups.[10]

Broad grants of administrative discretion to the "experts" seemed dangerously inconsistent with these newly discovered democratic virtues. Accordingly, the postwar intellectual and political agenda turned toward *reducing* administrative discretion rather than justifying and enlarging on it. But this proved no mean task. Given the complexities of modern government, legislatures could not simply reclaim responsibilities of the sort they had been delegating to administrators. At the same time, given the premises of pluralism and relativism, it was quite impossible to construct a set of substantive standards to guide administrators in discovering the public interest. For there was no longer assumed to be any unified "public interest" capable of discovery. What passed for the public interest at any moment was now thought to be the product of an ongoing competition among groups for power and influence.

One needed some means of reconciling the practical necessity of administrative discretion with this emerging pluralist norm—a way to retain the broadly delegated authority of administrators to make choices in the public interest, while radically limiting their substantive discretion over where the "public interest" might lie. The solution was found in the idea of administrative process. Henceforth, public administrators were to be managers of neutral processes designed to discover the best ("optimal") public policies. Their substantive expertise about a particular set of public problems was to be transformed into procedural expertise about a set of techniques applicable to all sorts of public problems. At the same time, new emphasis was to be given to the details of making administrative decisions. Public managers would have to follow certain preordained steps for gathering evidence and arriving at conclusions. The Administrative Procedure Act of 1946 and its subsequent amendments codified the prevailing expectations. The burgeoning field of administrative law thereafter concerned itself primarily with the procedural steps judges should demand of public administrators, rather than with the substance of what administrators ought to do. The effect was to treat administrative law as the consequence of judicial review rather than as a set of substantive standards of public administration.

Even the words used to describe the responsibilities of administrators subtly changed. Instead of finding the "common good" or the "public interest," the new language of public management saw the task in pluralist terms—making "tradeoffs," "balancing" interests, engaging in "policy choices," and weighing the costs and benefits. Graduate schools of public administration henceforth would pay less attention to the purposes and methods of governance than to the techniques of making and implementing public policy. Courses in "analysis" and "implementation" would frame the core curricula.[11]

THE TWO PARADIGMS

The postwar transformation of public administration centered on two related but conceptually distinct procedural visions of how public managers should decide what to do. The first entailed *intermediating among interest groups*; the second, *maximizing net benefits*. Intermediation was the direct intellectual descendant of pluralist theory. Maximization was a stepchild, claiming equal descent from decision theory and microeconomics. Together the two procedural visions embodied the postwar shift from a description of how democratic institutions work to a powerful set of norms for how public decision making should be organized.

Interest Group Intermediation

Interest group intermediation took as its starting point the prevailing pluralist understanding of American politics, along with its prescriptive tilt. The job of the public manager, according to this vision, was to accommodate—to the extent possible—the varying demands placed on government by competing groups. The public manager was a referee, an intermediary, a skillful practitioner of negotiation and compromise. He was to be accessible to all organized interests while making no independent judgment of the merits of their claims. Since, in this view, the "public interest" was simple an amalgamation and reconciliation of these claims, the manager succeeded to the extent that the competing groups were placated.

In time, as the rather self-congratulatory pluralist theories of the 1950s and early 1960s gave way to a deepening critique of the American "administrative state" for its insensitivity to less organized interests and its corresponding tendency to be captured by dominant interests, the job of the manager-as-intermediator was refined. The central challenge came to be understood as ensuring that *all* those who might be affected by agency action were represented in decision-making deliberations—including interests dispersed so widely and thinly over the population that they might otherwise go unexpressed.

The federal courts took an early, active role in this refinement. As early as 1966 the Court of Appeals for the District of Columbia Circuit ruled that, within a license renewal proceeding, the Federal Communications Commission was obliged to permit the intervention of spokesmen for significant segments of the listening public. The basis for the ruling was that, since consideration of such viewpoints was necessary to ensure a decision responsive to public needs, failure to allow intervention rendered decisions arbitrary and capricious. The court noted that in "recent years, the concept that public participation in decisions which involve the public interest is not only valuable but indispensable has gained increasing support."[12] Subsequent court decisions required that an agency seek out representatives of opposing views, that it affirmatively consider all such views, and that it also consider alternate policy choices in light of their impact on all affected interests.[13] State courts imposed similar requirements on state agencies. Public participation was further aided by several statutes that provided funding for interest groups to be represented in agency proceedings. The Federal Trade Commission Improvement Act of 1975, for example, authorized the FTC to pay attorneys' fees and costs of rule-making participation to any group representing an interest that "would not otherwise be represented in such a proceeding" and whose representation "is necessary for a fair determination of the rule-making proceeding."[14]

As opportunities for participation grew, the task of interest group intermediation became more open to public scrutiny—or rather to the scrutiny of organized groups with the resources to ferret out information from the government. Courts required, for example, that all relevant information from agency files or consultants' reports be disclosed to all participants for comment, that agency announcements of proposed rule making give the agency's view of the issues, and that agency decision makers generally refrain from communicating in secret with participants.[15] Moreover, in the 1976 Government in the Sunshine Act, Congress declared it "the policy of the United States that the public is entitled to the fullest practicable information regarding the decisionmaking processes of the Federal Government." The act required that, with limited exceptions, agencies make their decisions in public.[16]

These developments tended to formalize the administrative process, making it resemble a trial court proceeding. But their more consequential effect was to impose ever more severe penalties on a public manager who failed to reach a workable compromise with groups that had the resources to challenge his decision in the courts, on some procedural ground. The penalty they could threaten was delay; litigation could drag on for years. Procedural formality thereby upped the ante, making accommodation all the more important.

Accommodation was possible largely because participation was conditioned on specific, concrete, and self-serving claims, rather than on general views about what policies were in the "public interest." To be sure, these self-interested claims typically were encased within arguments appealing to general principles of law or public interest that tended to favor the claimants' position. But it was well understood that the purpose of the inquiry was not to discover the public interest directly, only to find it indirectly by identifying programs or solutions that accommodated most groups. The courts would not guarantee groups espousing so-called ideological interests—who had no selfish stake in the outcome—a right to participate in the proceedings. Participation was conditioned on a showing that the proposed agency action might cause some material "injury in fact" to members of the group, or that the group's interest was specifically protected by the statute in question.

This condition aided accommodation in two ways. First and most obviously, it limited participation. If the proceedings were open to anyone who claimed to know what was best for the public, there might be no efficient way of reaching agreement among so large a crowd. Even more importantly, the requirement that participants have experienced a concrete injury ensured that grievances could be remedied and compromises devised. There would be no efficient way to bargain with parties espousing purely "ideological" views about what was good for the community or the nation, because there would be no obvious means of compensating them for their potential loss. Their injuries would involve values rather than palpable harms. Such values are often impossible to measure or rank, and they have an all-or-nothing quality that makes them stubbornly resistant to tradeoffs. They cannot be compromised easily without losing their inherent moral character.[17]

Net Benefit Maximization

Net benefit maximization proceeded along a different route. This paradigm took as its starting point the decision-making tools that had been successfully applied in World War II for allocating resources and planning strategy, and added to them microeconomic theory, which supplied the idea of allocative efficiency. But the shift from description to prescription was as complete as in the preceding vision. How people acted in the market to satisfy their desires was taken as a model for how public managers should decide what to do. In this view government intervention was justified primarily when it would result in an allocation of goods and services better matched to what people want than the outcome generated by market forces alone (as under conditions of natural monopoly or other forms of "market failure"). Even when allocative efficiency was not the goal of a given intervention, consideration of economic effects presumably would lead to a more efficient intervention—that is, one that achieved its goal at minimal cost.

Here the public manager was less a referee than an analyst. HIs responsibilities were, first, to determine that the market had somehow failed and that intervention might improve overall efficiency; second, to structure the decision-making process so as to make explicit the public problem at issue, alternative means of remedying it, and the consequences and tradeoffs associated with each solution; and third, to choose the policy option yielding the highest net benefits—where there was the greatest social utility. Along the way he (or his staff) might employ a range of analytic tools: probability theory, to deal with uncertainty; econometric, queuing, diffusion, and demographic models, to help predict the remote consequences of particular actions; linear programming, to perform complex resource allocation computations; discounting, to measure future outcomes in terms of present values; and other variations on game theory, statistics, and mathematics. Social science data derived from empirical experiments and field studies might be applicable to these analytic processes, of course, particularly to anticipate the consequences of various alternatives. But unlike his prewar predecessors who wielded substantive expertise, the public manager who sought to maximize net benefits relied primarily on procedural expertise. His focus was on how to organize the process of discovering the optimal policy.

Net benefit maximization became a cornerstone of regulatory reform efforts. Between 1965 and 1980, Congress passed approximately forty new laws—on health, education, transportation, housing, the environment, and agriculture—that required evaluations of the economic impact of regulations proposed under them. Six of these laws specifically authorized funding of, or required that a fixed percentage of the agency program budget be set aside for, such evaluations.[18] In addition, the Ford, Carter, and Reagan administrations actively pursued economic impact analysis. Executive orders required that agencies subject major regulations to a "regulatory analysis" that contained a succinct statement of the problem requiring federal action, the major ways of dealing with it, analysis of the economic effects of the proposed regulation and of alternative approaches considered, and a justification of the approach selected. These analyses were to be reviewed by groups within the Office of Management and Budget, or affiliated with the Council of Economic Advisors, to ensure that major regulations were justifiable in terms of costs and benefits.[19] Similar efforts cropped up among the states. At the same time, and with increasing boldness, the courts also embraced net benefit maximization. They deemed evidence "insufficient" or the process of decision making "arbitrary and capricious" when an agency disregarded important economic effects of its actions, artificially narrowed options, failed to set forth its theories, or employed faulty analysis and a weak chain of analytic reasoning.[20]

Net benefit maximization shared with interest group intermediation the central premise that the "public interest" could—and should—be defined only by reference to the disparate, selfish preferences of individuals. But rather than uncritically accept the preferences articulated by and through group leaders, net benefit maximizers sought to measure preferences directly by observing how people behaved. If people were simply asked what they wanted, their responses would not necessarily reflect tradeoffs implied in the choice. A preferable course was to observe how people expressed their priorities within the numerous market transactions of their daily lives. If the policy at issue concerned something that was not traded on the market, like clean air, the net benefit maximizer would seek a surrogate measure of citizens' willingness to pay for such a good, like the price of homes in a non-polluted area of town relative to housing prices in a polluted section nearby.

Policies that would make one group of people worse off and another group better off posed a special problem. Interest group intermediators attempted to solve it by pitting the groups against one another, presumably until an accommodation occurred through which the gainers shared some of their benefits with the losers. This approach still left open the possibility that certain groups might have more organizational strength than others and thus could impose substantial (although perhaps widely dispersed) costs on the others for the sake of relatively small gains for themselves. Net benefit maximizers sought to solve the problem through cost-benefit analysis; policies would be chosen that conferred larger benefits on some than losses for others. Because there is no theoretically defensible means of determining that the wants of one group of people are either stronger or more worthy than those of another, net benefit maximizers felt more confident about these decisions if the two groups—the gainers and the losers—started in roughly equivalent circumstances or, if not, the resulting redistribution at least moved them closer together.[21] But such judgment ultimately rested on a pluralist vision as well—one that perceived individuals as members of groups, the members as possessing certain common characteristics, and the group existing in some specific and identifiable relationship to one another. These perceptions, in turn, could be drawn reliably only from the ways in which the groups actually organized themselves—what criteria defined their memberships, how they described their central purposes, and how they characterized themselves.

The Two Paradigms in Practice

These two approaches to policy making—interest group intermediation and net benefit maximization—have coexisted uneasily. Both have rested on the same pluralist vision and understood the "public interest" as nothing more (or other) than the disparate sentiments of diverse groups of people about what they want for themselves, combined with procedural norms for weighing and balancing such interests. And from a strictly theoretical perspective (ignoring agency and transaction problems) there is no difference in outcome between the two methods. After all, any "solution" whose benefits exceed its costs would enable those who gain from it to compensate those who lose (or who receive none of the direct benefits) and still come out ahead. Since actual compensation would cause losers and nongainers to acquiesce to the change, the mere fact of unanimous agreement to a compromise would signal that it is efficient.

As a practical matter, however, the two approaches ave diverged in several ways. The first involves the objectives to be sought by government intervention. Interest group intermediators have assumed that the objective will emerge only from the interactions of divergent participants and cannot be fully defined in advance. This lack of definition enables each of the participating groups to believe (or at least its leader to claim to his clients and constituents) that the intervention served the group's purposes. As a result, the public goal of the government action is established after the fact, if at all. But net benefit maximizers have required that the objective be articulated as specifically and narrowly as possible in advance, so that alternative (and less costly) means of attaining it can be considered.

A second divergence has to do with evidence. Interest group intermediators have assumed that the facts at issue are the articulated preferences of parties likely to be affected by the rule. Relevant evidence therefore properly includes a substantial amount of testimony by group representatives about what the group wants and needs. On the other hand, net benefit maximizers have not concerned themselves with articulated preferences. The facts at issue are the potential overall costs and benefits of the proposed action and its alternatives. Articulated preferences offer a poor means of measuring these values.

A final divergence concerns the criteria for a good decision. Interest group intermediators have believed the best decision is the one most acceptable (or least objectionable) to the groups affected—that outcome to which the greater number of participants ultimately subscribe most enthusiastically. But net benefit maximizers have believed the best decision is the most efficient one—that which maximizes benefits for a given cost or minimizes costs for a given benefit. Negotiation and compromise have nothing to do with it; an efficient solution might be unpopular with many participants.

To get a concrete sense of these differences, imagine a town in a river valley periodically subject to flooding. The public manager has a broad statutory mandate to "manage the environment" or "manage water resources"; or perhaps he is a city manager charged with overseeing the local government. If he views his role as interest group intermediator, he would listen to the complaints of various group representatives who came to his office—business and civic associations representing downstream merchants and householders who want a dam constructed. He also would listen to residents of the less populous area upstream, who would lose their businesses and homes if a dam turned the upstream area into a reservoir. The intermediator's objective is neither to stop the downstream flooding nor to save upstream homes, but only to reach an accommodation that basically satisfies the various groups. Our manager-as-intermediator also might solicit the participation of other, less organized groups, such as lower-income people who now rent houses on the flood plain (whose rents would substantially increase if the land value were to rise). The resulting decision would reflect a great deal of negotiation. The dam may be built; but if so, upstream owners will be paid for their land and their moving expenses, and perhaps given an additional "sweetener," and some of the poorer renters downstream will be allocated parcels of the new land made habitable as a result of the project.

A manager who viewed his role as net benefit maximizer would proceed quite differently. He would be open to the possibility of a dam project, since the market cannot be expected on its own to generate a "public good" like a dam. But he would carefully examine the costs and benefits of building it or taking any other measure to reduce downstream flooding. He might gather evidence of the market values of property on the flood plain, above it, and upstream—thereby discovering how much money people in principle would be willing to spend to avoid flooding, on the one hand, or to live in the rural area upstream that would be permanently flooded by construction of a dam. In the end, let us suppose, the administrator decides that the benefits of the dam far outweigh the costs. The dam will be built. But upstream landowners will not necessarily be paid anything (beyond the "just compensation" required by the Fifth Amendment to the Constitution) since actual compensation need not be paid to make the outcome efficient, and there is no particular income difference between upstream and downstream owners that might justify such a payment. Poorer renters downstream will receive a cash transfer instead of an allocation of the newly habitable public lands; such a transfer will represent a more efficient redistribution than a donation of the land, since the poor can then choose how they wish to spend it.

It is hardly surprising that these two different approaches have, in practice, resulted in something of a hybrid. While the formal language of policy making increasingly has borrowed forms of argument and analysis from net benefit maximization, the actual process of coming to a decision has rested ever more firmly on interest group intermediation. Each participating group typically submits its own data and analysis tending to support a definition of the problem and a proposed solution that best serves its wants. To return to our example, upstream homeowners could be expected to submit data and analyses suggesting that the periodic costs of downstream flooding are really quite minor, while the costs of damming the river and flooding upstream would be high, and that, in any event, the problem could be alleviated simply by building a drainage canal. Downstream owners, on the other hand, would submit data and analyses tending to show that the costs of failing to remedy the problem are higher than those of building the dam, and that there are no less costly alternatives. Typically the public manager would compromise among these competing estimates, choosing a set of valuations approximately halfway between those offered by the competing camps (thereby practicing interest group intermediation while applying the form of net benefit maximization.)[22]

Ironically, the hybrid of the two procedural visions occasionally has thwarted both. The strategic use of the *form* of net benefit maximization in the *process* of intermediation has tended to exacerbate a central problem of intermediation: the underrepresentation of poor and diffused interests. The very insistence on analytic argument has altered the rules of the game; proffered "views" are no longer assertions of preference for certain outcomes, but estimates of costs and benefits, and predictions about future consequences. Wealthy and well-organized groups have been able to offer sophisticated analyses and rebut alternative (often less sophisticated) analyses supplied by less well-endowed groups. The very complexity of the analysis has tended to discourage the involvement of a wider range of participants, who feel that they have nothing legitimate to add to this form of public debate.

At the same time, the commingling of the two approaches has aggravated a central problem of net benefit maximization, which is the interpersonal comparisons of utilities implied when some people gain and others lose from a policy deemed to maximize net social benefits. The analytic form of argument has obscured the actual patterns of group organization and membership lying behind it. This in turn has made it more difficult to judge whether groups of gainers and losers are in roughly equivalent circumstances to begin with, or whether the resulting redistribution brings them closer together.

The net result of these conceptual impasses has been to undermine further the legitimacy of administrative decision making and subject it to repeated criticism both for failing to respond adequately to affected interest *and* for failing to yield efficient solutions. Proposals for reform have cycled back and forth between interest group intermediation and net benefit maximization as the inadequacies of first one, then the other vision are exposed. Not surprisingly, the resulting policy decisions have often lacked broad and sustained public support.

THE PROBLEM OF NEUTRALITY

The muddle into which both types of policy making have fallen is due, I believe, to difficulties lying deeper than the problems of reconciling them or the technical challenges of accommodating diffused interests and comparing the utilities of different groups. These are symptoms of a more profound failure to reflect an authentic governmental character—that is, to inspire confidence among citizens that the decisions of public managers are genuinely in the "public interest."

Both procedural devices are premised on the view that democracy is simply (or largely) a matter of putting public authority to the service of what individual people want. These individual preferences in turn are assumed to exist apart from any process designed to discover and respond to them—outside any social experience with democratic governance. Both interest group intermediation and net benefit maximization share a view of democracy in which relevant communications all flow in one direction: from individuals' preferences to public officials, whose job it is to accommodate or aggregate them. The formal democratic process of electing representatives is only the most traditional manifestation of this communications system. Since elected representatives cannot or will not fully instruct public managers in what to do, the formal process has needed to be enlarged and supplemented by a separate system that links individual preferences more directly to administrative decision making: hence interest group intermediation and net benefit maximization.[23]

This view of the place of public management in a democracy suffers from two related difficulties. First, it is inaccurate. Individual preferences do not arise outside and apart from their social context, but are influenced by both the process and the substance of policy making. Communications move in both directions, from citizen to policy maker and from policy maker to citizen, and then horizontally among citizens. The acts of seeking to discover what people want and then responding to such findings inevitably shape people's subsequent desires. Occasionally these effects are so profound that neither interest group intermediation nor net benefit maximization can do its job, even in the limited terms of linking public authority to selfish wants. In addition, this view of policy making is normatively suspect. It leaves out some of the most important aspects of democratic governance, which involve public deliberation over public issues and the ensuing discovery of public ideas. As we will see, these two shortcomings are connected. For it is only through public deliberation that the shared understandings that animate public policy can be examined and the tacit assumptions about what is wanted can be revised.

Consider, first, the possible effects of interest group intermediation on the way a citizenry understands what is important to its collective life, what problems it must address, what is at stake in such decisions, and its capacities to deal with such problems in the future. Returning to our earlier example, suppose the intermediator has sought out the views of citizen groups on construction of a dam. He has been willing to listen to spokesmen of any established organization, and he has actively encouraged the leaders of other, less prominent groups to proffer their views as well. He has listened to the president of the local Chamber of Commerce, the head of the Downtown Merchant's Association, the chairman of the Board of Realtors, the leader of the Upper Valley Homeowners Association, and a variety of other groups representing homeowners and merchants, living upstream and downstream from the proposed dam. Each group leader has presented formal testimony; some have filed reports, analyses, and extensive commentary. The local media have duly reported their views. Editorialists, commentators, and political leaders have begun to take sides in the emerging controversy. It is soon understood as a contest between upstreamers and downstreamers.

But note that the controversy itself has been shaped largely by how representatives of the various groups have expressed their views about what their constituents want for themselves. These spokespeople have identified the key issues and arguments, defined the relevant constituencies, and structured the emerging debate. The public might have developed a very different understanding about what was at stake had a different set of representatives and groups participated—for example, downstream tenants or those who loved to fish and hike in the upstream woodlands. Rather than a contest between upstreamers and downstreamers, the controversy might have been understood as one between economic growth and environmental conservation, or between land speculators and poor renters, or all of these and more—a decision rich with implications, potentially creating all sorts of gainers and losers. Each of these frames would have caused a different set of issues to be explored in the media and in various public forums, a different set of arguments and questions to be considered by the public, and a different set of connections to be made to other issues and values lying at the perimeter.

The implicit selection of certain groups and leaders to participate has subtly altered the configuration of influence and political authority in the community. These groups and those who have spoken on their behalf are now seen as having access to power, and this perception feeds on itself. Earlier there were probably many *incipient* groupings in the community, since at any point in time there is a variety of ways in which citizens might join together to express different constellations of concerns. Many of these fledgling organizations and leaders were presumably weak—disorganized, lacking a clear focus, as yet incapable of generating strong support and a dedicated following. Those that become recognized as participants in the decision making process, however, find their roles legitimized and strengthened. The groups and leaders that were encouraged to participate have now become semiofficial channels through which community views are expressed; accordingly, their focus and support are both enhanced. As issues arise in the future, these groups and their leaders will be among the first to be consulted. Incipient groups and leaders that were not selected or encouraged to participate, on the other hand, suffer a corresponding decline in influence and status. Citizens have less reason to involve themselves in such groups or support such leaders next time because they are perceived to lack standing to articulate public views.

Finally, the act of participation has rendered the articulated concerns appropriate subjects of public debate and, by implication, public action. Their very expression has legitimized them. The concerns of downstream merchants now have a clear place on the public agenda; the periodic flooding to which they are exposed has been transformed from an act of nature causing private loss into a public problem open to public remedy. To the extent possible, these concerns must now be accommodated in the eventual decision. For under interest group intermediation, the primary criterion of a good decision is that it addresses such articulated concerns. There are no principled limits to, or goals for, public involvement apart from this. Once they become legitimate subjects of public debate and action, such concerns will remain on the public agenda, to be accommodated in future decisions as well. The welfare of downstream merchants has now become a public goal.

In all these ways, the interest group intermediator is an active participant in the political development of the community. By recognizing "established" groups and leaders, and subtly encouraging others to participate, the intermediator effectively shapes public understandings of what is at stake, perceptions of who has power in the community, and assumptions about what subjects merit public concern. In this way he alters the political future. To view him merely as a neutral intermediator dramatically understates his true role.

Net benefit maximization is no less influential. But here it is the initial selection of objectives to be achieved and options to be weighed, rather than the groups and leaders to participate, that shapes public perceptions about what is at stake; and it is the choice of proxy for "willingness to pay" that affects how the public values these stakes.

Let us return to our example, but this time with our public manager as a net benefit maximizer. To analyze the problem and measure public preferences for different solutions, he first must simplify it. Asking himself how the costs of downstream flooding can most efficiently be reduced, he estimates the costs and benefits of three alternatives: a dam, a drainage canal, and a dike along the edge of the river. The cost of the dam will include the loss of upstream wilderness that will be flooded. The manager estimates this loss by adding to the market value of the land its recreational value, calculated by estimating how many people visit the wilderness area in a given time period, how much money they spend to get there, and how much more they would have to spend to travel to alternative wilderness areas. Assume that after estimating the costs and benefits of each alternative he concludes that the dam will generate the greatest net benefits, and the dam is constructed.

The issue is not the "correctness" of his conclusion about the social utility of a dam relative to the other alternatives, although that will be how opponents of the dam will approach the subject. Any formal analysis necessarily entails a somewhat simplified characterization of reality and a host of choices about how and what to simplify. Of more enduring consequence is the effect of such choices on the social utility function itself. Like the intermediator's implicit choices of whom to encourage to participate, these net benefit maximizing choices reverberate through the community because they have public authority behind them. They influence the way people in the community come to think about the problem, its possible solutions, and the values at stake in the decision.

To state the objective as reducing the costs of downstream flooding, for example, constitutes an important public act. That technical objective is transformed into a public goal to which the community attaches its collective aspirations and around which citizens mobilize. Just as mere participation serves a legitimizing function in interest group intermediation, such a statement of objective legitimates a whole class of similar problems as appropriate subjects for public action—for example, acts of nature (rock slides, dust storms, tornadoes) that periodically imperil the area or hardships that periodically befall those who live downstream. It simultaneously makes other ways of thinking about the issue less legitimate—for example, the thought that periodic flooding is not really a public problem at all, since downstream owners have always coped with it.

The identification of alternative solutions also sends powerful social messages that will influence the way people think about, and act on, similar problems in the future. One such message is that appropriate solutions are to be found in complex engineering projects, rather than in social endeavors like organizing a voluntary brigade to clean up after each flood. Another, related message is that the identification of alternative solutions is primarily a technical task for which the average person has no particular competence or relevant knowledge. Together these messages may tend to discourage social responses that draw inspiration and energy from citizens' sense of their shared responsibility for community problems and their competence in devising solutions.

Finally, the methods used by the net benefit maximizer to evaluate the alternatives affect the way citizens come to view certain attributes of their lives. The official act of placing a monetary value on the upstream wilderness, for example, constitutes a powerful public statement that feelings toward such wilderness *can* be expressed in monetary terms. It thereby transforms wilderness areas into consumer goods whose worth depends on how well they satisfy us, rather than entities with their own constitutive values, whose worth to us is bound up in the belief that monetary value cannot be placed on them. The further assumption that "willingness to pay" to travel to such a wilderness area is the proper measure of how we value it, moreover, dismisses as irrelevant any positive feelings people have simply because the wilderness area exists there upstream. It suggests that the only grounds for complaint or despair, should the area disappear, derive from the direct and personal loss of access to it. Together, such ideas—that wilderness areas should be valued in terms of how well they satisfy people, and then only on the basis of people's direct and personal experience with them—are powerful social norms that may influence how citizens think about their environment in the future.[24]

The *substantive* decisions that emerge from both types of policy making, or some hybrid of the two, also influence future preferences. These decisions alter the world that people experience. To return to our example, the experience of future generations in the community will be quite different if the dam is constructed. People will then grow to adulthood without enjoying relatively easy access to the upstream wilderness. Not knowing what experiences they have missed, they will never learn to place the same high value on accessible wilderness as earlier generations did. Because their relationship with the environment is likely to be more attenuated, they will probably be more willing to make subsequent decisions that sacrifice the environment to other values. If the dam is not built, the experience of future generations will not change in this way. Over time, the divergence between the two paths of decisions (and the preferences on which they are based) would grow larger. Several generations hence, the descendants of the dam builders are likely to live in a profoundly different setting and to have different norms, espouse different causes, dream different dreams. The decision to build the dam, then, does not just reflect the values of the present generation; it sets a trajectory of future values.

Even the choice of a policy instrument can generate powerful social signals that shape future norms. As we have seen, for example, the net benefit maximizer typically prefers to give the poor cash rather than a scarce commodity—like a portion of the downstream lands rendered habitable by construction of the dam—on the rationale that it is more efficient to let individuals decide how to spend the cash than to give them something that might not exactly meet their needs. But this view ignores the quite different public perceptions attached to the two transfers. The transfer of newly habitable land has a clear social meaning. The land is indelibly "public"; it was created through public action aimed at improving the habitability of the entire downstream area. This particular parcel could have been used for a park or a school, but the public has chosen instead to give it to those in need. It is thus a particular gift, reflecting a particular sort of public generosity, linked to particular public purposes. The homes that the poor can now build in this area will continually remind the community of these purposes and thus shape the way the public thinks about future projects of a similar sort. A simple transfer of cash would be devoid of these social meanings—so devoid, in fact, that it might not summon sufficient political support to be authorized in the first place.[25]

In sum, both the process and the substance of policy decisions generate social learning about public values and set the stage for future public choices. They give rise to new understandings and expectations; they shape policy debates in other, related policy areas; they reconfigure social ideals. It is therefore misleading to view the job of public managers simply as responding to pre-existing preferences, expressed either through group leaders or market transactions. Their responsibility is much broader and more subtle.

CIVIC DISCOVERY

Within the context of either interest group intermediation or net benefit maximization, disagreements among people are assumed to derive from incompatible preferences—conflicts among selfish desires. The challenge to the public manager under these circumstances is thought to be a technical one: either to intermediate among groups until an accommodation is reached or to measure people's willingness to pay for certain things (and avoid other things) and then maximize their combined welfare. As we have seen, neither of these techniques is entirely neutral; both can alter how the initial problems are perceived and solutions understood. In addition, neither creates an opportunity for the public to deliberate about what is good for society. Yet it is through such deliberation that opinions can be revised, premises altered, and common interests discovered.

To return once again to our example, imagine now that the public manager eschews both types of conventional policy making. Instead of assuming that he must decide whether the dam should be built, he sees the occasion as an opportunity for the public to deliberate over what it wants. Accordingly, he announces that various people living and working downstream are complaining about periodic flooding of the river. He then encourages and instigates the convening of various forums—in community centers, schools, churches, and workplaces—where citizens are to discuss whether there is a problem and, if so, what it is and what should be done about it. The public manager does not specifically define the problem or set an objective at the start. He merely discloses the complaints. Nor does he take formal control of the discussions or determine who should speak for whom. At this stage he views his job as generating debate, even controversy. He wants to bring into the open the fact that certain members of the community are disgruntled and create possibilities for the public to understand in various ways what is at stake. He wants to make the community conscious of tensions within it, and responsible for dealing with them. In short, he wants the community to use this as an occasion to debate its future. Several different kinds of civic discovery may ensue.

The problem and its solutions may be redefined. During the course of such deliberations, people may discover that their initial assumptions about the nature of the problem and its alternative solutions are wrong or inappropriate. Through sharing information about what concerns them and seeking common solutions to those concerns, they come to see that the issue should not be defined as whether to build the dam, but how best to relocate people off the flood plain. Viewed this way, a potentially sharp conflict within the community is transformed into a project that almost everyone can support (even though it may be no one's most preferred outcome). Had the public manager sought to make the decision on the basis of the interest groups through which people express their wants, or through measurements of their willingness to pay, this possibility for redefining the issue and garnering widespread support would have been overlooked.

Voluntary action may be generated. Their consideration of the plight of the downstream residents and businesses may lead others to volunteer time and money to the effort—erecting dikes, digging drainage canals, or relocating people and businesses. This willingness to volunteer stems from the discovery that others are also willing to lend a hand. Had there been no such deliberation, individuals might not have recognized how they could voluntarily help remedy the situation. Those who were inclined to help might have assumed that their charitable impulses were not widely shared, so that it would have been futile to act on them. The discovery empowers people, together, to take voluntary action.

Preferences may be legitimized. Some people may discover that there are many others like them who have not visited the upstream wilderness, but who nevertheless share a deep feeling for it and wish it to be preserved. Had there been no such deliberation, each might have continued to assume that his feelings were somehow illegitimate since they were not based on direct experience—and for this reason were not measurable on a willingness-to-pay scale and did not fit within an established interest group. Indeed, people might have denied having such feelings, regarding them as invalid or immature. But the discovery emboldens these people to admit and express such views, and seek to persuade others of their validity.

Individual preferences may be influenced by considerations of what is good for society. Some people may discover a conflict between their personal, pecuniary interests in the problem and their hopes for their community. A downstream property owner who realizes that the dam would increase property values downstream, enhancing his personal wealth, may nevertheless believe it would be bad for the community. The dam would continue to be a divisive issue for years to come; future generations would no longer have access to the unspoiled wilderness areas upstream; and too many people would move to the downstream area, eventually overloading the roads, schools, and sewage lines. The citizen may still choose to favor his own pecuniary interest. Public deliberation does not guarantee that people will become more altruistic. But the deliberation at least creates the opportunity for such weighing and balancing. Had there been no such deliberation, the downstream owner might never have considered the future of the community.

Deeper conflicts may be discovered. People may discover that their disagreements run much deeper than previously imagined. Those who want to preserve the upstream wilderness also want to minimize downstream development and preserve parks and open spaces within and around the city; downstream owners who want the dam also favor extensive development. The discovery of this more fundamental conflict might have been avoided (or delayed, or denied) had the public manager decided whether to build the dam on the basis of interest group demands or willingness to pay.

In these ways, public deliberation provides an opportunity for people to discover shared values about what is good for the community, and deeper conflicts among those understandings. Deliberation does not automatically generate these public ideas, of course; it simply allows them to arise. Policy making based on interest group intermediation or net benefit maximization, by contrast, offers no such opportunity. The self-interested preferences of individuals as expressed through their market transactions do not reflect potential public ideas. Interest groups, for their part, are instrumental devices for fulfilling the individual desires of their members, not bodies for deliberating what is good for society; their leaders are paid to be advocates and conduits, not statesmen.

The failure of conventional techniques of policy making to permit civic discovery may suggest that there are no shared values to be discovered in the first place. And this message—that the "public interest" is no more than an accommodation or aggregation of individual interests—may have a corrosive effect on civic life. It may invalidate whatever potential exists for the creation of shared commitments and in so doing may stunt the discovery of public ideas. Such a failure may in turn call into question the inherent legitimacy of the policy decisions that result. For such policies are then supported only by debatable facts, inferences, and tradeoffs. They lack any authentic governmental character beyond accommodation or aggregation. Those who disagree with the procedures or conclusions on which the policies are based have every reason to disregard them whenever the opportunity arises. Under these circumstances disobedience is not a social act reflecting on one's membership in a community, but merely another expression of preference.

REAL-WORLD APPLICATIONS

Can public managers realistically hope to enhance public deliberation and social learning about what is good for society? Some real-world illustrations will suggest both the possibilities and limitations of such a role.

Ruckelshaus and Tacoma

Under the Clean Air Act Amendments of 1970, the Environmental Protection Agency (EPA) is required to issue national emissions standards for hazardous air pollutants, so as to provide an "ample margin of safety" to protect the public health.[26] Congress gave EPA no guidance for deciding how much safety is "ample," however. Even a small exposure to certain hazardous pollutants can pose substantial health risks. But to ban any air pollutant that caused even a small risk to health would substantially impair the national economy.

The problem received national attention in 1983 when the agency was trying to decide what, if anything, should be done about inorganic arsenic, a cancer-causing pollutant produced when arsenic-content ore is smelted into copper. The issue was dramatized especially in the area around Tacoma, Washington, where the American Smelting and Refining Company (Asarco) operated a copper smelter. The EPA had concluded that if Asarco's emissions were not controlled, approximately four new cases of lung cancer would be contracted each year in the area; even the best available pollution control equipment would still emit enough inorganic arsenic into the air to cause one cancer death a year. But the cost of such equipment would render the plant uneconomical, forcing the company to close it. The closing would have a devastating effect on the local economy: Asarco employed 570 workers with an annual payroll of about $23 million, and the company purchased $12 million of goods from local suppliers.

William Ruckelshaus, then administrator of the EPA, decided that the citizens of the Tacoma area ought to wrestle with the problem in a series of public meetings held during the summer of 1983. EPA officials began each meeting by explaining how the agency had estimated the health risks; they then divided the audience into three groups for more informal discussion with agency officials and staff. Some of the ensuing discussion concerned technical questions of measurement and emissions control, but many of the citizens' questions concerned the possible effects of the emissions on their gardens, animals, and overall quality of life. As the dean of the University of Washington School of Public Health observed, "the personal nature of the complaints and questions made a striking counterpoint to the presentations of meteorological models and health effects extrapolations."

These meetings, together with the national attention that Ruckelshaus had deliberately drawn to them, generated considerable and often unfavorable press coverage. In one editorial entitled "Mr. Ruckelshaus a Caesar," the *New York Times* argued that it was "inexcusable . . . for him to impose such an impossible choice on Tacomans." The *Los Angeles Times* pointed out the difficulties in "taking a community's pulse. . . . [Should he] poll the community . . . [or] count the pros and cons at the massive hearing?" Ruckelshaus was not surprised by the controversy. "Listen, I know people don't like these kinds of decisions," he said. "Welcome to the world of regulation. People have demanded to be involved and now I have involved them, and they say, 'don't ask that question.' What's the alternative? Don't involve them? Then you are accused of doing something nefarious."

By 1985, the EPA still had not promulgated regulations for arsenic emissions, but declining world copper prices in the interim had forced the closure of the Asarco smelter. What then did Ruckelshaus accomplish? For one thing, the problem was redefined. Instead of focusing on how best to control hazardous air pollutants, citizens began to ask how they could diversify a local economy and attract industry that would not generate such substantial hazards. Attendance at the meetings, along with massive media exposure, had personalized the controversy in ways that induced people to look at it differently. As area residents heard a tearful woman, diagnosed as ultrasensitive to arsenic, describe how she and her husband had to sell their farm at a severe loss and leave the area, or saw copper workers in danger of losing their jobs, energies shifted from "winning" to changing the way the problem was understood and finding workable solutions. As Ruckelshaus described it, "Even the residents of Vashon Island, who were directly exposed to the pollution and yet had no employment or financial stake in the smelter, began to ask whether there was a means of keeping the smelter going while reducing pollution levels. They saw the workers from the smelter—encountered them in flesh and blood—and began incorporating the workers' perspective into their own solutions."

Several participants attacked the fundamental perception of "the environment versus jobs issue," arguing that discussion should focus instead on the development of new pollution control technologies that could control arsenic emissions and allow the plant to stay open. Others argued that Tacoma would do better to diversify its employment base and that the real problem was the local economy's dependence on a few industries like copper. Gradually, for many participants, the goal came to be understood as finding new jobs for the Asarco workers and new industry for the region, by attracting and developing nonpolluting businesses.[27] This view gained substantial support. By 1985, when the Asarco smelter closed down, Tacoma already had begun the task of diversifying its economy.

For Ruckelshaus, the value of the Tacoma experiment also included social learning about the health risks of pollution and the enormous costs of eliminating them altogether, not only in Tacoma but also in other communities that saw what occurred there. The deliberation in Tacoma thus helped launch a national debate over environmental policy, giving the public a deeper understanding about what would have to be sacrificed to reduce risks to health. Looking back more than a year later, after he had left the EPA, Ruckelshaus assessed the Tacoma experiment:

> Perhaps I underestimated how difficult it would be to get people to take responsibility, to educate themselves and one another about such a difficult issue. Probably not more than a relatively few citizens of Tacoma learned that for issues like this there is no "right" answer. . . . They would have to decide what they wanted for their community. They would have to determine their own future. But even if a handful learned this lesson, then you have a basis for others learning it. You have the beginnings of a tradition of public deliberation about hard issues. And you also have all the other people in the country who watched what happened there in Tacoma, and indirectly learned the same lesson from it.[28]

Pertschuk and Children's Advertising

In 1914 Congress created the Federal Trade Commission (FTC) as an independent agency to ferret out "unfair and deceptive acts and practices in commerce," but it left to the agency the task of defining these vague terms.[29] In 1977, Senator Warren Magnuson, chairman of the Senate Commerce Committee, which oversaw the FTC, suggested that the agency, under the direction of its new chairman, Michael Pertschuk, should look into the issue of advertising directed at children as a possible "unfair act." Magnuson knew very little about the subject and had only vaguest of concerns. "Now, we've all been interested here in children's advertising," he said when Pertschuk first came to the Commission. "It's a difficult, complex subject. . . . I would hope that you would take a good, long look. . . . I hate to narrow this down, but the abuses seem to be in children's advertising, advertising directed to children."

Pertschuk saw in the issue a perfect means of raising consciousness about public susceptibility to advertising in general and in particular the vulnerability of young children to commercial inducements to buy sugary cereals and candy. Accordingly the Commission launched a preliminary investigation, and by April 1978 was considering several possible remedies: a ban on the number of advertisements for sugared products that could be directed at children during a certain period of time, or on a particular medium; controls on the kinds of advertising techniques that could be used; a requirement that nutritional information be disclosed in such advertisements; a ban on advertisements for sugar-coated products; and a ban on all children's advertising. The proposals drew significant media attention. Pertschuk received even more when he gave strongly worded speeches and provocative interviews about the dangers of advertising directed at children.

The proposals and Pertschuk's speeches and interviews set off a firestorm of criticism from industry groups. Broadcasters, advertisers, cereal manufacturers, grocery manufacturers, and sugar producers all felt threatened and counterattacked through the press and their lobbyists in Congress. The *Washington Post* editorialized that the FTC was aiming to be the "national nanny" and that it had no business interfering in an area of parental responsibility. One lobbyist felt that the Commission's confrontational strategy had contributed to the tumult. "We could have gotten some of the more enlightened companies to say, let's go in and bargain a little bit, and get half a loaf," he observed. "But they got everyone 100 percent against them, willing to commit war chests and time, the personal time of chief executive officers, saying, we cannot allow this to happen. They basically accused well-known businessmen of deliberately trying to foreshorten the lives of kids."

In the end, Congress reined in the FTC. Indeed the Commission's powers to issue all rules were curtailed; the agency's appropriations were reduced and its credibility severely crippled. What then did the campaign accomplish? Looking back several years later, Michael Pertschuk regretted the tactics, but not the goals.

> I suppose we made some mistakes. We came on too strong. If the goal was to preserve and develop the FTC's powers over the long haul, then Kidvid was a disaster. . . . But I'm not sure that was or should be the goal. After all, the FTC is merely a shell. It changes its color with every new administration. Why should I worry about its powers over the long term? The real goal was to get issues like children's advertising out there in front of the public. . . . I wanted to stir up a debate, get people thinking. You know, that's one of the most important things we can do, get the public to grapple with hard issues. And they did. The public had a chance to understand children's advertising, the press played it up. . . . We probably should have gone easier with it, give the issue more time to boil. But even so, you look around now in the stores, you see a lot less sugary cereal. You watch cartoons on Saturday morning, you see a lot fewer advertisements for sugary cereals and candy. Was consciousness raised about advertising directed toward children? Yes, and I think we contributed.[30]

Bennett and Educational Reform

Our final illustration concerns William Bennett, who became secretary of education in 1985.[31] The Department of Education administers a wide variety of programs, but they are tightly connected to individual congressional committees and to state and local programs. Most educational policy in the United States is determined at the state and local levels, where the bulk of the money is raised and spent. Accordingly a secretary of education has quite limited scope to affect change directly. Bennett, however, was determined to raise issues about American education that might affect change indirectly, through public debate. He began boldly, perhaps too boldly. At his first news conference, when announcing tighter standards for student loans, Bennett opined that students should help meet tuition by "stereo divestiture, automobile divestiture, three weeks at the beach divestiture." The speech infuriated many middle-class parents who relied on the student loan program and angered several members of Congress who had long supported it. By the end of Bennett's first month in office, the *Washington Post* ran an article entitled "Another Watt?" referring to the former secretary of interior's tendency to offend.

In subsequent months, however, Bennett's pronouncements were accompanied by detailed position papers and proposals for changes in various department regulations. Among other things, he advocated improved teacher training, higher standards for promoting students to the next grades, a return to "basics" in the classroom, educational vouchers as a means of generating competition among schools and giving students a choice of where to attend, a reconsideration of the place of religion in public education, and a rethinking of the tenets of bilingual education. Amid much press attention, Bennett traveled around the country, sitting and teaching in public classrooms and continuing to raise issues about educational policy. As his credibility increased, many of his ideas gained begrudging respect, even from groups that opposed him, like the National Educational Association and the American Federation of Teachers. Prominent politicians were picking up some of his themes. By March 1986, *Newsweek* remarked that Bennett's style was "guaranteed to win some enemies . . . but even critics recognize its usefulness. As Diane Ravitch, a professor at Teachers College of Columbia says: 'The main role of the Secretary of Education is to keep the attention of the country focused on education.' By that standard, Bennett has been a resounding success. He has turned his office into a bully pulpit . . . He has barnstormed the country." One of Bennett's assistants explained the overall strategy:

> Bennett sees himself as in the business of raising the level of debate, focussing the public's attention where it hasn't been focussed before. We've had to be sufficiently controversial to get the attention, but solid enough to gain the public's respect. It's a delicate balance. . . . It's okay to get the front-page story the next day, but you really want the feature stories that follow a few days or weeks later, that set out the arguments on both sides, and the editorials. The subject gradually becomes a respectable topic of debate. Politicians pick up the ideas. University presidents talk about them. . . . You know, most people think of speeches and position papers and all that stuff as being in the service of specific regulations or legislation. Around here, it's the other way around. The specific policies are in the service of raising issues.[32]

LESSONS

In each of the situations described above, a public manager sought to stimulate public deliberation over what was good for society rather than to decide specific policy. Each felt that public learning was at least as important a part of his job as policy making, because the public had to understand and decide for itself what value it was to place on certain issues lying within the manager's domain. Deliberation was worthwhile both in itself and because it could clarify ambiguous mandates and perhaps even move Congress to a different course of action. Rather than view debate and controversy as managerial failures that made policy making and implementation more difficult, these managers saw them as natural and desirable aspects of the formation of public values, contributing to society's self-understanding.

Were they successful? The answer depends on what is meant by success. Each succeeded in stimulating debate and focusing attention. There is some evidence—scattered, impressionistic—that each succeeded in altering the terms of public debate, engendering some sorts of civic discovery. Each insisted that such public deliberation was crucial to his mission. Ruckelshaus made the point explicitly: "My view is that these are the kinds of tough, balancing questions that we're involved in here in this country in trying to regulate all kinds of hazardous substances . . . [T]he societal issue is what risks are we willing to take and for what benefits? . . . For me to sit here in Washington and tell the people of Tacoma what is an acceptable risk would be at best arrogant and at worst inexcusable."[33]

But there were costs. Ruckelshaus's Tacoma experiment reduced his credibility with environmentalists, whose support he vitally needed on other EPA projects. Pertschuk almost destroyed the Federal Trade Commission. Bennett spent so much time and energy in instigating debate that he had none left for legislative battles. All three managers faced a hostile press.

The cases also suggest that public deliberation is not easy to manage well. Public managers and the public at large often tend to equate administrative effectiveness with active decision making and successful implementation. These are concrete achievements that can be measured and on which reputations can be built. The nurturing of social learning about public values, on the other hand, is an elusive undertaking. A manager who tentatively advances several proposals and stirs controversy about them may appear indecisive or indifferent at best, as did Ruckelshaus, or he may be cast as a villain, as was Pertschuk. Moreover the public will wish to avoid facing difficult issues and examining the values bound up in them. Many people will resent the tensions and ambiguities inherent in such deliberation. They would prefer that the public manager take responsibility for making such decisions, as did many Tacomans, or that unsettling problems and questions not be raised at all.

There will also be procedural obstacles. To instigate public discourse the manager will have to make speeches, stage events, and use the press artfully. But in doing so he may deflect public attention from the issue to himself. It is far easier to attract the public's curiosity to a personality than to a substantive problem. Ruckelshaus, Pertschuk, and Bennett all became the focus of the media. Ruckelshaus managed to refocus on the issues; Pertschuk never quite pulled it off; Bennett, at this writing, is still struggling with the problem.

The manager must also contend with well-established interest groups, whose strong advocacy can drown out any semblance of public thought. Their easy dominance of the media and of legislatures can push issues back off the table or reconfigure them into older debates. Ruckelshaus avoided this by staging his event in Tacoma, far from the center of organized group activity on the Potomac. Much of Pertschuk's message was jammed by the trade associations and major corporations that waged war against the FTC. Bennett took his show on the road, where established groups could not override his message, but teachers' lobbies and textbook manufacturers continually sought to define the issues he raised in ways they could control.

Public deliberation will take up inordinate time and resources (all three of our managers were almost consumed by it), and it can easily cycle out of control. There is no guarantee that the resulting social learning will yield a clear consensus at the end. Instead the process may exacerbate divisions within the community and make it more difficult to achieve consensus in the future. The FTC debacle made it more difficult for the Carter administration as a whole to gain the cooperation of the business community later on issues for which its support was needed.

The experience of public deliberation is not likely to be enjoyable for either politicians or agency employees. Politicians will resent a process that is beyond their control, often involving issues they would rather not have to deal with (that is why those issues were handed over to the public manager in the first place). All three of our public managers met with hostility from important congressional committees. Agency employees, for their part, are unlikely to understand the importance of fostering public discourse rather than getting on with the job of making policy. Their jobs and reputations depend on getting something done (or undone), and they will have little role in instigating or managing the debate. Furthermore, they will have to live with the results, often long after the top manager has left. Pertschuk's employees did not appreciate his willingness to sacrifice the agency's powers to the more immediate goal of raising the public's consciousness.

Lastly, there are lingering doubts about the propriety of nonelected bureaucrats' taking on this sort of responsibility. The line between ideological chest-thumping and the instigation of public debate can be a narrow one, easily missed even by managers who sincerely believe they are letting the public decide. Ruckelshaus stayed well to one side, but Pertschuk and Bennett both approached the line. James Watt, Reagan's errant secretary of the interior, seemed to have crossed it. Although there is no clear guide for where the line should be drawn, the cases examined here suggest a rule of thumb. The public manager may be in a better position than a legislator or senior elected official to foster a national debate over certain value-laden issues when the manager deals with specific applications of general principles. It is through detailed and vivid applications that the public comes to understand the principles and the tradeoffs and stakes they imply. Tacoma dramatically illustrated the principle that the cost of achieving zero health risk is prohibitive. Advertising directed at children was a less specific application, and Congress could have instigated a similar public deliberation. Similarly with many of the issues that Bennett sought to dramatize.

For all these reasons, prudence is advised. The public manager should not completely abandon interest group intermediation and net benefit maximization in favor of public deliberations. Each of the more traditional techniques has its place, especially for the vast majority of comparatively routine decisions, which are not fundamentally bound up with public values and are unlikely to have important effects on future choices.

But public managers must be willing to venture occasionally into the third sphere, in which public deliberation takes prominence. As we have seen, they have little choice in the matter. Enabling statutes are often vague, as was Congress's requirement that the EPA ensure an "ample margin of safety" for hazardous emissions or that the FTC ban "unfair" advertising. In certain areas of policy making, any decision is likely to have profound effects on how people understand and value the objects of policy. Instigating deliberation on controversial issues may sometimes be the only way for a public manager to effect change. In these circumstances, it is wise to allow, or even invite, some public discourse rather than to aim single-mindedly at making a decision. Public managers must understand that public debate and controversy over a domain within their control are not necessarily to be avoided. Although heated discourse may make their jobs somewhat less comfortable, it comes with the territory.

Notes

1. Alexander Hamilton et al., *The Federalist*, No. 78, B. Wright, ed. (Cambridge, MA: Harvard University Press, 1961), pp. 103–10.
2. Jurisprudential schools have risen and fallen with some regularity. Some have confined their concerns to constitutional norms, while others have taken on the whole corpus of judicial activity, including statutory construction and common law adjudication. But regardless of their precise field of vision, most have somehow addressed themselves to the fundamental question of how judicial discretion can be reconciled with democratic values.
3. Woodrow Wilson, "The Study of Administration," *Political Science Quarterly* 2 (June 1887): 197–217.
4. Progressives were no less confident about the capacity of managers in the private sector to discover the "single best way" of making and delivering goods and services. See, for example, Frederick Winslow Taylor, *The Principles of Scientific Management* (New York: Harper and Brothers, 1911), pp. 20–28. For a general discussion, see Robert B. Reich, *The Next American Frontier* (New York: Times Books, 1983), chap. 4.
5. See, for example, Ernst Freund, *Legislative Regulation* (New York: Commonwealth Fund, 1932).
6. See, for example, *Panama Refining Co. v. Ryan*, 293 U.S. 388 (1935); *Schechter Poultry v. United States*, 295 U.S. 495 (1935).
7. These arguments were advanced by Felix Frankfurter in *The Public and Its Government* (New Haven: Yale University Press, 1930), and James Landis, in *The Administrative Process* (New Haven: Yale University Press, 1938). See also James W. Fesler et al., *The Elements of Public Administration* (New York: Prentice-Hall, 1946), pp. 7–9.
8. For a thoughtful treatment of this issue, see Edward Purcell, Jr., *The Crisis of Democratic Theory: Scientific Naturalism and the Problem of Value* (Lexington: University of Kentucky Press, 1973).
9. See, for example, Robert A. Dahl, *A Preface to Democratic Theory* (Chicago: Uni-

versity of Chicago Press, 1956); David Truman, *The Governmental Process: Political Interests and Public Opinion* (New York: Knopf, 1951).

10. Joseph Schumpeter, *Capitalism, Socialism, and Democracy* (New York: Harper, 1942); Anthony Downs, *An Economic Theory of Democracy* (New York: Harper, 1957).

11. See Fesler et al., *The Elements of Public Administration*, pp. 37–41; *The John F. Kennedy School of Government: The First Fifty Years* (Cambridge, MA: Ballinger, 1986), pp. 25–48.

12. *Office of Communication of the United Church of Christ v. Federal Communications Commission*, 359 F. 2d 994, 1000-06 (C.A. D.C. 1966).

13. See, for example, *Scenic Hudson Preservation Conf. v. Federal Power Commission*, 354 F. 2d 608 (C.A. 2, 1965), cert. denied, 384 U.S. 941 (1966); *Friends of the Earth v. Atomic Energy Commission*, 485 F. 2d 1031, 1033 (C.A. D.C. 1973); and other cases cited in Richard Stewart, "The Reformation of American Administrative Law," *Harvard Law Review* 88 (1975): 1667.

14. 15 U.S.C. 57a(h) (1976).

15. For a summary of these and related reforms, see generally Stewart, "Reformation," and Colin Diver, "Policymaking Paradigms in Administrative Law," *Harvard Law Review* 95 (1981): 393.

16. 5 U.S.C. 552b (1976).

17. In *Sierra Club v. Morton*, 405 U.S. 727 (1972), the Supreme Court denied standing to the Sierra Club to contest an Interior Department ruling, on the ground that the club's asserted interest in the broad principle that wilderness areas should be preserved did not place the club or any of its members in jeopardy of a material injury by the department's proposed actions. The club's assertion in a subsequent proceeding that the rule would deny certain of its members the enjoyment of the wilderness area in question was deemed by the court to be sufficient to confer standing. Some commentators have criticized these seemingly inconsistent decisions as examples of legal legerdemain; they argue that almost any ideological group can contrive some material injury to one of its members sufficient to gain standing. But this critique misses the important difference between the two instances in these cases. A view about what constitutes a good society does not readily lend itself to hard bargaining; by contrast, a specific and identifiable injury, as to particular individuals' enjoyment of particular wilderness areas, lends itself to negotiation and perhaps compensation. In the latter case, the public manager-as-intermediator can do his job.

18. for example, the Consumer Product Safety Commission's product safety rules must "express in the rule itself the risk of injury which the standard is designed to eliminate or reduce" (15 U.S.C. 2058(b), 1976).

19. The Reagan order forbad any regulatory action, whether major or minor, by executive agencies unless "the potential benefits to society . . . outweigh the potential costs to society" and the alternative chosen to achieve the goal maximizes the aggregate net benefit to society. Executive order No. 12,291 46 Fed. Reg. at 13,193 (1981).

20. *Pilai v. CAB*, 485 F. 2d 1018 (C.A. D.C. 1973); *Portland Cement v. Ruckelshaus*, 486 F. 2d 375 (C.A. D.C. 1973), cert. denied 417 U.S. 921 (1974); *Aqua Slide N'Dive v. Consumer Products Safety Commission*, 569 F. 2d 831 (C.A. 5, 1978).

21. See Edith Stokey and Richard Zeckhauser, *A Primer for Policy Analysis* (New York: W.W. Norton, 1978), p. 281.

22. In one real-world example, the Civil Aeronautics Board (CAB) was presented with two conflicting estimates of the changes in air traffic that would result from a fare increase then under consideration. The CAB staff offered estimates based on an analysis of air traffic and prices over the previous twenty years. The industry, using an analysis that omitted certain years considered to be unrepresentative, offered a very different estimate. The CAB ultimately accepted neither estimate

completely, but found it could "form the basis for a reasonable judgment on the issue." Its "reasonable judgment," not surprisingly, fell between the two estimates. See *Domestic Passenger Fare Investigation, Phase 7*, Part 9, 1971.

23. It has been suggested that certain of these devices are applicable even in absence of formal democratic institutions. See, for example, Stokey and Zeckhauser, *Primer:* "Most of the materials in this book [concerning the techniques of policy analysis] are equally applicable to a socialist, capitalist, or mixed-enterprise society, to a democracy or a dictatorship, indeed wherever hard policy choices must be made" (p. 4).

24. See Steven Kelman, *What Price Incentives?* (Cambridge, MA: Arbor House, 1981). It should also be noted that market prices and expressions of willingness to pay depend on the current distribution of wealth and income. If the current distribution is deemed to be unfair, then a different set of prices and expressions of willingness to pay might be more appropriate.

25. See M. Landy, "Policy Analysis as a Vocation," *World Politics* (April 1981): 469; Steven Kelman, "A Case for In-Kind Transfers," *Economics and Philosophy* 2 (1986): 55–73.

26. This illustration is based primarily on Henry Lee, "Managing Environmental Risk: The Case of Asarco," John F. Kennedy School of Government Case Program, Harvard University, 1985.

27. *Seattle Times*, June 30, 1984, A10, col. 3.

28. William Ruckelshaus, interview with author, February 27, 1985.

29. This illustration is based primarily on Arthur Applbaum, "Mike Pertschuk and the Federal Trade Commission," John F. Kennedy School of Government Case Program, Harvard University, 1981.

30. Michael Pertschuk, interview with author, March 7, 1986.

31. This illustration is based primarily on Glen Tobin, "Creating Discussion in Modern America," unpub. ms. Kennedy School of Government, Harvard University, 1986.

32. Interview with author, June 4, 1986. The assistant's name is withheld at his request.

33. *Los Angeles Times*, August 13, 1983. 20, col. 3.

Accountability Battles in State Administration

WILLIAM T. GORMLEY, JR.

State bureaucracies have paid a price for their growing importance, and that price is a loss of discretion. In recent years, state bureaucracies have become more permeable, more vulnerable, and more manipulable. They are subject to a growing number of controls, as governors, state legislators, state judges, presidents, members of Congress, federal bureaucrats, interest groups, and citizens all attempt to shape administrative rule making, rate making and adjudication at the state level. Of equal significance, they are subject to tougher, more restrictive, and more coercive controls.

In other words, state bureaucracies have become more accountable for their actions. In a sense, this is both understandable and desirable. Even state bureaucrats concede the virtues of accountability, at least in theory. Yet accountability is a multidimensional concept. Increasingly, the question is not whether state bureaucracies shall be accountable but to whom. A related question is how accountability can best be structured to avoid damage to other important values, such as creativity and flexibility.

A variety of controls that limit the discretion of state bureaucracies recently has proliferated, primarily in the areas of legislative oversight, executive management, due process, and regulatory federalism. For example, "coercive controls" rely on coercion for bureaucratic performance, while "catalytic controls" may yield comparable progress with fewer adverse side-effects. The emergence of accountability battles pit competing claimants against one another, in bitter struggles over authority, with state bureaucracies as the ultimate prize. Courts increasingly are being asked to resolve these disputes, but the courts are not disinterested claimants. Often they wish to shape the behavior of state bureaucracies. Thus, judges have emerged as key arbiters and managers, deciding accountability battles in some instance, triggering them in others.

THE PROLIFERATION OF CONTROLS

During the 1970s and the 1980s, as state bureaucracies grew larger and more important, politicians, judges, and citizens strengthened their leverage over state bureaucracies by institutionalizing a wide variety of control techniques. Some of these techniques, such as sunset laws and ombudsmen, were new. Others, such as executive orders and conditions of aid, were old but not much utilized. Control techniques also differed in their directness, formality, durability, and coerciveness. However, they all shared a common purpose—to make state bureaucracies more accountable to other public officials or to the people.

Legislative Oversight

During the 1970s, state legislatures discovered oversight as a form of bureaucratic control. Legislative committees took an active interest in bureaucratic implementation or nonimplementation of state statutes and conducted hearings aimed at identifying and resolving problems. This became easier as the legislator's job became a full-time profession in most states and as legislative staffs became larger and more professional. More than their congressional counterparts, state legislators decided not to leave oversight to chance. Perhaps oversight needed an extra push at the state level. In any event, state legislatures established regular mechanisms for legislative review.

Following the lead of Colorado, approximately two-thirds of the state legislatures adopted sunset laws, which provide for the automatic expiration of agencies unless the state legislature acts affirmatively to renew them. Although the threat of extinction is far-fetched in the case of large agencies, the threat of review must be taken seriously by all agencies. The sunset review process is especially important for obscure agencies that might otherwise escape scrutiny by legislative committees.

In addition to sunset laws, many state legislatures substantially upgraded the quality of their legislative audit bureaus. Gradually, these organizations came to place greater emphasis on program evaluation and policy analysis, less emphasis on auditing and accounting. To ensure careful, well-crafted evaluations, state legislatures augmented the staffs assigned to these organizations.

Finally, the overwhelming majority of state legislatures provided for legislative review of administrative rules and regulations. In sixteen states, legislative vetoes enable the legislature to invalidate an administrative rule or regulation. Through the legislative veto process, state legislatures have exercised closer scrutiny of administrative rule making. The U.S. Supreme Court declared the legislative veto unconstitutional at the federal level,[1] and state courts have invalidated legislative vetoes in eight states.[2] Nevertheless, the legislative veto continues to be an important mechanism for legislative control in one-third of the states.

In thinking about legislative controls, a useful distinction can be made between inward-looking and outward-looking legislative changes. As political scientist Alan Rosenthal has observed, state legislatures have become more fragmented, more decentralized, and less cohesive in recent years. In some sense, this might be characterized as legislative decline. However, a fragmented legislature is not necessarily weaker in its dealings with other units of government, such as state bureaucracies. A highly fragmented legislature may provide more occasions for legislative oversight and more incentives for individual legislators to engage in oversight. Thus, as legislatures become weaker internally, they may become stronger externally. This is especially true of those forms of legislative control that do not require a legislative majority.

Executive Management

For years, governors have complained about the fragmented character of the executive branch. Many executive branch officials are elected or appointed to office for fixed terms that do not coincide with the governor's term. The number of state agencies, boards, and commissions can be overwhelming and disconcerting. Also, agencies have their own traditions and habits and may be reluctant to follow the priorities of a new governor. All of these factors have inhibited executive integration, coordination, and leadership.

During the 1970s and the 1980s, many governors took steps to deal with these problems. Most governors spearheaded major reorganizations of the executive branch, striving for greater rationality and for a reduction in the number of boards and commissions. Minor reorganizations also were commonplace. In Minnesota, for example, five governors issued a total of 155 reorganization orders between 1970 and 1988.[3]

Governors also institutionalized cabinet meetings, subcabinet meetings, or both to secure greater coordination and integration. During the 1970s, approximately fourteen governors established a cabinet for the first time and approximately twenty-five governors established subcabinets to advise and coordinate in broad policy domains.[4] The hope was that these meetings would ensure that key executive branch officials marched to the same drumbeat.

In addition, governors relied on new budget techniques, such as zero-based budgeting, to increase their control over agency budget submissions and, ultimately, agency budgets themselves. Under zero-based budgeting, the previous year's budget base is not taken for granted, although it may be incorporated into alternative budget submissions. During the 1970s, approximately twenty-five states adopted a modified form of zero-based budgeting.[5]

At the same time, governors fought successfully for shorter ballots to bring more top state officials under gubernatorial control. Between 1962 and 1978, the number of elected state executives declined by 10 percent.[6] As a result of these reforms, governors today are more likely to deal with state agencies headed more often by gubernatorial appointees in whom they can have confidence.

Finally, executive orders have become more popular in recent years. In Wisconsin, Gov. Lee Sherman Dreyfus issued more executive orders in 1979 than his predecessors had issued during the 1960s and 1970s.[7] Dreyfus's successor, Anthony S. Earl, issued even more executive orders than Dreyfus.[8] Similarly, in Massachusetts, the number of executive orders issued between 1965 and 1980 rose 206 percent over the preceding fifteen years.[9] Many of these executive orders were aimed at controlling state bureaucracies.

Interest Representation

Unable or unwilling to control state agencies directly in every instance, politicians relied on surrogates to ensure better representation for favored points of view, such as consumers, environmentalists, and the elderly. Political scientists Matthew McCubbins and Thomas Schwartz referred to this phenomenon as "fire-alarm oversight" because politicians in effect depend on citizen or other public officials to spot fires in the bureaucracy and help stamp them out.[10] During the 1970s and the 1980s, states took a number of steps to improve representation for broad, diffuse interests or other underrepresented interests, especially before state regulatory agencies—a "representation revolution" occurred.[11]

For example, many established "proxy advocacy" offices to represent consumer interests in state public utility commission proceedings, such as rate cases. In some instances, attorneys general served this function; in other instances, separate consumer advocacy offices were established. Wisconsin, meanwhile, established a Citizens Utilities Board, funded by citizens through voluntary contributions but authorized by the state legislature to include membership solicitations in utility bills.[12] State legislatures in Illinois, Oregon, and New York subsequently established similar organizations, though without provisions for inserts.[13]

Disappointed in the performance of occupational licensing boards, state legislatures mandated lay representation on the boards in the hope that fewer anti-competitive practices would result. Wisconsin law specifies that at least one public member shall serve on each of the state's occupational licensing boards. California goes even further. Since 1976, California has required that all occupational licensing boards have a majority of public members, except for ten "healing arts" boards and the Board of Accountancy.[14]

Many state legislatures require public hearings in various environmental policy decisions. Pursuant to the California Coastal Act of 1972, a coastal zoning commission must call for a public hearing whenever a developer submits a construction permit request for a project that might have an "adverse environmental impact" on coastal resources.

Some interest representation reforms that occurred on the state level were mandated by or encouraged by the federal government. For example, Congress required states to cooperate with the Environmental Protection Agency (EPA) in providing for public participation under the Federal Water Pollution Control Act; the Resource Conservation and Recovery Act; the Comprehensive Environmental Response, Compensation, and Liability Act; and other statutes. Through the Older Americans Act, Congress required states to establish long-term care ombudsman programs to investigate complaints by nursing home residents and to monitor the development and implementation of pertinent laws and regulations.

Regulatory Federalism

The dynamics of regulatory federalism differ significantly from those of interest representation reforms. In both cases, politicians exercise indirect control over state bureaucracies, relying on surrogates to articulate their concerns. However, regulatory federalism is much more intrusive. If a consumer advocacy group recommends a new rule or regulation, a state agency may consider and reject it. If a federal agency instructs a state agency to adopt a rule or face a sharp cutback in federal funds, the state agency does not have much of a choice.

Regulatory federalism is a process whereby the federal government imposes conditions on state governments that accept federal funding.[15] Regulatory federalism arose as an adjunct to the new social regulations of the 1970s and as an antidote to the laissez faire of general revenue sharing. Regulatory federalism includes a variety of techniques, such as direct orders (unequivocal mandates), crossover sanctions (threats in one program area if actions are not taken in another program), crosscutting requirements (obligations applicable to a wide range of programs), and partial preemptions (the establishment of minimal federal standards if states wish to run their own programs).[16] Some of these techniques apply to state legislatures; some apply to state agencies; many apply to both.

The number of federal statutes imposing significant new regulatory requirements increased dramatically during the 1970s. Given the Reagan administration's public support for federalism and deregulation, many observers expected regulatory federalism to decline during the 1980s. However, as political scientist Timothy Conlan has shown, the number of federal statutes with significant intergovernmental controls directed at the states increased even further.[17] Moreover, a disproportionate increase came about in the most coercive regulatory control techniques—namely, direct orders and crossover sanctions. In Conlan's words, "the 1980s rivaled the previous decade as a period of unparalleled intergovernmental regulatory activity."[18]

In some cases, Congress imposed new regulatory requirements on the states despite Reagan's philosophical reservations. This was especially true in environmental policy. In other cases, however, the Reagan administration fully supported tougher controls on the states. For example, in transportation policy, it endorsed a variety of crossover sanctions,[19] and in welfare policy, it advocated limits on eligibility to receive public subsidies.[20]

Several regulatory federalism initiatives of recent years have been challenged in court. However, the courts have routinely upheld the federal government's right to impose constraints on state governments accepting federal funds.[21] The courts also have upheld partial preemptions,[22] crossover sanctions,[23] and direct orders.[24]

Due Process

In addition to serving as arbiters in intergovernmental disputes, federal judges have been active participants in efforts to control state bureaucracies. They have intervened vigorously in pursuit of such constitutional rights as "due process of law" and freedom from "cruel and unusual punishment." Dissatisfied with progress at the state level, they have gone so far as to seize, for example, state prisons and homes for the mentally ill or the mentally retarded, substituting their managerial judgment for that of state public administrators.

Wyatt v. Stickney[25] was the first in a long line of institutional reform cases in which federal judges decided to play a strong managerial role. Alabama's homes for the mentally ill and the mentally retarded were overcrowded, understaffed, dangerous, and unsanitary. In response to a class action suit, Judge Frank Johnson held that mental patients have a right to adequate and effective treatment in the least restrictive environment practicable. To secure that right, he issued extremely specific treatment standards and ordered rapid deinstitutionalization.

Shortly after the *Wyatt* decision, Judge Johnson found himself embroiled in an equally bitter controversy over Alabama's prisons. By most accounts, conditions in the state's prisons were deplorable. Rapes and stabbings were widespread; food was unwholesome; and physical facilities were dilapidated. In response to inmate complaints, Judge Johnson issued a decree calling for adequate medical care, regular fire inspections, and regular physical examinations.[26] When conditions barely improved, he issued detailed standards, including cell-space requirements, hiring requirements, and a mandatory classification system.[27]

The Alabama cases set the stage for a large number of similar cases throughout the country. In state after state, federal judges mandated massive changes in physical facilities, staffing ratios, health services, and amenities. They specified the size of prison cells, the credentials of new employees, and plumbing and hygiene standards. They shut down facilities and prohibited new admissions, even where alternative facilities were not available.

The U.S. Supreme Court finally applied the brakes on mental health orders in *Youngberg v. Romeo.*[28] In that decision, the Court ruled that mentally retarded clients are constitutionally entitled to minimally adequate treatment and habilitation but that professionals, including state administrators, should be free to decide what constitutes minimally adequate training for staff. Thus, the decision was viewed as a partial victory for state administrators.

The Supreme Court has yet to focus on prison reform cases, which continue to drag on in many states. In Texas, for example, Judge William Justice has been locked in a bitter battle with the Texas Department of Corrections since he called for sweeping reforms in *Ruiz v. Estelle*.[29] By 1992, thirty-seven states were under some kind of court order for their prisons. In nine states, the entire state prison system was under court order.[30]

As Republican presidents have appointed more conservative judges to the federal bench, court takeovers of prisons and other public institutions would be expected to decrease. However, as political scientist Robert Bradley has noted, judges appointed by Republican presidents are no more likely than judges appointed by Democratic presidents to issue structural reform decrees in state prison cases.[31] Additional reasons exist to doubt that this phenomenon will diminish. As John DiIulio, Jr., has observed, "Demographic and sentencing trends make it likely that institutional overcrowding will worsen over the next decade. If that happens, and if prison and jail officials prove unable to maintain any semblance of safe and humane conditions behind bars, then sweeping judicial intervention into prisons and jails may be more of a growing prospect than a fading memory."[32]

TYPES OF CONTROLS

Useful in thinking about recent efforts to control state bureaucracies is to imagine a spectrum ranging from catalytic controls, at one end, to coercive controls, at the other end, with hortatory controls falling in between. Catalytic controls stimulate change but preserve a great deal of bureaucratic discretion. Coercive controls require change and severely limit bureaucratic discretion. Hortatory controls involve more pressure than catalytic controls but more restraint than coercive controls.[33]

Moreover, different types of controls have different types of effects. In their public policy implications, catalytic controls have been surprisingly effective and coercive controls have been notably counterproductive.

Catalytic Controls

Catalytic controls require state bureaucracies to respond to a petition or plea but do not predetermine the nature of their response. As a result, such controls are action-forcing but not solution-forcing. They alter bureaucratic behavior, but they permit the bureaucracy a good deal of discretion and flexibility. Examples of catalytic controls include public hearings, ombudsmen, proxy advocacy, and lay representation.

Public hearings have enabled environmentalists to win important victories in their dealings with state bureaucracies. For example, citizens have used public hearings on state water quality planning in North Carolina to secure important modifications of state plans concerning waste water disposal, construction, and mining.[34] Similarly, citizens used public hearings before the California Coastal Commission to block permits for development projects that would have an "adverse environmental impact" on coastal resources.[35]

Ombudsmen have been active in several areas but especially on nursing home issues. According to one report, [36] nursing home ombudsmen have been effective in resolving complaints on a wide variety of subjects, including Medicaid problems, guardianship, the power of attorney, inadequate hygiene, family problems, and the theft of personal possessions. Another study[37] found that nursing home ombudsmen provide useful information to legislators and planners.

Proxy advocates have effectively represented consumers in rate cases and other proceedings held by state public utility commissions. As a result of the interventions, utility companies have received rate hikes substantially lower than those originally requested. Proxy advocates also have been instrumental in securing policies on utility disconnections and payment penalties that help consumers who are struggling to pay their bills.[38] Even in complex telecommunications cases, proxy advocates have successfully promoted competition on behalf of consumers.[39]

Catalytic controls may be too weak in some instances. In several Southern states, for example, public hearing requirements in utility regulatory proceedings have been pointless because consumer groups and environmental groups have not materialized to take advantage of such hearings.[40] Lay representation on occupational licensing boards also has been a disappointment. Lacking expertise, lay representatives typically have deferred to professionals on these boards.[41]

Overall, though, catalytic controls have been remarkably successful in making state bureaucracies more responsive to a vast array of formerly underrepresented interests. In effect, they have institutionalized what political scientist James Q. Wilson refers to as "entrepreneurial politics"[42] or the pursuit of policies that offer widely distributed benefits through widely distributed costs. Moreover, catalytic controls have achieved results without engendering bureaucratic hostility and resentment. Studies show that state administrators welcome citizen participation[43] and interest group interventions.[44] At their best, catalytic controls provide state bureaucrats with ammunition to justify policies that promote the public interest.

Hortatory Controls

Hortatory controls involve political pressure or "jawboning," usually by someone in a position of authority. They strike a balance between bureaucratic discretion and bureaucratic accountability. Some, such as sunset laws and administrative reorganizations, are relatively mild; others, such as partial preemptions and crossover sanctions, are relatively strong.

The strength of hortatory controls depends primarily on two factors: their specificity (are the goals of the controllers clear?) and the credibility of the threat (how likely is it that penalties will be invoked?). Thus, sunset laws are relatively weak because the threat of termination is remote, except in the case of extremely small agencies.

To argue that some hortatory controls are mild is not to say that they are ineffective. A study of legislative audit bureau reports reveals that they do lead to changes in legislation, administrative practice, or both. Research by legislative audit bureaus is more likely to be utilized by state legislators than other types of research.[45] The literature on administrative reorganizations reveals that they do not reduce government spending but that they can promote coordination and integration if they are well-crafted and well-executed.[46] The key seems to be to put agencies with interrelated missions under the same roof.

Research on sunset laws roughly parallels the findings on administrative reorganizations. As a cost-containment device, sunset legislation has been a failure. However, as a mechanism for focusing legislative attention on agencies and issues low in visibility, sunset legislation has been a success. In a number of states, such as Connecticut and Florida, sunset laws have resulted in significant changes in statutes and agency rules.[47]

Stronger hortatory controls have been even more effective, though they also have been dysfunctional in some respects. In response to quality control systems in welfare, "errors of liberality" have declined, but "errors of stringency" have increased.[48] In effect, states have sacrificed accuracy for cost-containment. States also have enforced federal regulations that they know to be unreasonable, in response to partial preemptions in environmental policy. For example, the Minnesota Pollution Control Agency enforced a rigid EPA definition of hazardous waste, even though it meant that a lime sludge pile could not be removed from a highway site, could not be used for waste-water treatment, and could not be used to clean an electric utility company's smokestack emission.[49]

Strong hortatory controls place a premium on uniform standards and universal compliance with such standards. In some instances, such as civil rights, no practical alternative exists to strong controls, because local prejudices are too deeply ingrained to permit cooperation. In others, however, strong hortatory controls may impose premature closure, discouraging innovation and experimentation and proving difficult for the states to serve as "laboratories" for the nation and for other states.

Despite the new federalism, strong hortatory controls have been particularly prominent in intergovernmental relations. Although federal aid to state and local governments has declined, no commensurate decrease has taken place in federal regulations. Political scientist Richard P. Nathan cites state reforms in health, education, and welfare as evidence of a growing state role in a conservative era.[50] Yet state administrators cite precisely these issue areas, along with environmental policy, as ones where federal influence is relatively strong.[51] States can be both innovating and responding. Or perhaps the state legislatures are innovating, while the state agencies are responding. In any event, regulatory federalism has not abated in recent years, even if the goals and purposes of federal overseers have changed during the Reagan and Bush administrations.

Coercive Controls

Coercive controls rob state bureaucracies of their discretion. They compel a specific response, often within a specific time frame. Neither the solution nor the deadline may be reasonable, but the state bureaucracy does not have the luxury of responding reasonably. Immediate compliance becomes more important than rationality, and short-term "outputs" become more important than long-term "outcomes."

Coercive controls often trigger bureaucratic circumvention or resistance. In the former case, bureaucrats comply with the letter, but not the spirit, of a tough requirement. In the latter case, the bureaucracy goes to court. In both cases, an adversarial relationship develops that precludes cooperation, bargaining, and persuasion.

As a response to legislative vetoes, some state agencies have issued emergency rules, which are not subject to the usual legislative review process. In Wisconsin, for example, state agencies issued a total of fifty-four emergency rules during the 1985-1986 legislative session—a sharp increase over earlier years.[52] Reliance on emergency rules is especially unfortunate, because they do not involve public hearings. Thus, to escape highly threatening legislative vetoes, agencies have escaped less-threatening public hearings as well.

Court orders have triggered some of the more dysfunctional bureaucratic responses. When Judge Frank Johnson required state prisons to reduce their overcrowding, Alabama prison officials simply released large numbers of prisoners, forcing county jails to take up the slack. Unfortunately, county jails were poorly equipped for the task; they lacked adequate space and personnel. Consequently, many prisoners, shipped to county jails, were forced to endure conditions even worse than those they experienced in the state prisons.[53] Yet the state agency was technically in compliance with the court decree.

A key problem with coercive controls is that they place far too much emphasis on formal authority. Many state agencies depend considerably on a series of informal understandings. This is especially true of prisons, where quick-thinking guards and cooperative inmates help to maintain a delicate balance between order and chaos. When that balance is disrupted, tragedy may result. This is precisely what happened in Texas, where Judge Justice's court orders dissolved the informal networks that enabled the prisons to function on a daily basis. As guards became more timid, direct challenges to authority rose sharply. Disciplinary reports reveal abrupt and dramatic increases in incidents where a guard was threatened or assaulted.[54] Inmates also turned on themselves, with their fists or with makeshift weapons. By generating rising expectations and undermining bureaucratic morale, Judge Justice created a temporary power vacuum that prison gangs quickly filled. The tragic result was a series of riots and violent episodes that left fifty-two inmates dead within two years.[55]

ACCOUNTABILITY BATTLES

Accountability battles have become more prominent in state politics for three principal reasons: (1) the proliferation of controls; (2) the intensification of controls; and (3) the judicialization of controls. As controls multiply, some are likely to be contradictory. Competing claimants emerge. As controls intensify, contradictory controls generate more friction. Competing claimants press their claims. As controls spill over into the courts, disputes are resolved according to legal criteria. Moreover, the courts themselves become active participants in these battles. Frustrated with both state politicians and state bureaucrats, judges have decided that they can do a better job and that they are entitled to do so under the U.S. Constitution, the state constitution, or both.

State Legislatures versus Governors

Accountability battles between state legislatures and governors have erupted in recent years. Although such disputes are not new, they seem to focus increasingly on directives to administrative agencies and on questions of legal authority instead of political preference. As a result, state judges have found themselves playing a key role in arbitrating disputes between governors and state legislatures.

Legislative vetoes have aroused considerable conflict between state legislatures and governors, even when the same party controls both branches of government. In New Jersey, for example, the Democratic state legislature and Democratic governor Brendan T. Byrne clashed in court over a generic legislative veto and a more specific veto, whereby certain building authority proposals must be approved by both houses or the presiding offices of the legislature, depending on the nature of the proposal.[56] The New Jersey state supreme court upheld the specific legislative veto[57] but ruled the generic veto unconstitutional, citing violations of separation of powers and the presentment clauses of the state constitution.[58]

Executive orders also have triggered conflict between state legislatures and governors. In Pennsylvania, for example, Republican governor Dick Thornburgh issued an executive order "privatizing" the state's liquor control store system. The Democratic state legislature, which had just rejected such a plan, promptly took the governor to court. A Commonwealth Court judge ruled in favor of the legislature, noting that the governor's privatization plan was "without authority and contravenes the Sunset Act." He also accused both sides of playing an unseemly game of political football at the public's expense.[59]

Money, the "mother's milk of politics," has fueled many disputes between state legislatures and governors. In Wisconsin, Republican governor Tommy Thompson refused to accept a decision by the Democratic state legislature to maintain welfare benefits at existing levels. Stretching the outer limits of his line-item veto authority, Thompson vetoed two digits and a decimal point from the state legislature's benefit formula, thereby effecting a 6 percent reduction in welfare benefits. The legislature promptly took the governor to court, but the Wisconsin supreme court upheld a generous interpretation of the governor's line-item power.[60]

The most striking aspect of accountability battles between state legislatures and governors is that they often have a partisan edge, pitting a Republican governor against a Democratic state legislature or vice versa. As divided government has become more common at the state level, state agencies find determining whether they are in Democratic or Republican hands increasingly difficult. Thus, the voters' ambivalence has triggered important legal battles with high stakes.

Federal Politicians versus State Politicians

State bureaucracies increasingly are being asked to implement federal statutes, such as environmental protection statutes. Often these federal statutes contradict state statutes or the policy preferences of the state's governor.

Under such circumstances, a showdown is likely, with the federal government citing the "commerce clause" or the "take care clause" of the U.S. Constitution, while the state government cites the Tenth Amendment.

The U.S. Supreme Court and other federal courts have routinely sided with the federal government in accountability battles where the allocation of federal funds is at issue. If states accept federal funding, they also must accept the conditions the federal government attaches to those funds. However, many intergovernmental disputes do not involve federal funding but a federal effort to preempt state activity in a particular policy domain. Here, also, the U.S. Supreme Court has sided with the federal government, though with occasional exceptions.

In *National League of Cities v. Usery*,[61] the Supreme Court surprised many observers by rejecting the federal government's attempt to extend minimum wage and maximum hour provisions to municipal employees. In doing so, the Court said that the Tenth Amendment prohibited any federal action that impaired "the State's freedom to structure integral operations in areas of traditional governmental functions." Thus a key provision of the 1974 Fair Labor Standards Act Amendments was ruled unconstitutional. The decision was an important victory for both state and local governments.

In subsequent cases, the Supreme Court wrestled gamely with the "traditional governmental functions" criterion and offered further clarification. For example, in *Hodel v. Virginia Surface Mining and Reclamation Association*,[62] the Court articulated a three-fold test for determining when Tenth Amendment claims shall prevail. Specifically, the Court extended protection to the states if federal regulations: (1) regulate the states as states; (2) address matters that are indisputable attributes of state sovereignty; and (3) impair the states' ability to structure integral operations in areas of traditional function. In *Hodel*—a strip mining case involving a partial preemption statute—the Court concluded that Congress had acted properly and with restraint. Similarly, in *FERC v. Mississippi*,[63] the Court applauded Congress for imposing modest constraints on state public utility commissions, when it could have preempted the field entirely.

Finally, after years of painful efforts to distinguish between "traditional government functions" and other functions, the Supreme Court abandoned that doctrine outright in *Garcia v. San Antonio Metropolitan Transit Authority*.[64] Writing for the majority, Justice Harry A. Blackmun concluded that "State sovereign interests . . . are more properly protected by procedural safeguards inherent in the structure of the federal system than by judicially created limitations of federal power."[65] In effect, the states would have to protect themselves through vigorous lobbying on Capitol Hill. The Supreme Court no longer would invoke a rule that was "unsound in principle and unworkable in practice."[66]

Although most accountability battles between federal and state politicians have focused on the commerce clause, one celebrated dispute involved the constitutional provision (in Article I) that the states shall have the authority to train state militia. A number of governors, opposed to the Reagan administration's Central America policies, objected to White House orders, backed by Congress, to use the National Guard for training exercises in Honduras. The governors feared that their troops would directly or indirectly support the contras' efforts to overthrow the Sandinista government in Nicaragua. Gov. Rudy Perpich of Minnesota and ten other governors sued the federal government to protest the deployment of National Guard troops without gubernatorial consent. The governors did not dispute the president's authority to federalize the Guard to deal with a national emergency, but they noted pointedly that no state of emergency existed.

On August 5, 1987, a federal district court upheld the federal government's right to deploy National Guard units while the Guard is on active duty. In the words of Judge Donald Alsop, "All authority to provide for the national defense resides in the Congress, and state governors have never had, and never could have, jurisdiction in this area."[67] That decision was subsequently affirmed by the U.S. Court of Appeals and by the U.S. Supreme Court.[68] Here, as in other disputes between federal and state politicians, the federal government has been successful in establishing its preeminence.

Federal Judges versus State Politicians

In accountability battles between federal politicians and state politicians, federal judges have served as arbiters. In other disputes, however, federal judges have served as both arbiters and combatants. In numerous institutional reform cases, federal district court judges have ordered sweeping changes that are attainable only if state legislatures allocate more money than they wish to spend in a particular policy domain. These decisions have had tangible effects on state budgets.[69] The decisions also have raised important questions concerning both federalism and the power of the purse.

Confronted by shocking conditions in Alabama's prisons, Judge Frank Johnson ordered the entire prison system overhauled. He required immediate action to provide adequate food, clothing, shelter, sanitation, medical attention, and personal safety for inmates. He ordered individual cells, with each cell being at least 60 square feet. He required educational and rehabilitative services. And to ensure swift implementation, he established human rights committees.

Other federal judges have acted with equal vigor. Judge William Justice, appalled by conditions in Texas prisons, ordered an end to quadruple cells, triple cells, and double cells. He restricted the use of force by prison guards and ordered an end to the state's "building tender" system, in which inmates in effect guarded other inmates. In addition, he ordered sharp improvements in health care, fire and safety standards. He also insisted on prompt punishments for violations of constitutional rights.

In other institutional reform cases, federal judges have ordered sweeping changes in state treatment of the mentally ill and the mentally retarded. In New York, Judges Orrin Judd and John Bartels demanded more ward attendants, eighty-five more nurses, thirty physical therapists, and fifteen more physicians at the Willowbrook Developmental Center on Staten Island. They prohibited seclusion of patients and called for the immediate repair of broken toilets. They also ordered a sharp decrease in the Willowbrook population, stressing the advantages of deinstitutionalization. To implement these reforms, they appointed and preserved a Willowbrook Review Panel, which developed into a powerful agent of change.

In Pennsylvania, Judge Raymond Broderick went ever further, after learning of unsanitary, inhumane, and dangerous conditions at the Pennhurst State School and Hospital for the mentally retarded. In a strongly worded opinion, Broderick ordered the eventual closing down of the Pennhurst facilities, with residents being relocated in community facilities. In the meantime, he insisted on clean, odorless, and insect-free buildings, no new admissions, and less reliance on forcible restraint and unnecessary medication. To achieve these results, he appointed a special master and set deadlines for compliance.

More often than not, accountability battles between federal judges and state politicians have been won by federal judges. In reviewing lower court decisions, appeals court judges and the U.S. Supreme Court have agreed that "cruel and unusual punishment" is intolerable in state prisons and that the mentally ill have a constitutional right to "treatment" if admitted to a state facility. However, appeals courts also have raised questions about the extraordinarily detailed and specific remedies mandated by federal district court judges.

In *Newman v. Alabama*,[70] the U.S. Court of Appeals for the Fifth Circuit ruled that Judge Johnson went too far in specifying the size of new prison cells, in appointing human rights committees, and in insisting on rehabilitation opportunities for all prisoners. In the words of the court: "The Constitution does not require that prisoners, as individuals or as a group, be provided with any and every amenity which some person may think is needed to avoid mental, physical and emotional deterioration." In *Ruiz v. Estelle*,[71] the U.S. Court of Appeals for the Fifth Circuit ruled that Judge Justice went too far in outlawing double cells in Texas prisons (but supported his ban on triple and quadruple cells). In *New York State Association for Retarded Children v. Carey*,[72] the U.S. Court of Appeals for the Second Circuit concluded that Gov. Hugh Carey could not be held in contempt of court for failing to provide funding for the Willowbrook Review Panel. In *Pennhurst State School and Hospital v. Halderman*,[73] the U.S. Supreme Court ruled that a right to treatment exists only if a state accepts federal funds and if federal conditions of aid are clearly and unambiguously stated. In *Youngberg v. Romeo*,[74] the U.S. Supreme Court ruled that even when a right to treatment exists, it should be operationalized by qualified professionals, not judges.

Thus, accountability battles between federal district court judges and state politicians have given way to battles between federal district court judges and federal appeals court judges. On questions of constitutional rights, the appeals court judges generally have deferred to federal district courts, to the chagrin of the states. On questions of remedies, however, the appeals courts have cautioned lower courts against excessive specificity that stretches the limits of judicial expertise.

CONCLUSION

State administrative agencies once enjoyed considerable autonomy. Ignored by virtually everyone but clientele groups, they were "semisovereign" entities. In the early 1970s, that began to change. As state budgets grew and state bureaucracies increased in importance, this era came to a close. To make state agencies more accountable, politicians and judges institutionalized a wide variety of reforms. Through direct and indirect means, they attempted to bring state bureaucracies under control.

Ironically, this occurred at precisely the same time as the growing professionalization of state agencies. Thanks to civil service reforms, budget increases, rising education levels, and growing pressure for specialization, state bureaucracies acquired greater experience and expertise. They now are more adept at problem solving than ever before and arguably more deserving of discretion. Thus, they chafe at external pressure, particularly when it is highly coercive.

General agreement exists that state agencies ought to be accountable. Even state bureaucrats cheerfully concede that point. However, consensus on the need for bureaucratic accountability has given way to "dissensus" on lines of authority. If governors and state legislators both claim an electoral mandate, who is right? If presidents and governors both cite constitutional prerogatives, who is correct? If federal judges and state politicians disagree on spending priorities, who deserves the power of the purse?

In the 1990s, state agencies are living in a different world—one characterized by growing emphasis on hierarchy, oversight, and judicial review. State agencies are more accountable to their sovereigns than they used to be. Yet accountability has become a murky concept. Principal-agent theories of politics[75] work only when the principal's identity is clear to the agent. In numerous policy areas, state bureaucratic agents face dual principals or even multiple principals.

Thus, accountability battles rage, as competing sovereigns press their claims. As one might expect in a federal system, different actors have won accountability battles in different settings and at different times. Increasingly, however, federal judges are settling the most difficult of these battles. In the process of resolving disputes, federal judges have themselves become interested parties. Ultimately, federal judges decide how accountability shall be defined, how authority shall be structured, and how power shall be wielded in a federal system. If accountability battles persist, the judicialization of state administration is the most probable result.

Notes

1. *Immigration and Naturalization Service v. Chadha*, 462 U.S. 919 (1983).
2. L. Harold Levinson, "The Decline of the Legislative Veto: Federal/State Comparisons and Interactions," *Publius* 17:1 (Winter 1987): 115–132.
3. Thad L. Beyle, "The Executive Branch: Organization and Issues, 1988–1989," in Council of State Governments, *The Book of the States, 1990–1991* (Lexington, Ky.: Council of State Governments, 1990), 76.
4. Lydia Bodman and Daniel Garry, "Innovations in State Cabinet Systems," *State Government* 55:3 (Summer 1982): 93–97.
5. Thomas Lauth, "Zero-Base Budgeting in Georgia State Government: Myth and Reality," in *Perspectives on Budgeting*, ed. Allen Schick (Washington, D.C.: American Society for Public Administration, 1980), 114–132.
6. Larry J. Sabato, *Goodby to Good-time Charlie: The American Governorship Transformed* (Washington, D.C.: CQ Press, 1983).

7. Susan King, "Executive Orders of the Wisconsin Governor," *Wisconsin Law Review* 2 (1980): 333–369.

8. Justin Kopca, "Executive Orders in State Government," unpublished manuscript, Madison, Wis., May 1987.

9. E. Lee Bernick, "Discovering a Governor's Power: The Executive Order," *State Government* 57:3 (1984): 97–101.

10. Matthew McCubbins and Thomas Schwartz, "Congressional Oversight Overlooked: Police Patrols versus Fire Alarms," *American Journal of Political Science* 28:1 (February 1984): 180–202.

11. William Gormley, Jr., "The Representation Revolution: Reforming State Regulation through Public Representation," *Administration and Society* 18:2 (August 1986): 179–196.

12. Involuntary bill inserts later were ruled unconstitutional in a California case that effectively invalidated a key provision of the Wisconsin law. See *Pacific Gas and Electric v. Public Utilities Commission of California* 106 S. Ct. 903 (1986).

13. Beth Givens, *Citizens' Utility Boards: Because Utilities Bear Watching* (San Diego, Calif.: Center for Public Interest Law, University of San Diego Law School, 1991).

14. Howard Schutz, "Effects of Increased Citizen Membership on Occupational Licensing Boards in California," *Policy Studies Journal* 2 (March 1983): 504–516.

15. Regulatory federalism also may be used to describe the relationship between state and local governments. For more on the growing burdens placed by state governments on local governments, see Catherine Lovell and Charles Tobin. "The Mandate Issue," *Public Administration Review* 41:3 (May/June 1981): 318–331. See also Joseph Zimmerman, "Developing State-Local Relations: 1987–1989," in Council of State Governments, *The Book of the States, 1990–1991*, 533–548.

16. Advisory Commission on Intergovernmental Relations, *Regulatory Federalism: Policy, Process, Impact and Reform* (Washington, D.C.: Advisory Commission on Intergovernmental Relations, 1983).

17. Timothy Conlan, "And the Beat Goes On: Intergovernmental Mandates and Preemption in an Era of Deregulation," *Publius* 21:3 (Summer 1991): 43–57.

18. Ibid., 50.

19. James Gosling, "Transportation Policy and the Ironies of Intergovernmental Relations," in *The Midwest Response to the New Federalism*, ed. Peter Eisinger and William Gormley (Madison: University of Wisconsin Press, 1988), 237–263.

20. Sanford Schram, "The New Federalism and Social Welfare: AFDC in the Midwest," in *The Midwest Response to the New Federalism*, 264–292.

21. *Massachusetts v. U.S.*, 435 U.S. 444 (1978); and *Connecticut Department of Income Maintenance v. Heckler*, 105 S. Ct. 2210 (1985).

22. *Hodel v. Virginia Surface Mining and Reclamation Association*, 452 U.S. 264 (1981); and *FERC v. Mississippi*, 456 U.S. 742 (1982).

23. *South Dakota v. Dole*, Slip Opinion No. 86-260, U.S. Supreme Court, June 23, 1987.

24. *EEOC v. Wyoming*, 460 U.S. 226 (1983); *Garcia v. San Antonio Metropolitan Transit Authority*, 105 S. Ct. 1005 (1985); *City of New York v. FCC*, 108 S. Ct. 1637 (1988); and *Mississippi Power and Light v. Mississippi*, 108 S. Ct. 2428 (1988).

25. *Wyatt v. Stickney*, 324 F. Supp. 781 (M.D. Ala., 1971).

26. *Newman v. Alabama*, 349 F. Supp. 278 (M.D. Ala., 1972).

27. *James v. Wallace*, 406 F. Supp. 318 (M.D. Ala., 1976); and *Pugh v. Locke*, 406 F. Supp. 318 (M.D. Ala., 1976).

28. *Youngberg v. Romeo*, 102 S. Ct. 2452 (1982).

29. *Ruiz v. Estelle*, 503 F. Supp. 1265 (S.D. Tex. 1980).

30. Joel Rosch, "Will the Federal Courts Run the States' Prison Systems?" in *State Government: CQ's Guide to Current Issues and Activities 1987–1988*, ed. Thad L. Beyle (Washington, D.C.: Congressional Quarterly Inc., 1987), 165–168.

31. Robert Bradley, "Judicial Appointment and Judicial Intervention: The Issuance of Structural Reform Decrees in Corrections Litigation," in *Courts, Corrections, and the Constitution,* ed. John DiIulio, Jr. (New York: Oxford University Press, 1990), 249–267.

32. John DiIulio, Jr., "Conclusion: What Judges Can Do to Improve Prisons and Jails," in *Courts, Corrections, and the Constitution,* 288–289.

33. William Gormley, Jr., *Taming the Bureaucracy: Muscles, Prayers, and Other Strategies* (Princeton, N.J.: Princeton University Press, 1989).

34. David Godschalk and Bruce Stiftel, "Making Waves: Public Participation in State Water Planning," *Journal of Applied Behavioral Science* 17:4 (October–December 1981): 597–614.

35. Judy Rosener, "Making Bureaucrats Responsive: A Study of the Impact of Citizen Participation and Staff Recommendations on Regulatory Decision Making," *Public Administration Review* 42:4 (July/August 1982): 339–345.

36. Administration on Aging, U.S. Department of Health and Human Services, *National Summary of State Ombudsman Reports for U.S. Fiscal Year 1982* (Washington, D.C.: U.S. Government Printing Office, 1983).

37. Abraham Monk et al., *National Comparative Analysis of Long Term Care Programs for the Aged* (New York: Brookdale Institute on Aging and Adult Human Development and the Columbia University School of Social Work, 1982).

38. William Gormley, Jr., *The Politics of Public Utility Regulation* (Pittsburgh, Pa.: University of Pittsburgh Press, 1983).

39. Paul Teske, *After Divestiture: The Political Economy of State Telecommunications Regulation* (Albany: SUNY Press, 1990), 63–85.

40. Ibid.

41. Gerald Thain and Kenneth Haydock, *A Working Paper: How Public and Other Members of Regulation and Licensing Boards Differ: The Results of a Wisconsin Survey* (Madison, Wis.: Center for Public Representation, 1983).

42. James Q. Wilson, ed., *The Politics of Regulation* (New York: Basic Books, 1980).

43. Cheryl Miller, "State Administrator Perceptions of the Policy Influence of Other Actors: Is Less Better?" *Public Administration Review* 47:3 (May/June 1987): 239–245.

44. Glenn Abney and Thomas Lauth, *The Politics of State and City Administration* (Albany: SUNY Press, 1986).

45. David Rafter, "Policy-Focused Evaluation: A Study of the Utilization of Evaluation Research by the Wisconsin Legislature," Ph.D. dissertation, University of Wisconsin, Madison, Wis., 1982.

46. Kenneth Meier, "Executive Reorganization of Government: Impact on Employment and Expenditures," *American Journal of Political Science* 24:3 (August 1980): 396–412; and Karen Hult, *Agency Merger and Bureaucratic Redesign* (Pittsburgh, Pa.: University of Pittsburgh Press, 1987).

47. Doug Roederer and Patsy Palmer, *Sunset: Expectation and Experience* (Lexington, Ky.: Council of State Governments, June 1981).

48. Evelyn Brodkin and Michael Lipsky, "Quality Control in AFDC as an Administrative Strategy," *Social Service Review* 57:1 (March 1983): 1–34.

49. Eric Black, "Why Regulators Need a Don't-Do-It-If-It's-Stupid Clause," *Washington Monthly* 16:12 (January 1985): 23–26.

50. Richard P. Nathan, "The Role of the States in American Federalism" (Paper delivered at the annual meeting of the American Political Science Association, Chicago, September 3–6, 1987).

51. Richard Elling, "Federal Dollars and Federal Clout in State Administration: A Test of 'Regulatory' and 'Picket Fence' Models of Intergovernmental Relations" (Paper delivered at the annual meeting of the Midwest Political Science Association, Chicago, April 17–20, 1985).

52. Douglas Stencel, "Analysis of Joint Committee for Review of Administrative Rules Caseload 1985–1986," unpublished manuscript, Madison, Wis., April 1987.
53. Tinsley Yarbrough, *Judge Frank Johnson and Human Rights in Alabama* (University: University of Alabama Press, 1981).
54. James Marquart and Ben Crouch, "Judicial Reform and Prisoner Control: The Impact of *Ruiz v. Estelle* on a Texas Penitentiary," *Law and Society Review* 19:4 (1985): 557–586.
55. Aric Press, "Inside America's Toughest Prison," *Newsweek*, October 6, 1986, 46–61.
56. Levinson, "The Decline of the Legislative Veto," 121.
57. *Enourato v. New Jersey Building Authority*, 448 A. 2d 449 (N.J. 1982).
58. *General Assembly v. Byrne*, 448 A. 2d 438 (N.J. 1982).
59. Gary Warner, "Despite Ruling, Future of Liquor Stores Up in Air," *Pittsburgh Press*, December 30, 1986, 1.
60. Charles Friederich, "Lawmakers to Sue Thompson over Budget Vetoes," *Milwaukee Journal*. September 2, 1987, B3; and Doug Mell, "Thompson Vetoes Win in Court," *Wisconsin State Journal*, June 15, 1988, 1.
61. *National League of Cities v. Usery*, 426 U.S. 833 (1976).
62. *Hodel v. Virginia Surface Mining and Reclamation Association*, 452 U.S. 264 (1981).
63. *FERC v. Mississippi*, 456 U.S. 742 (1982).
64. *Garcia v. San Antonio Metropolitan Transit Authority* 105 S. Ct. 1005 (1985).
65. 105 S. Ct. 1018 (1985).
66. 105 S. Ct. 1016 (1985).
67. Robert Whereatt, "State Loses Guard Suit," *Minneapolis Star and Tribune*, August 5, 1987, 1.
68. *Perpich et al. v. Department of Defense*, Slip Opinion NO. 89-542, U.S. Supreme Court, June 11, 1990.
69. Linda Harriman and Jeffrey Straussman, "Do Judges Determine Budget Decisions?" *Public Administration Review* 43:4 (July/August 1983): 343–351.
70. *Newman v. Alabama*, 559 F. 2d 283 (5th Cir., 1977).
71. *Ruiz v. Estelle*, 679 F. 2d 1115 (1982).
72. *New York State Association for Retarded Children v. Carey*, 631 F. 2d 162 (1980).
73. *Pennhurst State School and Hospital v. Halderman*, 101 S. Ct., 1531 (1981).
74. *Youngberg v. Romeo*, 102 S. Ct. 2452 (1982).
75. Jonathan Bendor and Terry Moe, "An Adaptive Model of Bureaucratic Politics," *American Political Science Review* 79:3 (September 1985): 755–774.

Accountability in the Public Sector: Lessons from the Challenger Tragedy

BARBARA S. ROMZEK
MELVIN J. DUBNICK

On January 28, 1986, the space shuttle Challenger exploded in mid-flight and seven crew members lost their lives. The widely known details of that tragic event need not be retraced here. Opinion is growing, however, that the official explanations offered by the Presidential Commission on the Space Shuttle Challenger Accident (the Rogers Commission) fail to provide full answers to why the disaster occurred. We offer an alternative explanation which addresses institutional factors contributing to the shuttle accident.

I. SEEKING AN INSTITUTIONAL PERSPECTIVE

Two common threads ran through public discussions of the Challenger incident. First was the urge to pinpoint the technical problems contributing directly to the booster rocket explosion on the shuttle. Second was the desire to uncover human and managerial errors that might have caused National Aeronautics and Space Administration (NASA) officials to overlook or ignore those technical flaws. By the time the Rogers Commission issued its findings on June 9, 1986, those technical and managerial issues dominated its conclusions.

On the first point, the verdict of the commission was unequivocal:

> The consensus of the commission . . . is that the loss of the space shuttle Challenger was caused by a failure in the joint between the lower segments of the right solid rocket motor. The specific failure was the destruction of the seals that are intended to prevent hot gases from leaking through the joint during the propellant burn of the rocket motor. The evidence assembled . . . indicates that no other element of the space shuttle system contributed to this failure.[1]

The commission was equally explicit about managerial problems at NASA being a "contributing cause" of the accident:

> The decision to launch the Challenger was flawed. Those who made the decision were unaware of the recent history of problems concerning the O rings [seals] and the joint and were unaware of the initial written recommendation of the contractor advising against the launch at temperatures below 53 degrees Fahrenheit and the continuing opposition of engineers at [Morton] Thiokol after the management

had reversed its position. . . . If the decision-makers had known all the facts it is highly unlikely that they would have decided to launch [the shuttle] on January 28, 1986.[2]

The commission's report was notable for its conclusive tone regarding these specific findings. More interesting, however, is the untravelled investigative path which asks if the problems at NASA and in the space shuttle program were institutional as well as technical or managerial. The institutional perspective is familiar to students of organizational theory who, following the lead of Talcott Parsons and James D. Thompson, note three levels of organizational responsibility and control: technical, managerial, and institutional.[3]

At the *technical level*, organizations focus on the effective performance of specialized and detailed functions. At the *managerial level*, an organization provides for mediation among its technical components and between its technical functionaries and those "customers" and "suppliers" in the organization's "task environment." At the *institutional level*, the organization deals with the need for being part of the "wider social system which is the source of the 'meaning,' legitimation, or higher-level support which makes implementation of the organization's goals possible."[4]

Applying this framework to the study of specific program or project failures such as the Challenger, one can argue that critical problems can arise at any or all three levels. Thus, an investigation of such events would be incomplete without considering the possible implications of activity at each level. The fact that NASA and other public agencies must constantly contend with the institutional forces that surround them (i.e., the "wider social system" of which they are part) is worthy of attention because agency efforts to deal with those forces may contribute to shaping the outcomes of agency action.

Investigators might ignore the role of institutional factors for several reasons. Attention to such factors might raise questions that are too basic and too dangerous for the organization or its supporters. Thus, a commission composed of individuals committed to the enterprise under investigation[5] and to the political system in general[6] is unlikely to open up the Pandora's box of institutional factors. In contrast, institutional factors might be overlooked because analysts lack a conceptual framework that facilitates such considerations. Assuming the latter explanation, we offer a framework useful for highlighting the institutional factors that might have contributed to the Challenger disaster.

II. AN "ACCOUNTABILITY" PERSPECTIVE

While often regarded as a unique public organization,[7] NASA has institutional characteristics similar in very important respects to other public sector agencies. As such, NASA has to deal with the diversity of legitimate and occasionally conflicting expectations emanating from the democratic political system of which it is a part (its institutional context). In the following pages we present a framework of public accountability as a means for examining NASA's management of its institutional pressures and its implications.

Managing Expectations

Accountability is a fundamental but underdeveloped concept in American public administration. Scholars and practitioners freely use the term to refer to answerability for one's actions or behavior. Administrators and agencies are accountable to the extent that they are required to answer for their actions. Beyond this basic notion of answerability, there has been little refinement of the term. Most of the discussion in the literature centers on the "best" strategy for achieving accountability, with the Friedreich-Finer exchange of the 1940s being the most cited example.[8]

From an alternative perspective, accountability plays a greater role in the processes of public administration than indicated by the idea of answerability. In its simplest form, answerability implies that accountability involves limited, direct, and mostly formalistic responses to demands generated by specific institutions or groups in the public agency's task environment. More broadly conceived, *public administration accountability involves the means by which public agencies and their workers manage the diverse expectations generated within and outside the organization.*[9]

Viewed as a strategy for managing expectations, public administration accountability takes a variety of forms. The focus here is on four alternative systems of public accountability, each based on variations involving two critical factors: (1) whether the ability to define and control expectations is held by some specified entity inside or outside the agency; and (2) the degree of control that entity is given over defining those agency's expectations. The interplay of these two dimensions generates the four types of accountability systems illustrated in Figure 4-1.

Regarding the first dimension, the management of agency expectations through accountability mechanisms calls for the establishment of some authoritative source of control. Internal sources of control rely on the authority inherent in either formal hierarchical relationships or informal social relationships within the agency. External sources of control reflect a similar distinction, for their authority can be derived from either formalized arrangements set forth in laws or legal contracts or the informal exercise of power by interests located outside the agency.

A second ingredient in any accountability system is the degree of control over agency choices and operations exercised by those sources of control. A high degree of control reflects the controller's ability to determine both the

Figure 4-1. Types of Accountability Systems

		Source of Agency Control	
		Internal	External
Degree of Control over Agency Actions	High	1. Bureaucratic	2. Legal
	Low	3. Professional	4. Political

range and depth of actions which a public agency and its members can take. A low degree of control, in contrast, provides for considerable discretion on the part of agency operatives.

Bureaucratic accountability systems (cell 1) are widely used mechanisms for managing public agency expectations.[10] Under this approach, the expectations of public administrators are managed through focusing attention on the priorities of those at the top of the bureaucratic hierarchy. At the same time, supervisory control is applied intensively to a wide range of agency activities. The functioning of a bureaucratic accountability system involves two simple ingredients: an organized and legitimate relationship between a superior and a subordinate in which the need to follow "orders" is unquestioned; and close supervision or a surrogate system of standard operating procedures or clearly stated rules and regulations.[11]

Legal accountability[12] (cell 2) is similar to the bureaucratic form in that it involves the frequent application of control to a wide range of public administration activities. In contrast to bureaucratic accountability, however, legal accountability is based on relationships between a controlling party outside the agency and members of the organization. That outside party is not just anyone; it is the individual or group in a position to impose legal sanctions or assert formal contractual obligations. Typically, these outsiders make the laws and other policy mandates which the public administrator is obligated to enforce or implement. In policy-making terms, the outsider is the "lawmaker," while the public administrator has the role of "executor."

The legal accountability relationship between controller and the controlled also differs from that found between supervisor and subordinate in bureaucratic accountability forms. In the bureaucratic system, the relationship is hierarchical and based on the ability of supervisors to reward or punish subordinates. In legal accountability, however, the relationship is between two relatively autonomous parties and involves a formal or implied fiduciary (principal/agent) agreement between the public agency and its legal overseer.[13] For example, Congress passes laws and monitors a federal agency's implementation of those laws; a federal district court orders a school board to desegregate its classrooms and oversees the implementation of that order; the local city commission contracts with a private firm to operate the city refuse dump. In each case the implementors are legally or contractually obliged to carry out their duties, and the enforcement of such obligations are very different from those found in situations where bureaucratic accountability systems are applied.[14]

Professional accountability[15] (cell 3) occurs with greater frequency as governments deal increasingly with technically difficult and complex problems. Under those circumstances, public officials must rely on skilled and expert employees to provide appropriate solutions. Those employees expect to be held fully accountable for their actions and insist that agency leaders trust them to do the best job possible. If they fail to meet job performance expectations, it is assumed they can be reprimanded or fired. Otherwise they expect to be given sufficient discretion to get the job done. Thus professional accountability is characterized by placement of control over organizational activities in the hands of the employee with the expertise or special skills to get the job done. The key to the professional accountability system, therefore, is deference to expertise within the agency. While outside professional associations may indirectly influence the decision making of the in-house expert (through education and professional standards), the source of authority is essentially internal to the agency.

Typically the professional accountability organization will look like any other public agency with a manager in charge of a set of workers, but the relationships among them are much different. Under a bureaucratic accountability system, the key relationship would be that of close supervision. In contrast, under professional accountability the central relationship is similar to that found between a layperson and an expert, with the agency manager taking the role of the layperson and the workers making the important decisions that require their expertise.[16]

Political accountability (cell 4) is central to the democratic pressures imposed on American public administrators. If "deference" characterizes professional accountability, "responsiveness" characterizes political accountability systems (cell 4).[17] The key relationship under these systems resembles that between a representative (in this case, the public administrator) and his or her constituents (those to whom he or she is accountable). Under political accountability, the primary question becomes, "Whom does the public administrator represent?" The potential constituencies include the general public, elected officials, agency heads, agency clientele, other special interest groups, and future generations. Regardless of which definition of constituency is adopted, the administrator is expected to be responsive to their policy priorities and programmatic needs.

While political accountability systems might seem to promote favoritism and even corruption in the administration of government programs, they also serve as the basis for a more open and representative government. The urge for political accountability, for example, is reflected in open meetings laws, freedom of information acts, and "government in the sunshine" statutes passed by many state and local governments.

Table 4-1 summarizes the principal features of the four general types of accountability systems. Under the bureaucratic system, expectations are managed through a hierarchical arrangement based on supervisory relationships; the legal accountability system manages agency expectations through a contractual relationship; the professional system relies on deference to expertise; while the political accountability system promotes responsiveness to constituents as the central means of managing the multiple expectations.

Table 4-1
Relationships within Accountability Systems

Type of Accountability System	*Analogous Relationship (Controller/Administrator)*	*Basis of Relationship*
1. Bureaucratic	Superior/subordinate	Supervision
2. Legal	Lawmaker/law executor Principal/agent	Fiduciary
3. Professional	Layperson/expert	Deference to expertise
4. Political	Constituent/representative	Responsiveness to constituents

Preferences for Accountability Systems

Given these alternative means for managing expectations, what determines the preference for one accountability approach over others in any particular situation? The appropriateness of a specific accountability system to an agency is linked to three factors: the nature of the agency's tasks (technical level accountability); the management strategy adopted by those heading the agency (management level accountability); and the institutional context of agency operations (institutional level accountability).[18] Ideally, a public sector organization should establish accountability mechanisms which "fit" at all three levels simultaneously.

In the American political system, all four accountability types offer potentially legitimate means for managing *institutional level* expectations.[19] Under current institutional norms, no single type of accountability system is inherently more acceptable or legitimate than another. *In theory*, each of the four accountability systems can insure agency responsibility at the institutional level. Thus, in theory an agency might manage its expectations using the accountability system most appropriate in light of relevant institutional considerations. The same potential flexibility may not exist at the technical or managerial levels where the appropriateness of accountability mechanisms is more closely tied to specific tasks or the strategic orientations or idiosyncrasies of individual managers.

In reality, most U.S. public agencies tend to adopt two or more types of accountability systems at any time depending on the nature of existing environmental (institutional) conditions as well as their technical tasks and management orientations. We argue, however, that institutional pressures generated by the American political system are often the salient factor and frequently take precedence over technical and managerial considerations.[20] If this is the case, the challenge of managing expectations changes as institutional conditions change. If the environmental changes are drastic enough, they may trigger a different type of accountability system, one which attempts to reflect those new institutional conditions.

III. ACCOUNTABILITY UNDER DIFFERENT CHALLENGES: THE CASE OF NASA

NASA was an organizational initiative born in the midst of a national crisis and nurtured in the relatively protective shelter of an institutional consensus that lasted until at least 1970. That nurturing consensus focused attention on President Kennedy's mandate to land an American on the moon by the end of the 1960s. In addition, it fostered the belief that achieving that objective required complete deference to those experts who could get the job done. In short, it was a consensus which supported a professional accountability system.

Over time, the pressures to develop a politically responsive agency strategy became dominant. Even before the successful lunar landing of Apollo 11, changing institutional conditions were creating an organizational setting that encouraged more reliance on bureaucratic and political accountability mechanisms. This reliance on bureaucratic and political accountability systems produced circumstances which made the agency ill-equipped to contend with the problems that eventually led to the Challenger disaster. Furthermore, institutional reactions to the Challenger tragedy itself may be creating new pressures that are moving the agency toward a greater reliance on legal and bureaucratic accountability methods for managing expectations.

The Professionalization of the Space Program

NASA's earliest programs had three important characteristics: they involved clearly defined outcome objectives, highly technical methodologies for achieving those goals, and almost unqualified political (and therefore budgetary) support.[21] The task of overcoming the technical barriers to space exploration was central to the agency's mission, and NASA was able to invest its expenditures primarily in research and development projects associated with its missions.[22]

Those early conditions had a significant impact on the development and management of NASA. The agency's structure and recruiting practices reflected an institutional willingness to respect the technical nature of NASA's programmatic tasks. NASA's form of organization emphasized deference to expertise and minimized the number of political appointments at the top of the administrative structure (in this case, two political appointees with extensive professional expertise in public management).[23] NASA's initial staff consisted almost entirely of individuals with the relevant substantive knowledge, primarily aeronautical engineers.

These circumstances afforded NASA the opportunity to become among the most innovative organizations (public or private) in recent American history and a classic example of an agency operating under a professional accountability system. The locus of control over agency activities was internal; NASA's relationship to outside sources (including Congress, the president, and the general public) was that of expert to layperson. Internally, NASA developed a matrix structure in which managers and technicians were assigned to project teams based on the expertise they could offer to the particular task at hand. Technical experts in NASA were expected to make decisions based upon their expertise. Thus, within the agency the degree of control exercised over NASA technical personnel was relatively low. Much of this deference to NASA's technical experts was based on trust in their judgment as well as their expertise. The early managers at NASA "were highly technical people, who knew the spacecraft from the ground up, and they were all very conservative." If "an order to launch came down from on high, they wouldn't do it without first giving everybody the bottom line."[24]

The professional accountability system was evident in the three centers under the Office of Manned Space Flight (OMSF): the Marshall Space Flight Center (Alabama), the Manned Spacecraft Center (Texas; later renamed the Johnson Space Center), and Kennedy Space Center (Florida). During the early 1960s, OMSF and its subunits acted with considerable autonomy. NASA's top management in Washington did occasionally pull in the organizational reins. In several cases (1961, 1963, and 1965), reorganizations were intended to redirect several key units toward new program goals as NASA moved from project Mercury toward Project Apollo. Each of these changes led to a short-term centralization of control which was intentionally relaxed once programmatic arrangements were in place. In 1967, however, a major long-term effort was made to reduce the autonomy of the manned space flight centers in light of the agency's first major budget constraints and the launch pad fire that killed three astronauts.[25]

The Politicization and Bureaucratization of Accountability

Although many of the technical tasks facing NASA have not changed significantly over the past 30 years, institutional pressures on the agency have undergone considerable change. In the late 1960s, NASA faced a leveling off of both its political and financial support. Beginning in the early 1970s there was more concern about the managerial challenges inherent in making NASA into an operational agency—a concern arising from pressures to make the shuttle system a full operational program.[26] The result of these pressures was a reconfiguation of the accountability systems used by some of the agency's key units. Ironically, the very success of NASA's early programs generated those changes.

NASA's apparent victory in the "space race" coincided with an end to the nurturing consensus that permitted the agency to rely almost exclusively on professional accountability for managing expectations. With America's attention turned increasingly toward Vietnam and economic issues, the space program no longer took priority. A new consensus had to be constructed around some new programmatic mission, and in the late 1960s the idea of a space shuttle began to take form. According to its proponents, the shuttle would represent "a whole new way of space flight," one that would transform NASA from an agency committed to accomplishing specific and discrete program goals within given time constraints (e.g., Apollo) to an agency obligated to the continuous operation of a commercial-like enterprise.[27]

The effort to gain presidential endorsement for the space shuttle program made NASA more aware of and responsive to key actors in the political system. Building the necessary consensus was not easy in the highly volatile and competitive institutional context of the early 1970s. James Fletcher, NASA's Administrator from 1971 to 1977 (and the individual President Reagan brought back to head the agency after the Challenger disaster), needed to sell the space shuttle effort to Congress and the American public as well as the White House. Most of the opposition to the shuttle came from the Office of Management and Budget and was supported by negative assessments of the program by a presidential scientific advisory committee and the RAND Corporation.[28]

During this period NASA entered into political coalitions with groups that it had previously ignored or fought in the policy-making arena, as well as with its traditional supporters in government and among its contractors. The shuttle program, for example, was designed to attract the support of those who might take advantage of its capacity to launch satellites and conduct unique scientific and technological experiments in space. Aided by the military, the scientific community, and parts of the business community, NASA was able to get President Nixon's backing for the program in 1972 despite

OMB's opposition. Political accountability was no longer secondary or peripheral to NASA.[29] It became a critical ingredient in guaranteeing its maintenance as a viable agency. In more recent years, that urge for public and political support was implicit in NASA's widely publicized efforts to include members of Congress and nonagency civilians on its shuttle flights. These programs represented NASA's efforts to cultivate or maintain general support for its activities.

Another important (and related) set of institutional constraints emerged in the form of major budget cutbacks and (in the late 1970s) greater pressures for privatization. From the height of its support in the late 1960s to the mid-1970s, NASA's budget was cut in half (in constant dollars). Recent estimates indicate that NASA went through a staff cut of 40 percent from the big-budget days of Apollo, and that NASA's safety and quality control staff alone were cut by 71 percent between 1970 and 1986.[30] Operating with fewer resources, the agency had to economize; it became just like most other agencies in Washington. NASA experienced a new-found interest in efficiency and thus became more willing to use bureaucratic means for dealing with its financial problems.

NASA officials intended to accommodate these new institutional pressures by reducing the organizational costs that characterized NASA in the "old days" when external support and availability of resources were not major concerns. NASA has "had to pinch pennies to protect the shuttle, accepting lower-cost technologies and making what seem to have been extravagant claims for its economic potential."[31] Agency decentralization and field center specializations continued, and decentralization brought with it increasing reliance on bureaucratic accountability mechanisms. The shift allowed for economies due to a careful division of labor and compartmentalization of authority based on position. While professional accountability systems survived *within* some of the field centers, for the agency as a whole professional accountability patterns characteristic of the early NASA nearly disappeared. With decentralization in NASA came an isolation and competition among field centers.[32]

NASA's use of contractors was, to a certain extent, a manifestation of its efforts to manage changing institutional expectations. In addition to any technical and financial benefits they provided NASA, contractors had always proved very helpful politically in establishing support for the agency's programs and annual funding requests. During the 1970s the link between contract decision and political support became increasingly critical to NASA.[33]

Bureaucratically, contracting out established the ultimate superordinate/subordinate relationship between NASA's top managers and those carrying out the specific parts of the shuttle program. A contract establishes clear responsibilities and gives top management considerable leverage to apply pressures for better performance. It also allows top management to avoid the problems and costs associated with directly maintaining professional accountability mechanisms. Thus, contracting out not only enhanced the bureaucratization process at NASA; it also reduced the reliance on deference to expertise characteristic of professional accountability systems.

Changing institutional conditions altered the locus of control over NASA's activities as well as the degree of control over agency activities. The result was a shift in the types of accountability systems relevant to NASA's operations. In place of the dominant professional accountability systems of the pre-Apollo 11 era, NASA created an elaborate mixture of accountability mechanisms that stressed the political and bureaucratic. It was under these conditions that decisions regarding the general schedule of space shuttle flights and specific launch times were being made when the Challenger lifted from its Kennedy Space Center pad on January 28, 1986.

The Case of the Challenger

Evidence gathered by the Rogers Commission report and through the mass media illustrate the various forms of accountability in operation in NASA before the launch of the Challenger. The principal question is whether (and to what extent) the Challenger accident resulted from the efforts by NASA's leadership to manage changing institutional expectations through political and bureaucratic forms of accountability. Did NASA's emphasis on these accountability mechanisms eventually take precedence over the professional system of accountability that characterized NASA in the early 1960s? Were the problems that eventually led to the Challenger accident linked at all to the poor fit between agency tasks and agency accountability mechanisms? In our view, the answer to both questions is "yes."

Political Pressures   The contention that NASA was feeling considerable political pressure to launch the Challenger on January 28 was widely rumored just after the Challenger accident, particularly stories about direct pressure emanating from the White House. The Rogers Commission emphatically denied the truth of those rumors.[34] Nonetheless, similar pressures existed and came from a variety of sources outside of NASA, including the White House.

On the official policy level, President Reagan announced in July 1982 that the first priority of the shuttle program was "to make the system fully operational." Given the costs involved in supporting the program, additional pressures emanated from an increasingly budget-conscious Congress.[35] Other pressures on NASA were due to widespread reporting of shuttle delays in the mass media. One top agency official argued that the press, in giving major coverage to numerous shuttle delays over the previous year, had "pressured" the agency to jeopardize flight safety. "I don't think it caused us to do anything foolish," he said. "But that's where the pressure is. It's not from anywhere else."[36]

These external pressures were easily translated into internal decisions that set an overly ambitious launch schedule.[37] In short, NASA set that schedule for the purposes of reducing the program's cost factors and appeasing various attentive publics, including the White House, Congress, the media, and the agency's military and private sector "customers" who were important actors in NASA's supportive political coalition.

These political pressures may not have been specifically addressed to the Challenger launch, but there is little doubt they were felt throughout the agency. The increasing emphasis on political accountability was bound to cause attitudinal as well as operational problems. "The pressure on NASA to achieve planned flight rates was so pervasive," concluded a congressional report, "that it undoubtedly adversely affected attitudes regarding safety."[38] An agency official noted that NASA's organization culture changed "when NASA felt itself under pressure to demonstrate that the shuttles were operational vehicles in a 'routine' transportation system."[39] Part of that "routinization" took the form of "streamlining" the reporting requirements for safety concerns. Less documentation and fewer reporting requirements replaced previous directives that all safety problems and responses were to be reported to higher levels in NASA's hierarchy. The "old requirements," it was argued, "were not productive for the operational phase of the Shuttle program."[40]

The same political accountability pressures had an impact on NASA's key shuttle program contractor, Morton Thiokol. The assent of Morton Thiokol management (and the silence of their engineers) to the Challenger launch recommendation was influenced in part by NASA's importance as a primary customer—a customer who was in the process of reviewing its contracts with the firm. The company's management did not want to jeopardize their relationships with NASA. As a result, rather than emphasizing deference to the experts who worked for them, Morton Thiokol deferred to the demands of NASA's top managers who, in turn, were under a self-imposed, politically derived launch schedule.

Bureaucratic Pressures Indications of preference for bureaucratic rather than professional forms of accountability in NASA are evident in the agency's shuttle program operations. By the early 1980s, NASA's managers were having difficulty coordinating their projects.[41] They came to rely increasingly on hierarchical reporting relationships, a clear manifestation of bureaucratic accountability. This had two effects. First, it increased the potential for "bureaupathological" behavior which the professional accountability system attempted to minimize.[42] Second, it reduced the crosscutting communications channels which once characterized the less hierarchical and flexible matrix structure at NASA.

The failure of NASA's management system is a fundamental theme of the Rogers Commission. Supervisors were criticized for not passing on up the hierarchy their subordinates' recommendations. Managers were criticized for judgments that were contrary to those suggested by the available data. The commission reported that its investigation revealed "failures in communication that resulted in a decision to launch [the Challenger] based on incomplete and sometimes misleading information, a conflict between engineering data and management judgments, and a NASA management structure that permitted internal flight safety problems to bypass key Shuttle managers."[43] But what the Rogers Commission perceived as a failure of the agency's management system was, in fact, an inherent characteristic of the bureaucratic accountability system adopted by NASA in order to meet the institutional expectations of the post-Apollo 11 era.

Under NASA's shuttle program, responsibility for specific aspects of the overall program was allocated to supervisors at lower levels in the reporting hierarchy, and the burden for giving the go ahead to launch decision makers shifted from the engineers and experts toward those supervisory personnel. As scheduling and other pressures increased, so did the reluctance of those supervisors to be the individual who threw a monkey wrench into the shuttle program machinery. Thus it is not surprising that lower-level managers tried to cope on their own instead of communicating their problems upward.[44]

The relevance of this problem to the Challenger disaster was illustrated time and time again in the testimony given before the Rogers Commission. NASA officials noted that individuals higher up in the agency had not been informed about the Rockwell engineers' reservations about ice on the launch pad nor the concerns of Morton Thiokol's personnel about weather conditions and the O-rings.[45] In another instance, when asked why he had not communicated the Thiokol engineers' concerns about the O-ring seals to the program manager of the National Space Transportation System, the manager of the Solid Rocket Booster Project (based at the Marshall Center) answered that he believed it was an issue that had been resolved at his level in the organization.[46] As one reporter observed, "no one at Marshall saw any reason to bother the managers at the top of NASA's chain of command—the normal procedure in the face of disturbing new evidence." This bureaupathological behavior reflects an attitude among employees at Marshall who feel they are competing with Johnson and the other centers. "Nothing [sic] was ever allowed to leave Marshall that would suggest that Marshall was not doing its job. . . ."[47]

The impact of the bureaucratic accountability system is also evident in testimony about discussions between NASA representatives and Thiokol engineers on the night before the Challenger launch. During an "off-line" caucus between Morton Thiokol management and their engineers (while NASA prelaunch review officials were "on hold"), a member of management asked one of his colleagues

> to take off his engineering hat and put on his management hat. From that point on, management formulated the points to base their decision on. There was never one comment in favor . . . of launching by any engineer or other nonmanagement person in the room before or after the caucus. . . . [The engineers were] never asked nor polled, and it was clearly a management decision from that point. . . . This was a meeting where the determination was to launch, and it was up to [the Thiokol engineers] to prove beyond a shadow of a doubt [to Thiokol management and NASA] that it was not safe to do so. This is in total reverse to what the position usually is in a preflight conversation or a flight readiness review. It is usually exactly opposite that.[48] (emphasis added)

A final example of the bureaucratic accountability system's relevance to the failure of the Challenger focuses on an incident occurring in 1984. Problems with the O-rings were noticed and noted by Morton Thiokol engineers in February that year after the tenth shuttle mission had been completed, and a report on the problem was ordered by the Office of the Associate Administrator for Space Flight before the launch of the eleventh flight in late March. A decision was made to launch the shuttle, but not before it was determined by the associate administrator, James Abrahamson, and NASA's deputy administrator, Hans Mark, that the O-ring problem had to be solved. A meeting to discuss the problem with relevant officials from the different NASA centers was called for May 30. It was a meeting that would have drawn attention to the technical factor that would later cause the shuttle tragedy; it was a meeting that never took place. By May 30, Abrahamson had left the agency to work on President Reagan's Strategic Defense Initiative, and Deputy Administrator Mark cancelled the meeting to visit Austin, Texas, where he was being considered for the position of university chancellor. Abrahamson's successor, Jesse A. Moore, was never informed of the problem, and Mark's successor was not appointed for a full year. Thus, the O-ring problem was never communicated to the relevant experts for action. In Mark's words, it was "a classic example of having something fall between the 'cracks.'"[49] In our terms, it was another instance of bureaucratic accountability applied in inappropriate circumstances.

IV. A POST-COMMISSION ERA: THE NEW INSTITUTIONAL PRESSURES

Given the technical and managerial focus of the Rogers Commission report and other investigations of the Challenger accident, it is not surprising that calls for changes in the space program tend to favor two objectives: punishing those in NASA who were to blame for the tragedy, and instituting reforms that would guarantee that a similar event would not occur in the future. In both form and content, these efforts represented increased institutional pressures for NASA, pressures likely to lead the agency to develop new legal accountability mechanisms as well as increase its reliance on bureaucratic accountability mechanisms.

The search for scapegoats and legal responsibility for the Challenger accident are unsavory but perhaps unavoidable by-products of the Rogers Commission's focus on technical and managerial problems. If a technical problem existed, why was it not discovered in time; and if it was discovered in time, why was it not taken seriously by those in charge?[50] These are the questions which have led to personnel actions within NASA (and Thiokol) ranging from reassignments and resignations to early retirements. Beyond these actions, the families of most Challenger crew members either filed lawsuits or accepted legal settlements from the government and its subcontractors.[51]

On less personal levels, suggestions for reforms in the space agency have proliferated. On the surface many of these seem to signal a return to professional accountability. Some recommendations call for improving the role and voice of certain classes of individuals within NASA with special or unique insight into the risks associated with space exploration. There is, for example, a proposal for placing ex-astronauts in management positions at NASA.[52] At first glance, this looks like an attempt to reinvigorate the role of experts and professionals in the agency, but bringing former astronauts into NASA does not guarantee improvement in technical expertise and actually looks more like a thinly veiled attempt to use highly visible symbols of the space program to enhance the agency's damaged credibility.

Another proposal that at first seems to involve a return to professional accountability calls for the establishment of explicit guidelines and criteria for use in making launch decisions. Supposedly these criteria would represent the accumulated wisdom of many experts in the field, but they can just as easily be regarded as another step away from deference to professional engineering judgments and toward imposing accountability that carries with it threats of legal liability if such checklists are not properly followed.

Legal accountability mechanisms are also manifested in the emphases in many other proposed reforms on establishing independent or external oversight bodies capable of vetoing decisions by agency personnel regarding safety issues. For example, the Rogers Commission called for the creation of an independent Solid Rocket Motor Design Oversight Committee to review the rocket design and make recommendations to the administrator or NASA.[53] Similarly, the commission called for creation of a separate Office of Safety, Reliability and Quality Assurance outside the normal lines of the agency hierarchy to report directly to the NASA administrator.[54] In both instances, actors outside the normal lines of the agency hierarchy would oversee key decision-making points within NASA dealing with the design and launch of future manned space flights.[55] While these bodies are not intended to exercise direct control over the day-to-day operations of NASA's space shuttle program, such bodies would have jurisdiction over a wide range of agency actions.

It is also evident that congressional oversight of NASA activities is likely to focus a great deal more on details of technical and managerial matters than in the past.[56] In the past, Congress' role regarding NASA was that of patron rather than overseer. For the most part, congressional concerns about NASA were limited to the general priorities of the agency and its potential as a source of pork-barrel projects. In the near future, at least, members of relevant congressional committees and their staffs will become more involved in the details of NASA's operations.[57]

Other suggested reforms (some already being implemented) attempt internal changes in NASA that would complement this movement toward changing accountability. For example, recommendations for reorganizing the shuttle management structure include redefining the program manager's responsibilities to enhance that official's decision-making role. In addition, units within NASA are being reorganized to improve intraorganizational communications. Operationally, suggested reforms include a call for refinement of decision criteria used in equipment maintenance, landing safety, and launch abort procedures. These changes reinforce or legitimize the influence of bureaucratic structures within NASA by formalizing organizational relationships and operational procedures. In form and function, they attempt to move the bureaucratic structures of NASA closer to a centralized system more easily held legally accountable for the agency's future actions.

It was inevitable that the Challenger disaster would generate strong institutional pressures for NASA, and those pressures are creating new demands and expectations for the agency. Ironically, the direction of those pressures has been toward enhanced bureaucratic structures and growing reliance on legal accountability mechanisms which stress NASA's formal responsibilities for the safety of its astronauts. Since President Reagan ordered NASA to terminate its commercial operations temporarily, a major source of political pressure and support has been removed. Thus, we might expect a decline of political accountability in the space agency's operations. Nevertheless, political factors have not disappeared. At present, NASA lacks a clear sense of direction and faces programmatic competition from the military and commercial sectors. At the end of 1986, Dr. Fletcher's view was reported as follows: "The policymaking process is not so straightforward because there are 'so many players.'"[58] In addition, there is little likelihood that Challenger-related reforms will reflect the need for NASA to reestablish the priority of professional accountability systems which held sway in the agency during pre-Apollo 11 heydays.

V. CONCLUSION

The primary contention of this [article] is that the Rogers Commission was shortsighted in focusing exclusively on the failure of NASA's technological or management systems. The problem was not necessarily in the *failure* of those systems, but rather in the *inappropriateness* of the political and bureaucratic accountability mechanisms which characterized NASA's management approach in recent years. The agency's emphasis on political and bureaucratic accountability was a relevant response to changing institutional expectations in NASA's environment, but they were inappropriate for the technical tasks at hand. To the extent that these accountability mechanisms were ill-suited to the technical nature of NASA's agency task, they comprised a major factor in the Challenger tragedy.

In more prescriptive terms, if the professional accountability system had been given at least equal weight in the decision-making process, the decision to launch would probably not have been made on that cold January morning. Had NASA relied exclusively on a professional system of accountability in making the decision to launch the Challenger space shuttle, perhaps deference would have been given to the technical expertise of the engineers. Their recommendation against launch might never have been challenged by the project manager for the solid rocket booster.[59] Instead, the Thiokol engineers' initial recommendation against launch was ignored by their hierarchical superiors. Decision makers relied upon supervisors to make the decision rather than deferring to professional experts.

Will the post-accident push for greater emphases on the legal and bureaucratic accountability systems improve NASA's ability to successfully pursue its mission? If this assessment of the role of institutional factors in the success and failure of NASA's programs is correct, then the proposals for reform increase the chances of other failures. This conclusion is consistent with the thesis that adding safety mechanisms to already complex systems in fact may increase the chances that something can go wrong.[60] As NASA gets drawn further away from what it can do best—namely, mobilizing the expert resources needed to solve the technical challenges of space exploration—its chances for organizational success are diluted. Ideally, NASA needs to return to what it does best, using the form of accountability that best suits its organizational mission, i.e., a professional accountability based on deference to expertise.[61] The reality of NASA's institutional context, however, makes achievement of this ideal highly improbable. NASA no longer enjoys a nurturing institutional context; instead it faces increased environmental pressures calling for the adoption of political, bureaucratic, and legal accountability mechanisms. Such is the dilemma facing NASA and the challenge confronting all American public administrators.

Notes

The authors gratefully acknowledge the helpful comments of Dwight Kiel, John Nalbandian, Laurence J. O'Toole, Jr., and anonymous referees.

1. *Report of the Presidential Commission on the Space Shuttle Challenger Accident* (Washington, D.C.: June 6, 1986), p. 40; hereafter cited as *Rogers Commission Report*.
2. *Rogers Commission Report*, p. 82.
3. See James D. Thompson, *Organizations in Action: Social Science Bases of Administrative Theory* (New York: McGraw-Hill Book Co., 1967), pp. 10–11.
4. Thompson, *Organizations in Action*, p. 11.
5. Besides current astronaut Sally Ride and former astronaut Neil Armstrong, the commission membership included: Eugene Covert, an MIT professor and frequent consultant to NASA who received the agency's Public Service Award in 1980; Robert W. Rummel, an aerospace engineer and private consultant who was also a recipient of a NASA public service award; and Major General Donald J. Kutyna, director of the U.S. Air Force's Space Systems program and former manager of the Defense Department's space shuttle program.
6. For example, Commission Chair Rogers was attorney general for President Eisenhower and secretary of state for Richard Nixon. David C. Acheson, a well-known Washington lawyer, had previously served as a U.S. Attorney, counsel for the Atomic Energy Commission, and senior vice president of COMSAT. Other members of the Commission were two physicists, Richard P. Feynman and Albert D. Wheelan (executive vice president, Hughes Aircraft); astronomer Arthur B. C. Walker, Jr.; test pilot Charles E. Yeager; aeronautical engineer Joseph F. Sutter; and Robert B. Hotz, former editor of *Aviation Week and Space Technology Magazine*.
7. See Paul R. Schulman, *Large-Scale Policy Making* (New York: Elsevier North Holland, Inc., 1980), pp. 22–41; James E. Webb, *Space Age Management* (New York: McGraw-Hill Book Co., 1968); Leonard R. Sayles and Margaret K. Chandler, *Managing Large Systems* (New York: Harper and Row, 1971); and Peter F. Drucker, *Management: Tasks, Responsibilities, and Practices* (New York: Harper and Row, 1974), chapter 47.
8. See discussion in Herbert A. Simon, Donald W. Smithburg, and Victor A. Thompson, *Public Administration* (New York: Alfred A. Knopf, Inc., 1950), especially chapters 24 and 25. Also, Carl Joachim Friedrich, "Public Policy and the Nature of Administrative Responsibility," in C. J. Friedrich and Edward S. Mason, eds., *Public Policy, 1940* (Cambridge: Harvard University Press, 1940), pp. 3–24; and Herman Finer, "Administrative Responsibility and Democratic Government," *Public Administration Review*, vol. 1 (Summer 1941), pp. 335–350.
9. This view of accountability is developed more fully in Barbara Romzek and Mel Dubnick, "Accountability and the Management of Expectations: The Challenger Tragedy and the Costs of Democracy," presented at the annual meeting of the American Political Science Association, the Washington, D.C., Hilton, August 28–31, 1986.
10. See Max Weber, *Economy and Society: An Outline of Interpretive Sociology*, edited by Guenther Roth and Claus Wittich (Berkeley: University of California Press, 1987), chapter XI.
11. See Alvin Gouldner, *Patterns of Industrial Bureaucracy* (New York: The Free Press, 1954), pp. 159–162.
12. Philosophically and ideologically, the basis of legal accountability is found in the "rule of law" concept; see Friedrich A. Hayek, *The Road to Serfdom* (Chicago: University of Chicago Press, 1944), chapter VI; also see Theodore J. Lowi's call for "juridical democracy" in *The End of Liberalism: The Second Republic of the United States*, 2d ed. (New York: W. W. Norton and Co., 1979), chapter 11.

13. For a comprehensive application of the theory of agency, see Barry M. Mitnick, *The Political Economy of Regulation: Creating, Designing, and Removing Regulatory Forms* (New York: Columbia University Press, 1980).

14. While bureaucratic accountability relies on methods available to members, such as close supervision and rules and regulations, legal accountability is limited to the tools available to outsiders, such as monitoring, investigating, auditing, and other forms of "oversight" and evaluation.

15. See Carl Joachim Friedrich, "Public Policy and the Nature of Administrative Responsibility."

16. For an example of a professional accountability system, see the story of the Manhattan Project offered in Peter Wyden, *Day One: Before Hiroshima and After* (New York: Warner Books, 1985), Book One.

17. See Emmette S. Redford, *Democracy in the Administrative State* (New York: Oxford University Press, 1969); also see works by Paul Appleby and Herman Finer.

18. See James Thompson, *Organizations in Action.*

19. See Robert C. Fried, *Performance in American Bureaucracy* (Boston: Little, Brown and Co., 1976).

20. It is possible (at least theoretically) for different accountability mechanisms to operate within one agency at different levels of the organization. For example, a professional accountability mechanism may be in operation at the technical level of an organization while a legal accountability mechanism may be used to manage external expectations at the institutional or boundary-spanning level. See Thompson, *Organizations in Action.* For an application of this notion in a related area, see Donald Klingner and John Nalbandian, "Values and Conflict in Public Personnel Administration," *Public Administration Quarterly* (forthcoming).

21. See Hans Mark and Arnold Levine, *The Management of Research Institutions: A Look at Government Laboratories* (Washington, D.C.: National Aeronautics and Space Administration, 1984), pp. 117–118. On the political support for NASA in those early years, see Don K. Price, *The Scientific Estate* (Cambridge, MA: The Belknap Press, 1965), pp. 222–223. On the effects of its budgetary support through 1966, see Paul R. Schulman, *Large-Scale Policy Making* (New York: Elsevier North Holland, Inc., 1980), pp. 87–88.

22. Through the Apollo program, NASA spent over 80 percent of its funding on research and development (R&D) efforts. See Philip N. Whittaker, "Joint Decisions in Aerospace," in Matthew Tuite, Roger Chisholm, and Michael Radnor, eds., *Interorganizational Decision Making* (Chicago: Aldine Publishing Co., 1972), p. 272.

23. On the early history of NASA by an "insider," see John D. Young, "Organizing the Nation's Civilian Space Capabilities: Selected Reflections," in Theodore W. Taylor, ed., *Federal Public Policy: Personal Accounts of Ten Senior Civil Service Executives* (Mt. Airy, MD: Lomond Publications, Inc., 1984), pp. 45–80. Some analysts have defined that "nurturing consensus" as little more than a "political vacuum" in which the agency got to define its own programmatic objectives. See John Logsdon, *The Decision to Go to the Moon,* cited in Lambright, *Governing Science and Technology* (New York: Oxford University Press, 1976), pp. 41–42.

24. Henry S. F. Cooper, Jr., "Letter from the Space Center," in *The New Yorker* (November 10, 1986), p. 93.

25. Mark and Levine, *The Management of Research Institutions,* pp. 60, 200–202.

26. Schulman, *Large-Scale Policy Making,* pp. 62–74. Also Cooper, "Letter from the Space Center," p. 99.

27. Schulman, *Large-Scale Policy Making,* pp. 74–76; also Mark and Levine, *The Management of Research Institutions,* pp. 117–118.

28. Lambright, *Governing Science and Technology,* p. 43. Also see Wayne Biddle, "NASA: What's Needed To Put It On Its Feet ?" *Discover,* vol. 8 (January 1987), pp. 36, 40.

29. It is incorrect to think that NASA was apolitical even during its early years. Tom Wolfe describes a heated argument between John Glenn and NASA Administrator James Webb when Glenn bitterly complained of the number of trips he had to take at the request of members of Congress or the White House. See Wolfe's *The Right Stuff* (New York: Bantam Books, 1979), p. 331. See also Mark and Levine, *The Management of Research Institutions*, p. 82, for a discussion of the importance of generating "new business" for the agency. The politics surrounding the shuttle are reflected in investigations of the role Fletcher played in awarding contracts for the shuttle project in 1973; see William J. Broad, "NASA Chief Might Not Take Part in Decisions on Booster Contracts," *New York Times* (December 7, 1986), pp. 1, 14.

30. W. Henry Lambright, *Governing Science and Technology*, pp. 21–22; and U.S. Congress, House Committee on Science and Technology, *Investigation of the Challenger Accident*, Report, 99th Congress, 2d Session (Washington, D.C.: U.S. Government Printing Office, 1986), pp. 176–177.

31. John Noble Wilford, "NASA May Be a Victim of Defects in Its Own Bureaucracy," *New York Times* (February 16, 1986), p. 18E.

32. See Cooper, "Letter from the Space Center," especially pp. 85–96.

33. See Mark and Levine, *The Management of Research Institutions*, pp. 122–123, on NASA contracting. NASA's use of "pork barrel" politics dates to the agency's earliest years; see Amitai Etzioni, *The Moon Doggle* (Garden City, NY: Doubleday and Co., 1964), and Price, *The Scientific Estate*, pp. 21–23. The continuation of political considerations in NASA's contracting practices during the 1970s is demonstrated by the circumstances surrounding the competition for the shuttle's booster rocket contract which was eventually awarded to Thiokol in 1973; see Broad, "NASA Chief May Not Take Part in Decisions on Booster Contracts."

34. *Rogers Commission Report*, p. 176.

35. *Rogers Commission Report*, pp. 176, 201. Also Cooper, "Letter from the Space Center," pp. 99–100, and U.S. Congress, House, *Investigation of the Challenger Accident*, pp. 119–120.

36. William J. Broad, "NASA Aide Assails Panel Investigating Explosion of Shuttle," *New York Times* (March 16, 1986), p. 23.

37. U.S. Congress, House, *Investigation of the Challenger Accident*, p. 120.

38. U.S. Congress, House, *Investigation of the Challenger Accident*, p. 122. Richard P. Feynman, a member of the Rogers Commission, speculated about agency attitudes regarding safety. He believed the agency might have downplayed the riskiness of the shuttle launching to "assure" Congress of the agency's "perfection and success in order to ensure the supply of funds." See David E. Sanger, "Looking Over NASA's Shoulder," *New York Times* (September 28, 1986), p. 26E.

39. John Noble Wilford, "NASA Chief Vows to Fix Problems," *New York Times* (June 10, 1986), p. 22.

40. *Rogers Commission Report*, pp. 153–154.

41. Laurie McGinley and Bryan Burrough, "Backbiting in NASA Worsens the Damage from Shuttle Disaster," *Wall Street Journal* (April 2, 1986), p. 1.

42. See Victor A. Thompson, *Modern Organization*, 2d ed. (University, AL: University of Alabama Press, 1977), chapter 8.

43. *Rogers Commission Report*, p. 82.

44. On the factors which make it difficult for employees to pass bad news to upper levels of the organization, see Chris Argyris and Donald A. Schon, *Organizational Learning: A Theory of Action Perspective* (Reading, MA: Addison-Wesley Publishing Co., 1978).

45. *Rogers Commission Report*, p. 82.

46. Testimony of Lawrence Mulloy, *Rogers Commission Report*, p. 98.

47. Cooper, "Letter from the Space Center," pp. 89, 96.

48. Testimony of Roger Boisjoly, *Rogers Commission Report*, p. 93. Also see testimony of R. K. Lund, *Rogers Commission Report*, p. 94.
49. David E. Sanger, "Top NASA Aides Knew of Shuttle Flaw in '84," *New York Times* (December 21, 1986), pp. 1, 22.
50. See William J. Broad, "NASA Had Solution to Key Flaw in Rocket When Shuttle Exploded." *New York Times* (September 22, 1986), p. 1; and David E. Sanger, "NASA Pressing Shuttle Change Amid Concerns: Fear of Short-Circuiting Safety Search Raised," *New York Times* (September 23, 1986), p. 1.
51. In July 1986, the family of shuttle pilot Michael Smith filed a "wrongful death" suit against NASA and some of its top managers. Later settlements with other families were announced. See William J. Broad, "4 Families Settle Shuttle Claims," *New York Times* (December 30, 1986), p. 1.
52. *Rogers Commission Report*, pp. 199–201.
53. *Rogers Commission Report*, p. 198.
54. *Rogers Commission Report*, p. 199.
55. *Rogers Commission Report*, pp. 198–199.
56. Members of Congress criticized the Commission for not going deeply enough into the question of which individuals bore direct responsibility for the accident. See Philip M. Boffey, "Shuttle Panel is Faulted for Not Naming Names," *New York Times* (June 11, 1986), p. 16.
57. Philip M. Boffey, "NASA Challenged on Modification That Rockets Met Requirements," *New York Times* (June 12, 1986), p. 18.
58. John Noble Wilford, "Threat to Nation's Lead in Space is Seen in Lack of Guiding Policy," *New York Times* (December 30, 1986), p. 18.
59. *Rogers Commission Report*, p. 96.
60. See Charles Perrow, *Normal Accidents: Living with High Risk Technologies* (New York: Basic Books, Inc., 1984).
61. Our suggestion that a professional system of accountability is the most appropriate to NASA should not be construed as an endorsement of professional accountability under all circumstances. Rather, our point is to indicate that the type of accountability system needs to suit the agency task.

Public Administration and Ethics

DWIGHT WALDO

"No process has been discovered by which promotion to a position of public responsibility will do away with a man's interest in his own welfare, his partialities, race, and prejudices."—James Harvey Robinson

"You are welcome to my house; you are welcome to my heart . . . my personal feelings have nothing to do with the present case. . . . As George Washington, I would do anything in my power for you. As President, I can do nothing."—George Washington, to a friend seeking an appointment

"There is not a moral vice which cannot be made into relative good by context. There is not a moral virtue which cannot in peculiar circumstances have patently evil results."—Stephen Bailey

"The big organization dehumanizes the individual by turning him into a functionary. In doing so it makes everything possible by creating a new kind of man, one who is morally unbounded *in his role* as functionary. . . . His ethic is the ethic of the good soldier: take the order, do the job, *do it the best way you know how,* because that is your honor, your virtue, your pride-in-work."—F. William Howton

"It seems to be inevitable that the struggle to maintain cooperation among men should destroy some men morally as battle destroys some physically."—Chester Barnard

"The raising of moral considerations in any discussion on organizations usually causes discomfort. . . . Nonetheless, if morality is about what is right and wrong, then behavior in organizations is largely determined by such considerations."—David Bradley and Roy Wilkie

"The first duty of a civil servant is to give his undivided allegiance to the State at all times and on all occasions when the State has a claim on his service."— Board of Inquiry, United Kingdom, 1928

. . . The several heterogeneous epigraphs are directed toward emphasizing the central theme of this presentation, namely, that moral or ethical[1] behavior in public administration is a complicated matter, indeed, *chaotic*. While some facets of the matter have been treated with insight and clarity, nothing in the way of a comprehensive and systematic treatise exists—or if so I am unaware of it.[2] This situation may not reflect just accident or lack of interest. What may be reflected is the fact that a systematic treatise is impossible, given the scope, complexity, and intractability of the material from which it would have to be constructed and given an inability to find acceptable or defensible foundations of ideas and beliefs on which it could be grounded.

In this discussion I hope to indicate some of the subjects that might be given attention in a systematic treatise. I appreciate that even this hope may represent pretentiousness.

PUBLIC MORALITY AND PRIVATE MORALITY

An appropriate beginning is to note a distinction between public and private morality and the possibility of a conflict between them.[3] This is a very elementary distinction, but much evidence indicates that it is little understood. As presented in the media, including the columns of the pundits, morality in public office is a simple matter of obeying the law, being honest, and telling the truth. *Not so.*

Public morality concerns decisions made and action taken directed toward the good of a collectivity which is seen or conceptualized as "the public," that is, as an entity or group larger than immediate social groups such as family and clan. Conventionally, "the public" in the modern West is equated with "the nation," or "the country." Thus when decisions are made and actions taken vis-à-vis other nations or countries a public interest is presumed to be in view. Similarly, when the decision or action is directed inward toward the affairs of the nation-state, a public or general interest is presumed to come before private or group interests.

In either case a decision or action justified as moral because it is judged to be in the interest of the public may be immoral from the standpoint of all, or nearly all, interpretations of moral behavior for individuals. The most common example is killing. When done by an individual it is, commonly, the crime of homicide. When done in warfare or law enforcement on behalf of the public it is an act of duty and honor, perhaps of heroism—presuming the "correct" circumstances. All important governments have committed what would be "sins" if done by individuals, what would be "crimes" if done under their own laws by individuals acting privately.

Those in government who decide and act on behalf of the public will from time to time, of *necessity* as I see it, be lying, stealing, cheating, killing. What must be faced is that all decision and action in the public interest is inevitably morally complex, and that the price of any good characteristically entails some bad. Usually the bad is not as simple and stark as the terms just listed signify; but sometimes it *is*, and honesty and insight on our part can begin with so acknowledging.

Ironically, the concept of "the public" is regarded, and I believe properly, as a good and even precious thing. It is a heritage from Greek and Roman antiquity. Its projection, elaboration, nurture, and defense are generally represented as the work of inspired thinkers, virtuous statesmen, and brave warriors. How can this be, when sins and crimes are committed in the name of the public? The answer is twofold. First, my favorite question: Compared to what? Assuming government is desirable, or at least inevitable, what legitimating concept is better? At least the idea of government in the name of a public advances that enterprise beyond purely personal and often tyrannical rule. Second, once in motion, so to speak, the concept of the public becomes invested with, a shelter for, and even a source of, goods that we identify with words such as citizenship, security, justice, and liberty.

THE STATE AND HIGHER LAW

To see the matter of public and private morality in perspective it is necessary to understand the complicated relationship of both moralities to the concept of *higher law*. The concept of higher law, simply put for our purposes, holds that there is a source and measure of rightness that is above and beyond both individual and government. In our own history it is represented prominently in the justification of the Revolution against the government of George III, and it inspired the Declaration of Independence.

The classical Greek philosophers, from whom much of our tradition of political thought derives, sought a moral unity. Are the good man and the good citizen the same? Both Plato and Aristotle answered the question affirmatively, though Plato more certainly than Aristotle. In the comparatively simple world of the city-state this answer could be made plausible, given the Greek conviction of superiority and the elitist nature of citizenship: the polity creates citizens in its admirable image and is thus the source of man's morality; there can be no legitimate appeal from what it holds to be right.

But as Sophocles' *Antigone* signifies, the idea of a higher law—in this case the laws of Zeus as against those of the king, Creon—existed even in Athens. During the Hellenistic period, after the decline of the city-state, the idea of a natural law above and beyond the mundane world was elaborated, especially by the Stoics. A sense of personhood apart from the polity, and of the essential equality of humans *as* humans was developing, and this was accompanied by a growing belief that right and wrong rested on foundations beyond the polity. As Sabine put it in his history of political theory: "Men were slowly making souls for themselves." With Christianity these ideas were of course broadened and deepened. The idea of God's law, or natural law—and characteristically the two became conflated—was to become a powerful force in relation to both private and public morality.

For more than a millennium after the fall of Rome, during a period in which government all but disappeared in the West, the relationship of the two powers, the sacred and the secular—for most purposes to be equated with Church and secular authority—was at the center of political philosophy and political controversy; but the theoretical and logical supremacy of the higher law was seldom questioned. With the emergence of the modern state a new era opened. The authority of a state, even a secular state, to determine right and wrong for its citizens was powerfully asserted by political theorists, notably Machiavelli and Hobbes. On the other hand, the long era of higher-law thinking had left an indelible imprint on thought and attitude. That there is something to which one's conscience gives access and which provides guidance on right and wrong remains a strong feeling even among those who regard themselves as completely secular.

The discussion of higher law has indicated that the initial duality of public morality and private morality was simplistic. There *is* an important, and insufficiently appreciated, distinction between the two, as I hope was demonstrated. But two important matters are now apparent. One is that higher law does not equate with or relate only to private morality as against public. Its sanction can be claimed by the polity if the polity represents the sacred as well as the secular, that is, if there is no separation of church and state—or perhaps even if there is.

The other matter is that the public-private distinction is but one example, albeit a crucial one for our purposes, of a class of relationships that can be designated *collectivity-person*. The biological person is of course distinguishable from any collectivity: nation, party, union, family, whatever. But whether the person can have or should have moral standing apart from the collectivities that have created him and given him meaning is a large part of what ethics is about; for all collectivities of any durability and significance will claim, explicitly or implicitly, to be the source of moral authority. While the state may well, and in some cases inevitably will, claim moral supremacy, the individual will have to weigh its claims against his or her interpretations of competing claims of other collectivities *and* the claims of higher law and "conscience."

Plainly, the ethical landscape is becoming very cluttered and complex. More to this shortly. But first a few words on *reason of state*. Reason of state is public morality at its extreme reach. Plainly put, it is conduct that violates all or nearly all standards of right conduct for individuals; this in the interests of the creating, preserving, or enhancing state power, and rationalized by "the ends justify the means" logic. A few years ago I had occasion to review the literature on this subject in Political Science in the United States. Significantly, what I found was very little, and this mostly by émigré scholars. Unbelievably, there is no entry for this important subject in the seventeen-volume *International Encyclopedia of the Social Sciences,* even though it was planned and executed during the moral-ethical hurricane of the Vietnam War. A number of historical factors, beyond exploring here, have led us to gloss over and even deny the complexities and contradictions that exist when public and private morality conflict, as inevitably they sometimes will.

A MAP—OF SORTS

A few years ago, attempting to address the subject "Ethical Obligations and the Public Service," I made a rough sketch of the ethical obligations of the public administrator as seen from one point of view. Later, this sketch was somewhat elaborated and refined in collaboration with Patrick Hennigan in a yet unpublished essay. It will serve present purposes to indicate the nature of this endeavor.

The sketch, or "map," as we called it, is of ethical obligations of the public administrator with special reference to the United States. The perspective taken is that of the *sources* and *types* of ethical obligations to which the public administrator is expected to respond. We identify a dozen, but as we indicate, the list is capable of indefinite expansion and does not lend itself to logical ordering.

First. Obligation to the Constitution

This is a legal obligation of course, but it is also a source of ethical obligations, which may be symbolized and solemnized by an oath to uphold and defend the Constitution. The upholding of regime and of regime values is a normal source of public-service obligation, and the Constitution is the foundation of regime and of regime values for the United States. But note: not an unambiguous foundation. A great deal of our history, including a civil war, can be written in terms of different interpretations of the Constitution.

Second. Obligation to Law

Laws made under the Constitution are a source not just of legal obligation but also of ethical obligations, as public-service codes of ethics normally underscore. Note again the ambiguities and puzzles. What if the law is unclear? What if laws conflict? What if a law seems unconstitutional, or violates a tenet of higher law? What is the ethical status of regulations made under the law?

Third. Obligation to Nation or Country

By most interpretations, a nation or country or people is separable from regime, and plainly this sense of identity with a nation, country, or people creates ethical obligations. Indeed, in many situations the obligation to country—

Fatherland, Motherland, Homeland, however it may be put—overrides the obligation to regime. Lincoln, justifying his actions in 1864: "Was it possible to lose the nation, and yet preserve the constitution?"

Fourth. Obligation to Democracy

As indicated in previous discussions, this is separable from obligation to Constitution, granted that the relationship is complicated and arguable. Whatever the intent of the Framers—and I do not expect agreement on that, ever—democracy happened: it came to be accepted as an ideology or ethic and as a set of practices that somewhat overlie and somewhat intertwine with the Constitution. The emotional and intellectual acceptance of democracy creates obligations that are acknowledged and usually felt by the public administrator. But again, note the ambiguities: Is the will of the people *always* and *only* expressed in law? If in other ways, how? And how legitimated? Is the *will* of the people, however expressed, to be put ahead of the *welfare* of the people as seen by a public official with information not available to the people?

Fifth. Obligation to Organizational-Bureaucratic Norms

These may be logically divided between those that are *generic* and those that are *specific*. The generic obligations are deeply rooted, perhaps in human nature, certainly in history and culture. They are associated with such terms as loyalty, duty, and order, as well as, perhaps, productivity, economy, efficiency. Specific obligations will depend upon circumstance: the function, the clientele, the technology.

Sixth. Obligation to Profession and Professionalism

The disagreements among sociologists as to what precisely *profession* entails may be disregarded here. All would agree that a profession, indeed a well-developed occupation, has an ethos that acts to shape the values and behavior of members. This ethos concerns actions pertaining to fellow professionals, clients, patients, employers, and perhaps humanity in general. We have become much more aware of the strength and effects of professional values and behavior in public administration since the publication of Frederick Mosher's *Democracy and the Public Service*.

Seventh. Obligation to Family and Friends

Obligation to family is bedrock in most if not all morality. But in countries shaped by the Western political tradition it is formally accepted that *in principle* obligation to country and/or regime as well as to the public is higher than that to family. While the newspaper on almost any day will indicate that the principle is often breached, we are very clear and insistent on the *principle*, and on the whole we believe that the principle prevails. But in countries in which the concept of public is recent and inchoate and in which family or other social group remains the center of loyalty and values, the principle is breached massively, so much so that the creation of an effective government may be impossible.

Friendship is less than family, but shares with it the immediate, personal bond; and friendship as well as family is honored in moral tradition. To indicate the ethical problems that may arise from this source one has only to set forth a name: Bert Lance.

Eighth. Obligation to Self

Yes, to self: this is a respectable part of our moral tradition, best epitomized in the Shakespearean "This above all, to thine own self be true." Selfishness and egocentrism are by general agreement bad. The argument for *self* is that self-regard is the basis for other-regard, that proper conduct toward others, doing one's duty, must be based on personal strength and integrity. But, granting the principle, how does one draw the line in practice between proper self-regard and a public interest?

Ninth. Obligation to Middle-Range Collectivities

In view here is a large and heterogeneous lot: party, class, race, union, church, interest group, and others. That these are capable of creating obligations felt as moral is quite clear, and that these obligations are carried into public administration is also quite clear. When, and how, is it proper for such obligations to affect administrative behavior, to influence public decisions?

Tenth. Obligation to the Public Interest or General Welfare

This obligation is related to Constitution, to nation, to democracy. But it is analytically distinct. It is often explicitly embodied in law, but also has something of a separate existence. The concept is notoriously difficult to operationalize, and has been repeatedly subject to critical demolition. But presumably anyone in public administration must take it seriously, if only as a myth that must be honored in certain procedural and symbolic ways.

Eleventh. Obligation to Humanity or the World

It is an old idea, and perhaps despite all a growing idea, that an obligation is owed to humanity in general, to the world as a total entity, to the future as the symbol and summation of all that can be hoped. All "higher" religions trend in this direction, however vaguely and imperfectly. It is certainly an ingredient in various forms of one-world consciousness, and it figures prominently in the environmental ethic and in ecological politics.

Twelfth. Obligation to Religion, or to God

Immediately one must ask, are these two things or the same thing? The answer is not simple. But that obligations are seen as imposed by religion or God is not doubted even by atheists. One could quickly point to areas of public administration in which these felt obligations are at the center of "what's happening"—or possibly not happening.

A NEED FOR MAPS

Obviously, this listing of sources and types of ethical obligations involved in public administration is rough. The number, twelve, is plainly arbitrary. Perhaps some of the items were wrongly included, or should be combined. Perhaps some should be further divided and refined. Certainly other items might be included: *science,* for example, since science is interpreted not just to require a set of proper procedures but to be an ethos with accompanying ethical imperatives. As we know, *face-to-face groups* develop their own norms and powerfully influence behavior, but were not even mentioned. And what of *conscience?* Is it to be regarded as only a passive transmitter of signals or as in part at least an autonomous source of moral conduct?

You will have noticed that I did not attempt to order the twelve types of obligations, that is, list them in order of importance or ethical imperative. This was neither an oversight nor—I believe—a lack of intelligence on my part, but rather reflected the untidiness of the ethical universe. Perhaps the list included incommensurables. In any event, we lack the agreed beliefs which would enable us to construct an order of priority, one to twelve, with the higher obligation always superior to the lower.

How are we to proceed? How can we achieve enough clarity so that we can at least discuss our differences with minimum confusion, the least heat and the most light? My own view is that a desirable, perhaps necessary, preliminary activity is to construct more and better maps of the realm we propose to understand. Granted that this expectation may reflect only the habits of academia; professors are prone to extensive preparation for intellectual journeys never undertaken. But I do not see how we can move beyond a confused disagreement until there is more agreement on what we are talking about.

If I am essentially correct, then what would be useful would be a serious and sizable mapmaking program. We need various types of maps, analogous to maps that show physical features, climatic factors, demographic data, economic activity, and so forth. We need maps of differing scale, some indicating the main features of a large part of the organizational world, some detailing particular levels, functions, and activities. Despite common elements, presumably—no, certainly—the ethical problems of a legislator are significantly different from those of a military officer, those of a regulatory commissioner different from those of a police chief, those of a first-line supervisor from those of a department head.

Simply put: If we are going to talk about ethics in public life it would be useful to know what we are talking about.

A NEED FOR NAVIGATION INSTRUMENTS

The metaphor of maps may not have been the most apt, but I now use one that may be less felicitous, that of navigation instruments. But at least the second metaphor is complementary: given maps, how do we navigate? How do we find our way through what the maps show us? Let me indicate the nature of some navigation equipment that would be of use.

First, it would be useful to have an instrument to guide us through the historical dimensions of our ethical problems in public administration. Above all, it would be useful to have an explication of the implications and consequences of the disjunction, noted in earlier discussions, between the rise of political self-awareness and the rise of administrative self-awareness. Both as a part of that inquiry and independently, what do we know about the rise and growth of administrative morality, of notions of stewardship, duty and obligations, reciprocal or unilateral? With respect to estate management, which has been so large a part of administrative history, have rules of proper conduct been widely divergent, or has the nature of the function disposed toward uniformity? Since estate management has been centrally involved in royal governance, from Sumer to the Sun King—and beyond—what effect has this had on bureaucratic morality? Perhaps it is worth more than mere mention that *estate* and *state* are cognates, both derived from the Latin *stare:* "to be or stand"; the essential notion in both cases is of substance, firmness, an organizing center.

Second, it would be useful to have instruments provided by the social sciences or derived from a survey of them. Immediately, we face the fact indicated in the epigraph from Bradley and Wilkie at the head of this chapter: "The raising of moral considerations in any discussion on organizations usually causes discomfort." In addressing organizational behavior as in contemporary social science generally, ethics is not just a neglected interest, it is a rejected interest. I shall return to this point; but what I have in mind presently need not cause serious discomfort, though it no doubt would strike many as a peculiar interest and a waste of energy. What I have in view is not an addressing of ethical issues as such, but rather a survey to determine what the several social sciences have to say about ethical matters, either directly or indirectly. For example, are ethical issues present in disguise—morality pretending to be science? We can see that the *yes* answer has often been true in the past, and not a few claim it is true now. What would the most honest, nonideological view reveal? Aside from this question, do the paradigms and tools of the several social sciences offer any handles for ethical inquiry?

Political Science, presumably, would be most centrally involved. And that brings me, inevitably, back to the theme of disjunction: what are the consequences for both Political Science and Public Administration, more broadly, *politics* and *administration,* of the fact that politics reached self-awareness in classical Greece and administration not until the late nineteenth century—this despite the fact that, even (especially?) in small and simple polities, politics and administration were inevitably intermingled.

The other social sciences, even Anthropology, need also to be surveyed. "Even Anthropology?"—an argument could be made that its determined lack of normativeness plus its comparativeness make it particularly germane. Sociology—beginning with its ancestry in Montesquieu and others, and certainly decisively in Comte, Spencer, Durkheim, Weber, Parsons, and other major figures—is rich with relevant material; whether in spite of or because of its scientific stance is hard to say. And Economics? One should not, of course, be put off with its scientific aura and impressive technical apparatus.

Adam Smith, in his own view and that of his contemporaries, was a moral philosopher; and Irving Kristol has recently reminded us that Smith's *An Inquiry into the Nature and Causes of the Wealth of Nations* was not intended as a defense of the *morality* of free enterprise. Economics, both in what it attends to and in what it refuses to attend to, in the behavior it licenses and in the behavior it forbids, is very central to any inquiry into ethical conduct in administration: As a random illustration, the recent realization that noxious waste chemicals simply have been dumped in tens of thousands of locations. What sins are committed in the name of externalities and exogenous variables?

Third, ethics as a self-aware enterprise, together with the philosphic matrices from which differing ethical theories are derived, needs to be searched and ordered for the purposes of ethical analysis and judgment in public administration. It may be thought peculiar, to say the least of it, that only well into this discussion ethical theory as such is brought to the fore. But as I view the matter it deserves no high priority. For ethics has little attended to proper behavior in large-scale organization. Its central interests have been elsewhere, tending to oscillate between the probing of traditional relationships such as those of family and friendships and rather abstract and bloodless general principles of conduct. While there is to be sure a great deal in the literature that is relevant, its relevance becomes clear only by extrapolation and application.

Fourth, religion also needs to be surveyed with the object of determining what instruments of navigation it can provide. For our purposes attention should be centered on the Judeo-Christian stream of religious thought and practice, but all major religions should be included. Among the many subjects on which I am not expert are theology and religious history. However, it takes only a little knowledge and understanding to appreciate three things. The first is that theology as such, like ethics to which it is linked in many ways, has attended very little to proper conduct in formal organizations, at least those not religious. Second, as with ethics, there is in theology a great deal that can be made relevant by extrapolation and application. In fact, the writings of Reinhold Niebuhr moved vigorously in this direction; and perhaps I do less than justice to others of whose work I may be unaware. Third, the history and effect of religious institutions and the second, third and X-order effects of religious thought and practice are of so great import for organizational life that one could devote a career to the matter without doing more than explore a few areas. The point is made simply by referring to the work under the heading of Protestant Ethic.

THE PYRAMID PUZZLE

Not surprisingly, many of the most interesting and significant questions concerning administration and ethics concern the theory and practice of hierarchy. Some of these questions are generic, in the sense that they apply to business and nonprofit private organizations as well as to public administration. But some have a special relevance to public administration, as they concern governmental institutions and political ideology. It will be instructive to focus briefly on this pyramid puzzle in the public context.

Central, at least to my own interest, is the fact that hierarchy is represented both as a force for morality and a source of immorality. Both cases are familiar to us, though perhaps not in the context of ethics.

The affirmative case has it that hierarchy is a force that works both for the soft values of democracy and the hard values of effectiveness, efficiency, and economy; indeed, that the achievement of the soft and hard values is complementary, not two things but a single thing. This is a central theme of old-line Public Administration, and the reasoning and conclusions are familiar: Democracy is, realistically, achievable only if power is concentrated so that it can be held accountable, and this is possible only through hierarchy. Otherwise, responsibility bleeds into the social surround. The devices for focusing citizen attention so that it could be made effective—devices such as the short ballot and party reform—were part of the old-line package. Responsibility was viewed as owed upward, subordinate to superordinate, to the top of the pyramid, then bridged over by the electoral principle to the people. Authority was viewed as moving the other direction, upward from the people through their elected representative, then bridged over to the top of the pyramid and descending, echelon by echelon, to every officer and employee.

That this way of viewing things has considerable logic and force strikes me as self-evident. It is plausibly, though hardly unarguably, based on Constitution and history, and can be bolstered with much evidence. It can be, and has been, buttressed by arguments from foreign experience and from business practice. Able and honorable persons have supported the main tenets of the argument. Thus Paul Appleby in his *Morality and Administration in Democratic Government:*[4] The hierarchical principle forwards effective government, but above all it is necessary to democratic government, insuring through its operation the triumph of the general interest over special interests. Thus Marver Bernstein in "Ethics in Government: The Problems in Perspective,"[5] arguing that serious ethical irregularities as well as inefficiencies are all but assured through the absence of hierarchical control in the arrangements for some regulatory agencies, which create conflicts of interest or in effect make the regulatory agencies captives of the interests to be regulated. Thus Victor Thompson in his *Without Sympathy or Enthusiasm: The Problem of Administrative Compassion,*[6] where he argues that the prescriptions for participation equal an invitation for the unauthorized to steal the "tool" of administration from its "owners," the public.

The case against hierarchy in turn has considerable logic and force. It also has roots in Constitution and history, and can be bolstered with much evidence. In this case persons who are able and honorable have stressed the contradictions involved in using hierarchy as a means of promoting democracy, the limitations of hierarchy as a means of achieving effectiveness and efficiency, and its complicity in forwarding immorality. Thus Vincent Ostrom in his *The Intellectual Crisis in American Public Administration,*[7] arguing the spuriousness of the case for centralization, and the greater democracy achievable by organizing public administration into smaller units more in accord with "consumer" will and control. Thus the advocates of a New Public Administration,[8] who take social equity as guiding principle and seek to achieve it "proactively," through client-oriented and client-involving devices. Thus F. William Howton—quoted in one of the epigraphs[9]—who speaks for many who believe that hierarchy with its accustomed corollaries creates deformed humans with deadened consciences. Thus Frederick Thayer in his *An End to Hierarchy! An End to Competition!* [10] who finds hierarchy implicated in immorality as well as promoting inefficiency, and necessarily to be abolished if there is to be a tolerable future—indeed, perhaps, a *future*.

My aim is not to weigh the arguments, much less render a verdict, but rather to emphasize the tangle of ethical problems in and related to the principle and practice of hierarchy; this by way of illustrating the central position of ethical concerns in our professional business—whether or not we care to attend to them *as* ethical questions. But before passing on, let me pose one question that many would regard as the paramount one: What difference does democracy make with respect to the morality of actions taken by government? Rousseau, if I understand him correctly, argued that while the people can be *mistaken*, they cannot be *wrong*. Two examples to ponder, the first from history, the second hypothetical. (1) If the bombing of Haiphong was "immoral," was the firebombing of Hamburg and Dresden—which was massively greater—also immoral? If not, why not? (2) If the Holocaust had been carried out under a democratic government rather than a dictatorship, would an Eichmann have been any more or less immoral? In reflecting on this, bear in mind Herman Finer's notable essay on "Administrative Responsibility in Government," [11] in which he holds with regard to the public servant: "The first commandment is subservience."

OBSERVATIONS AND REFLECTIONS

. . . At most I can hope to point to some of the matters that would be worthy of attention in a more serious and systematic inquiry. In conclusion, the following further observations and reflections. I shall proceed discontinuously, serially.

First

The twentieth century has hardly been distinguished either by its observance of agreed moral codes or by its concentration on ethical inquiry. On the contrary, it has been distinguished by a "decay" of traditional moral codes, a widespread feeling that morality is "relative" if not utterly meaningless, and a disposition to regard ethical inquiry as frivolous, irrelevant. These currents of thought and feeling have been associated with a "falling away" from religious belief and a concomitant rise of "belief" in science and its philosophical—or antiphilosophical—aura.

These developments have coincided with the Organizational Revolution: an unprecedented increase in the variety, number, size, and power of organizations, at the center of which is government, public administration. It has coincided also, and relatedly, with the arrival of administrative self-awareness, with a new type of "scientific" interest in administrative study and a resulting increase in administrative technology.

So we confront this historical situation: Just at the time the organizational world is thickening and thus the need for ethical guidance increasing, not only does old morality erode but no serious effort is made to create new codes of conduct appropriate to the new situation; and the scientific mentality that is largely responsible for the Organizational Revolution simultaneously makes it difficult to take ethical matters seriously.

Second

In no country does the level of conscious ethical conduct in government reach the level of complex reality, but the United States may have one problem to an unusual degree. It has often been observed that Americans tend to view morality very heavily if not exclusively in sexual and pecuniary terms: in the public area, Elizabeth Rays on payrolls and Tongsun Parks passing envelopes of currency behind closed doors.

As I see it, a concern for *public* morality must indeed include a concern with the ordinary garden varieties of sexual and pecuniary misconduct within or affecting public life; we would have to be ignorant of history and oblivious to contemporary political life to think otherwise. However, as even my few shallow probes indicate, the matter of ethically proper conduct reaches far, far beyond the popular images of sex and money. It presents problems of conduct for which traditional morality, growing in and shaped to simpler times, provides little guidance. Or worse, it provides *mis*guidance.

Third

Some of the better writings bearing on our subject emphasize the prevalence, perhaps even the necessity, of "moral ambiguity" in organizational life. Thus Stephen Bailey in his "Ethics and the Public Service";[12] I refer back to the epigraph from this essay emphasizing the "contextuality" of good and evil. Thus Melville Dalton in his *Men Who Manage*,[13] who concluded that persons from a middle-class background are more likely to become successful managers than persons from a working-class background, not because of superior ability or technical skill but because of a socialization that better prepares them to cope with moral ambiguity.

If we cannot *clarify* the ethics of the organizational world, perhaps it will help if we can advance *understanding* of the complexity and confusion. If ambiguity cannot be eliminated, then a "tolerance for ambiguity" becomes an essential operating skill. A *moral* quality as well as an operating skill? I shall not try to answer that.

Fourth

The following seems to be true, almost axiomatically: Moral complexity increases as memberships in organizations increase; persons in formal organizations in addition to traditional/nonformal organizations face greater moral complexity than those only in the latter; those in formal *public* organizations face more moral complexity than those in nonpublic organizations; and moral complexity increases as responsibilities in an administrative hierarchy increase.

If this is a correct view, then high-placed administrators (managers, executives) in public organizations are at the very center of ethical complexity. In this connection I refer you to the probing of morality in relation to administration in Chester Barnard's *The Functions of the Executive*[14]—from which comes the epigraph at the head of this chapter. *The Functions* is of course widely and correctly viewed as a seminal work. But it is a commentary on the interests of the past generation that this discussion of morality has been generally ignored.

Barnard believed that "moral creativeness" was an essential executive function. As the quoted sentence indicates, he believed also that the burden assumed could lead to moral breakdown. In a similar vein Stephen Bailey, in the essay cited in observation Third above, uses the metaphor "above the timber line" to signify the severe moral climate in which the high executive must operate and the dangers to which he is exposed.

Fifth

We have recently seen, and we presently see, the growth of a gray area, an area in which any clear distinction between the categories of *public* and *private* disappears, disappears in a complex and subtle blending of new organizational modes and legal arrangements. In this gray area, hierarchy is diminished, but does not disappear; new lateral and diagonal relationships grow up and operate along with it, making it formally and operationally difficult to answer the question: Who's in charge here?

As I view it, our ethical problems are compounded in this growing gray world. Who will be responsible for what to whom? In what will duty consist and by what can honesty be judged? One view is that, with hierarchy relaxed and freedom increased, the way is open for the development of authentic *personal* morality. Harlan Cleveland seeks a solution in the hope and prescription that managers in the "horizontal"[15] world that is emerging will regard themselves as "public managers"–because in fact they will be. I confess that on most days I find it hard to share either of these two varieties of optimism.

Sixth

As the epigraph from David Bradley and Roy Wilkie indicates, "the raising of moral considerations" in the study of organizations has not been popular. Indeed, the chapter on Morality and Organizations in their *The Concept of Organization*[16] is, to my knowledge, without a parallel in the scores of general treatments of organizational behavior or theory.

A number of factors, some pertaining to American public affairs and without need of mention, and some pertaining to the general climate of our intellectual life that are beyond explicating here, suggest that there may be a change in the situation, that we will begin to address seriously the ethical dimensions of our organizational world—here I allow myself a bit of optimism. This may be best done—perhaps it can be done only—by working from the empirical base legitimated in recent social science. It might begin, for example, with mapmaking, along the lines suggested earlier. Later, just possibly, we may be able to address the ethical as such.

One point of view has it that ethical inquiry is dangerous. Samuel Butler put it this way: "The foundations of morality are like all other foundations: if you dig too much about them, the superstructure will come tumbling down." But in our case, the digging has been done; the superstructure is already down. But then, the old superstructure was not to our purpose anyway. Perhaps on a new foundation we can use some of the fallen materials to build a superstructure that *is* to our purpose?

Notes

1. Strictly speaking, *moral* signifies right behavior in an immediate and customary sense; *ethical* signifies right behavior as examined and reflected upon. But no warranty is given that this distinction is always made in what follows.
2. Certainly Robert T. Golembiewski's *Men, Management, and Morality: Towards a New Organizational Ethic* (New York: 1965) is an able and useful work, and I do not wish to demean it. But the picture in my mind is of a work even broader in scope, one taking into account developments of the past decade. Neither do I mean to slight the useful work of Wayne A. R. Leys, done when ethics was *really* unfashionable: *Ethics and Social Policy* (New York: 1946), and *Ethics for Policy Decisions: The Art of Asking Deliberative Questions* (New York: 1952).
3. The analysis set forth in this section is a brief version of that in my "Reflections on Public Morality" (*6 Administration and Society* [November 1974], pp. 267–282).
4. Paul Appleby, *Morality and Administration in Democratic Government* (Baton Rouge, La.: 1952).
5. Marver Bernstein, "Ethics in Government: The Problems in Perspective" (*61 National Civic Review* [July 1972], pp. 341–347).
6. Victor Thompson, *Without Sympathy or Enthusiasm: The Problem of Administrative Compassion* (University, Ala.: 1975).
7. Vincent Ostrom, *The Intellectual Crisis in American Public Administration* (University, Ala.: 1973).
8. See the symposium, H. George Frederickson, ed., "Social Equity and Public Administration" (*34 Public Administration Review* [January/February 1974], pp. 1–51).
9. F. William Howton, *Functionaries* (Chicago: 1969).
10. Frederick C. Thayer, *An End to Hierarchy! An End to Competition! Organizing the Politics and Economics of Survival* (New York: 1973).
11. Herman Finer, "Administrative Responsibility in Democratic Government" (*1 Public Administration Review* [Summer 1941], pp. 335–350).
12. Stephen Bailey, "Ethics and the Public Service" (*23 Public Administration Review* [December 1964], pp. 234–243).
13. Melville Dalton, *Men Who Manage* (New York: 1959).
14. Chester Barnard, *The Functions of the Executive* (Cambridge, Mass.: 1947). See especially Chapter 17, The Nature of Executive Responsibility.
15. Harlan Cleveland, *The Future Executive: A Guide for Tomorrow's Managers* (New York: 1972).
16. David Bradley and Roy Wilkie, *The Concept of Organization: An Introduction to Organizations* (Glasgow: 1974).

PART THREE

The Management of Government Agencies

5

ORGANIZATION THEORY AND PUBLIC ADMINISTRATION

In this part of *Current Issues in Public Administration*, attention shifts from external relations to the internal dynamics of public agencies. Chapter 5 introduces organization theory, the many different approaches and theories to help explain behavior in organizations.

As it turns out, and as you may have expected, what goes on outside administrative agencies and what goes on inside are not easily separated. In the first article in this chapter, Harold Gortner, Julianne Mahler, and Jeanne Bell Nicholson examine what are for them the four pivotal controversies in public organization theory: legal authority, rationality and efficiency, psychological and social relations, and politics and power relations. Gortner and associates speculate that legal authority and politics may play a smaller role in the behavior within business organizations. Along their way, these authors also nicely survey the ideas of some of the key organizational theorists, including Max Weber, Frederick Taylor, Luther Gulick, Chester Barnard, the human relations school, Talcott Parsons, Irving Janis, and Herbert Kaufman.

In the second article, Lee Bolman and Terrence Deal see four approaches (or "frames") for understanding organizational behavior. In some ways similar to and in other ways different from Gortner's controversies, these approaches are structural, human resource, political, and symbolic. Most of their examples are from public schools, a context most of us readily understand. Education is an important part of public administration; over half of all state and local employees are employed in education.

Bolman and Deal take on the slipperiest of all organizational topics—leadership. They seek to clarify the definition of leadership and effective leader behavior in terms of their four frames.

The final article in this chapter focuses on, you guessed it, *mal*administration: sick organizations and poor administrative practices. While bureaucracy-bashing is quite common in our regular lives, there have been few systematic attempts to sort out what we mean by maladministration. If public agencies are going to do better, says author Gerald Caiden, first we must take seriously the common forms of organizational diseases, his "bureaupathologies."

Some questions to think about here include:

- While Gortner, Mahler, and Nicholson discuss four controversies, isn't one of these far more important than the other three? In your opinion, which one, and why?

- Consider together the four approaches to understanding public organizations from three different articles—Romzek and Dubnick (in the last chapter), Gortner and associates, and Bolman and Deal. What do they suggest about a multidimensional approach to understanding public agencies?

- What do Bolman and Deal tell us about effective leadership? Would you recognize it if you saw it? Do you have an example of an effective leader in your community, or state, or university?

- What about Caiden's bureaupathologies? Are they real? Do you have examples? (We will return to this in Chapters 8 and 10.)

Organization Theory: The Pivotal Controversies

**HAROLD F. GORTNER
JULIANNE MAHLER
JEANNE BELL NICHOLSON**

. . . Organization theory is a disorderly and fascinating field (Waldo, 1978). Each theory starts with a unique set of assumptions, asks a different set of basic questions, and, not surprisingly, arrives at different—sometimes diametrically opposed—answers. Nevertheless, certain themes are constantly addressed as the frantic debate among "public" organization theorists goes on. These controversies about, or perspectives on, organization in the public sector can be categorized under the following four general headings:

1. *Law and/or legal authority.* . . .
2. *Rationality and/or efficiency.* . . .
3. *Psychological and social relations.* . . .
4. *Politics and/or power relations.* . . .

THE CONTROVERSY AROUND FOUR PERSPECTIVES

Law and Legal Authority

We take it for granted that bureaus operate on a legal basis, or according to the law. We also recognize that the purpose of the bureau is to execute the law. However, we may fail on occasion to recognize that the effort to execute the law according to structures and processes established by law may cause great difficulty for bureaus. The most obvious example of this difficulty is seen in law enforcement's attempt to control organized crime, where the strict limits placed on surveillance and collection of evidence and the broad interpretation of individual rights create problems for the police. Derided for not doing a better job of controlling organized crime, police officers also work under procedural proscriptions, strongly ascribed to by most citizens, that limit their ability to control that crime. Law enforcement must find a way to meet the goals established for it by society while staying within the procedural limits placed on it by that same society.

In a similar vein, it is not uncommon for legislative adversaries, once aware that they cannot block passage of a new program, to attempt to place it in an already existing organization that is inimical or at best, coldly neutral, to that program. Another ploy regularly used by enemies of programs is to create, in the enabling act, procedures or structures that will hobble or make inefficient the delivery of the service or good in the hope that they may reopen the debate about the issue at a later date with "proof" that the decision to create the program was a mistake in the first place because of the problems that have been shown to exist in administering it.

That government and its bureaus should operate according to law is a widespread belief. Even in a totalitarian state such as the Soviet Union, the government and its agencies at least pay lip service to this idea and function under a constitution and laws that, while failing to guarantee some of the most important human rights, justify the legality of the imposed order to the citizenry. In our society, those few public organizations that we suspect may not always operate according to the law of the land (the Central Intelligence Agency, for example) cause considerable discomfort to interested observers because such activity, while perhaps necessary, is considered amoral. Even though it is endured, attempts are made to limit the amounts and types of covert activity, and various checks are created to oversee the organizations. As a result, leaders of such organizations sometimes complain of being hamstrung in their operations and of being unable to respond to, or counter, similar organizations in the communist world or, as noted above, in organized crime.

The concept of the laws as the basis of authority is relatively new in organization life. Authority, according to Max Weber, was based on charisma and/or tradition at earlier points in history. While examples of increasing dependence on legal authority can be invoked from earlier times (the Athenian democracy, the Magna Carta, and canon law), the concept became fully developed and widely accepted only during the last few hundred years. Today, however, we take for granted Abraham Lincoln's statement that we have a government of laws, not of men. The public bureaucracy is the administrative or implementation and service arm of government, and it is based on laws. Laws establish the policy direction, or the goals, of bureaus, thereby spelling out what is expected in the way of output or results. Likewise, laws define proper organizational structure, due process, reporting procedures, and conflict of interest. In other words, the law clarifies both structural and procedural questions. It even establishes the system by which personnel are selected, rewarded, or punished within the bureau.[1] Public bureaucracy and dependence on the law grew together, as is noted by Herbert Spiro.

> Modern law and modern bureaucracy were created to fill the same needs. On the Continent, especially, the birth and growth of each cannot be conceived of without the other. Administrative law was designed to make responsible conduct possible for the ruler's new instruments, the bureaucrats, by giving them reasonable expectations of the probable consequences of their acts. . . . In the days of the youth of modern bureaucracy, the bureaucrat's accountability normally stood in fair proportion to his causal responsibility. He knew the extent of his accountability, i.e., it was explicit. What he should or should not do, and how he should go about his tasks, were laid down for him with greater exactness perhaps than for anyone else who acts politically. The statutes creating or regularizing his position told him from the outset what would happen to him if he committed "nonfeasance, malfeasance, or overfeasance." (1969, 86–87)

The centrality of law and the concomitant responsibility for the execution of the law required the development of the modern public bureau. This is especially true if it is assumed that bureaus should react to and fulfill citizen desires and demands rather than create social objectives because the bureaucracy is geared toward objectivity, independence from personal pressure, and control over discretionary actions by bureaucrats. Looking back at Max Weber's model of bureaucracy, or at his description of the internal characteristics of bureaucratic organizations, one can see how these characteristics help to guarantee that public agencies will "automatically" obey the law.

Weber argues that organizations of this type exist in both the private and public sectors—and this is certainly true; however, public organizations probably tend to match this model more closely than private ones. In the first place, public agencies, having been established by the legislature to achieve certain objectives through specified processes—all spelled out by the law—are creatures of the law.

A second aspect of the relationship between the law and bureaucracy becomes overwhelmingly apparent as we look at Weber's model and the ways in which it guarantees that the law will be the basis for bureau action. By examining Weber's criteria, we can clarify the way in which the bureaucratic system guarantees an inordinate focus by public employees on the law. Central to this point is the fact that each office has a clearly defined sphere of competence. . . . And where is that sphere defined? In the law—if not in the enabling act, then in the rules, regulations, and other materials that are based on and interpret the inert law as it is put into action. Note also that bureaucratic officials are subject to authority *only* when it applies to their offices . . . ; these offices are at least their primary occupation . . . ; and the officials are entirely separated from ownership. . . . These factors limit the possibility of conflict of interest; thus, bureaucrats are under no other pressure except to know and obey the law. Furthermore, the fact that positions in the bureaucracy are filled by free contractual relationships . . . after being selected on the basis of technical qualifications . . . and are then paid fixed salaries in money . . . guarantees their loyalty. The officials are not forced to participate and their rewards are fixed; therefore, no *person* has an undue claim on their services. They are not distracted by personal claims from the objective administration of the law. Finally, the hierarchical structure of offices . . . and the natural desire to advance in a career . . . mean that all officials are held accountable for their actions. Strict accountability breeds close adherence to the law, and deductive rules and rigorous control are the major objects of design and management. . . .

Within the public sector, adherence to the law is central to all activities. Accountability and control, especially as spelled out in the law, are ensured by the structure of organizations. Structure, as portrayed in the organizational chart, is the formal aspect of organizational life, and if the chief executive or an external body such as the legislature wishes to have an impact on the operation of an agency, the primary line of attack is through changes in the law that force reorganization. Likewise, the easiest and most direct way for top officials to make an imprint on their agencies is through reorganization. The result is instantaneous and visual, whereas attempts to influence the informal portion of a bureau take an indeterminate amount of time and often cannot be concretely measured. Nor are these officials often able to get the enabling law changed to accomplish the shift in agency direction that they would like. In addition, appointed officials, bringing with them a portfolio of experience from their prior positions (sometimes from the private sector), are convinced that by restructuring the bureau they can streamline operations and improve on the effectiveness of the public agency. Changes and "improvements" always appear, ultimately, in formal rules and regulations or some similar "lawlike" format.

Interest in the effect of organizational structure on the success of public organizations as executors of law actually existed before the time of Max Weber, but no one had formalized the theory. Apparently, the structure of the governmental bureaucracy was *not* an issue of importance to the framers of the Constitution (Wilson 1887); little mention is made of such factors in records of the day—including the record of debates at the Constitutional Convention or the explanatory and laudatory *Federalist Papers* (1961). However, while the founders may not have recognized it, the civil service reformers who became active in the second half of the nineteenth century did. They argued that in order to improve the efficiency and effectiveness of government, a structural change was needed in public organizations and that such change had to occur through the establishment of law (the Civil Service Act and similar reform legislation). Interest in the public sector can then be traced through a series of reorganization commissions (the Brownlow Commission and the first and second Hoover Commissions being the prime examples), each of which led to new laws up to the present, with major political battles having recently been waged over the establishment and dissolution of the federal Departments of Energy and Education.

Efficiency and Rationality

The principles of efficiency and rationality are grouped together here because many social theorists, especially during the first third of the twentieth century, used the terms almost interchangeably. Whether they realized the synonymity of the two concepts is unclear, but their recognition, or lack thereof, is not important to the major thrust of our argument. In the interest of clarity, we will first discuss the two principles separately. Then we shall point out how they overlap.

Efficiency   In its simplest sense, efficiency equals maximization of productivity, or the greatest possible output for the least input. The founders of this school of administrative study came from both industry and public administration, with their ideas being adapted in both sectors. Let us look at the two approaches to this principle and then note the common assumptions from which the founders operated.

Frederick Taylor was interested in increasing productivity because everybody benefited from the result.

> It is perfectly clear that the greatest permanent prosperity for the workman, coupled with the greatest prosperity for the employer, can be brought about only when the work of the establishment is done with the smallest combined expenditure of human effort, plus nature's resources, plus the cost for the use of capital in the shape of machines, buildings, etc. (1947, 11)

Productivity was achieved by applying Taylor's interpretation of the scientific method to the man/machine system in industry. Since little had been done up to that time by way of systematically examining how men and machines interacted as a single task or process (series of tasks) was carried out, Taylor zeroed in on this most obvious factor.

Industry had moved from the production of goods by tradespeople who made complete items to production by specialization where items were produced by a combination of machines and workers, each of whom performed part of a complex process that yielded finished items more rapidly and in a more standardized form. The specialization occurred somewhat randomly, however, and no careful scientific analysis of how jobs were done was carried out. Machines were responsible for much of the improvement in productivity; they would continue to account for much of the improvement because there appeared at that time to be an almost infinite potential for technical development. However, little effort went into examining how the weak link in the system—man—could be made to operate more efficiently, either in conjunction with the machines he operated or in those jobs that tended to require his attention without the aid of technology (either because it was not appropriate to the job or was not yet developed).

Taylor's approach to the study of work soon became known as "scientific management." He best defines the central concepts of this approach at the end of his treatise when he says that

> It is no single element, but rather [a] combination, that constitutes scientific management, which may be summarized as:
> Science, not rule of thumb.
> Harmony, not discord.
> Cooperation, not individualism.
> Maximum output, in place of restricted output.
> The development of each man to his greatest efficiency and prosperity. (1947, 141)

By using his version of the scientific method, Taylor was convinced that it was possible to discover the "one best way" to structure any job or process. With the discovery of the one best way, the principle of efficiency was realized.

Another group of individuals was attempting to apply scientific principles to administration, which Luther Gulick defined as "the phenomena of getting things done through co-operative human endeavor" (1937). Whereas politics is concerned with the process of getting elected to office and setting objectives for the country, Gulick argues that "administration has to do with getting things done; with the accomplishment of defined objectives" (1937, 191). If administration is removed from the value-laden field of politics, then a science of administration becomes possible.

> In the science of administration, whether public or private, the basic "good" is efficiency. The fundamental objective of the science of administration is the accomplishment of the work in hand with the least expenditure of man-power and materials. Efficiency is axiom number one in the value scale of administration. (1937, 192)

The way to achieve that efficiency is by "scientifically" examining the structure of organizations, and this is what is done throughout Gulick's and Urwick's *Papers*. Questions such as what is the proper span of control for a supervisor, what should be the basis for assigning supervisors over workers, and what principles should control the division, or structure, of large organizations are analyzed throughout the book in one of the first attempts to find the "one best way" to structure organizations to guarantee efficiency in both administration and production of goods or services.

The followers of Taylor, Gulick, and the other expounders of the principle of efficiency are legion. Industrial engineering, which has as its goal the improvement in efficiency and productivity, traces its beginning in the United States directly to Frederick Taylor (1911). While the techniques that are used have become more sophisticated, industrial engineers still accept the basic premises postulated by Taylor at the turn of the century. Likewise, many current students of work flow and office design are convinced that there is one best way to establish the physical layout of a workplace so that all of the tasks can be completed with optimum efficiency. On a larger scale, information scientists are striving to achieve the greatest possible efficiency in the flow, impact, and use of information; this requires an acceptance of the idea that there is, if not one best way, at least an optimal way to structure both organizations and information systems. The principle of efficiency lives on.

Rationality The principle of rationality was accepted as an undisputed law by all of the writers mentioned above. When Weber defines the phenomenon that he calls bureaucracy, he is simply describing the organizational construct that has been established to guarantee rationality. Taylor, Gulick, Urwick, and the other proponents of scientific management and scientific administration prescribe rational procedures and structures. Both groups, whether descriptive or prescriptive, accept the idea that what organizations seek and need is rationality. Rationality (the quality or state of having or being based on reason) is central to all organizations in our modern, technological, interdependent world. Nowhere is this idea more alluring than in the public sector due to the government's influence on all of society.

However, these theorists are overly simplistic in their definition and perception of essential elements. This simplicity is best understood by examining the term *rationality* and by recognizing the narrowness of their definitions as opposed to the complexity that exists when a full explication of the concept is given.

First, there are two levels of rationality: instrumental and substantive (Weber 1947). Substantive rationality is concerned with the ends that an organization attempts to achieve—what are the right, appropriate, or best goals to be sought? Instrumental rationality is concerned not with ends, but means, or *how* an organization attempts to achieve a given end or set of ends. The two levels are both essential, but the types of logic and analytic tools that are involved differ dramatically. Second, Paul Diesing (1962) defines five types of rationality that currently exist in our society: technical, economic, social, legal, and political. He discusses the social conditions in which they exist, conditions that, as Diesing points out, they partially help to create. Careful consideration leads to even more "rational systems" based on other premises (axioms) commonly accepted by major active sectors of society. For example, the major religious groups in our society have their own "rationalities" that determine both the substantive and instrumental decisions of their organizations.

Weber recognizes the need for rationality as one of the central causes for the development of bureaucracy. Bureaucracy is a necessary result of the development of modern technology, with its incredible level of interdependence among all parts of society. Technological interdependence creates a requirement for stable, strict, intensive, and calculable interactions, and "it [bureaucracy] is superior to any other form [of organization] in precision, in stability, in the stringency of its discipline, and in its reliability" (Weber 1947, 339). Like them or not, bureaucracies are rational, and since that principle is central to our lives, bureaucracies will continue to exist until a form of organization is discovered that improves on the delivery of this particular characteristic. All of this discussion, however, focuses on instrumental rationality—getting things done efficiently—rather than focusing on "what should be done," which is determined by the superior powers (i.e., the legislature, courts, and so on) outside the bureaucracy. This is especially true in the public sector.

On the other hand, students of scientific management and administration prescribe rationality rather than describe it. It is significant that Gulick referred to efficiency as "axiom number one in *the value scale* of administration." (Emphasis added.) The use of the term *axiom* was not accidental. Axioms are a part of science and these people believed that by building a full set of axioms, or propositions regarded as self-evident truth, administration could become a part of science just as geometry became a part of mathematics. The axioms that were sought by the scientific administration group were related to the structures of organizations as those structures related to the functions of administration—or as Gulick referred to them, the functions of the chief executive—because all administrators simply fulfilled roles and exercised the powers delegated to them by the chief executive, either directly or indirectly. Through the use of axioms and rationality, many important problems could be solved by finding the one best way to organize; and the one best way was considered the most efficient way (a value judgment). A similar type of logic applied to the followers of Taylor.

In comparison to the publicly oriented theories that we have been discussing, the model presented by Peters and Waterman, which applies more directly to business organizations, begins with a very special definition of rationality and efficiency, a "bottom-line" definition that says rationality and efficiency are measured by how successful the organization is in achieving the goals of profit, size, and growth. These ends are usually not appropriate for the public manager. Substantive rationality is an important part of the internal decision-making process in the private sector, but the decisions about "what ought to be" are biased by the basic assumptions about what the goals of businesses are.

In order to achieve the bottom-line success that is assumed to be the goal of all organizations, Peters and Waterman encourage structures and procedures that would be highly questionable in the public sector. For example, they argue that it is rational to break the corporation into small, competing units and that the organization should cater to its customers. Both of these eminently rational suggestions for corporations would raise howls of protest if implemented by many of their public counterparts. It can also be suggested to private managers that they remain in the business the company knows best and that the administrative structure be kept lean and simple. Private managers can do this because they control their own destiny in this area. However, public managers often do not have the luxury of deciding such matters; therefore, such advice may very well be useless to them.

Rationality-Efficiency By closely examining the two approaches to organization theory, and by probing for the more basic assumptions on which the approaches are built, it becomes clear that while two different terms are used, they are used in almost identical ways. The theorists discussed above—Weber, Taylor, Gulick et al.—consider only the instrumental level of rationality and they define rationality and efficiency identically. According to these theorists, "The efficient achievement of a single goal is technical rationality (Taylor), the maximum achievement of a plurality of goals is economic rationality (Gulick; Weber), and no other types of rationality are admitted" (Diesing 1962, 1). Substantive rationality is irrelevant; goals are established somewhere outside the organization, or the part of the organization being considered. Technical rationality, as developed by Taylor, was specifically geared toward increased output for the same amount of input; that equals efficiency. Gulick, Urwick, and the others who were scientifically examining administration were interested in *efficient* organization or structures that maximized the managerial functions; good management guaranteed efficiency in operation and maximum return for tax dollar spent. Weber argues throughout his writing that *technical efficiency*, a term he uses interchangeably with *rationality*, is the major benefit to be gained from bureaucracy and the reason that bureaucracy developed in the first place.

The issues of rationality, efficiency, or both, if they are in fact one and the same, are of great importance in the study of public organizations. Attempts to achieve rationality and efficiency must not be downplayed. However, focusing on such concepts inspires us to ask only *some* of the vital questions, and our horizons must expand, even when we are considering the place of reason or rationality in organizations. Both levels of rationality, and at least the five types of reason mentioned by Diesing, are required to understand or operate in a public organization.

Psychology and Social Relations

Interest in the social relations of organizations developed in part as a reaction to the formalistic approaches emphasized by the early students of management and organization and in part as the logical evolution of interest or curiosity by those who desired to examine all aspects of organizational life. The reaction to the formal emphasis and the ensuing recognition of the fact that informal relations within an organization are equal in importance to the structures and processes established by law or in writing occurred for at least three reasons. Some manager/scholars such as Chester Barnard (1938) began to point out that both a formal and an informal side of life existed side by side, if not intertwined, in the structure and functions of any organization, and that both aspects of organizational life had to be considered. At the same time, some of the programs attempting to reach the goals of increased productivity and rationality did not achieve the expected results (e.g., the Hawthorne experiments, Roethlisberger and Dickson 1939). At least part of the reason for the failure of such efforts was the fact that after a certain point in the development of productivity programs and increasing rationality in structures, the individuals operating in the organizations began to resist further change. To comprehend the attitudes and reactions of employees, it became important to focus on both the individuals and groups in the organizations and how they interacted outside the formal structures and procedures. Finally, with the developing interest and skill in testing and evaluation of individuals, and to a certain extent groups, which was especially hastened and increased by the coming of World War II, it became obvious that the informal side of organization theory could add a great deal to our knowledge about the total field.

The interest in the informal aspects of organization led to two major categories of theories: (1) those dealing predominantly with individuals, and (2) those concerned with groups. The first can be considered the psychological approach and the second the sociological approach. Each obviously deals with an important aspect of the organization, and each has presented us with theories that try to explain and predict what has happened or will happen in organizations as different elements change. After examining both types of theories, we shall go one step further and note how, by combining the two, a third level of theory appears that adds even more to our understanding.

Focus on Individual Behavior (the Psychological Approach)   The focus on individual behavior is, in many ways, a continuation of the interests noted by Frederick Taylor as he emphasized the study of individual jobs and how the "man-machine system" could be made to function more efficiently. However, the new focus on the individual recognized an aspect of human nature that Taylor tended to overlook, even though students of psychology were emphasizing it. At the same time that Taylor was expounding on the principles of scientific management (which, in part, accepted as its basis the rationality of man), Walter Dill Scott, a psychology professor at Northwestern University, was arguing that man was *not* fundamentally a reasoning creature. Scott argued that the power of suggestion was very important in influencing human decisions and that it was therefore essential to study individuals for the purpose of understanding their personal makeup, which might, in turn, influence their habits.

The importance of examining the individual's skills and aptitudes (issues also important to Taylor) is recognized by everyone, but equally important is the study of individual traits and attitudes, with the second gaining major impetus from the "surprises" at Hawthorne. Central to the examination of individual skills and aptitudes is the area of testing and measurement. Personnel selection, for instance, has been one of the principle areas of interest to industrial and organizational psychologists since the field's earliest days. The goal of those involved in testing and measurement is to choose, from a larger group, the best individual or group of individuals to fill positions within an organization. These decisions are frequently based on tests that purport to measure one's ability to perform specified mental or physical tasks or to measure attitudes and personality traits or attributes that are believed to predict future success on the job. With the evolution of demands for equal employment opportunity, this field in the study of individual behavior has come under increased scrutiny and attack.[2] In this area psychologists cannot lose for winning even though they cannot win for losing: the more tests—usually prepared with the help of psychologists—are challenged, the greater the demand for psychologists skilled in test validation to examine the testing procedures.

Central to this issue is a series of questions, a sample of which are: What is the impact of the civil service system on recruiting top-notch individuals and then motivating them to do good work? How do bureau structures affect communication, decision making and other functions? How do people interact with the new technologies being introduced into bureaus? Organization structure, job design, and even the physical layout of offices have an impact on the way that individuals interact and carry out their tasks. All of these factors then must be considered as organizational managers decide what is appropriate job preparation for applicants, and, for those already in the bureau, what kinds of preparation, training, and knowledge/skills are required for the new jobs being created by technological change or for promotion to higher positions.

The researchers at the Hawthorne experiments, who set out to examine the impact of the immediate physical surrounding on worker productivity, came to the conclusion that one of the most important factors influencing individual behavior was the morale or motivation of the subject workers; in other words, the most important factor influencing the workers was not the physical environment, but the attitudes that resulted from the workers seeing themselves as important to the ongoing experiment. Even though the Hawthorne research is methodologically suspect in retrospect (Carey 1967; Roethlisberger 1941), it started a line of inquiry that continues today. In the ensuing decades a variety of theories about motivation and about the impact of motivation on productivity have been developed. Indeed, a great deal of work continues in this area and is the theme of a later chapter. The relationships between job satisfaction, material rewards, productivity, the physical and psychic environment of work, and numerous other factors associated with individual attitudes have been found to be correlated with the success of organizations, but in varying ways and degrees. In addition, the unique aspects of public organization environments create peculiar challenges for those interested in this sector of society.

The focus on the individual extends to the examination of the functions and/or processes of organizations. The functions of management are described in numerous ways; but however described, it is essential that one understand how an individual thinks, acts, and reacts to the various stimuli that constantly bombard him or her. When a public official, whether Prime Minister Margaret Thatcher or city auditor Sally Smith, has to make decisions, she normally goes through a series of steps, and a variety of individual factors determine how she sees the problem, what alternatives she believes are possible, which ones are acceptable, and which one is ultimately chosen. These and other issues are examined by psychologists, economists, decision scientists, and others. Indeed, Herbert Simon, whose intellectual roots are in public administration, has been awarded the Nobel Prize in Economics because of his work in decision theory which, in part and in a very sophisticated way, deals with the issues just noted. The role of the individual in other management activities, such as communication, coordination, planning, and objective setting, also plays an important part in the theory of the individual in the organization.

Finally, the study of leadership focuses much attention on the individual; considerable effort has gone into the attempt to discover the personality characteristics or traits of leaders. Do individuals who become leaders have certain traits in common? Are certain traits always necessary in particular types of situations? These and similar questions are examined by students of leadership. When one examines history, it appears that some individuals were destined to become leaders while others would never have risen to the top, no matter how hard they tried. This phenomenon has piqued the interest of all those who examine the leadership role.

Focus on Group Behavior (the Sociological Approach) The common thread in every case above is the researchers' interest in the individual. A parallel interest exists in the role of the *group* and how it affects and is affected by the organization. The informal organization, which is composed of groups that form outside of or in spite of the formal structure, plays a significant part in determining the perceptions and attitudes of group members, as well as in establishing the values and norms of behavior. One of the early discussants of the importance of the informal aspects of organization was Chester Barnard (1938), who argued that informal organization preceded the formal in existence. Barnard also pointed out that each type of organization needed the other if both were to continue existing for a significant period of time because each fulfilled functions that could not be accomplished by the other.

Of course, the recognition of the importance of informal groups meant that a new fact of organization life had to be examined if we were to be fully cognizant of *all* the forces that influence organizations. The most inclusive term for this study is *group dynamics*, which is defined by Cartwright and Zander as "a field of inquiry dedicated to achieving knowledge about the nature of groups, the laws of their development, and their interrelations with individuals, other groups, and larger institutions" (1968, 4). From this research came numerous explanations of and theories about group behavior.

Of special interest is the recognition of the importance of informal groups in establishing values, norms, roles, and status. *Values*, the ideas that are considered to have intrinsic worth or desirability and that are the basic standards and principles that guide action, are greatly influenced by groups. Individuals do not create their values in a vacuum; instead, values are developed in a group context. Thus, the result is inevitably different than it would be if an individual did not interact with numerous groups of varying persuasions. *Norms*, the social rules or authoritative standards or patterns against which attitudes and behavior can be measured, are directly related to group interactions. Without groups, norms could not be developed. *Roles*, the behavior that is expected from an individual by the others in the group, are assigned to the person or position by the other group members. While a formal role may be spelled out by the official organizational chart, job description, and official pronouncements, there is just as assuredly an informal role established by the group or groups with which the individual interacts and the two roles may or may not coincide. Likewise, groups develop roles that they play in the larger institutional setting and that develop both formally and informally. Finally, the whole idea of *status*, one's position or rank in relation to others, is again only possible as a concept in a group setting.

These and other similar concepts help to describe the workings of the informal side of an organization, which is essential since it has become apparent that formal structures and processes are always matched by informal systems. When, for example, an agency establishes a hierarchy that spells out who an employee is to seek help from and who is to evaluate that employee's work (usually an "immediate supervisor"), a second system develops that allows an employee to go to selected peers for help and advice—usually people with recognized expertise (Blau 1955). Peer evaluations of work performance are often considered just as, or more, important than the opinions of the boss. This type of informal structure is apparent in a factory setting or a government office and is a key element in such matters as job satisfaction and morale, as well as efficiency and productivity. These kinds of factors are especially important for public managers because of the limitations placed on them by formal rules and regulations. One of the ways that public managers can motivate their employees is by using the informal system that exists in every agency to foster esprit de corps and reinforce appropriate behavior.

The recognition of this fact led to the development of the "group" side of the Human Relations School, which emphasizes the importance of employee morale in productivity. The keynote theme of the school is that successful organizations generally have satisfied employees, or employees who are happy with and challenged by the organization's environment. The applied approach to the field is organization development (OD), in which behavioral scientists have begun to use the findings about organizational culture in an attempt to make changes so that bureaus will be "better" (more democratic) places to work and more effective in serving the public. Behind the theories of OD lie a complex set of values that can only be summarized here by using Robert Simmons' phrase, "humane organization," about which he says:

> The first essential step in provisioning humane organization is to confront the full meaning of groups, organizations and bureaucracies in the context and fabric of our political, social and personal lives. . . . The attainment of humane bureaucratic organizations is crucial for the full achievement of human dignity in industrial urban society. The social "payoff" is creative and producing human beings fulfilling their own capabilities, contributing to stable social institutions, and challenging the unknown horizons of human existence and understanding. (1981, 241)

Closely related to the idea of organization culture and its impact is the understanding of leadership in the group context. Success in changing the attitudes and habits of individuals and groups usually depends on the commitment of the leaders: If they support change it has a chance; if they do not support change it probably will not occur. The relationship between groups and their leaders has become an increasingly important aspect of organization theory. Social exchange theory, for example, bases leadership effectiveness in a group not on formal position, but on the benefits the leader can generate for the group in return for his or her acceptance in the position (Jacobs 1971). In other words, leadership is a role or position granted by the group in exchange for services rendered. This and other similar theories point out the difference between management and leadership, the first being based on one's position in the bureaucratic hierarchy and the second on power relationships in a social situation (French and Raven 1958).

Group behavior is also a major focus when examining the processes of organizations. Much effort has gone into noting how decisions are influenced by groups. Irving Janis (1972), for example, has looked at what he refers to as the dangers of groupthink, while other students of decision making, attempting to find productive ways to use groups, have promoted the use of group decision-making techniques, such as synectics, brainstorming, and Delphi. Likewise, all of the processes discussed by Gulick (POSDCORB) or other writers about public management have a group aspect to them. Only by understanding the group aspects of these processes can anyone claim to be knowledgeable about the theory of organizations or about how to apply that theory to group management.

Combining the Individual and the Group Our understanding of organizations increased immensely by examining the individual, or the group, and how s/he or they interact with the organization. Perhaps even greater progress has been made by combining the various theories into a more comprehensive network. When one looks at theories about individuals in organizations, then adds the element of individuals in informal groupings that also are operating within the formal organization, and finally recognizes that the formal organizations themselves operate in larger environments where each organization may be thought of as an individual within the larger system, the complexity of organization theory is brought home rather forcefully. The results of such a "weltanschauung" create an incredibly rich tapestry that allows greater detail to be developed at multiple levels. It also enables one to see the interrelationships between numerous factors that, when considered singly, do not provide an appropriate or adequate explanation of how or why they occur.

In looking back at the two models presented at the beginning of the article, we find that Weber seems to separate consideration of the individual and the group (although he does look at both). This separation occurs because of the strictly formal view he takes of bureaucracy. Social relations—at least the formal ones—within the bureau are spelled out by the criteria of each job and the structure of the organization while the informal side of the organization is ignored.

On the other hand, Peters and Waterman take a broader view of both individuals and organizations that focuses on informal social relationships. (To use the vernacular, organizational "culture" is their "bag".) They encourage a formal structure (lean and simple with lots of individual and group autonomy) that allows the informal aspect of the firm to flourish; management's job is to guarantee that the relevant aspects of the informal organization are focused on the major values of the firm (which should be simple and direct). By recognizing that productivity occurs through people, this model emphasizes the importance of motivating employees. Peters and Waterman recognize, as do most current organizational model builders, that a broad and multifaceted view of the psychological and social principles is necessary. The problem becomes one of figuring out what parts of their ideas can be applied in the public sector and how, and then using them.

A good example of this more inclusive approach to organization theory is presented in the systems theories of Kenneth Boulding, an economist, and Talcott Parsons, a sociologist. Parsons, for example, argues that

> Like any social system, an organization is conceived as having a describable structure. This can be described and analyzed from two points of view, both of which are essential to completeness. The first is the "cultural/institutional" point of view which uses the values of the system and their institutionalization in different functional contexts as its point of departure; the second is the "group" or "role" point of view which takes suborganizations and the roles of individuals participating in the functioning of the organization as its point of departure. (1956, 67)

Other scholars, notably March and Simon (1958), Katz and Kahn (1982), and Thompson (1967) also use the systems approach in their consideration of complex organizations.

Finally, the much-touted area of "organization development" is based on an attempt to apply all of the theories in a way that will open communication channels, increase trust, and create a more democratic environment in organizations. While there is a fierce debate about the feasibility and propriety of the objectives and about the methods used to achieve them, the debate is one that includes all of the various aspects of organization theory. Therefore, it encourages a scope of integration that is beneficial to those wishing to improve their understanding of how public bureaus work, regardless of what happens to the ideas generating the debate.

Politics and Power

Public organizations, which we refer to as bureaus, are unlike most others in one important way: The difference is the political setting in which public organizations function. In this area, most of the generic or universal models have failed; they simply do not deal with the issue of politics, and they interpret power as an internal phenomenon usually related to the area of leadership. Weber, for example, spends little time in discussing power, and to the extent that he does discuss it, internal power relations are defined by the law and its formal interpretation in the hierarchy and in individual spheres of competence. Ultimate power and the relationship of each bureau with the others in society are determined either totally outside of the organization or are considered by only those few in formal positions at the top of the hierarchy where such matters fall within their sphere of competence.

Peters and Waterman, in their model of the excellent organization, speak even less to the subject of power and politics. Power relationships within the corporation (based on the idea of maximum delegation of all but the most basic authority related to the most central values of the firm) are carefully described as minimal, and nothing is said about the political environment within which the organization operates.[3]

Public employees operating at lower levels of bureaus, especially those in nonboundary-spanning positions, may not recognize or care much about the political environment because the way they work may be somewhat similar to the way an employee in the private sector works. However, when one examines positions at higher levels of the bureau, or when the behavior of the public organization as an entity is the focus of attention, the political environment becomes an essential element in the equation. In this case, it is necessary to note the development of theories related to political values and power, which in turn have an impact on resource distribution, coalition building, and political goal setting and decision making. A grasp of these theories is essential to an understanding of the political factors that profoundly influence public organization.

The oldest of the continuous studies of politics—political philosophy—has much to say that is relevant to students of organizations. Herbert Kaufman (1964) points out that organization theory and political theory have produced findings and inferences that are "closely parallel in many important respects." . . . The values espoused by the political system also have a dramatic impact on the way that bureaus' structures actually operate. Basic premises about the state and the citizen vary significantly depending on whether organizations with identical structures are located in a democratic-socialist state, an authoritarian-communist state, or a democratic-capitalist state because their objectives will operate quite differently.

Just as one must consider political philosophy when examining public organizations, so must one look at the "culture" of government. Included in culture are such factors as (1) the history of government, or how it developed; (2) the role of government as perceived by members of society; (3) the structures and processes considered proper to government; and (4) the values, mores, and habits of the primary actors, especially the elected and appointed officials and the bureaucrats working beneath those officials. All of these factors help to "define reality" for public officials, employees, and the organizations they represent. Even relatively small differences in political culture may create important variations in the way bureaucrats perceive the world and the way they operate in it. . . .

Political culture may lead to results that are the opposite of the objectives stated in the law. Weisband and Franck (1975) note that top officials in the

United States are guaranteed by the Constitution the right to resign and use whatever nonclassified information is available to them to fight policies proposed by the president if they are convinced those policies are wrong. On the other hand, in Great Britain, cabinet officials operate without a formal guarantee of protection if they release information that is damaging to the government. However, in almost every case, officials in the United States resign quietly, without taking up the battle against the policy that caused them to resign. In the few cases where these officials have protested publicly, they have tended to be viciously attacked and their public careers ruined, if not their private careers as well. In Great Britain, on several occasions where officials not only resigned but also released information damaging to the government's cause, the officials were not punished for the infraction, and in fact, they often found themselves at a later date holding equal or higher posts in the cabinet (Weisband and Franck 1975, 95–98). By looking only at the law or the formal rules and by not understanding the cultural context in which the law and the relevant public organization operates, an observer would be totally bewildered.

The culture of a political system is inextricably bound up with the existing governmental structure. A mayor-council or a council-manager form of government exists in a city not by chance, but because of the size of a community, the heterogeneity of its population, and the political values of the citizens in the community. (Smaller and middle-sized communities that are socioeconomically homogenous tend to have city manager-council governments, while larger and more socioeconomically heterogeneous communities tend to have mayor-council systems.) To a great extent, the structure of local government is a formalized statement of the citizens' values as they relate to such vital issues as political decision making, communication, conflict resolution, and control. The structure, in turn, influences the procedures around and in the bureaus established to carry out city policy. Therefore, theories about how the political system works, who has access where, and what is considered "proper" within the political sphere are vital to understanding how public structure develops and is maintained. . . .

The Impact of the Political Setting on Public Organization Theory Undoubtedly some readers are not convinced that the political setting is important to a discussion of organization theory. It may be impossible to convince those who do not wish to agree, but a brief history of the interaction between the political arena and public organization theory may help to make the point. What is important to note in the following review is that every time a new historical development occurred, a concomitant new perspective of public organization was introduced. No attempt to prove a cause and effect relationship is made here. The authors simply wish to note that the two factors—political developments and public organization theory—were and are interconnected.

At the very beginning of the formal study of organizations, for example, the two major theories (those of Weber and Taylor) melded perfectly with the major thrust of the reformers.[4] Reformers were trying to remove the "business of government," as Woodrow Wilson referred to it, from the political arena, at least to the extent that decisions and actions could be made independent of politicians. Second, a major claim of reformers was that, by separating politics and administration, efficiency and neutrality could be dramatically improved. The theories of Wilson and Taylor gave rational and powerfully persuasive support to the reform movement, which, in turn, gave impetus to the development of the civil service system, the anchor point of the reform movement. If one examines the merit personnel system from beginning to end, it is obvious that it almost perfectly matches the bureaucratic system as described by Weber—even if the reformers were not aware of Weber's writings. The structure also allowed the specialization and development of expertise as defined by Taylor. In spite of temporary setbacks, such as the refusal of civilian naval employees to allow stopwatches in the armories, the technological complexity of society led to an increasing acceptance of specialization and its focus on efficiency.

With the arrival of President Roosevelt's New Deal, two major political facts of life (the Great Depression and World War II) influenced the development of organizations and the way scholars thought about them in government. For the first time, government was expected to be responsible for the state of the economy and to help those people who were out of work or had other chronic and/or serious economic needs. The increased charge led to two phenomena, the first of which was the general growth of government and new agencies. Government could not take on all of the new functions that became part of its sphere without growing immensely; therefore, the magnitude of public organizations became increasingly important as a part of the total society. Along with growth came an influx of new people into public service, many of whom were well-educated and highly specialized individuals who would obviously be leaders of public organizations for the next two generations. Second, many of these people had been trained in political science, economics, history, and other disciplines by scholars who wholeheartedly accepted the politics-administration dichotomy as presented by Woodrow Wilson, Frank Goodnow, and numerous others writing between 1880 and 1930.

The storm of World War II, which broke over the United States with the Japanese attack on Pearl Harbor, also attracted many highly talented and well-trained individuals to federal government positions. After the war, many of these people either continued their careers in government or began a routine of moving regularly between government and academic or private sector positions. Not only did the government benefit from the infusion of intellectuals, but scholarly understanding of public administration was expanded dramatically because many of these intellectually inclined individuals, upon returning to the more objective and neutral environment of the university, grasped at the opportunity to thoughtfully consider their experiences as practitioners.

From this group, a quite different view of the public organization emerged, a view that included the bureau and its top managers as active participants— by necessity as well as desire—in the overall public policy process. The idea that politics and administration were separate and autonomous functions was put aside and a more viable theory that recognized the overlap of the two fields became the standard doctrine of public administration. The concepts of efficiency and effectiveness and the belief that public bureaucracies were just like private ones were rethought and enriched by the addition of political theory, both in philosophical terms and in terms of "political system mechanics" and the roles of public organizations and administrators in that process.

At the same time, the demands of the Cold War, space exploration, and technological development in general required a larger and more sophisticated public bureaucracy to carry out the government's work. Even the social programs needed greatly expanded capabilities in information science to keep pace with increased demands for record keeping, much less for any planning or decision making based on the most rudimentary models of facts, trends, and potential outcomes. Thus, when examining public organizations, the theories of the information and decision sciences firmly established themselves as a major component of a required knowledge base.

As the bureaucracy grew in size and scope, and the growth replicated the impact of government on everyone's life, the inevitable occurred: People became distrustful of the organization for which they had clamored. To carry out the functions that the citizens demanded of government, it grew; and as it grew there was increasing fearfulness of big government. Of course, the same phenomenon was occurring throughout society. Even though most organizations were becoming larger and more bureaucratic, people saw largeness in the government as a threat to their everyday lives because government played such a central and visible role, especially at the national level. . . .

PUBLIC ORGANIZATION THEORY TODAY

All of the forces just discussed have led to an intense interest in organization theory as it applies to the public sector bureaucracy, and this discussion is a greatly simplified review of the environment in which both scholars and managers have to work. It is no wonder that a large number of theories has appeared, given the multitude of perspectives from which to examine organizations. In most cases we have a situation similar to that of the group of blind men who examined the elephant. Any one theory about public organizations may appear to be wrong, even ludicrously wrong, at least in part because the theory focuses too closely on one particular aspect of the organization at the expense of the others.

By examining the full range of theories, we can move toward the creation of a set of perspectives useful to public administrators and students of public management. [Some] readers of this [article] are primarily looking for a basis of knowledge that will help them accomplish the daily task of managing public organizations. To accomplish this task, all four perspectives presented in this [article] must be considered, and it is the fourth dimension—the political environment of public management—that is usually missing as organization theory is studied. Likewise, the legal dimension is downplayed in the private sector. While focusing on rationality and efficiency, it is important to recognize that political and economic definitions of these terms may be, and in fact usually are, dramatically varied. An understanding of these differences and how to either bring them together or accept the impossibility of doing so, and discovering ways to survive in the resulting conflictual environment is essential to managing public organizations.

In a similar vein, it is not enough for public managers to know all about the psychological and sociological theories related to complex organizations.

When any attempt is made at application of these theories (and that is the prevalent goal), it is essential to understand the legal and political environment in which that attempt is being made. For example, public managers cannot use all of the methods of motivation that are open to managers in the private sector. Likewise, many other theories about organization, when applied in the public sector, must be adjusted to meet the demands of the general political culture and the specific political actors that are relevant to the bureau in question. Public organization theory must address all four perspectives in the controversy to develop a comprehensive picture of the bureau and how it works.

Notes

1. While the laws specify all the elements of organization mentioned here, it must be understood that the elements may not, indeed cannot, be complete, concise, and clear in many if not most cases.
2. In the public sector, an examination of the testing and selection process for either police or fire department employees will serve as a fine example of the development of, the complexity of, and the challenge to, the idea of tests and measurement as the chief tool for decisions about hiring.
3. Private organizations also must pay attention to the political setting. An example that shows the difficulty that may be caused when two sociopolitical systems are involved is the case of international corporations giving bribes to government officials in foreign countries to gain contracts. Such behavior is a common practice in some countries, but it caused an uproar in the United States and several business officials lost their jobs as a result. They should have been more politically sensitive and astute in their actions. Industries that are regulated by government or that depend on government for much of their business are naturally much more cognizant of the principles of politics and power; however, these are generally seen as *external* factors, only peripherally affecting *internal* operations. . . .
4. While Weber's writings were not translated from German to English until the 1940s, it is probable that the intellectual leaders of the reform movement were familiar with the writings of his intellectual predecessors. Wilson, for example, notes the import of German sociologists on the progressives of his day. It is not possible at this point to debate the questions of intellectual causality and to attempt to decide whether the reform movement was a result of the developments in the social sciences or if the two developed coterminously but independently.

Bibliography

Barnard, Chester. *The Functions of the Executive.* Cambridge, Mass.: Harvard University Press, 1938.

Bentley, Arthur F. *The Process of Government; A Study of Social Pressures.* Chicago: University of Chicago Press, 1908.

Blau, Peter M. *The Dynamics of Bureaucracy.* Chicago: University of Chicago Press, 1955.

Carey, Alex. "The Hawthorne Studies: A Radical Criticism," *American Sociological Review* 32, 1967: 403–16.

Cartwright, Dorwin, and Alvin F. Zander. *Group Dynamics: Research and Theory.* New York: Harper & Row, 1968.

Dahl, Robert. *Who Governs? Democracy and Power in an American City*. New Haven: Yale Univ. Press, 1961.

Dahl, Robert, and Charles E. Lindblom. *Politics, Economics and Welfare: Planning and Politico-Economic Systems Resolved into Basic Social Processes*. New York: Harper, 1953.

Diesing, Paul. *Reason in Society: Five Types of Decisions and Their Social Conditions*. Urbana: Univ. of Illinois Press, 1962

Dye, Thomas R., and Harmon Ziegler. *The Irony of Democracy: An Uncommon Introduction to American Politics*. 6th ed. Monterey, Calif.: Brooks/Cole Publishing, 1984.

French, John R. P., and Bertram Raven. "The Bases of Social Power." In *Studies in Social Power*, ed. Dorwin Cartwright. Ann Arbor, Mich.: Institute for Social Research, 1958: 150–67.

Gulick, Luther H., and Lyndall Urwick, eds. *Papers on the Science of Administration*. New York: Institute of Public Administration, 1937.

Hersey, Paul, and Kenneth H. Blanchard. *Management of Organizational Behavior: Utilizing Human Resources*. 4th ed. Englewood Cliffs, N.J.: Prentice-Hall, 1982.

Hummel, Ralph. *The Bureaucratic Experience*. 2d ed. New York: St. Martin's Press, 1982.

Hunter, Floyd. *Community Power Structure: A Study of Decision Makers*. Chapel Hill: Univ. of North Carolina Press, 1953.

Jacobs, T. O. *Leadership and Exchange in Formal Organizations*. Alexandria, Va.: Human Resources Research Organization, 1971.

Janis, Irving L. *Victims of Groupthink*. Boston: Houghton Mifflin, 1972.

Katz, Daniel, and Robert L. Kahn. *The Social Psychology of Organizations*. 3d ed. New York: John Wiley & Sons, 1982.

Kaufman, Herbert. *The Forest Ranger*. Baltimore: The Johns Hopkins Univ. Press, 1960.

Kernaghan, Kenneth. *Ethical Conduct: Guidelines for Government Employees*. Toronto: Institute of Public Administration, 1975.

March, James, and Herbert A. Simon. *Organizations*. New York: John Wiley & Sons, 1958.

Parsons, Talcott. "Suggestions for a Sociological Approach to the Theory of Organizations." *Adminstrative Science Quarterly* 1, 1956: 63–85.

Peters, Thomas J., and Robert H. Waterman, Jr. *In Search of Excellence: Lessons from America's Best-Run Companies*. New York: Harper & Row, 1982.

Roethlisberger, Fritz J. *Management and Morale*. Cambridge, Mass.: Harvard Univ. Press, 1941.

Rossiter, Clinton, ed. *The Federalist Papers: Alexander Hamilton, James Madison, John Jay*. New York: New American Library, 1961.

Scott, Walter Dill. "How Suggestion Works on the Prospect's Brain." *Advertising & Selling* (May 1914): 11, 59.

Simmons, Robert H. *Achieving Humane Organization*. Malibu, Calif.: Daniel Spencer Publishers, 1981.

Spiro, Herbert. *Responsibility in Government; Theory and Practice*. New York: Van Nostrand Reinhold, 1969.

Stokey, Edith, and Richard Zeckhauser. *A Primer for Policy Analysis*. New York: W. W. Norton, 1978.

Taylor, Federick W. *Principles of Management*. New York: Harper & Row, 1911.

———. *Principles of Scientific Management*. New York: W. W. Norton, 1947.

Thompson, James. *Organizations in Action*. New York: McGraw-Hill, 1967.

Truman, David. *The Governmental Process; Political Interests and Public Opinion*. New York: Alfred A. Knopf, 1951.

Waldo, Dwight. "Organization Theory: Revisiting the Elephant." *Public Administration Review* 38, 1978: 589–97.

Weber, Max. *The Theory of Social and Economic Organization.* Trans. and ed. A. M. Henderson and Talcott Parsons. New York: Oxford Univ. Press, 1947.

Weisband, Edward, and Thomas M. Franck. *Resignation in Protest.* New York: Grossman Publishers/Viking Press, 1975.

Wilson, Woodrow. "The Study of Administration." *Political Science Quarterly* 2 (June 1887): 197–222. In *Classics of Public Administration,* ed. Jay M. Shafritz and Albert C. Hyde. Oak Park, Ill.: Moore Publishing Co., 1978.

Reframing Organizational Leadership

LEE G. BOLMAN
TERRENCE E. DEAL

America's quest for better public organizations is also a plea for better leadership. Whenever an organization is not working, people look for leadership to make it better. Leadership is a hardy perennial that returns season after season to offer hope of reliable and effective ways to improve organizations. Yet the hopes have been repeatedly dashed. Is the promise of leadership illusory? Or have we not yet understood it well enough to bring it to fruition? Despite countless books and studies, no one has developed a widely accepted definition of what leadership is, nor what makes some leaders effective and others ineffectual. Yet Americans remain optimistic:

> For many—perhaps for most—Americans, leadership is a word that has risen above normal workaday usage as a conveyer of meaning and has become a kind of incantation. We feel that if we repeat it often enough with sufficient ardor, we shall ease our sense of having lost our way, our sense of things unaccomplished, of duties unfulfilled. (Gardner, 1985, p. 1)

COMMON-SENSE IDEAS OF LEADERSHIP

In the absence of any consensual view of leadership, a series of common-sense views of leadership have arisen. Debates about which is better confuse leaders and followers alike. The problem is that each view captures only part of what leadership is about.

The most prevalent common-sense conception equates leadership with power: "Leadership is the ability to get others to do what you want." This definition is too broad because it includes coercion and the naked exercise of force, very different from leadership. It is too limited because it omits the art and poetry of leadership: such things as values, vision, and passion.

A second lay definition suggests that leaders "motivate people to get things done." This idea emphasizes persuasion and example rather than force or seduction, and implies that leadership is to be judged by its product. But how do we assess leadership outcomes? Still missing from the definition is the question of purpose and values.

A third definition sees leadership as a participative, democratic process that helps followers to find their own way. Leaders help followers do what *they* want, rather than what the leader wants. This view rejects images of powerful leaders who manipulate sheep-like followers, but it risks turning leaders into weathervanes who simply turn in the direction of the prevailing winds.

A fourth common-sense definition is that "leaders provide a vision." This adds needed elements of meaning, purpose and mission, but it implies that vision is the solitary creation of a brilliant, forward-looking prophet. It also neglects to ask what happens if no one else shares or supports the leader's vision. This definition can be intimidating to potential organizational leaders who wait expectantly for the brilliant flash of insight that will finally free them to lead.

These views are only a sample of existing images of leadership. If this array is not confusing enough, consider the definitions offered by experts, scholars, and famous leaders in Table 5-1. The idea of leadership has survived for centuries, and almost everyone believes that it is important. The public keeps

Table 5-1
Conceptions of Leadership

"Leadership is any attempt to influence the behavior of another individual or group." (Paul Hersey in *The Situational Leader*)

"Managers do things right. Leaders do the right thing." (Warren Bennis and Burt Nanus in *Leaders: Strategies for Taking Charge*)

"Leadership is the ability to decide what is to be done and then get others to want to do it." (Dwight D. Eisenhower)

"Leadership is the process of moving a group in some direction through mostly non-coercive means. Effective leadership is leadership that produces movement in the long-term best interests of the group." (John Kotter in *The Leadership Factor*)

"Leadership is the process of persuasion or example by which an individual (or leadership team) induces a group to pursue objectives held by the leader or shared by the leader and his or her followers." (John Gardner in *On Leadership*)

"Leadership over human beings is exercised when persons with certain motives and purposes mobilize, in competition or conflict with others, institutional, political, psychological, and other resources so as to arouse, engage and satisfy the motives of followers." (James MacGregor Burns in *Leadership*)

"Leadership is a particular kind of ethical, social practice that emerges when persons in communities, grounded in hope, are grasped by inauthentic situations and courageously act in concert with followers to make those situations authentic." (Robert Terry in "Leadership—A Preview of a Seventh View") searching for more of it to solve the great social problems, including those in education. Yet the concept remains shrouded in controversy and confusion. School leaders, like leaders in other sectors, are often bewildered and puzzled. When they look to academics and consultants for help, they encounter a cacophonous chorus that adds to the confusion. In this article, we attempt to decompose the concept of leadership, and to distinguish it from related ideas. Our purpose is to provide a way out of the continuing conceptual confusion and give organizational leaders at least a rough map of the territory. We present several propositions that outline our view of what leadership is, what it is not, and what it might become. Our examples are primarily from education, our principal area of research, but the concepts here are applicable to a wide variety of other public and nonprofit organizations.

1. Leadership and power are not the same.

Most images of leadership suggest that leaders get things done by getting people to do something. Yet powerful people are not always leaders. Armed robbers, extortionists, bullies, traffic cops, prison guards, and used-car dealers all get people to do things, but few would see them as "leaders." We expect leaders to influence noncoercively and to generate cooperative effort toward goals that transcend the leader's narrow self-interest.

2. Leadership is different from authority.

Leadership is also distinct from authority, even though leaders may have authority and authorities may be leaders. In many ways, the concept of authority is as controversial as leadership. Max Weber (1947) linked it to legitimacy. People voluntarily obey authorities when they believe their requests are legitimate and cease to obey if legitimacy is lost. Legitimate authority comes from three sources (Weber, 1947):

a) Traditional—we obey a particular custom or official because our ancestors did

b) Legal-rational—we obey people who hold certain offices, such as school principals, because we believe that they have the right to make decisions, a right based on the premise that the system will work better if we follow their directives

c) Charismatic—we obey a particular person because of an "uncommon and extraordinary devotion of a group of followers to the sacredness or the heroic force or the exemplariness of an individual and the order revealed or created by him" (Weber, 1947, pp. 358–359)

A leader cannot lead without legitimacy. The cooperation that leaders get must be primarily voluntary rather than coerced. But authority refers broadly to the phenomenon of voluntary obedience, including many examples (such as obedience to law) that fall outside the domain of leadership. As Gardner (1985, p. 7) put it, "The meter maid has authority, but not necessarily leadership."

3. Leadership and management are not the same.

One can be a leader without being a manager, and many managers could not "lead a squad of seven-year-olds to the ice cream counter" (Gardner, 1989, p. 2). The fact that managers are *expected* to lead can make it more likely that they will. But many teachers will attest vehemently that, if anyone in their school is providing leadership, "it sure isn't the principal."

Gardner argues against contrasting leadership and management too sharply because of the risk that leaders "end up looking like a cross between Napoleon and the Pied Piper, and managers like unimaginative clods" (Gardner, 1989, p. 3). He suggests several dimensions for distinguishing leadership from management. Leaders think longer-term and look beyond their unit to the larger world. They reach and influence constituents beyond their immediate jurisdictions. They emphasize vision and renewal. They have the political skills to cope with the challenging requirements of multiple constituencies (Gardner, 1989, p. 4).

4. Leadership is not always heroic.

Popular images of John Wayne, Bruce Lee, and Sylvester Stallone provide a distorted, romanticized, male-dominated view of how leaders function. Murphy (1988) wisely calls for recognition of the unheroic side of leadership. We need to recognize that leadership is always situational and relational, and that leaders are often not the most potent or visible force for change or improvement. Leaders may exemplify and represent important values without being flamboyant. Often, their most important and heroic achievement is to recognize and anoint unsung heroes and heroines whose day-to-day actions are the real basis for an organization's success.

5. The demands for leadership vary by context.

Images of the solitary, heroic leader focus too much on the actors and too little on the stage. We often overemphasize the influence of stars and underemphasize the significance of the supporting cast or the people backstage. Against the assumption that "leaders make things happen," it is important to consider the alternative proposition that "happenings make leaders." That proposition is reflected in Figure 5-1.

Requirements for effective leadership differ greatly in different situations. The Chancellor of the New York City Public Schools and the Superintendent of Schools in Cosmos, Minnesota (who is also principal of the district's elementary school) face very different challenges. Brookline High School (in a wealthy suburb of Boston) and Jamaica Plain High School (in inner-city

Figure 5-1

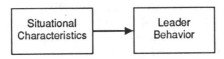

Boston) are about two miles apart geographically, but light years apart in the problems facing their respective principals. No single formula for leadership is possible or advisable for the great range of situations that school leaders encounter.

6. Leadership is relational.

Leadership is often seen as a one-way process: leaders lead and followers follow. In reality, leadership is fundamentally a complex relationship between leaders and their constituents. Despite its many contributions, the "effective schools" tradition has sometimes added to the confusion by emphasizing "strong leadership" from principals, while deemphasizing collegiality and collaboration (Barth, 1990). Even the most sophisticated current models of school leadership typically accept the "one-way" assumption. Ames and Maehr (1989) and Bossert, Dwyer, Rowan, and Lee (1982) present one-way causal models. They depict principals' instructional leadership as a consequence of factors *external* to the school, but solely as an independent variable with respect to *internal* school variables. Such an assumption misleads both research and practice. Cronin (1984) captures this issue well:

> The study of leadership needs inevitably to be linked or merged with the study of followership. We cannot really study leaders in isolation from followers, constituents or group members. The leader is very much a product of the group, and very much shaped by its aspirations, values and human resources. The more we learn about leadership, the more the leader-follower linkage is understood and reaffirmed. A two-way engagement or two-way interaction is constantly going on. When it ceases, leaders become lost, out of touch, imperial, or worse (Cronin, 1984, pp. 24–25).

Experienced public administrators feel and know all too well that leaders are not independent actors, and that their relationship with those they lead is not static. It is a two-way street: leaders both shape and are shaped by their constituents. Leaders often promote a new idea or initiative only *after* large numbers of their constituents already favored it (Cleveland, 1985). Leaders respond to what is going on around them. Their actions generate responses from others that, in turn, affect the leaders' capacity for further influence (Murphy, 1985). Leadership never occurs in a vacuum. It requires an organic relationship between leaders and followers.

7. Leadership is different from position.

It is common to regard "school leadership" and "school administration" as synonymous. Although we look to administrators for leadership, it is both elitist and unrealistic to look *only* to them (Barth, 1988). Assuming that leadership is solely the job of administrators relegates everyone else to the pale and passive role of "follower." It also encourages managers to try to do everything, taking on more responsibility than they can adequately discharge.

Administrators are leaders only to the extent that others grant them cooperation and see them as leaders. Conversely, one can be a leader without holding an administrative position. There are opportunities for leadership from a variety of roles or groups. Good schools are likely to be those that encourage leadership from many quarters (Kanter, 1983; Bolman, Johnson, Murphy, and Weiss, 1990; Murphy, 1990):

> The relationship between teacher and principal is currently under sharp scrutiny. The top-down model is too unwieldy, is subject to too much distortion, and is too unprofessional. Problems are frequently too big and too numerous for any one person to address alone. Schools need to recognize and develop many different kinds of leadership among many different kinds of people to replace the venerable, patriarchal model. While much of the current literature suggests that effective principals are the heroes of the organization, I suspect that more often effective principals enable others to provide strong leadership. The best principals are not heroes; they are hero makers (Barth, 1990, pp. 145–146).

8. Good leaders need the "right stuff."

The last decade has spawned a series of studies of "good leadership," both in education (Brookover and others, 1987; Lezotte and others, 1980) and in the private sector (Bennis and Nanus, 1985; Clifford and Cavanagh, 1985; Conger, 1989; Kotter, 1982, 1988; Kouzes and Posner, 1987; Levinson and Rosenthal, 1984; Maccoby, 1981; Peters and Austin, 1985; Vaill, 1982). The literatures in the two sectors have followed divergent methodological paths, and each has reached somewhat different conclusions.

Research on school leadership has been mostly correlational and based primarily on survey data. Test scores in reading and mathematics have served almost exclusively as the dependent variable (Bossert, 1988; Chubb, 1988; Murnane, 1981; Persell, Cookson, and Lyons, 1982; Rowan, Bossert, and Dwyer, 1983). By comparing schools with similar demographics but dissimilar test scores, researchers have concluded that effective schools are likely to have a principal "who is a strong programmatic leader and who sets high standards, observes classrooms frequently, maintains student discipline, and creates incentives for learning" (Bossert, 1988, p. 346).

The flurry of recent leadership in the private sector consists almost entirely of qualitative studies of organizational leaders, mostly corporate executives. Methodology has varied from casual impressions to systematic interviews and observation. Vision is the one characteristic of effective leadership that is universal across the private-sector reports. Effective leaders help to establish a vision, to set standards for performance, and to create a focus and direction for organizational efforts. While no other characteristic is universal, several appear repeatedly. One that is explicit in some studies (Clifford and Cavanagh, 1985, Kouzes and Posner, 1987, Peters and Austin, 1985) and implicit in most of the others is the ability to communicate a vision effectively to others, often through the use of symbols. Another frequently mentioned characteristic is commitment or passion (Clifford and Cavanagh, 1985; Vaill, 1982; Peters and Austin, 1985). Good leaders care deeply about whatever their organization or group does. They believe that nothing in life is more important than doing something well, and they communicate that belief to others. A third frequently mentioned characteristic is the ability to inspire trust and build relationships (Kotter, 1988, Maccoby, 1981, Bennis and Nanus, 1985). Kouzes and Posner (1987) found that "honesty" came first on a list of traits that managers said they most admired in a leader.

Beyond vision, the ability to communicate the vision, and the capacity to inspire trust, consensus breaks down. The studies cited above, along with extensive reviews of the leadership literature (Bass, 1981; Hollander, 1978; Gardner, 1989), provide a long list of attributes associated with effective leadership: risk-taking, flexibility, self-confidence, interpersonal skills, "managing by walking around," task competence, intelligence, decisiveness, understanding of followers, and courage, to name a few. The problem is that nearly everyone has a different list.

9. School leadership takes place in organizations.

Research on school leadership is often disconnected from research on school organization. Bossert (1988) correctly notes that "a classical model of bureaucratic organization underlies much of the thinking about school effectiveness." Bossert argues for a "multi-level" view of the principal's leadership that emphasizes the leader's role in shaping instructional organization and school climate. Yet, even this view takes only partial account of the significant organizational features affecting school leadership.

Bolman and Deal (1984;1991) argue that organizational research and administrative practice are seriously impaired because scholars and practitioners focus on only one or two of four critical aspects of multidimensional organizations. They propose that organizations need to be understood through four perspectives: structural, human resource, political, and symbolic. The *Structural Frame* emphasizes the importance of formal roles and relationships. Structures—commonly depicted in the form of organization charts—are created to fit an organization's environment and technology. Organizations allocate responsibilities to participants and create rules, policies, and management hierarchies to coordinate diverse activities.

The *Human Resource Frame* starts with the premise that organizations are inhabited by people who have needs, feelings, prejudices, skills, and limitations. They have great capacity to learn, and an even greater capacity to defend old attitudes and beliefs. From a human resource perspective, the key to effectiveness is to tailor organizations to people—finding an organizational form the enables people to get the job done while still feeling good about what they are doing.

The *Political Frame* views organizations as arenas where different interest groups compete for power and scarce resources. Conflict arises because of differences in needs, perspectives, and lifestyles among different individuals and groups. Bargaining, negotiation, coercion, and compromise are all part of everyday life in organizations. Every practitioner knows that politics are a major part of the school leader's job, yet much of the literature on the principalship says little about these issues. Even the intensely political features of the superintendency have been largely ignored by educational researchers (with a few significant exceptions, such as Cuban, 1988). A recent wave of "critical," "postmodern," and "deconstructionist" theory *is* explicitly political, but primarily offers a critique of existing institutions rather than offering guidance to practitioners wondering how to get on with the job in an imperfect world.

The *Symbolic Frame* abandons the assumptions of rationality that appear in the other frames. It treats organizations as tribes, theaters, cathedrals, or carnivals. In this view, organizations are cultures, propelled more by rituals, ceremonies, stories, heroes, and myths than by rules, policies, and managerial authority. Organization is theater: the drama engages actors inside, and outside audiences form impressions based on what they see occurring onstage. Myer and Rowan's (1977, 1978) work on formal structure as myth and ceremony, and Cohen and March's (1974) model of garbage-can decision-making are among the clearest applications of the symbolic frame to educational organizations, but such concepts have only partially been integrated into research and theory on school leadership.

10. Effective leaders are flexible thinkers.

Each of the four organizational frames offers a different view of leadership (summarized in Table 5-2). Structural leadership is reflected in the calls for more attention to instruction (Bossert, 1988). Structural leaders lead through analysis and design rather than charisma and inspiration. Their success depends on developing the right blueprint for the relationship between their school's goals and structure, and on their ability to get that blueprint widely accepted. Successful structural leaders create schools with high expectations and a clear sense of direction. Structural leaders who pay too little attention to other dimensions of organizational life are likely to be dismissed as short-sighted tyrants or insensitive bureaucrats.

Human resource leadership focuses on school climate, interpersonal relationships, and the values of shared governance, participation, and openness. Successful human resource leaders are catalysts and servant leaders. They build organizations whose success derives from highly committed and productive employees. Calls for the principal to build a positive school climate (Bossert, Dwyer, Rowan and Lee, 1982), to create a community of learners (Barth, 1990), and to empower teachers (Johnson, 1989) reflect the human resource view. But it is abundantly clear that many school adminis-

Table 5-2
Reframing Leadership

	Effective Leadership		Ineffective Leadership	
Frame	Leader is:	Leadership Process	Leader is:	Leadership Process
Structural	Social architect	Analysis, design	Petty tyrant	Management by detail and fiat
Human resource	Catalyst, servant	Support, empowerment	Weakling, pushover	Abdication
Political	Advocate	Advocacy, coalition-building	Con artist, hustler	Manipulation, fraud
Symbolic	Prophet, poet	Inspiration, framing experience	Fanatic, fool	Mirage, smoke and mirrors

Source: Adapted from Bolman and Deal, 1991.

trators fear the negative side of this perspective: being labeled as wimp and weakling.

Most practicing school administrators recognize the political nature of the job. A group of big-city superintendents, gathered at a conference at the Harvard Graduate School of Education in early 1989, were asked, "What is the most vexing challenge that you currently face in your job?" Consider some of their responses:

> Getting a board of seven diverse people to become visionaries for the school district, while addressing their own personal and political needs—getting them to recognize that they are leaders for the entire district.

> I thought first of the vexing problem of giving a school board vision, but it's like teaching a pig to sing: the results are poor and it annoys the pig. I think the biggest challenge is the issue of minority achievement. Urban schools catch the dark and the different. I often talk about the relentless intractability of the job. Most of the problems don't seem to have solutions. You're choosing between the lesser of two evils, and that has personal costs.

> One of my critical problems is getting people to love and care for these young people—having high expectations and being committed—and getting various publics to care about these young people, when 70 percent of our population does not have children in the schools.

> My most critical problem is developing a comprehensive vision of what needs to be done to improve schooling in America, and getting stakeholders to buy into it. Having a vision does not help unless stakeholders buy it, add to it, make it their own.

All of those descriptions reflect central dimensions of political leadership: the need to deal with multiple publics with diverse interests and agendas, the ubiquity of conflict, and the problematic nature of the superintendent's capacity to influence. Only a few studies of school leadership have begun to deal with this reality (examples include Blumberg and Greenfield, 1988; Cuban, 1988; Murphy, 1990). Effective political leaders, like many of the superintendents quoted above, know how to develop agendas, build coalitions, and move their organizations forward. But political dynamics play themselves out on an elusive and slippery slope. Less effective or principled political leaders are likely to be seen as manipulators and con artists.

In the private sector, visionary leadership became the great fad of the late 1980s. Like many corporate fads, it seeped rapidly into discussions of school leadership but produced almost no careful discussion of what symbolic leadership is really all about. Several accounts of visionary and charismatic leaders in the private sector have appeared (for example, Carlzon, 1987; Conger, 1989; Kouzes and Posner, 1988), but comparable studies of school leaders are scarce. A few case studies of charismatic school leaders (examples include Lightfoot, 1983; Stahl and Johnson, no date; Kaufer and Leader, 1987a, 1987b) demonstrate that such leaders exist. Much more research is needed on the process by which vision emerges, and on the relationship of symbolic to other elements in leadership. Faith and meaning are central problems in education. The key dilemma for symbolic leaders is how to bring vision and inspiration without being seen as fools or shamans who use smoke and mirrors to create empty hope.

Each of the frames has its own vision or image of reality. Each is incomplete, but each captures a significant and powerful slice of organizational reality. Only when both scholars and practitioners can use all four are they likely to appreciate the depth and complexity of organizational life.

NEW POSSIBILITIES

Leadership is indispensable to significant improvement and reform in America's public schools and many other public agencies. It plays a central role in shaping missions, articulating values, setting directions, and building motivation. Leadership helps people move forward in the face of uncertainty about what to do, disagreement about how to do it, and doubts that it can be done. But leadership is a very challenging and arduous enterprise. When leaders in the public sector look for help on how to lead, they encounter a jangled, cacophonous chorus of ideas. Both academic literature and commonsense ideas about leadership confuse and frustrate highly motivated, well-intentioned administrators who want to do whatever they can to help their organizations succeed.

This article tries to sketch a better map of the terrain of organizational leadership. The map is incomplete, because the territory is only partly charted. We hope that readers can take the map, study it, revise it, fill in some of the gaps, and make it their own. In the process, they will experience both the joy of discovery and the satisfaction of knowing more clearly where they have been and where they might go next. *Far Side* creator Gary Larson once drew a cartoon showing dozens of heavily armed sheriff's deputies and police officers on a manhunt. They enthusiastically follow a single bloodhound who charges forward, nose to the ground, with only one unspoken thought: "I can't smell a damn thing!" School and governmental leaders need better maps. Otherwise, like the bloodhound, they may take a lot of people with them even when they have no idea where they are going. With the help of their colleagues and constituents, leaders will need to find or blaze new paths. Better maps make it easier to know which paths are likely to be roads to hell, and which might lead to the promised land of real and lasting improvement in educational and other public organizations.[1]

Note

1. This article is based in part on the research of the National Center for Educational Leadership, funded under a grant from the Office of Educational Research and Improvement of the U. S. Department of Education. Some ideas in this paper originally appeared in *Reframing Organizations: Artistry, Choice and Leadership* (Bolman and Deal, 1991). We are grateful to our colleagues in NCEL, whose insights and counsel have enriched and expanded the ideas in this paper.

Bibliography

Ames, R. and Maehr, M. A research agenda for the Center for Research and Development on School Leadership. Paper presented at AERA, San Francisco, March, 1989.

Barth, R. "Principals, Teachers, and School Leadership." *Phi Delta Kappan,* **69** (9), May 1988, 639–642.

Barth, R. *Improving Schools from Within.* San Francisco: Jossey-Bass, 1990.

Bass, B. M. *Stogdill's Handbook of Leadership: A Survey of Theory and Research.* New York: Free Press, 1981.

Bennis, W. and Nanus, B. *Leaders: Strategies for Taking Charge.* New York: Harper, 1985.

Blumberg, A. and Greenfield, W. *The Effective Principal: Perspectives on School Leadership.* Boston, MA: Allyn and Bacon, 1988.

Bolman, L. G. and Deal, T. E. *Modern Approaches to Understanding and Managing Organizations.* San Francisco: Jossey-Bass, 1984.

Bolman, L. G. and Deal, T. E. *Reframing Organizations: Artistry, Choice and Leadership.* San Francisco: Jossey-Bass, 1991.

Bolman, L. G., Johnson, S. M., Murphy, J. T., and Weiss, C. H. Re-Thinking School Leadership. Cambridge, Massachusetts: National Center for Educational Leadership, Harvard University, Occasional Paper No. 1, 1990.

Bossert, S. T., Dwyer, D. C., Rowan B. and Lee, G. "The Instructional Management Role of the Principal." *Educational Administration Quarterly,* **18,** 1982, 34–64.

Bossert, S. T. "School Effects." In Boyan, N. J. (Ed.) *Handbook of Research on Educational Administration.* New York: Longman, 1988.

Brookover, W., Bready, C., Flood, P., Schweitzer, J., & Wisenbaker, J. *School Social Systems and Student Achievement: Schools Can Make A Difference.* New York: Praeger, 1987.

Burns, J. M. *Leadership.* New York: Harper, 1978.

Carlzon, J. *Moments of Truth.* Cambridge, MA: Ballinger, 1987.

Chubb, J. E. "Why the Current Wave of School Reform Will Fail." *Public Interest,* **90,** Winter 1988, 28–49.

Cleveland, H. *The Knowledge Executive: Leadership in an Information Society.* New York: Dutton, 1985.

Clifford, D. K. and Cavanagh, R . E. *The Winning Performance.* New York: Bantam Books, 1985.

Cohen, M., and March, J. G. *Leadership and Ambiguity.* New York: McGraw-Hill, 1974.

Conger, J. A. *The Charismatic Leader.* San Francisco: Jossey-Bass, 1989.

Cronin, T. E. "Thinking and Learning about Leadership." *Presidential Studies Quarterly,* 1984, 22–34.

Cuban, L. *The Managerial Imperative and the Practice of Leadership in Schools.* Albany, NY: State University of New York Press, 1988.

Gardner, J. *The Nature of Leadership.* Washington, DC: The Independent Sector, 1985.

Gardner, J. *On Leadership.* New York: Free Press, 1989.

Hersey, P. *The Situational Leader.* New York: Warner, 1984.

Hollander, E. P. *Leadership Dynamics.* New York: Free Press, 1978.

Johnson, S. M. Teachers, power, and school change. Paper presented at Conference on Choice and Control in American Education, University of Wisconsin-Madison, May, 1989.

Kanter, R. M. *The Change Masters.* New York: Simon and Schuster, 1983.

Kaufer, N. and Leader, G. C. "Diana Lam (A)." Boston: Boston University, 1987a.

Kaufer, N. and Leader, G. C. "Diana Lam (B)." Boston: Boston University, 1987b.

Kotter, J. P. *The General Managers.* New York: Free Press, 1982.

Kotter, J. P. *The Leadership Factor.* New York: Free Press, 1988.

Kouzes, J. M. and Posner, B. Z. *The Leadership Challenge: How to Get Extraordinary Things Done in Organizations.* San Francisco: Jossey-Bass, 1987.

Levinson, H., and Rosenthal, S. *CEO: Corporate Leadership in Action.* New York: Basic Books, 1984.

Lezotte, L., Hathaway, D. V., Miller, S. K., Passalacqua, J., & Brookover, W. B. School Learning Climate and Student Achievement: A Social Systems Approach to Increased Student Learning. Tallahassee: The Site Specific Technical Assistance Center, Florida State University Foundation, 1980.

Lightfoot, S. L. *The Good High School.* New York: Basic, 1983.

Maccoby, M. *The Leader.* New York: Ballantine, 1981.

Meyer, J., and Rowan, B. "Institutionalized Organizations: Formal Structure as Myth and Ceremony." *American Journal of Sociology,* **30,** 1977, 431–450.

Meyer, J., and Rowan, B. "The Structure of Educational Organizations." In M. W. Meyer and Associates, *Environments and Organizations: Theoretical and Empirical Perspectives.* San Francisco: Jossey-Bass, 1978.

Murname, R. J. "Interpreting the Evidence on School Effectiveness." Teachers College Record, **83**(1), Fall 1981, 19–35.

Murphy, J., "Preparing school administrators for the twenty-first century: The reform agenda." In B. Mitchell & L. L. Cunningham (Eds.), *Educational Leadership and Changing Contexts of Families, Communities, and Schools,* (the 1990 NSSE yearbook). Chicago: University of Chicago Press, 1990.

Murphy, J. T. *Managing Matters: Reflections from Practice.* Monograph, Harvard Graduate School of Education, Cambridge, Massachusetts, 1985.

Murphy, J. T. "The Unheroic Side of Leadership: Notes from the Swamp." *Phi Delta Kappan,* **69**(9), May 1988, 654–659.

Murphy, J. T. "Searching for Leadership: From Hacksaw to Pogo." *Phi Delta Kappan,* in press.

Persell, C. H., Cookson, P. W., & Lyons, H. "Effective Principals: What Do We Know From Various Educational Literatures?" Paper Prepared for the National Conference on the Principalship, convened by the National Institute of Education, October 1982.

Peters, T. J. and Austin, N. *A Passion for Excellence.* New York: Random House, 1985.

Rowan, B., Bossert, S. T., and Dwyer, D. C. "Research on Effective Schools: a Cautionary Note." *Educational Researcher,* April 1983, 24–31.

Stahl, E. and Johnson, S. M. "The Josiah Quincy School." Cambridge, MA: Harvard Graduate School of Education, no date.

Terry, R. "Leadership: A Preview of a Seventh View." Minneapolis: Humphrey Institute of Public Affairs, University of Minnesota, 1986.

Vaill, P. B. "The Purposing of High-Performance Systems." *Organizational Dynamics,* Autumn 1982, 23–29.

Weber, M. *The Theory of Social and Economic Organization.* Translated by T. Parsons. New York: Free Press, 1947.

What Really Is Public Maladministration?

GERALD E. CAIDEN

Ask people what "public administration" means and either their faces will cloud over or everyone will give a different answer. This question of meaning has always bedeviled the subject and remains unresolved. Yet ask people what is wrong with public administration, i.e., public *mal*administration, there is likely to be an immediate and lively response and the recalling of instances of mistreatment that they personally have experienced or know happened to somebody else. So it should be easier to define public maladministration. Yet, one looks in vain for an extensive treatment in the literature of this obverse side of public administration.

In the United States, this neglect of the obvious may well be because most public arrangements now hum along so well that they are taken for granted and most people do not have to think about them at all, unless they falter. Even so, institutionalized fail-safe procedures kick in for instantaneous correction. Yet every so often, things do go wrong, sometimes horrendously. Malfunctioning goes undetected for too long. The fail-safe devices prove inadequate. No matter how well-performing, somewhere in every administrative system, things are going wrong, mistakes are being made, and justifiable grievances are being ignored.

As administrative practices are part of everyday life in modern society, one would expect that obvious malpractices would be a popular topic among public administrators and that correcting them would be a key concern to researchers. Alas, this has not been the case. Despite major efforts that once in the 1950s went into identifying bureaucratic dysfunctions, there are few studies of particular dysfunctions and no typology of administrative pathologies and morbidities appears in any major text on administration, organization, and management nor even in books that purport to explore the phenomena of counter-productive organizational behavior (Brown, 1987).

IDENTIFYING SELF-DESTRUCTIVE ADMINISTRATIVE BEHAVIOR

As administrative malpractices occur so often, can they be inherent in large-scale administration? Christopher Hood (1974), seeking to classify and explain some of the key mechanisms of such counter-intuitive behavior in British public administration, has identified at least five distinctive types of administrative failure:

- overkill or diseconomy: results are achieved at unnecessary high cost;

- counter productivity: results are contrary to those desired;

- inertia: nothing happens in response to stimulus;
- ineffectiveness: responses evoked merely rearrange inputs and outputs achieving little or nothing; and
- tail chasing: the more is supplied, the more is demanded.

He also identifies:

- under- and over-organization: red-tape (ritualized procedures) and bribery (corruption);
- wastage: revolving door employees;
- big-stick syndrome: self-defeating controls and threats;
- negative demonstration: actions trigger antagonistic or perverse responses;
- time-lags: delayed responses (fighting yesterday's war);
- reorganization: structural changes as symbolic responses, tokenism leaving substance untouched;
- suboptimization: component units defeat overall purpose; conflicting objectives; lack of coordination; and
- professional fragmentation: shuffling problems and costs around.

In a more light-hearted vein, Thomas Martin (1973) consolidated all the then laws of administrative misbehavior (kludgemanship) in the world of bureaucracy (blunderland). He cited gems already assimilated into English managerial parlance such as *Murphy's Laws, Parkinson's Law, The Peter Principle,* and their many corollaries and variations.

More seriously, Robert Kharasch (1973), investigating the laws of institutional behavior (or rather of U.S. federal agency misbehaviors), blunders, and gamesmanship concluded that their malfunctioning was systematic, consistent, and accelerating such that "Our great institutions are out of control" (p. 245). Peter Drucker (1980) came to similar conclusions and stated that "malperformance is increasingly being taken for granted. . . . All we really expect now . . . is more expenditure, a bigger budget, and a more ineffectual bureaucracy" (p. 103). Whereas Kharasch attributed malfunctioning to self-justificatory axioms, Drucker blamed "six deadly sins in public administration":

- giving lofty (unspecified) objectives without clear targets, which could be measured, appraised, and judged;
- doing several things at once without establishing and sticking to priorities;
- believing that "fat is beautiful," i.e., that abundance, not competence, got things done;
- being dogmatic, not experimental;
- failing to learn from experience and feedback; and
- assuming immortality and being unwilling to abandon pointless programs (p. 103).

Whereas Kharasch believed that public organizations were programmed for failure and could be programmed for success, Drucker was more sanguine. Avoiding the sins would not guarantee performance and results, but at least it would be a prerequisite as "most administrators commit most of these 'sins' all the time, and indeed, all of them most of the time" due to the cowardice of practitioners and the lack of concern with performance by theorists.

William Pierce (1981) went further in listing comprehensive types of bureaucratic failure besides malperformance. He listed corruption (theft of materials, misuse of time on the job, bribery, misuse of office, conflicts of interest), misallocation of resources, technical inefficiency (waste, diseconomies, poor management, inappropriate investments, lack of innovation), ineffectiveness (useless activities, quiet ineffectuality, bad advice, egregious errors), subservience to clients, lack of coordination, conflicting objectives, spoils system, displacement of mandated objectives, favoritism, foot-dragging, arbitrariness, and inflexibility. His study was based on 11 cases of administrative failures in U.S. federal government, variously attributed to inadvertent legislation (written without forethought), ambiguous goals, inappropriate sanctions, incompetence, incompatible tasks, interorganizational conflict, defective management, turnover, excessive workload, and haste to spend. He put forward 75 hypotheses, each beginning with "Failure is more likely. . . ."

He went beyond fairly standard American public organization theory by combining these hypotheses within major themes relating to miscommunication, immeasurable outputs, technical difficulties (environmental uncertainty and task complexity), ineffectual coordination, disregard of costs imposed on others, political problems, governmental turbulence, role conflicts, incompetent personnel, nonaccountability, and inappropriate mandates. Presumably all these factors were recipes for administrative disaster if left uncorrected.

Defining Public Maladministration

The breakdowns of individual policies, programs, and organizations do not constitute an indictment of a whole administrative system. They could always be aberrations, although none of the quoted analysts thought so. They implied that whole administrative systems could self-destruct. Studies of postcolonial administrations in several newly independent states had indicated that systemically sick administrations did exist, which caused the societies they served so badly to fail to develop and even deteriorate. Unless they were turned around and turned around quickly, their future was bleak. Montgomery (1966) had gone some way in the mid-1960s to catalogue complaints against such obstructive administrative systems:

> . . . resistance to change, rigid adherence to rules, reluctance to delegate authority, sycophancy toward superiors, "target" mentality, indifference to the standards of efficiency, ignorance of the purposes behind regulations, generalist-elitist orientation combined with hostility toward technology . . . insistence on status and prestige symbols, "formalism" or adherence to traditional relationships while desiring to appear modern; and . . . jobstocking and overstaffing, corruption, xenophobia, and nepotism (p. 262).

But these were often-heard criticisms of public bureaucracies the world over and read remarkably similar to those of William Robson (1964):

. . . an excessive sense of self-importance on the part of officials or an undue idea of the importance of their offices; an indifference towards the feelings or the convenience of individual citizens; an obsession with the binding and inflexible authority of departmental decisions, precedents, arrangements or forms, irrespective of how badly or with what injustice or hardship they may work in individual cases; a mania for regulations and formal procedure; a preoccupation with particular units of administration and an inability to consider the government as a whole; a failure to recognize the relations between the governors and the governed as an essential part of the democratic process (p. 18).

Robson quoted from the 1944 Parliamentary committee on civil service training:

. . . over devotion to precedent; remoteness from the rest of the community, inaccessibility and faulty handling of the general public; lack of initiative and imagination; ineffective organization and waste of manpower; procrastination and unwillingness to take responsibility or to give decisions (p. 18).

Could there be a theory of public maladministration? Although individual administrative maladies have been identified for many centuries, no one has ever tried to combine them systematically. The closest attempt was made by F. H. Hayward (1917) who referred to comon criticisms made of professionalism or the dangers of professionalism or professional depravity. Since government service was also a profession, public administration shared them:

- *perversity*—professionalism became the enemy of the ends which it should serve and resisted innovations;

- *treason*—professionalism opposed the great aims of humanity as a whole in mistaken defense of its own procedures;

- *self-seeking*—professionalism sought to acquire power, privileges or emoluments for itself;

- *cultivation of complexity and jargon*—development and retention of complicated and laborious methods of work and jargon, the tendency to create work and jargon as means of maintaining or expanding professional importance;

- *fear of definiteness*—professionalism opposed definition and preciseness because they would allow standards by which it could be judged;

- *hatred of supervision*—particularly from the uninformed general public;

- *self praise*—vanity, exaggerated claims made for past professional achievements;

- *secrecy*—professionalism resisted prying eyes;

- *uncreativeness*—improvements mostly came from the laity and were opposed by professionals;

- *abuse of power*—professionalism was unchivalrous, tyrannical or cruel towards the weak in its care; and

- *malignity*—professionalism waged a war of slander and spite against innovators, suggesting they were defective, unpractical, weak, unbalanced, without judgment, ignorant, hasty, plagiarizers, and motivated by self-seeking, self-achievement or private gain (Warner, 1947, p. 63–65).

In these respects, public administrators were the same as everybody else, and they were subject to the same failings.

The study of public maladministration as such had to await the spread of the institution of ombudsman from its native Scandinavia into the English-speaking world. Here, after 1960, was an organization established by governments to receive and investigate public complaints against government administration, a veritable gold mine of information about public maladministration. In 1973, Kenneth Wheare (1973) chose maladministration for special study, specifically showing how remedies for maladministration in Europe were superior to those in the United Kingdom. He believed that maladministration was present in all social organization, that the more administration there was, the more maladministration there would be. While maladministration was difficult to define, most people could describe it by examples (illegality, corruption, ineptitude, neglect, perversity, turpitude, arbitrariness, undue delay, discourtesy, unfairness, bias, ignorance, incompetence, unnecessary secrecy, misconduct, and high handedness). The best that could be done was to quote an ombudsman's definition of maladministration: "administrative action (or inaction) based on or influenced by improper considerations or conduct."

Bernard Frank (1976) elaborated on this position in his view of the ombudsman as an office to prevent:

> . . . injustice, failure to carry out legislative intent, unreasonable delay, administrative error, abuse of discretion, lack of courtesy, clerical error, oppression, oversight, negligence, inadequate investigation, unfair policy, partiality, failure to communicate, rudeness, maladministration, unfairness, unreasonableness, arbitrariness, arrogance, inefficiency, violation of law or regulation, abuse of authority, discrimination, errors, mistakes, carelessness, disagreement with discretionary decisions, improper motivation, irrelevant consideration, inadequate or obscure explanation, and all the other acts that are frequently inflicted upon the governed by those who govern, intentionally or unintentionally (p. 132).

Based on actual complaints investigated by the British version of the ombudsman, Geoffrey Marshall (1975) concluded that maladministration was both a matter of instinct and an acquired technique. But the ombudsman office deals only with singular rather than institutionalized instances of maladministration. None of them include crimes committed by people in organizations either on their own behalf against organizational norms (theft, violation of trust, fraud, tax evasion, embezzlement) or at the behest of their organization (genocide, torture, murder, robbery, coercion, terror, intimidation, crimes against humanity, etc.) (Smigel and Ross, 1970).

A novel experiment was tried in the early 1970s at the Institute of Administration at the University of Ife, Nigeria, where 72 Nigerian civil servants wrote case studies of malpractices. Factor analysis pointed to six leading causes preventing initiative—corruption and lack of integrity, community conflict and aggression, inefficiency, sectarian conflict, misconduct and indiscipline, and bad authority relationships. Specific cultural items—"rumor, accusations, denunciations, suspicion, intrigue, threats, blackmail, coercion, malice and inequitable treatment of individuals without cause"—suggested a paranoid personality in "a social climate of pervasive anomie, distrust, and lawlessness" (Bowden, 1976, p. 392). As Yoruba culture was "dysfunctionally distorted toward a schizoid-paranoid form of culture personality," there could be little room for initiative where suspicion, intrigue, and insecurity were combined with the stultifying effect of authoritarianism in which deference was paid to age and rank. Here was a culture of maladministration akin to repressive authoritarianism found throughout history and exemplified in Nazism, Stalinism, and Latin American fascism.

Blaming Bureaucratization

Elsewhere, institutionalized maladministration is not attributed so much to authoritarian cultures or psychotic individuals as to increasing reliance in human arrangements on the bureaucratic form of administration, i.e., the process of bureaucratization. The critics of bureaucratization see it as being inherently defective and a curse on modern society. They dislike bureaucratization altogether or for what it does to society, organizations, and individuals. They object variously to authority, technocracy, meritocracy, materialism, consumerism, capitalism, state power, complexity, mass culture, elitism, large organizations, self-serving administration, impersonality, complexity, legalism, specialization, careerism, formalism, dependency, and anything else they attribute to bureaucratization. They seek to reverse the process of bureaucratization, that is, to turn back the clock to before the organizational society or to advance the clock to a debureaucratized (or postbureaucratic) society, to liberate people from organization, and to eliminate rule by officials, to reduce administration by experts, to minimize public sector administration, and this way to make public organizations less dysfunctional and reduce malpractices by reducing individual dependence on bureaucratic administration.

Bureaucratization, according to critics, has been a wrong step for humanity. To reform bureaucracy, to improve it, to make it work better, would only make things worse. It should be replaced altogether with alternatives that are not so inherently bad (O'Leary, 1988). For a start, big government should be decentralized, public organizations made more representative, self-management encouraged, demarchy (Burnheim, 1985) boosted. Both political extremes want to get rid of the administrative state and bureaucratic government (Peters, 1981). While the Right prefers to rely almost exclusively on private initiatives and market forces, the Left prefers autonomous self-governing communities. Less politically motivated opponents of bureaucratization believe that the process of bureaucratization can be reversed. The rigid hierarchical structure of bureaucracy will eventually be replaced by more flexible, participatory, temporary organizations beyond bureaucracy (Bennis, 1973) as machines replace human labor altogether in the postindustrial world. The adhocracy of the future (Toffler, 1971) will be smaller, less hierarchical, more professional, less routinized, more innovative, providing more creative, meaningful, stimulating work and more collaborative, personalized, responsive management. Computers spell the death of bureaucracy. They will reduce the number of clerical functionaries and blue-collar workers, ensure the accurate dissemination of information, eliminate much job fragmentation, place people into electronic networks, minimize paperwork, decentralize decisionmaking, broaden effective participation, and free people from much bureaucratic maladministration.

Meanwhile, bureaucracy has not declined, and the process of bureaucratization has not been halted. Big has not turned out to be so ugly. On the contrary, as people wake up to their rights all over the world and raise their expectations, so they insist on constitutionalism, rule of law, equal consideration, due process, equity, protection, access, competence, regularity, quality, fairness, responsibility, accountability, openness, and those other factors that have promoted bureaucracy, bureaucratization, and bureaucratic abuses. Undoubtedly some cherished values of the past—self-reliance, individual initiative, independence, integrity, the work ethic, altruism, competitiveness—have suffered in the process of bureaucratization, and bureaucracy has been carried too far in some areas, but this does not mean that other equally cherished values have not gained more and that bureaucracy cannot be readjusted (Hummel, 1982). Yet, there is no denying that bureaucratization carries with it a high propensity for maladministration.

That bureaucracy has inherent dysfunctions has long been known. Its unanticipated dysfunctional consequences have been subject to much sociological analysis. Karl Marx identified the maintenance of the status quo, promotion of incompetence, alienation, lack of imagination, fear of responsibility, and rigid control over the masses. Robert Michels recognized that democratic participation was technically impossible in complex organizations. Max Weber perceived that bureaucracy threatened democracy by demanding the sacrifice of freedom. But it was Robert Merton (1936) in the 1930s who first emphasized dysfunctions that impeded effectiveness when conflicting or displacing organizational goals, i.e., means became ends in themselves. He later identified rigidity, while Selznick (1949) added bifurcation of interests and Gouldner (1954) punitive supervision. These and other dysfunctions (mediocrity, officiousness, stratification, gamesmanship) sabotaged bureaucracy.

Studies of over-bureaucratized organizations such as multinational corporations, armed forces, prisons, legal systems, mail services, and welfare agencies indicate how the functional elements of bureaucracy—specialization, hierarchy, rules, managerial direction, impersonality, and careerism—if overdone turn dysfunctional and counter productive, alienating employees and clients. Its virtues become vices. Whereas specialization was supposed to increase production, too much specialization entailed dull, boring, routine soul-destroying work that brought about careless performance, soldiering and sabotage, which resulted in low productivity. Similarly, reliance on written rules led to excessive red-tape and legalism that actually resulted in goal displacement, group norm substitution, corruption, and discrimination. The career service concept, which was supposed to ensure competence, could result in narrow-minded, time-serving mediocrities. An organization can start out with all the virtues of bureaucracy and soon decline with all its vices, a process which James Boren (1975, p. 7) described as *mellownization* "as dynamic action is replaced by dynamic inaction."

Jack Douglas (1989) believes that contemporary bureaucracies go through cycles similar to those experienced by ancient dynasties. They begin dynamically and grapple with real problems directly, simply, and successfully. They have vigorous administration and entrepreneurial bureaucrats uplifted with ideas and bounding confidence bending the rationalistic, legalistic forms to achieve their goals. Because they work or work better than any predecessors, people demand more and get hooked on entrepreneurial bureaucracy. They

grow, adopt increasingly formal-rational methods of recruitment and administration and become increasingly distant from the people, and stifling. Their
efficiency declines and they subvert their resources and power, becoming corrupt and usurpatory, succumbing to machinations that eventually give way to
self-serving, change resistant, devious, ineffective, and corrupt bureaucrats.
They decline into bureaucratic factionalism, inertia, "the fluorescence of (useless) reform movements" (that mostly rationalize their appeals for more
power, money, and personnel), irresponsibility, and self-directing fiefdoms,
invoking rebellion by the populace and conquest by new entrepreneurial
bureaucrats who repeat the cycle. He compared the dynamism of the
Roosevelt New Deal social welfare bureaucrats such as Harry Hopkins with
contemporary social welfare agencies:

> . . . some of the bureaucrats are still dedicated, at least when they begin, but they
> soon burn out from the immensity of the rules, the relative inflexibility of the regu-
> lations, and the apparent uselessness and unprofitability of all their
> efforts. . . . Careerism, alienation, factionalism, inefficiency, and displacement of
> goals are their most important products (Douglas, 1989, pp. 407–408).

He largely blamed the informational pathologies inherent in bureaucracy,
such as the divorce of income from expenditure and inputs from outputs, the
lack of marketing price and profit signals, the absence of proportioned feedback, information distortions and blockages, the emphasis on conformity, the
propensity for sabotage, hyperinflexibility, elongated chains of command,
enfeudation, conspiracy to defraud and deceive, disinformation, and sheer
size. But they are not the only bureaupathologies that attack public administration.

BUREAUPATHOLOGIES

These vices, maladies, and sicknesses of bureaucracy constitute bureaupathologies. They are not the individual failings of individuals who compose organizations but the systematic shortcomings of organizations that cause
individuals within them to be guilty of malpractices. They cannot be corrected by separating the guilty from the organization for the malpractices
will continue irrespective of the organization's composition. They are not
random, isolated incidents either. Although they may not be regular, they
are not so rare either. When they occur, little action is taken to prevent
their recurrence or can be taken as in the case of anorexia (debilitation) and
gattopardismo (superficiality) (Dunsire and Hood, 1989). They are not just
physical either; organizations also suffer definite mental illnesses or neuroses
too—paranoid, compulsive, dramatic, depressive, and schizoid (deVries and
Miller, 1985).

Altogether, some 175 or so common bureaupathologies are listed in
alphabetical order for convenience (see Table 5-3). They are the most frequently found and identifiable. Any public organization that claims to be free
of them is remarkable and probably deceiving itself. All mar performance but
none prevent a public organization performing, although if left uncorrected
for any length of time and institutionalized, they will eventually cripple the

organization and give rise to serious public complaint. Each is fairly easily defined and can be readily identified. Each has its own peculiarities. Each has different origins, takes different forms, has different effects and consequences, and each has to be tackled differently. Taken together, they constitute a checklist for organizational diagnosticians, a checklist that is by no means exhaustive but should cover most administrative malpractices.

These common bureaupathologies can be variously grouped and classified as to administrative activity, external or internal cause, extent of organizational collusion, symptoms, and so forth and could be mapped or arranged similar to a Gray's anatomy of public organizations if such a compendium could be devised and universally accepted. Like diseases of the body, some are quite similar but each is distinct and takes slightly different forms. Some are simple but others are quite complicated. Contrast "account padding" with corruption. Account padding is claiming more expenses than actually incurred. It can or cannot be fairly common practice in an organization to which a blind eye is turned because it costs too much to control, or accuracy is impossible, or the organization needs to build a hidden reserve to cover unexpected contingencies that are bound to occur, or it is criminally motivated and the organization is being deliberately exploited by its members at public expense. It could be corrupt; however, corruption takes on so many forms of which account padding is only a symptom of something much more sinister, hidden, conspiratorial, and immoral if not illegal and certainly dysfunctional. The way one would tackle *paperasserie* (too much paperwork) is quite different from tunnel vision, or tokenism, or ineptitude, or empire-building, or sabotage. The only thing they all have in common is that they run counter to correct administrative norms, or what public administrators believe they ought to practice.

Possibly, the greatest obstacle for public administrators to overcome is that of organizational complacency and inertia. Bureaupathologies often create a comfortable, serene, and relaxed atmosphere in which work is performed after a style and everything on the surface looks fine (Levin, 1970; Warwick, 1975). But dig below the surface, as ombudsman and whistleblowers reveal, and maladies abound and persist. The people in the diseased organization agree that what is being done is unsatisfactory and capable of considerable improvement. As individuals, they all welcome change and reform. They may even be agreed on the specific changes they would like to see made. Plans may have been made, guidelines readied, staff prepared, but they are still waiting for a more opportune moment that never seems to arrive. Or they have kept abreast of discoveries in their field and are keen to try some new ideas. But nobody is prepared to take the first step and the same ideas are discussed repeatedly without any action being taken. Or some people do take upon themselves the responsibility for initiating change and design suitable, feasible, doable proposals, which they know beforehand are acceptable. But they never hear again what happened to their proposals. Nobody knows why. They have been lost in the works.

In such inert organizations, the people are not lazy. On the contrary, they work hard and keep busy coping with daily demands. Everybody appears to be fully occupied, carrying out their set tasks and observing the directions issued to them. Each is loyal to the organization, each approves of its mission,

Table 5-3

Common Bureaupathologies

Abuse of authority/ power/position	Favoritism	Lack of coordination	Red-tape
Account padding	Fear of change, innovation, risk	Lack of creativity/ experimentation	Reluctance to delegate
Alienation	Finagling	Lack of credibility	Reluctance to take decisions
Anorexia	Footdragging	Lack of imagination	Reluctance to take responsibility
Arbitrariness	Framing	Lack of initiative	Remoteness
Arrogance	Fraud	Lack of performance indicators	Rigidity/brittleness
Bias	Fudging/fuzzing (issues)	Lack of vision	Rip-offs
Blurring issues	Gamesmanship	Lawlessness	Ritualism
Boondoggles	Gattopardismo (superficiality)	Laxity	Rudeness
Bribery	Ghost employees	Leadership vacuums	Sabotage
Bureaucratese (unintelligibility)	Gobbledygook/jargon	Malfeasance	Scams
Busywork	Highhandedness	Malice	Secrecy
Carelessness	Ignorance	Malignity	Self-perpetuation
Chiseling	Illegality	Meaningless/make work	Self-serving
Coercion	Impervious to criti- cism/suggestion	Mediocrity	Slick bookkeeping
Complacency	Improper motivation	Mellownization	Sloppiness
Compulsiveness	Inability to learn	Mindless job per- formance	Social astigmatism (failure to see problems)
Conflicts of interest/ objectives	Inaccessibility	Miscommunication	Soul-destroying work
Confusion	Inaction	Misconduct	Spendthrift
Conspiracy	Inadequate rewards and incentives	Misfeasance	Spoils
Corruption	Inadequate working conditions	Misinformation	Stagnation
Counter- productiveness	Inappropriateness	Misplaced zeal	Stalling
Cowardice	Incompatible tasks	Negativism	Stonewalling
Criminality	Incompetence	Negligence/neglect	Suboptimization
Deadwood	Inconvenience	Nepotism	Sycophancy
Deceit and deception	Indecision (decidophobia)	Neuroticism	Tail-chasing
Dedication to status quo	Indifference	Nonaccountability	Tampering
Defective goods	Indiscipline	Noncommunication	Territorial imperative
Delay	Ineffectiveness	Nonfeasance	Theft
Deterioration	Ineptitude	Nonproductivity	Tokenism
Discourtesy	Inertia	Obscurity	Tunnel vision
Discrimination	Inferior quality	Obstruction	Unclear objectives
Diseconomies of size	Inflexibility	Officiousness	Unfairness
Displacement of goals/objectives	Inhumanity	Oppression	Unnecessary work
Dogmatism	Injustice	Overkill	Unprofessional conduct
Dramaturgy	Insensitivity	Oversight	Unreasonableness
Empire-building	Insolence	Overspread	Unsafe conditions
Excessive social costs/complexity	Intimidation	Overstaffing	Unsuitable premises and equipment
Exploitation	Irregularity	Paperasserie	Usurpatory
Extortion	Irrelevance	Paranoia	Vanity
Extravagance	Irresolution	Patronage	Vested interest
Failure to acknowl- edge/act/answer/ respond	Irresponsibility	Payoffs and kickbacks	Vindictiveness
	Kleptocracy	Perversity	Waste
	Lack of commitment	Phony contracts	Whim
		Pointless activity	Xenophobia
		Procrastination	
		Punitive supervision	

each is keen to do a good job. All are aware of its shortcomings and deficiencies. They know of its mistakes and errors and can recount horror stories they know about. Between them, they have a pretty good idea how it can be improved, and they personally are willing to try something different to improve its performance. Yet, somehow nothing changes. The same old patterns and routines are preserved; the shortcomings and deficiencies are perpetuated; mistakes and errors are repeated. When the organization does change, it moves slowly, incrementally, predictably, and then not always in the right direction.

Such inert organizations fail to adjust in time to changes in their environment. They become insensitive to criticism. They appear not to know or want to know what is really going on. Everything stays pretty much the same. Nobody knows why. Nobody admits responsibility. Nobody confesses error. Nobody ends wrongdoing. It is as if the organization has a mind of its own, a mind closed to any other way of doing things. In fact, by failing to anticipate, recognize, avoid, neutralize, or adapt to pressures that threaten their long-term survival, inert organizations are in a serious state of decline, threatening enormous social repercussions to the economy and society and to the individuals dependent on them for products and services and jobs (Weitzel and Jonnson, 1989). A good shake-up may suffice to reinvigorate them, but already they may be too blind to recognize threats, too inert to decide on a remedial course of action, too incompetent to make and implement the right actions, too crisis ridden to accept the need for major reform, and perhaps even too far gone to save. This truly is public maladministration in extremis. Although by no means confined to the public sector, it is the kind of public maladministration that lowers the reputation of public administration and leaves a bad taste in people's mouths. The first step to reform and improvement is to admit bureaupathologies and take them seriously. Otherwise, public maladministration will persist and continue to damage.

Bibliography

Bennis, W. 1973. *Beyond Bureaucracy*. New York: McGraw-Hill.

Boren, J. 1975. *Have Your Way With Bureaucrats*. Radnor, PA: Chilton Book Co.

Bowden, E. 1976. "Maladministration: A Thematic Analysis of Nigerian Case Studies in the Context of Administrative Initiative." *Human Organization*, vol. 35 (Winter), p. 392.

Brown, D. 1987. *Management's Hidden Enemy and What Can Be Done About It*. Mt. Airy, MD: Lomond.

Burnheim, J. 1985. *Is Democracy Possible?* Cambridge: Polity Press.

deVries, F. R. Kets and D. Miller. 1985. *The Neurotic Organization*. San Francisco: Jossey Bass Publishers.

Douglas, J. 1989. *The Myth of the Welfare State*. New Brunswick, NJ: Transaction Publishers.

Drucker, P. 1980. "The Deadly Sins in Public Administration." *Public Administration Review*, vol. 40 (March/April), p. 103.

Dunsire, A. and C. Hood. 1989. *Cutback Management in Public Bureaucracies*. Cambridge: University of Cambridge Press.

Frank, B. 1976. "The Ombudsman and Human Rights Revisited." *Israel Yearbook on Human Rights*, vol. 6, p. 132.

Gouldner, A. W. 1954. *Patterns of Industrial Bureaucracy.* Glencoe, IL: Free Press.
Hayward, F. H. 1917. *Professionalism and Originality.* London: Allen & Unwin.
Hood, C. 1974. "Administrative Diseases: Some Types of Dysfunctionality in Administration." *Public Administration,* vol. 52 (Autumn), pp. 439–454.
Hummel, R., 1982. *The Bureaucratic Experience.* New York: St. Martin's Press.
Kharasch, R. N. 1973. *The Institutional Imperative.* New York: Charterhouse Books.
Levin, A. 1970. *The Satisficers.* New York: McCall Publishing Company.
Marshall, G. 1975. "Technique of Maladministration." *Political Studies,* vol. 23, pp. 305–310.
Martin, T. 1973. *Malice in Blunderland.* New York: McGraw-Hill.
Merton, R. 1936. "The Unanticipated Consequences of Purposive Social Action." *American Sociological Review,* vol. 1, pp. 894–904.
———. 1940. "Bureaucratic Structure and Personality." *Social Forces,* vol. 18, pp. 560–568.
Montgomery, J. and W. J. Siffin, eds. 1966. *Approaches to Development: Politics, Administration and Change.* New York: McGraw-Hill.
O'Leary, B. 1988. "The Limits to Bureaucide: A Critical Analysis of Three Visions of Debureaucratization." Paper presented to the Round Table on Administration Without Bureaucracy. International Institute of Administrative Sciences, Budapest.
Peters, B. G. 1981. "The Problems of Bureaucratic Government." *Journal of Politics,* vol. 43 (Feburary), pp. 56–82.
Pierce, W. S. 1981. *Bureaucratic Failure and Public Expenditure.* New York: Academic Press, Harcourt Brace Jovanovich.
Robson, W. 1964. *The Governors and the Governed.* London: Allen & Unwin.
Selznick, P. 1949. *T.V.A. and the Grass Roots.* Berkeley: University of California Press.
Smigel, E. O. and H. L. Ross, eds. 1970. *Crimes Against Bureaucracy.* New York: Van Nostrand Reinhold Co.
Toffler, A. 1971. *Future Shock.* New York: Bantam Books.
Warner, R. 1947. *The Principles of Public Administration.* London: Pitman, pp. 63–65.
Warwick, D. 1975. *A Theory of Public Bureaucracy.* Cambridge: Harvard University Press.
Weitzel, W. and E. Jonnson. 1989. "Decline in Organizations: A Literature Integration and Extension." *Administrative Science Quarterly,* vol. 34, pp. 91–109.
Wheare, K. 1973. *Maladministration and Its Remedies.* London: Stevens & Sons.

6

PUBLIC PERSONNEL MANAGEMENT AND LABOR RELATIONS

In government, we really have *three* public personnel systems: the patronage system, based on political appointments to positions; the merit or civil service system, designed to employ the ablest in public jobs; and the labor relations or collective bargaining system, the most recent.

Most public employees in America are employed under a merit system. The concept of a merit system is really quite elitist, suggesting that citizens prefer "the best and the brightest" individuals to be employed in government.

The determination "where to draw the line" between patronage and merit systems is always difficult, and there is almost always conflict between the staffing purposes of political groups and civil service systems. Official contempt for the civil service and federal civil servants probably reached its height under President Nixon, when there was a conscious effort to subvert the federal civil service system.

What constitutes a modern merit personnel system? The U.S. Office of Personnel Management suggests two dozen elements for any governmental jurisdiction of about five hundred employees or more. These are:

Provision for *equal employment opportunity applicable to all personnel actions* without regard to political affiliation, race, color, national origin, sex, age, religious creed, marital status, or physical handicap.

A plan for systematic *job analysis* involving collecting data and making certain judgments about the nature of individual jobs to provide a basis for such things as classifying positions, developing minimum qualification requirements, constructing job-related tests, identifying training needs, and reviewing individual performance. Job analysis is a major component of affirmative action for equal employment opportunity. The courts have specifically cited job analysis as a required basis for qualification standards and written tests.

Grouping or classification of positions by occupation according to similarities or differences in duties, responsibilities, and qualification requirements.

238

A realistic *pay system* tied to sound job analysis and position classification, which assures equity within the system and comparability with pay offered by other employers in the same labor market area for similar work.

Job-related *minimum qualification requirements* which describe the nature and amount of experience, training, knowledge, and skills needed for successful performance as well as a means for determining that applicants possess such requirements.

Recruiting, examining, rating certification, and selection procedures which reach all parts of the labor market; which apply the established qualification requirements in a fair, job-related fashion in testing and selecting the best-qualified persons from among all eligible candidates; and which make special affirmative action provisions for assuring equal opportunity to members of minority groups, women, and those disadvantaged by educational, economic, physical, or social handicaps.

A *placement* system which not only assures the sound initial placement of new employees but also provides for follow-up and for remedial placements.

An adequate *probationary period* which must be satisfactorily completed before permanent tenure or status is conferred.

A continuing *performance evaluation* system providing employees and managers feedback aimed at strengthening employee and oarganizational performance.

An *incentive awards* program which provides recognition for exceptional performance and successful ideas for improving operations.

A *training and career development program* which, among other things, fills the gaps between the qualifications required for the positions in question and the qualifications possessed either by employees already in or on the career ladder for such positions or by outside candidates for such positions; which prepares employees to meet the future needs of the public service; and which keeps the public service up-to-date in its use of modern techniques, technology, and equipment.

A *promotion* system which provides for fair and objective consideration of eligible employees for the promotion opportunities which arise; and which assures that selection for promotion is job-related and based on merit, not political or personal patronage or racial or other favoritism.

Provision for lateral *transfers and reassignments* of employees among different agencies or parts of agencies, and for *details and temporary duty* assignments to meet short-term needs.

Provision for *reprimands, suspensions, demotions, and removals* of employees for disciplinary reasons or unsatisfactory performance.

Objective and effective *appeals and grievance* systems for employees.

A *labor-management relations* provision which enables employees to be involved in personnel policies and practices affecting their employment consistent with merit principles, the preservation of management rights, and the protection of the public interest.

An orderly and fair method of making necessary *cutbacks in the work force* due to budget reductions, decrease in workload, reorganizations, or other reasons.

Fringe benefits, such as *age and disability retirement, group life and health insurance, vacation and sick leave, paid holidays, and employees' compensation for job-connected injuries and sickness.*

An *occupational safety and health program* and provision for employee counseling and guidance services.

A statutory or executive code of *ethical conduct* for all public service personnel which includes prohibitions against conflict of interest, nepotism, and political coercion.

A system of *policy, regulatory, and operational issuances* published by the central personnel agency for the direction and guidance of employing agencies of the government.

A system of *personnel records, reports, and statistics* as needed for legal or personnel management purposes.

Provision for *personnel planning, overall program planning, and continuing program evaluation* which recognizes the critical role of effective personnel management in the delivery of government services to the public.

A sound basic *public personnel law*, positive *support from top management, adequate financial resources* for essential operations, *and competent professional personnel staffs* both in the central personnel agency and in the line departments.

However, merit goals have not always brought meritorious results. There are many critics of contemporary civil service procedures—federal, state, and local. They claim that there is little scientifically supportable evidence that many civil service examinations are directly related to later on-the-job performance, that too much job security for public employees limits managerial effectiveness, that past performance receives too little credit for promotions as opposed to the reliance on written examinations, and that salary increases are virtually automatic, thereby eliminating an important possible incentive for improved performance. To this some critics would add that collective bargaining systems in state and local government have the tendency to reinforce some of the worst aspects of civil service systems.

In this chapter's first article, Patricia Ingraham and David Rosenbloom look at the condition of the federal government's merit personnel system. They provide a short history of the civil service and then examine hiring, classification and pay, and training. They also examine relevant court rulings and the meaning of "merit" in the federal government.

Collective bargaining in government in this country is usually dated from 1954 in New York City and from 1959 in Wisconsin, which was the first state to authorize public employees to organize and bargain collectively.

Especially when there are strikes—legal or illegal—we are aware that collective bargaining plays an important role in personnel management and in public administration generally, especially at the state and local levels.

Labor-management relations in the federal government have changed a great deal since 1962, when President Kennedy fulfilled a campaign promise by allowing federal employees to organize unions. Today, as a result of the Civil Service Reform Act of 1978, the Federal Labor Relations Authority monitors federal bargaining activity. In 1981 President Reagan took a strong stand against a strike by the Professional Air Traffic Controllers Organization (PATCO), which was stripped of its right to represent air traffic controllers.

However, it is principally at the state and local levels that this relatively recent phenomenon has had its greatest impact. Public employees are often highly organized and exert considerable political clout, although under conditions of fiscal stress they appear to be less influential.

Collective bargaining, particularly by state and local employees, is the topic of this chapter's second article. Joel Douglas focuses on the compatibility between collective bargaining systems and merit systems in the 1990s.

In an increasingly diverse country, managing diversity is a topic of growing importance. Beyond affirmative action and equal employment opportunity, Walter Broadnax tells us it is critical in the 1990s to appreciate and value diversity in public administration. Broadnax recounts the State of New York's experience with diversity; he is the former head of the State of New York's civil service system.

Finally, there is an increasing awareness of the problems of gender in the workplace, the "glass ceiling" for women executives, and even the problems of men and women just talking to one another. No gender issue has received greater public attention in recent years than sexual harassment. In the fourth article, Rita Mae Kelly and Phoebe Stambaugh synthesize what is known about sexual harassment and explore its prevalence and impact in five states, including Arizona, their own state.

Personnel issues are some of the most important in public administration. A few of the questions raised here are:

- Ingraham and Rosenbloom conclude that "neither the essential definition of merit nor fundamental merit principles is clear" today. If the Pendleton Act was approved in 1883 and the Civil Service Reform Act passed in 1978, how can that be?

- What effect does collective bargaining have on merit personnel systems? On public sector supervisors?

- Whether it is women or members of diverse racial and ethnic groups, why are diversity and especially managing with diversity such troublesome issues in America today? How can we do better? Why is it important?

The State of Merit in the Federal Government

PATRICIA W. INGRAHAM
DAVID H. ROSENBLOOM
(with the research assistance of
JOHN P. KNIGHT)

> The merit system, by raising the character and capacity of the subordinate service, and by accustoming the people to consider personal worth and sound principles, rather than selfish interest and adroit management as the controlling elements of success in politics, has also invigorated national patriotism, raised the standard of statesmanship, and caused political leaders to look more to the better sentiments and the higher intelligence for support.
>
> The Eaton Report to President Rutherford B. Hayes, 1879

THE PROBLEM

For over one hundred years, the American civil service has been guided by merit principles. Those principles, underpinning a system intended to protect federal employment and employees from partisan politics, were simple and direct: fair and open competition for federal jobs, admission to the competitive service only on the basis of neutral examinations, and protection of those in the service from political influence and coercion. The system that has grown from these principles, however, is not simple and direct. Today, rules and regulations related to federal personnel administration fill thousands of pages. Today, the federal government's merit system *does not work*. These procedures have created a system in which the recruitment, testing, and hiring of employees is often conducted independently of those who will manage and be responsible for the employees' performance. The personnel function is often viewed independently—indeed, often in isolation—from management concerns and priorities. Many continue to define merit only in terms of entrance to the federal service through centralized neutral and objective examinations, but in a diverse and complex society, tests alone are not an accurate measure of merit. It is abundantly clear that the construction and administration of such examinations create as many problems as they solve. Many federal managers argue that the time spent trying to understand the system overshadows whatever benefits the merit system provides.

In 1978, President Jimmy Carter declared that there was "no merit in the merit system." Others have argued that there is no system in the merit system. Incremental laws and procedures, accumulating over a one-hundred-year period, have created a jerrybuilt set of rules and regulations whose primary emphasis is on negative control of federal personnel, rather than on a positive affirmation of merit and quality in the federal service. The design of a system intended to screen large numbers of applicants for a limited number of positions is outdated and inappropriate for contemporary technology and the changing demographics of the twenty-first century. The elimination of the discriminatory Professional and Administrative Career Examination (PACE) in 1982 demonstrated how entrance procedures should not look, but failed to specify how they should. The gradual accretion of often conflicting objectives, rules, and regulations has created, not a coherent national system of merit, but a confusing maze of procedure. At the same time, the long-term effectiveness of the federal government rests on the ability to recruit and retain a quality workforce. The many restrictive components of the contemporary merit system severely inhibit that ability. Merit has come to signify a narrow and negative focus on positions and jobs, rather than competence, accountability, and effective public service.

It is not the intent of this article to propose or endorse specific reforms, although there are many. Instead, the purpose is to describe the disjointed evolution and current state of the federal merit system—the status quo from which future reforms must proceed. Very clearly, those reforms cannot build on a clear and coherent foundation, for no such foundation exists. Future reforms, therefore, must address fundamental questions: What does "merit" mean for contemporary federal personnel administration?[1] What are the critical components of a merit system for the future? Is it possible to replace rules and regulations with flexibility and discretion for federal personnel, but still to ensure accountability and responsiveness to the public and to elected officials? Without this fundamental analysis, current proposals for reform may only contribute to the system's baggage; the ability of the federal government to be an effective and competitive employer will not be addressed.

THE ORIGINS

The passage of the Pendleton Act in 1883 began the process of creating a civil service based on merit for the American national government. Strongly anchored in the experience of the British civil service, the American system nonetheless reflected uniquely American politics and government. The public excesses of the patronage system were viewed as a national disgrace and as a serious burden on the presidency. The assassination of President James Garfield by a demented office seeker dramatically demonstrated the problem. The glut of office seekers in Washington and their constant demands on the president and his staff created other problems; they reportedly led President Abraham Lincoln to request, when he contracted smallpox, that all the office seekers be sent to him, for "now I have something I can give to each of them."[2]

The passage of the legislation reflected political realities as well. There were strong civil service leagues in many states. They had successfully placed personnel reform on the agenda for the 1882 congressional elections. The support expressed for reform in those midterm elections ensured that it would become a national issue. Political demands, however, were tempered by a serious constitutional question: Did the creation of a centralized personnel system and Civil Service Commission violate the powers of both the president and Congress over personnel matters?[3]

The dilemma posed by the political need to act and questions of constitutional legitimacy produced a classically political solution: The initial legislation covered only 10 percent of the federal workforce. But Congress granted the president power to include additional federal employees in the classified civil service by Executive Order. Patronage would be controlled, but slowly. Van Riper notes, "If the act permitted an orderly retreat of parties from their prerogatives of plunder, it made possible as well the gradual administrative development of the merit system."[4]

At the heart of the new merit system was one fundamental principle: Admission to the classified civil service would be *only* through open competitive examinations. Unlike the British system, which relied on formal academic training, the American system hailed the practical American spirit; the examinations would focus on common sense, practical information, and skills. The examination system would be designed to provide all who desired federal employment a fair, equal, and objective opportunity to enter the civil service. The act created decentralized Boards of Examiners to administer the tests and specified that they "be so located as to make it reasonably convenient and inexpensive for applicants to attend before them."[5]

The American system also differed from its British heritage in its definition and treatment of neutrality. Very clearly, political neutrality was to be a hallmark of the new classified civil service. The need for a competent civil service that would serve either political party well was widely accepted. At the same time, neither members of Congress, the president, nor the reformers were willing to commit to the British tradition of an elite higher civil service whose members were active participants in policy debates. Policy participation was not viewed as a legitimate administrative function. For the American civil service, neutrality was a protection against politics, but also an exclusion from policy. Herbert Kaufman offered the following assessment: "the civil service was like a hammer or a saw; it would do nothing at all by itself, but it would serve any purpose, wise or unwise, good or bad, to which any user put it."[6]

THE GROWTH OF THE CLASSIFIED SERVICE

The origins of the merit system in the federal government are important for a number of reasons. First, because the system had a purposefully limited beginning, growth could, and did, occur in an unplanned and unpredictable way. Second, the system was formed in a way designed to gather the largest possible number of applicants for a limited number of government jobs. The "fair and open competition" principle was interpreted from the outset to be national competition for what were then largely Washington-based jobs (postmasters were not included in the original legislation). The system was, in short, designed to be a screening system and was based on the fundamental assumption that there would be many more job seekers than jobs. Further, since most positions would be in Washington, centralizing the personnel function within the Civil Service Commission made good sense. Third, despite the emphases on objective merit and free and open competition, the Pendleton Act included provisions whose intent and impact was to attenuate those emphases. The act specifically noted, for example, that veterans were to continue to be given preference in federal hiring, a practice that had been formally established in 1865. In addition, the Pendleton Act reaffirmed the nation's commitment to a geographically "representative" federal workforce, an emphasis first articulated during George Washington's presidency. Merit, veterans' preference, and geographic representativeness did not necessarily coincide, even in 1883. In the ensuing years, veterans' groups, in particular, have often pursued objectives clearly at odds with those of federal personnel experts and managers.

Finally, the provision for presidential determination of increased coverage did not remove politics from the development of the civil service system; instead, it ensured that the growth of "merit" would be dependent on political cycles. Presidents who chose to extend the merit system often came under attack from their own parties for doing so; each extension of civil service coverage meant fewer patronage appointments and fewer payoffs for party loyalty. As a result, commitment by presidents to merit and the classified civil service fluctuated dramatically in the early years. Generally, presidents such as Theodore Roosevelt (also a former civil service commissioner) who succeeded a president of their own party found advancing merit to be somewhat easier than those who did not. President William McKinley, for example, included 1700 additional employees in the classified service by Executive Order, but also exempted about 9,000 employees through rollback and new exemption procedures.[7] Woodrow Wilson took the reins of a federal government that had been controlled for sixteen years by Republicans. Despite his association with the National Civil Service Reform Association, the Wilson administration was under intense pressure for patronage. President Wilson said of this pressure, "The matter of patronage is a thorny path that daily makes me wish I had never been born."[8]

Congress, too, retained a keen interest in patronage. As new governmental tasks and functions were approved, Congress could choose to place the jobs created outside the classified service. From the time of the first Wilson term to the New Deal, that option was often pursued. It was pushed to new heights—this time at presidential initiative—in Franklin Roosevelt's New Deal. The experience of the civil service in the New Deal years is treated differently by different analysts; Van Riper, for example, offers an exceedingly harsh assessment. More pragmatically, Kaufman notes that Franklin Roosevelt managed to "kill two birds with one stone," when he "put into effect all of the programs and projects he considered vital for the welfare of the country. And he excepted the positions in these agencies from the classified service, thus enabling him to fill many of the patronage demands threatening the merit system."[9] In any case, prior to Roosevelt's election in 1932, approximately 80 percent of federal employees were in the competitive civil service. By 1936, that proportion had declined to about 60 percent.[10]

The percentage of the federal workforce under merit protection gradually increased during and after World War II. That time period also saw notable efforts to bring cohesion to the previously haphazard development of the civil service system. The Ramspeck Act in 1940, for example, gave the president the authority to eliminate existing exemptions, including those created by the Pendleton Act. By 1951, about 87 percent of total federal employment was in the classified service.[11] The percentage expanded still further throughout the 1960s and 1970s, so that, by 1980, well over 90 percent of the federal workforce was covered by civil service laws and regulations.

THE GROWTH IN COMPLEXITY

The Pendleton Act itself contained the seeds for the disjointed growth, internal contradictions, and enormous complexity of the American merit system. The very limited initial coverage and the presidential power to extend merit created "blanketing in" procedures. As each new group of employees was thus included in the system, employees who had been appointed by patronage became members of the merit system. As the Civil Service Commission noted, "Although the practice represents a deviation from the merit principle, it makes future appointments to the 'blanketed in' positions subject to merit rules."[12] In addition, the provisions for veterans' preference flatly repudiated the merit principles that applied to everyone else in the competitive system. It was not until 1953, for example, that veterans were required to achieve a passing score on the competitive examinations before having their five- or ten-point veterans' preference added.[13] All other applicants, of course, were not considered for federal employment if they failed the examination.

HIRING

There were other deviations from merit principles. Almost from the beginning, the Civil Service Commission divided the classified civil service into "competitive" (competitive exam required), "noncompetitive" (noncompetitive exam required) and "excepted" (no exam required). Schedule A authority, which exempted from examination some positions that were technically within the classified service, formalized these distinctions. Until 1910, all noncompetitive and excepted categories were lumped under Schedule A authority. In 1910, Schedule B was created to include all noncompetitive positions. In 1953, an Executive Order from President Dwight Eisenhower removed confidential and other policy-sensitive positions from Schedule A and placed them in the newly created Schedule C, whose intent was to permit the president greater numbers of political appointees in policy-sensitive posts (as well as in other lower-level positions, such as chauffeurs and receptionists).[14] Although Schedule A authority is now used primarily for appointing in specialized professions such as law and accounting, Schedule B authority became the primary vehicle for federal hiring in the period immediately following the abolition of PACE. Because federal hiring during this period was limited to a few major agencies with the greatest employment needs, most federal agencies had no systematic hiring authority available to them and little, if any experience with Schedule B. In 1985, one of the last years of heavy reliance on Schedule B, 98 percent of all appointments under the authority were made by nine of the twenty-one largest departments and agencies.[15] The use of Schedule C, although fairly limited initially, has also expanded in the past twenty years, primarily at upper grade levels.[16]

It is also important to consider the large number of special authorities under which federal agencies now hire. Reliance on such authorities (as well as on Schedule B) was necessitated by the abolition of the Professional and Administrative Career Examination (PACE) in 1982. PACE, which replaced the earlier Federal Service Entrance Examination (FSEE), had provided a single centralized means of recruitment and entry for many federal jobs. When PACE was abolished with no replacement, it became necessary for the Office of Personnel Management (OPM) and the many federal agencies to fall back on existing limited authorities and to use them for purposes for which most had never been intended.

Temporary appointment authority, intended to simplify hiring and separation, as well as to limit the expansion of government, is one such special authority. Temporary appointments have increased substantially in both numbers and duration in recent years, particularly since 1984, when the OPM permitted expansion of their use. Of equal significance, methods of appointing to temporary positions have increased dramatically. At the present time in the federal government, there are *thirty-five* ways to appoint to temporary positions alone.[17] Part-time appointments are an additional option; they, too, are not consistently made through competitive examination procedures.

Direct-hire authority was created for hard-to-hire occupations such as engineers, nurses, and scientists. Direct-hire appointments are made on the basis of unassembled examinations. In 1989, a new direct-hire authority was created for Vietnam veterans. The Outstanding Scholar authority permits on-the-spot hiring of college graduates who have completed four-year degrees with a GPA of 3.5 or better. Simplified hiring procedures also exist for affirmative-action hires, for returned Peace Corps volunteers, and for students enrolled in the Cooperative Education Program, among others. A precise and current list of the many authorities available to federal employers is difficult because the OPM has not updated and distributed such a list since 1980. It is important to note, however, that in 1989, 45 percent of federal career appointments were made under provisions that delegated either examining or hiring authority (or, in some cases, both) to the individual agencies. Another 25 percent were direct-hire appointments in hard-to-hire occupations, while about 15 percent were specialized mid- to senior-level appointments for which there was no register. Only about 15 percent of the appointments were made through "traditional" civil service procedures; that is, through centralized examination or from central registers administered by OPM.[18]

Finally, the federal merit hiring "system" is made more complex by the inclusion of entire agencies (FBI, CIA, Postal Service) in excepted authorities and by the creation of separate but parallel merit systems in others (TVA, for example). The Foreign Service operates with a separate system; so too does the Public Health Service. In some organizations, such as the Department of Health and Human Services and the State Department, more than one system is in place.

In 1978, major civil service reform legislation was passed. A centerpiece of Carter administration domestic policy, the Civil Service Reform Act of 1978 (CSRA) was intended to simplify federal personnel policy through decentralization and delegation, as well as to increase the accountability and responsiveness of federal employees through performance appraisal and evaluation. CSRA created financial incentives linked to performance for top career executives and mid-level managers. The act created the Senior Executive Service (SES) in an effort to make the senior management cadre of the federal career service more flexible and more responsive. It codified federal labor-management practices for the first time, reaffirmed the federal government's commitment to representativeness and affirmative action, and provided new protection for whistleblowers. The act abolished the Civil Service Commission and replaced it with the Office of Personnel Management, the Merit Systems Protection Board, and the Federal Labor Relations Authority. These new institutions were to be leaders in shaping a new and more coherent federal personnel and human resource management strategy.

Because CSRA was the first comprehensive reform of the civil service in nearly a hundred years, expectations for improvements were high. In fact, however, many of those expectations have not been met.[19] This is due to a modest understanding and shallow level of support for many of the reforms; the new political environment of the Reagan administration also had a profound impact on many of the primary implementation activities. The budgetary cutbacks in the early years of the Reagan administration accompanied implementation of critical components of the reform. Much of the political rhetoric accompanying proposed policy changes was directed at the career bureaucracy: the "permanent government." Morale was very low. Delegation, decentralization, and simplification proceeded in fits and starts; attention was again paid to this issue only because the abolition of PACE removed the major central means of recruiting and testing for the federal service.

Most significantly, however, for all its emphasis on greater clarity and simplicity in the federal merit systems, the Civil Service Reform Act did not replace the tangle of procedures related to federal personnel practices. In many respects, it merely added another layer of complexity and confusion to an already complex system. Decentralization and delegation of recruiting and hiring, for example, is not simplification if 6,000 pages of rules, regulations, and guidelines remain in effect. The ability to understand and monitor such a system is extremely difficult, and probably impossible in the absence of any central guiding principles and objectives. The ability to understand and manage effectively in such a system is made even more difficult when other characteristics of the federal personnel system are considered.

CLASSIFICATION AND COMPENSATION

Classification of federal employees was formally authorized in 1923 with the passage of the Classification Act. This legislation not only classified positions according to duties and responsibilities but also assigned salary levels to those positions. It therefore established in law the principle of nationally uniform compensation levels. The act was passed shortly after the Budget and Accounting Act of 1921, and clearly fell under the umbrella of the economy and efficiency movement so prevalent in government at that time. Van Riper notes that "the Bureau of the Budget [created by the 1921 act] tended to emphasize economy at the expense of almost everything else. But the pressing need for careful estimates of personnel and personnel costs, if any budget was to really mean anything, stimulated further concern with the standardization . . . of federal wages and functions." [20]

The administration of the new act was supervised by a newly created Personnel Classification Board.

In addition, the act established in law the American principle of "rank in job," rather than the European practice of "rank in person." This meant that the salary or wages for each job was determined solely by the position and by the necessary qualifications for that position, not by the personal qualifications of the person filling the position (although presumably they matched fairly closely). Finally, the act institutionalized the very specialized nature of the American civil service. The jobs to be classified were narrow and specific; again, in keeping with the economy and efficiency movement, flexibility and discretion were limited whenever possible.

Although an analysis of the Classification Act's effectiveness in 1929 indicated that it had not created a "consistent and equitable system of . . . pay for positions involving the same work," [21] there was no additional reform in this area until 1949. There were, however, fairly consistent calls for change during that twenty-year period. The Commission of Inquiry on Public Service Personnel noted in 1935, for example, that "the most obvious fault to be found with all classifications made on the American plan is their complexity— the great number of classes and occupational hierarchies that are set up. What seem to be the most trifling differences in function or difficulty are formally recognized and duly defined. . . ." The commission noted further that "classifications of such complexity are to be condemned because of the fetters that they place upon department heads in the management of their business." [22]

The Ramspeck Act extended the Civil Service Commission's authority for classification to the entire field service in 1940; in 1945 a presidential order directed the commission to begin that task. By that time, the commision was responsible for about half of the total federal civil service positions. [23] The complexity of the federal personnel system was now much in evidence. The absence of a comprehensive wage-and-salary policy had become a notable problem. The final report of the first Hoover Commission detailed the issues related to pay and personnel and concluded: "Probably no problem in the management of the Government is more important than that of obtaining a capable and conscientious body of public servants. Unfortunately, personnel practices in the federal government give little room for optimism that these needs are being met." [24]

In 1949, at least partially in response to Hoover Commission recommendations, the Classification Act of 1949 was passed. The act created the "supergrade" system, which preceded the Senior Executive Service, and simplified the occupational series by merging the previous five into two. The Classification Act of 1949 is important for another reason: It marked an early point on what has now come to be considered the "cycle" of centralization and decentralization in federal personnel policy. Excessive centralization of classification activities was perceived to be a major cause of an overly rigid and slow system. As a result, the 1949 act delegated classification authority for positions below the supergrades back to the agencies. It gave the Civil Service Commission postaudit review authority for those delegations. With other authority such as examining still residing with the Civil Service Commission, with very limited experience in classification activity at the agency level, and with extensive central regulations and procedures still governing the activity, however, this delegation set the precedent for others to follow. Authority was gradually pulled back into the commission until, when the Civil Service Reform Act of 1978 was written, excessive centralization was again perceived to be the problem.

Despite the centrality of classification activities to federal personnel policy and pay, classification has not been thoroughly analyzed since before the passage of the 1949 act. In the intervening forty years, the procedures and regulations associated with classification—most notably the classification and qualification standards[25]—have become seriously outdated and burdensome. The Merit Systems Protection Board recently found, for example, that *63 percent* of the white-collar classification standards currently in use were issued before 1973.[26] In addition, for the 1982–84 period, OPM declared a moratorium on writing new classification standards and the problem was exacerbated. Because grade levels flow directly from classification and qualification standards (or they *should*), the link between these standards and pay is immutable. Obsolescent standards inevitably influence the ability to determine fair pay for an occupation or grade. There are more than 900 occupations in the federal classified service and over 30 different pay systems. The links between the two cannot be ignored in reform, and simplification or total redesign of federal classification schemes is also necessary.

The Civil Service Reform Act of 1978, which did not address the issue of pay, did give the Office of Personnel Management authority to delegate classification activities to the agencies. It did so, however, without addressing or eliminating the plethora of rules and regulations that had accumulated over the years and without directly reforming the Classification Act of 1949. As noted earlier, this failure to address the procedural "baggage" added yet another layer of complexity to a very murky system. To date, OPM has limited such delegation to a very small number of demonstration projects. "Reform" of classification and qualification standards has occurred primarily through efforts to write "generic" standards, which provide greater flexibility. Without a fundamental reexamination of classification procedures, however, other efforts at personnel and pay reform necessarily remain somewhat tangential to change.

TRAINING AND DEVELOPMENT

Training and development of the federal workforce has had a somewhat checkered history. Although a limited number of agencies created education and training programs for their employees, general direction and support was clearly lacking until the passage of the Government Employees Training Act of 1958. Indeed, Van Riper notes that, before 1940, "the excess of applicants compared to available jobs had suggested to both Congress and many administrators that extensive in-service training programs were essentially wasteful."[27] The very limited supply of labor during World War II mandated that federal personnel policy include provisions for training and retraining of federal personnel. At the end of the war, however, many of these activities were cut back or eliminated. The training void was duly noted by the first Hoover Commission and, partly in response to the Hoover Report, President Truman directed the Civil Service Commission to attack what the commission itself called the "curse of excessive specialization."[28] By most accounts, this attack garnered only modest results.

During the presidency of Dwight Eisenhower, whose military training convinced him of the benefits of the enterprise, training began to achieve more credibility. In Eisenhower's first term, the Federal Training Policy Statement was issued. This directive advocated formulation of training plans and emphasis on employee development opportunities. The Civil Service Commission was given lead responsibility for these training efforts. In 1958, during the second Eisenhower term, his administration followed up with the Government Employees Training Act of 1958. Although passage of the act involved intense political negotiation, this act legitimized the training function and provided funds for training and centralized training programs. In its 1974 report, *Biography of an Ideal,* the Civil Service Commission argued that the provisions of the 1958 act "make the training function in the United States Government the envy of even the most advanced of nations."[29] That statement was undoubtedly an exaggeration in 1974; it is clearly not accurate today.

Like much else in the federal personnel system, training and development have not grown in a systematic and coherent way. Despite the provisions of the 1958 act (which has never been revisited), training has remained a fairly low priority. In times of budget cuts and constraints, training costs are often the first to be eliminated from the budget. In its report to the National Commission on the Public Service, the Task Force on Education and Training said, "There are significant shortcomings in federal government human resource policies. Government agencies spend far too little on training of all kinds and concentrate their efforts on meeting narrow, short-term needs. The area of greatest concern is the plainly inadequate attention paid to the development of management and executive leadership in the civil service."[30]

The Civil Service Commission and, later, the Office of Personnel Management, did not develop a government-wide training strategy until Constance Newman assumed the directorship of OPM in the Bush administration. Financial support for training at both central and agency levels remains very limited. At the same time, the need for training and retraining has never been more clear. The demographics of the twenty-first century, changing skill demands, and dramatic technological progress all point to new development needs. Merit and competence are inextricably intertwined.

THE COURTS AND THE MERIT SYSTEM

In the 1970s and 1980s, the federal judiciary played a substantial role in defining and redefining the merit system. The Supreme Court, in particular, has been an ardent supporter of two historical tenets of merit: (1) depoliticization of the public service, and (2) assuring that operational definitions and applications of merit in public personnel administration are strongly job related.

Depoliticization

A major goal of the merit system has been to remove partisan politics from public personnel management. George William Curtis, a leading nineteenth-century civil service reformer, noted that the merit system made it possible to take "the whole non-political public service out of politics." [31] The effort had two prongs: to prohibit public employees from taking an active part in partisan political management and campaigning, and to eliminate patronage hiring and dismissal from the public service. The Supreme Court has embraced both elements of depoliticization.

The effort to remove public employees from partisan politics has been most generally embodied in the first and second Hatch Acts (1939 and 1940) and in various state and local equivalents. The first Hatch Act applies only to federal employees; it prohibits them from using their "official authority or influence for the purpose of interfering with or affecting the result of an election," or from taking an "active part in political management or political campaigns." The second Hatch Act applies similar restrictions to state and local government employees whose positions are at least partially funded by the federal government. These measures carve out a legal and political status for public employees that is remarkably different from that of ordinary citizens. While partisan political participation is considered virtuous for citizens generally, it is simply illegal for public employees. Not surprisingly, both acts have been subject to challenge in the courts on the grounds that they violate the First and Fourteenth Amendment rights of public employees. They have also been attacked for vagueness because both acts lack a comprehensive definition of the activities they proscribe.

The constitutional arguments against the Hatch Acts and similar political neutrality statutes have filled volumes of law reviews and many court briefs. In 1973, however, the Supreme Court seemed to put the constitutional issues to rest in an opinion that strongly supported depoliticization of the public service and afforded Congress great latitude in seeking to achieve that end. In *U.S. Civil Service Commission* v. *National Association of Letter Carriers (NALC)*,[32] the Court held:

> We unhesitatingly reaffirm . . . that Congress . . . has the power to prevent [federal employees covered by the first Hatch Act] from holding a party office, working at the polls and acting as party paymaster for other party workers. . . . Our judgment is that neither the First Amendment nor any other provision of the Constitution invalidates a law barring this kind of partisan political conduct by federal employees.
>
> Such a decision on our part would no more than confirm the judgment of history, a judgment made by this country over the last century that it is in the best interests of the country, indeed essential, that federal service should depend upon meritorious performance rather than political service.

The *NALC* decision effectively allows Congress to take virtually any reasonable steps to remove the federal service from partisan political activity. The Court went even further in supporting depoliticization when, in *Elrod* v. *Burns* (1976),[33] it ruled patronage dismissals from ordinary public-service positions *unconstitutional*.

Elrod concerned the constitutionality of patronage dismissals from the Cook County, Illinois, Sheriff's Office. The discharged employees claimed that their First and Fourteenth Amendment rights to freedom of belief and association had been violated. A majority of the Supreme Court's justices agreed that the dismissals were unconstitutional, but the Court was unable to reach a majority opinion as to precisely why.

The issue was more fully clarified in *Branti* v. *Finkel* (1980),[34] in which the Court came close to "constitutionalizing" merit. In assessing the patronage dismissal of two public defenders in Rockland County, New York, Justice John Paul Stevens, speaking for the Court's majority, reasoned that patronage dismissals are unconstitutional unless "the hiring authority can demonstrate that that party affiliation is an appropriate requirement for the effective performance of the public office involved." As Justice Lewis Powell argued in dissent, however, the only logical alternative to a patronage system is one that is merit oriented: "Many public positions previously filled on the basis of membership in national political parties now must be staffed in accordance with a constitutionalized civil service standard that will affect the employment practices of federal, state and local governments."

An important aspect of the *Branti* ruling is that the Court reasoned that merely labeling positions "policy making" or "confidential" is not enough to justify patronage dismissals from them. In practice, this means that some traditional public personnel classifications, such as "excepted" and "exempt," will no longer be synonymous with "at the pleasure" of the political official at the head of an agency or government.

In sum, the Supreme Court has been very sympathetic to the nineteenth-century civil service reformers' ideal of taking politics out of the public service and the public service out of politics. It has declared that patronage dismissals will generally be unconstitutional and has held that the Constitution can easily accommodate restrictions on public employees' partisan political activities. At the same time, it must be noted that Congress has recently raised questions about the overall utility of the Hatch Act and about its infringement on the rights of public employees. Each of the last several sessions has seen the introduction of legislation intended to roll back Hatch provisions. Those in favor of reform argue that federal employees are severely disadvantaged by the inability to participate in politics on their own behalf. Those opposing reform argue that continued political restrictions on federal employees are essential to maintaining any semblance of a merit system. It is important to note that the strength of the proreform group has increased recently; in fact, some observers predicted reform of the Hatch Acts before the end of 1990.[35] The Supreme Court's view of such legislation, should it pass, could be an important redefinition of merit.

Making Sure That the Merit System Assures Merit

A second aspect of the judiciary's involvement in public personnel administration has concerned the very meaning of *merit*. Here, too, the thrust of judicial activity has been two pronged.

All merit systems afford covered employees protection against arbitrary, capricious, illegal, or unconstitutional dismissals. These same systems provide for dismissals in the interests of the efficiency of the public service. During the aftermath of the loyalty-security programs of the late 1940s and early

1950s, the federal judiciary began to look more closely at the government's claims that particular dismissals promoted efficiency. In *Board of Regents* v. *Roth* (1972),[36] the Supreme Court held that public employees are constitutionally entitled to procedural due process protection when dismissals abridged their constitutional rights or liberties, damaged their reputations, seriously impaired their future employability, or infringed upon a property interest, such as tenure, in their jobs. By 1985, the Court had expanded the application of due process considerably. In *Cleveland Board of Education* v. *Loudermill*,[37] it found that a public employee had a "property right" in a job because the Ohio civil service statute made him a "classified civil service" employee, who was entitled to retain his position "during good behavior and efficient service."

Constitutional due process in dismissals from the civil service does not necessarily require elaborate procedures. It does require that the government, as employer, state its reasons for the dismissal and allow the public employee to try to rebut its claims. Once the record contains each side's perspective, review by an administrative official or a court is generally possible. Unsubstantiated claims that dismissals will promote efficiency have been vulnerable to successful challenge. Thus, where there is a merit system, the government cannot simply purport that dismissals serve efficiency objectives; it must demonstrate conclusively that they do so.

The federal judiciary has also sought to assure that merit systems yield merit by requiring, under some circumstances, that standard civil service examinations be strongly job related. In a series of cases beginning in the early 1970s, the courts have held that employment practices having a negative impact on the employment interests of members of minority groups and women are illegal unless they are valid in the sense of being job related.[38] These rulings have been under the Civil Rights Act of 1964, as amended, and the Constitution's equal protection clause (limited to the public sector). There have been numerous instances in which public agencies have been unable to demonstrate sufficient job relatedness to make the practices at issue legally or constitutionally acceptable. One remedy that the judiciary may impose in such cases is quota hiring from among qualified minority-group members for a limited period of time, as in *United States* v. *Paradise* (1987).[39]

These cases have forced public-sector jurisdictions to rethink their definitions and applications of merit principles and to attempt to eliminate cultural bias in their hiring and promotional procedures. In *Johnson* v. *Santa Clara County* (1987),[40] the Supreme Court accepted a broad definition of merit that included an effort to establish a socially representative workforce. It specifically embraced the principle that exam scores do not have to be the sole determinant in promotions. Instead, jurisdictions are free to consider a range of factors, including sex and minority-group status. In *Johnson*, the Court noted that merit systems can be flexible because "there is rarely a single, 'best qualified' person for a job. An effective personnel system will bring before the selecting official several fully-qualified candidates who each may possess different attributes that recommend them for selection."[41]

Thus the federal judiciary and the Supreme Court have strengthened two aspects of the merit system. They have protected depoliticization by upholding regulations prohibiting federal employees from engaging in partisan political activity. They have required depoliticization by finding that patronage dismissals from the public service will generally be unconstitutional. The courts have also strengthened the merit system by requiring that dismissals, selections, and promotions done in the name of merit actually embody merit.

THE MERIT SYSTEM AND MERIT PRINCIPLES

This, then, is the procedural and legal environment of the contemporary federal "merit system." The remarkable growth of complexity in both the environment and the system has been reflected in restatements of the underlying principles: Not surprisingly, there are more merit principles today than there were in 1883. After a long period of formal silence about what the merit principles actually ensured, they have been enunciated in legislation twice in the past twenty years. In 1970, the Intergovernmental Personnel Act formally listed the merit principles for the first time:

1. Hiring and promoting employees on the basis of relative ability, with open consideration for initial appointment.
2. Providing fair compensation.
3. Retaining employees on the basis of performance, correcting inadequate performance and separating those whose inadequate performance cannot be corrected.
4. Training employees as needed for high quality performance.
5. Assuring fair treatment of applicants and employees in all aspects of personnel administration without regard to political affiliation, race, color, national origin, sex, or religious creed, and with proper regard for their privacy and constitutional rights as citizens.
6. Protecting employees against partisan political coercion; and prohibiting use of official position to affect an election or nomination for office.[42]

It is worth noting that the Intergovernmental Personnel Act, by using the lever of federal funding, applied these merit principles to state and local governments, just as the second Hatch Act had earlier prohibited state and local employees from partisan political activity.

In 1978, the principles were restated and somewhat redefined again in the Civil Service Reform Act. Now there were nine, much more complex, principles:

1. Recruitment should be from qualified individuals from appropriate sources in an endeavor to achieve a workforce from all segments of society, and selection and advancement should be determined solely on the basis of relative ability, knowledge and skills, after fair and open competition that assures that all receive equal opportunity.
2. All employees and applicants for employment should receive fair and equitable treatment in all aspects of personnel management without regard to political affiliation, race, color, religion, national origin, sex, marital status, age, or handicapping condition, and with proper regard for their privacy and constitutional rights.

3. Equal pay should be provided for work of equal value, with appropriate consideration of both national and local rates paid by employers in the private sector, and appropriate incentives and recognition should be provided for excellence in performance.
4. All employees should maintain high standards of integrity, conduct, and concern for the public interest.
5. The federal workforce should be used efficiently and effectively.
6. Employees should be retained on the adequacy of their performance, inadequate performance should be corrected, and employees should be separated who cannot or will not improve their performance to meet required standards.
7. Employees should be provided effective education and training in cases in which such education and training would result in better organizational and individual performance.
8. Employees should be (a.) protected against arbitrary action, personal favoritism, or coercion for partisan political purposes, and (b.) prohibited from using their official authority or influence for the purpose of interfering with or affecting the result of an election or a nomination for election.
9. Employees should be protected against reprisal for the lawful disclosure of information that the employee reasonably believes evidences (a.) a violation of any law, rule, or regulation, or (b.) mismanagement, a gross waste of funds, an abuse of authority, or a substantial and specific danger to public health and safety.[43]

Whatever else might be said about the merit principles as we near the year 2000, they are no longer simple and straightforward. Even the principles without their baggage do not provide clear guidance to the federal manager or personnel director who seeks to ensure merit within the overarching objective of effective service delivery. Further, the principles themselves now contain conflicting purposes and objectives. They are more comprehensive, but they are much, much more confusing.

COPING WITH THE MERIT SYSTEM

How do federal managers deal with the constraint, confusion, and complexity of merit as it exists today? In an effort to examine this question, staff members of the National Commission conducted a series of interviews with personnel directors and others in agencies that have made extensive and recent use of existing hiring procedures. Representatives from different agencies, different regions of the country, and central and field offices were interviewed to determine whether and where differences in attitudes toward merit existed. Many persons interviewed requested confidentiality. To honor those requests, no persons or agencies are identified [here]. In the interviews, commission staff focused on entrance to the federal service, rather than on promotion once inside.

Two findings from our interviews are paramount: first, there continues to be remarkable support for the merit *principles*. Second, there is almost unanimous dissatisfaction with the merit *system*. Furthermore, although there is strong support for reforming and removing what many refer to as the "procedural baggage" of the merit system, there is a continuing awareness of the potential for political and other abuse of the merit system and for the need for some protection of career employees and positions. There was, nonetheless, a very strong conviction that federal personnel directors and other federal managers, left on their own, would actively pursue merit. One group of managers said, "If the slate were clean, most of the agencies, most of the time, would create procedures that make good sense. Those procedures that they would re-create would look like the merit principles."[44]

Other managers affirmed this commitment, but emphasized that both the definition of merit and the means of pursuing it need to be examined. Arguing that managers must focus on purpose, not problems, one personnel director said, "The merit system has come to be a way of life, but we must remember that the principles are the basis."[45] Another noted that merit "is confused and it is struggling, but it is there. The system, however, is beyond repair; it needs to be totally rethought. Delegating bad procedures to us does not solve problems; we need to go back to the fundamental principles and guidelines."[46]

The central agency personnel directors interviewed were unanimous in their assessment that the basic design of the current merit system is not appropriate for either current or future recruiting and hiring needs. One director said, "The days of national recruiting are over; the reality is that if you waste the time advertising nationwide, you lose the opportunity to hire the people you really need."[47] Representatives of an agency noted for its innovation and foresight in relation to personnel summarized the situation in these terms: "the goal is to find the best person for the job. The principles are fundamental and they shape the process, but you cannot control merit in a centralized way. . . . The system is arcane and archaic and we have not done a good job of articulating the new realities."[48]

The interviews uncovered strong differences between central agency staff and field staff in relation to the status of merit. The view of the merit system as archaic and procedure bound was echoed in the field office interviews, but those interviews reflected serious concerns about protecting merit as well. One manager put it in the following terms, "The merit system has little credibility . . . only a few remaining bureaucrats and a few conscientious managers are keeping it from being totally disregarded."[49] Another manager said, "Until merit is defined as something other than test scores, we will continue to reach merit goals, but the quality of the workforce and the quality of the work, will go steadily down."[50]

Underlying many of these concerns is the conviction that while the merit system does not work well or consistently anymore, no coherent replacement or direction has been advanced. Without that replacement and additional guidance, field managers fear replacing even an unworkable system. Indeed, a recent report of the General Accounting Office found that in the face of extensive decentralization and inadequate central-to-field communication, many field managers simply did not know how they were supposed to operate in relation to merit. There has been virtually no systematic monitoring of field experience and precedent; GAO found that even keeping adequate records was problematic.[51]

Overall, then, while there continues to be strong support for the fundamental principles of merit, dissatisfaction with and confusion about the current system is high. Further, the split between central agency personnel and field personnel in terms of how well agencies are coping in the current environment is cause for concern. The inability, or unwillingness, of central personnel to trust and train other personnel in their own agencies is damning evidence of the problems with merit today. The problem highlighted by National Commission interviews has been noted elsewhere. A recent MSPB survey reported that "personnel specialists view delegation of authority from agency personnel offices to line managers somewhat less favorably than they view delegation from OPM to agencies. Whereas 83 percent of respondents believe that delegation of authorities from OPM to agency personnel offices can lead to improved personnel management, only 60 percent believe the same is true of delegation from personnel offices to line management."[52]

It may be that, lacking confidence in field managers, central agency personnel have failed to take the responsibility of decentralization and delegation seriously. The same may be said of the Office of Personnel Management. The ensuing lack of reporting and monitoring is a serious deficiency that needs to be corrected. A more accurate record of experience with decentralized merit is necessary for effective reform. In addition, the need for training and education—about the new environment, the new accountability, and the new responsibility—is very clear. It must be given high priority.

CONCLUSIONS AND RECOMMENDATIONS

Today, neither the essential definition of merit nor fundamental merit principles is clear. Merit cannot mean, as one would assume from examining the system, excessive constraint and blind obedience to a nearly unintelligible maze of procedure. No manager or personnel director can work consistently or effectively in a system defined by over 6,000 pages of rules and regulations. One hundred years of accumulated rules and regulations are the baggage of merit. They do not clarify and define; they obscure. The current system essentially assumes that public managers must be coerced into meritorious behavior; there is no presumption that, left to their own skills and conscience, members of the federal service will nonetheless pursue quality and effective service.

The basic components of the system continue to reflect demographic realities of the late nineteenth century. For many federal agencies, many occupations, and many regions of the country, the contemporary reality is that personnel systems cannot screen out potential employees, but must gather them in. Demographic projections for the next twenty years demonstrate very clearly that to be competitive in these activities, the federal government must be flexible, aggressive, and innovative. The current system is set up precisely to discourage such qualities.

Key components of the current system have not been reexamined for many years. Classification and training are leading examples. A crazy quilt of rules and regulations, patched together as new needs and demands appeared over the past hundred years, provides false assurance that important protections are in place. Rhetoric creates both complacency about the status quo and an unnecessarily negative view of the career civil servants the system is intended to protect.

Today, it is inconceivable that a major nation could govern well, resolve social and economic problems, or play an effective global role in the absence of a strong civil service that is well integrated into its political institutions and culture. Throughout the world, national civil services are being reformed and restructured. Virtually everywhere, government is considered a tool for formulating and implementing public policies. But as Alexander Hamilton noted two centuries ago in *The Federalist Papers*, "the true test of a good government is its aptitude and tendency to produce a good administration."

Good government in the United States requires much better public administration. There is no doubt that public personnel administration, always the cornerstone of public administration, must be redesigned—or perhaps designed for the first time—if the United States is to meet the challenges of the present and the future. There is no "quick fix" for the civil service and public administration. There is a dramatic need to decide, for the first time in over a hundred years, what kind of public service the American national government needs and deserves. Proceeding from that base, future reforms must provide the map and the tools for a new system.

Notes

1. Throughout this [article], "merit" is defined primarily in terms of entrance to the federal service. Very clearly, promotion and protection of employees' rights are also part of the merit mosaic. Both, however, are worthy of separate treatment.
2. Civil Service Commission, *Biography of an Ideal* (Washington, D.C.: CSC, 1974), 28.
3. Paul P. Van Riper, *History of the United States Civil Service* (Evanston, Ill.: Row, Peterson, 1958), 106.
4. Ibid., 105.
5. The Civil Service Act of 1883 (Pendleton Act), *Statutes at Large of the United States of America*, vol. 20, p. 403, sec. 3.
6. Herbert Kaufman, "The Growth of the Federal Personnel System," in The American Assembly, *The Federal Government Service* (New York: Columbia University Press, 1954), 36.
7. Stephen Skrowronek, *Building a New American State: The Expansion of National Administrative Capacities, 1877–1920* (New York: Cambridge University Press, 1982), 70–71.
8. Woodrow Wilson, quoted in Van Riper, *History of Civil Service*, 234.
9. Herbert Kaufman, "Growth of Federal Personnel System," 39. For Van Riper's dissenting view, see Van Riper, *History of Civil Service*, chap. 13.
10. See the Civil Service Commission, *Biography of an Ideal*, 66.
11. See the discussion of the Ramspeck Act and its implementation in Van Riper, *History of Civil Service*, 344–46.
12. Civil Service Commission, *Biography of an Ideal*, 49.
13. Ibid., 89.
14. Van Riper, *History of Civil Service*, 207.
15. Merit Systems Protection Board, *In Search of Merit: Hiring Entry Level Federal Employees* (Washington, D.C.: MSPB, September 1987), i.
16. The greatest increase occurred in the Carter presidency; the elevated levels from that administration were increased still further under President Reagan. See

Patricia W. Ingraham, "Building Bridges or Burning Them? The President, the Appointees and the Bureaucracy," *Public Administration Review*, September/October 1987, 425–35.

17. This number is based on research conducted by the U.S. Navy, Office of Civilian Personnel.
18. Data from the U.S. Office of Personnel Management, Office of Career Entry.
19. For extensive discussion of CSRA, see Patricia W. Ingraham and David Rosenbloom, Co-Editors, "Symposium on Ten Years of Civil Service Reform," *Policy Studies Journal*, Winter 1989.
20. Van Riper, *History of Civil Service*, 298.
21. Ibid., 304.
22. Lucius Wilmerding, Jr., *Government by Merit* (New York: McGraw-Hill, 1935), 57.
23. See Van Riper, *History of Civil Service*, 426–27.
24. *Final Report of the First Hoover Commission*, in *Basic Documents of American Public Administration, 1776–1950*, ed. Frederick C. Mosher (New York: Holmes and Meier, 1976), 210.
25. Standards are the tools actually used to describe a job and the necessary qualifications for it. The Merit Systems Protection Board notes that "typically, each occupation is covered by a standard that describes the work of the occupation at various grade levels . . . to function, the classification process must bring together three elements—position descriptions, classification standards, and human judgment—to arrive at appropriate conclusions. . . . OPM's qualification standards determine what skills are needed and evaluate whether candidates who apply are basically qualified to perform the work." Merit Systems Protection Board, *OPM's Classification and Qualification Systems: A Renewed Emphasis, A Changing Perspective* (Washington, D.C.: MSPB, November 1989), 6–7.
26. Ibid., 12.
27. Van Riper, *History of Civil Service*, 380.
28. Ibid., 432.
29. Civil Service Commission, *Biography of an Ideal*, 97.
30. Task Force on Education and Training, National Commission on the Public Service, *Investment for Leadership: Education and Training for the Public Service* (Washington, D.C., 1989), 120.
31. George William Curtis, *The Situation* (New York: National Civil Service Reform League, 1886), 17.
32. 413 U.S. 548 (1973).
33. 427 U.S. 347 (1976).
34. 445 U.S. 507 (1980).
35. For a full discussion of the issues surrounding Hatch reform, see chap. 2 of [*Agenda for Excellence: Public Service in America*, ed. Patricia Ingraham and Donald F. Kettl (Chatham, NJ: Chatham House Publ., 1992)].
36. 408 U.S. 564 (1972).
37. 470 U.S. 532 (1985).
38. See David H. Rosenbloom, "What Every Public Personnel Manager Should Know about the Constitution," in *Public Personnel Administration*, ed. Steven Hays and Richard Kearney (Englewood Cliffs, N.J.: Prentice-Hall, 1990), 49–52, for a brief recent analysis.
39. 94 L. Ed.2d 203 (1987).
40. 94 L. Ed.2d 615 (1987).
41. 413 U.S. 548 (1973).
42. This summary of the principles contained in the Intergovernmental Personnel Act is taken from Civil Service Commission, *Biography of an Ideal*, 99–100.
43. P.L. 95–454, 13 October 1978, Civil Service Reform Act of 1978, Title I.

44. Personal interview, National Commission on the Public Service staff, February 1990.
45. Ibid.
46. Personal interview, National Commission on the Public Service staff, March 1990.
47. Ibid.
48. Personal interview, National Commission on the Public Service staff, February 1990.
49. Telephone interview, National Commission on the Public Service staff, December 1989.
50. Ibid.
51. General Accounting Office, *Federal Recruiting and Hiring* (Washington, D.C.: GAO, May 1990).
52. Merit Systems Protection Board, *Federal Personnel Management Since Civil Service Reform* (Washington, D.C.: MSPB, November 1989), 10.

Public Sector Collective Bargaining in the 1990s

JOEL M. DOUGLAS

THE REQUIREMENT TO BARGAIN COLLECTIVELY

Requiring public employees to bargain collectively is one of the most far-reaching developments in public administration and public personnel management in the twentieth century. The evolution and institutionalization of collective bargaining in government have generated new responsibilities and challenges for public administrators and have drastically changed the practice and delivery of public personnel administration in the United States. In political subdivisions where the work force is unionized, virtually every aspect of personnel systems and associated administrative procedures is affected by this process.[1]

Although public sector labor relations (hereinafter "PSLR") was noted to a limited degree in the nineteenth century, it began to expand at the federal level in the pre-World War I period.[2] However, it wasn't until the 1950s, when public employees began to insist on their rights, that PSLR was extended to municipal and state government in any systematic way. The first collective bargaining statute for state workers was reported in Wisconsin[3] in 1959, although municipal workers, most notable in New York City, bargained in the mid-1950s.

As of 1990, approximately 17% of the total labor force is organized or represented by collective bargaining agreements. Of that total, 12% are employed in the private sector and 5% in the public sector. These include approximately 6.3 million public employees, or 37% of those who work for federal, state, and local government and related agencies and support systems.[4] The extensive unionization of public employees was not predicted in either size or intensity. That this period of growth occurred at a time when private sector union membership was in a period of decline further documents the uniqueness of this phenomenon.

The public sector growth rate, which was substantial in the 1970s and 1980s, has stabilized and, in some parts of the country, has begun to decline. For the purpose of their employment relationship, approximately 65% of public sector employees are unrepresented and not covered by a union contract. Of this group, the number protected by civil service merit systems (hereinafter "CSMS" or "civil service") is estimated to be modest because states with well-developed civil service systems are also among those with heaviest union density.[5] However, union membership figures in isolation belie the political and economic strength of the public sector labor movement. In many jurisdictions, unionized public employees, through their representatives and bargaining agents, possess the greatest amount of knowledge as to the workings of government and by collaborative action have the ability to monitor organizational operations and influence elected officials and other policy-makers.

LEGISLATIVE / LEGAL FRAMEWORK—AN OVERVIEW

The outcomes of labor relations frequently depend on the legislative provisions that established the regulatory framework for bargaining. Consistency among public sector labor relations laws is not imperative, and accordingly variety and experimentation have occurred. In accordance with the doctrine of federalism, the public sector labor relations legislative framework encourages experimentation and legislative diversity. PSLR in the United States at the beginning of the 1990s is a conglomeration of private sector labor relations theory, experience, and law, less reliant on market forces and more heavily regulated than its private sector counterpart. The prototype is relatively young in its emerging stage, but shows little, if any, signs of erosion. There is no evidence to suggest that any jurisdiction that has enacted collective bargaining legislation has subsequently repealed it. Furthermore, public sector workers have not, to any large degree, voluntarily chosen to decertify their unions and reject the collective bargaining process. Once prescribed, public sector collective bargaining legislation becomes institutionalized and remains an integral component of human resources and public personnel systems.

The present PSLR legislative and legal framework is based on an adversarial relationship rooted in the National Labor Relations Act (NLRA) and is structured on private sector principles.[6] These include narrow unit determination requirements, bargaining agent election procedures, exclusive union representation, a series of unfair labor and employment practices, and a decentralized bargaining structure. Reliance on the private sector model was successful in developing the PSLR legal framework in which employees, subject to restrictions, most notably the anti-strike ban, negotiate with government the terms and conditions of employment. Although the private and public sectors contain many similarities, a distinct difference is noted in the public sector, since the government is both employer and regulator at the bargaining table. Other differences include the private sector's reliance on market forces, distributive bargaining, and the use of strikes and lockouts.

PSLR is regulated by a variety of state laws, municipal and local ordinances, and federal wage, hours, health and safety, and affirmative action statutes. There is no national public sector collective bargaining statute; each state and political subdivision is free to enact its own legislation. These statutes and regulations compromise the total PSLR legislative/legal judicial fabric.[7] Public employees in approximately 40 states, the federal government, and the Virgin Islands have the right to bargain collectively under the protection of various federal, state, and local statutes. Comprehensive collective bargaining legislation for all or selected groups of employees is found in 34 states.[8] In addition, three states[9] limit bargaining to police and firefighters while two others[10] authorize "meet and confer" discussions. In one state,[11] negotiations are conducted under the authority of executive order. Two additional categories of quasi-labor relations statutes, grievance procedures, and payroll deduction plans exist. Legislated, as opposed to negotiated, employee grievance procedures are found in seven states.[12] In some, they supplement a statewide labor relations system (hereinafter "LRS"); in others the reason for their enactment is less clear. Nine states provide for payroll deduction plans, which employees may use to support employee associations or unions.[13] Public policy in three states sets forth a prohibition against collective bargaining, public employees joining a labor organization advocating public sector bargaining, and forbids employers from recognizing a union in the absence of enabling legislation. Additional PSLR enabling legislation is found in selected cities, counties, special districts, and other jurisdictions. At the opposite end of the spectrum there exists state and local prohibitions against public sector collective bargaining.[14]

With the exception of demographic data and legislation, the federal government collective bargaining model is not included here. The limited scope of bargaining in the federal sector, as well as other distinguishing features including the ban against negotiating salary and other economic issues, creates a pattern different from other public sector labor relations systems, and while this is not to suggest the superiority of either approach, in an attempt to standardize this discussion the federal model was excluded. Federal sector employees bargain pursuant to a series of presidential executive orders and statutes. Executive Order 10988[15] gave federal employees the basic right to organize and form unions and encouraged their participation in noneconomic matters. An enlarged, although still severely restricted, scope of bargaining and the creation of the Federal Labor Relations Commission was provided for in Executive Order 11491.[16] It is estimated that approximately 1.2 million, or over 50% of the executive branch federal workers are covered by collective bargaining agreements. Additionally, nearly 600,000 postal workers, 90% of the postal work force, are unionized or covered by labor agreements.[17] The enactment of the Federal Service Labor Management and Employee Relations Law as part of Title VII of the 1978 Civil Service Reform Act[18] elevated previous executive orders to the level of statutory law and served to encourage and facilitate the development of federal sector labor relations. This Act created the Federal Labor Relations Authority, which has jurisdiction to direct the collective bargaining process for federal employees. The Act also provided binding arbitration as the last step in all grievance procedures.

THE RIGHT TO STRIKE

Public sector collective bargaining legislation contains a universal strike prohibition. No statute confers upon public employees an unqualified right to strike. Although approximately a dozen states have enacted limited right-to-strike legislation for public employees, this option becomes operable only after exhausting existing impasse procedures and other administrative remedies. The states with the limited legal right-to-strike option include Alaska, California, Hawaii, Illinois, Minnesota, Montana, Ohio, Oregon, Pennsylvania, and Wisconsin. Rhode Island and Vermont have adopted a "qualified right to strike" that prohibits only those strikes that cause an imminent danger to public health.[19] In these states, public unions are free to strike upon giving adequate notification and after exhausting all impasse procedures. While there are still certain critical functions, such as protective services, that are generally not afforded the right to strike, the universal strike ban has been reversed.

The strike or the threat thereof, once considered labor's strongest weapon, has eroded to the extent that in many jurisdictions it is irrelevant. The effectiveness of the strike ban is difficult to assess and, although the data reveals a decrease in work stoppages of unionized government employees, it is unclear whether this is the result of strike prohibitions or is attributable to unfavorable market conditions.[20]

The Professional Air Traffic Controllers Organization (PATCO) strike, in which federal air traffic controllers were permanently replaced, has profoundly transformed the rules of the game.[21] A scenario that pitted a recalcitrant employer against a union leadership that overestimated its strength and underestimated its adversary created problems that were insolvable. Never again could a union threaten a strike against government and back the chief executive into a no-way-out position without fully understanding the consequences of its actions. Heretofore, while employers possessed the right to replace strikers, this prerogative was seldom exercised. The use of replacement workers was limited. A typical strike scenario ensued that involved either ceasing operations or remaining open through the use of supervisory/managerial workers. When replacement workers were used, striking workers were returned to work upon conclusion of the strike. This was not done in the PATCO case and, accordingly, the ground rules of the strike scenario dramatically changed.

At the crux of the strike issue is the authority of the employer to permanently replace striking workers. The United States Supreme Court upheld the unqualified right of private employers to replace economic strikers.[22] Workers who were permanently replaced after participation in a work stoppage were not considered to have been discharged and, as such, retained preferential recall rights when and if vacancies occurred. Replacement workers were not required to be fired in order to reinstate strikers. The increased use of replacement workers during the 1980s in private sector and, to a limited extent, in public sector work stoppages has resulted in a legislative attack by organized labor on this principle. Bills protecting the right to strike in the private sector by prohibiting or limiting the use of replacement workers have been introduced into the Congress.[23] The thrust of the proposed legislation is to prevent or severely limit the use of replacement workers as strike breakers. Employers who hire replacements at the outset of, or during the first weeks of, a stoppage would be guilty of an unfair labor practice. Critics argue that the legislation does not distinguish between legal and illegal strikes and favors strikers over those who remain on the job. Other issues center on the inconsistency between job security rights for strikers, the right to join unions and bargain collectively, and the choice to strike or refrain from striking. The effect of the proposed legislation on public sector strikes is unknown; however, it is expected that, if enacted, similar legislative protections will be sought by public sector unionists.

THE SCOPE OF BARGAINING

The scope of bargaining (hereinafter "scope") delineates topics which may or may not be collectively negotiated. Scope is based on the premise that certain subjects are critical to the well-being and efficiency of the enterprise and, if collective bargaining was permitted, the nature and mission of the organization might be threatened. Unlike the private sector, where the scope of bargaining is broad and has become almost a non-issue, scope is primarily a public sector consideration. Public sector scope ranges from expansive, in which the parties bargain nearly all aspects of the employment relationship, to limited, the type found in the federal government where negotiations are restricted primarily to non-economic matters. Public sector legislation delineates scope into three categories: (1) mandatory subjects, which must be bargained, (2) prohibited subjects, which must not be bargained, and (3) permissive subjects, which may be bargained. It is within the "permissive" category that most scope litigation occurs. Demands to enlarge the scope of bargaining and negotiate permissive and/or prohibited subjects, thereby making inroads into managerial prerogatives, have been attempted by unions.

Confrontation over control of specific scope-of-bargaining subject areas has been litigated in several forums, including administrative agencies, state legislatures, courts, and public employment relations boards (hereinafter "PERBs"). Employers have argued that a topic is beyond the scope of bargaining and attempt to remove it from bargaining and potential union control. Restrictions on scope are often subsumed in the "management rights" provisions of collective bargaining agreements. Absent a statutory ban, the parties in a unionized relationship are free to negotiate those subjects that they believe constitute the whole of the employment relationship.

While the debate concerning the scope of bargaining has diminished, there are those that argue against scope provisions, claiming that to permit collective bargaining and subsequently to superimpose constraints as to what is negotiable does a disservice to both parties. Not only is scope adjudication and litigation a timely and costly process, it allows the parties to seek refuge behind the "scope shield" instead of directly confronting a problem. Managers, reluctant to address a workplace concern, frequently claim it lies outside the scope of bargaining, while their union counterparts, unwilling or unable to bargain a demand, often profess that it is nonnegotiable. While the creation of a national public sector scope-of-bargaining standard is not recommended, these examples are illustrative of the wide range of scope diversity that exists. Scope remains a complex area within PSLR.

THE STATUS OF SUPERVISORS

After more than thirty years of PSLR, the question of collective bargaining rights for public sector supervisors (hereinafter "PSS") remains unresolved.[24] The debate centers on whether PSS should be afforded comprehensive collective bargaining rights or what limits, if any, should be imposed on them. Private sector supervisors do not have the right to bargain collectively, although in some industries, most noticeably maritime, they do so on a voluntary basis. The NLRA does not include supervisors under the definition of employee nor does it compel employers to treat supervisors as employees for the purposes of bargaining. The definition of supervisor is similar in both the private and public sectors. A supervisor is defined in the National Labor Relations Act as:

> . . . any individual having authority, in the interest of the employer, to hire, transfer, suspend, lay off, recall, promote, discharge, assign, reward, or discipline other employees, or responsibly to direct them, or to adjust their grievances, or to effectively recommend such action, if in connection with the foregoing their exercise of such authority is not of a merely routine or clerical nature, but requires the use of independent judgment.[25]

In public sector legislation the presumption in favor of coverage is controlling in the case of statutes that make no mention of supervisors. As distinguished from protecting a right to bargain, most PSLR statutes do not forbid supervisors from becoming members of labor organizations nor do they prohibit employers from voluntarily recognizing bargaining units of supervisors. Specific job functions are more controlling than job titles. Managers do not have the right to bargain in either sector.[26]

Arguing in support of PSS collective bargaining rights are those who assert that PSS do not exercise responsibilities associated with supervisory status, are powerless as supervisors, have meaningless titles, and as such, should be afforded the same bargaining rights as nonsupervisory employees. They contend that PSS have job-related needs compatible with unionization and, since many were promoted from the rank and file, they have a continuing community of interest. Furthermore, since many PSS have prior organizational affiliations with public sector organizations such as the National Education Association, American Nursing Association, Police Benevolent Associations, and certain civil service unions, supporters claim they should be allowed to continue that relationship.

Those against collective bargaining rights for supervisors argue for complete exclusion, asserting that if public management is to be strengthened a clearly defined cadre of supervisors is needed. They claim that unionized PSS are unable to meet their conflicting roles as rank-and-file employees and as members of management, thus leading to divided loyalties and a potential conflict of interest. Contending that supervisors are agents of the employer, opponents maintain that PSS must assume a managerial role in both collective bargaining and in the event of work stoppages. Allowing these groups to negotiate would allow them to sit on both sides of the bargaining table. An accommodation position suggests that PSS should neither be excluded from collective bargaining nor included in bargaining units with rank-and-file employees but should instead be placed in autonomous supervisory bargaining units.

There is presently a modest trend in public sector legislation and case law toward PSS bargaining restrictions that suggests a movement toward the private sector exclusionary model.[27] While a presumption in the public sector in favor of PSS coverage is still widespread, the right to bargain is no longer absolute. While PSLR can be characterized as being in an emerging and formative stage, it appears that the practice of allowing broad bargaining rights, even in a manner different from rank-and-file employees, has lessened. The trend toward exclusion should assist both labor and management in formulating long-term collective bargaining policies. Unions may no longer be faced with issues that are of interest to a minority of the membership, and public administrators may be able to reshape management teams to include clearly designated supervisors. PSS, caught in the middle, may have to develop new employment relationships consistent with the exclusionary trend, remain in non-nonsupervisory categories, abdicate their duties that render them supervisory, or opt to forgo union representation.

CIVIL SERVICE VERSUS COLLECTIVE BARGAINING— THE NATURE OF THE CONFLICT

The relationship between collective bargaining legislation and civil service merit systems has generated challenges and obstacles for public personnel administration.[28] For discussion purposes, civil service systems are defined as statutorily enacted personnel rules and regulations designed to implement merit principles such as recruitment and selection on the basis of knowledge, skills, ability, nondiscrimination, and testing. Characteristics of CSMS include independent bipartisan commissions, government-wide central personnel agency responsibilities, control of the examining function, and enforcement of rules pertaining to staffing the bureaucracy.

The function of civil service as an impartial arbiter has been called into question. In most unionized jurisdictions, the role of the civil service commission has been diminished and its traditional unilateral rule-making authority reduced to an appellate capacity. Some employees and unions view CSMS as an arm of the administration and not a neutral body, and have characterized it as an employer liability in the bargaining process. Questions persevere as to the impact of collective bargaining on preexisting CSMS and the continued authority of public managers to unilaterally prescribe the terms and conditions of employment. CSMS continue to regulate traditional personnel functions; however, in jurisdictions with public employee unions, fringe benefits, compensation programs, time and attendance standards, union membership requirements, and grievance procedures are being negotiated between labor and management. In some jurisdictions, labor relations systems along with conventional CSMS serve as integral components of public personnel administration, while in others there are jurisdictional clashes, functional overlap, and election of forum questions. Disagreements remain as to the ability of CSMS and LRS to coexist. Proponents of civil service submit that CSMS are robust healthy organizations and remain the only means to properly staff the bureaucracy. Those arguing in support of LRS claim that civil service has been unable to adapt to recent pressures confronting personnel systems.

The primary questions addressed in this section are to what extent, and in what manner, have labor relation systems been accommodated with preexisting civil service merit systems. In order to assess the relationship between CSMS and LRS, four types of statutory provisions within LRS legislation were surveyed. They were: (1) the existence of statutorily protected CSMS, (2) subjects reserved exclusively to CSMS and not within the scope of bargaining, (3) statutorily protected LRS and/or collective bargaining agreements that supersede existing CSMS, and (4) subjects reserved exclusively as management rights and not within the scope of bargaining. The results of this investigation are discussed below.

The evolution of CSMS as unilateral centralized personnel systems with control over merit rules and regulations, and almost every facet of the employment relationship, remained virtually unchallenged until the mid-1960s when public sector collective bargaining legislation began to emerge. Many CSMS were not adaptable to this new labor relations environment. During this period of collective bargaining growth, tension between civil service and union advocates was evident. Unlike organized labor, civil service has a narrow constituency that has remained relatively passive-reactive. The political strength of public sector unions was largely responsible for the passage of collective bargaining legislation and other structural changes in the organization, implementation, and delivery of personnel services. This is not meant to suggest that the erosion of CSMS can be attributed solely to the growth of unionization; however, the increase in collective bargaining played a major role in this development.[29]

The attempt to integrate collective bargaining statutes within state civil service merit systems is contradictory. CSMS do not evolve into LRS; certain fundamental characteristics inherent in each militate against juxtapositioning. Merit principles based on individualism, open competitive examinations, fitness and efficiency, probationary evaluation periods, and a politically neutral bureaucracy form the cornerstone of civil service. While merit principles may be acknowledged and supported by unions, they are not, nor can they be, the building blocks of unionism. The union is an instrument rooted in collectivism, designed to counterbalance the employer and ensure equality and uniform treatment of employees. So long as determinations of merit and fitness possess subjective elements, they cannot be considered legitimate union objectives. While these characteristics are associated with both public and private sector unions, the absence of CSMS in the private sector minimizes the difficulty.

The enactment of collective bargaining statutes requiring negotiations and execution of written collective bargaining agreements is evidence of the legislative response to the demand of public employees to alter the nature and structure of employment relationships. Collective bargaining legislation was not enacted in a vacuum. The statutes enable public employees to embark upon new forms of governance and bilateral negotiations as to the terms and conditions of employment. The system that previously regulated the employment relationship was CSMS; if that system was still viable in terms of fulfilling its historical mission, collective bargaining legislation would have been unnecessary. No one collective bargaining model setting forth the relationship between CSMS and LRS emerges as dispositive, yet certain commonalities are evident. In every situation, LRS has superseded, but not replaced, existing CSMS. The failure of state legislatures to implement termination procedures for CSMS or to successfully integrate LRS and CSMS has resulted in numerous problems including duplicative services.

The doctrine of exclusive primary jurisdiction, the rule statutorily specifying the agency charged with responsibility for issuing initial decisions, has been ignored. There is no evidence to document the revocation of existing civil service statutes in favor of more recent LRS legislation. In two states, Ohio and Illinois, that enacted collective bargaining laws during the 1980s, CSMS were not eliminated.[30] The structural pattern between civil service and labor relations legislation is consistent. In each instance the civil service statute predates the collective bargaining law. While administrative law principles suggest that the more recent legislation applies, few have a legislative commitment to that effect. In instances where language supportive of maintaining CSMS is found in collective bargaining legislation, the enforceability of such provisions remains unclear. Support for merit systems is a relatively safe position for policy-makers to assume, but whether CSMS are stronger because of stated legislative commitment is debatable. Furthermore, such pledges may be hyperbole at best, because the incompatibility of the systems may be beyond repair.

Subjects identified in collective bargaining legislation as reserved to the CSMS category relate to pre-pre-employment issues; however, in those jurisdictions where strong LRS exist and the subject is negotiable, there appears to be a practice of leaving these tasks to civil service. Other topics cited as reserved to CSMS are performance rating, position classification, and promotion. While unions are aware of the importance of these issues, they have been unable to make substantial headway negotiating these subjects into labor agreements.

Contract supremacy clauses reinforce the position of those who argue that LRS have replaced CSMS as the primary force within public personnel. It is arguable that statutory contractual supremacy is indicative of union political strength and statutory silence a matter of individual lawmakers' convenience; however, without an examination of the legislative history of each jurisdiction, this point is unknown.

Legislative silence on the scope of negotiations reflects a policy of allowing issues to be litigated, while designating them as a management right eliminates the risk of erosion through collective bargaining. Included as statutorily reserved subjects are traditional civil service functions such as recruitment, hiring, selection, transfer, and promotion. Granting control over pre-employment functions to management and not civil service is considered more detrimental to CSMS than LRS since most unions are willing to forgo negotiations for workers not yet hired. Their primary concern remains negotiating and protecting benefits and job security for the existing rank and file. The statutory designation of management right subjects has been at the expense of civil service and further weakens that system. It is difficult to ascertain from a legislative analysis whether the employer actually performs the tasks reserved to it or if CSMS continues to be the vehicle to implement and administer the process. It is unknown if the removal of topics from civil service control is a transfer of function from what may be perceived as one arm of management to another. CSMS have been derogated by the widespread existence of LRS; however, on the macro level, it is difficult to quantify as to what extent. An analysis of each jurisdiction's scope of bargaining case law is necessary to further assess this issue.

Topics previously under the exclusive contol of CSMS and now categorized by statutes or administrative agencies as nonmandatory subjects of bargaining continue to have an impact on the terms and conditions of employment. "Impact bargaining," the requirement to bargain the effect of implementing nonmandatory subjects on the terms and conditions of employment, is commonplace and permits a broader range of bargaining than might have been originally intended. Topics included under impact bargaining are often contested, and litigation frequently occurs. States that statutorily constrain the scope of bargaining may raise false employee expectations while deterring union political strength. Scope limits may be critical to the preservation of civil service or management rights yet weaken collective bargaining.

Causal inferences should be questioned when assessing the deterioration of CSMS. One might question if the passage of LRS legislation weakened civil service, or was the system so infirm that it was beyond resuscitation? Causality is difficult to measure; however, it is evident that the collective bargaining legislation did little, if anything, to strengthen CSMS. At best the legislation appears to reflect a tacit understanding to allow CSMS to continue within the parameters of LRS. The best causality evidence would be case studies on the relationship between the two systems.

A LOOK AT THE 1990s—THE EMERGENCE OF DUAL PERSONNEL SYSTEMS

An analysis of PSLR suggests the emergence of dual personnel systems (hereinafter "DPS"), which may be defined as shared systems that attempt to integrate competing elements of civil service merit systems and labor relations systems. They are found in jurisdictions where collective bargaining laws have been enacted as an addition to, or part of, civil service statutes, and where the scope of bargaining is broad. DPS may exist as the result of competition between CSMS, LRS, and public employers over control of subjects designated as management rights. Employee promotion is illustrative of this conflict. In some jurisdictions this subject is considered within the purview of CSMS, while in others it may either be reserved as a management right or negotiated between the parties. The issue may be further aggravated if the

CBA contains promotion criteria rooted in seniority, contradicting the CSMS requirement of promotions based on fitness and competitive exams. Another seniority-related issue could occur as political subdivisions consolidate services, thereby requiring the dovetailing of seniority lists. Would civil service requirements prevail over negotiated agreements? Within DPS confusion over primary and concurrent jurisdiction, scope of bargaining, and election of forum is commonplace. Questions of a substantive nature regarding employee classification status and procedural questions, once within the exclusive authority of state civil service commissions, now may be litigated in multiple forums. If CSMS have traditionally exercised control over employee time and attendance procedures and the parties subsequently collectively bargain alternative systems, which forum controls? If union demands for wage increases are met with employer support for employee reclassification, can it still be said that position classification remains outside the scope of bargaining? Disputes over performance ratings, licensing and credentialing, public safety training, certification requirements, and performance ratings may also arise when both CSMS and LRS simultaneously attempt regulation. Concurrent jurisdiction between CSMS and LRS exists either as a theoretical position or at the tolerance of the union. Some unions may support CSMS for a variety of reasons including using them as a means of limiting management rights. In those political subdivision areas where CSMS have authority over some aspect of the terms and conditions of employment, that is, retirement and health care benefits, unions might perceive a greater opportunity to effectuate their goals by lobbying a weakened CSMS in lieu of negotiating with an adversarial employer.

The development of DPS is evidenced by the widespread enactment of public sector collective bargaining statutes. This has resulted in the creation of an inconsistent legislative framework, one that is difficult to implement and might not accurately reflect existing personnel policy and practice. The task of uniting collective bargaining statutes within existing CSMS has been largely ignored.

Inconsistent personnel policies have created problems beyond the unionization question. Policy-makers must reassess the delivery of human resource services within the parameters of a unionized employment relationship and must consider legislation to alleviate the DPS problem. While it may have been expedient not to address the issue when public sector unionism was in its early stages, avoidance is no longer a viable policy.

DPS have damaged civil service merit systems and, while they continue, the data support the contention that for public employees, LRS, more than CSMS, have become the primary force in human resource policy formulation and implementation. Although CSMS retain their legislative basis, in unionized states they have become supporting players and no longer possess a monopoly over public personnel administration. In jurisdictions where collective bargaining laws have been implemented, civil service merit systems have become tired institutions, are in a period of decline, and may be at the twilight of their existence. This is evidenced by the widespread diffusion of their authority and the emergence of strong labor relations systems. In some jurisdictions, the collective bargaining agreement has become a central component of the personnel function. Bilateralism has replaced unilateralism in the decision-making process. The problems identified as characteristic of dual personnel systems are political in nature and will remain so long as policy makers see no advantage to change. Living with dual personnel systems is an option widely followed yet not recommended. Collective bargaining does not fit within civil service merit systems. The task ahead is the enactment of statutory revocation provisions for those state civil service merit systems that conflict with labor relations systems, and the preservation of merit principles within the context of collective bargaining.

Notes

1. This article is a synthesis of three studies conducted by the author: "Collective Bargaining and Public Sector Supervisors: A Trend Towards Exclusion?," *Public Administration Review*, November/December 1987, 47:6, pp. 485–497; "State Civil Service and Collective Bargaining: Systems in Conflict," *Public Administration Review*, March/April 1992, 52:2, pp. 162–172; and "Public-Sector Labor Relations in the Twenty-first Century: New Approaches, New Strategies," *Public Personnel Management*, C. Ban and N. Riccucci, eds. (New York: Longman Press, 1991), pp. 207–223.

   Additionally, several of the suggestions and concepts contained herein have been addressed in Joel M. Douglas, "Labor Law as an Impediment to Labor Relations Reform: Leveling the Playing Field," *International Journal of Public Administration*, Winter 1993, in press, and Melvin J. Dubnick and Joel M. Douglas, "A Trashy Situation: Collective Bargaining in the Public Sector," *Doing Public Administration*, 3rd ed., Nicholas L. Henry, ed. (Dubuque, IA: William C. Brown, 1991), pp. 83–107.

2. The passage of the *Lloyd-LaFollette Act* in 1912 gave federal sector employees the right to organize but did not afford bargaining rights to employee organizations.

3. *Wisconsin Municipal Employment Relations Act*, WISC. STAT. ANN., Chap. III, Ch. 509, L. 1959.

4. For union membership, density, and number of employees covered by collective bargaining agreements data, see: U.S Department of Labor, Bureau of Labor Statistics (BLS), *Current Wage Developments* reports and bulletins (February 1992).

5. For a discussion of civil service systems, see Joel M. Douglas, "State Civil Service and Collective Bargaining: Systems in Conflict," *Public Administration Review*, March/April 1992, 52:2, pp. 162–172.

6. *National Labor Relations Act*, P. L. 198, 74th Congress (1935).

7. Amending the *NLRA* to include public employees has been suggested by those favoring national public sector collective bargaining legislation. In addition to specific labor relations statutes, the laws frequently cited as part of the PSLR legislative/legal fabric include *The Fair Labor Standards Act of 1938, The Equal Pay Act of 1963, Title VII of The Civil Rights Act of 1964*, and *The Age Discrimination in Employment Act of 1967*.

8. States with enabling public sector legislation covering all state/municipal employees or selected occupational groupings are: Alaska, California, Connecticut, Delaware, Florida, Hawaii, Idaho, Illinois, Iowa, Kansas, Maine, Maryland, Massachusetts, Michigan, Minnesota, Montana, Nebraska, Nevada, New Hampshire, New Jersey, New Mexico, New York, North Dakota, Ohio, Oklahoma, Oregon, Pennsylvania, Rhode Island, South Dakota, Tennessee, Vermont, Washington, Wisconsin, and Wyoming.

9. States that restrict collective bargaining to police and firefighters in selected municipalities are Georgia, Kentucky, and Texas.

10. States with "meet and confer" statutes are Alabama and Missouri.

11. The *Indiana Public Employment Relations Act* was declared unconstitutional by the Indiana Supreme Court in *IEERB* v. *Benton Community School Corp.*, 77–78 PBC (1977). Indiana public employees now bargain pursuant to a governor's executive order.

12. Suggestions have been made that legislated employee grievance procedures are part of a union avoidance policy. Establishing these programs in a nonunion environment enables employers to weaken union organizing drives by granting employees a benefit frequently associated with unionized employment relationships. Another reason for the existence of these processes may be found in federal grant requirements that mandate employee grievance systems in order to qualify for funding. Legislated employee grievance procedures are found in states with and without enabling collective bargaining legislation. These states include Colorado, Maryland, Massachusetts, North Dakota, South Carolina, Utah, and Virginia.

13. In addition to those states with comprehensive collective bargaining statutes whereby dues deduction is within the scope of bargaining, the following states without comprehensive labor relations legislation permit payroll deduction or dues checkoff plans: Arizona, Arkansas, Louisiana, Nevada, North Carolina, Tennessee, Texas, Utah, and West Virginia. While it is arguable that payroll deduction plans provide a neutral employee benefit, they may also be construed as a means of union development.

14. See *Texas Public Employee Collective Bargaining Ban*, Ch. 135, L. (Art. 5154c, Title 83) (1947), *North Carolina Public Employee Membership in Labor Unions Act*, Ch. 95, Art. 12, Sec. 97-100, Gen. Stat., Ch. 958, L. (1981), and *Virginia Strikes by State Employees Act*, Sec. 40.1-55 and 40.1-57, Code of VA (1970).

15. *Executive Order 10988* (1962).

16. *Executive Order 11491* (1969). See also *Executive Order 11616* (1971) and *Executive Order 11838* (1975), which extended federal employee rights to partake in the labor relations process.

17. For data pertaining to the unionization of federal sector and postal employees, see "U.S. Office of Personnel; Management, Union Recognition in the Federal Government," Annual Reports.

18. *Civil Service Reform Act*, P. L. 95-454, 92 Stat. 1111 (1978) Title 5, Part III, Subpart F, Chapter 71, United States Code.

19. For states with a limited legal right to strike, see ALASKA STAT. Sec. 23.40.200(d) (1984); HAWAII REV. STAT. Sec. 89-12 (1976 and Supp. 1984); ILLINOIS ANN. STAT. Ch. 48 Sec. 1713; MINNESOTA STAT. ANN. Sec. 179A.18; MONTANA REV. CODES, Title 39, Sec. 39-31-101-409 (1973); OHIO REV. CODE. ANN. Sec. 4117.14 (D) (2); OREGON REV. STAT. Sec. 243.726 (1979); PA. LEGIS. Title 43, Sec. 1101.1001; WISCONSIN STAT. ANN. Sec. 111.70 (4) (1987). For states with a qualified right to strike, see RHODE ISLAND General Laws, Ch. 9.3, Title 28, Sec. 28-9.4-16 and VERMONT STAT. ANN. Ch. 20, Title 21, Sec. 1730. The California State Supreme Court held in *County Sanitation District* v. *Los Angeles County Employees Association* (699 P.2d 835, 1985) that a work stoppage would be considered legal unless it was expressly prohibited by case law or legislation. The ruling does not apply to police or firefighters.

20. For strike data, frequency, and number of employees involved in work stoppages, see U.S. Department of Labor, Bureau of Labor Statistics strike data as reported in *Monthly Labor Review*, 1981–1992.

21. For an analysis of the PATCO work stoppage, see "Air Traffic Controllers," Harvard Business School, Case Study 9-482-056, 1982.

22. *NLRB* v. *Mackay Radio & Tel. Co.*, 304 U.S. 333 (1938).

23. See Senate Bill Number 55 (S. 55), United States Senate, 1991. At the time of this writing the Senate had not voted on this bill; however, similar legislation passed the United States House of Representatives (H.R. 5).

24. For a discussion of public sector supervisors, managers, and confidential employees and their right to collectively bargain, see "Collective Bargaining and Public Sector Supervisors: A Trend Towards Exclusion?," *Public Administration Review*, November/December 1987, 47:6, pp. 485–497. See also Joel M. Douglas, "At the Bargaining Table: The Status of Public Sector Supervisory, Managerial and Confidential Employees," *Public Employees Relations Library*, Monograph #70 (Alexandria, VA: International Personnel Management Association, 1987), 96 pp.

25. *National Labor Relations Act*, P. L. 198, 74th Congress (1935), Sec. 2 (11).

26. No definition of manager is contained in the NLRA; however, the federal courts rely on standards set forth in the case law. Managerial employees are those ". . . executives who formulate and effectuate management policies by expressing and making operative decision of their employer . . ." *Palace Dry Cleaning*, 75 N.L.R.B. 320 (1947). The U.S. Supreme Court subsequently affirmed this definition in *N.L.R.B.* v. *Bell Aerospace Company Division of Textron Inc.*, 416 U.S. 267 (1974).

27. For an analysis of the trend toward PSS exclusion from collective bargaining and/ or the placement of supervisors in autonomous units, see Joel M. Douglas, "Collective Bargaining and Public Sector Supervisors: A Trend Towards Exclusion?," *Public Administration Review*, November/December 1987, 47:6, pp. 485–497.

28. See Joel M. Douglas, "State Civil Service and Collective Bargaining: Systems in Conflict," *Public Administration Review*, March/April 1992, 52:2, pp. 162–172.

29. It is arguable that the decrease in CSMS effectiveness contributed to the development of LRS. This theory may be correct; however, in the absence of any supporting documentation, it remains untested. One is reminded of the statement by Fritz Mosher when he wrote about the relationship between civil service and collective bargaining: "The founders of civil service did not bargain on collective bargaining." *Democracy and the Public Service* (New York: Oxford Univ. Press, 1968), p. 176.

30. See *Ohio Senate Bill 133, Public Employee Bargaining Law*, Ohio Revised Code, Ch. 4117, 1984, and *Illinois Public Labor Relations Act*, Public Act 83-1012, L. 1983.

Managing Diversity: From Civil Rights to Valuing Differences

WALTER D. BROADNAX

The United States has been racially, ethnically, sexually, religiously, and philosophically diverse since its earliest beginnings. As the early Europeans and Africans began arriving, they were met by native Americans who had established various cultures and communities across the land. Many of these cultures were internally quite complex, and there was substantial diversity within the overall native American population itself. There were Iroquois, Sioux, Cherokee, Seminoles, Blackfeet, Navajos, Apaches, and numerous other groups and tribes.

Our history is one of the many stresses and strains between different groups over time. There have been wars fought that sprang from those differences. We have moved forward but, at times, it has been with great difficulty. Now, it is late in the 20th century, and we must once again find the reoslve and the resources to cope positively with societal change. It is widely known that women, minorities, and immigrants will constitute a much larger proportion of the work force by the year 2000. Moreover, it is reported that

> . . . white native born men are no longer a majority in the American workplace. Today, more than half the work force is comprised of women, people of color, and immigrants.[1]

Given our history, these facts indicate that we could be facing one of the greatest challenges in the life of the republic. Can we find appropriate means to help us value and manage diversity in the work place successfully?

The New York state government experience is an example where we find tremendous variety in language, culture, race, religion, ethnicity, sexual orientation, politics, and philosophy. New York is a veritable cauldron of differences; thus, it faces some difficult challenges in the years ahead as the state tries where necessary to reconcile and implement policies derived from concepts such as civil rights, human rights, affirmative action, equal opportunity, desegregation, and now, diversity.[2] If we look at New York state government from several different perspectives, as it wrestles with various ideas and prescriptions for valuing and managing diversity, there are some lessons and experiences that may be useful for others, including public policy and management professionals.

EQUAL OPPORTUNITY AND AFFIRMATIVE ACTION

As in other parts of the country, the road from civil rights to valuing diversity has been long and sometimes very difficult to travel in New York. In many ways, New York's struggles with regard to equal employment opportunity (EEO) and affirmative action (AA) are no different than those same struggles taking place in other states across this country.

However, New Yorkers pride themselves on being innovative and out front in the human rights, equal opportunity, and affirmative action debate. It remains a debate because there are still disagreements about what equal opportunity and affirmative action mean and how they should best be implemented. There are often even more complex disputes and wrangling about how these policies should be approached within the context of the state's human rights law, which predates both.

To the extent that procedures and protections are still needed to facilitate minority entrance to the work force, their existence often limits our ability to focus on the more promising messages embedded in notions of valuing and managing diversity. Many white males in New York view affirmative action and equal opportunity as ways to cheat them out of what is rightfully theirs. On the other hand, many minorities view the emerging focus on diversity as a means to dilute and even derail equal opportunity and affirmative action initiatives and programs.

Initiatives

In 1988, the Governor's Executive Committee on Affirmative Action, which I chaired, met to discuss the status of various gubernatorial equal opportunity and affirmative action initiatives. The entire meeting was devoted to how state government could best respond to all of the competing demands from various groups, e.g., homosexuals, African-Americans, women, native Americans, Hispanics, Chinese, Jews, white women, African-American women, etc. How could we promote the interest of one group without being accused of subverting the interests of another group?

During this same meeeting, we also discussed anticipated worker shortages and how this might increase opportunities for all groups. The participants were initially attracted to this notion, but the natural tendency to worry about who is possibly winning and who is possibly going to be the loser prevailed and the discussion returned to how to ensure equal opportunity and affirmative action related results.

Reactions

The meeting described above presaged the difficulties we would have later on as we began developing the state's first work force plan. Various groups were afraid that human resource strategies laid out in the plan did not explicitly address the need for a continuing emphasis on EEO/AA processes and procedures. Rather, many of the strategies developed within the work force plan were based on notions related to increased diversity in the work place. But, even though representatives of the different interests really wanted to embrace and value diversity, it just did not seem to be as compelling as those concepts which promoted inclusion first.

What the New York experience seems to indicate is that even though people want to value diversity and embrace it as an approach to managing differences in the work force, they are afraid that the gates to good jobs and upward mobility will not be opened without strong policies, procedures, and controls. Most minority group members are suspicious of any discussion that suggests that white males will easily change their attitudes, beliefs, and actions toward them. Therefore, it will be important for people to begin to see that diversity is being valued and that managers are becoming interested in managing differences before equal opportunity programs and affirmative action procedures can be supplanted successfully by other means and methods for bringing all people successfully into the New York state work force.

VALUE ADDED THROUGH DIVERSITY

During the late 1960s and 70s, the idea that public bureaucracies might be able to perform their missions better if those who worked within them were more representative of the society at large received a good deal of attention. Moreover, there were some who believed that there was something intrinsically valuable about the perspectives that would be rendered in the policymaking and decision processes by the inclusion of minorities and women.[3] Embedded in the concept of representativeness was the notion of value added to state government by the potentially positive influence women and minorities might have on the policy and decisionmaking processes of government. Either implicitly or explicitly, the belief was that including those who are different will enrich and strengthen what government is as well as what government does.

It is difficult for some people to believe that there could be any value in differences. Recently, it has become chic to point to Japan's success as an industrial power and explain that success by calling attention to her relatively homogeneous population. When this subject arises, rarely does anyone proceed to explain and substantiate this bit of conjecture. Rather, there is usually a pause in the exchange and the conversation or presentation continues. The implication seems to be that we all understand and agree with the notion that sameness (homogeneous populations) produce better products more efficiently.

New York state is many things to many people but it could never be referred to as homogeneous. In fact, it was estimated that in 1980, 16 percent of the state's labor force, 37 percent of its physicians, and 20 percent of its nurses were foreign born.[4]

The state has the largest Jewish population in the world outside of Israel and the largest African-American population in the United States. Putatively, there are over 50 different languages represented within the student body of the City University of New York. The streets of Manhattan are teeming with differences.

Oath of Allegiance

Any state as diverse as New York must constantly search for ways to include people in the processes of business and government. The benefits to be gained from this inclusion can be seen in some very practical and concrete outcomes that have been achieved through the value added derived from diversity. For example, the state had struggled for years with the refusal of native Americans to take an oath of allegiance to the United States. This created a very big problem in that the oath was required in the civil service law covering state employment and the state education law which covered teachers and others under the jurisdiction of the education commissioner. Many attempts had been made over the years to find a solution to this problem so that native Americans would no longer be disadvantaged in the hiring process and officials could be satisfied that they did not wish to undermine the government.

In 1989, the first native American was hired in the affirmative action office of the New York State Department of Civil Service. There was all of the expected discomfort with this action in many parts of the department, but the leadership believed that in order for the state to become seriously inclusionary with regard to native Americans, it would be necessary to create a focus for those interests within the Civil Service Department by hiring a native American. Over the course of several months, this one individual was able to generate support within his own department and find allies within the Department of Education and the state legislature. He worked tirelessly to build rapport and understanding between himself and others across various agencies and units of government. Through this process, he was able to bring the commissioners of Education and Civil Service together around a piece of legislation which established an alternative oath of office for native Americans. This legislation removed a significant legal obstacle to native American employment by the state of New York.

Tangible and Intangible Benefits

In this situation, the value added came in tangible ways, such as the new legislation and revised regulations regarding the oath of office but there were also certain intangible benefits. One such benefit was that nonminorities were able to experience a point of view, a culture, a policy perspective that, in many ways, differed substantially from their own. These differences and the feelings they sometimes generated, often helped them to understand some of the reactions they may have gotten themselves from traditional minorities. Differences, when accepted as legitimate, can keep us from becoming smug. Creating a situation where everyone is considered with dignity and treated with respect empowers more people in the work place. More people empowered translates into a more powerful work place.

EDUCATION AND HUMAN RESOURCE DEVELOPMENT NEEDS

In the 60s and 70s, many government managers were being exposed to sensitivity training. The objective then was to help white managers deal with what appeared to be a rapidly increasing minority presence in the workplace. Quickly added to the mix was the increasing presence of women, especially in professional and managerial roles. There are many stories about sensitivity training where participants felt things got out of hand. However, the objective was usually a laudable and sound one—to help people cope successfully with change.

The Supreme Court decision in Brown vs. The Topeka Board of Education had only recently stated that separate but equal was a fantasy and, therefore, public facilities, schools, colleges and universities, and public transportation would have to be desegregated. The decision was handed down in 1954, but it was not until the 1960s that we saw desegregation beginning to unfold seriously. As desegregation accelerated, many people were being asked to shift from a situation where it was legal and common practice to keep minorities out to one where they were being told they should work together in peace and harmony. Something more than saying that it was a good idea was needed.

NEW CHALLENGES

Today, public managers and government officials face yet another education and development challenge spawned by societal, and to some extent, global change. Some managers, within the space of a 30-year career, have come from a situation where they rarely saw minorities in positions of respect and authority in the workplace, to one where there are large numbers of minority and women technicians, professionals, and managers.

Columbia University's School of Business is developing a comprehensive "Managing Diversity" course. The program, which is being produced by psychologist and diversity consultant, Dr. Anna Duran, is designed for executives and managers who are faced with increasing cultural diversity in their organizations and it will examine the best methods for incorporating approaches to cultural diversity into routine management activities.[5]

Looking closely at recent training efforts, we can find themes and strains that remind us of experiences from the old sensitivity training workshops. A vignette from a training workshop run by Terrance Simmons reveals the following insights.

> The 13 senior-level UNISYS managers sitting in a Norcross, Georgia, training center look uneasy. As part of a day-long diversity management workshop, they have just been instructed to compile a list of negative and positive stereotypes that are normally associated with various groups—including blacks, Hispanics, women, and white males . . .
>
> The consultant running the seminar politely asks that the participants be as candid as possible. Just jot down things you have heard or that you have seen. After working for 10 minutes, the group which has been divided into three teams, reads their list aloud.
>
> Although several positive stereotypes were listed for white males—they were labeled leaders and decisionmakers—the group appears disturbed that a number of negative stereotypes were listed for the other groups. For example, women were viewed as pushy, bitchy, and too emotional. Hispanics were seen as lazy, emotional, and unskilled. African-Americans described as uneducated, slow workers, and militant. When asked, almost all managers in modern organizations will say they are not racists or sexists.
>
> The purpose of the exercise is to allow managers safely to recognize and admit, to themselves and their peers, that they really do still harbor some biases against minorities and women. Once this happens, we have made a quantum leap ahead because it becomes obvious that those biases are adversely affecting their ability to manage a diverse workforce productively.[6]

Training

It appears that objectives of the 60s and 70s are similar to those of the 90s and education and training are fundamentally important to reaching them. The National Association of State Personnel Executives has recognized this need for training and education relaterd to diversity. As a result, each semiannual and annual conference has devoted a substantial proportion of the program to providing educational and training opportunities in this area for the state's chief personnel and human resources executives. Regretfully, New York state, like almost every other state, provides too few seminars, workshops, lectures, or experientially-based training and educational programs focusing on cultural diversity for its managers and executives. This can be partially explained by an increasingly difficult financial situation.

Because New York state's human resources system is driven by the fact that its workforce is 97 percent unionized and a civil service approach that requires examinations for most entry-level jobs as well as promotions, diversification of the workforce has been relatively slow. Moreover, training those from minority groups so that they might be able to meet the standards set for most jobs has been cumbersome at best, although some progress has been made over the last few years.

For example, the Civil Service Employees' Association negotiated with the state for the creation of the Civil Service Employees' Advancement Program (CSEAP). This program has helped hundreds of female employees move out of clerical poisitions and into managerial and professional positions through on-the-job training opportunities. There have also been some smaller successes with transitional programs such as the School-to-Work Bridge Program which provides experiential opportunities for minorities as they are leaving high school or college, thus improving their performance on examinations required for appointment.

Again, the New York experience is one of successes as well as obstacles yet to be overcome, but one where there is an increasing awareness that much remains to be done in order successfully to diversify its workforce. In areas such as mental health, mental retardation and developmental disabilities, and correctional services, there is a rapidly increasing population of minority clients and a situation that is quickly escalating into one that will demand a more diversified workforce.

WHAT MANAGERS MUST UNDERSTAND

As was discussed earlier in this essay, managers sometimes may need help finding out what the problem is before they can be expected to solve it. The process of discovering what the problem is and where it comes from is what many would call education. Education is cognitive but it is also very much affective or emotional in character as well. Black is not necessarily black and white is not necessarily white until people are able to understand such factual information in terms that are useful to them in a personalized way. For example, the fact that white males are no longer in the majority within the workforce is factually true. But, this may mean something different for each individual.

The challenge is to help managers and those they manage to come to value differences. This means that both those who manage and those who are managed must receive assistance in learning what the objectives of the organization are in regard to diversity and then they must receive skills training that will help them achieve those organizational goals. As is true for any organization, the commitment must begin at the top and it must be sustained from the top.

Typically, excellent managers have developed outstanding human resource management skills. They have learned how to create situations for getting the best out of each individual within his or her organization. Yes, this is much more difficult than proceeding as though everyone was the same or as though everyone could become the same. It means that each organization and each leader within his or her organization must take seriously the fact that the world is changing and come to understand that these changes do not have to mitigate against individual aspirations or ambitions. However, if managers are going to take organizational goals related to diversity seriously, they must be treated like all other goals that are important to top management. There must be rewards for those who do well. The behaviors desired must be reinforced.

In a very practical sense, we see organizations like XEROX, where David T. Kearns, the former chairman and chief executive officer (currently deputy secretary of the Department of Education), was able to diversify his corporation culturally. He took it seriously and those working with him were compelled to take it seriously as well.[7] If the person at the top is only paying lip service to the value of diversity, everyone will know it because they will be able to see it. The work place will not have changed.

Tragically, in managing diversity, there are many who still ask what is it that women and minorities want. Complete success would be when there is no need to ask this question because it would be understood that they basically want what we all want and that those wants are tempered and shaped by individual differences and desires. A more conceivable indicator of success would be the existence of increasingly visible public and private organizations across the land where the inclusion of differences was the rule, rather than the exception. Once differences are included, we can then work toward valuing those differences.

CONCLUSION

Valuing differences has not been something that has come easily in the United States. We have struggled with a host of concepts, notions, and approaches to dealing with differences; they range from legalized perpetual servitude to America the melting pot. But each time we have seriously reached for a solution we have made incremental progress. Today, it seems that the stage may be set for us to take a major step toward valuing diversity by fully embracing the notion of including differences. Once organizations have reached a critical mass in terms of having brought people from different backgrounds and experiences into the working environment, the most important ingredient necessary for learning to value diversity will be in place. The sine qua non of any meaningful discussion of diversity is the successful inclusion of differences.

Notes

1. Loden, Marilyn and Ronne Hoffman Loeser, "Working Diversity: Managing the Differences," *The Bureaucrat*, Spring 1991, p. 21.
2. See *Public Service Through the State Government Workforce: Meeting the Challenge of Change*. Task Force on the New York State Public Workforce in the 21st Century.

Nelson A. Rockefeller Institute, February 1989, and New York State Department of Civil Service Work Force Plan 1989: Preparing Today's Work Force for Tomorrow, Spring 1989.

3. See Broadnax, Walter D., "Role Orientations of Minority and Nonminority Urban Administrators: Forces for Convergence and Divergence." Dissertation, 1975.

4. New York State Department of Civil Service, New York State Workforce Plan 1990: Building a State Workforce in the 1990s, Spring 1990.

5. Thompson, Kevin D., "Back to School," *Black Enterprise*, November 1990, p. 57.

6. Ibid., p. 56.

7. Thomas, R. Roosevelt, "From Affirmative Action to Affirming Diversity," *Harvard Business Review*, March-April 1990, p. 115.

Sexual Harassment in the States

RITA MAE KELLY
PHOEBE MORGAN STAMBAUGH

This article outlines the current discourse concerning sexual harassment. It compares and contrasts the experience of sexual harassment between genders, between occupations (traditional versus nontraditional occupations), and between sectors (private versus public), and finally focuses on sexual harassment at the state level. Data from the surveys of public administrators in the states are analyzed[1] and policy implication areas are discussed. Analysis focuses on Kanter's thesis that structural and systemic characteristics play an important role in the experience of sexual harassment.

WHAT IS SEXUAL HARASSMENT?

The term "sexual harassment," coined by activists in the mid-1970s, was first used in reference to the imposition of unwanted sexual attention endured by women at their place of work (Backhouse and Cohen 1981; Farley 1978). In 1976, the public's interest was sparked by a *Redbook* survey that reported an incidence rate of more than 80 percent among its readership (Safran 1976). While the emergence of sexual harassment as a concern may coincide with the sharp increase of middle- and upper-class women in the labor force, evidence indicates that since colonial times sexual harassment has been the working woman's nightmare (Bularzik 1978; MacKinnon 1987).

Many feel that efforts to remedy the problem have been thwarted by the lack of an agreed-upon definition. In terms of social science research, the lack of a narrow definition has resulted in a wide range of findings (Gruber 1989). Thus, the validity and reliability of scientific explanations and definitions are often suspect (Gillespie and Leffler 1987). The lack of a consensus among social scientists reflects the subjective nature of the experience of sexual harassment as well as the impact of sex role ideology in the identification of unwanted sexual attention.

In 1980, the Equal Employment Opportunity Commission (EEOC) issued guidelines for employers in the development of policies to forbid sexual harassment policies. These guidelines portray sexual harassment as a discriminatory action that is sexual in nature and that negatively affects an individual's experience of equality in his or her work environment. To put it another way, defined as a violation of Title VII, sexual harassment is an act of sex discrimination and violates a constitutional right to equality in the workplace. Thus, the EEOC definition is the one most commonly used by policy makers. For example, the Office of the Civil Rights Commission adopted the EEOC guidelines almost verbatim for application under Title IX. As a result, sexual harassment is also a violation of one's right to equal access to education. This is most important because the application of EEOC guidelines in the development, dissemination, and implementation of sexual harassment policies is the primary consideration in the assignment of liability once sexual harassment claims enter the judicial arena.

WHO GETS SEXUALLY HARASSED?

Since the emergence of the concept in the late 1970s, sexual harassment has been considered a "woman's issue." Evidence indicates a disproportionate number of women report sexual harassment. As previously mentioned, in the *Redbook* survey more than 80 percent of the women reported having experienced sexual harassment. In a random survey of the working population at large, 21 percent of the women claimed they had been harassed (Gutek 1985). And in the largest and most comprehensive survey to date of governmental employees, the U.S. Merit Systems Protection Board found in 1981, and again in a 1987 replication, that 42 percent of all women employed by the federal government had experienced sexual harassment within two years of each study (U.S. Merit Systems Protection Board 1987).

Gender disparity in sexual harassment is very evident. Men do report sexual harassment, but the incidence—from 8 percent to 16 percent—is significantly lower than it is for women (Gutek 1985; U.S. Merit Systems Protection Board 1987). Interestingly, sexual harassment of most men is perpetrated by men (Gutek and Morasch 1982). Studies of sexual harassment in the private sector reveal comparable trends (Personnel Policies Forum 1987). In all fifty-seven companies surveyed by the Personnel Policies Forum, 96 percent of the complaints were filed by a female employee against a male offender (Personnel policies forum 1987, p. 17).

One explanation for the gender disparity is that men are more likely than women to find sexual behaviors to be positive (Powell 1986). Another explanation is said to rest with the disparity of organizational power between men and women. Women are more likely to be troubled by unwanted sexual attention and more likely to feel helpless to stop it because working women are outside the dominant power group (Kanter 1977). While women may have organizational status, they may still lack organizational power. Female teachers have reported harassment by male students (Herbert 1989), female supervisors by male employees (Clarke 1986), and female sales executives by their male customers (Nemec 1988). Female managers and administrators are no exceptions (Powell 1986).

This gender disparity in reactions to unwanted sexual attention has contributed to the 1991 judicial interpretation in *Ellison* v. *Brady* that the standard for assessing whether sexual harassment exists must be a reasonable woman's judgment, not a reasonable man's judgment. The decision in this case argues that women are disproportionately affected by sexual harassment and that women react differently than men to unwanted sexual advances. The decision also reaffirmed that an employer's failure to remove a perpetrator of sexual harassment from the workplace creates and perpetuates a hostile environment. The employer must be held accountable for this failure.

Evidence shows that sex segregation by occupation and workplace not only contributes to the prevalence of sexual harassment but also figures into how it is experienced (Gutek and Morasch 1982; Hemming 1985; Kanter 1977). For example, women working at jobs traditional for their sex role (such as secretary, clerk, receptionist, waitress) may experience sexual harassment as "sex role spillover" (Gutek and Morasch 1982). In other words, their traditional social roles as wife, girlfriend, mother, or daughter become inseparable from their work duties. When this happens, interactions with women in these occupations are more often sexual in nature than professional. And, as previously mentioned, this type of behavior in the workplace tends to be viewed positively by men but negatively by women.

Women working in nontraditional occupations often find themselves removed from women working in more traditional jobs in the organization and are assigned minority status in a culture dominated by men. In the role of "tokens" or "pioneers" (Kanter 1977), these women must often negotiate the resentment, anger, confusion, and frustration generated by their "invasion" of the masculine domain. When these negative responses to their entrance into nontraditional areas are manifested in sexual behavior, then they become sexual harassment.

WHAT IS THE COST OF SEXUAL HARASSMENT?

The price paid by individuals, organizations, and society cannot be overestimated. "Sexual harassment syndrome" may manifest itself in the form of depression, chronic physical illness, and the deterioration of self-esteem and self-worth. Many victims of sexual harassment must take extended sick leave without pay (U.S. Merit Systems Protection Board.1987). A large portion are forced to quit their jobs (Coles 1986), forfeiting years of seniority, security, and benefits. Some even become suicidal (Gacioch 1987). Those few who risk filing a grievance rather than quit are stigmatized as "whistle-blowers" (Dandekar 1990) or malcontents (Branson and Branson 1988). Those who make it to a court of law and are awarded restitution, usually in the form of back pay, find that the award rarely compensates for the financial as well as emotional losses experienced.

At the organizational level, the cost in lost productivity, training, and support services and the cost of litigation are substantial. For example, the American Broadcasting Company paid $15 million to settle a claim made by one of its female executives (Garvey 1986). In 1987, it was estimated that sexual harassment cost taxpayers $189 million per year in employee turnover alone (U.S. Merit Systems Protection Board 1987). As one executive stated, "the cost [for employers] is high since many women just quit. There goes the kilobucks you just spent to train and market her" (Kiechel 1987, p. 20).

SEXUAL HARASSMENT AND THE PUBLIC SECTOR

The public sector, especially the federal government, has taken the lead in addressing sexual harassment. At the federal level, the U.S. Postal Service and the civil service initiated the development and implementation of organizational responses at the agency level (Neugarten and Miller-Spellman 1983). Ironically, one of the first court cases involving claims of sexual harassment was filed against the EEOC (*Rogers* v. *EEOC 1972*).

At the state level, responses have been slow and diverse. In 1979, surveys of the employees of Illinois and Florida (McIntyre and Renick 1982) indicate the prevalence of sexual harassment of state employees to be near that experienced by federal workers. In Illinois, 59 percent of the women reported having been sexually harassed at their present job. In Florida, the rate was 42 percent. "Fear of deterioration in their working conditions, losing promotions or pay raises, poor references and loss of their jobs prevented resistance to unwanted sexual attention" (McIntyre and Renick 1982, pp. 284–85). At the time these surveys were in progress, Maryland was the only state with specific provisions for handling sexual harassment of state employees (McIntyre and Renick 1982).

By 1987, however, thirty-three states had published statewide sexual harassment policies (Ross and England 1987). About one-half of these policies were in the form of executive orders issued from the office of the governor. For example, in 1980, Utah's governor, Scott M. Matheson, declared sexual harassment to "be prohibited in any and every workplace in which public employees are required to conduct business" (as cited in McIntyre and Renick 1982). In each case, state policy reflected the use of the EEOC employment guidelines and included the commission's definition (Ross and England 1987).

In 1981, California not only issued a statewide policy but also required each agency and department to develop sexual harassment guidelines within their own organizations. During that same year, Texas approved a proscriptive statute and Wisconsin's governor issued an executive order that included educational systems as well. Both Arizona and Alabama have executive orders prohibiting sexual harassment of all state employees. Given that the majority of states in the nation now have policies specific to sexual harassment, the question remains, how prevalent is sexual harassment at the state level? How is it experienced, and who reports it?

PATTERNS OF SEXUAL HARASSMENT

Table 6-1 presents the findings from our empirical assessment of the extent of sexual harassment in the five states of Alabama, Arizona, Texas, Utah, and Wisconsin. The data reveal several consistent patterns across these states as the following description explains.

Women in substantially higher proportions than men have experienced all forms of sexual harassment. Specifically, from 6 to 16 percent of high-level female public administrators have experienced unwelcome sexual advances, while almost none of their male counterparts have. While 11 to 24 percent of the females experienced requests for sexual favors, only 1 to 7 percent of males in any of these same states did. Whereas 14 to 36 percent of the women experienced offensive physical contact, only 1 to 5 percent of the men did. In addition, whereas 33 to 60 percent of the women experienced offensive verbal behavior, only 16 to 36 percent of the men did.

Similarly, women reported hearing about these types of sexual harassment at higher levels than men. Specifically, the percentage of women hearing about unwelcome sexual advances ranged from 29 percent in Texas to 67 percent in Arizona; for men the range went from 19 to 45 percent. In terms of requests

Table 6-1
Type of Sexual Harassment Experienced and Heard About (%)

	Women		Men	
Type and State	Experienced	Heard About	Experienced	Heard About
Unwelcome sexual advances				
Alabama	11	46	1	45
Arizona	10	67	0	39
Texas	7	29	0	19
Utah	16	46	1	32
Wisconsin	6	39	1	22
Requests for sexual favors				
Alabama	12	42	1	46
Arizona	24	57	7	34
Texas	11	27	2	21
Utah	21	38	1	30
Wisconsin	12	36	4	18
Offensive physical contact				
Alabama	24	42	1	42
Arizona	14	62	3	42
Texas	16	28	2	15
Utah	36	38	2	37
Wisconsin	19	43	5	31
Offensive verbal behavior				
Alabama	57	54	36	49
Arizona	57	50	36	45
Texas	33	41	16	39
Utah	46	34	31	39
Wisconsin	60	53	36	50

for sexual favors, a low of 27 percent of the women in Texas heard about such requests and a high of 57 percent in Arizona did. Among the men, the range was a low of 18 percent in Wisconsin to a high of 46 percent in Alabama. The range of women hearing about offensive physical contact was about the same: 28 percent in Texas to a high of 62 percent in Arizona. For the men, the range was 15 percent in Texas to 42 percent in Alabama and Arizona. The differences between the men and women in each state hearing about offensive verbal behavior was 34 percent in Utah to 54 percent in Alabama for the women; and 39 percent in Texas and Utah to 50 percent in Wisconsin for the men.

BACKGROUND CHARACTERISTICS AND HARASSMENT

It is evident from the variation in the data that not all women experience or hear about sexual harassment. To assess the extent to which background variables other than one's sex are related to sexual harassment, an index of the level of harassment experienced was created and compared to management rank for the women in the Arizona study. Data from Arizona and Wisconsin are used in this analysis because the sampling procedures in these two states make it possible to separate the respondents by managerial rank. This separation into middle and upper ranks allows comparisons between women and men at graduated ranks. Although it is not possible to generalize broadly from these two states, the insights obtained from this more microscopic view ought to be helpful. The general comparability of findings across the states reported in Table 6-1 indicate that the variations to be anticipated among the states are likely to be differences of degree rather than of kind.

The index was an additive one scored as follows: those respondents who had not experienced any form of either verbal or other harassment were assigned a score of 0; those who had experienced verbal harassment only in the form of jokes and snide remarks were assigned a score of 1; those who had experienced any or all of the other possible options (other offensive physical conduct of a sexual nature, requests for sexual favors from work colleagues, or unwelcome sexual advances in exchange for an employment opportunity by a superior) were assigned a score of 2. This scoring procedure creates an ordinal scale of gradations of the sexual harassment experienced.

Table 6-2 shows the severity of harassment experienced by the women in Arizona and Wisconsin by mid-level versus high-level ranks. About one-third of the women in each sample had experienced no harassment, one-third had experienced verbal harassment only, and another one-third had experienced more severe forms of harassment. Having risen in the administrative ranks provides no apparent protection against harassment. In fact, the pattern in Table 6-2 suggests that upper-level women might actually experience both more verbal and more severe forms of physical harassment than do the middle-level women.

For the State of Arizona, the harassment index was run against various background characteristics (age, race, religion, parental social class, income, political party affiliation, years of service, and marital status) to assess whether any of these characteristics were associated with higher or lower levels of harassment. Only race and current marital status had any relationship with harassment levels.

Table 6-2

Harassment Experienced by Sex and Management Level for Arizona and Wisconsin Administrators (%)

	Women		*Men*	
Arizona	*18–22*	*23–30*	*18–22*	*23–30*
Grades	*(n =53)*	*(n =42)*	*(n =118)*	*(n =206)*
None	35.8	26.2	60.2	61.2
Verbal only	28.3	33.3	33.9	29.6
Other forms	35.8	40.5	5.9	9.2
Wisconsin	*13–17*	*18–24*	*13–17*	*18–24*
Grades	*(n =104)*	*(n =50)*	*(n =135)*	*(n =73)*
None	38.5	30.0	60.7	64.4
Verbal only	37.5	46.0	33.3	24.7
Other forms	24.0	24.0	5.9	11.0

Contrary to what might be expected, white women at all levels were more likely to experience harassment than nonwhite women. In the mid-level sample, whereas 30 percent of the forty-four white women did not experience any harassment, 67 percent of the nine non-white women did not. Among the upper-level group the key difference in sexual harassment experience by race/ethnicity was in terms of its severity. About one-fourth of each racial grouping did not experience any harassment, whereas 27 percent of the thirty-four white women but 63 percent of the eight black women experienced verbal harassment only; 43 percent of the white women but only 13 percent of the non-white women experienced the more severe forms of harassment.

The small sample size for both of these racial groups requires caution in extrapolating these percentages to other populations. Nonetheless, because the sample does include almost all of the women at the upper level in Arizona's state government, it does reflect the pattern of harassment in this state.

As one would expect, women not currently married were more subject to harassment than women who were. Among the mid-level women, about one-third of both the married and unmarried did not experience harassment, but 48 percent of the unmarried experienced the more severe forms of harassment whereas only 25 percent of the married women did. Apparently, marriage still connotes that a woman "belongs to" someone else and, therefore, has some additional protection from harassment by the men with whom she works.

IMPACT OF HARASSMENT ON JOB PERFORMANCE AND EFFECTIVENESS

J. L. Pereia (1988), a lawyer for the Securities and Exchange Commission in the 1980s, characterized sexual harassment as "psychological warfare with an old-boy network," stressing both the harm that can be done to women and the gender power differential undergirding such harassment. The argument that sexual harassment is a serious form of sexual discrimination derives from the assumption that it has a critical impact on a woman's ability to perform a job and to be an effective employee.

To examine the impact harassment has on job performance and effectiveness, analyses of variance were completed using twenty-two types of job functions and competencies. Given the probability that harassment is likely to have a greater impact on job performance of the mid-level than the higher-level women, we kept the two data sets separate for this analysis. Sexual harassment, or the possibility of it, is often a component of the invisible barriers that keep numerous mid-level women from "breaking through the glass ceiling" to the upper levels in both public and private sector management. These functions and/or competencies encompassed the following: communication abilities; organizational coalition formation/conflict management; specialized expertise (e.g., engineering, law); adaptability/flexibility, ability to balance short- and long-term considerations; the collection/assessment/analysis of information and making judgments; sensitivity to the environment; focusing on results/goal achievement; taking initiative/showing creativity; leadership; competency in interpersonal relations; personnel management; affirmative action/EEO management; budgetary resource management; keeping up with agency policies/priorities, external issues/trends; keeping subordinates informed regarding agency policies, issues, and trends; selling/defending work unit activities to supervisor and external groups; coordinating and integrating work activities with those of other organizations; identifying policy and program alternatives; managing programs (planning, coordinating, guiding staff); monitoring program compliance/program evaluation; and research and program development.

The results indicate that a substantial variation in the impact of sexual harassment on job performance and effectiveness exists by level within the hierarchy. The mean scores show that the importance of focusing on results and goal achievement is lower for mid-level women experiencing higher levels of harassment ($n = 53$; mean $= 4.1$; $F = 3.01$; $p < 0.10$) than it is for the mid-level women who experience lower levels of harassment ($n = 53$; mean $= 4.1$; $F = 4.32$; $p < 0.05$). At this same mid-level, the women experiencing high levels of harassment also perceive "taking the initiative/showing creativity" as not being very important for their job effectiveness ($n = 53$; mean $= 4.3$; $F = 3.83$; $p < 0.05$).

At this mid-level in the Arizona public service it appears that sexual harassment sharply reduces a female employee's perception that focusing on results and goal achievement and taking the initiative on the job is important for her effectiveness as an employee. Over time it is obvious that such attitudes are likely to affect the quality of performance and to reduce the probability of promotion for these women. Managers typically must take the lead in setting goals, defining a unit's strategy, and launching new projects. Employees who do not show promise in engaging in these activities are unlikely to be considered managerial material. To the extent that sexual harassment contributes to deterring substantial numbers of women from being visible in these positive ways, sexual harassment is a concrete manifestation of institutional sexism and a major factor in enforcing the "glass ceiling" beyond which women find it hard to move.

At these same mid-level ranks, women who experienced the more severe forms of sexual harassment rated the importance of affirmative action and equal employment opportunity for both their job performance and effectiveness lower than did the women who experienced no or less severe harassment. The mean score on the importance of AA/EEO as it relates to job performance for women experiencing no verbal harassment was 2.53 (S.D. = 1.5); for the women experiencing verbal harassment only it was 3.27 (s.d. = 1.58); for the women experiencing the more severe forms of harassment the mean score was 2.00 (s.d. = 1.08). The means for the effectiveness data were comparable. It seems that the women experiencing less harassment sense a connection between the absence of harassment and the presence of AA/EEO policies. Perhaps the women who experience verbal harassment rate the importance of these policies higher than either the women experiencing no harassment or those who experience more severe forms because they think the harassment would be worse if no such policies existed.

Among these same mid-level women, those experiencing the most severe sexual harassment also rated "keeping subordinates informed regarding agency policies, issues, and trends" as less important for their job performance ($n = 53$; mean = 3.3; $F = 3.16$; $p < 0.05$) and effectiveness ($n = 53$; mean = 2.84 $F = 2.84$; $p < 0.10$). Women who experienced more severe harassment also indicated that identifying policy and program alternatives was less important for their job effectiveness than women at the same mid-levels who experienced less severe harassment ($n = 53$; mean = 3.6; $F = 2.6$; $p < 0.10$). The degree of sexual harassment that women experience appears to be related to the connection (or lack of it) a woman sees between her decision-making functions and her ability and effectiveness in performing her job.

Among the upper-level women administrators (GS 23–30), higher levels of sexual harassment had a different impact on their responses to the questions regarding job functions and competencies. These women seemed to have overcome some of the problems sexual harassment poses for attaining results and achieving goals.

The upper-level women administrators who had experienced more severe sexual harassment were more likely to indicate that coalition formation and conflict management were less important for their job performance than did those who experienced no harassment ($n = 42$; mean = 3.6; $F = 2.97$; $p < 0.10$). Although not reaching statistical significance, the upper-level women who experienced more severe levels of harassment also indicated that the functions of coordinating and integrating unit activities with other organizations were less important than did the women who experienced less harassment.

The findings of these two items suggest one of two things: either the majority of the upper-level women who experienced harassment had significantly less need to perform these functions, or harassment affected their perception of the importance of performing these functions. Because we have no reason to believe that the former situation is the case, we are inclined to think that sexual harassment does impact high-level female administrators negatively in the performance of integrating and coordinating functions. Given that conflict management and coalition formation are critical for managerial success at the upper levels, these data suggest, as the previous data have, that sexual harassment is indeed one of the barriers contributing to the creation of the "glass ceiling" in public organizations.

Table 6-3 details the relationship between job functions and competencies for higher-level women in Arizona. The results show a statistically significant increase or decrease in the average importance rating as the level of harassment increases (0 indicates no harassment experienced; 1 = verbal harassment; 2 = other more severe forms; importance was ranked from a low of 1 to a high of 5).

Table 6-3 shows the following: (a) that specified expertise, ability to balance short- and long-term considerations, and sensitivity to the environment were perceived as more important by those who experienced higher levels of sexual harassment; and (b) that AA/EEO declined in perceived importance as the level of sexual harassment increased. We also explored the relationship of the type of training desired to enhance job performance and sexual harassment. The women experiencing no harassment indicated that getting more training to improve their communication abilities would be helpful for their job performance (mean = 3.56 s.d. = 0.73); the women experiencing verbal harassment were least inclined to think training in communications abilities would be helpful (mean = 2.46 s.d. = 1.05); and the women experiencing the more severe forms of harassment were in between the other two groups (mean = 2.93 s.d. = 1.27).

These Arizona women administrators who experienced higher levels of harassment also indicated a desire for training to be sensitive to the environment, whereas the women experiencing lower levels indicated lower levels of interest in this type of training. No differences existed among mid-level women in terms of how sexual harassment experiences influenced their desire for training.

Table 6-3
Importance of Job Functions and Competencies (Arizona Data, Grades 23–30)

	Mean Harassment Scores				
Job Functions and Competencies	*0*	*1*	*2*	*n*	*Tau C*
Specialized expertise					
Importance for performance evaluation	3.18	3.46	4.00	39	0.25 ★★
Importance for job effectiveness	3.50	3.90	4.30	40	0.24 ★
Ability to balance short- and long-term					
considerations					
Importance for job effectiveness	4.18	4.36	4.30	42	0.18†
Sensitivity to the environment					
Importance for performance evaluation	3.40	3.90	4.00	40	0.23 ★★
Interpersonal relations/sensitivity					
Importance for performance evaluation	4.10	3.80	3.60	41	−0.19 ★★
AA/EEO management					
Importance for performance evaluation	3.50	3.20	2.90	39	−0.16
Importance for job effectiveness	3.70	3.50	2.60	40	−0.35 ★

★$p < 0.05$
★★$p < 0.01$
†$p < 0.10$

IMPACT OF HARASSMENT ON PERCEPTION OF SUCCESS

If sexual harassment is indeed some type of psychological warfare in the workplace, then the women experiencing its worst forms ought to react differently to it as a barrier to their career success than women not experiencing it so severely. To examine this possibility, the factors that have been important for their career success were correlated with the sexual harassment index. Given the status differential between the middle and upper levels, we explored each separately. Table 6-4 displays the relationship.

Among the mid-level women, those scoring higher on the harassment index indicated at significantly higher levels than the other women that their work style was the factor most important for their career success. Among the higher-level women, those scoring higher on the harassment index indicated at significantly higher levels than the other women that their personal attitude, self-concept, and motivation, and their mentors were most important for their career success. The mid-level women seem to rely on their behavior to protect themselves and their careers from the negative effects of harassment. The upper-level women, most of whom have advanced degrees, appear to rely on internal self-definition and supportive mentors to deal, apparently successfully, with more severe forms of harassment.

Harassment derives, in part, from a gender power differential and gives males an unfair advantage in the workplace. It is likely that women experiencing more severe harassment will view the factors contributing to the success of males and females differently than women who experience less harassment. Indeed, we find that the mean scores for the women indicating they think male career success is related to ability and hard work declines as the harassment level rises. Among higher level women, the perception that male success is related to hard work also declines as harassment levels

Table 6-4
Tau C Correlations of Factors Contributing to Career Success and Level of Sexual Harassment

	Grade Level	
	18–22 (n = 53)	23–30 (n = 42)
Attitude/self-concept/motivation	0.10	0.17*
Education	−0.34*	−0.08
Skills and abilities	−0.05	−0.09
Work style	0.44*	−0.10
Promotional opportunities offered	−0.10	0.03
Financial support from others	0.00	0.00
Training opportunities	−0.05	0.00
Mentor(s) or sponsorship	0.05	0.24*
Emotional support of others	0.00	−0.10
Having distinct career goals	−0.10	−0.08
Whom respondent knows	0.05	0.00

*$p < 0.05$

increase. Among the higher-level women, those who are more harassed also rate the importance of ability and hard work higher as a contributor to female success than those women who experience less harassment.

To determine if sexual harassment is related to individual perceptions of career success and satisfaction, the harassment index was correlated with items asking how successful and how satisfied each respondent felt. No significant differences were found for either the mid- or upper-level female administrators on these measures.

CONCLUSION

These data from the State of Arizona indicate that substantial percentages of both middle- and high-level female administrators in state government experience sexual harassment and that these experiences impact their job performance and behavior. Such harassment appears to affect work style, self-perception, and a woman's ability to perform particular job functions, such as managing conflict and organizing coalitions. Such harassment remains a contributor to the "glass ceiling effect," which keeps women both out of upper levels of management and from seeking entrance to those levels.

The fact that such harassment continues in the state civil service reflects quite negatively on the perception that state governments are dedicated to ending gender discrimination and gender power differentials. We recommend that all states re-examine the effectiveness of their sexual harassment policies so that progress can be made in ending this particular form of gender "psychological warfare."

Note

1. We wish to thank Robert Schwartz (Arizona), Mary Ellen Guy (Alabama), and Cathy Johnson and Georgia Duerst-Lahti (Wisconsin) for their assistance in completing the data analyses for their respective states.

Bibliography

Backhouse, C., and Cohen, L. 1981. *Sexual Harassment on the Job.* Englewood Cliffs, NJ: Prentice-Hall.

Branson, H., and Branson, R. 1988. The supervisor and sexual harassment. *Supervision* 50(2): 10–12.

Bularzik, M. 1978. *Sexual Harassment at the Workplace—Historical Notes.* Somerville, MA: New England Free Press.

Clarke, L. W. 1986. Women supervisors experience sexual harassment, too. *Supervisory Management* 31(4): 35–36.

Coles, F. S. 1986. Forced to quit: Sexual harassment complaints and response. *Sex Roles* 14(1): 81–95.

Dandekar, N. 1990. Contrasting consequences—Bringing charges of sexual harassment compared with other cases of whistle blowing. *Journal of Business Ethics* 9(2): 151–158.

Ellison v. *Brady.* 59 Law Week 2455 (9th cir). Jan. 23 (1991).

Farley, L. 1978. *Sexual Shakedown: The Sexual Harassment of Women on the Job*. New York: McGraw-Hill.

Gacioch, L. 1987. Employing fear. *Arizona View:* 1–9.

Garvey, M. S. 1986. The high cost of sexual harassment suits. *Personnel Journal* 65: 75–78.

Gillespie, D. L., and Leffler, A. 1987. The politics of research methodology in claims-making activities. *Social Problems* 34(5): 490–498.

Gruber, J. E. 1989. Sexual harassment research: Problems and proposals. Paper presented at the American Sociological Association Annual Meeting, August 1989.

Gutek, B. A. 1985. *Sex and the Workplace*. San Francisco: Jossey-Bass.

Gutek, B. A., and Morasch, B. 1982. Sex-ratios, sex-role spillover, and sexual harassment. *Journal of Social Issues* 38(4): 33–54.

Hemming, H. 1985. Women in a man's world: Sexual harassment. *Human Relations* 38(1): 67–79.

Herbert, C. 1989. *Talking of Silence: The Sexual Harassment of Schoolgirls*. London: Falmer.

Kanter, R. M. 1977. *Men and Women of the Corporation*. New York: Basic.

Kiechel, W. 1987. The high cost of sexual harassment. *Fortune* 116: 147–148.

MacKinnon, C. A. 1987. Sexual harassment: Its first decade in court. In *Feminism Unmodified: Discourses on Life and Law*, ed. C. A. MacKinnon. Cambridge: Harvard University.

McIntyre, D. I., and Renick, J. C. 1982. Protecting public employees and employers from sexual harassment. *Public Personnel Management Journal* 11: 282–292.

Nemec, J. 1988. Give salespersonship a high priority. *American Salesman* 33(9): 20–23.

Neugarten, D. A., and Miller-Spellman, M. 1983. Sexual harassment in public employment. In *Public Personnel Administration: Problems and Prospects*, ed. S. W. Hays and R. C. Kearney. Englewood Cliffs, NJ: Prentice-Hall.

Pereia, J. L. 1988. Women allege sexist atmosphere in offices constitutes harassment. *Wall Street Journal*, February 10, sec. B, p. 23.

Personnel Policies Forum. 1987. Sexual harassment: Employer's policies and problems (PPF Survey no. 144). Washington, DC: Bureau of National Affairs.

Powell, G. N. 1986. What do tomorrow's managers think about sexual intimacy at work? *Business Horizons* 29(4): 30–35.

Rogers v. *EEOC*. 454 F.2 234 (5th Cir. 1971), cert. denied, 406 U.S. 957 (1972).

Ross, C., and England, R. E. 1987. State government's sexual harassment policy initiatives. *Public Administration Review* 47(3): 259–262.

Safran, C. 1976. What do men do to women on the job? *Redbook* 149: 217–23.

U.S. Merit Systems Protection Board. 1987. *Sexual Harassment in the Federal Workplace: Is It a Problem?* Washington, DC: Government Printing Office.

7

PUBLIC BUDGETING AND FINANCIAL MANAGEMENT

Budgeting is one of the most important games in government, complete with players, roles, strategies, and prizes. And how the game is played determines what government does (or does not do). The budget may be the most important document in public administration. It is a statement, more or less, of what government is going to do for the next year—with price tags attached.

Budgets have two basic parts: revenues and expenditures. Without taxes, there is little to spend. A great deal of uncertainty and instability pervades the budget process these days, what with federal tax reform and balanced budgets (the Gramm-Rudman-Hollings Act); the fiscal crises of cities like New York, Cleveland, and Detroit; and taxpayer "revolts," as in Proposition 13 in California and Proposition 2½ in Massachusetts.

The politics of the budgetary process normally brings only modest (or incremental) changes in a budget from one year to the next. Over several years, of course, budget changes may add up to significant, even fundamental alterations of governmental resource allocation and public programs.

In the first article of this chapter, an expert on national budgetary politics, Dennis Ippolito, examines the federal budgetary process and recent attempts at its reform. His focus is the seeming inability to deal with growing budget deficits, to balance revenues and expenditures, the heart of any budget.

The issue of budget deficits raises a related problem for public administration: "hollow government." By this, we mean the increasing inability of governments at all levels to operate approved programs because of several consecutive years of austere budget reductions.

Next, Irene Rubin looks carefully at budget reforms in six cities. She observes how the state of political reform and budget reform are related, but also how budget innovation is often brought about by the need to deal with city problems. Rubin surveys Boston, Dayton, Phoenix, Rochester, St. Louis, and Tampa. In these cities, we learn a great deal about the different approaches to municipal budgeting and their impact.

Budgeting not only includes annual operating revenues and expenditures, it also includes paying for large capital projects, like bridges and airports. In the third article in this chapter, economist Alan Blinder examines America's nagging *infrastructure* problem. Much of this has to do with shortcomings and budget difficulties in states and localities, but, as Blinder notes, it does not preclude a federal role.

Budgeting is inseparable from other aspects of governmental financial management. Financial management is concerned with a wide variety of other issues:

- Accounting, auditing, and financial reporting

- Budget execution and control

- Cash management, involving the handling of cash receipts, investment of idle funds, relations with financial institutions like banks, cash flow, and general treasury management

- Risk management and insurance, preventing and reducing a governmental unit's exposure to the accidental loss of its assets

- Revenue and expenditure forecasting

- Capital improvement planning and debt management, particularly long-term indebtedness and bonds

- Appraising the financial condition of a governmental jurisdiction

- Determining the actuarial soundness of financial schemes, like pension systems

- Purchasing and procurement

Some questions to discuss about public budgeting are:

- Who are the participants in the budgetary process—federal or local— and what roles do they play?

- Although both President Bush and President Clinton talked about it during the last presidential election, are budget deficits all that bad? And exactly why is it so difficult to reduce the annual federal deficit? How successful has the federal government been in doing this in the 1990s, and why?

- Cities too often require budget reform. Describe what you think is the best approach to city budgeting of the six covered in the Rubin article. Why was this approach implemented in a particular city? How well did it work?

- How would you describe America's public infrastructure problem and possible solutions?

- Looking back on this chapter, why is budgeting more difficult in periods of fiscal stress?

The Budget Process and Budget Policy: Resolving the Mismatch

DENNIS S. IPPOLITO

The federal budget process is in disarray. Despite a series of major reforms, the federal government's deficit record has steadily worsened, and the nation now faces "a new and more dangerous deficit dynamic" (General Accounting Office, 1992, pp. 2–3). Along with deficits have come breakdowns in budget procedure, violations of budget accounting, and a "malaise [that] has spread from legislative chambers to executive offices" (Schick, 1990, pp. 1–3). The intensity and persistence of budgetary stalemates have encouraged hyperbole about failures of governance, making it more difficult to focus attention on specific budget policy issues (Haas, 1990; Kettl, 1992).

According to Fisher (1990), the recent failures of the budget process are the direct, if unintended, results of budget reforms that have fed on "institutional weaknesses," rather than taking advantage of the "institutional strengths of Congress and the President" that undergirded the Budget and Accounting Act of 1921 (pp. 693–694). The competing congressional budgets mandated by the Budget Act of 1974, for example, reduced the President's "personal and visible responsibility for submitting a national budget" (Fisher, 1990, p. 693). The resulting vacuum in leadership has not, and cannot, be filled by Congress.

Reestablishing the primacy of the President's budget and of presidential leadership is an "essential first step in reshaping and controlling budgets" (Ippolito, 1991, p. 252). This will necessitate, however, restoring the comprehensiveness of the President's budget. As Kettl (1992) has argued, the new structure of entitlements, debt financing, and mandatory spending means that the "share of the budget open to discretionary choices by budget makers is shrinking steadily" (p. 158). These structural changes in budget policy have reduced the comprehensiveness of the President's budget (and of the budget process generally). Reviving the President's role in budgeting, therefore, will require an integration of the institutional insights of the Budget Act of 1921 with the evolving structure of budget policy. One way to accomplish this integration may be through an expanded budget reconciliation process.

DIMENSIONS OF THE DEFICIT PROBLEM

The balanced-budget rule, states Savage (1988), "is so deeply rooted in the nation's political culture that neither full-employment economics nor the presence of the huge deficits created during the Reagan presidency has shaken American politics free from its constraining influence" (pp. 235–236). Although concern over deficits is not a uniquely modern preoccupation, the dimensions of current deficit problems dwarf those of earlier periods. During the 1980s, for example, average annual deficits reached an unprecedented level of nearly $160 billion, and the federal debt held by the public more than tripled to $2.2 trillion. During the 1990s, average annual deficits are expected to exceed $250 billion (Congressional Budget Office, 1992, p. 30).

Important technical disagreements exist over how to measure accurately budget deficits and public debt (e.g., Eisner, 1986). Uncertainty also exists about the impact of deficits on the economy and about the economy's capacity to absorb current debt levels.[1] Nevertheless, certain aspects of the deficit issue are straightforward.

First, over the past two decades, deficits and public debt have grown much more rapidly than the economy. Second, the escalation in deficit and debt levels, combined with high interest rates, has increased significantly the cost of servicing the debt. Net interest costs have averaged more than 3 percent of gross domestic product (GDP) since the mid-1980s, more than double the GDP share for most of the post-World War II period.[2] With interest payments on the debt now absorbing such a significant share of annual outlays, discretionary spending choices have narrowed. The corollary rise of entitlements and mandatory spending programs has further tightened the squeeze on discretionary programs, both defense and nondefense.

SPENDING GROWTH AND SPENDING CONTROL

One side of the deficit debate insists that spending is out of control, an argument with intuitive appeal given the sheer size of recent budgets. When the spending side of the budget is analyzed in terms of program categories, however, evidence of long-term spending control exists for the most politically contentious policy areas—discretionary defense and domestic programs. Where control has been noticeably absent, by comparison, is in retirement and healthcare entitlements whose growth has been heavily influenced by factors outside the budget process.

The discretionary portion of the budget—defense and nondefense— has shrunk significantly since the early 1960s (Table 7-1). Discretionary spending as a percentage of GDP actually has fallen to its lowest point since the late 1940s, and future estimates show a continuing decline. By the late 1990s, projected discretionary spending will have dropped to approximately one-third of the total budget, compared to roughly two-thirds during the early 1960s.

Because spending levels for discretionary programs are usually determined through annual appropriations, the traditional budget process appears to have operated effectively for these programs. Spending control has tightened over time, while tradeoffs between defense and nondefense programs have accommodated shifts in political priorities. The correspondence between these shifts and presidential spending initiatives, moreover, suggests that presidential budgets retain considerable influence over discretionary spending programs (Ippolito, 1991, pp. 193–227).

The record on nondiscretionary spending is very different. The long-term

Table 7-1

Outlays for Major Spending Categories, Selected Years 1962–1997
(as a percentage of GDP)

Fiscal Year	Discretionary Defense/Nondefense		Entitlements and Mandatory	Net Interest
1962	9.5	4.0	5.8	1.2
1965	7.6	4.6	5.4	1.3
1970	8.3	4.3	7.0	1.5
1975	5.8	4.9	10.9	1.5
1980	5.1	5.4	11.0	2.0
1985	6.4	4.1	11.3	3.3
1990	5.5	3.6	10.4	3.4
1995 (est.)	7.6*		12.1	3.5
1997 (est.)	7.2*		12.5	3.5

*These estimates are based on the aggregate spending cap for FY 1995 under the Omnibus Budget Reconciliation Act of 1990 and upon the Congressional Budget Office's extrapolation for FY 1997.

Source: Congressional Budget Office, 1992. *The Economic and Budget Outlook: Fiscal Years 1993–1997.* Washington, DC: CBO, pp. 50, 119, 121.

expansion in entitlements and other mandatory spending programs and in net interest outlays has more than offset the discretionary spending decline. By the mid-1980s, for example, total nondiscretionary spending had risen to approximately 14 percent of GDP. Projected levels for the 1990s are even higher.

The impetus behind this expansion has come almost exclusively from programs to assist the elderly. In the early 1960s, federal retirement programs accounted for about 3 percent of GDP, while current outlays for Social Security, medicare, and other retirement and disability programs are just under 8 percent of GDP. Thus, about 80 percent of the long-term expansion in entitlements and mandatory spending has been accounted for by the rising cost of income and medical benefits for the elderly, with much of the remainder accounted for by medicaid.

Programs for the elderly have grown sharply even when demographic and economic factors are taken into account. Over the past three decades, the growth in all federal entitlements has been more than double the rate needed to keep pace with inflation, population, and economic growth (Howe, 1991, p. A-5). The disparity is even more pronounced for retirement and healthcare programs, whose budget share continues to rise, despite legislative efforts to curb their growth rates.[3]

From the perspective of deficit reduction, the structure of current and future spending budgets poses formidable problems. Long-term discretionary spending has been held well below economic growth, but budget deficits have increased dramatically. The spending budget is now dominated by a few very popular and costly entitlements, whose growth is tied to demographic and economic factors. Moreover, in order to finance these entitlements, revenue policy has been skewed, making it more difficult to reduce deficit levels through increased taxes.

TAX LEVELS AND DEFICITS

Some deficit critics argue that federal taxes are too low, but budget receipts have rarely exceeded the outlay-GDP levels of recent years. Only twice since World War II has the receipts-GDP level climbed even slightly above 20 percent, and on both occasions (fiscal years 1969 and 1981), the level dropped sharply over the next two years. Even during World War II, receipt levels peaked at approximately 22 percent of GDP.

Revenue levels under the Reagan and Bush administrations have been slightly higher than average levels in earlier decades (see Table 7-2). As White and Wildavsky (1989) have emphasized, "If a normal level of revenues is 19 percent of [GDP] . . . then the long-term budget problem [is] not simply an artifact of the Reagan tax cuts" (p. 333). Even with the multiyear tax increases enacted in 1990, revenue levels are expected to remain well below 20 percent for the remainder of the decade (Congressional Budget Office, 1992, p. 68).

The relative stability of revenue levels over time reflects economic policy as well as political constraints, and neither of these appears to be easing. It seems unlikely, for example, that significantly higher revenue levels would be viewed by many economists as an appropriate fiscal policy response to the economic growth and productivity problems facing the nation. More to the point, long-term trends in the composition of revenues have raised the political barriers to significant tax increases.

Over the past three decades, the share of total budget receipts generated by the two most politically sensitive taxes—individual income and social insurance taxes—has risen by about one-third, to a current level of more than 80 percent. As a share of GDP, individual income taxes are slightly higher than in the early 1960s, while social insurance taxes have more than doubled. The federal government's direct tax burden on individuals, then, has increased dramatically.

Given the composition of federal revenues, it would be difficult to design a major tax increase that did not include higher taxes on individuals. Social Security tax levels, however, already have been raised above outlays in order to build the massive surpluses needed to finance future benefits. In order to preserve this surplus accumulation, Social Security is officially off-budget, insulated from deficit calculations and deficit-reduction controls. This leaves an average annual on-budget deficit, excluding Social Security, estimated at more than $300 billion over the next decade. Erasing any substantial part of

Table 7-2
Receipts as a Percentage of GDP, Fiscal Years 1962–1997

Fiscal Years	Annual Average Percentage of GDP
1962–69	17.5
1970–79	18.3
1980–89	19.0
1990–97 (est.)	19.0

Source: Congressional Budget Office, 1992. *The Economic and Budget Outlook: Fiscal Years 1993–1997*. Washington, DC: CBO, pp. 68, 115.

this on-budget deficit with current revenue sources would obviously necessitate a huge increase in individual income taxes.[4]

Finally, just as the indexing of entitlement benefits has made spending control more difficult, indexing provisions have raised the political barriers to tax increases. The indexing of individual income tax brackets, standard deductions, and personal exemptions has essentially eliminated inflation-boosted tax liabilities, so any future increases in real tax liabilities will require legislative action. It is not surprising that peacetime income tax increases over the past half-century have been rare (Witte, 1985). It would be surprising if tax increases sufficient to accomplish significant deficit reduction could be adopted and maintained, given the relatively high burdens already affecting taxpayers.

GRAMM-RUDMAN-HOLLINGS AND OBRA

In response to its growing deficit-control problems, the government has experimented with two legislative approaches. The first approach, the Gramm-Rudman-Hollings (GRH) bills of 1985 and 1987, was designed to bring the budget into balance through declining deficit ceilings enforced, if necessary, by automatic spending cuts. The second approach, the Omnibus Budget Reconciliation Act of 1990 (OBRA) and the accompanying Budget Enforcement Act, attempts to control deficits through procedural constraints on spending programs and tax policy.

The GRH approach ultimately failed. For several years, generous deficit ceilings and fortuitous economic conditions made compliance with GRH possible through a variety of short-term expedients, but in 1990 the room for accommodation abruptly disappeared. The President and Congress faced a deficit reduction of more than $100 billion for FY 1991 in order to comply with the GRH deficit ceiling. This amount of deficit reduction could not be achieved through a one-year budget agreement or through the automatic spending cuts prescribed under GRH.

As a result, the Bush administration and Congress negotiated a new long-term deficit-reduction agreement. The Omnibus Budget Reconciliation Act of 1990 contains multiyear spending cuts and revenue increases. The Budget Enforcement Act of 1990 establishes budget process controls to enforce these deficit reductions. The budget agreement's estimated $500 billion in deficit reduction includes more than $180 billion in discretionary spending baseline cuts for fiscal years 1991–1995. These discretionary spending cuts are enforced through straightforward statutory ceilings on budget authority and outlays for each fiscal year.

The revenue increases and entitlement spending reductions in the budget agreement, however, are enforced through a complex pay-as-you-go requirement. In any given year, new legislation affecting revenues and entitlement programs must be, in total, deficit-neutral. An entitlement increase or tax cut, for example, requires an offsetting change in other entitlements or taxes. No offset is required, however, in response to demographic, economic, or other external factors that increase entitlement spending, nor is any action necessary when economic or other factors reduce revenues below baseline projections.

The budget agreement also creates a special off-budget category for the Social Security retirement and disability trust funds.

The control points in the post-OBRA budget process are not actual deficit levels, but rather any new legislative actions that contribute to deficits. If these procedural controls had been superimposed upon a budget already in balance, there might be some optimism about balance being maintained. Unfortunately, the effect on current budget trends will likely make balance more difficult to achieve. The strongest controls now apply to discretionary spending programs, which are at most a minor element in deficit growth, while the weakest controls affect entitlements, particularly Social Security and Medicare.

What has been termed the entitlement "explosion" is a relatively recent phenomenon, and it has been fueled in part by economic and demographic, as well as legislative, changes (e.g., Thane, 1987). These changes and their corollary social policy problems are affecting all of the advanced industrialized democracies, none of which has, as yet, found a completely satisfactory resolution. The policy issues that must be addressed are complicated, and policy makers have very limited experience on which to draw.

Nevertheless, shaping a budget process that will highlight entitlement control problems is a necessary first step in effective budget reform. The GRH approach failed to accomplish this, and OBRA is, at best, a modest improvement. The budget process implemented under OBRA lessens the risk of future legislative actions that will exacerbate deficit problems, but it ignores the inherited policy commitments that have caused chronic and growing deficits.

A COMPREHENSIVE BUDGET PROCESS

During its heyday, the balanced budget norm did not stand alone but was complemented by other prescriptive criteria, particularly comprehensiveness.

> A commitment to budget balance meant acceptance of a de facto spending limit. . . . Adherence to the norm of comprehensiveness meant that almost everything was in the same pot. When restraints had to be exercised in the name of balance, therefore, both substantial revenues and expenditures were vulnerable to the ratcheting up and down by political authorities (Wildavsky, 1988, p. 424).

Comprehensiveness is now lacking, with the largest spending programs automatically programmed for growth and a significant portion of revenues earmarked to support these programs.

Congressional Reconciliation Process

The need for a comprehensive budget process that can bring entitlements and revenue policy onto the annual budget-balancing agenda has been acknowledged through changes in the congressional budget process. Reconciliation procedures were established under the Budget Act of 1974 to allow Congress to enforce the spending and revenue levels in its budget resolutions. Once Congress agrees to an overall budgetary program, it can direct its committees to report spending reductions and tax increases needed to comply with congressional budget totals and spending priorities.

Since the early 1980s, reconciliation has been used repeatedly to package entitlement savings and tax increases into omnibus legislation governed by special rules (Gilmour, 1990, pp. 107–130). The omnibus format has allowed Congress to avoid highly divisive votes on specific provisions and instead to focus attention on overall savings, while special procedures have facilitated reconciliation action whenever a budget resolution has assumed changes in the permanent laws governing entitlements and taxes. Reconciliation is also available to Congress to enforce the pay-as-you-go provisions for entitlements and revenues contained in the 1990 budget agreement.

The reconciliation process is a potentially vital part of future deficit-reduction strategies, but it has substantive and institutional flaws. The most important substantive flaw is the statutory exclusion of the off-budget Social Security trust funds from reconciliation coverage. In order to broaden the scope of deficit control, reconciliation's substantive reach must extend to the broadest possible range of entitlements and revenue sources, particularly programs as large as Social Security.

Presidential Reconciliation Process

The institutional flaw is that reconciliation is a formal and required part of the congressional budget process; the President's role in initiating or developing a reconciliation bill is entirely discretionary. Although the President must sign a reconciliation bill if it is to become law, he is under no obligation to submit reconciliation proposals as part of his annual budget. In addition, Congress is under no obligation to consider reconciliation proposals if they are submitted. Indeed, Congress has actively resisted presidentially initiated reconciliation since the first year of the Reagan presidency (Gilmour, 1990).

This peripheral presidential role is incompatible with budget policy leadership. As Fisher (1990) emphasizes, presidential responsibility is an institutional prerequisite for budgetary control; the budget process "works best when Congress receives from the President a budget which presents responsible totals for aggregates (especially total spending and the level of the deficit), with the understanding that Congress will generally live within those aggregates while rearranging the priorities" (p. 693).

When the Budget Act of 1921 was enacted, however, national budgets were primarily comprised of the discretionary expenditures of executive departments. The discretionary appropriations recommendations in today's presidential budget account for less than half of federal spending. The bulk of the budget includes spending for entitlements (and, of course, for interest payments on the debt), most of which is provided by permanent appropriations. The President is not required, however, to integrate discretionary appropriations recommendations with entitlements savings proposals and tax policy changes into a comprehensive and comprehensible budget program. Even if the President were to submit such a program, Congress need act only on discretionary appropriations.

The President's budget now includes detailed information on his discretionary appropriations requests. An additional reconciliation section, mandated by law, would include detailed entitlement and tax proposals making up the remainder of the President's budget program. A parallel statutory requirement would then make congressional action compulsory on this reconciliation addendum as part of the annual budget process. Making congressional action mandatory while reserving Congress's full authority to reject or to amend the President's proposal would establish, in effect, an automatic spending analogue to the regular appropriations process. The President would propose, Congress would respond, and accountability for results could be readily determined. Many proposed budget reforms would deliberately affect the balance of power between the President and Congress (e.g., Shuman, 1992, pp. 336–337). An expanded reconciliation process, however, would fully respect the separation of powers. It would simply adapt the institutional arrangements of the Budget Act of 1921 to the structure of modern budgets.

A statutory requirement for presidential reconciliation would thus eliminate an option the President currently enjoys—eschewing responsibility for preparing a truly comprehensive budget. Making reconciliation mandatory would also eliminate Congress's option of ignoring major parts of the President's program. As a result, it would be considerably easier to establish accountability for the budget policy results. In effect, the separation of powers would be reinvigorated in terms of the federal budget process.

Presidential leadership is only the first step in a revived federal budget process. Effective budget control will require many additional steps, by Congress and the public, over an extended period. As difficult policy solutions are debated, it is entirely possible that deficits will, in the end, be deemed preferable to entitlement cuts or tax increases. What would nevertheless be gained would be a clearer public understanding of the policy disagreements between the two branches, and of the policy costs of deficit reduction. It is this type of responsibility and accountability that the federal budget process should legitimately be expected to provide.

Notes

1. As a percentage of GDP, gross federal debt dropped from a World War II peak of nearly 130 percent to less than 35 percent in 1980. Since then, the level has risen to nearly 60 percent and is expected to rise to nearly 70 percent by the mid-1990s.
2. Beginning with the FY 1993 budget, federal agencies have switched from gross national product (GNP) to gross domestic product (GDP) as the basic measure of the nation's economic activity. From 1979 to 1991, for example, growth of real GDP averaged 0.1 percent a year higher than growth in real GNP (Congressional Budget Office, 1992, p. 5).
3. The Social Security benefit formula, for example, was adjusted in 1977 to eliminate a technical flaw that had artificially boosted benefits for new retirees. In 1983, a portion of Social Security benefits was made subject to taxation, effectively reducing benefits for affected beneficiaries. Efforts to control medicare costs have been a regular feature of the budget process for over a decade. It should also be noted that what has turned out to be the very costly indexing of Social Security benefits in 1972 was in large part a response to a series of discretionary increases that had outpaced inflation rate increases during the preceding several years.
4. This would be further complicated by the more than 150 trust funds for which income is earmarked. The federal funds deficit projected for FY 1995, for example, is $335 billion, while a trust fund surplus of $140 billion is projected for that year.

Bibliography

Congressional Budget Office, 1992. *The Economic and Budget Outlook: Fiscal Years 1993–1997*. Washington, DC: CBO.

Eisner, Robert, 1986. *How Real Is the Federal Deficit*. New York: Free Press.

Fisher, Louis, 1990. "Federal Budget Doldrums: The Vacuum in Presidential Leadership." *Public Administration Review*, vol. 50 (November /December), pp. 693–700.

General Accounting Office, 1992. "Budget Policy: The Budget Deficit and Long-Term Economic Growth." Testimony Before the Joint Economic Committee, United States Congress. Washington, DC: GAO.

Gilmour, John B., 1990. *Reconcilable Differences? Congress, the Budget Process, and the Deficit*. Berkeley: University of California Press.

Haas, Lawrence J., 1990. *Running on Empty: Bush, Congress, and the Politics of a Bankrupt Government*. Homewood, IL: Business One Irwin.

Howe, Neil, 1991. *Entitlements and the Aging of America*. Washington, DC: National Taxpayers Union Foundation.

Ippolito, Dennis S., 1991. *Uncertain Legacies, Federal Budget Policy from Roosevelt through Reagan*. Charlottesville: University Press of Virginia.

Kettl, Donald E., 1992. *Deficit Politics*. New York: Macmillan.

Savage, James D., 1988. *Balanced Budgets and American Politics*. Ithaca, NY: Cornell University Press.

Schick, Allen, 1990. *The Capacity to Budget*. Washington, DC: Urban Institute Press.

Shuman, Howard E., 1992. *Politics and the Budget*, 3d ed. Englewood Cliffs, NJ: Prentice-Hall.

Thane, Pat, 1987. "The Growing Burden of an Ageing Population?" *Journal of Public Policy*, vol. 7 (October-December), pp. 373–387.

White, Joseph and Aaron Wildavsky, 1989. *The Deficit and the Public Interest*. Berkeley and New York: University of California Press and Russell Sage Foundation.

Wildavsky, Aaron, 1988. *The New Politics of the Budgetary Process*. Glenview, IL: Scott Foresman.

Witte, John F., 1985. *The Politics and Development of the Federal Income Tax*. Madison: University of Wisconsin Press.

Budget Reform and Political Reform: Conclusions from Six Cities

IRENE S. RUBIN

BIG CITY BUDGETING

Municipal budgeting, especially in larger cities, has changed over the last 20 years. A variety of tools like program formats, long-term revenue and expenditure projections, management-by-objectives (MBO), zero-based and target-based budgets, capital budgeting, and strategic planning have become commonplace (Poister and Streib, 1989). A surprisingly large number of cities are using some performance monitoring (Poister and Streib, p. 242).

Why does budgeting change? Budget formats and processes develop over time, as new tools are adopted, altered, and incorporated into the standard repertory in response to changes in resources levels and the spirit of the times. The relative emphasis on spending controls, managerial efficiency, and program planning (Schick, 1966) is influenced by the current rate of growth in revenues, the rate of growth of expenditures in the previous period, and the pressure on government to solve infrastructural and social problems.

Literature about changing budget formats and processes emphasizes trends across time rather than variation between governmental units. Yet some cities responded earlier and more wholeheartedly to program budgeting, zero-based budgeting, or performance measures than others. The topic of this article is how cities differ in their use of budget reforms depending on the level of their political reform.

The concept of political reform is multidimensional. In this study, a city with a council-manager form of government and at-large elections for council seats is considered more reformed. Less-centralized cities with weak mayoral control and strong department heads are considered less reformed. The importance of patronage employees and the choice of friends of the mayor as key administrators are also considered indicators of the level of political reform. More politicized cities, where electoral politics play an important part in policy and administrative decisions, are considered less reformed. Political reform also has a historical dimension; a city that has alternated between a manager and a mayor or that has recently given up the manager form of government is considered less reformed than a city that has a long, unbroken tradition of city-manager government. In less-reformed cities, accountability is provided more through elections and the person of the mayor; in more reformed cities, accountability is provided more through the openness of administrative processes and documents.

Budget reforms have been adopted in cities with varying degrees of political reform, but they do not seem to fit decentralized, highly political cities. The reforms have included central financial controls over departments and evaluation of departmental performance, and they have emphasized openness and accountability. They have linked the budget with policy-based planning goals. Long-term financial planning challenges the ad hoc nature of political deal making. The top-down nature of some of the reforms defies the independence of powerful departments. The openness of evaluation creates political vulnerability to the press and opposition candidates, and the transparency and comprehensiveness of reformed budgeting threatens the traditional secrecy of decision making in more political cities.

If this image of a mismatch between less-reformed cities and budget reform is correct, one would expect cities with a weaker reform tradition to avoid budget reforms or adopt them selectively or implement reforms in ways that reduce their potential threat value. However, the possibility remains that the level of political and structural reform may make little difference to the adoption of budget innovations. Cities with different levels of political reform may adopt the same budget reforms because they are responding to similar environmental pressures. Or they may adopt similar budget reforms, but for different reasons. This article explores the relationship between political reform and the adoption of budget reform by examining these four alternatives (see box).

The first alternative is that cities avoid some reforms and pick others that suit their political characteristics. Target-based budgeting, with its more

---

THE STUDY

The four alternatives grew out of (but were not tested in) six case studies representing varying degrees of political reform. Two were city-manager cities with traditions of reform (Dayton, Ohio, and Phoenix, Arizona); two were mayor-council cities, with some reformed elements (Rochester, New York, and Tampa, Florida); and two were traditionally decentralized, politicized mayor-council cities (Boston, Massachusetts, and St. Louis, Missouri). Each pair of cities represented different regions of the country.

The case studies combined interviews with documentary materials, such as charters, budgets, capital improvement plans, constitutional constraints, and newspaper accounts. There were 38 interviews, with several informants interviewed twice. Key informants included the staff members who were most responsible for the introduction of major budget changes, current budget directors, department heads and/or their assistants, city managers and/or their assistants, and the mayors and/or their assistants. The questions asked included the role in the budget process of the mayor, the council, the departments, and the budget office; the timing and nature of any changes in the budget process or format; the reasons for these changes; and how the changes were implemented.

The reforms studied included Planning-Programming-Budgeting Systems (PPBS), performance evaluation, productivity programs, zero-based (ZBB) and target-based budgets (TBB), and capital budgeting. The study also looked at the extent to which all municipal spending was described in one budget (consolidation) in a relatively easy to understand format.

lump-sum allocations, might be welcome in cities with strong departments and weak budget offices. More centralized cities would presumably choose budget processes that made explicit tradeoffs between programs. Cities with strong departments may be unable to adopt budget systems that request extensive information from the departments, especially information that departments see as threatening.

The second alternative is that cities adopt the same reforms, but implement them at different levels, depending on the degree of political reform. Less-reformed cities might not fully implement reforms that require more control over the departments, or that expose politicians to negative publicity. Performance measures might be implemented in such a way that departmental goals are always achieved 100 percent, so the departments are not threatened and politicians are not vulnerable to public criticism. Reforms requiring more openness of decision making may be less fully implemented in more politicized cities. For example, the budget may be less integrated, with more separate decision processes, each addressing a separate political constituency.

The third alternative is that, regardless of the level of political and structural reform, cities have been experiencing similar environmental threats, including declining federal aid, recessions, and tax revolts, and have adopted similar patterns of budgeting to help them solve these problems. Different budget reforms are intended to solve particular problems, and, when the problems change, an informed staff picks the appropriate budgeting system. For example, if lack of public confidence in government fuels a tax revolt, then budget processes may need to emphasize public accountability and more public input into budget priorities.

The fourth alternative is that cities with different levels of reform have been adopting similar budget reforms, but for different reasons. For example, a more-reformed city may adopt target-based budgeting because it helps deal with financial uncertainty, whereas a more decentralized city might adopt it because it helps deal with conflicts between the budget office and the departments. Cities that are less reformed might adopt program and performance measures because they give the mayor more policy control over the departments. Cities that are more reformed might adopt program and performance measures because they promise to improve efficiency.

THE CASE STUDIES

Reformed Cities: Dayton and Phoenix

Dayton was the first of the large cities to adopt the council-manager form of government, in 1913, and it has maintained this form of government to the present. The five-member commission (which serves as a council) is elected at large. The mayor, who is separately elected, is one of the five commissioners. Central control over the departments is very strong. Throughout the years, Dayton has been an early adopter of new management techniques.

The City of Dayton's major budget changes began in 1968, when it was chosen (because of its reputation for good management) as part of a national experiment to introduce the Planning Programming Budgeting System

(PPBS) to five states, five counties, and five cities. The city had automated its financial system and recast the budget in program format, with descriptions of activities and work-load measures by 1971. The budget split people between programs, which became problematic when the city had to make cutbacks. Cutting a program meant cutting a part of a person's salary (Woodie, 1989). The city reorganized in early 1975, so that programs did not include fractional people.

The public, irritated at service cuts, refused to support tax increases, forcing more cuts. In 1974, after taxes were put in the budget office, the budget director decided to spell out the level of services the city would provide and the taxes necessary to provide those services at that level for five years. The proposal was approved by the public, and the city was bound by a five-year plan.

The city had to demonstrate that it had done what it promised over the last five years in order to get public approval of revenue for the next five years. The city manager set up a series of measurable, verifiable, and attainable objectives in 1974. Quarterly reports of accomplishments were circulated to the neighborhoods and the press. High-level objectives were printed in the budget; level-two objectives were reported to the manager and department heads; and level-three objectives were reported only to program directors. Initially, the budget director chose the most important issues, then that decision shifted to the council. The program budget was then restructured around council goals so council members could see how their goals were being accomplished in the budget.

By 1975, as part of the effort to make budgets accountable, the budget process was consolidated. The capital and operating budget processes were integrated and any separate funds were brought on budget. Capital projects and departmental equipment were listed separately in the budget, but capital projects were also listed with each program so the total expenditures of each program were clear.

To make the budget reflect public priorities, the city gathered citizen input on budget priorities. As the former budget director put it, "we wanted to pass the tax, so we were going to become responsive" (Woodie, 1989). The public continues to approve tax levels by wide majorities.

Most of Dayton's budget changes were in place by 1975 and remained, with minor tinkering, until 1990. Between 1989 and 1990, property tax revenues declined and grant revenue declined sharply, while other key revenue sources grew slowly. The city responded by drawing down a rainy day fund. By spring of 1991, the city adopted spending targets (target-based budgeting) to help keep expenditures down. The budget office used revenue estimates to help fashion ceilings for the departments; within those limits, substantial decision making authority was decentralized to the departments.

To summarize, Dayton's early adoption of PPBS reflected the reformed nature of city management and willingness to try new techniques. The city modified the program budget structure to facilitate cuts. When tax increases were rejected by the public, the city responded by making budgeting more open and bringing citizens into the budget process earlier in the decision making. The city set goals, costed them out, and got public approval for them. Performance measurement was a required part of the agreement; the city had to be able to show it had done what it promised to do. The recession of the early 1990s caused several years of draw downs in reserves. The city responded by changing the budget system to one that would systematically hold down expenditures to the level of revenues—target-based budgeting.

Phoenix is a little less politically reformed than Dayton. It adopted the council-manager form of government in 1914; it was among the first dozen cities to do so (Luckingham, 1989). However, the first city manager proved too reformed for the business elite, as he attacked patronage positions, introduced competitive bidding, encouraged municipal ownership, and actually collected license fees. He was fired, and the powers of the city manager scaled back (Luckingham, 1989, p. 71). In 1948, the powers of the manager were again strengthened, and members of the business and social elite formed the Charter Government Committee to slate candidates. This coalition dominated city government until about 1975 (p. 150). In 1982, the city voted to change from at-large to district elections in an effort to make government more responsive and democratic (Luckingham, p. 223). The level of reform is still high. As one department head described it,

> The mayor here is the chairman of the council, but the manager runs the city. The council members are prohibited from giving directions to the departments heads, they have no appointments, everything is professional staff. We win recognition every year, we run like a business. It's the opposite of the older, eastern cities, with patronage and political intervention (Public Works Director, Phoenix, December, 1990).

Phoenix's budget changes began in 1970, as part of an effort to improve productivity. A group of engineers was added to the budget department, doubling its size. In 1971 and 1972, as part of the continuing effort to enhance productivity, PPB was introduced. The industrial engineering continued while staff tried to produce citywide goals and program analysis reviews, which were effectiveness studies. The effectiveness studies stayed with the budget office, but the engineering studies later went to the auditor's office.

In 1977, the city adopted zero-based budgeting. This changed to a target-based budget only to revert to zero-based budgeting during fiscal stress of the late 1980s and early 1990s.

The citywide goals statement, which had been part of PPB, evolved into two parts, an MBO type performance achievement system and a long range strategic plan. Work on the strategic plan began in 1985. Currently, there are three levels of planning, which are only loosely integrated with each other and the budget. One is a departmental planning process, the second is a citywide corporate plan, and the third is a community-based long-term plan which only partly involves the city in implementation.

The engineering focus on productivity gradually changed to an employee-development focus with quality circles. At the department level, Phoenix's five-year plans replaced the old program analysis reviews and are focused less on effectiveness and what the departments are doing and more on where they are going.

Why were these changes adopted? One informant described the initial engineering efficiency drive as a response to fiscal stress in the late 1960s (Manion, 1990). Private sector people on the council said that business handled its problems using industrial engineering so the city should too. Once in place, the efficiency emphasis suggested the importance of studying effectiveness as well. The same consultants who recommended efficiency measures in the late 1960s, also recommended the adoption of PPB. PPB was getting a lot of publicity then, so the city picked it up; it fit their need to judge effectiveness.

PPB did not give the city adequate tools to handle cutback. The oil embargo and the recession of 1973 and 1974 forced the city to make cuts by attrition and reduce the number of vehicles purchased, without much reflection on the impact on operations. By 1976, the city tried to raise the sales tax. The voters rejected the $10 million tax hike in February 1977, the middle of a fiscal year. The budget director at the time, Charles Hill, argued, "We needed a new way to set priorities, so I educated myself to use zero-based budgeting" (Hill, 1990). He used the ability of PPB to delineate service impacts in order to implement zero-based budgets.

The recession of 1980 and 1981–1982 caused another round of cutbacks. The at-large council cut out some popular neighborhood projects. These specific service cuts combined with underfunding of service expansion as the city rapidly increased its area. Many neighborhoods and areas of the city felt neglected. These citizens wanted services; many of them supported the change to election of councilmembers by district in 1982 because the district system promised more responsiveness to neighborhood needs.

> The former budget director argued that the change to district elections did have some impact on budgeting. "Neighborhood coalitions became more powerful, and affected budgeting. Capital budget on construction—we began to produce reports on each district. We informally set aside a sum for council add-ons after the manager's budget, for recreation, school officer, and the like. That is the way the council adapted their budgets, add-ons after the manager's budget. With the manager's full understanding that that was the way it would work. It grew each year until last year it reached $2 million in add-ons for various programs" (Hill, 1990).

If there are difficult policy choices in the budget, a budget hearing takes place in every district. The Public Information Office works up a sound and slide show to present the budget. The budget officer attends to answer questions, and the mayor and the district council member listen to the public comments. The elected officials can take what they hear from the public to help them formulate their moderate add-ons to the manager's proposal.

> The capital budget process, which is somewhat separate, reflects a desire to get public support early in the budget process. "There is a 200 member citizen bond committee. The departments prepare needs studies and take them to the citizens' councils, there are 10 or 12 of them, for different areas, like police. They review the departments' needs and develop recommendations for what is taken to the voters. The council then decides. . . . The budget office updates the capital improvement plan for the council. . . . We continue to work with the citizens committee as advisory. We take the preliminary capital improvement plan to them, to see that it meets with the citizens' intent" (Tevlin, 1990).

When the city manager was asked what factors influenced budget processes, he offered three. First, the city staff try to keep up with national trends and modern practice. Second, the city tried to adapt to pressures from the council or the community to respond to community needs. Third, the staff continually evaluated their own budget processes to see what could be improved. The manager elaborated on the second of these reasons for changing the budget process. "As community needs have arisen, and trust has ebbed and flowed between the community and the city . . . we try to make the process more open when trust is low and give the council more input. When there is more trust, we have short cut the process" (Fairbanks, 1990).

The city manager downplayed the importance of fiscal stress in determining the budget process, in part because some fiscal stress had been present during each of the preceding 12 years. He agreed, however, that the budget process did help find different ways to cut the budget.

Phoenix's zero-based budgeting evolved into target-based budgeting. Prioritization occurred at the margins with new revenue, but most of the base remained intact from year to year. However, Phoenix was particularly hard hit by overbuilding in real estate and a drop in real estate values and was further threatened by the possibility of declining state aid in the early 1990s. As the city wrestled with financial problems, the Chamber of Commerce warned that there could be pet projects in the base budgets and departments might be bringing projects to the council that the council could not cut. In response, the mayor called for a comprehensive budget review. The departments were divided into five groups; all the programs in one group would be examined in year one, all the programs in a second group would be reviewed the next year, and so on, until all the programs had been reviewed. Staff portrayed the process as an opportunity to educate the council, but the council surprised them by cutting an additional $20 million during the first year of the more intensive review.

The comparison between Dayton and Phoenix is interesting. Both were early adopters of PPB. During the middle 1970s, each city responded to recession and price increases with a proposed tax increase and both were defeated at the polls. Dayton reacted by strengthening the planning end of PPB, setting goals with the public, and linking them to the budget, creating a kind of contract. Phoenix, in a similar situation, strengthened its capacity to rationally cut back and engaged in nearly continual cuts of some sort for the next 12 years. It alternated between a zero-based and a target-based budget system. It did not add strategic planning until 1985, and it took five years to get the process running. Even then, the planning process was only loosely linked to the budget. Although Phoenix was generally ahead of the curve in anticipating and reacting to fiscal stress, it was sometimes behind the curve in planning for its enormous, rapid growth and in responding to community demands.

Intermediate Levels of Reform: Rochester and Tampa

From the turn of the century to 1922, Rochester was a Republican city under a political boss. Supporters of the manager system were able to take advantage of the boss's death and the disarray in the Republican party to push through the council-manager system in 1925. By 1931, the city's expenditures increased greatly as a result of the unemployment burden of the depression and an ambitious capital improvement program. Republicans, pointing to greatly increased debt, failure to balance the budget, and increased tax bills, won the election, restoring the old political machine (Mosher, 1940).

When the machine-oriented administration refused to accept the financial advice of the business community in 1932, bankers and businessmen successfully demanded a new city manager, a mayor of their choice, and a continuing voice in the affairs of the city. "The bankers had the whip hand, since they could refuse the city credit" (Mosher, 1940, p. 44). The manager system lasted from 1932 until 1986.

Most of the staff and many of the procedures from the manager period were retained after 1986, so the city is part way between the council-manager and mayor-council forms of government. This in-between status is reinforced by a council that has four district and five at-large seats. The city council was openly partisan until the early 1980s, when an open meetings law forbade decision making by party caucus. Departments were powerful under the managers and remained powerful under the mayor.

Staff changed the budget format in the late 1960s, but by 1970, the budget returned to a straight line-item format. Program and performance budgeting were adopted in 1974-75. Fiscal problems had begun several years earlier, but a short interlude of Republican dominance had been characterized by denial of fiscal problems. When the Democrats reassumed dominance in 1974, they inherited a fiscal mess.

One informant described the need for a changed budget format as a response to fiscal stress and a large tax increase. The fiscal problems created a need for a better understanding of the budget. The existing document and systems could not answer the questions that the manager and the budget bureau were asking. Moreover, the need to explain to the council and the public why taxes were being raised so high so quickly required a budget that was open and simple to understand (Myers, 1989). The city also needed to explain its financial problems to the county and the state legislature in order to get some financial relief (City of Rochester, 1974, p. M-4).

The new budget format included a program structure, useful descriptions of programs, explanations of changes in programs between the past year and the current year, and workload measures. Over the next few years, measures of success were gradually added. One participant described, "Our attitude was, we would do what worked, we were not wedded to any theoretical system. . . . We borrowed from other budgets. If it was good, we took it" (Myers, 1989).

In the mid-1970s, as the city was working on program structures and workload measures, it adopted an engineering-oriented innovation and productivity program. Then the city adopted productivity bargaining with labor, a huge tax hike to balance the budget, and reductions in staffing levels by attrition. However, the city was unable to stabilize finances by 1979. The city was particularly hard hit by the rapid inflation that characterized the end of President Carter's regime. The New York Court of Appeals ruled in the spring of 1978 that the city had improperly excluded certain expenditures from the constitutional tax limit, forcing a last minute revision of the fiscal year 1979 operating budget that resulted in expenditure reductions, service cutbacks, employee terminations, and new user charges, taxes, and special assessments.

Preparing for 1980, the city found that the level of state aid was uncertain, wage levels depended on arbitration decisions not yet made, and the size of the tax refund the city would have to pay depended on a forthcoming court decision. The county refused to create a refuse district to alleviate the city's burden, and assessed valuation began to decline. The manager wrote in his budget letter, "It was clear we had to prepare for a wide variety of alternatives and produce a budget that could be adjusted to reflect changes in the City's economic situation that were largely outside our direct control. Departments were, therefore, instructed to prepare basic budgets which would enable us to make further reductions if necessary or restore priority items if additional resources became available" (City of Rochester, 1980, p. 2).

This statement in the budget was the first reference to the target-based budgeting that characterized Rochester's budget in the 1980s. Target-based budgeting was initiated as a response to intense uncertainty, but it also handled cuts in a decentralized departmental structure. "They [the departments] understood reductions had to occur. They could be more painful or the best reductions they could get with less pain and more efficiency. We rarely told the departments how to change their budgets . . . they could choose their own poison. They had better knowledge of their operations and were responsible for continuing operations [despite cuts]" (Myers, 1989).

After 1986, concurrent with the shift to the mayor-council system, the budget office simplified the budget, eliminating measures that were not being used and working on the performance measures. Although the budget contained good demand and workload measures, only a few programs included results measures in the budget (City of Rochester, 1990). The budget director suggested that the city was unlikely to ever have good results measures. "The resources to develop them are not there." He argued, "impact measures take a lot of research, and we may not be ready to share" (Sette, 1989).

One informant explained that the political orientation of the city shows up in the performance measures, which are oriented more to workload than to efficiency or outcomes. "You get 25 calls for potholes [demand] you fill 25 potholes [workload]. You used X tons of fill, at $100 a ton [efficiency]. But so what? You filled 25 potholes and that is what matters to citizens. Re-election is the result" (Sette, 1989).

Another reason that performance evaluation never became an integral part of the budget was that the departments often did not go along with it. During the 1970s, the city did program evaluations as part of federal grants. Reportedly, the evaluation process caused a lot of anxiety. When the federal grants disappeared, so did the evaluation process. A former budget director described, "The limitation was we couldn't outrun departments that could generate meaningful numbers and understand what it was we were doing. . . . But it wasn't installed from the top down. They had to accept the need" (Robert Myers, October, 1989).

The change to a mayor-council city had relatively little impact on the budget process, but there were indications that the budget document itself was considered a little more political and a little more sensitive. The mayor reportedly opposed the inclusion of a list of city goals in the budget because he thought it would look bad if the goals were not accomplished. In the absence of council and public participation, the budget document is a major tool of accountability in Rochester, but it is not clear to city staff if the mayor will continue to keep the budget open.

To summarize, Rochester used budget reform to help explain the city's financial problems to itself, to the public, and to other governmental bodies.

After some 15 years with a performance budget, the city has yet to work out a reasonable set of measures of outcomes. The budget document itself is the major tool of public accountability. It covers most city operations and is reasonably open, reflecting its origins as an attempt to explain the city's financial status. This openness is in tension with the mayor's concerns about leaving his administration vulnerable to public criticism.

The City of Tampa is a somewhat reformed, strong-mayor city. The council is composed of three at-large representatives and four district representatives. Department heads and "superchiefs" who manage several departments and link the political and administrative systems are professionals rather than political appointees. Patronage hiring is not a major issue.

The changes in Tampa's budgeting originated with the federal Model Cities program, which required planners to do needs assessments. The planners had to devise city standards for service delivery, so they could know whether a neighborhood was above or below the standard. Then the planners recommended to the mayor a list of projects to meet the needs they had uncovered (Wehling, 1991).

In the mid-1970s, Mayor Poe decided to expand the needs assessments and standards of service from grant-funded programs to the whole city, not just to the low-income neighborhoods. The planning office was expanded. The planners wanted program budgets so they could see if the spending they had recommended was resulting in higher service levels. They managed to get program descriptions in the budget in 1975, but the rest of PPB was not implemented. There were no measures of accomplishment or impact, and no analysis (Wehling, 1991).

> By the late 1970s, the city was facing financial problems and had to cut the budget. A lot of games were played during cutback. The fire chief would close a fire station in a wealthy neighborhood, knowing it would be restored during the year. Recreation would close a recreation center, or transit would eliminate 10 busses. There was no more justification than that, just 10 busses. They would negotiate, and take a cut of five instead (Wehling, 1991).

At the beginning of the administration of Mayor Bob Martinez in 1979, the budget office adopted target-based budgeting. The new mayor reportedly liked the target-based system because it gave him more control over the departments and because it was a new process he could identify his administration with. The budget director implemented target-based budgeting because it put the management decisions where he felt they belonged (in the departments) and helped reduce gameplaying between the departments and the budget office (Desilet, 1990). Target-based budgeting gave the departments maximums for their budget requests; the department heads had to decide what to put into the request and what to leave out.

A former staff member in the budget office explained that the year before target-based budgeting was adopted, a midyear shortfall had developed, which was made up from operating lines in the departments that still had unspent funds. Police and public works were especially hard hit. Departments felt the cuts were arbitrary and the budget office staff reportedly felt a little guilty. Target-based budgeting gave credibility to the cutback process because the budget office showed the departments that it had taken a variety of factors into consideration in the assignment of targets. The result was more cooperation and less antagonism between the departments and the budget office.

The current budget director argued that TBB made it easier to prioritize cutbacks. "You get basic policy decisions from the mayor, how to favor the departments, and go from there, how people can manage with that amount, what do they say they can't do, and how critical is that. The powers that be look at that and say how important the unfunded parts are" (Stephan, 1990).

Although the city never fully implemented PPB, the needs assessment and service levels analysis that developed under the aegis of planning were integrated into the budget process during Mayor Poe's administration in the later 1970s. The planners made sure the mayor had a list of projects he could recommend that were responsive to the things he gave priority to. Planners created that list by combining policy statements made by the mayor with their own assessments of needs based on service level analyses (Wehling, 1991).

Early in his administration, Mayor Martinez discarded this process because many departments opposed the planning department's overly large role. After one budget cycle without any way of judging the department's requests, Mayor Martinez reestablished much of the process, but without the dominance of the planning department. The departments had to establish their own standards and document their current needs with respect to the standards. During Martinez' administration, the service-level analysis was closely linked to funding; departments would promise to do a particular amount of service for a particular amount of funding. The mayor could ask for higher standards, or reduce the targets, but budget and performance were linked. Key departments, such as public works, knew almost exactly how much service they could deliver in various programs for particular amounts of money (City of Tampa, 1991).

The linkage between the budget and service levels was reportedly weakened under the next mayor, Sandra Freedman, who imposed higher service requirements without additional funding and cut spending targets while expecting service levels to remain the same. Mayor Freedman was familiar with city operations so she found the many hours of meetings with department heads over relatively unchanging service targets tedious. She also opposed service-level analysis because it made her politically vulnerable. When she was running for mayor, "She took the SLA [Service Level Analysis] system and looked at the unmet needs, using them as if the budget should have corrected all of them. It was unfair. But she is so aware of this tactic, and it was used against her, she wants to get rid of it" (Wehling, 1991).

Reportedly, what she wanted to put in its place was a simpler list of political goals, such as greater use of partnerships or more emphasis on prevention. There would be no reference to unmet needs. Proposals from the departments would be judged for their contribution to these goals. The mayor could go out to the public and say, "I got the private sector involved, and I got people involved in designing policy." The direction of the shift was from greater emphasis on comprehensive planning to more emphasis on strategic planning.

The difference between mayors is important. Martinez built his popularity on budget cutting, tax reductions, and downtown development. He used the service-level analysis and the target-based budgeting system to achieve those goals. Freedman was more interested in building support by addressing problems such as crime or dirty streets. She took her set of problems from public perceptions, from the people she talked to in the neighborhoods, and from housing, civic, and environmental groups. She did not want some other list of needs. She needed to be able to spend on priority items without destroying the budget, and target-based budgets helped her do that, creating some flexibility for policy redirection within tight budgets. Both mayors were able to use TBB to achieve their goals, but they had different needs for the service-level analysis.

The Least Reformed Cities: Boston and St. Louis

Boston is a strong mayor city, with a very weak council. The council has alternated between at-large and district elections. As of 1983, the city changed to a 13 person council, in which 9 seats are from districts, and 4 are at large (Schabert, 1989, p. 133 fn.). Political patronage has been an important part of the municipal government. Mayor Kevin White, who was mayor from 1968 to 1984, reportedly merged his personal machine with the city government. At one time, he employed about 825 people directly loyal to himself, often funded by federal grants and located in different departments and programs (Schabert, 1989, pp. 58–60). Superchiefs, who played the role of liaison between the political level and the technical and managerial levels, were generally political appointees and mayoral loyalists, rather than long-term professional employees. Despite the tradition of strong mayors, power has remained fragmented, and some departments have had considerable autonomy.

Boston was one of the early adopters of PPB in 1969 and 1970, but within a few years, the budget returned to a line-item format. In 1986, the city adopted a program and performance budget. Capital budgeting, which has been a separate function in Boston for many years, had a similar pattern of start and stop. Informants attributed the start-and-stop pattern largely to fiscal stress. With respect to the disappearance of PPB, one informant reported,

> The focus at the time was on obtaining more revenue. They were desperate. They were in survival mode. It is hard to think of evaluating programs when you aren't fine tuning. They were making wholesale changes. . . . We got the budget balanced in 1986 and it has been balanced since then. The relatively stable finances gave us a chance to look at program budgeting. The budget was no longer acting as a triage system (Robert Ciolek, 1989).

Similarly, lack of funds derailed the capital budget (Nee, 1989). However, the stop-and-go pattern of budget reform also had political roots. "That is life in the big city . . . the Mayor gets out a press release, you have to do it, you don't touch all the bases you need to make it work" (Anonymous, 1989).

The city's departments were not consulted before the major budget changes in 1986. The performance budget was introduced from the top down. Mayor Flynn, reacting to a reputation of being uninterested in management and responding to a long string of municipal deficits, convened a private-sector task force shortly after his election in 1985. The task force made hundreds of suggestions for improving the accounting system and the operating and capital budgets, most of which the mayor implemented. When asked how the budget office got departmental cooperation, the budget director responded, "We tell the departments they have to do it" (Gottschalk, 1989).

Departments resisted the newly centralized capital budgeting process. The director of the capital planning office described, "I was criticized a thousand times over. The mayor always backed me up. . . . The structure had been decentralized and they had their own agendas. I changed the playing field a lot. Most people now see and understand the benefits [of a more centralized system]" (Mary Nee, November, 1989).

The implementation of the new budget system depended on the mayor's support. A talented political appointee, the deputy director of fiscal affairs, translated the task force's recommendations into a budget process that matched the personality and needs of Mayor Flynn. He described some of the advantages of the program and performance budget:

Robert Ciolek: You can make better political decisions when you have good facts. it gives you effective controls over the bureaucracy. It informs and it controls. The budget office can respond to the mayor's direction.

Author: Are you saying that the budget process makes the departments more responsive to the mayor?

Ciolek: Yes, that is one of the major reasons why we did it (Ciolek, 1989).

The idea was to help the departments improve their management simultaneously with making them more accountable to the strategic goals of the mayor. The departments listed their goals and then the policy office of the mayor met with each department head. The mayor's goals were incorporated with the performance measures. The departments tried to figure out how to measure the mayor's goals. Several informants reported tension between the mayor's short-term policy objectives and the longer-term objectives of the program budget.

The report on performance measures was treated somewhat politically. It was not widely circulated, because of the fear that the press would pick up the negative aspects and ignore the rest. Despite the limited circulation of the document, departments have set goals low so they can meet all the goals 100 percent. This problem seems to be slowly abating.

Most of the implementation of the program and performance budget was done in one year. The departments and the budget office continued to weed out useless measures and add better ones, but as they were doing that, the city's revenues again became shaky, largely as a function of the state's deteriorating financial condition and a large drop in state aid to the city. The program budget gave little guidance on how to cut the departments, and competition to avoid or minimize cuts was intense. The budget office switched to a target-based budget to help control and minimize this competition for the 1990 budget.

The target-based budget requires the departments to report the impacts of proposed reductions on service levels. These impacts are evaluated for acceptability and for conformity to the mayor's goals. This process gives the departments the opportunity to demonstrate how they will be hurt, and to make a plea for more funds; it also preserves the mayor's policy priorities during cutback.

The initial budget reform was implemented too quickly. Some performance measures were weak, and the budget remained somewhat fragmented. Grants were not incorporated into the operating budget, and a line-item budget alternated with the program budget, page by page. Much attention was focused on making the budget format visually attractive, but there is more to the new budget process than a change in appearance. ". . . the process helps in the tactical relationship between the budget office and the departments. It arms the budget office with facts. . . . Its biggest value is to the departments, to help them manage. It also helps the mayor's office tactically . . ." (Ciolek, 1989).

St. Louis is the least reformed of the six cities. Budget decisions are primarily the responsibility of the Board of Estimate and Apportionment, composed of the mayor, the comptroller, and the President of the Board of Aldermen, all elected at-large. The council is elected from districts, with no at-large seats. The city government is merged with the county government, the latter controlled by the state. The county positions, referred to as the patronage positions, are not under civil service. Patronage is a hotly discussed issue. The city is poor, and the need for jobs considered so high that some council members do not push for staff that could help them read the budget because they fear the quality of the appointments and the acrimony of the fight to see who will get the jobs.

A highly fragmented power structure and unreformed government are reflected in a highly fragmented budget. The budget director in 1988, Steve Mullin, described the level of fragmentation:

> The municipal government also administers other programs which, at this time, are not subject to review through this primary budget process. They include the Community Development Block Grant Program (approximately $20 million annually), various programs for economic development, various State and Federal health programs, the City's revenue collection functions (approximately $3 million annually), the Parking Meter Fund (approximately $2 million annually), the Street Improvement-St. Louis Works Fund (approximately $5 million annually), SLATE Federal training programs, and programs for the elderly. Each of these functions is developed independently during the year, and appropriation ordinances are passed by the Board of Aldermen (City of St. Louis, 1989, p. 8).

Despite this fragmentation and severe fiscal problems, in 1989 the budget office introduced a program-and-performance budget that was somewhat integrated with a strategic planning process. However, the budget continued to include a line-item budget.

Although the budget document emerged suddenly, budget changes had been occurring over a long period that gave the mayor some centralized control over a limited set of departments. The first of these changes was a gradual shift from having the budget office report to all three members of the Board of Estimate and Apportionment to having the budget director report only to the mayor. This shift began in the early 1970s and was completed by the early 1980s. The second change had a number of the department heads appointed by and report to the mayor. "St. Louis in the early 1980s was still characterized by department heads who determined their own budgets. Mayor Vincent Schoemehl picked his own department heads and weakened the independence of the commissioners. . . . The mayor transferred some of the commissioners and he persuaded others to be more amenable" (Rubin and Stein, 1990, p. 423).

Once the mayor had some control over the department heads, he strengthened the budget director's control over reviewing departmental proposals and allowed the budget director to formulate the executive budget proposal. The Board of Estimate and Apportionment then reviewed that proposal rather than dealing individually with each department's request. The mayor hand picked young professional budget directors who were familiar with modern budgeting techniques.

When Mayor Schoemehl was first elected in 1981, he brought with him a modified version of MBO. At first, the system did not work very well, because the departments set goals that were too low, the same problem that occurred in Boston. With the help of a consultant, the MBO plan was turned into a motivational tool, to help personnel see the kind of progress they were making toward goals. The goals were not linked directly to pay and evaluation, which may have helped reduce the tendency to set easily achieved goals.

Sometime around 1987, the budget director decided to link the performance measures to the budget and create a program-and-performance budget. By then, the departments had had several years of nonthreatening experience with performance measures, and city staff had experience using visual displays to show progress over time. The performance budget that emerged in 1989 had a multiyear planning dimension and short-term component. Although the budget staff and departments are still struggling to put together additional measures of outcomes, the existing ones are reasonably useful.

During 1987, a new capital budget process was developed. The capital budget process, initiated by an alderman, was in part a response to the declining infrastructure of the city and the difficulty of maintaining a capital budget in the face of pressing operating needs. It was not based on establishing standards or citywide needs; rather, it gathered lists from the departments of their future capital needs and tried to prioritize them. The membership of the capital committee reproduced to some extent the fragmentation of the Board of Estimate and Apportionment, with the mayor, the comptroller, and the president of the Board of Aldermen each having probable control of two or possibly three votes. The five-year plan the capital committee put together was so expensive in comparison to the funds available that it was more a wish list than a budget. Nevertheless, the committee did select projects for the current year's budget and did formulate criteria by which to judge projects.

Part of the motivation for creating the list of projects was to help pass a half-cent sales tax to help pay for capital projects. A consultant had advised the city that voters were more likely to vote for a tax if they knew what they would be getting for it. Despite the existence of the list, the tax was rejected. Without funding, most of the list remained to be carried out; the urgency to meet again and revise the list for the next time was small.

A strategic planning process was also begun in 1987. The strategic planners divided the city into functions and then set goals and achievable, measurable targets for each function. The mayor and his staff chose from among the list of achievable targets a set of projects that could be funded in the near term.

The mayor had been cutting city staff virtually since his inauguration, especially in health and hospitals, and fiscal stress had resulted in delayed maintenance and deteriorating infrastructure. Much grant money went into large downtown economic development projects. These choices resulted in faltering service levels and considerable opposition to the mayor, ultimately contributing to a rejection by the public of the continuation of the ⅜ cent sales tax, forcing further service cuts.

The mayor must have been aware of the percolating criticism of how he had chosen to cut the budget. The strategic planning process was put in place "to improve the methods of allocating and managing resources to achieve the stated mission of city government" (City of St. Louis Budget 1988–1989, p. 13). Its intent was to find out the needs of the community, focus government efforts on those needs, and improve effectiveness and efficiency of those efforts. The format of the program and performance budget linked directly to the goals and targets formulated by the strategic planning process, to show how the city was addressing the goals that the public wished the city achieve. The evaluation of performance was not linked directly to the strategic plan, however, although some components of the performance measures addressed some of the goals in the plan. As of 1990, the program and performance report, which had the possibility of demonstrating what the city was doing with public money and possibly helping to win support for a tax increase, was not widely distributed, and the council remained generally unaware of its existence.

ANALYSIS

The case-study cities used similar budget reforms to meet and help handle common environmental threats to some extent, but no one-to-one relationship existed between environmental threats and budget reforms. Environmental threats had little to do with the adoption of PPB or program-and-performance budgets. A stronger case can be made for linking fiscal stress and the adoption of target-based or zero-based budgeting. Budget directors facing cutbacks looked for ways to select and implement cuts. They also sought to defuse the intense budgetary competition resulting from eroding tax bases, reduced state funding, recessions, and defeated tax referenda. Target-based budgeting was also used to hold down property taxes; it responded to a strong antitax sentiment. However, once target-based or zero-based budgeting was in place, the linkage between environmental threat and budget systems was weakened. ZBB and TBB prioritize for either growth or decline. Once cities adopt this form of budgeting, they keep it through good and bad times.

Although the direct link is not that strong, a good case can be made for an indirect link between environmental threat and changes in budgeting process and format. When environmentally caused fiscal stress led a city to go for a tax increase or petition the county or legislature for new revenue sources, the result was an effort to tidy up the budget, to make it clearer, to establish and make concrete the need. This effort often included consolidation of the budget, a five-year revenue and expenditure projection, and larger print, readable formats, glossaries, tables, charts, and narrative descriptions. When the tax increase was turned down by the public in Dayton, and to some extent in St. Louis, the city shifted to trying to get the public more involved in budgetary decision making. In Phoenix, the city tried to live within the narrower revenue limits after a tax increase was turned down, but the public rebelled against the cutbacks in services and slow expansion of services to newer areas of the city, forcing a change in governmental structure and more attention to neighborhood needs in the budget process. Fiscal stress thus creates pressure to improve the accountability of the budget and expand meaningful public involvement in the budget process.

Although some of the similarity in the case-study cities' budget systems resulted from the choice of similar techniques to resolve similar, environmentally imposed problems, the case-study cities sometimes adopted the same budget reforms for different reasons. Dayton adopted PPB as part of a national experiment; Phoenix adopted PPB as part of a productivity drive in response to a stalled economy. Program and performance budgeting was used in less-reformed cities to provide the mayor additional control over the departments in the area of short-term policy goals while it was used in more reformed cities to increase efficiency.

More-reformed cities often adopted reforms because either staff or council members were eager to try out the newest budget practices and make them work. Less-reformed cities were more eclectic, borrowing selectively from other cities to solve specific problems faced by the mayor or the budget office. Budgeting systems were chosen not only for their technical viability and ease of implementation, but also for their match to the personalities and political needs of mayors.

The budget reforms may have looked more similar than they were. In particular, program and performance measures were implemented differentially. Performance measures were fully implemented in Dayton, Phoenix, and Tampa and only partially implemented in Rochester and Boston, neither of which had good measures of outcomes or impact. Generally, more-reformed cities were more determined to implement performance measures and better able to get the departments to cooperate.

Implementation was more problematic in less-reformed cities partly because the budget changes had to be prepared in a hurry, when a new mayor wanted a new system. It took Phoenix five years to implement a strategic planning process; it took Dayton some six years to get its PPB system fully functional, but it took Boston only two years to get its Program and Performance budget up, and most of the implementation was done in the first year. Similarly, the major work of implementing St. Louis' new program and performance budget was over a two-year period. Because of the speed, loose ends were left hanging.

Another problem with implementation of performance measures in less-reformed cities is the fear that they will be used against the mayor or the departments. Mayors in Rochester and Tampa felt vulnerable to bad publicity from opposition on the council if unfilled performance targets were reported in the budget or to the public. In Boston, departments often felt vulnerable if they achieved less than 100 percent of their targets, and performance reports were given limited circulation for fear of bad publicity.

In addition to performance measures, less-reformed cities also implemented program budgeting less fully. Dayton, Phoenix, and Rochester have integrated program budgets. Tampa tried program budgeting briefly and dropped it. St. Louis divided up the budget into two volumes. Volume one is the program budget, with performance measures but no line items; volume two is a departmental line-item budget with lists of personnel positions by program. Boston's budget presentation gives departmental line-item budgets first and then program expenditures.

The dual budgets of the less-reformed cities can be interpreted in different ways. The dual budgets may represent a compromise in which the professional staff improve technical matters and relations between the departments and the budget office while the city-wide political decisions are made independently of the budget process much as they always have been. Or the dual structure may include a real (incremental) budget and a symbolic budget intended to improve the appearance of the cities' financial management. Less-reformed cities were generally more likely to use the budget format to communicate symbolically or strategically to the legislature or the county, to get changes in laws or additional revenue, or to shift spending.

Over time, the six cities adopted many of the same reforms, but their overall budget systems evolved in different directions at different times. Dayton and Phoenix adopted PPB; the other cities either tried it and dropped it or did not try it at all. Boston and St. Louis, for much of the period, had traditional line-item budgets. Comprehensive planning characterized Dayton. Tampa recently shifted from comprehensive to strategic planning, while Boston and St. Louis went without a capital plan for years. Boston's recent capital plan was developed under the gun of court mandates. Phoenix adopted a ZBB approach very early, alternating with target budgeting; this fit the city's continuing fiscal stress and inability to raise taxes. Tampa and Rochester were early adopters of target-based budgeting, making this form dominant in the middle group of case studies.

Choices among budget reforms were generally consistent with the level of political reform. More-reformed cities adopted budget reforms that were heavier on planning and comparative programmatic analysis. Cities in the middle generally emphasized techniques that controlled departmental totals and kept the peace with the budget office, while holding down property taxes. The less-reformed cities, until recently, maintained line-item budgeting and virtually no planning. Moreover, when the less-reformed cities did adopt budget reforms, they were more likely to start and stop, based on the availability of revenue and the preferences of the mayor.

The differences in the choice, emphasis, and implementation of budget reforms in cities of varying degrees of political reform is suggestive, but, with the addition of program and performance budgets in Boston and St. Louis and the adoption of target-based budgets in Boston and Dayton, the cities' budget systems have looked more like each other in the last few years. What might this mean?

One interpretation is that expectations that the level of political reform would structure the adoption of budget reform missed an important dynamic, namely that the level of budget reform may be consciously used to modify the level of political reform, at least in the sense of curtailing highly independent departments. In St. Louis, Mayor Schoemehl used budget reform to help gain some control over the departments; in Boston, the new capital budget process, which had the power of several court mandated changes behind it, forced a new level of centralization on departments. That is not to argue that departments did not resist the changes, or that implementation was not affected, or that the changes might not yet be reversed; only that budgeting can influence the level of centralization. In light of this finding, the fact that the two least reformed cities, St. Louis and Boston, have both dramatically modified their budgets in the last few years, including performance measures, is less difficult to interpret.

The widespread adoption of target-based budgeting reflects not only the widespread conditions of fiscal stress and the usefulness of this budgeting form in setting priorities for expenditures, but also the general applicability of a budgeting system that centralizes fiscal totals and ensures budget balance while decentralizing decision making to the departments and essentially ends budget games between the departments and the budget office. The advantages fell differently depending on whether the city was initially centralized or not. In decentralized cities, it gave the budget office more control over totals; in centralized cities, it gave the departments badly needed autonomy over spending choices. Target-based budgeting builds in the possibility of reallocation, and careful setting of priorities of budget requests at the margins, but it can easily—and comfortably—deteriorate into incremental allocations. Thus it fits in both more- and less-reformed cities, and in the same cities as they choose to be more or less incremental in their decision making. Although the choice of five out of six cities for this type of budgeting seems impressive, it may mask a great deal of variation in how the system is being used and for what purpose.

Some of the most suggestive similarities were not in fact between the particular budget reforms adopted but in the similarities in the pattern of variation within cities between more and less openness to the public and citizen input into the budget. The city manager of Phoenix emphasized the variability of the need to respond to community demands as a major force changing budget processes; neighborhood pressures and the need for citizen participation were important in other cities as well. These pressures resulted not only from declining tax bases and rejection of proposed tax increases, but also from allocation decisions that slighted the neighborhoods, or that weighed business demands for lower taxes more heavily than citizen demands for more services. Dayton seems to have met and resolved that problem with a budget system that endured throughout the period, but other cities experienced more alternation.

CONCLUSIONS

Allen Schick (1966) described patterns of changing budgeting from the origin of budgeting in the United States through the adoption of PPB. This article carries the examination forward by looking at budgeting changes in six cities over the last 20 years. The study investigates the variation between cities in their adoption of budget innovations, as well as their evolving similarities. The analysis suggests that the more-reformed cities adopt budget reforms much more quickly, followed by the intermediate, and finally, the least reformed cities. These early, intermediate, and late adopters tend to differ in their motivations and use of reforms. The most reformed cities adopt budget reforms because they are there and to help them adapt to particular environmental threats. The intermediate cities wait to see what works, what can be easily implemented, and what seems to address the specific environmental and technical problems they confront without overly threatening or changing the political structure. The last group, the least politically reformed, use budget reforms to address immediate environmental problems but also to help change the political structure, towards more central control and policy accountability of the departments.

Schick's description of the evolution of budgeting from financial control to managerial emphasis and then to planning, in a developmental sequence, did not apply the shorter time span of my study. The more-reformed cities were more interested in comprehensive planning, the intermediate cities in strategic planning, and the least reformed planned only when forced by the courts. The managerial orientation, as reflected in program budgeting and analysis and the potential tradeoffs between programs was also strongest in the most reformed cities, but tradeoffs for policy reasons, as opposed to for efficiency reasons, were dominant in the least reformed cities. How to make the budget responsive to the mayor's short-term policy directions without causing deficits or wreaking havoc with the departments was a key focus of budget reform in the less politically reformed cities. This is not to challenge Schick's formulation, only to add that there may be more than one line of evolution. As budget innovations reach the least politically reformed, the budget reforms are called upon to do different things, which complicates the notion of evolving towards a single goal or model. The second pattern of evolution emphasizes increased accountability of the departments to the mayor and increased accountability of the mayor to the public.

To the extent that the analysis presented here is correct, it provides good news for both budgeters and budget reformers. Budget reforms are widely adopted. They are not just used as window dressing; they are used by pragmatic managers and politicians to solve problems. Moreover, budget reforms turn out not to always be cabooses behind political reform; sometimes, they head the train. They provide an expanded set of options for elected officials who despair of controlling independent departments, and who do not know how to bring back a disaffected public to supporting city government.

Note

This is a revised version of a paper given at the American Political Science Association Meeting, Washington, DC, September, 1991. Some of the field research was funded by the Graduate School at Northern Illinois University.

Bibliography

Anonymous, 1989. Asked not to be identified other than as an employee who worked for the city for ten years, interview November 8.
Ciolek, Robert, 1989. Acting director of administrative services and former budget director City of Boston, interview November 13.
City of Rochester, 1974. Budget letter from the city manager, from City Manager Elisha C. Freedman to the city council, May 28, in the City of Rochester Budget for fiscal year 1974–75, p. M-4.

City of Rochester, 1979. Budget letter from the city manager, from City Manager Joe L. Miller to the city council, May 15, in the City of Rochester Budget for fiscal year 1979–1980, p. 2.

City of Rochester, 1989–1990. Approved budget.

City of St. Louis, 1988–1989. Budget Summary.

City of Tampa, 1991. Public works department budget coordinator, interview January 12.

Desilet, Al, 1990. Former budget director, City of Tampa, interview October 4.

Fairbanks, Frank, 1990. City manager City of Phoenix, interview December 11.

Gottschalk, Barbara, 1990. Budget director, City of Boston, interview November 9.

Hill, Charles. Former budget director City of Phoenix and more recently in charge of strategic planning, interview December 10.

Luckingham, Bradford, 1989. *Phoenix: The History of a Southwestern Metropolis.* Tucson: University of Arizona Press.

Manion, Pat, 1990. Deputy city manager, City of Phoenix, interview December 8.

Mosher, Frederick, 1940. "City Manager Government in Rochester, New York." In Frederick Mosher, Arthur Harris, Howard White, John Vieg, Landrum Bolling, A. George Miller, David Monroe, and Harry O'Neal Wilson, eds., *City Manager Government in Seven Cities.* Chicago: Public Administration Service.

Myers, Robert, 1989. Budget analyst City of Rochester from 1972–1974 and budget director from 1976–1982, interview October 6.

Nee, Mary, 1989. Director of capital budgeting City of Boston, interview November 13.

Poister, Theodore and Gregory Streib, 1989. "Management Tools in Municipal Government: Trends over the Past Decade." *Public Administration Review,* vol. 49 (May/June), pp. 240–248.

Public works director, 1990. Phoenix, interview December 10.

Rubin, Irene and Lana Stein, 1990. "Budgeting in St. Louis: Why Budgeting Changes." *Public Administration Review,* vol. 50 (July/August), pp. 420–426.

Schabert, Tilo, 1989. *Boston Politics, Creativity of Power.* Berlin: Walter DeGruyter.

Schick, Allen, 1966. "The Road to PPB: The Stages of Budget Reform." *Public Administration Review,* vol. 26 (November/December), pp. 245–256.

Sette, Al, 1989. Budget director City of Rochester, interview October 5.

Stefan, Jim, budget director, City of Tampa, interview October 4, 1990.

Tevlin, Andrea, 1990. Acting budget director City of Phoenix, interview December 10.

Wehling, Roger, 1991. Planner for the City of Tampa, interview January 8.

Woodie, Paul, 1989. Head of the planning department and former head of the budget office when all the changes in budget format took place, interview October 20.

The Public's Capital

ALAN S. BLINDER

One day in the early 1980s, I spoke at a business conference along with Amitai Etzioni, the noted sociologist. As I awaited my turn to speak, I listened to Etzioni talk of togetherness, or rather its lack, in contemporary American society. His catalog of unmet collective needs included our inadequate public infrastructure, and he concluded with a remark that struck me as hilarious at the time: "On your way home, if you come to a bridge, don't cross it."

Not long afterward, a portion of the bridge over the Mianus River on the Connecticut Turnpike—a bridge I had often crossed—collapsed. The remark no longer seemed so funny. Within the next few years, a number of other not-very-funny incidents occurred: a New York State Thruway bridge collapsed, killing 10 motorists; a dam burst in Georgia, flooding a Bible school and drowning a number of children; and so on.

Tragedies like those helped focus public attention on America's crumbling infrastructure. But they were also misleading. Only a morbid individual worries about drowning from a collapsing bridge or a bursting dam. But all of us deal frequently with more mundane hazards like being stuck in traffic jams, jarred by pothole-ridden roads, or delayed at crowded airports. Many of us also worry about the quality of our municipal water supplies. In a sense less dramatic than the bridge over the Mianus River, public health, safety, and convenience—and national productivity—are imperiled by the way America starves its public sector.

Contrary to a recent cliché, we have no infrastructure *crisis*. We are not on the verge of a cataclysm nor at a dramatic historical crossroads. But we do have a nagging infrastructure *problem*. America's bumpy roads, teetering and sometimes closed bridges, and congested airports symbolize a seriously deteriorating public capital stock. Fifteen years of policy aimed at boosting private investment and stinting on public investment has left America with what has aptly been called a third deficit—a serious imbalance between relatively abundant private capital and relatively scarce public capital. And we have no one to blame but ourselves.

The third deficit is sizable, as are its ill effects. A few years ago, the Federal Highway Administration estimated that 53 percent of nonlocal roads were in fair or poor condition. Substandard road surfaces cost Americans upward of $30 billion a year in vehicle damage and excess fuel consumption alone; no one knows how to put a price tag on the aches and pains and annoyance. Across the nation about 136,000 bridges are rated structurally deficient. The estimated bill for bringing them all up to par exceeds $50 billion.

Roughly half of all urban interstates and a third of other urban arterial highways are congested, making traffic jams a shared ritual of modern American life. During the 1980s, commuting delays into Manhattan doubled, and rush-hour driving speeds on the Washington, D.C., beltway fell by 15 to 50 percent. The U.S. Department of Transportation (DOT) estimated that 722 million person-hours and three billion gallons of gasoline were wasted in urban freeway delays in 1985. The total cost of this congestion: about $9 billion. And things keep getting worse.

The nation's airports are also choked with traffic. No wonder. While air traffic has risen about 9 percent a year, the nation has not opened a single major airport since 1974. (Denver is building one now.) According to the DOT, all 21 of the nation's primary airports, which together handle 80 percent of the traffic, are seriously congested. The Federal Aviation Administration estimated that in 1986 air-travel delays cost airlines $1.8 billion in additional operating expenses and cost travelers $3.2 billion in lost time.

All this does not constitute a crisis. But it is certainly a colossal waste. The total cost may run to $50 billion or more a year. More to the point of this book, America's shortage of infrastructure capital may also be retarding productivity growth. By one estimate, it accounts for more than half of the total productivity slowdown since the early 1970s. This estimate, produced by economist David Aschauer, is quite controversial. So we should pause a moment to understand precisely what it means and just how stunning it is.

According to Aschauer's research, the slowdown in the rate of investment in *public* capital was a major cause of the slowdown in *private-sector* productivity growth. The implication is clear: If the government would invest more in core infrastructure—roads and bridges, water and sewer systems, airports and mass transit, electrical and gas facilities—productivity growth would accelerate. At one level this conclusion is unremarkable. I have observed several times [previously] that workers with more capital are more productive. Why should public capital be different from private capital in this respect? Just as a truck driver can produce more work per hour if his truck is bigger and more reliable, so can he be more productive if the roads are smoother and less congested—not to mention passable.

Why, then, has Aschauer's work ignited a tempest in the Washington think-tank teapot? Because his estimates of the productivity-enhancing effects of public capital are so large that many people refuse to believe them. They imply, for example, that productivity growth since 1970 would have been 50 percent higher if we had held the rate of public investment (relative to GNP) at 1950–1970 levels. They also imply that public investment would now contribute more to private-sector productivity growth than private investment—as anti-Reaganesque a conclusion as you are likely to encounter.

Critics have attacked Aschauer's work on a variety of technical grounds, and others have scurried to its defense. This is not the place to join the technical debate. Perhaps his estimates are too high. But all the fuss seems to have missed an obvious and fundamental point. The conclusion that the nation should invest more in infrastructure may well be right even if Aschauer's estimates of the productivity impacts are wrong. Why? Because many, if not most, of the benefits from public-infrastructure capital do not even count in the GNP.

Some years ago, my wife and I bumped into an example. We were driving home late at night from a lovely restaurant on the Pennsylvania side of the Delaware River when our car, which was new at the time, hit what must have been one of history's great potholes. It was new no longer. The resulting impact not only flattened a tire and ruined our evening but bent two wheels out of shape and destroyed the front-end suspension. Had Pennsylvania better maintained its public infrastructure, the Blinder family would have benefited. But the GNP would not have recorded our gain. In fact, GNP would have been smaller because we would have spent less on auto repairs.

Now suppose I had been a truck driver returning from a delivery. Because of the time spent changing the flat, my delivery might have taken four hours instead of two. Pennyslvania's shoddy infrastructure would have reduced my productivity (GNP per hour of work), and therefore better infrastructure would have boosted GNP.

The general point is clear: smoother road surfaces lead to less maintenance and faster travel not only for trucks on business trips but also for cars in personal use. But while the former are reckoned into the GNP, where they appear as productivity improvements, the latter are not. (In fact, they may actually lower the GNP, as my example suggests.) And other benefits of better roads—like the fact that people with backache suffer less pain—do not affect the productivity statistics at all. The only benefits that enter into Aschauer's calculations of the worth of public capital are the ones that boost GNP. So his calculations miss much of consequence.

The same point applies to infrastructure investments that alleviate congestion. If expanded highway and airport capacity enables truckers and pilots to accomplish more work in an hour, productivity will rise. That is precisely what Aschauer measures—and what his critics dispute. But if families on vacation endure fewer traffic jams and airport delays, or if millions of commuters cut minutes from their morning drive times, the GNP statistics will record no gain.

The upshot: Aschauer's estimate that public capital is more productive than private capital is astonishing—once you realize how much it leaves out. Only some of the returns on public capital actually get counted in GNP. That these alone might exceed the total returns on private capital is truly remarkable. Even if Aschauer overstates the effects of infrastructure on GNP by a factor of two, the nation might still be well advised to start pouring cement.

Or would it? There is at least one important reason to question this conclusion. And it has major implication for the debate over infrastructure and productivity.

MAKING SOMETHING FROM NOTHING

What the nation really wants and needs is not more roads, bridges, and airports but more trucks, cars, and aircraft carrying more passengers and freight more smoothly, conveniently, and in less time. Building additional physical facilities is the most obvious way to achieve that goal. But it is not the only way. And it is a very expensive way. Advocates of greater infrastructure spending have bandied about figures on "unmet needs" that run as high as $2 trillion and more. That is a titanic sum—enough to sink several budgets. Not only that, the solution sows the seeds of its own destruction because, for example, more roads will surely attract more drivers to damage and crowd the greater volume of pavement.

Fortunately, a team of economists has recently proposed two more subtle and less costly means to the same end. Instead of building more highways, Kenneth Small, Clifford Winston, and Carol Evans argue, we should make better use of the ones we've got. Build our roads better and charge more intelligently for their use, they claim, and the American public will get more and better highway services at lower cost. Let us see how.

To start, the trio finds that current building practice makes roads too thin, so they begin crumbling too soon. Building roadways to last longer costs more initially but yields substantial savings in maintenance and repair costs later. The economists estimate that thicker pavement—for example, about two more inches on interstates—would eventually save taxpayers at least $4 for every $1 of public expenditure, including interest. Even if their calculations err by a considerable margin, this simple change in policy has much to recommend it. Other experts point out that rubberized asphalt—created by adding rubber from old tires to asphalt—lasts longer and decreases vehicle wear and tear.

But what about pricing? Elementary economic principles suggest that the fee each vehicle pays for road use ought to approximate the costs that vehicle imposes on society. There are two principal costs: damage to the roadway and congestion. Loosely speaking, trucks cause the damage and cars cause the congestion. So each requires a different approach.

Trucks pay considerable road-use taxes, as we all know. Indeed, they must be the only pieces of capital that wear their tax bills on their rear ends. Unfortunately, taxes on trucks ignore important engineering evidence that the damage a vehicle does to a roadway depends not on its total weight but on its weight per axle. This is, after all, just common sense. (Or is it common physics?) The weight of a truck is not distributed evenly over the road but concentrated at points where tire meets pavement. Distributing the same weight over more points (more axles) eases the strain on the pavement. So we should encourage the use of trucks with many axles.

Yet what do we do now? First, we charge for road use principally through a gasoline tax that actually penalizes multi-axle trucks, which are generally larger and less fuel-efficient. Then we levy a special excise tax on tires, so multiwheeled vehicles pay more. Finally, many toll roads charge by the axle— precisely the reverse of what they should be doing. If road-use fees were based on vehicle weight per axle, America's truck fleet would be redesigned in ways that do less damage to both our roads and our pocketbooks.

With cars, the principal concern is congestion, not road damage. When Joe Commuter decides to drive to work rather than take the train, he presumably takes account of the traffic delays he will encounter on the road. But he ignores the fact that his decision to drive slows down the progress of every other driver on the congested roads. Because Joe does not weigh the full *social* costs of his decision, he drives too much and at the wrong hours.

The economic remedy is simple in principle, and modern technology makes it much more practical than it once was: drivers should pay more for using roads during rush hours than during slack periods. The gasoline tax makes a slight nod in this direction, because fuel economy declines in heavy traffic. But economists who have studied the matter conclude that charges for road use in peak periods should be much higher than they are now. With more appropriate pricing, traffic would spread itself out more evenly over the day, and the existing road network would accommodate more cars traveling at higher speeds.

The same principles apply to our overcrowded airports, where pricing can only be called wacky. Airport landing fees generally depend on weight. But the main cost of accommodating an additional plane at a busy airport is not the damage it does to the runway but the delays it imposes on other aircraft. Thus, while a tiny Beechcraft costs society about as much to land as a Boeing 747, airports charge it much less. And even though it costs vastly more to handle any plane at 6 p.m. than at 1 p.m., landing fees rarely vary by time of day.

Rational airport pricing would make landing fees depend on time of day rather than on aircraft weight. If airport services were priced this way, much general aviation trafific would voluntarily divert itself to smaller reliever airports rather than land at Kennedy, O'Hare, and LAX. Commercial airlines would spread their traffic out more evenly through the day. Delays would shorten and the nation would suddenly find its existing airports able to handle more traffic. It would be as if we got something for nothing. Correction: We *would* have gotten something for nothing.

Some people have used the preceding analysis to argue that we should not build any more infrastructure; instead, we should utilize what we have more efficiently. This conclusion seems to me illogical. We should always use whatever resources we have more efficiently. But that does not preclude building more. There are at least four reasons why I believe America should invest more in its roads, bridges, airports, and water-treatment facilities.

The first is their apparently dramatic effect on national productivity. It is true that the nation could—and should—get more out of the capital already on hand. But if such large benefits flow from such inefficiently used infrastructure, there is a strong presumption that efficiently used infrastructure would offer real bonanzas.

Second, the share of infrastructure spending has declined from about 2 percent of GNP in the 1960s to about 1 percent in the 1980s, which suggests underinvestment. Critics of greater infrastructure spending point out that real GNP has grown about 70 percent in two decades; so 1 percent of today's GNP buys almost as much as 2 percent of GNP did then. But we must remember that economically speaking America is now a much bigger place. There are, for example, 23 percent more Americans living now than 20 years ago, about half again as many cars and trucks on the road, and about twice as many aircraft in the skies. Why should we think that the 1970 absolute spending levels are appropriate today?

Third, America has accumulated private capital much more rapidly than public capital for several decades now, making private capital relatively more abundant and public capital relatively more scarce. According to the so-called (and widely misunderstood) law of diminishing returns, this dramatic shift in relative supplies should have raised the productivity of public capital compared with that of private capital. So there are two possibilities: Either the productivity of public capital was exceedingly low in 1970, or it is exceedingly high today. You choose.

Fourth, when given a choice at the ballot box, Americans vote overwhelmingly in favor of more infrastructure spending. Despite the vaunted tax revolt, voters in the 1980s approved more than three-quarters of all bond referenda for infrastructure. And the typical outcome was lopsided—about a two-to-one margin in favor. The message seems clear: Americans are willing to tax themselves to build roads, bridges, sewage-treatment plants, and the like. Maybe they know what they're doing.

WHOSE PROBLEM IS IT?

Careless discussions of the infrastructure shortage often proceed as if it were all a federal problem. It is not. A large portion of the nation's infrastructure is, in fact, the responsibility of state and local governments, and the conditions of highways and bridges vary enormously across the 50 states.

The Federal Highway Administration estimates that 13 percent of all the deficient bridges covered by the federal aid system are in a single state: New York. More than 54 percent of the Empire State's bridges that receive federal aid are deficient, while just across the river (if you can get across a bridge), New Jersey's deficiency rate is only 21 percent. New York and New Jersey receive federal aid according to the same formulas, have similar weather, and buy concrete at similar prices. The difference presumably reflects New Jersey's superior performance on bridge repair.

Even larger discrepancies exist in road conditions. Whereas about 12 percent of the interstate highway system was in poor condition at the end of 1987, the figure was a stunning 40 percent in Missouri but less than 5 percent in neighboring Illinois and 1 percent or less in eight particularly tidy states. Again, the suspicion is that different state maintenance policies are at the bottom of this.

That a good part of the infrastructure problem has its roots at state and local levels does not preclude a federal role. State and local governments respond to both political and economic incentives. And the economic incentives, at least, are heavily influenced by federal matching grants that lower the price of infrastructure for states. If the federal government offers to match state expenditures on a three-for-one basis, for example, a $40 million span of highway will cost the state that builds it just $10 million. The other $30 million comes from Washington. Economists have found, not surprisingly, that such incentives encourage more construction. There are two problems, however.

One is that federal grant programs are typically capped, and spending in many states is at or beyond the cap. In such cases, the state becomes ineligible for further federal aid, and the inducement to spend more disappears. The remedy, of course, is to uncap the programs. But Congress is naturally worried about open-ended commitments. Perhaps a good solution, recently suggested by a group of congressmen, is to lower the matching rate but eliminate the caps.

The second problem is more worrisome. Nowadays many of our most acute infrastructure needs are for maintaining and repairing existing roads and bridges, not for building new ones. The interstate highway system, for example, is nearly complete; but parts of it are in sorry shape. Unfortunately, state and local politicians who send road crews out to repair potholes and reinforce bridges earn no photo opportunities, cut no ribbons, and get no sound bites on the TV news. But when local politicians announce plans for a new bridge, the local media lavish attention and compliment them on their ability to pry money out of Washington.

Such political incentives produce what has been called an edifice complex— a bias in favor of building new rather than fixing up. This bias was not created by the federal government. But if Washington ignores it, the nation may develop an ever-increasing imbalance in its stock of public infrastructure. One thing we certainly do *not* need is more and more decrepit bridges. What to do? One idea is for the federal government to provide more generous matching grants for maintenance and repairs and less generous ones for new construction.

If public investment is to live up to its potential as a source of productivity growth, it is imperative to get the incentives right. State and local governments must be given appropriate incentives to build the right types of capital, and individuals and businesses must be given appropriate incentives to utilize infrastructure efficiently. In addition to all this, however, we probably need to build more.

And public infrastructure has a final virtue—one I have not yet mentioned but that bears on a central theme of this [article]. Unlike a private home, office building, or factory, a publicly owned bridge, road, or airport is neither mine nor yours. It is everybody's. We own it together. Upgrading our shabby stock of infrastructure will contribute to the sense of social cohesion and even of togetherness that we need to take to other spheres of life—like the workplace.

Note on Sources

The facts and figures on infrastructure come from four main sources: David A. Aschauer's article "Public Investment and Private Sector Growth" (Economic Policy Institute, 1990); Aschauer's "Why Is Infrastructure Important?," a paper prepared for the Federal Reserve Bank of Boston, 1991; Heywood T. Sanders' article "Public Works and Public Dollars" (The House Wednesday Group, February 1991); and Carol A. Evans, Kenneth A. Small, and Clifford Winston's, *Road Work* (Brookings, 1989). Aschauer's papers summarize his more technical work on the impact of public infrastructure on productivity. Sanders' paper emphasizes the role of state and local governments and was background for the House Wednesday Group's statement on highway policy, "Rules of the Game" (February 4, 1991). The book by Small et al. is the source of the analysis of efficient highway construction and pricing.

8

POLICY ANALYSIS, PLANNING, AND STRATEGIC MANAGEMENT

A great deal of current effort in public administration deals with management improvement in the operation of public agencies. This chapter deals with the strategic management of public agencies and the planning, implementing, and evaluating of public services.

Much management improvement is predicated on the practice of planning: deciding in advance what an agency is going to do and how it is going to do it. In public administration today, the emphasis is on *strategic* planning. As depicted in Figure 8-1, strategic planning involves the "matching" of three kinds of considerations:

- A review of an organization's history and current mission, stated and actual

- An analysis of current and future *external* factors having the greatest impact on an organization—political, economic, social, technological—and particularly the opportunities, challenges, and obstacles they represent

- An assessment of internal organizational capabilities and resources, stressing current and projected strengths and weaknesses.

Besides examining alternative goals, strategic planning involves an assessment of the prospects of acquiring the resources necessary to achieve those goals. Goals without resources are meaningless, and the resources an agency can obtain often depend on which goals it pursues and how it pursues them.

As Figure 8-1 shows, strategic planning has four different "products": a mission statement, reaffirming current goals or creating new goals for an agency; a "strategy," the overall blueprint for future changes, including how to get there; a plan, a document detailing the changes sought, with attention to the roles of key organizational units and participants; and changes in organizational policy—structures, standard operating procedures, and other rules—necessary to accomplish the plan.

Figure 8-1. Strategic Planning

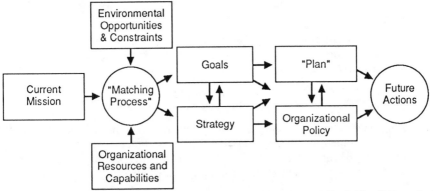

Source: Madeleine Wing Adler and Frederick S. Lane, "Why Colleges Don't Plan," *Journal of the College and University Personnel Association* (Summer, 1988), p. 29.

Strategic planning is intended to produce different future organizational actions. Without actual implementation, even the best planning process is a failure. In this sense, planning provides a basis for accountability: Did the organization actually carry out the agreed-upon goals and courses of action?

Closely related to planning is policy analysis—the careful, systematic consideration of issues to improve governmental decision-making. The policy issue involved can range from improving the nation's health care system to the most efficient routing of school buses. In the first article in this chapter, Laurence Lynn explains policy analysis and its potential. He also observes that there are different kinds of policy analysts with different combinations of analytical and political skills.

Most of the literature on strategic management focuses on business firms. In the second article here, Barton Wechsler and Bob Backoff analyze strategic management approaches in Ohio state agencies. They find four distinctive public sector strategies: developmental, transformational, protective, and political.

The final two articles in this chapter are reports of management success stories in two different jurisdictions, the State of Minnesota and the city of Madison, Wisconsin. In the first of these two, Sandra Hale, former State Commissioner of Administration and a senior member of the governor's cabinet, tells us about implementing the award-winning STEP program (Strides Toward Excellence in Performance) and other management improvement programs. Commissioner Hale also describes ALLTECH, which involves a public-private partnership.

Finally, Joseph Sensenbrenner describes his concerns and problems as the elected mayor in bringing Total Quality Management (TQM) to Madison, the state capital of Wisconsin. Sensenbrenner today is a public sector consultant specializing in TQM.

Here are just a few questions to think about in connection with Chapter 8:

- The word "strategic" is used a great deal in the management literature these days. What is meant by *strategic* planning? By *strategic* management?

- Policy analysis is increasingly important in public administration. What is policy analysis? Assess its potential in improving governmental decision-making.

- As seen in Ohio, how can strategic management improve public administration? What distinctive public sector strategies are there?

- Both Hale and Sensenbrenner talk about confronting maladministration in their respective jurisdictions, and they use practices more common in business administration. Describe the difficulties of implementing new management approaches in Minnesota and Madison.

- If you knew a new city manager in a nearby city, would you recommend any particular management practice you read about in this chapter? Which one or ones, and why?

Policy Analysis

LAURENCE E. LYNN, JR.

Because policy analysis is both a specialized and a controversial activity, it is useful to introduce the basic ideas and approaches that distinguish its practitioners. The evolution of policy analysis as both an intellectual discipline and an institutional process has been shaped by the tension between two conflicting points of view, one supportive and one critical.[1]

THE IDEA

Advocates of the analytic perspective argue that the typical public policy issue is so complex, value-laden, and unstructured that policy analysis is essential if policymakers are to sort through the issues, the alternatives, and the costs and consequences of those alternatives to reach a thoughtful position. As Charles Schultze, former director of the Bureau of the Budget and chairman of the Council of Economic Advisers, puts it: "The most frustrating aspect of public life is . . . the endless hours spent on policy discussions in which the irrelevant issues have not been separated from the relevant, in which ascertainable facts and relationships have not been investigated but are the subject of heated debate, in which consideration of alternatives is impossible because only one proposal has been developed, and, above all, discussions in which nobility of aim is presumed to determine the effectiveness of the program."[2]

A meaningful resolution of policy disagreements, in this view, can be achieved only if the relationships between inputs (or means) and outputs can be established. Schultze argues that a primary function of policy planning is identifying "social production functions," that is, the ways in which inputs, such as teachers, school facilities, and curriculum materials, are transformed into outputs, such as specific educational attainments.[3] He goes on to say that policy analysis is necessary to translate values, such as an educated citizenry, into specific objectives, such as eliminating financial barriers to attending college. The policy planner supports the formulation of strategy by saying to the public executive, "If these are your values (say, ensuring equality of opportunity), here are policy objectives consistent with those values (say, improved access to public education by handicapped children), and here are alternative programs together with the costs necessary to achieve these objectives. Now you can make an informed choice."

In this supportive view, [political] conflict . . . cannot be intelligently resolved without systematic analysis of the net effects and costs. . . . Politics inescapably reflects a balancing of economic interests; to remain oblivious to whose wants are satisfied and at whose expense makes no sense.

Criticism of the analytic perspective takes two contrasting forms. According to the first type of criticism, public policymaking is too political to benefit from the formal techniques of policy analysis.[4] Ours is a society of divergent and often conflicting values. The reconciliation of these conflicts often depends on suppressing discussion either of underlying values and goals or of the overall consequences of governmental actions. Focus is concentrated instead on budgets, programs, or "inputs," about which differences of opinion can be adjusted and agreement can be reached. A good decision is one to which every participant can attach satisfactory meanings and thus accept as consistent with particular goals and values. A process that forces debate on the goals, outputs, costs, and priorities of alternatives may be disruptive to the orderly adjustment of conflicting interests. Policy analysis is incompatible with, or irrelevant to, the give-and-take of partisan mutual adjustment.

In this critical view, the impasse over the Simpson-Mazzoli bill should have been resolved not by analysis but by the striking of a bargain between supporters and opponents in which both get something of value.

An alternative criticism of policy analysis takes the opposite tack: public policymaking should be more rather than less principled. Policy analysis takes the process in the wrong direction, making it too narrowly political. In the view of Laurence H. Tribe, policy analysis, with its methodological bias in favor of economic models and concepts, reflects a "wants orientation to public choices and a value system built on ever changing perceptions of immediate self-interest, of benefits and costs expressed in monetary terms."[5] Tribe believes that public policy should instead be founded on bodies of principle to which we are committed or obligated rather than on calculations of who gains and who loses by specific government actions. The discovery and integration of our values rather than repeated reference to analytic frameworks built on self-interest should lie at the heart of policymaking.

In this view, the debate between Reagan and Mondale was as it should have been. Are we to be a nation in which citizens must be issued identity cards by the government? Are we to be a nation in which rapacious employers exploit powerless workers? It is those principles, rather than the matter of net benefits or costs, that are rightly at stake.

Who is right, advocates or critics? In general, the value of substantive policy planning and analysis depends on one's answers to the kinds of questions raised in the first half of this book: How are public policies actually determined? (Do ideas, evidence, and argument make a difference?) Do public executives have a significant role in policy formation? (Do we care about their intellectual competence in policy debate?) What kinds of factors influence the behavior of government organizations? (Do research and analysis help shape the premises for organizational action?) How do personality and cognitive styles influence the performance of executive roles in government? (Is competence in complex substantive matters associated with managerial competence?) How do individuals make choices? (Do they ever refer to analysis of alternatives?)

Since the answer to most of the parenthetical questions is "yes," the question of whether systematic policy analysis should be part of the policymaking process is really not an issue. Charles Lindblom observes that "in all governments all over the world, a standard routine for reaching a policy decision is to gather and analyze facts, doing so with at least implicit theory. If analysis is often hurried and sometimes superficial, it is never wholly absent."[6] Successful public executives no more question the value of analytic support than they question the contributions of other specialists—lawyers, auditors, comptrollers, political tacticians—in their organizations.

THE DISCIPLINE

What is policy analysis?

The short answer is that policy analysis is conducted in whatever way is appropriate to the problem and the circumstances.[7] Policy analysis is often relatively simple, done, as practicing policy analysts like to say, on the backs of envelopes and using "naive" methods. It may be no more extensive, for example, than a list of effects and costs accompanied by rough and partial orders of magnitude. Occasionally—the analysis of national energy policy alternatives is an example—more elaborate approaches are called for in which large-scale policy models are constructed and used to evaluate a sophisticated range of policy choices. The spirit motivating all such work is the same, however: to clarify issues and alternatives for the benefit of policymakers.

Whether simple or elaborate, policy analysis proceeds in a disciplined, logical way. It is worth laying out the general structure of policy analysis to serve as a model by which to determine what might be done in any given circumstance. This structure has four elements: identifying the purposes of government actions; identifying and evaluating alternative ways of achieving given purposes; choosing specific designs for governmental actions; and evaluating the capacity of the government to execute particular actions.

Identifying Purposes

A comprehensive policy analysis begins with a clear formulation of possible justifications for government action. A problem exists—social or economic conditions are not what they should be—and government action of some kind may be justified to correct or ameliorate the situation. Justifying government action (or inaction) is, of course, a fundamentally philosophical and political matter—a high game. It is not self-evident that policy analysts have any special competence in addressing it. Indeed, many experienced political executives forbid their policy planners to take up such large questions, especially if they believe the answers ought to be determined by a consensual process among high-game participants. For several reasons, however, that is a short-sighted view.

First, because controversy is usually associated with justifying public policy, effective public executives devote considerable thought to the rationale for particular proposals. Such preparation enables them to be more persuasive and, by revealing logical or philosphical problems, makes them less vulnerable to unanticipated partisan criticism.

Second, even at a philosophical level, there are many ways of articulating the purposes of governmental activity and many different principles justifying government action. Those principles may have widely different, even conflict-ing, implications for what kind of action ought to be undertaken. Systematic analysis, as Schultze pointed out, can reveal the principles at stake and the costs and consequences of embracing them or of choosing one principle over another.

Finally, officials are often judged on the consistency of their views and actions. By insisting that policy analyses begin with principles, officials gain some measure of protection against inconsistent, uncoordinated, thoughtlessly expedient actions. They can better communicate the sense of having a bigger picture within which specific issues should be understood. This sense may be an advantage in partisan policy debate.

Evaluating Alternatives

How should government go about achieving its purposes? What means should it employ to achieve desired ends or specific effects? More than any other, those questions challenge the intellectual creativity and the political and bureaucratic sophistication and communications skills of policy analysts. The most important contribution of a policy analysis is often the extent to which it broadens the range of realistic alternatives from among which policymakers can choose a course of action.

The key concept here is "alternatives." To an analytical mind, the idea that one should evaluate alternative ways of achieving a given objective comes naturally; it is the "right" way to approach the making of a choice. Many, perhaps most, policymakers, however, do not think this way. They may view policymaking as reacting to particular proposals for action that "experts" have created rather than solving problems or pursuing substantive goals. Moreover, they are apt to approach policy issues with definite predispositions about how government ought to act. These predispositions may spring from intellectual conviction, but more often they reflect the policymakers' intuitive judgments about what is politically feasible, what is ideologically acceptable, or what "works" in practice.

Nonetheless, in principle and usually in fact, there are alternatives or options for achieving policy goals and for dealing with a pressing problem. Analysis of the alternatives may reveal opportunities for creative contributions to public policy that would otherwise go unrecognized. Actively calling for and paying attention to this kind of analysis can be an important factor in public executive effectiveness.

Designing Specific Actions

When the means have been chosen, the design of public policies is far from complete. This is nowhere more clearly indicated than in legislation that authorizes the performance of a service, actions to control a private activity, or the awarding of grants in accordance with regulations or guidelines established by the relevant public official. It is evident in countless instances of executive decision making during which, in the quest for agreement or under the pressure of deadlines, detailed questions as to how the action is to be designed are postponed until "later." Nothing can happen, however, and no results can be produced until those details have been worked out.

It can be sensed from the foregoing that the bureaucratic problems of resolving these questions confront public executives with difficult issues. For one thing, because of their specialized or technical nature, such matters are of necessity delegated to specialized agencies or staffs or contracted to consultants. For another, the choices to be made may be especially difficult or controversial; had they been easy to resolve, they would have been resolved. Thus, the public executive must be able to supervise the design process without becoming consumed or coopted by it.

An experience in Joan Claybrook's administration of the National Highway Traffic and Safety Administration illustrates the complications associated with designing specific government actions and the problems these pose for public executives.

> There was continuing battle going on between me and many of my assistant administrators over the level of detail that it was necessary for me to know. I felt they didn't have the same kind of judgment as I did about what was and was not important.
>
> For example, when I read the department regulation on odometers, it stated that if an odometer could be turned backwards it would have to have an indication on it that would register the action. . . . Well, I thought, why have the indicator option—why not just say you couldn't turn it backwards? So I wrote a note saying the regulation was not properly written and somebody dutifully knocked out the indicator option and reissued the regulations.
>
> A month later a spinner—a guy who spins odometers backwards—went to see Wendell Ford, the senator who chairs one of the Senate commerce subcommittees that authorizes NHTSA's programs. The spinner showed the senator how our regulation was deficient, since the clip that manufacturers would put in to prevent turning the odometer backwards would stop a normal person but not a spinner. Well, that's a very deficient regulation so I hurried over to the rulemaking engineer who had handled it and asked him, "Why didn't you write the regulation so that it

wouldn't be easy for a spinner to avoid?" He said, "Well, it would cost more money." I told him, "Who's the decision maker in the agency? You should tell me you have several different ways to accomplish a goal." We might have, for example, written the regulation so that the whole odometer would be destroyed if you turned it backwards. . . .

As a result of all this, . . . Senator Ford held a public hearing at which I had to testify about why we did this dumb thing. I had to spend five times as much time studying the details of the odometer regulations because this guy made a pre-judgment. . . .[8]

The fact that there were alternative ways to write an odometer regulation and that each had different costs and consequences was not evident to Claybrook until she was confronted by time-consuming political controversy over her regulation. While it is impossible to consider every alternative for every detail of policy design, the discipline of asking, "Are there significant alternatives that should be considered?" will improve executive performance.

Assessing Government Capacity

Based on his experience as a public official in New York City, the late Gordon Chase asserted that "an agency head is well advised to consider . . . whether a proposed new or expanded program will be relatively difficult to implement—and therefore eat up a lot of his best staff—or whether it will be relatively inexpensive in drawing down scarce managerial resources."[9] Before deciding on a particular policy design, a good public executive will ask, "How hard will it be to implement?"

Following experiences in the 1960s and 1970s when the expectations of many social policy advocates as to what government could do were disappointed, students of public policy increasingly turned their attention to problems of implementation. The emphasis on implementation is intended to highlight the value to sound decision making of being able to consider governmental capacity when choosing a policy design. Chase, for example, identified three sources of difficulties in implementing public programs:

- operational demands on program agencies and field workers implied by a particular program concept;

- the nature and availability of resources necessary to run the program;

- the extent to which authority over the program would be shared with other political and bureaucratic actors, that is, the extent to which the program administrator would have control over program implementation.

Richard F. Elmore has christened the class of approaches that includes Chase's "backward mapping."[10] "The logic of backward mapping," says Elmore, "begins with a statement of specific behavior at the lowest level of the implementation process that generates the need for a policy." The analysis then states "an objective . . . as a set of effects, or outcomes." Next, "the analysis backs up through the structure of implementing agencies, asking at each level two questions: What is the ability of this unit to affect the behavior that is the target of the policy? And what resources does this unit require in order to have that effect?" Finally, the analyst describes the policy that will produce the necessary resources.[11]

The importance of this kind of thinking is that it brings to the foreground issues of organizational capacity to produce concrete results, issues of critical importance to public executives whose goal is to contribute to public policy. It will not always be possible to complete a comprehensive backward map. It is expensive in terms of staff resources, and the kinds of questions that arise cannot always be answered with available information in a reasonable time. Nonetheless, the discipline of visualizing desired outcomes and anticipating obstacles to achieving them is an effective preventer of policy failure.

THE ANALYSTS

Public executives are often uncomfortable around the policy analysts who do the kind of work just described. Part of that discomfort stems from ignorance or misconceptions concerning policy analysts' professional motivations and methods of work.

The key characteristic of good policy analysts is their intellectual versatility. Policy analysts employ whatever intellectual and computational approaches will clarify issues and alternatives, thereby sharpening and focusing policy debate and choice. In choosing an approach to analyzing a policy issue, policy analysts will, of course, consider the nature of the problem, the public executive's interest, the amount of time available, the availability of data and other information, and their own skills and abilities as well as those of coworkers whose cooperation will be needed. Even though they may be trained in an academic discipline or technical field, good policy analysts are not first and foremost economists, engineers, statisticians, or sociologists who happen to be interested in policy. Rather, they are technically versatile, inquisitive, naturally interdisciplinary individuals whose first loyalty is to clarifying policy issues and alternates for public executives.

In the flesh, policy analysts, like public executives, display wide variations in talents, interests, and styles, which reflect differences in training, experience, and competence. Arnold Meltsner, who has studied policy analysts at work, observes that "they come to their jobs with different incentives. They have different internalized standards of accomplishment and success, and even those with a common education rely on different skills or strengths in the performance of their tasks."[12] As with public executives, it is the peculiar characteristics of their operating style that are often most consequential to their effectiveness in particular roles.

Meltsner has devised a revealing scheme for classifying policy analysts. He ranks them as high or low in two separate dimensions: analytical skill, the ability to do technically competent work, and political skill, the ability to function effectively in a government organization and to communicate with public officials. The classification scheme that results is shown in Figure 8-2.[13]

At first glance, it might be thought that a public executive would want to assemble a policy analysis staff that contains no pretenders and as many entrepreneurs as possible, with politicians and technicians (the one-dimensional analysts) included only out of necessity. In fact, as noted previously, many public executives distrust policy analysts with high political skill, whether technically capable or not. Technicians, who can produce the numbers on

Figure 8-2. Classification of Policy Analysts

Political Skill

Analytical Skill		High	Low
	High	Entrepreneur	Technician
	Low	Politician	Pretender

Source: From Arnold S. Meltsner, *Policy Analysts in the Bureaucracy* (Berkeley: University of California Press, 1976). Reprinted by permission.

demand and who are apt to be comfortable in a role that requires no political acumen, fill the bill nicely for these public executives.

Many policy analysts are unquestionably entrepreneurial, seeing the social function of policy analysis as broadly educational and prescriptive. Beyond improving the basis for specific decisions by specific officials, policy analysis would help a wide audience think about and make judgments concerning what government should do. Many policy analysts believe they should produce ideal policies that can serve as standards by which to judge the performance of policymakers. The social value of policy analysis can, in this view, be unacceptably compromised if analysts lose their independence of view. In other words, if public executives reject sound advice, they, not the policy analysts, are in error.

Many analysts who work in or consult for government have been trained to adopt a vision that transcends the responsibilities of political superiors. Some go so far as to view policy analysis as a substitute for partisan political processes rather than as an adjunct to them. Many policy analysis shops maintain staff morale through changing political seasons by adopting the role of a counterculture, advocating "the public interest" rather than a narrow or parochial organizational or political interest. They would prefer a definition of policy analysis framed in terms of the nature of the intellectual tasks to be performed: identifying objectives; developing distinctive ways of accomplishing the objectives; evaluating alternatives in terms of benefits, losses, and risks; and determining the sensitivity of results to key assumptions. Good policy analysis, in this view, is necessarily produced by experts possessing neutral and professional competence.

Public executives are right to be skeptical of such claims and distrustful of the analysis that often accompanies them. Policy analysts may profess to be politically neutral, but the implications of their work are hardly ever neutral. Effective policy analysts are craftsmen, working with the materials of particular policy problems, rather than social scientists seeking universal truth. Public executives are nonetheless well advised to harness the idealism and enthusiasm for ideas and evidence that are characteristic of policy analysts. Breaking away from the status quo, even if only incrementally, often depends on identifying an alternative course of action or a new premise for action that originates in analytic insight stimulated by devotion to the public interest. Original minds may be hard to manage, but the effort is often worth it. . . .

Notes

1. Giandomenico Majone, "Applied Systems Analysis: A Genetic Approach," in *Handbook of Systems Analysis,* edited by Edward S. Quade and Hugh J. Miser, vol. 1 overview (Laxenburg, Austria: International Institute for Applied Systems Analysis, 1981, processed).
2. Charles L. Schultze, *The Politics and Economics of Public Spending* (Washington, DC: The Brookings Institution, 1968), p. 75.
3. Ibid., pp. 57 ff.
4. See, for example, Aaron Wildavsky, *The Politics of the Budgetary Process,* 3rd ed. (Boston: Little, Brown, 1979), chapter 6; Charles E. Lindblom, "The Science of 'Muddling Through,'"*Public Administration Review,* XIX (Spring, 1959), pp. 79–88 and Lindblom's subsequent works.
5. Laurence H. Tribe, "Policy Science: Analysis or Ideology?" *Philosophy and Public Affairs* 2:1 (Fall, 1972), pp. 66–110 and "Ways Not to Think About Plastic Trees," in Laurence H. Tribe, Corinne H. Schelling, and John Voss, *When Values Conflict: Essays on Environmental Analysis, Discourse, and Decision,* edited by Laurence H. Tribe, Corinne H. Schelling, and John Voss (Cambridge, Mass.: Ballinger, 1976), pp. 61–91.
6. Charles E. Lindblom, *The Policy-Making Process* (Englewood Cliffs, NJ: Prentice-Hall, 1968), p. 6.
7. The best explication of the spirit of policy analysis is in Giandomenico Majone, "An Anatomy of Pitfalls," in *Pitfalls of Analysis,* edited by Giandomenico Majone and Edward S. Quade (Chichester, England: Wiley, 1980), pp. 7–22.
8. Joan Claybrook and NHTSA, (C), a teaching case prepared by David Whitman, Kennedy School of Government Case Program, C95-81-385, copyright 1981 by the President and Fellows of Harvard College, pp. 14–15.
9. Gordon Chase, "Implementing a Human Services Program: How Hard Will It Be?" *Public Policy,* 27:4 (Fall, 1979), pp. 385–435.
10. Richard F. Elmore, "Backward Mapping: Implementation Research and Policy Decisions," in Walter B. Williams, et al., *Studying Implementation: Methodological and Administrative Issues* (Chatham, NJ: Chatham House, 1982), pp. 18–35.
11. Ibid., p. 21.
12. Arnold Meltsner, *Policy Analysts in the Bureaucracy* (Berkeley: University of California Press, 1976), p. 14.
13. Ibid., p. 16.

Policy-Making and Administration in State Agencies: Strategic Management Approaches

BARTON WECHSLER
ROBERT W. BACKOFF

The concept of strategy has been employed by business policy and management researchers for more than two decades.[1] Common usage of the term captures a variety of images, including "adaptation," "learning," "evolution," and "coalignment."[2] In this extensive literature, strategic management is seen to encompass strategic planning, direction setting for the organization as a whole, and the formulation, implementation, and evaluation of specific organizational strategies.[3] Organizational strategies reflect the actual pattern of choices and actions made in guiding the organization through time.

Although the strategy literature has largely focused on business organizations, public agencies also engage in strategic management, as reflected in a variety of policy-making and administrative activities. Agencies regularly engage in cycles of planning and goal setting, adopt and implement new policies, develop new programs or change the relative emphasis within a portfolio of programs, reorganize their internal structure, alter their service delivery systems, and seek new sources of funding and external support. Building on evidence of important differences as well as similarities between public and private organizations,[4] scholars have begun to develop a literature specifically concerned with the distinctive nature and characteristics of strategy and strategic management in public organizations.[5] This paper extends that emerging literature by reporting the results of field studies of strategic management in four Ohio agencies and providing a preliminary classification of public organization strategies.

THE STRATEGIC MANAGEMENT APPROACH

A strategic management approach to the study of public organizations focuses on the nature of human choice and action taking in the public sector. From a strategic perspective, the critical function in any public organization and the primary responsibility of its general managers is the coalignment of streams of institutionalized action designed to achieve a basic balance among purpose, present conditions, desired future outcomes, and inner and outer environments.[6] While explicitly accounting for the political, economic, and legal factors that shape public policy, the strategic management approach recognizes that organizational purpose, striving, and capacity also serve as determinants of the strategic direction of public organizations.

Because most theories of strategic management have been concerned with private-sector organizations, market-driven competition has been treated as the main source of strategic conceptualization.[7] Since public organizations operate in a governmental authority system rather than in a market system, strategic choices and actions in the public sector emanate from sources other than market competition. Rather than maneuvering in markets, public organizations act within relatively complex multilateral power, influence, bargaining, voting, and exchange relationships.

The strategic management task for the general purpose government agency (GPGA) involves not only the development of strategies for implementing policy and for the internal and external management of the agency, but also for the establishment of organizational purpose and character. The available strategies and forms of action are restricted at the GPGA level by various factors including constitutional arrangements, legislative and judicial mandates, governmentwide rules and regulations, jurisdictional boundaries, resource constraints, political climate factors, and client and constituent interests.[8] In this context, strategic choice and action taking by individual agencies is highly dependent on external influences and environmental forces. Since the primary goal of strategic management in public organizations is to provide direction for the organization through the coalignment of internal and external strategic variables, strategic management at the agency level involves the joining together of external demands, constraints, and mandates with agency-specific goals, objectives, and operational procedures.

THE OHIO STRATEGIC MANAGEMENT STUDIES

The Study

Related literatures in public policy-making and administration, organization theory, and strategic management suggest that the nature of strategy in public organizations and characteristic patterns of strategic management vary among agencies within and across political jurisdictions, depending on various organizational and environmental conditions.[9] To explore these relationships, this research focused on two central questions regarding the strategic management of public organizations:

1. What are the patterns of strategy and strategic management in public organizations?
2. What are the factors associated with the pattern of strategy and strategic management in a specific agency?

The first of these questions addresses the nature of specific strategies and the variations found among strategies. The second research question is concerned with the factors that influence or condition the pattern of strategic choice and action taking for any specific public organization. The identification of these factors and of the relationships among factors and specific patterns of strategy have potentially important implications for understanding the environment and tools of policy-making and administration in public organizations.

Research Design

Since January 1983, intensive field studies have been conducted in four agencies of state government in Ohio: the Department of Natural Resources, the Department of Mental Retardation and Developmental Disabilities, the Department of Public Welfare, and the Public Utilities Commission of Ohio. These studies focused on agency-level strategic management during the second administration of Governor James A. Rhodes (1974–1982).

In many ways, Ohio is a prototypical American state. It has large numbers of both urban and rural residents, sizeable ethnic and minority populations, and a diverse, albeit troubled economy. During the period 1974–1982, state government experienced first expansion and then cutback, relative fiscal well-being and extended budget crises, and simultaneous demands for new programs and services and for greater efficiency and reduced expenditures. The agencies selected for inclusion in this research are representative of a variety of policy and service types and account for a significant portion of state government activity and budgetary expenditure in Ohio. Moreover, in terms of both program and management responsibilities, they are generally representative of the population of Ohio and other state government agencies.

Multiple sources of data and methods of qualitative analysis were employed in the field studies. Unstructured, intensive interviews were conducted with directors, deputy directors, division chiefs, and other agency informants actually involved in the formulation and implementation of strategy. Key stakeholders of the agency from government and various constituency and clientele groups were also interviewed. These interviews took place in several waves over a period of 18 months. Also, annual reports, budgets, and other documents from the agencies, the State of Ohio Archives, and other sources were collected, and the contents were systematically analyzed.

From these various sets of data, extensive accounts of agency strategy and strategic management were prepared and analyzed.[10] These accounts proved highly suggestive of the varied patterns of strategy found in the four Ohio agencies. In addition to identifying specific strategic patterns, the analysis disclosed a number of factors which seemed to influence strategic choice and action taking in the agencies.

ANALYTICAL FRAMEWORK

Eight dimensions were employed in the analysis of the original accounts of strategic management in the Ohio agencies. While the dimensions are not completely independent, each captures a distinctive feature or element of the strategies of public agencies. The process of analyzing the original accounts and rating the agencies on each of the dimensions involved the authors as well as several colleagues and graduate students. Initial decisions about ratings were tested with informants in later stages of the research.[11]

Strength of external influence describes the extent to which external actors attempt to influence the strategy of an agency. This dimension measures the level of effort made by various stakeholders in the influence process.

Locus of strategic control reflects the outcome of influence processes, locating the control over strategic direction either with organizational actors (internal) or extraorganizational stakeholders (external). Where the level of external influence effort is moderate to high, this dimension captures the ability or inability of the agency to resist external direction.

Impetus for strategic action indicates whether the agency's strategy is crafted in anticipation of events (proactive) or in reaction to them (reactive).

Strategic orientation refers to the objectives of an agency's strategy: political, organizational, or policy. Organizations with a political orientation pursue strategic outcomes designed to serve the political interests of organizational actors, jurisdictional policy makers or controllers, or external stakeholders. An organizational orientation aims to add resources, improve performance, and/or develop capacity. Policy oriented strategies derive from membership in a specific policy community and support for its policy orientation.

Orientation toward change reflects the agency's intention toward itself and its environment. For example, agency strategies may be designed to produce fundamental change in program, structure, or relationships with stakeholders, or they may be designed to maintain the status quo.

Scope of strategic management refers to the range of concerns addressed by the agency's strategic management activity. The scope or domain of strategic choice and action may be broad or narrow, depending on organizational capacity, the preferences of key stakeholders, and various environmental circumstances.

Level of strategic management activity describes the effort expended by an agency to achieve its strategic objectives. A high level of strategic management activity is associated with significant effort and attention to specific strategic issues. An organization with low strategic management activity does not devote much energy to strategic management or to a strategic agenda and may appear to be passively drifting.

Direction of strategic movement refers to the target(s) of the agency's strategic management actions. Strategic actions can be directed internally toward achieving control, increasing efficiency, or building capacity; they may be focused externally as a means of responding to or transforming the environment; or, strategic actions may have both internal and external targets.

PATTERNS OF STRATEGY

Table 8-1 presents each of the agency strategies in terms of the eight dimensions defined immediately above. The patterns identified by this analysis are characteristic of the strategies of public organizations, but they do not necessarily exhaust all possible strategies. As noted in the concluding section, further research is required to complete the development of a strategic taxonomy for public organizations. The remainder of this section describes each of the strategies, with appropriate illustrations drawn from the agency studies. In the next section, factors associated with specific patterns of strategy are identified and discussed.

Analysis of strategic management in the Ohio agencies revealed four distinctive public sector strategies: developmental, transformational, protective, and political.

Table 8-1
Ratings of the Ohio Agencies on Strategic Dimensions

	DNR	DMRDD	DPW	PUCO
Strength of External Influence	Weak	Strong	Strong	Moderate
Locus of Strategic Control	Internal	External	External	Internal
Impetus for Strategic Action	Proactive	Reactive	Reactive	Reactive
Strategic Orientation	Organizational	Policy	Political	Political
Orientation toward Change	Incremental	Fundamental	Status Quo	Incremental
Scope of Strategic Management	Broad	Moderate	Narrow	Narrow
Strategic Management Activity Level	High	Moderate	Low	Low
Direction of Strategic Movement	Mixed	Internal	Mixed	Mixed

The Developmental Strategy—Department of Natural Resources

Operating in the developmental mode, organizational strategists purposefully craft strategies to enhance organizational status, capacity, resources, and impact, and to produce a new and different organizational future. The strategy is based on an awareness of and even attention to external actors and forces, but the impetus for strategic action is internal, as is the locus of strategic management control. Strategic choice and action taking range over a broad agenda, reflecting the various issues and concerns affecting the organization.

The developmental strategy characterized the Department of Natural Resources (DNR). During the Rhodes administration, DNR developed new and expanded programs, constructed new facilities, purchased land for state nature preserves, initiated a "People to the Parks" program, established a Youth Conservation Corps, and introduced a statewide litter-control program.

Under the leadership of Director Robert Teater, DNR sought to integrate its diverse and often-competing constituencies around core departmental objectives to secure independent sources of funding and to create an organizational climate and culture emphasizing individual and organizational performance. DNR's leadership shared a common vision of the department, of its future, and of the strategies for achieving departmental goals. Communication of this vision was instrumental in securing broad support for the DNR program within the department, in other parts of state government, and among constituency groups. At the same time, programs were developed to enhance the skills and competencies of DNR employees and to increase their commitment to the organization. Both internally and externally, DNR attempted to expand and build on its strengths so that it could realize opportunities for organizational and program development.

DNR's strategy was derived from a number of factors related to organizational capacity and environment. Because of the diversity of their demands and DNR's independent funding sources, external actors had relatively little control over DNR's strategic direction. On the other hand, the department was able to develop the necessary resources (financial, reputational, professional) to largely determine and control its strategic agenda. This agenda was broad in scope, encompassing virtually all aspects of capacity building. At the same time, objectives of DNR strategy were based on long-term incremental development rather than on fundamental change in program lines and service delivery. The department's strategic management team was capable, energetic, and highly cohesive.

The Transformational Strategy—Department of Mental Retardation and Developmental Disabilities

Transformational strategies are principally conditioned by a commitment to fundamental change, either internal or external. Typically, external actors and forces wield considerable influence over the organization. Strategic direction emerges from responses to this influence process and may be more congruent with external demands and pressures than with organizational aspirations. Because of the high level of external control, organizations with a transformational strategy usually have a policy or political orientation. Ratings of an agency on the other dimensions are not especially significant in the characterization of this strategy.

The transformational strategy was found in the Department of Mental Retardation and Developmental Disabilities (DMRDD). Developments in the decade preceding the creation of DMRDD had a major impact on its strategic direction. Among the most significant of these were fundamental changes in professional opinion regarding appropriate and effective care and treatment for the mentally retarded, the development of new behavioral science technologies for training and retarded individuals for normalized living environments, and a national legal rights movement which established basic principles of more humane treatment for the retarded.

These developments provided the impetus for a major change in the concept of service delivery to Ohio's MR/DD population. This new approach emphasized movement from a residential, service-delivery system to community-based care and treatment. Pressures from organized constituent groups, MR professionals, and legal rights advocates were a major source of pressure for rapid deinstitutionalization. By 1980, there was general commitment within Ohio to reduce state-operated programs, close residential centers, and develop and emphasize DMRDD's new regulatory role. The evolution of strategy in the Rhodes administration can be traced through DMRDD documents portraying the changing state role in direct service delivery. Over time, DMRDD came to describe itself not as a primary service provider, but rather as a monitor and regulator of the service-delivery system. Program statistics show decreasing numbers of residential clients and increasing enrollment in community programs. Similarly, DMRDD budgets reflected increasing expenditures for community programs and facilities.

Strategic management in DMRDD was largely conditioned by external factors, including legal mandates, advocacy group pressures, professional norms and standards, and state budgetary conditions. New service delivery technologies made it possible for many retarded individuals to adapt to normalized living environments.

The Protective Strategy—Department of Public Welfare

A hostile and potentially threatening environment, combined with limited organizational capacity, produces the protective strategy. This strategy seeks to accommodate strong external influence, while maintaining the organizational status quo. Although the protective strategy is motivated by an organizational or policy orientation, it is often played out in political terms. Strategic decisions and actions are formed in reaction to, and controlled by, external actors, causing internal observers to question the capacity and commitment of senior management. Relatedly, the organization may be seen as lacking vision, purpose, and energy. The image conveyed by this strategy is consistent with certain academic and popular notions of public organization behavior and performance.

The protective strategy typified the Department of Public Welfare (DPW). During the Rhodes administration, the major factors influencing DPW strategy were external in nature. Hostile relationships with legislators and other key stakeholders, nearly continuous media attention, tremendous increases in human service needs, decreased resource availability, and changing federal policy and program mandates were among the most important variables affecting departmental strategy. These conditions led to an environment that was perceived as threatening to the department, its programs, and clients. In response to this situation, senior management attempted to "bring peace to the place and get it out of the newspapers."[12]

Faced with political and fiscal threats from varied sources, the strategic agenda of the department was dominated by efforts to protect its core programs and to prevent substantial benefit reductions. The strategy devised to achieve these objectives required that DPW reestablish good relationships with the Ohio General Assembly and other constituents, lower its public profile, and impose tight controls over internal operations. Execution of this strategy was enhanced by an internal environment in which political considerations and relationships took precedence in policy and operational decision making.

The Political Strategy—The Public Utilities Commission

Political strategies may take more than one form. One type emerges from changing environmental conditions and is designed simply to accommodate a new balance of power among external influencers and to limit pressures for organizational change. Organizational strategists have more internal control in crafting this strategy than do strategists operating in the protective mode. Another form of the political strategy conceives of the organization as an instrument of partisan politics and as a means of rewarding political supporters. Often, execution of this strategy entails substantial changes in organizational arrangements, including staffing and structure, and in policy and program emphases.

The political strategy characterized the Public Utilities Commission of Ohio (PUCO). Historically, regulation by PUCO was a routine activity involving primarily technical questions related to the rate base and the calculation of a company's rate of return. Because of technological improvements, economies of scale, and the availability of low-cost and plentiful energy supplies, the regulated utility companies were able to maintain or even reduce the unit costs of their services. In this generally benign environment, it was possible for the PUCO to produce regulatory outcomes that were satisfactory to both producers and consumers.

Since 1973, a succession of events, including the Arab oil embargo, problems in the nuclear power industry, high rates of inflation, and changing federal energy and telecommunications policy, combined to produce a fundamentally different climate of regulation in Ohio. Changes in the Ohio statutes governing PUCO activities, creation of the Office of Consumers' Counsel, and increasing politicization of utility-related issues contributed to this general destabilization. As a consequence, PUCO came under intense pressure to modify its traditional regulatory approach, which was widely perceived as favoring utility interests. Following from its mandate to ensure service at the lowest possible rates while allowing the utility companies a fair rate of return, the commission employed a regulatory strategy aimed at balancing the competing interests of producers and consumers. As negative reactions to this approach increased, PUCO decisions retained a rhetorical commitment to the concept of balancing competing interests but produced results more favorable to consumers.

Strategic management in the PUCO has been a product of many factors, including the legal charter under which the commission operates, changing preferences and shifts in the balance of power among stakeholders, increasing politicization of regulatory issues, economic conditions which made neutral balancing less feasible, and the absence of strong leadership from the appointed members of the commission. Despite legal requirements and circumstances which seemingly constrained its strategic approach, the PUCO showed a remarkable capacity to reinterpret its environment and to develop a strategy more consistent with existing political conditions. While proclaiming faithfulness to its mandate, the commission demonstrated that balance, like beauty, is in the eye of the beholder.

FACTORS INFLUENCING THE STRATEGIES

As suggested in each of the preceding examples, a set of factors or variables was associated with each of the agency strategies. Among the external variables affecting the patterns of strategy were (1) resource constraints; (2) stakeholder preferences; (3) jurisdiction-level political agendas; (4) level of public support for the agency and its programs; (5) government budgetary conditions; (6) balance of constituent power; and (7) legal mandates. Internal factors included (1) organizational leadership; (2) organizational capacity; (3) internal policy consensus; (4) amount of discretion allowed by political controllers; (5) availability of alternative funding sources; (6) policy type; and (7) changes in service-delivery technology. Table 8-2 arrays the variables

Table 8-2
Strategic Factors in the Ohio Agencies

	DNR	DMRDD	DPW	PUCO
External				
Resource Constraints	−		+	
Stakeholder Preferences		+		
Political Agenda			+	+
Public Support	+		−	
Fiscal Conditions		+	+	
Balance of Power	+			+
Legal Mandates		+	+	
Internal				
Leadership	+		−	−
Competence and Capacity	+		−	−
Consensus	+	+		
Discretion	+			
Alternative Funding	+			
Policy Type			+	+
Service-Delivery Technology		+		

+ = presence of factor influenced pattern of strategy.
− = absence of factor influenced pattern of strategy.

across agencies and indicates the influence of factors on specific agencies. Interestingly, no single factor affected the strategy of all of the agencies. However, organizational leadership and capacity were significant in three out of four agencies, while resource constraints, fiscal conditions, political agenda, legal mandates, balance of power, internal consensus, and policy type each influenced the strategy of two agencies.

It should be apparent that certain factors are closely connected to specific strategic patterns. In the case of the developmental strategy, both internal and external factors serve as resources from which the agency constructs its strategy. Transformational strategies are driven by external factors, especially those promoting substantial change in the organizational status quo and which dominate in the absence of countervailing internal capacities that might allow the organization to maintain its direction. This pattern is even more pronounced in the protective and political strategies. For the protective strategy, however, it is the threatening character of external factors which shapes the agency's strategic response. While this may also be true for one variant of the political strategy, in others external actors are valued and rewarded.

IMPLICATIONS FOR PUBLIC ADMINISTRATION

This research contributes to public administration theory in three ways. First, the empirical studies of the Ohio agencies produce a significant body of knowledge regarding the strategic management of public organizations. Prior to this study, little evidence had been compiled about the character of strategic choice and action taking in a diverse set of public organizations. Relatedly, this research has identified specific patterns of strategy in public organizations, described a set of strategies, and suggested how these strategies were conditioned by internal and external factors. Finally, identification of a set of specific dimensions allows both researchers and practicing managers to analyze strategy in any public organization.

In-depth interviews with more than 50 informants provided ample evidence of the practical importance of the strategic management function in public organizations. While the research suggests that external factors play a major role in determining the strategy of public organizations, close examination of the agency studies and the strategic factors in each case demonstrates the significance of managerial choice and action taking in directing the course of public organizations. Strategies crafted by the public managers in the Ohio agencies represent solutions to fundamental organizational problems. The strategic management approach developed in this paper begins to suggest the full complement of conditions and considerations affecting strategic management and provides a framework for analyzing and building strategies in public organizations. In both analytical and action-taking modes, public managers can usefully employ this framework to assess their strategic situation and develop appropriate strategic programs.

From the perspective of action research methodology, this study confirms experiences of other researchers. Managers in the Ohio agencies not only understood the nature of the inquiry, but generally saw the research process as an opportunity for learning. Intensive interviewing led to the establishment of general rapport between researchers and informants. This produced a spirit of openness that allowed both researchers and research subjects to gain a deeper appreciation of the strategic management task in the Ohio agencies. Importantly, the Ohio research experience confirmed that multiple methods of qualitative data collection applied to multiple classes of informants are necessary to achieve a firm basis for discovery and confirmation.

Qualitative methods were employed in this research because they were clearly most appropriate given the objectives of the study and the state of knowledge about strategic management in public organizations. This "strategy" for strategic management research had several virtues. Constant interplay between observation and conceptualization allowed for more complete involvement in and understanding of the agencies and their environments. Also, through several waves of field study, it was possible to provide significant opportunities for surfacing disconfirming evidence and to achieve some measure of theoretical grounding.

Despite the precautions taken in the design of the studies, readers should retain some skepticism about the reliability and validity of the findings. Although the research subjects seemed generally truthful in their responses, the issue of informant reliability can never be fully resolved. Similarly, the retrospective nature of this inquiry has the potential for errors in various causal attributions. While the utilization of multiple sources and kinds of data and the use of explicit strategies for producing disconfirmation of initial conclusions minimize these problems, they will always be present to some degree.

Recognizing the importance of these issues points up the need for additional research. The rich data generated by these studies can best be seen as a foundation for ongoing scholarly research and debate. Additional research is especially necessary to determine the full range of strategies available to public organizations. Second-generation studies of strategic management in public organizations would also begin to extend the methodology and test the generalizability of the Ohio findings.

Notes

1. Among the many citations which might be provided are Russell L. Ackoff, *A Concept of Corporate Planning* (New York: John Wiley and Sons, 1970); H. Igor Ansoff, *Corporate Strategy* (New York: McGraw-Hill, 1965) and *Implanting Strategic Management* (Englewood Cliffs: Prentice-Hall International, 1984); Alfred D. Chandler, Jr., *Strategy and Structure* (Cambridge: M.I.T. Press, 1962); Charles W. Hofer and Dan E. Schendel, *Strategy Formulation: Analytical Concepts* (St. Paul: West Publishing Company, 1978); Raymond E. Miles and Charles C. Snow, *Organizational Strategy: Structure and Process* (New York: McGraw-Hill, 1980); Danny Miller and Peter Friesen, "Archetypes of Strategy Formulation," *Management Science*, vol. 24 (May 1978), pp. 921–933; Henry Mintzberg, "Patterns of Strategy Formulation," *Management Science*, vol. 24 (May 1978), pp. 934–948; Dan Schendel and Charles W. Hofer (eds.), *Strategic Management* (Boston: Little, Brown and Company, 1979); and Arthur A. Thompson, Jr. and A. J. Strickland, *Strategy Formulation and Implementation* (Plano, TX; Business Publications, Inc., 1980).
2. B. S. Chakravarthy, "Adaptation: A Promising Metaphor for Strategic Management," *Academy of Management Review*, vol. 7 (March 1982), pp. 35–44; Donald N. Michael, *On Learning to Plan and Planning to Learn* (San Francisco: Jossey-Bass, 1973); V. K. Narayanan and Liam Fahey, "The Micro-Politics of Strategy Formulation," *Academy of Management Review*, vol. 7 (March 1982), pp. 25–34; and James D. Thompson, *Organizations in Action* (New York: McGraw-Hill, 1967).
3. Schendel and Hofer, *ibid.*
4. Graham T. Allison, Jr., "Public and Private Management: Are They Fundamentally Alike in all Unimportant Respects?" prepared for the Public Management Research Conference, Brookings Institution, Washington, D. C., November 1979; M. Fottler, "Is Management Really Generic?" *Academy of Management Review*, vol. 6 (March 1981), pp. 1–12; Michael A. Murray, "Comparing Public and Private Management: An Exploratory Essay," *Public Administration Review*, vol. 35 (July/August 1975), pp. 364–371; and Hal G. Rainey, Robert W. Backoff, and Charles H. Levine, "Comparing Public and Private Organizations," *Public Administration Review*, vol. 36 (March/April 1976), pp. 233–244.
5. Louis Bragaw, *Managing a Federal Agency: The Hidden Stimulus* (Baltimore: Johns Hopkins University Press, 1980); John Bryson and Kimberly Boal, "Strategic Management in a Metropolitan Area," *Academy of Management Proceedings* (August 1983), pp. 332–336; Douglas C. Eadie and Roberta Steinbacher, "Strategic Agenda Management: A Marriage of Organizational Development and Strategic Planning," *Public Administration Review*, vol. 45 (May/June 1985), pp. 424–430; Charles H. Levine, "Police Management in the 1980s: From Decrementalism to Strategic Thinking," *Public Administration Review*, vol. 45 (November 1985); and Peter S. Ring and James L. Perry, "Strategic Management in Public and Private Organizations: Implications of Distinctive Contexts and Constraints," *Academy of Management Review*, vol. 10 (March 1985), pp. 276–286.
6. James D. Thompson, *ibid.*

7. Michael Porter, *Competitive Strategy: Techniques for Analyzing Industries and Competitors* (New York: The Free Press, 1980).
8. That these factors might constrain the strategies of general purpose government agencies is consistent with much of the literature related to public bureaucracy and management. See, for example, Laurence E. Lynn, Jr., *Managing the Public's Business* (New York: Basic Books, Inc., 1981); Francis E. Rourke, *Bureaucracy, Politics, and Public Policy*, 3d ed. (Boston: Little, Brown and Company, 1984); and Donald P. Warwick, *A Theory of Public Bureaucracy* (Cambridge: Harvard University, 1978).
9. Hal G. Rainey, Robert W. Backoff, and Charles H. Levine, *ibid.*; Peter S. Ring and James L. Perry, *ibid.*; Randall Ripley and Grace A. Franklin, *Bureaucracy and Policy Implementation* (Homewood, IL: The Dorsey Press, 1982); and Martha W. Weinberg, *Managing the State* (Cambridge: Harvard University Press, 1977).
10. Complete version of the accounts can be found in Barton Wechsler, *Strategic Management of Public Organizations; Studies of Public Policy Making and Administration in Ohio* (Columbus: unpublished doctoral dissertation, The Ohio State University, 1985).
11. A more complete description of the methodology employed in these studies is provided in Barton Wechsler, "Logic of Inquiry for Strategic Management Research: Standards of Good Practice From the Qualitative Tradition," *New Directions in Public Administration Research*, forthcoming. Analytical procedures were similar to those employed by Mintzberg and his colleagues. See Henry Mintzberg, Duru Raisinghani, and Andre Theoret, "The Structure of 'Unstructured' Decision Processes," *Administrative Science Quarterly*, vol. 21 (June 1976), pp. 246–275.
12. This quotation comes from a personal interview with Kenneth Creasy, former director of the Department of Public Welfare, July 1984.

Reinventing Government the Minnesota Way

SANDRA J. HALE

When I became Minnesota's commissioner of administration, in 1983, my agency had a history of forty-some years of bureaucracy—and our critics said "entrenched bureaucracy." State employees knew the Department of Administration as DOA, and there were lots of jokes about DOA meaning "dead on arrival." But we have been working hard to turn that perception around and to counteract at least twelve years of government bashing, from the federal level on down. Carter did it. Reagan did it in spades. Nixon had done it before, and of course it has had enormous fallout on all of us.

One of my major long-term goals has been to "expose" good government. The purpose of exposing good government is to build on the strengths of our employees. We have introduced marketplace dynamics into Minnesota state government. Wherever possible, we have changed our methods of doing business. We invite competition for our services instead of spending valuable time and staff on enforcement. The legislature does not always like that. We invite state agencies to find a better or cheaper or faster source for a wide range of services, from management consulting to office supplies, because we know they will have quite a search to find the quality and pricing we offer.

Can government business keep pricing down better than private business? We have. If one of our department's operations fails to be self-supporting (and we would prefer it to be profit making), we do not go back to the legislature for a larger appropriation. We take a long, hard look at our operation and find ways to improve. If it is not going to be self-supporting, we often eliminate the service altogether. This approach may sound like suicide to some people. But last year our books showed $80 million in annual sales, which is a lot for a state the size of Minnesota. All of this started in 1983, when Governor Rudy Perpich had just returned to the governorship after a four-year hiatus in private industry. His primary task was to pull state government out of the problems created by the global recession. Perpich wanted to infuse state government with productivity, quality, and cost-effectiveness.

We started with STEP, the Strive Toward Excellence in Performance program, where state employees themselves are instrumental in introducing and managing changes in the way things have been done. We steered away from the traditional productivity improvement methods. In fact, we changed our original words. Our acronym, STEP, remained the same, but the original name was going to be Strides Toward Efficiency and Productivity. *Productivity* became such a negative word for the unions in the early 1980s, and *excellence* became such a major new concept that, right about the time we devised the acronym, but before we announced the program, we changed its name to Strive Toward Excellence in Performance. Also, STEP was an insider joke, because a previous productivity program in Minnesota was called LEAP. State employees did not like LEAP, because it merely allowed the private sector to point out all of the problems.

We steered away from the traditional productivity improvement methods. We certainly used some of them, but to begin with we did not call in loaned executives from the private sector to tell state employees where they had gone wrong. This is always an unpopular approach, and it is almost always unsuccessful. STEP is a long-term, experimental program to improve the productivity and quality of Minnesota state government services. Its goal is to increase quality, quantity, and cost-effectiveness. It did not immediately show cost savings. Nobody, we believe, is willing to come up with major, long-term, important changes if they are immediately going to cut budget or staff. Long-term cuts, yes; short-term cuts, no.

We test each project in the manner of a scientific model: test, experiment, evaluate, adjust, test again. Most of the six methods in the STEP program will be very familiar to most of you. Our first is called *closeness to the customer*. It creates an awareness that public sector employees have customers, from their own colleagues to the members of the public who use their services. It gives employees a different perspective on their jobs, permitting them to examine how services are provided to the customers. The usual result is that services are redesigned to meet customers' needs.

Our second STEP method is called *employee participation*, another buzzword of the 1980s. This approach, of course, is attributed to the Japanese management style of relying on employees' expertise to identify and solve problems. It overcomes some of the shortcomings of decision making and traditionally hierarchical work cultures, where the distance between the decision makers and the customers can interfere with good public service.

The third STEP method is *managerial discretion*, which means empowering front-line employees to solve customer problems as they surface. Managerial discretion is based on the idea that everybody is a manager of, at least, his or her own job. Although we do not always follow these steps precisely, these are at least our guiding principles and our guiding goals.

Partnerships are the fourth STEP method. Partnerships are not new. The STEP approach involves the voluntary use of partners. The partners come from many sectors: public, private, not-for-profit, labor, and academe. The steering committee is composed of the governor and a succession of CEOs from the state's major companies, mostly Fortune 500 companies. We also have on our steering committee the heads of three top state labor unions and an assortment of other CEOs, public sector leaders, and academic leaders, most of whom have had government service. The difference is enormous if people understand government. STEP partnerships also work for the benefit of everyone involved; knowledge and expertise are shared both ways. We are finding that our private sector partners are learning. One of my purposes is this hidden agenda of exposing good government. Members of the committee are always surprised and impressed with the quality, hard work, and creativity of government employees.

The fifth STEP method is *productivity improvement*. These are state-of-the-art techniques to speed up the discovery and use of newer processes, materials, and equipment.

The last STEP method is *work measurement*. Again, although not a new concept, work measurement has not been used uniformly in government services. It is difficult, as we all know. Services are difficult to define, let alone quantify. But improved work measurement provides a base for improved service and gives employees information about their performance.

Four of these methods—employee participation, partnerships, productivity improvement, and work measurement—are the topic areas for this productivity conference. This is no coincidence. The 1980s were a time of massive change in organizational leadership, and these management techniques were in the forefront not only in the private sector but also in many places in local, state, and federal government. They have been successful in the private sector, and they are successful also in the public sector. The reason that they have succeeded and are increasingly part of today's management practice is because they have resulted in substantial results, a bottom line of productivity improvement.

The number of formal STEP projects in Minnesota government is about sixty. But we also have innumerable "STEP children." These are not formal STEP projects; they did not necessarily fit the six criteria, and they did not necessarily need the STEP umbrella. One of our big challenges always is not to put the STEP stamp on everything, because then we are competing with our goal of empowering employees. But if you do not say that such projects came out of the STEP program, people will say, "Prove to me what STEP did."

Some of the results have been substantial. Our Department of Natural Resources (DNR), for example, developed a marketing program that boosted state park attendance in the first year alone by 10 percent, and attendance is constantly increasing. Most important, the program helped park employees discover that their primary customers were not trees and deer, but people—a 180-degree shift.

In 1985 DNR was facing declining use of the state park system and an ever-tightening budget. At that year's conference for park managers, a presentation on marketing services started people talking about "marketing" the state parks. At the same time, we were soliciting proposals for the first round of STEP programs. DNR's dilemma was a natural for the STEP program. They brought their problems, they started working on their problems, and our STEP staff helped them. Marketing state parks became one of the first projects, and this year it will be the winner of the annual Governor's Award for Excellence, given by the Minnesota Business Partnership (the state's eighty top CEOs).

The project team quickly discovered that their first challenge would be a top-to-bottom, or bottom-to-top, attitude adjustment on the part of management and employees. The prevailing belief of managers in Natural Resources was that their sole job was to manage the sixty-four parks in our state system. If the public was interested in recreation there, fine, as long as they did not damage the natural resources or appear in great numbers. Thus park use was unintentionally, or intentionally, discouraged. Such an attitude was fine for the wildlife management part of the division, but the Parks and Recreation Division would get nowhere, of course, with that philosophy.

The first step was to sell the marketing idea to the people working in the department. Park managers were brought together at a workshop, where customer service was introduced. For the first time, the managers as a group began to think of the visitors' needs, and they themselves generated customer-oriented ideas.

Next, the first quality service workshop was held for all park employees. More ideas were generated, including—it sounds simple, but it was not—arranging for the use of credit cards to buy park memberships and a great expansion and use of credit cards at the park gift shops. Both those ideas, the credit cards and the gift shop expansion, were developed with the use of partnerships—one with another state agency, the other with a private business. In both cases, the contributions from the partners were equally valuable. The private sector certainly contributed, but it contributed no more than the other state agency did. New ideas and new attitudes were put into effect quickly, and they showed good results quickly.

Another notable STEP example also points up the value of partnerships. In 1985, the timing was also right to address a major problem in Minnesota's Human Rights Department. This time the idea had been around for a while, but it was constantly pushed to a low priority because of an enormous backlog of cases and a great deal of public criticism of the management of that agency. Once it was given the status of a STEP project, though, the project moved ahead and was able to be implemented.

The project was a discrimination testing program for investigations. Discrimination testing, where trained people pose as home seekers or job applicants to verify complaints of discrimination, has been used successfully for years by civil rights agencies throughout the country. It is considered by many people to be the most effective tool a human rights agency can use to prove discrimination. Although it had been used occasionally in Minnesota, a human rights investigator wanted to make it a regular part of the department's procedures.

What this investigator needed was the time to create a workable program, but media attention to the department's large backlog of discrimination investigations had embarrassed the management and demoralized the staff. Eliminating the backlog became the one and only focus of the department. It was the STEP program, with the personal involvement of Governor Perpich at a key time, that gave the human rights employees the edge they needed to proceed with their idea. In the long run, it was also an asset in controlling future case backlogs.

Partnerships were, again, key to the project. The division needed volunteer testers from various protected minority and other classes; private sector employers, who would provide real-life employment verification; the state's Department of Public Safety, to provide investigative resources to aid in the testing; and the state Department of Finance to set up a revolving account to provide rental deposits.

Within three months the training was done, and the human rights staff members were thinking of using discriminatory testing when handling new cases. It has now spread from two divisions to the entire department. The time needed to resolve cases has been reduced, and the cases that are tested are moving through the system far more rapidly.

The Minnesota Housing Finance Agency is the third of the projects I will describe briefly. A STEP project built around a survey to determine the value of housing programs for the elderly has resulted in a significant broadening of the agency's mission. Today the agency, which is a very well run agency in Minnesota, is working with owners and managers of housing for the elderly to put together a personalized service package for their tenants. A long-term goal is to keep tenants in their apartments rather than move them to more expensive, more impersonal nursing homes. Housekeeping, personal care, nutrition—these are coordinated according to the needs of each tenant. The agency is testing this program now in the Twin City counties. Again, this project represents partnerships between levels of government.

At the same time, the Housing Finance Agency is training owners and managers of housing for the elderly all over this state to identify the various problems of aging in order to better help families and tenants locate the services they need wherever they live.

All of these projects faced obstacles. I am not going to say that every STEP project has been as successful and outstanding as these. Nor was STEP an instant success. It ran into barriers in every direction. First, it is a customer-driven program. Most state employees, however, had never thought of their captive audiences as customers. It is also run from the bottom up. The frontline employees initiate and manage the projects and are given discretionary powers unheard of in most bureaucracies. Only strong managers will step aside and give employees this authority. Finally, STEP has no specific state appropriation. Its resources must come from existing budgets and personnel.

STEP has always been viewed as an experiment, so we have been permitted to make mistakes without considering ourselves failures. But this attitude is especially difficult in the public sector, because the press is interested only in the problems. Good news is no news in the public sector. We learned many lessons along the way, and we made many changes in the program. We have done it with the help of more than two hundred partners in the private sector, many of them from Minnesota's top, Fortune 500 companies.

STEP was a first-year winner of the Ford Foundation Innovations Award and was the first case study on innovations in their program. Part of the award money, at the request of the foundation, was used to produce a how-to book documenting the program. The Urban Institute Press in Washington D.C. then published it as *Managing Change: A Guide to Producing Innovation from Within*. Minnesota and its STEP program are also featured, along with seven others of the thirty award-winning innovations (from approximately three thousand to four thousand) in a new paperback book and video just released by the Ford Foundation, *Innovating America*.

Something is inherently irritating about a Department of Administration. Nobody gets excited about an agency that tells you what you cannot do, and that is what most administration philosophies have been in the past. That approach had been demanded and requested as part of the reform in the 1930s. But there is a natural connection, we thought, between STEP, the customer-driven operation, and what we now call enterprise management, our public version of privatization. We were about to break tradition, at least in Minnesota.

Not every program can be modeled into a discretionary service and placed into these competitive markets, but many of them can. Management consulting, office supplies, computer operations, micrographics, printing, and office leasing lent themselves to a market-oriented approach. In fact, about two-thirds of our programs are run as successful small enterprises.

We had to get legislative authority for these programs to operate on a self-supporting basis, something you would think would come easily. We had to persuade our managers and employees that the enterprise approach could be successful. We had to provide employee training, to introduce new attitudes, and to encourage independent thinking and decision making.

The result has been that prices in these activities have increased an average of only 0.8 percent annually over the last five years, while inflation has been at the level of 4.7 percent. And delivery turnaround times have been cut by more than half in those areas that are delivering supplies.

How did we achieve these results? Number one, we began by restructuring the department to separate the regulatory functions from the service functions. For instance, we separated our various information functions. We now have something called the Intertechnology Group, a large group of three hundred or so employees, which provides data processing, voice mail, electronic mail, and so on and sells these services to other state agencies. We also have a new, small Information Policy Office that performs the regulatory functions, sets standards, and reviews budgets for the legislature. The end result is that we do a better job of both support and control. Although they are both in the Department of Administration, the two groups are under two separate assistant commissioners. Often the head of the Information Policy Office says no to our own internal budget requests.

Number two, we then introduced marketplace dynamics to the service functions. There is a case study on this, too, called "Introducing Marketplace Dynamics into Minnesota State Government"—our early stages of enterprise management. We encouraged our customers to consider us as an option to private business and to expect us to be competitive. And our customers took us seriously. It was not long before we knew that such services as systems design and programming did not and could not have competitive rates, and we closed those businesses.

On the other hand, our micrographics services, office supplies, vehicle leasing, data processing, and printing are very competitive with private sector vendors. In fact, some of these are growth businesses. When I first came to the department, people would do anything to avoid using the state printer; they would do elaborate specifications. They would do anything to avoid renting a state car from the central motor pool (which is not the largest of the motor pools but is one of the central ones for small automobiles). Now they have proven to be very competitive. We have had to add another shift in printing. People are choosing to use state services, because they are customer-oriented. They are usually successful. Not every employee has the service orientation we would like, but most of them do.

Number three, we now use incentives and education to encourage compliance for our regulatory functions. We are trying to lead by example; punishment is not the best way to regulate.

Finally, we have powerful new tools for accountability, based on appropriate structural relationships and outputs. We have found this method to be much more successful than the old methods of controlling inputs. As I said, "Do not count my use of pencils if my quality is better and my prices are lower and my delivery time is better, or whatever." Whether I use eight pencils or one does not matter, if my results are better and my costs are lower. For services, our customers are usually the other agencies, sometimes the public. For regulation, our customers are the legislature and the governor.

Before competition entered the picture, our customers, as a rule, did not like us. As captive customers, they had little say in how we conducted our business. Today they have a lot to say about our methods. In cases where we do not have a strictly marketplace function, we operate more like a utility, with our customers serving as rate setters and with contract service agreements. Because we listened and began to give them what they wanted, we strengthened our operations. We had to streamline in order to become self-supporting. We had to become accountable in order to become profitable.

Finally, one of our latest and most exciting innovations is called ALLTECH, which stands for Alliances for Technology Development with Business, Government, and Education. ALLTECH may become, we are told, a model for public-private partnership. (ALLTECH is the basis for a new case study at Harvard, called "Minnesota's Knowledge Systems Center.") ALLTECH may become a model for these public-private partnerships, combining government and private technology resources to create artificial intelligence systems, in the case of expert systems, and state-of-the-art technology, such as microchip-embedded plastic cards, called Smart Cards, for public service improvement.

Smart Cards, demonstrated at this year's Minnesota State Fair, are automatic teller machine-type cards. Citizens could use them for a variety of services, such as vehicle and boat registration, hunting and fishing licenses, and human service programs. We had an expert system at the state fair asking people what, if any, services they would like on this card, what they would be willing to have on a card.

The expert systems aspect of artificial intelligence is being applied in the state; four private companies are working with us to research this project. Only one person in Minnesota state government knows how to identify routes for overweight trucks being driven through Minnesota. The demand for this information, as you can imagine, frequently results in long waits for the truckers. So this state employee's knowledge is being translated into sophisticated expert-system computer software. Anywhere in the state, now, Department of Transportation or public safety employees will be able to simply enter destination information into a computer and immediately determine the authorized route for the truckers. Another project we are undertaking is an expert system to help parents identify the best school for their child.

These are some of the expert systems being created by different agencies, in partnership with IBM and a Minnesota firm called PIG Solutions, a high-tech firm that was a spinoff of Unisys's artificial intelligence program. This is called a solution factory. We are about to sign a contract with IBM, which is contributing more than $900,000 in goods and services; we, in turn, are providing expertise and knowledge from my department's new Knowledge Systems Center. Forty other expert systems are being developed, and we know that there are thousands of other potential applications. The state will receive a percentage of the royalties as IBM and PIG Solutions and others sell these systems elsewhere.

We know these cooperative ventures are part of the new wave for the nineties, and we believe they are going to blossom in this decade, as limited resources become the catalyst for cooperation to replace competition. New technology that will be developed in this framework is going to make traditional ideas about the separation of public and private sectors obsolete.

These changes, as we learned with the STEP program, come with listening to the customer, and this is done first by the employees themselves. We have tried to empower them to serve customer problems on the spot, to suggest ways to improve their own services. As Charlie Brown once said, "The world is full of people eager to serve in *advisory* capacities." We have reached across the outside experts. We have listened to people who make the real difference: our customers and our employees.

We have replaced the once valuable bureaucratic-reform model of the 1930s with the enterprise model. Instead of controlling our employees, we try to empower them. Instead of managing input, we manage output. Consistency has been replaced with opportunity, uniformity with flexibility. Purpose has replaced rules. Competition has replaced administrative procedures. It is our customers' needs that come first, not our department's.

Innovative government is not a contradiction in terms. We began the shift toward enterprise with STEP and are continuing the shift away from bureaucracy with enterprise management. Both approaches provide us fresh insights into government service.

Quality Comes to City Hall

JOSEPH SENSENBRENNER

Government may be the biggest and the oldest industry in the world, but the statement "I'm from the government, and I'm here to help you" is universally considered a bad joke. Increasingly, people don't believe that government knows how to help or wants to bother. They find concepts like "total quality," "customer-driven," and "continuous improvement" foreign to everything they know about what government does and how it works. They wish government would be more like a well-run business, but most have stopped hoping it ever will be.

Today, fortunately, a new channel has opened through which business and progressive business practices can have an impact on the cost, efficiency, and overall quality of government. This channel is the quality movement—the rapidly growing acceptance of the management practices that W. Edwards Deming developed and persuaded Japanese industry to implement after the end of World War II. As more and more U.S. industries work with and profit from Deming's techniques, we have to wonder whether it's not possible to develop a public sector that offers taxpayers and citizens the same quality of services they have come to expect from progressive businesses like Motorola and Westinghouse.

My answer to that question is yes, it is possible. Moreover, while I was mayor of Madison, Wisconsin from 1983 to 1989, I took several steps to make it happen.

I acted in response to a changing climate. Just as major corporations like Ford and Harley-Davidson have had to improve or perish, so too the marketplace now confronts governments with shrinking revenues, taxpayer revolts, and a new insistence on greater productivity and better services.

"People are making comparisons," says one quality expert. "They can call American Express on Monday and get a credit card in the mail by the end of the week, but it takes six weeks to get a lousy driver's license renewed. You might not think the motor vehicles division competes with American Express, but it does in the mind of the customer."

WELCOME TO MADISON

These problems came alive for me when I was elected to the first of three two-year terms as mayor of Madison in 1983. As state capital and home of the University of Wisconsin, Madison smolders politically even in quiet times. Although life had returned to relative normalcy after the upheavals of the Vietnam War, government was still on the defensive. The Reagan revolution was cutting sharply into revenues (the city lost 11% of total revenues between 1983 and 1989) even as our service area continued to grow and costs continued to rise.

Madison's property-tax base is constrained in two ways—naturally by the city's location on a narrow isthmus, artificially by the volume of land and buildings devoted to the university and to county and state government. By 1983, we were taxing taxable property nearly to its limit and beginning to turn to controversial measures like ambulance fees to make up the difference.

Budget hearings were becoming an annual nightmare. The people of Madison did not want their services cut or their taxes raised. In their view, city services were in a steady decline already, even as they paid more for them. From what I could see, in many cases they were right.

But I felt boxed in. My previous managerial experience—as the governor's chief of staff and as deputy state attorney general—was nearly useless in getting a handle on the mixed operations of municipal government. As deputy state attorney general, I had run an office where I was an expert on every aspect of the work, and I practiced a good deal of participatory decision making. As mayor, I could not run an executive office, deal with the city council, and also be an expert on lawn cutting, snow removal, and motor vehicle maintenance. And it was out there on the front lines that systems were breaking down.

For example, a 1983 audit disclosed big problems at the city garage: long delays in repair and major pieces of equipment unavailable for the many agencies that used Madison's 765-unit fleet of squad cars, dump trucks, refuse packers, and road scrapers.

The audit gave a depressingly vivid and complete picture of the symptoms of the problem (for example, vehicles spent an average of nine days in the garage every time they needed work), but it offered no clear explanation of why things were so bad. Like other managers in similar situations, I felt inclined to call in the shop boss, read him the riot act, and tell him to crack the whip and shape up his department.

Just about then, an assistant in my office suggested I attend a presentation by W. Edwards Deming, the then 82-year-old statistician and guru of the Japanese industrial miracle.

Deming's approach is no doubt familiar to many businesspeople, but it was unlike anything I had ever heard. It sounded like common sense, but it was revolutionary. American industry, he said, had been living in a fool's paradise. In an ever-expanding market, even the worst management seems good because its flaws are concealed. But under competitive conditions those flaws become fatal, and that is what we are witnessing as U.S. companies lose market share in one area after another.

If there was a devil in the piece, Deming said, it was our system of make-and-inspect, which if applied to making toast would be expressed: "You burn, I'll scrape." It is folly to correct defects "downstream"; the critical issue, he said, is to get your "upstream" processes under control so you can guarantee the outcome every time. To do this, an organization must create a culture of quality; it must master proven quality techniques. Most important, it must define quality—first, as continuous improvement in pleasing customers and second, as reducing the variation in whatever service or product it offers.

As Deming described the organizational changes required to produce his culture of quality, I found myself thinking that this was, perhaps, what I had been searching for. It also occurred to me that it would take a revolution to get it. Autonomous departments are the virtual essence of government bureaucracy, so how was I going to implement Deming's command to break down barriers? "Cover your ass" and "go along to get along" are ancient tenets of the civil service, so how was I going to follow Deming's admonition to drive out fear and license more workers to solve problems? Most daunting of all was his command to install continuous improvement not just as a goal but as a daily chore of government. My God, government *invented* the status quo! And what were the voters going to think of "quality" as a cost item in a city budget?

THE FIRST STREET GARAGE

These were some of my thoughts as I headed back to city hall. But I had another: there was nowhere else to go. I had already seen that management by objective and threats of audits were not going to produce change. I might as well try it, I thought. And the city garage, where the rubber hit the road, seemed a likely place to start.

The manager and mechanics at the First Street Garage were surprised to see the mayor and a top assistant show up to investigate their problems; most previous mayors had shown their faces only when they needed a tankful of gas. Over the next few years I learned again and again the crucial importance of the top executive getting personally and visibly involved on the battlefield of basic change.

For the most part, the crew at the garage were doubters. But when I met Terry Holmes, the president of Laborers International Union of North America, Local 236, I looked him squarely in the eye, pledged my personal involvement, and confirmed his membership's central role. He agreed to participate. We formed a team and gathered data from individual mechanics and from the repair process itself. We found that many delays resulted from the garage not having the right parts in stock. We took that complaint to the parts manager, who said the problem with stocking parts was that the city purchased many different makes and models of equipment virtually every year. We discovered that the fleet included 440 different types, makes, models, and years of equipment. Why the bewildering variety? Because, the parts manager told us, it was city policy to buy whatever vehicle had the lowest sticker price on the day of purchase.

"It doesn't make any sense," one mechanic said. "When you look at all the equipment downtime, the warranty work that weak suppliers don't cover, the unreliability of cheaper machines, and the lower resale value, buying what's cheapest doesn't save us anything."

Our next trip was to the parts purchaser. He agreed with the mechanic. "It would certainly make my job easier to have fewer parts to stock from a few reliable suppliers. But central purchasing won't let me do it." Onward to central purchasing, where we heard this: "Boy, I understand what you're saying because I hear it from all over the organization. But there's no way we can change the policy. The comptroller wouldn't let us do it."

Enter the comptroller. "You make a very strong case," he admitted. "But I can't let you do it because the city attorney won't let me approve such a thing." On to the city attorney. "Why, of course you can do that," he said. "All you need to do is write the specifications so they include the warranty, the ease of maintenance, the availability of parts, and the resale value over time. Make sure that's clear in advance, and there's no problem. In fact, I assumed you were doing it all along."

This was a stunning disclosure.

Here was a major failure of a city service whose symptoms, causes, and solution were widely known but that had become chronic because government was not organized to solve it. No doubt there are dozens of large corporations that have made similar discoveries about their own bureaucracies. (Indeed, Deming would not be famous in the business world if this were not the case.) But for me—and, I later learned, for local governments all over the country and the world—this kind of discovery was eye-opening.

This first exercise confirmed point after point of Deming's paradigm and suggested strongly that what worked for business would work for government. To begin with, the source of the downtime problem was upstream in the relationship of the city to its suppliers—not downstream where the worker couldn't find a missing part. The problem was a flawed system, not flawed workers.

Second, solving the problem required teamwork and breaking down barriers between departments. The departments were too self-contained to be helpful to one another, and helpfulness itself—treating the people you supplied or serviced as "customers"—was an unknown concept.

Third, finding the solution meant including frontline employees in problem solving. The fact of being consulted and enlisted rather than blamed and ignored resulted in huge improvements in morale and productivity. When we actually changed our purchasing policy, cutting a 24-step process with multiple levels of control to just 3 steps, employees were stunned and delighted that someone was listening to them instead of merely taking them to task.

They were so enthusiastic, in fact, that they began to research the possible savings of a preventive maintenance program. They discovered, for example, that city departments did not use truck-bed linings when hauling corrosive materials such as salt. Mechanics also rode along on police patrols and learned that squad cars spend much more time at idling speeds than in the high-speed emergencies mechanics had imagined and planned for in tuning engines.

Various city departments—streets, parks, police—helped the First Street mechanics gather data, and we ultimately adopted their proposals, including driver check sheets for vehicle condition, maintenance schedules for each piece of equipment, and an overtime budget to cut downtime and make sure preventive maintenance work was done.

The result of these changes was a reduction in the average vehicle turnaround time from nine days to three and a savings of $7.15 in downtime and repair for every $1 invested in preventive maintenance—an annual net savings to the city of Madison of about $700,000.

THE SECOND WAVE

Despite the satisfying outcome of this first foray into public-sector quality, I understood that we were far from having enough knowledge and experience to develop a program for the entire city work force.

I attended a second, four-day seminar with Deming, and I enlisted the support of university faculty and local and national quality consultants. I also helped found the Madison Area Quality Improvement Network and recruited academic, professional, and corporate members. Today it is the largest and most active community quality council in the world. In the years that followed, corporate and academic experts provided the city with in-kind services that were worth hundreds of thousands of dollars.

I went about setting up a formal quality and productivity (QP) program that would eventually function citywide. I hired a full-time quality and productivity administrator—the first such public-sector position in the country—even though that meant giving up one of the four policy positions on my staff. I also organized a QP steering committee of top managers to direct the effort. Originally, the committee itself was a throwback to an older, hierarchical tradition: all top managers. Within two years, it replaced eight of its own original eleven members with two union presidents—Firefighters and AFSCME—three middle managers, two of our most enthusiastic frontline workers, and the president of the city council.

The steering committee issued a mission statement that envisioned employee involvement, customer input, continuous improvement, creativity, innovation, and trust. On a more practical level, it said that the hallmarks of quality in Madison city government would be excellence "as defined by our customers," respect for employee worth, teamwork, and data-based decision making. We called this foursquare commitment the Madison Diamond.

Finding the lofty words was the easy part; now we had to live up to them. The first task was to recruit the initial cadre of what we hoped would become a quality army. We set out to identify pioneers in several city departments—managers and frontline employees with the imagination and motivation to lead the way. Their most important characteristic, I found, regardless of political philosophy or training, was a strong ego: the capacity to take responsibility for risks, share credit for success, and keep one eye on the prize. We found enough of these people to begin a new round of experiments like our successful First Street prototype.

This second wave included projects in the streets division, the health department, day care, and data processing. We expanded the lesson we'd learned about purchasing at the First Street Garage to create a citywide "Tool Kit" program that got workers directly involved in choosing the most cost-effective tools and materials for their jobs. City painters picked the most durable, long-lasting paints for city housing projects, for example, and police officers chose the equipment they would be using every day in their patrol car "offices." Selections had to be made on the basis of hard data, however, so running the comparisons became quality projects for the employees.

In the health department, the challenge was simply to give citizens quicker, better answers to their questions about clinics and programs. Employees began to sample and analyze the questions that were coming in, then on the basis of that data they set up briefings for phone receptionists so they could answer most questions directly. They also created a clear system of referrals for more complicated requests. Follow-up studies showed considerable improvement in the department's level of "customer" satisfaction.

By gathering and analyzing data, the day care unit shortened its waiting list for financial assistance by 200 names, while data processing customized and thus greatly improved its relations with internal customers.

As with our first experiments at the garage, the second wave of quality initiatives worked minor wonders in productivity and morale, and they met with little resistance—so long as the projects stayed small. But as the program grew to involve more departments and demand more time of managers, opposition began to emerge. I had expected problems from structural sources: the 14 different unions that represented 1,650 of Madison's 2,300 employees; the strong civil service system that included and protected all of the city's mid-level managers and most of its department heads; the 22-member, nonpartisan city council (meaning no partisan bloc for the mayor's program); and Madison's "weak-mayor" system of government that invested little authority in the chief executive.

But it turned out that the city council supported the program, and the unions grew increasingly helpful. The real opposition was not structural but bureaucratic. There were individual managers who could not tolerate the idea of bringing their employees into decisions or who resented taking time to reassess tried and true procedures. There were employees who scorned the program as faddish and who looked on enthusiastic colleagues as management finks. There were cynics who tried to exploit the program by packaging their pet projects as QP initiatives, and I had political opponents in a few departments who tried periodically to entice some reporter into probing the "QP boondoggle."

Most surprising and disappointing to me were the barriers I discovered between work units, including even units in the same department. One department head told his middle managers that he expected them to deal with quality problems while he, as he put it, "protected" the department from the rest of city government! He could hardly have devised a better way to nip cooperation in the bud and help problems multiply.

The most unsettling indication of how far we had to go came early in the program when all the individual team members in our second wave of projects independently resigned. They felt their managers, who should have been giving them guidance and support, were simply cutting them adrift and thus setting them up for failure and blame. For their part, the managers believed that all they had to do was make an initial statement of support and invite subordinates to "call if you have a problem." Employees, of course, took this to mean, "I expect you to take care of it."

I addressed this problem by discussing it directly with all the people involved. I then restructured our procedures to require specific work plans and regular, scheduled meetings between the frontline project teams and their managers. Contacts had to stop being intrusions into a manager's schedule. They had to become predictable exchanges of information and assistance to which team members were entitled.

INTERNAL AND EXTERNAL CUSTOMERS

The parts-purchasing and preventive-maintenance improvements I described at the First Street Garage are examples of projects in one department that helped other departments do their jobs more efficiently. Another example involved trash collection workers analyzing the pattern of injuries in their own work, weighing and measuring the refuse put out at the curb by residents, and studying the lifting requirements of the refuse-packer trucks. Their proposals for restrictions on the size of bundles and better design of new trucks reduced neck and lower back injuries, saved lost time, and made working conditions safer, at no extra cost to the city.

In another project, seven city departments that used maps in their work got together, identified duplications of effort, and created a computerized database and a uniform map bank available to all departments as well as to Madison's private gas and electric utilities.

Long lines of trash-filled trucks at the city's recycling plant gave rise to another project. Employees clocked truck arrival times, noted how they clustered, and proposed a staggered schedule of trash collections that would cut waiting time. This proposal not only made the system more efficient; it also saved the money we were thinking of spending on an expanded dumping floor. But until the data had been gathered, no manager was in a position even to consider such a solution.

In projects that serve internal customers, government workers benefit directly at the workplace while taxpayers benefit from cost efficiencies and more smoothly functioning institutions. But such initiatives rarely make headlines, which go instead to projects that serve external customers and visibly change public-service delivery. In Madison, the most celebrated example was the creation of the experimental police district.

During the late 1960s and early 1970s, violent antiwar demonstrations turned Madison into a kind of battleground. At one point, the governor called in the Wisconsin National Guard to secure the university campus. The harsh tactics used to put down these demonstrations left much of the community with a distrust of the police.

The officers themselves felt battle scarred and alienated from the city they were hired to protect. When a young police chief named David Couper arrived in 1972 with newfangled philosophies of conflict management and citizen service, he was assailed with a series of grievances and lawsuits from veterans on the force.

Couper, a former marine, responded to these tests with what he now calls a typical military approach: "You'll be nice to citizens, or you'll have hell to pay!" This got him nowhere, of course, and after several frustrating years he took a sabbatical, rethought his management approach, and familiarized himself with Deming's quality gospel. He then decided, as he puts it, "to run the department for the 95% who did their jobs well, rather than write the rules for the 5% who were difficult."

He identified progressive officers interested in transforming the department and rebuilding community confidence. Together they created an elected employee policy-making council, a committee to look at the department's future, and a police mission statement that made peacekeeping the department's primary role and put law enforcement second.

This was a risky move, considering the probable reaction if people thought the police were neglecting detection and apprehension, but the new strategy had broader implications. It meant the department could deploy resources to work on the underlying causes of crime, interact with schools and neighborhood organizations, develop relationships with minority and student leaders, and put a higher priority on outreach. Most important, perhaps, it created the "constancy of purpose" that Deming has always put first on his list of techniques for achieving total quality.

In 1986, Couper and 50 police volunteers decided to test the new mission statement. They believed that a decentralized police district with a neighborhood headquarters would lead to more effective peacekeeping by giving better service to residents and by encouraging officers to "adopt" the neighborhood and vice versa. Police precincts were an old idea, but this was different: officers in the district would elect their own captains and lieutenants, determine their own staffing and work schedules as a team, and network with neighborhood associations to set law-enforcement priorities. Having worked with Couper for 14 years, the union had learned to trust him, and it accepted the idea.

Several months of surveys and data analysis resulted in the Madison Experimental Police District on the city's South Side, with its station house located in the aldermanic district of a relatively junior member of the city council. Because the officers had done their homework, they were able to nip in the bud an effort by the council president to locate this political plum in her own ward. They could show that their proposed location provided the best service to priority areas and populations, including the elderly, as well as the fastest access to all parts of the district.

Soon, South Side residents were seeing their police on the streets, at neighborhood meetings, and at their doorsteps to interview them about their concerns. Home burglaries decreased 28% between 1986 and 1989, while the rest of the city saw a 15% increase. Other statistics were equally impressive. Dollar savings included the reduction of overtime to 200 hours for the whole experimental district in 1988, compared with 980 hours for an equivalent number of officers from the central office. This savings was achieved after officers in the district ran a study of the kinds of calls that kept police on duty beyond their regular shifts. They discovered that a high percentage of such calls were not urgent, so they arranged with dispatchers to put these calls on a "B" list if they came in less than 45 minutes before the end of a shift. When new officers came on, they would take those calls first and attend to them at regular pay.

Although this triage meant some delay in police response for some police customers, I never received a single complaint about it. Tax dollars were saved, and surveys showed that citizens were satisfied with police service and that 85% of officers in the special district had higher levels of job satisfaction than in their previous assignments.

REMAKING CITY GOVERNMENT

. . . Deming-style quality is not a quick fix or a magic bullet; it is a top-to-bottom revolution in the definition of "business as usual" that takes years to accomplish. There's no reason in the world to think it can be done more quickly or easily in government than in industry. But in Madison, we saw encouraging gains in just a few years.

Some wary union leaders and members turned out to be among my strongest backers. Terry Holmes, the tough master mechanic and long-time union president, became a staunch ally. "Before the quality program, all we did was put out fires," he once told me. "Morale was low. The message from management was, 'You don't know what you're talking about. Do as you're told.'" Once the program was well under way, however, the message became, "You and your teammates understand your work better than management can. Tell us how to help you do it better."

Some managers who were initially highly skeptical became advocates of the program over time. Speaking of his own subordinates' quality team, one department head told me, "I had a 'show-me' attitude for three years—and they finally showed me."

In 1987, I offered my five best managers merit raises from a special pool of money I had set aside for recognition. To my astonishment, all five refused the money. To single them out as heroes, they said, would be setting up a star system and, by implication, denying credit to the efforts of their teams. What people wanted and needed was regular, daily feedback about the things they were doing well, pats on the back, notes from the CEO or, in this case, the mayor. They were performing as teams and they wanted to be recognized as teams.

We made immense progress in the six years I was in office. By the end of 1988, we had trained 75 team leaders (who have a stake in the outcome of team decisions and who lead team meetings), and facilitators (who come from other divisions or departments, have no stake in decisions, and take special responsibility for maintaining group process). We had also developed nearly two dozen projects and produced good enough results to warrant inviting all of the city's departments to apply for what we called "transformation status."

Transformation status meant a long-term, departmentwide commitment to the new management practices, including continuous quality improvement and training for all employees in quality-improvement skills and data-gathering techniques. The first two departments to accept the challenge were the police department and the Madison metro bus system. A year later, the streets division and the health department joined them.

When I left office in 1989, Madison city departments were running between 20 and 30 quality improvement projects at a time, five agencies were in transformation, the city was giving training in quality to every municipal employee, joint efforts were under way with several state agencies eager to follow our lead, and city workers left and right were continuing to invent service improvements for internal and external customers. If I ever had questioned the feasibility of applying Deming's principles to public-sector services, my doubts had long since vanished.

In politics as in business, however, nothing is simple. On the plus side, my quality program was streamlining Madison city government, and—though I insisted on giving credit to the people who earned it—producing political capital for me. In my 1989 reelection campaign, I received the rare combined endorsement of the unions representing police officers, sheriff's officers, firefighters, and street maintenance workers. Local papers praised my efforts to modernize public-sector management, and the nationwide State and Local Government Labor-Management Committee, organized by AFSCME, the AFL-CIO, and the U.S. Conference of Mayors, singled out Madison's accomplishments in a television documentary that was broadcast across the country on Labor Day.

But this recognition was not enough to win me a fourth term. Other political factors were more compelling. There was my incumbency itself—no Madison mayor had been elected to a fourth term in more than 50 years. There was the reemergence of a popular mayor of yesteryear in the field of candidates. And, most fatefully of all, there was a major money referendum on the ballot. The issue was a lakefront convention center expected to cost $46 million. I believed the center was important for the city; many others did not. I campaigned hard for the center as well as for my reelection, and we both went down to defeat by nearly identical margins.

I take consolation in the fact the election was not a referendum on the quality and productivity program. To the degree that QP played a role, it was an asset, and even though I lost, I believe the culture of quality that my administration introduced into city government will survive, maybe even flourish. The city departments that embraced it and saw its power are still active believers, and my successor has given QP his cautious support.

Implementing a Deming quality strategy is not simply a matter of adopting a new set of slogans or a new accounting system. It's a matter of radical restructuring—part sociology, part systems theory, and part statistics—all aimed at liberating human ingenuity and the potential pleasure in good work that lie at least partially dormant in every organization.

It may appear that corporations are in a stronger position to implement Deming's methods than are governments. Market forces exert great pressure on businesses to undertake fundamental change for the sake of efficiency and survival. But governments today are under equally ferocious pressure to economize. Deep federal deficits, state and local budget-balancing requirements, and the trials of finding revenue in times of economic contraction or slow growth will make life challenging for state and local government managers for years to come.

My experience in Madison convinces me that quality-oriented businesses can contribute to keeping the public sector strong and efficient. As taxpayers, as providers of goods and services to government, and as community citizens, businesses have a direct interest in lending a hand. If businesses insist on quality, offer their expertise, share their training programs with government executives and team leaders, and search for quality programs to translate into public operations, the payback can be substantial. Who knows—we may actually get governments that *are* there to help us.

PART FOUR

Public Administration and Change

9

WORKING TOGETHER: RELATIONS AMONG THE PUBLIC, BUSINESS, AND NONPROFIT SECTORS

Few topics dealing with public administration in the last few years have generated as much controversy and public debate as the relations between business and public administration. The issues are many and varied. They range from the size of government in American society to joint private-public ventures in promoting economic development; from contracting out to private firms for public services to greater governmental scrutiny to protect the environment; from occupational and health safety rules to industry advisory committees for government agencies.

One of the most dramatic examples during the Bush administration was the federal bailout of the savings and loan institutions. Hundreds of financially weak savings and loan associations were closed or taken over. The price tag will be in the hundreds of billions of dollars, primarily to support the government's commitment in guaranteeing the security of depositors' money. The Office of Thrift Supervision in the U.S. Department of the Treasury was created to more closely monitor the S & L industry. Funds are now insured by the Federal Deposit Insurance Corporation, which formerly covered only commercial banks. And a new organization, the Resolution Trust Corporation, was established to liquidate failed savings institutions.

In recent years, we have often heard in the United States that government, or bureaucracy, is too big, is too bloated. One way to measure this is to compare the size of government in this country with the size in other countries. One standard measure of this is governmental expenditures as a percent of gross domestic product (GDP), the total of goods and services produced in a country. For the United States, this involves adding together federal, state, and local expenditures.

The results of comparing the United States with a set of ten other industrialized democracies are shown in Figure 9-1. Although public expenditures

Figure 9-1. Government Sector's Total Outlays as a Percentage of the Nation's Gross Domestic Product (1987)

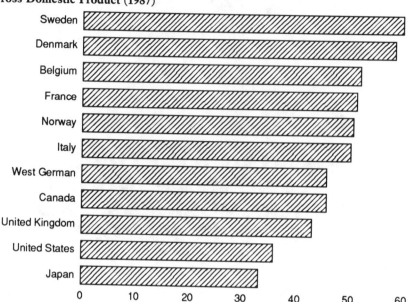

Source: Organization for Economic Cooperation and Development, *OECD Economic Outlook*, 46 (December, 1989), p. 179, Table R-14. As shown in James W. Fesler and Donald F. Kettl, *The Politics of the Administrative Process* (Chatham, NJ: Chatham House Publ., 1991), p. 2.

total about one-third of GDP in this country, all the other nations, except one, have governments *larger* than that in the United States.

A second way to measure would be to examine the extent of public ownership of basic industries. This is depicted for a broader set of countries in Figure 9-2. This approach also confirms that the United States is at one extreme in terms of the importance of its market economy.[1]

In the first article in this chapter, Norman Augustine, a corporate CEO with Defense Department experience, talks about international and technological imperatives for business and government to start working together more than they have in the past. To be competitive, says Augustine, U.S. business cannot go it alone.

The next two articles are by knowledgeable advocates of the increased use of the private marketplace; both of these authors served in the Reagan administration. The second article in this chapter is by Murray Weidenbaum, a distinguished economist, who surveys issues surrounding government regulation of business. Weidenbaum himself calls for continuing the deregulation of the Carter, Reagan, and Bush years, even as the Clinton administration wrestles with these issues.

The third article is by E. S. Savas, one of the most articulate advocates for increased privatization of public services. Many others, of course, would dis-

Figure 9-2. Who Owns How Much?

Privately owned: ○ all or nearly all

Publicly owned: ◔ 25% ◑ 50% ◕ 75% ● all or nearly all

	Postal service	Telecommunications	Electricity	Gas	Oil production	Coal	Railways	Airlines	Motor industry	Steel	Shipbuilding	
Australia	●	●	●	●	○	○	●	◑	○	○	na	Australia
Austria	●	●	●	●	●	●	●	●	●	●	na	Austria
Belgium	●	●	◕	◕	na	○	●	●	○	◑	○	Belgium
Brazil	●	●	●	●	●	●	●	◔	○	◕	○	Brazil
Britain	●	●	●	●	◕	●	●	◑	◑	◕	●	Britain
Canada	●	◕	●	○	○	○	◑	◕	○	○	○	Canada
France	●	●	●	●	na	●	●	◑	◑	◕	○	France
West Germany	●	●	◕	◑	◕	◑	●	●	◕	○	◕	West Germany
Holland	●	●	◕	◕	na	na	●	●	◑	◕	○	Holland
India	●	●	●	●	●	●	●	●	○	◕	●	India
Italy	●	●	◕	●	na	na	●	●	◕	◑	◕	Italy
Japan	●	●	○	○	na	○	◑	◕	○	○	○	Japan
Mexico	●	●	●	●	●	●	●	◑	◕	◕	●	Mexico
South Korea	●	●	◕	○	na	◕	●	○	○	◕	○	South Korea
Spain	●	◑	○	◕	na	◑	●	●	○	◑	◕	Spain
Sweden	●	●	◑	●	na	na	●	◑	○	◕	◕	Sweden
Switzerland	●	●	●	●	na	na	●	◕	○	○	na	Switzerland
United States	●	○	◕	○	○	○	◕*	○	○	○	○	United States

na - not applicable or negligible production   * including Conrail

Source: *The Economist*, December 30, 1978. Used with permission of *The Economist*.

agree, or at least disagree in the context of American society (for example, as opposed to some of the countries that were part of the Soviet Union).

Business and government are just two sectors of American society. There is also a third sector, the *nonprofit sector*. Nonprofit organizations consist of the nearly one million private, voluntary, charitable, human service, religious, and arts organizations so distinctive in American society. In the final article in this chapter, Michael Lipsky and Steve Smith describe the close and complex relationships between nonprofit organizations and government, everything from policy advocacy to contracting for human services.

When we talk about the public, business, and nonprofit sectors working together and arrangements such as public-private partnerships, many questions are raised:

- In the size of its public and private sectors, how does the United States compare with other developed democracies?

- How do global pressures promote cooperation between business and government today?

- Although the states regulated businesses first, federal regulation of business began with the Interstate Commerce Commission in the 1880s. Why does government regulate business, and why has there been a tendency toward deregulation in the last fifteen years? Do you favor greater deregulation or any reregulation?

- State and critique the case for contracting out many public services in this country.

- What are nonprofit organizations? Give some examples. How are they related to public administration?

Note

1. This is to acknowledge the work of Harvard Business School Professor Thomas K. McCraw in using this approach to assess the relative scope of the public and business sectors and in identifying the analysis by the staff of *The Economist*.

Public Employees and the Global Landscape

NORMAN R. AUGUSTINE

Events are moving so swiftly in today's topsy-turvy world that one is reminded of the predicament of the Red Queen in *Alice in Wonderland*—we are asked to believe three impossible things before breakfast each morning. The Berlin Wall is gone; Germany is united; Eastern Europe is free; and the Soviet Union is defunct. What took generations of violent history to create has been reversed peacefully in a matter of months.

Managing in such a dynamically changing environment requires extraordinary people—people with vision, adaptability, and the talent and commitment to see the job through. To some, such enormous changes bring disruption and disorientation, to others, opportunity. The challenge for our country, both in government and in the private sector, is not merely to adjust to these changes, but to anticipate them and turn them to an advantage.

CHALLENGE OF TECHNOLOGY

The upheavals we are experiencing are upsetting not only the political landscape, but the economic, technological, and social environment as well. The pace of technological change, for instance, seems to be striving to match the geopolitical changes we have seen. In my own field of aerospace engineering, the trajectory of the famous first flight of the Wright brothers in 1903 could easily fit inside the huge external fuel tank used on today's space shuttle.

The world's first electronic digital computer, the ENIAC, was constructed when I was a youth. It had 18,000 vacuum tubes occupying a large room, weighed 30 tons, and consumed the same power that is needed to illuminate some 1,700 light bulbs. Today, a few chips of silicon, each a quarter-inch square, have greater computing capacity than the original ENIAC. Computers in many homes today can process—in the time it takes the human heart to beat once—the same amount of information it would have taken ENIAC 192 years to process!

Robert Goddard's history-making rocket flight of the 1920s reached a peak altitude about half that of the Apollo moon rocket—while the latter was still affixed to its launch pad!

We have several thousand scientists, engineers, and mathematicians at Martin Marietta who are working in fields of specialization that did not even exist when I graduated from college. Software is a prime example. In fact, over half the scientists who have ever lived are alive today.

That is, of course, the challenge of technology. It simply will not sit still long enough to be dissected, packaged, and neatly delivered. Studies of the utilization of scientific publications and the content of university catalogs show that in most modern technical fields, the half-life of information is less than 10 years.

That means an otherwise excellent teacher who fails to continue the pursuit of new knowledge becomes professionally middle-aged by the time he or she is 30 years old. The situation is much like the epitaph on the old tombstone at Boot Hill Cemetery: "I was expecting this," it records, "but not so soon."

GLOBAL ECONOMY

The technology of instant communications has helped the globalization of our national economy arrive a lot faster than most anyone expected. We have not yet reached the point where in the movie "Network" Ned Beatty tells Peter Finch that nations don't exist anymore, only corporations. But that line of dialogue does dramatically illustrate how much we need to think about competing in the new global economy.

Market boundaries around the world no longer coincide with geopolitical boundaries. This is a profound change, indeed. Today, about one-half of all US imports and exports are transactions between US firms and their foreign affiliates or parents. About one-half of all products made in the US contain some foreign components. Indonesia is now building airliners and Malaysia is one of the world's largest manufacturers of computer chips.

These dramatic changes bring to mind the old Chinese curse, "May you live in interesting times,"—or the opening lines of Charles Dickens' *A Tale of Two Cities*, . . . "It was the best of times. It was the worst of times." And from a business person's standpoint, events around the world are changing so rapidly that they remind one of the situation in an area in Texas where I used to live. It was said to be so barren that a cow had to graze at 60 miles an hour just to stay alive!

IMPORTANCE OF PEOPLE

Adam Smith published *The Wealth of Nations* in 1776, the same year our country was founded. Smith wrote the book to explore why some nations grew to become economic giants while others stagnated. He found nations with abundant natural resources that were poor. He found other nations with few natural resources that had become rich. Why? After years of study, Adam Smith concluded a nation succeeds not because of its natural resources, but because of its human resources.

What was true in Adam Smith's day remains true in our own dynamic world. And in the words of Paul Volcker, former chairman of the Federal Reserve System: "Show me a nation with a second-rate civil service and I'll show you a second-rate nation." It's the people who make the difference. You can't run a good horse race without good horses. The same is true for running a government, especially in these constantly changing, demanding times.

It should perhaps be obvious that the quality of our government depends directly on the quality of the people who serve it. Yet one of the great myths about public employment is that there is no need to worry about what we pay government workers, how we recruit them or how we treat them, because "there are lots of folks around who would be willing to take those jobs." Doubtless there are. Just as there are probably lots of people who would be willing to take out your appendix or represent you in court for far less money than respected physicians or attorneys charge.

The real issue is: Do we want "just anyone" to carry out these important tasks, or do we want highly qualified people? As a former vice president of the United States once asked, "Is 'okay' enough for those who direct the next Shuttle mission? After Three Mile Island and Chernobyl, what level of competence do we want inspecting our nuclear plants? The next time you take an air flight, do you tell your family not to worry—'the controllers aren't the best, but they are okay?'"

At nearly every level of government, public workers are involved in making multi-billion dollar, sometimes even life-and-death decisions in this enormously dynamic world. It's time that our country recognizes its public workers as the vital resource they are.

In my own experience, as someone who proudly served the federal government for a decade in five different jobs, I look back on those years as among the most exciting, challenging, and thoroughly demanding in my life. I have never worked harder than I did in my years as a public servant. While in government I worked alongside some of the finest, most competent, thoroughly committed people I have ever known.

That experience left me with an abiding and continuing respect for the men and women who serve our nation as public employees. It also heightened my impatience with those who use the term "bureaucrat" in a demeaning and pejorative manner.

PUBLIC AND PRIVATE SECTORS

As a corporate executive with government experience, I often am asked my views of the differences between the public and private sectors. There are some obvious differences, but what strikes me most are the not-so-obvious similarities. For openers, people in both the public and private sectors today have the responsibility of running quality programs in austere times—with highly constrained resources.

Short-Term Perspectives

Further, both industry and government need to place greater emphasis on long-term considerations and goals. We have far too much short-term thinking in both American government and business. The average share of stock in corporations in the United States is held for about two years. In other words, ownership of publicly held companies on average turns over every 24 months. That encourages management not to look much beyond the next quarter's earnings.

At my own company, some years back, we proudly announced to a group of security analysts an extremely promising set of new research projects we intended to pursue. Rather than applaud our actions, the analysts, who wanted a short-term gain, rushed out of the room and advised their clients to sell our stock. In just five days, our stock dropped over eleven percent—and then continued to slide for two years. Later, when the results of our research and development were paying off with large production programs, the same analysts applauded how smart we were to invest in R&D!

American business needs to do more long-term thinking, but government tax laws encourage shareholders to demand short-term gains. We need to change those laws so business can concentrate more on developing and marketing technology. One way to do that would be to tie the capital gains tax to the length of time an investment is held, with declining tax rates for assets held for a longer period. Another is to provide meaningful tax incentives for investment in R&D.

Similarly, it's noteworthy that in government, high-ranking political appointees below cabinet level change positions on average every 18 to 22 months. That changes like this in senior government positions can occur in such a short period of time makes it vital that we rely on the managerial level within the civil service to provide continuity, institutional memory, and operating expertise so necessary to ensure the smooth running of government. The alternative is the equivalent of reinventing the wheel every two years.

Need for Partnership Approach

There are many other areas where the concerns and experiences of government and business organizations converge. I believe that in the final analysis there are many lessons we can learn from one another. But one lesson we can never learn too well is that today's changing environment requires that government and industry, as well as labor and academia, work much more closely together to serve the nation and assure its prosperity in our increasingly competitive world.

The country gains when we work together in a spirit of cooperation rather than against each other in adversarialism. Nowhere is this more essential than in the economic sphere. Individual US firms today are being required to compete against foreign governments—with all the resources the latter can muster. I believe no individual US company can by itself compete successfully in such a situation . . . the private sector's individual pockets simply aren't deep enough.

Not only are American firms required to operate in what is on occasion not a level playing field, but it has been pointed out that at times the playing field is not even well lit. The most blatant example of this is when foreign governments simply target a US industry and, through predatory pricing, dumping, and other illicit practices, set out to destroy it. This kind of competition suggests, as a last resort, a rather straightforward response; namely, strong retaliatory measures imposed at the government level.

No Accounting for It

Another form of unfair competition is more subtle. Let me give an example from the US commercial space launch industry where the overseas sale of one large booster rocket creates about 3,000 jobs for a year and offsets the import of some 10,000 Toyotas. Yet Chinese firms sell their launch vehicle, the "Long March," at a price equal to 20-to-40 percent of US manufacturers' cost.

When in China, I once asked a Chinese industrialist, "What percentage of your launch vehicle cost is attributable to medical insurance for retired employees?" "What are your expenditures for environmental activities?" "How much do you spend on third-party liability insurance?" Needless to say, my questions were greeted with genuine incredulity. Such questions of course have no relevance to the Chinese system of cost accounting. There is nothing necessarily nefarious involved. They just don't keep the books the way we do—and must.

Pay Scale

A third form of unfair competition results from the fact that there are large numbers of capable workers in many parts of the world who are ready to give a good day's work for a fraction of the pay we Americans take for granted. South Koreans generally make about 26 percent of the wages of their American counterparts. Workers in Mexico often earn about 12 percent and workers in India about three percent of the going rate.

There are some who argue that American businesses should counter this kind of foreign competition by relocating our factories to the world's low rent districts; or by reducing wages to the lowest common international denominator; or by building walls of protection around our country that deny Americans access to sought-after foreign goods.

ROLE OF GOVERNMENT

Obviously, we cannot and should not do any of these things. How, then, does American business compete in this challenging economic environment?

One thing is certain: US business cannot do it alone. For America to be competitive in the global market requires cooperation and support from the US government. This does not mean government intervention on the day-to-day affairs of business. It does mean that the government should concentrate on those things that cannot be satisfactorily performed in the private sector. This includes, for example, taking a leadership role in the pursuit of leading-edge, high-cost research with uncertain or long-term payoff; planning and providing specialized joint-use facilities; providing a world-class educational system; and seeking international agreements that assure a level playing field. These areas all require a strong partnership between government and the private sector.

When we look at Japan or any of our other world-class competitors, we realize that they have not stolen the march on us because of their superb investment bankers, arbitrageurs, takeover specialists, or any other eminent species of dealmakers. The Japanese miracle was forged right on the factory floor just like the long-running "American miracle" before that. That's where the real competition takes place. It's the people "on the factory floor" who will determine how well our country maintains its economic leadership position in the years ahead. It's up to those of us in supporting roles in both government and the private sector to assure they are given the opportunity to compete to the fullest possible extent.

Regulation as a Consumer Issue

MURRAY WEIDENBAUM

. . . All types of government regulation of business can affect the health of the economy. Thus, any comprehensive effort to achieve a stronger and more competitive economy must include an agenda for regulatory reform.

GOVERNMENT REGULATION AND THE CONSUMER

At first glance, the government imposition of socially desirable requirements on business appears to be an inexpensive way of achieving national objectives. It seems to cost the government little (aside from the expenses of the regulatory agencies themselves, usually overlooked) and therefore is not recognized as much of a burden on the taxpayer.

But the public does not escape paying the full cost. Every time an agency, in its attempt to safeguard occupational safety and health, imposes on business a more expensive method of production, the cost of the resultant product will necessarily rise. Whenever a commission supervising the safety of products imposes a standard that is more costly to attain, some products will increase in price. The same holds true for the activities of agencies protecting the environment, monitoring the food and drug industries, and so forth.

Although the costs of compliance with the directives of government agencies are buried in corporate cost accounts, such costs amount to a substantial hidden tax on the consumer. If consumers knew how much they were paying for regulation, they would probably be very upset. The high cost generated by rule making results in large part because government agencies do not feel great pressure to worry about it. Compliance costs show up not in their budgets but in those of the private sector.

At issue is not the desirability of the objectives of regulatory agencies; that subject will be examined a little later. Rather, the point is that the public does not get a "free lunch" by imposing government requirements on private industry. Although the costs of complying with regulation are not borne by taxpayers directly, they show up in higher prices of the goods and services that consumers buy and, often, in reduced product variety.

Perhaps more important than the amount of money involved is the increasing intervention by government in the daily lives of its citizens. Decisions by one or more government agencies alter, influence, or even determine what we can buy, how we may use the goods and services we own, and how we earn our daily living. Government decisions increasingly affect what we wear, what we eat, and how we play.[1] Few items of business or consumer expenditures escape regulation by one or more national, state, or local government agencies. Table 9-1 gives a representative sample limited primarily to the federal level.

Table 9-1
The Broad Scope of Government Regulation

Category	Regulatory Agency
Air travel	Federal Aviation Administration
Automobiles	National Highway Traffic Safety Administration
Bank deposits	Federal Deposit Insurance Corporation and Comptroller of the Currency
Boats	Coast Guard
Bus travel	Interstate Commerce Commission
Cigarettes	Public Health Service
Consumer credit	Federal Reserve System
Consumer products generally	Consumer Product Safety Commission
Consumer products containing chemicals	Environmental Protection Agency
Cosmetics	Food and Drug Administration
Credit union deposits	National Credit Union Administration
Drinking water	Environmental Protection Agency
Drugs (prescription and over-the-counter)	Food and Drug Administration
Eggs	Department of Agriculture
Election campaigns	Federal Election Commission
Electricity and gas	Federal Energy Regulatory Commission and state public service commissions
Exports	Departments of Commerce and Treasury
Firearms	Bureau of Alcohol, Tobacco, and Firearms
Flood insurance	Federal Insurance Administration
Food	Food and Drug Administration and Department of Agriculture
Housing	Federal Housing Administration and local building codes
Imports	International Trade Commission and Department of Treasury
Land	Office of Interstate Land Sales Registration and local agencies
Livestock and processed meat	Packers and Stockyards Administration
Meat and poultry	Animal and Plant Health Inspection Service
Milk	Federal and state departments of agriculture
Narcotics	Drug Enforcement Administration
Newspaper and magazine advertising	Federal Trade Commission
Pensions	Internal Revenue Service and Department of Labor
Petroleum and natural gas	Department of Energy
Potatoes	State Agricultural Agencies
Medical fees	Professional Standards Review Organizations
Radio and television	Federal Communications Commission
Railroad and bus travel	Interstate Commerce Commission
Savings and loan deposits	Federal Home Loan Bank Board
Stocks and bonds	Securities and Exchange Commission
Telephone service	Federal Communications Commission and state public service commissions

REGULATION AND THE BUSINESS FIRM

The pervasive expansion in the regulation of business that has been occurring in the United States in recent years is also altering fundamentally the relation between business and government. The concept of a regulated industry has become archaic. We now live in an economy in which every company feels the power of government in its day-to-day operations.

If we could accurately measure the pervasiveness of government intervention, we would not find the economists' favorites—electric utilities and railroads—at the top of the list. More likely, it would be such giants of the manufacturing sector as automobile, aerospace, and chemical companies, with the oil industry and health services not too far behind.

It is hard to overestimate the rapid expansion and the great variety of the American government's involvement in business. The major growth of government regulation is not in the traditional independent regulatory agencies, such as the Federal Communications Commission. (As will be discussed later, significant "deregulation" is occurring in the old-line regulatory commissions.) Rather, federal power over business is expanding by use of the operating bureaus of government—in the Departments of Agriculture, Commerce, Energy, Health and Human Services, Interior, Justice, Labor, Transportation, and Treasury—and by means of separate executive branch units, such as the Environmental Protection Agency. Approximately 85 percent of the budgets for federal regulation is assigned to social regulation and only 15 percent to the older forms of economic regulation.[2]

No business today, large or small, can operate without obeying a myriad of government restrictions and regulations. Entrepreneurial decisions fundamental to the business enterprise have become subject to government influence, review, or control—such decisions as what lines of business to go into, what products and services to produce, which investments to finance, how to produce goods and services, where to make them, how to market them, what prices to charge, and what profit to keep.

Virtually every major department of the American corporation has one or more counterparts in a government agency that controls or strongly influences its internal decision making. There is almost a "shadow" organization chart of public officials matching the formal structure of each private company. The scientists in corporate research laboratories now do much of their work to ensure that the products they develop are not rejected by lawyers in regulatory agencies. The engineers in manufacturing departments must make sure the equipment they specify meets the standards promulgated by Labor Department authorities. Marketing staffs must follow procedures established by government administrators in product safety agencies. The location of business facilities must conform with a variety of environmental statutes. The activities of personnel staffs are geared in large measure to meeting the standards of the various agencies concerned with employment conditions. Finance departments bear the brunt of the rising paperwork burden imposed on business by government agencies.

Few aspects of business escape government review or influence. As a result, important internal adjustments have been taking place in the structure and operation of the typical corporation. Each major business function has undergone an important transformation. These changes have increased the overhead costs of doing business and often deflected management and employee attention from the conventional tasks of designing, developing, producing, and distributing new and better or cheaper goods and services. The cost of complying with domestic regulation can be a significant handicap in competing against foreign firms that produce under less burdensome regulatory regimes.

Numerous chief executives report that one-third or more of their time is now devoted to governmental and public policy matters—dealing with the many federal, state, and local regulations that affect the company, meeting with a wide variety of civic and special-interest groups that make demands on the organization's resources, and increasingly participating in the public policy arena. Donald Rumsfeld, former chief executive of a major pharmaceuticals company, has described very personally the pervasiveness of government involvement in business:

> When I get up in the morning as a businessman, I think a lot more about government than I do about our competition, because government is that much involved—whether it's HEW, IRS, SEC, FTC, FDA. I always understood the problem intellectually, but the specific inefficiencies that result from the government, injecting itself into practically every aspect of our business—that is something one can feel only by being here.[3]

The impetus for most of the expansion in government power over business does not come from the industries being regulated; generally, they have shown a minimum of enthusiasm for EPA, OSHA, EEOC, ERISA, and the rest of the government's alphabet soup. If anything, companies claim that their "benefits" from these regulations are negative. The pressures for the new style of regulation come, rather, from a variety of citizen groups concerned primarily with noneconomic aspects of national life—environmentalists, consumer groups, labor unions, and civil rights organizations.

To say or write that the regulated industry is "capturing" its regulators is, to put it kindly, a quaint way of viewing the fundamental shift in business decision making taking place, the shift of power from private managers to public officials. Yet, the core of the economist's version of the "capture" theory still holds—public policy tends to be dominated by the organized and compact pressure groups that attain their benefits at the expense of the more diffused and larger body of consumers.

But the nature of those interest groups has changed in recent years. Rather than the railroad baron (a relatively easy target for attack), the villain of the piece has often become a self-styled representative of the public interest who has succeeded in identifying his or her personal prejudices with the national well-being. It is fascinating—and perhaps ironic—how much business firms, in performing the traditional middleman function, serve the unappreciated and involuntary role of proxy for the overall consumer interest. That is most apparent in the case of retailers opposing restrictions on imports that would raise the prices of the goods they buy—and sell.

EXAMINING THE BENEFITS OF REGULATION

The benefits of regulation should not be overlooked. To the extent that government rules result in healthier workplaces, safer products, and so forth, these benefits are very real. These words have been chosen very carefully. The mere presence of a government agency does not automatically guarantee that its worthy objectives will be achieved, nor are we justified in jumping to the opposite conclusion that no government agencies can achieve any good. The difficult and double-barreled question that needs to be answered is, How much benefit does the regulation produce and is it worth the cost? Society's bottom line is not the impact of regulatory actions on government or on business but the effect on consumers and on citizens generally.

The relevant issue is therefore not a broadly philosophical one: Are you for or against government intervention? Rather, it involves a very practical question: Does this specific type of government activity work? The sad reality is that it often does not or that it works against the interest of the consumer. This reality has been recognized in some areas. As is pointed out later in this chapter, deregulation of the airlines has reduced the costs of traveling substantially. Cutting back the regulation of railroads and trucking has likewise benefited consumers, albeit indirectly, by permitting competition to hold down the cost of shipping commodities.

Consider drug regulation by the Food and Drug Administration (FDA). A look at the mortality data—rather than at the rhetoric—shows that, for decades, the leading causes of death in this country have been heart attacks and strokes. There exists a series of new drugs for these illnesses called beta blockers, which were in widespread use in the United Kingdom and other developed nations for many years before they could be purchased in the United States.

This nation, however, lagged in the introduction of these drugs because of the antiquated procedures of the FDA. According to the research performed at the University of Rochester Medical School by Dr. William Wardell, one of these beta blockers, practolol, can save ten thousand lives a year in the United States.[4] That is a real measure of the cost of the delayed introduction as a result of the slow pace of FDA approval of new pharmaceuticals.

Beta blockers are not the only drugs whose use has been delayed by the FDA. Dr. Wardell examined the list of drugs actually approved as safe and effective. In case after case, the United States was one of the last countries to permit their introduction. It was the twenty-second country in the case of the anti-inflammatory drug fenoprofen, the thirty-ninth country for the oral cephalosporin cephalexin, and the fortieth country for the antitubercular antibiotic capreomycin.[5]

These delays are not surprising, given the cardinal rule for bureaucratic survival: Do not stick your neck out. If you were an FDA reviewer and had approved practolol quickly, you would have been taking a risk. If anybody suffered an adverse reaction, you might have borne the responsibility. On the other hand, if you delay approving the drug, the potential users are unlikely to complain, since they do not know about it and quickly pass from the scene. As a result, the cautious regulator asks for more studies—and more delay.

Consider the results of this bureaucratic process of decision making: if sixteen people are harmed by the side effects of a drug in use, that becomes front-page news. If ten thousand people die prematurely because approval of a new drug has been delayed, the public is unaware. This is one example from among many where the real costs of regulation are expressed in terms not of dollars but of lives—and where tougher choices on the part of government officials would enhance consumer welfare.

DEREGULATION IS WORKING

Progress has been made during the last decade in cutting back some of the older forms of economic regulation, where competition in the marketplace can do a better job of protecting the consumer than the imposition of bureaucratic judgments on private enterprise. A brief review of how this came to pass is instructive.

The partial deregulation of American transportation, telecommunications, energy, and financial markets over the past ten years has been a triumph of ideas over entrenched political interests. For ninety years, from the establishment of the Interstate Commerce Commission (ICC) in 1886 to the passage of the Toxic Substances Control Act in 1976, government regulation of American economic activity continually expanded, and it created in its wake powerful constituencies who benefited from the regulation.

Yet, this trend in government rule making has changed dramatically and perhaps irrevocably during the past decade, resulting in remarkable benefits for the American economy. Deregulation has lowered the cost of producing goods and services. It has offered most American consumers a wider array of choices. And it has substantially bolstered the international competitiveness of the economy.

What caused the shift toward deregulation was not a realignment of political forces. The most significant developments were supported by a bipartisan coalition in both the legislative and the executive branches of the federal government. Consumer activists offered support at vital points, as did leaders of both political parties. But the most important role was played by a very unusual set of actors in the public policy arena: economists, political scientists, legal scholars, and similar purveyors of ideas.

The Intellectual Support for Deregulation

Three streams of research dealing with different aspects of regulation reached a confluence in the early 1970s.[6] The first focused on the heavy and widely distributed burdens that economic regulation imposed on the economy, especially in the field of transportation, and the smaller and far more concentrated distribution of any benefits that resulted. The second research effort dealt with the fundamental nature of the regulatory process, especially the relations between regulators and those regulated. The third area of research focused on the cost of regulation, especially to the consumer.

It was in the airline industry that the research results were most widely accepted. The clearest example of the heavy cost of regulation was demonstrated by the price differences for trips on regulated and nonregulated airlines. Interstate travel was under the jurisdiction of the Civil Aeronautics

Board (CAB); intrastate travel was beyond the CAB's jurisdiction. Because of regulation, someone flying 300 miles from Portland, Oregon, to Seattle, Washington, was paying more than a traveler flying 500 miles in California, going from San Diego to San Francisco.[7]

Most American economists writing in this field also concluded during the 1970s that Interstate Commerce Commission (ICC) regulation was protecting the carriers (railroads, truckers, and their unions) while increasing costs to shippers by billions of dollars a year.[8]

A consensus gradually emerged. Transportation regulation in the United States did not protect its purported beneficiaries—consumers—but instead benefited the employees, executives, and shareholders of the companies being regulated. Government rule making shielded entrenched firms from potential new competitors, and that kept a high-price umbrella over the regulated industry.

A second, and related, stream of research focused on the notion that regulation resulted primarily from the efforts of key interest groups and ultimately benefited those regulated (the now widely held "capture" theory of regulation). In this view, as the only political force in the regulatory agency's environment with any stability, the industry eventually forced the agency to accommodate to its needs.[9] In developing and refining that notion, Professor George Stigler and his colleagues at the University of Chicago contended that regulatory policy reflects the interests and the power of the concerned groups, not necessarily the consumers.[10] In 1982, Stigler was awarded the Nobel Prize in economic science for his pioneering work in this field.

By the mid-1970s, the connection was complete. On both theoretical and empirical grounds, the fundamental justification for much of the existing body of regulation, especially of the economic type, was demolished. Particularly in the case of transportation, it was demonstrated that the rule-making process succeeded primarily in protecting entrenched companies from new competition. Rather than being helped, consumers suffered the higher prices reflecting the "dead weight" losses resulting from regulation. Although specific estimates of the economic cost of airline regulation varied widely, it became clear that the burden on the traveling public was substantial.[11]

The third line of research, focusing on costs to consumers, saw the topic move from the academic journals and the business pages to the front pages and the nightly news. That occurred in the mid-1970s with the publication of widely distributed research on the high cost of regulation.[12] The issue hit a responsive chord with the media, influential policy groups, and, finally, the Congress.[13] A few simple concepts made it attractive. First, in a period of escalating inflation, a strategy of deregulation presented policymakers with an opportunity to deal with that critical issue in a way that did not involve a trade-off with jobs. Indeed, reduced regulation would cut both costs and barriers to production and employment.

Second, the burdens of regulation were summed up as a hidden tax on the consumer ($63 billion in 1976 for a sample of federal regulatory programs).[14] This cost increase was buried in the form of higher prices, but it was very real and often regressive. Third, the notion of benefit-cost analysis, which had been used to screen out clearly uneconomical expenditure projects for decades, also proved to be useful when applied to regulation. Although the implementation required dealing with many difficult conceptual and statistical problems, the general notion of weighing costs against benefits generated a positive reaction.

Finally, a variety of carefully researched examples of regulatory silliness and nonsense reached the public consciousness. Perhaps the first was the dead haul—the requirement that resulted in trucks returning empty, despite ample opportunity to fill them with cargo. The public needed no great expertise to resent the waste that resulted.

This unusual form of applied research focused increasingly on the Occupational Safety and Health Administration. OSHA jokes (based on that research) became a staple of business conversation. Did you hear the one about the OSHA rule that spittoons have to be cleaned daily? Is it true that OSHA made one little company build separate "his" and "her" toilets even though the only two employees of the firm were married to each other? Did OSHA really issue a bulletin to farmers telling them to be careful around cows and not to step into the manure pits? [15]

Clearly, by the late 1970s, support for regulatory reform had become widespread. It included business executives who found themselves pestered with a flood of rules to follow and reports to file, lawyers and political scientists who thought that the regulatory agencies often were captured by the industries being regulated, and economists who believed that regulation reduced competition and increased costs. Some congressional hearings on the subject yielded support for less regulation from such disparate groups—and surprising allies—as the American Conservative Union and the Consumer Federation of America.

Progress on Deregulation

Actual progress on deregulation was slow until dramatic momentum developed in the middle and late 1970s (see Table 9-2). In 1968, an obscure Supreme Court decision permitted non-AT&T equipment to be hooked into the Bell telephone system. In the following year, the Federal Communications Commission (FCC) allowed a non-Bell company to connect its long-distance network with local phone systems. Although these two actions attracted little attention at the time, they triggered the forces that ultimately led to the breakup of the Bell system.

In 1970, interest rates on deposits of $100,000 and over were deregulated. Again, one move toward deregulation ultimately led to another. As securities firms took advantage of that "loophole," banks responded. Thus, a process was set in motion that has resulted in the lifting of interest rate ceilings, the payment of interest on consumer demand deposits, and enhanced competition among financial institutions.

Two important regulatory changes took place in 1975. The Securities and Exchange Commission (SEC) ordered an end to the practice of fixed brokerage fees for stock market transactions, and the ICC prohibited rate bureaus for trucking firms and railroads from protesting independent rate filings by members. Clearly, the regulatory ice was breaking.

In 1977, the Civil Aeronautics Board (CAB), under the chairmanship of the economist Alfred Kahn and with the support of the economist member

Table 9-2

Landmarks in Deregulation

1968	Supreme Court permits non-AT&T equipment to be hooked up to Bell System.
1969	MCI is allowed to connect its long-distance network with local phone systems.
1970	Interest rates on deposits of $100,000 and over are deregulated.
1972	FCC sets domestic satellite open-skies policy.
1975	SEC ends fixed brokerage fees for stock market transactions.
1975	Rate bureaus for trucking firms and railroads are prohibited from protesting independent rate filings.
1977	Air cargo is deregulated; airlines are given more freedom in pricing and easier access to new rates.
1978	Congress partially decontrols natural gas.
1978	OSHA revokes 928 "nitpicking" rules.
1978	CAB is phased out, ending its control over airline entry and prices.
1978	EPA begins emissions trading policy.
1980	FCC eliminates most federal regulation of cable TV and of consumer premises equipment.
1980	Motor Carrier Act removes barriers for new entries and lets operators establish fares and routes with little ICC interference.
1980	Depository Institutions law phases out interest rate ceilings and permits S&Ls to offer interest-bearing checking accounts.
1980	Staggers Rail Act enables railroads to adjust rates without government approval and to enter into contracts with shippers.
1981	President Reagan decontrols crude-oil prices and petroleum allocations.
1981	FCC eliminates much radio regulation.
1982	New bus regulatory statute allows intercity bus companies to change routes and fares.
1982	Garn–St. Germain Act allows S&Ls to make more commercial and consumer loans and removes interest rate differentials between banks and S&Ls.
1984	AT&T agrees to divest local operating companies as part of antitrust settlement.
1984	Individual ocean shipping companies are allowed to offer lower rates and better service than shipping conference.

Elizabeth Bailey, instituted several changes that ultimately led to deregulation. The CAB gave airlines increased freedom in pricing and easier access to routes they had not previously served. The results were spectacular. Fares for tourists fell drastically, planes filled up, and airline profits soared. The CAB experience provided a striking example of how regulation had been hurting the consumer (the traveling public) and how any gains to the regulated industry had long since been dissipated. In 1978, a bipartisan coalition in Congress passed legislation phasing out the CAB and its authority to control entry and prices.

The year 1980 was an extremely eventful one for economic deregulation. In that year, the FCC eliminated most federal regulation of cable television. The economist Darius Gaskins became chairman of the ICC, and the economist Marcus Alexis was appointed a member of the commission. That, in turn, encouraged (or scared) the trucking industry into supporting congressional assumption of leadership in the reform of regulation in this field, in the expectation that the results would be less drastic than desired by the ICC. Later in the year, a new trucking law provided much more freedom to individual truckers in pricing, made entry much easier, and eliminated many costly ICC restrictions—but the ICC presence was retained. Also passed in 1980, the Staggers Rail Act provided the railroads with new pricing freedom.

In 1981, the executive branch took the leadership on regulatory reform. Building on the groundwork of the Ford and Carter administrations, President Reagan issued a new executive order directing the regulatory agencies under his jurisdiction to perform cost-benefit analyses prior to issuing new rules.[16] A formal review process was placed under the auspices of the Office of Management and Budget.

As a result of these efforts, the rapid rate of regulatory expansion in the 1970s was followed by a substantial deceleration in the 1980s. No new regulatory agencies have been created since 1981.[17] Staffing for regulatory agencies is down, as are their expenditures in real terms.[18] Progress toward deregulation was made in a few areas. President Reagan decontrolled crude-oil prices and petroleum allocations and quietly terminated the Council on Wage and Price Stability. The FCC eliminated much regulation of the radio industry.

Although the Reagan administration virtually stopped the growth in the issuance of new rules, it did not make any significant cutbacks in the structure of regulation. For the most part, it left laws unchanged. A backlash in the environmental area (fueled in part by the controversial personalities of some of the administration's appointees, such as James Watt and Anne Burford) put the regulatory-reform movement on the defensive after the initial burst of change in early 1981. The initial effort to rewrite environmental protection statutes, for example, was abandoned in the face of strong congressional opposition. If the political environment shifts again to favor more regulation, the various federal agencies are in a position to adapt to that reversal quite readily.

Although regulatory reform was one of the four original pillars of "Reaganomics" (along with tax reduction, budget cutting, and anti-inflationary monetary restraint), it never received as high a priority as the other three. Nevertheless, some modest progress has continued to be made. Banking legislation enacted in 1982 allowed savings and loan associations to make more commercial and consumer loans. Also, the interest rate differentials between banks and thrift institutions were removed.

The Bus Regulatory Reform Act of 1982 allowed bus companies to change routes and fares. In 1984, the Shipping Act permitted individual ocean shipping companies to offer lower rates and better service than did shipping "conferences." Also in that year, AT&T agreed to divest local operating companies as part of its historic antitrust settlement with the Justice Department.

In one key area, the regulation of foreign trade, substantial backsliding has occurred. Since 1981, the Reagan administration has renewed or extended restrictions on the import of automobiles, meat, motorcycles, sugar, steel, textiles, and many other products. Simultaneously, control over exports, often justified on foreign policy or national-security grounds, has been tightened.

In environmental and safety rule making, wholesale deregulation has not been the reformers' goal in either the Carter or the Reagan administration. The emphasis here has been on relating the costs of regulation to their benefits and thus reducing the economic burdens of the regulatory process. Responding to the critics of its regulatory approach, the Occupational Safety and Health Administration (OSHA) eliminated or modified 928 of its "nitpicking" rules. The Environmental Protection Agency (EPA) experimented with "bubble" or "offset" policies designed to give companies more flexibility in complying with environmental standards.

The courts have often been barriers to the adoption of more economically efficient regulations. For example, in 1981 a federal court ruled out cost-benefit tests performed for a proposed cotton dust standard, because it held that the law did not provide for basing OSHA rulings on economic criteria. Nevertheless, the increasing support for reviewing the costliness and desirability of proposed new regulations—an approach started by President Ford, continued under President Carter, and expanded under President Reagan—has clearly slowed down the pace of federal rule making.

Consumer Protection through Deregulation

The general impact of deregulation on the American economy has been positive. The lessened government intervention has expanded the role of competition and market forces. Virtually every study of the changes has concluded that they have resulted in lower costs, thus raising demand and creating new opportunities for both producers and consumers of the previously regulated activities.[19]

Competition among airlines has been especially vigorous; twenty-six new carriers entered between 1978 and 1985, and nineteen have left. This has exerted great downward pressure on labor and overhead costs. Airline productivity has risen, average air fares have declined greatly, and volume has gone up sharply. The number of city pairs served by more than one airline increased by 55 percent from 1979 to 1984. While some passengers no longer have direct flights, the proportion of passengers changing planes actually decreased from 27 percent in 1978 to 25 percent in 1984.[20]

Moreover, despite several highly publicized air crashes and "near-misses," the overall safety record of air travel has improved since deregulation. . . .[21] The accident rate declined 26 percent, from the average of 2.35 accidents per 100,000 flight hours during 1972–78 to 1.73 per 100,000 hours during 1979–86.

A recent Brookings Institution study shows that airline deregulation has saved consumers $6 billion a year through lower fares and better service. At the same time, the airline industry has generated an additional $2.5 billion in annual profits.[22] Not expected by many proponents of deregulation, however, was the tendency for consolidation of airlines. Initially, the number of carriers in the United States rose, from thirty-six in 1978 to ninety-eight in 1983, but subsequently declined, to seventy-four in 1986.[23]

As of late 1987, a handful of major trunk lines were coming to dominate passenger air traffic, and passenger complaints about flight delays and lost luggage were rising. In specific central hubs, the dominant carrier's market share was quite high: Northwest had an 87 percent share of the Memphis departures, US Air 83 percent in Pittsburgh, TWA 82 percent in St. Louis, and Continental 72 percent in Houston.[24]

The structure of the industry is still evolving, and the long-term effects of the merger movement on price and service have yet to be determined by the newly unleashed competitive forces. In any event, new potential for competition does now exist in the industry. Moreover, airlines remain subject to the scrutiny of the federal government's antitrust authorities and to the possibility of renewed regulatory legislation on the part of the Congress.

For the railroads, revenue per ton-miles (a good measure of unit cost) has been declining in recent years while volume (total revenue ton-miles)—and operating income—have been on an upward trend line. For trucking, comprehensive data are harder to come by; 65 percent of a large sample of shippers recently reported lower trucking rates and improved services. The number of new firms entering the industry has far exceeded the loss of older companies. The number of ICC-authorized carriers increased from 18,000 in 1980 to 33,000 in 1984.[25]

Reduced regulation, ranging from outright deregulation to the simplification and streamlining of rule making, has enabled the competitive process to work better. Depositors in financial institutions have been receiving higher interest rates on their money than they would otherwise have gotten as a greater variety of companies compete for their business. Long-distance telephone users find that greater competition has resulted in lower rates. Simultaneously, the traditional subsidies to local service have been eliminated. Moreover, the deregulated industries experienced far-above-average rapid increases in productivity. Compared with a little more than 3 percent yearly growth in manufacturing productivity—and less than that in the service sector generally—airlines, railroads, and telecommunications averaged productivity increases of 5–10 percent a year during 1980–86.[26]

Inevitably, the wrenching changes brought about by deregulation have generated counterpressures by the interest groups that have lost the benefit of government protection.[27] The managements of many deregulated firms have seen their pay and perquisites decline to the competitive norm. Some companies have not been able to survive in the new competitive environment and have gone bankrupt or have been acquired by stronger firms.

Overall, the cost of producing goods and services in the United States is lower today than it would be if deregulation had not occurred. Opportunities have been created for new enterprises and for their employees. The position of American industry in an increasingly competitive global economy has been strengthened, and, most fundamentally, the welfare of the consumer has been enhanced. These positive accomplishments outweigh the transitional costs incurred in moving from a more regulated to a more competitive environment. In any event, a decade of active reduction of economic regulation seems to have drawn to a close. The deregulatory momentum developed during the 1970s has been lost in the 1980s.

Some observers anticipate a flood of new social regulation beginning in 1989 that will swamp that of the early 1970s. The environmental economist Lester Lave of Carnegie-Mellon University believes that the accumulating pressure of inaction on this front during the Reagan years "is about to explode." This is not a development that he welcomes.[28]

Lave notes that the scientific basis of the social-regulatory decisions of the 1970s was slim and often reflected outmoded or even incorrect science. Billions of dollars were wasted on sewage treatment plants that were never operated, tall stacks that merely diffused air pollution over larger areas, and jerry-built auto-emission controls. "In the haste to be responsive to public demands," Lave has written, "Congress and the regulators guessed rather than wait for facts and analysis to guide multi-billion dollar decisions."

How do we avoid repeating the errors of the 1970s and 1980s? Doing so will not be easy. For one thing, the Reagan administration's term *regulatory relief* should be promptly abandoned. The sensible goal is not to reduce the burden on business by easing the enforcement of existing regulation but to ensure that the regulations that are enforced benefit the consumer. Nor is it desirable to impose regulatory burdens on the economy merely because such actions enable elected officials to show they are "responsive." Rather, the objective should be to determine which regulations make economic sense, which should be modified, and which lack sufficient justification in an economy in which efficiency and equity are both dominant concerns. Let us try to develop such a useful approach.

ANOTHER WAVE OF REGULATORY REFORM

The First Step Toward Regulatory Reform Is Educational   The public must come to understand that it is paying very substantially for the supposedly good things that government regulators are doing.

Economists are prone to take measurements of economic phenomena. The numbers, of course, are not an end in themselves but an input to decision makers. The measurement of the costs and benefits that flow from government regulation is not merely a technical matter. This information can be used to show the public and the government the large amounts of resources being devoted to meeting federal mandates. Such analysis also helps shift the public dialogue onto higher ground. The pertinent policy questions are no longer absolutes: Are you for or against clean air or safe products? Increasingly, the public discussions are in terms of less emotional and long-neglected questions: How well is the regulatory process working? and Are there better ways of achieving the public's desires?

Congress needs to curtail its traditional response of creating a new bureau whenever it confronts a difficult problem. The symbolism involved may be good politics, at least in the short run, but such empty gestures undermine citizen confidence in government—and also contribute to the budget problem. It would be helpful if the Congress endorsed the kind of common sense embodied in the federal appeals court decision that stopped OSHA from issuing new benzene regulations. The court's language is instructive: "Although the agency does not have to conduct an elaborate cost/benefit analysis . . . it does have to determine whether the benefits expected from the standards bear a reasonable relationship to the costs imposed by the standard."[29]

The Second Step Is to Recognize That Merely Creating a Government Bureau and Giving It Large Amounts of Money and Power Does Not Necessarily Mean That the Air Will Be Any Cleaner or the Water Any Purer   The results may be the opposite. The environmental label has been used to justify subsidies to politically powerful regions of the country, notably producers of soft ("dirty") coal. As we noted earlier, in a misguided effort to keep off the market medicines that may generate any adverse side effects, the regulatory authorities often deprive patients of newer, more effective products.

In fact, regulatory activity can generate unexpected negative effects, such as the stifling of innovation. The engineer-lawyer Peter Huber questions whether Henry Ford's original Model T could have survived today's environmental challenges: "Darn thing was dangerous; why you could break your arm cranking it."[30]

The Third Step Is to Sort Out Regulatory Programs That Are Worth the Costs They Impose from Those That Fail a Benefit-Cost Test   The regulation of entry and pricing in the airline market by the now defunct Civil Aeronautics Board (CAB) was an example of regulatory activities not worthwhile. The elimination of the CAB has lowered the real cost of air travel and increased the travel choices available to most passengers. Simultaneously, however, the resultant greater volume of air travel has increased congestion, airline delays, lost baggage, and so on.

On the other hand, despite their many shortcomings, social regulatory agencies such as OSHA and the FDA conduct a variety of activities that contribute to the public welfare. That does not necessarily mean that every OSHA or FDA rule and requirement is optimally conceived or even necessary.

Environmental protection, product safety, and other regulatory efforts should be related to costs to the consumer, availability of new products, and employment. A parallel can be drawn to macroeconomic matters, where important and conflicting objectives are recognized and attempts to trade off are made (for example, as between rapid growth and inflation). This reconciliation of regulatory and broader goals can be made at the initial stages of the government process, when the President proposes and the Congress enacts new regulatory programs. In structuring regulatory programs, emphasis should be placed on the development of basic principles to guide the companies subject to regulation (such as economic incentives). This approach contrasts sharply with the traditional case-by-case adjudication so beloved by generations of attorneys.

A formal requirement for all regulatory agencies to perform benefit-cost analysis of proposed regulations is a useful check on expansions of government activity that would not help the average citizen.

Benefit/cost analysis has been used for decades in examining government spending programs. Its application to regulation has been attacked by both ends of the political spectrum—by the far left, because not every proposal for government intervention passes a benefit/cost test, and by the far right, because benefit/cost analysis can be used to justify some types of government intervention. No analytical approach is totally value free, but benefit/cost analysis has less ideological baggage than other alternatives do. To an economist, *overregulation* is not an emotional term; it is merely shorthand for regulation for which the costs to the public are greater than the benefits.

Critics who are offended by the notion of subjecting regulation to a benefit/cost test unwittingly expose the weakness of their position. They must fear that their pet rules would flunk the test. After all, showing that a regulatory activity generates an excess of benefits is a strong justification for continuing it. Benefit/cost analysis is a neutral concept, giving equal weight to a dollar of benefits and a dollar of costs. The painful knowledge that resources available to safeguard human lives are limited causes economists to become concerned when they see wasteful use of those resources because of regulation.

Fundamentally, the task is not to perform statistical tests on proposed rules, helpful though that may be. More basically, the public—and its legislative representatives—must come to a better understanding of the limits to the effective use of governmental power over private decision-making.

Regulatory reform is not really based on a concern with technical measurements or administrative procedures. Government decision makers need to view the regulatory mechanism differently than they do now. Rather than relying on regulation to control every facet of private behavior, the regulatory device needs to be seen as a powerful tool to be used with great care and discretion. Basically, it is attitudes that need to be changed. Experience with the job safety program provides a cogent example. Although the government's safety rules have resulted in billions of dollars in public and private outlays, the goal of a substantially safer work environment has not been achieved.

A more satisfying way of improving the effectiveness of government regulation of private activities will require a major change in the approach to regulation, and one not limited to the job safety program. Indeed, I cite that program merely as an illustration. If the objective of public policy is to reduce accidents, then public policy should focus directly on the reduction of accidents. Excessively detailed regulations are often merely a substitute—the normal bureaucratic substitute—for hard policy decisions.

Rather than placing emphasis on issuing citations to employers who fail to fill forms out correctly or who do not post the required notices, stress should be placed on the regulation of those employers with high or rising accident rates. Fines could be levied on those establishments with the worst safety records. When the accident rates decline toward some sensible standard, the fines could be reduced or eliminated. But the government should not be overly concerned with the way a specific organization achieves a safer working environment. Some companies may find it more efficient to change work rules, others to buy equipment, and still others to retrain workers. Making this choice is precisely the kind of operational business decision making that government should avoid but that now dominates regulatory programs.

The Fourth Step in Reforming Federal Regulation Is to Change or Repeal the Basic Statutes For starters, here is a modest agenda for revising the basic statutes that authorize and govern the regulation of business in the United States:

1. *Environmental law should make much more use of market-based approaches.* The legislation on water pollution control should be overhauled. Rather than specifying effluent standards based on a presumed degree of technology that may not be achievable in the future, government authorities should be authorized to charge per unit of effluent. This approach uses the price system to provide an incentive for reducing pollution. Increases in prices of high-polluting products would provide a spur to innovation in techniques to reduce the amounts of wastes discharged; those antipollution efforts would stem not from idealism but rather from a straightforward desire to maintain competitive positions. This would be more cost-effective than the present reliance on standards, which are almost invariably postponed because of court battles or lack of sufficient technology.

Economic approaches to pollution can produce substantial savings for taxpayers and consumers. A study of the Delaware Estuary showed that effluent fees could achieve the desired degree of water purity at half the cost of conventional regulatory methods.

2. *Progress on deregulation of transportation should be accelerated.* The agencies that still regulate prices and the entry and exit of firms in the transportation industry—the Interstate Commerce Commission and the Federal Maritime Commission—should be eliminated. Their interment would end the CAB's monopoly of the federal graveyard for regulatory commissions. Reliance on the competitive forces of the marketplace will ensure more efficient and less costly transport for business and personal travelers. Similarly, cabotage laws (such as the Jones Act, which limits shipping between American ports to U.S. flagships) should be repealed.

3. *Regulation of financial institutions should be reduced.* Statutes that unduly restrict competition in the banking system should be repealed, especially the McFadden Act, which limits the geographic expansion of commercial banks, and the Glass-Steagall Act, which inhibits their entry into other types of financial services.

4. *Remaining vestiges of energy price regulation should be repealed.* Recent history is instructive. In spite of the howls of outrage at the time, the elimination by President Reagan in 1981 of price and allocation controls over gasoline and petroleum products was followed, with the inevitable lag, by lower prices. The deregulation of natural gas is likely to have similarly beneficial results.

5. *The regulation of exports should be cut back drastically.* While export controls on highly classified military equipment are likely to remain—and they should—such restrictions should not be imposed merely as an effort to achieve foreign or domestic policy objectives. The embargoes on grain exports were exercises in futility. The restriction of exports of items readily obtainable in world markets does not hurt the foreign buyer as much as it punishes domestic producers and their employees.

6. *The regulation of imports through quotas should be terminated.* Study after study demonstrates that quotas and other quantitative restrictions on imports hurt the total domestic economy more than they benefit the specific industrial sector they are designed to protect—and they do so even more than tariffs. At least tariffs work through the price system and, unlike quotas, allow some of the benefits to accrue to the U.S. Treasury and ultimately to American taxpayers.

Under all forms of trade restriction, consumers wind up paying higher prices. Those other domestic industries that purchase the now higher-priced products become less competitive, and they often then join the chorus for government intervention. Moreover, the incentive of the "protected" companies to become more efficient is reduced in the process.

7. *A fundamental rewriting of the statutory framework for social regulation should be undertaken.* Unrealistic goals and objectives, such as "zero discharge," should be modified or, better yet, eliminated. Their continued presence undermines confidence in the overall effectiveness of government activities. The strongest proponents of government intervention in the marketplace conclude that such tasks are simply not possible.

Likewise, in giving the EPA the task of overseeing the cleansing of the nation's water, the Congress established the goal of "zero discharge" of untreated waste by 1984. In retrospect, the task was impossible, and there is considerable evidence that Congress realized this at the time.[31]

Reforming the regulatory process is an uphill battle. An insight into the difficulty involved is provided by the results of a nationwide Gallup poll that shows how poorly informed the American public is on these matters. Half of those interviewed could not name even one federal regulation that affected them or their family. Only 17 percent knew that the executive branch is responsible for issuing regulations; 47 percent thought Congress was. More than half could not name any difference between laws and regulations. Among those who did name a difference, the most popular response was that laws were mandatory, while regulations were optional.

The most fundamental need is to help the public understand the limits of government rule making. Even if the EPA were staffed entirely with Newtons and Einsteins, it could not meet the present statutory expectations of cleaning all of the water, air, and land surfaces in and around the United States, nor could the Consumer Product Safety Commission effectively regulate the two million companies producing the ten thousand products within its jurisdiction. The need is not for greater compassion, commitment, or technological expertise—those we have in abundance. What we require now is the willingness and the courage to make difficult choices among the many alternative demands for government regulation of private activity.

Notes

1. For detail, see Murray L. Weidenbaum, *The Future of Business Regulation* (New York: Amacom, 1980); Murray L. Weidenbaum, "The Hidden Tax of Government Regulation," *Economic Affairs*, December 1986–January 1987, pp. 14–18.
2. Paul N. Tramontozzi with Kenneth W. Chilton, *U.S. Regulatory Agencies under Reagan* (St. Louis: Washington University, Center for the Study of American Business, 1987), table 1.
3. Quoted in an interview in *Fortune*, September 10, 1979, p. 94.
4. William M. Wardell, "Therapeutic Implications of the Drug Lag," *Clinical Pharmacology and Therapeutics*, January 1974, pp. 73–96.
5. William M. Wardell, *Testimony before the Senate Committee on Labor and Public Welfare, Subcommittee on Health*, Washington, D.C., September 27, 1974.
6. This section draws on material in Murray L. Weidenbaum, "Liberation Economics: The Benefits of Deregulation," *Policy Review*, Summer 1987, pp. 12–16.
7. See George W. Douglas and James C. Miller III, *Economic Regulation of Domestic Air Transport* (Washington, D.C.: Brookings Institution, 1974).
8. John R. Meyer et al., *The Economics of Competition in the Transportation Industries* (Cambridge: Harvard University Press, 1959); Thomas Gale Moore, *Freight Transportation Regulation* (Washington, D.C.: American Enterprise Institute, 1972).
9. Marver Bernstein, *Regulating Business by Independent Commission* (Princeton: Princeton University Press, 1955).
10. George J. Stigler, "The Theory of Economic Regulation," *Bell Journal of Economics and Management Science*, Spring 1971, pp. 3–21; Sam Peltzman, "Towards a More General Theory of Regulation," *Journal of Law and Economics*, August 1976, pp. 211–40.
11. Theodore Keeler, "Airline Regulation and Market Performance," *Bell Journal of Economics and Management Science*, Autumn 1972, pp. 399–424; W. A. Jordan, *Airline Regulation in America* (Baltimore: Johns Hopkins University Press, 1970).
12. Murray L. Weidenbaum, *Government-Mandated Price Increases* (Washington, D.C.: American Enterprise Institute, 1975).
13. Martin Derthick and Paul J. Quirk, *The Politics of Deregulation* (Washington, D.C.: Brookings Institution, 1985), pp. 257–58.

14. Murray L. Weidenbaum and Robert DeFina, *The Cost of Federal Government Regulation of Economic Activity* (Washington, D.C.: American Enterprise Institute, 1978).

15. "Dick and Jane Visit the Farm: Editorial," *Omaha World-Herald*, June 15, 1976.

16. Executive Order 12291, November 27, 1974 (President Ford); Executive Order 12044, March 24, 1978 (President Carter); Executive Order 122191, February 17, 1981 (President Reagan).

17. George C. Eads and Michael Fix, eds., *The Reagan Regulatory Strategy* (Washington, D.C.: Urban Institute Press, 1984), pp. 15–41.

18. Tramontozzi and Chilton, *Regulatory Agencies*, tables 1 and 2.

19. David R. Graham and Daniel P. Kaplan, "Airline Deregulation Is Working," *Regulation*, May–June 1982, pp. 26–32; Comptroller General, *Increased Competition Is Making Airlines More Efficient and Responsive to Consumers* (Washington, D.C.: General Accounting Office, 1985); Robert E. Mabley and Walter D. Strack, "Deregulation—A Green Light for Trucking Efficiency," *Regulation*, July–August 1982, pp. 36–42; Theodore E. Keeler, *Railroads, Freight, and Public Policy* (Washington, D.C.: Brookings Institution, 1983); Thomas G. Moore, "Rail and Truck Reform—The Record So Far," *Regulation*, November–December 1983; Andrew S. Carron, "The Reorganization of Financial Regulation," *Brookings Review*, Spring 1984.

20. James L. Gattuso, "What Deregulation Has Meant for Airline Safety," *Heritage Foundation Backgrounder*, November 12, 1986, pp. 1–11.

21. Richard B. McKenzie and William Shughart II, *Has Deregulation of Air Travel Affected Air Safety?* (St. Louis: Washington University, Center for the Study of American Business, 1986).

22. Steven Morrison and Clifford Winston, *The Economic Effects of Airline Deregulation* (Washington, D.C.: Brookings Institution, 1986).

23. "Airlines Before and After," *National Journal*, June 20, 1987, p. 1586.

24. Agis Salpukas, "The Crunch at Airlines' Hubs," *New York Times*, October 12, 1987, p. 23.

25. Kenneth Labich, "Blessings by the Truckload," *Fortune*, November 11, 1985, pp. 138–44; James L. Gattuso, "Time to Complete Trucking Deregulation," *Heritage Foundation Backgrounder*, January 16, 1986, pp. 1–12.

26. Sylvia Nasar, "Productivity Perks Up," *Fortune*, September 28, 1987, p. 62.

27. Robert D. Hershey, Jr., "Airline Deregulation Debated," *New York Times*, August 28, 1986, p. 21; James L. Gattuso, "The Consumer Rail Equity Act: Returning to the Dark Days of Regulation," *Heritage Foundation Backgrounder*, June 5, 1987, pp. 1–10.

28. Lester Lave, "A New Wave of Environmental Laws Looms," *Wall Street Journal*, December 17, 1986, p. 20.

29. *American Petroleum Institute v. OSHA*, No. 78-1253 (5th Circuit, 10-5-78).

30. Peter Huber, "Who Will Protect Us from Our Protectors?" *Forbes*, July 13, 1987, p. 57.

31. The discussion between Senators Griffin and Muskie on the Clear Air Act of 1970 furnishes an insight into the contemporaneous congressional attitude. Here is a sample (*Congressional Record*, September 21, 1970, pp. S16095–96):

    Muskie: We think . . . this is a necessary and reasonable standard . . . if the industry cannot meet it, they can come back. . . .
    Griffin: . . . without the kind of scientific knowledge that is needed—without the hearings that are necessary and expected, this bill would write into legislation concrete requirements that can be impossible. . . .

On Privatization

E. S. SAVAS

"Privatization" is a clumsy neologism, but no one has come up with a better word to capture the essence of the current debate on the role of government in society. Privatization means relying more on private institutions and less on government to satisfy societal needs. Its opponents deride it as a simplistic and primitive call to turn government property and government functions over to private business. Its uncritical enthusiasts are sometimes guilty of blindly advocating precisely that. In fact the idea is much deeper and broader than that and encompasses many familiar forms.

For example, one way to privatize is to "contract out" to firms and nonprofit organizations; this is done for services that range from repairing roads and collecting trash to delivering meals on wheels for elderly shut-ins. Issuing food stamps and housing vouchers to the poor is another way to privatize and is better than having government-run grocery stores and more public-housing ghettos. Letting the competitive marketplace fill a perceived need is also privatization. Urban dwellers practice privatization when they form neighborhood safety patrols, and so do suburbanites who join volunteer fire departments.

One driving force behind privatization is primarily ideological in its roots: It derives from the widespread feeling that government has become too big, too powerful, too costly, too inefficient, and overly intrusive and dominant in daily life. According to this reasoning, although collective action clearly is necessary in a complex world, even more than in simpler tribal communities, government is not the only institution that society has for acting collectively. There are many different and versatile institutions: civic and neighborhood associations, religious institutions, charitable and fraternal organizations, ethnic clubs, businesses, unions, and so forth. Nor should one neglect the most basic institution in society, the family; after all, the family is the original department of health, education, welfare, housing, and human services. All of these are non-governmental, societal institutions in the private sector that express collective choices and take actions that benefit many. In short, they can perform many of the activities assumed by government.

But another driving force behind privatization, one that arouses much less ideological fervor, is also at work. It derives from the pragmatic notion that one can improve the performance of government functions by finding alternative ways to carry them out.

After a half century of rapid government expansion and government's assumption of numerous societal roles, it is time to pause and inspect the changed boundary line between government and the other societal institutions. It is appropriate to seek a better division of responsibilities and a better functional balance between government and private-sector institutions, so as to take advantage of the strengths of each sector, to overcome the limitations of the other, and to avoid unwarranted overdependence on either. In this way, society can best satisfy its needs.

GOVERNMENT MONOPOLIES

The starting point for determining the best roles for the public and private sectors is to compare the approaches used by each to provide services or to perform functions. When government does it, the work is carried out by government employees and it is paid for by taxes, user charges, or both. The critical weakness of traditional public services is their often unnecessary reliance on government monopolies. Considering how vigorously we oppose monopolies in the private sector, and conspiracies that would restrain competition, it is remarkably perverse that in the public sector we have done just the opposite. We have operated under the unspoken and unchallenged assumption that total reliance on a single supplier is the best way to assure satisfactory delivery of public services, if the supplier is the government itself. Yet we know how difficult it is to make any monopoly—public or private— serve the interests of its customers rather than its owners or employees. The fiction that government agencies exist solely to serve the public has long been discredited; as in all organizations of human beings, other less lofty but understandable interests are at work as well.

To justify government monopolies it is frequently asserted that "government can do it cheaper because it doesn't make a profit"; however, a growing body of empirical evidence refutes this simple-minded generality. Economists despair at the ignorance of those who mouth this myth, for competition tends to bring about efficiencies that far offset profits and therefore benefit the public.

Total and permanent dependence on one supplier, whether a government agency or a private organization, can be harmful. Without effective freedom of choice the citizen-consumer of public services can be exploited. People should have alternatives whenever possible, because when choice is replaced by compulsion, the basic relationship between citizens and public employees is drastically altered; there are no public servants anymore. Anyone who has been in the Soviet Union and dealt with officious bureaucrats, surly waiters, or rude retail clerks—all government employees—has experienced this problem in its endemic and most extreme form.

How can competition be introduced? What functions lend themselves to competition? What functions are best performed by government monopolies despite the potential hazards?

To begin with, there are some obvious functions that ought to continue in the hands of the government, even if there is some waste and inefficiency. For example, nobody would want the nation defended by Joe's Air Defense, Inc.—"Missiles Intercepted or Your Money Back!" Nevertheless, there are many ancillary functions that can be handled by contractors or franchisees, including base and equipment maintenance, office chores, and most of the activities involved in feeding, housing, and providing for the daily needs of military personnel and their families.

Aside from national defense, however, there is hardly any function that cannot be privatized, at least partly. Police protection is the local analogue of national defense, and yet there is ample room for private guards, private alarm services, and voluntary neighborhood patrols, as well as private custodial services for precinct station houses and private repair shops for police cars and radios.

Of course, not all government activities are true monopolies. For example, state schools are not the only schools: there are private schools of various kinds. Nevertheless, the government-supplied service is dominant and unavoidable; it must be bought and paid for by a family even if the latter does not want it and chooses an alternative supplier instead. In effect, then, the government service exhibits most of the properties of a monopoly.

PRIVATIZATION ALTERNATIVES

Privatization offers a way out, for it provides alternatives to unnecessary government monopolies and to other activities that need not be performed by government. There are seven different structural arrangements for providing so-called public services under privatization:

1. Contract work, where the government chooses a private contractor—whether for-profit or not-for-profit—to perform the service and the government pays the contractor.
2. Franchises, awarded by government to private organizations that perform the work and charge their customers directly.
3. Voucher systems, where the government issues vouchers (scrip or cash) to eligible recipients, who then obtain the needed service in the marketplace.
4. Producer subsidies, given by the government to service producers so that they will supply the desired service at a discount to eligible recipients.
5. The marketplace, where entrepreneurs see the need for goods and services and supply them for a price to those who want them.
6. Voluntary arrangements, where organizations recognize a need and undertake the job, through volunteers or fund raising.
7. Self-service, where a family or individual performs the service directly.

There are numerous current examples of each of these methods of privatization. The first one, contracting for service, is widely used at all levels of government. Indeed, a list of more than one hundred services that are provided by private organizations under contract to municipalities appears in Table 9-3.

Franchise service is the second form of privatization. Although in some communities local governments supply utilities, in many others franchises are awarded to provide electric power, gas, water, bus service, taxis, cable television, and hot dogs in stadiums. Increasingly franchises are used for operating recreational facilities on public property, such as tennis courts, golf courses, swimming pools, and skating rinks.

Vouchers, the third form of privatization, have been used for food, rent, medical care, cultural events, and education. Witness the extraordinary

Table 9-3
Some Municipal Services Supplied by the Private Sector under Contract

adoption service	microfilming
air pollution abatement	mosquito control
ambulance service	noise abatement
animal control	nursing services
assessing	park maintenance
auditorium and convention center	parking lots
management	parking meter collections and main-
bridge construction and maintenance	tenance
building demolition	parking ticket processing
building and mechanical inspection	patrol service
bus shelters	payroll processing
cafeteria operation	personnel services
catch-basin cleaning	planning
cemetery operation	plumbing inspection
child protection	police communications
civil defense communications	public health service
communications maintenance	public relations
crime laboratory	records maintenance
custodial services for buildings and	recreation facilities
grounds	rehabilitation of addicts and alcoholics
data processing	rehabilitation of buildings
day care	school buses
election administration	secretarial and clerical work
electrical inspection	sewage treatment
electric power	sewer maintenance
elevator inspection	snow removal
engineering services	soil conservation
family counseling	solid-waste collection
fire communications	solid-waste disposal
fire prevention	street construction
fire service	street lighting
foster-home care	street maintenance
guard service	street sweeping
homemaker service	tax collection
hospital management	test scoring
housing	towing of illegally parked autos
hydrant repair	traffic control
industrial development	traffic markings
institutional care for the disabled and	traffic sign and signal maintenance
retarded	training of municipal employees
irrigation	transit management
jail and detention	treasury functions
juvenile delinquency programs	tree planting, pruning, removal, and
keypunching	stump removal
laundry service	urban renewal
lawn maintenance	utility billing
leaf collection	vehicle maintenance
legal aid	voter registration
legal services	water-meter maintenance
library operation	water pollution abatement
licensing	water supply
management consulting	weed abatement
mapping	welfare
mental health services	zoning and subdivision control

success of the GI Bill, which was in essence a voucher program that enabled veterans to get college educations. Compelling proposals have been offered to use vouchers for elementary and secondary education, for vocational and job training, to replace wasteful an degrading forms of housing assistance, and as a form of unemployment insurance, where the job-seeker has a valuable voucher to offer a potential employer.

The fourth method of privatization, subsidies to producers, has been used for mass transit, for health care, and to build housing for below-market rental to low-income families.

The market system is the fifth and most common form of privatization. The marketplace is relied on by most Americans to provide food, clothing, shelter, and most other daily needs, as well as health care, recreation, transportation, and so on. In addition, as the demand for social services has grown, the market has been quick to respond with child-care centers, adult education, nursing homes, senior-citizen communities, and even singles bars and dating services, for example. Privatization through the market mechanism can be advanced by selling surplus government property and facilities, such as wastewater treatment plants, that might be better utilized or operated by the private sector.

The sixth privatization arrangement, voluntary service, spans the gamut from neighborhood organizations that clean streets, maintain parks, and run Little Leagues, to labor unions that distribute surplus food and fix up the homes of retirees, to charities that rehabilitate addicts and help the handicapped. Some corporations give time off to their employees to encourage their participation in such efforts.

Self-service is the final approach to privatization. The individual who brings his newspapers to a recycling center, bandages a cut, drives to his destination, or gives vocational guidance to his child is practicing self-service.

WHO SHOULD DO WHAT?

It is evident from this brief synopsis that most so-called public services can be provided either by government or by one or more of the seven privatization arrangements discussed above. How, then, does one sort through the myriad human activities in modern society and decide which ones ought to be handled in which manner? Clearly some general principles are needed.

Two characteristics of goods and services, *access* and *consumption*, suffice to sort all the goods and services into useful categories. Access refers to the ease or difficulty of denying someone the particular good. For instance, it is easy to prevent someone from taking a fish from the supermarket, unless he pays, but it is almost impossible to stop him from taking a fish from the sea. The other characteristic, consumption, can be exclusive at one extreme or common at the other. For example, consuming a slice of bread is an exclusive act, for the bread is no longer available to anyone else, but a TV broadcast is "consumed" in common, for no matter how many TV sets are tuned to a particular program, that program remains available for everyone else and has not been diminished one iota.

These two examples can be combined to define four classes of goods, as

Table 9-4
Definitions of the Four Types of Goods

	Exclusive Consumption	*Common Consumption*
Easy to Deny Access	Private goods	Toll goods
Difficult to Deny Access	Common-pool goods	Collective goods

shown in Table 9-4. *Private goods* are consumed exclusively and can be denied to anyone who does not pay for them; most store-bought goods and services are in this category. *Toll goods*, such as telephone service, are consumed in common, and the more subscribers the better, but someone who does not pay can be denied access to the network. Therefore the market will readily supply private and toll goods, and government involvement is generally not needed except to establish ground rules for market transactions, assure safety, and regulate those toll goods that are natural monopolies.

On the other hand, *common-pool goods*, like the fish in the sea, are consumed on an exclusive basis, as defined above, but access to them cannot readily be denied to anyone. In other words, they are virtually free for the taking. As a result, they can be squandered and destroyed, like whales and rhinoceroses. The market won't supply such goods and therefore collective action is needed to protect the supply.

The most problematic of all are *collective goods*, for their consumption is common and ready access is available to all. National defense is the classical good (as were city walls in earlier days), and so are lighthouses, city streets, and common grazing grounds. Many people avail themselves of such goods, but no one has to pay directly to benefit from them. Obviously, the goods won't exist for long, or at all, without collective action, and hence coercion— in the form of taxes—is needed to make everyone pay a fair share. Collective action is also needed to provide those private and toll goods that society decides are to be subsidized and provided as though they were collective goods, such as education.

Now we can join the discussions about service arrangements and types of goods, for we've seen that some arrangements cannot be used to supply some types of goods. Table 9-5 shows the arrangements that can be used to provide

Table 9-5
Types of Goods and the Arrangements That Can Be Used to Supply Them

Arrangement	*Private Goods*	*Toll Goods*	*Common-Pool Goods*	*Collective Goods*
Government	X	X	X	X
Contract	X	X	X	X
Franchise	X	X		
Voucher	X	X	X	
Producer subsidy	X	X	X	
Market	X	X		
Voluntary	X	X	X	X
Self-service	X			

each type of good. Note that collective goods can be provided by government, contract, or voluntary arrangements.

Finally, we can complete the picture by noting that each service delivery arrangement has distinctive features. No one arrangement is universally best; each has a unique combination of attributes that make it better or worse for a particular activity.

Table 9-6 describes each of the different service delivery arrangements in terms of ten important characteristics, namely, the extent to which the arrangement (1) promotes competition; (2) is responsive to consumer preferences; (3) relates costs to benefits, which influences efficiency; (4) achieves economy of scale; (5) permits redistribution of wealth to the extent desired, as determined by democratic means; (6) can be used to further other public purposes; (7) can handle services for which clear specifications cannot be written; (8) requires that there be more than one supplier or potential supplier of the service; (9) is relatively invulnerable to fraud; and (10) limits the number of government employees.

Inspection of Table 9-6 should dispel any concern that privatization inevitably imposes a greater burden on the poor. That is not the case at all. Contracts, vouchers, and subsidized franchises (for example, subsidized private bus lines) permit as much redistribution of wealth as direct government service does and as much as the public desires, because in each case government sets the terms and pays the bill. Many who oppose privatization on the grounds that it is unfair to the poor assume incorrectly that privatization requires a pure market arrangement, and they conjure up the vision of every family, rich and poor alike, having to pay individually for their children's basic schooling.

THE EVIDENCE OF PRIVATIZATION

What is the empirical evidence concerning the relative performance of these different arrangements, particularly comparing government service against the privatized alternatives? Careful studies have been carried out in the United States and in several other countries for many of the more tangible, physical (and hence relatively easy to measure) services. Detailed comparisons of government and contract work show unamiguously that the latter is significantly and substantially less costly for the same level of service, and the contract work is of equal or better quality as measured both objectively and by citizen opinion surveys. The particular services subjected to this kind of close scrutiny include fire protection, refuse collection, bus transportation, air transportation, street and highway maintenance, street cleaning, janitorial services, traffic-signal maintenance, payroll preparation, and data processing. The cost of government service in all these studies generally runs from 30 to 120 percent higher than the equivalent work performed for governments by private contractors.

Other privatization successes are reported in dispute resolution, where private firms have emerged in the marketplace for a fee; disputants save money because of speedier resolution, compared to the slow and stately pace of civil actions in government courts.

Table 9-6
Characteristics of Different Institutional Arrangements

Characteristic	Govern- ment	Con- tract	Fran- chise	Voucher	Producer Subsidy	Market	Volun- tary	Self- service
Promotes com- petition		X	partly	X	partly	X	partly	
Is responsive to consumer preferences				X	partly	X	X	X
Relates costs to benefits			X	X	X	X	X	X
Achieves econo- mies of scale		X	X	X	X	X		
Permits redistri- bution of wealth	X	X	X	X	X			
Can further other purposes	X	partly	partly	partly	partly			
Handles poorly specified services	X			X		X	X	X
Requires multiple suppliers		X		X	X			
Is relatively invulnerable to fraud							X	X
Limits the num- ber of govern- ment employees		X	X	X	partly	X	X	X

Market-oriented mail services and private "post office boxes" have joined the older, successful United Parcel Service in competing with the U.S. Postal Service. The rapid growth of this industry testifies that firms in it are satisfying the public's needs.

The Congressional Budget Office, in a major study, concluded that 80 percent of current in-house work in the federal government could be shifted to the private sector, with annual savings reaching $870 million and with a reduction of 165,000 in the number of government employees. Detailed analysis of all 235 contracts awarded by the Defense Department between October 1980 and October 1982 showed that the actual cost of in-house work had been 28 percent greater than the cost of the same work done subsequently by contractors.

The evidence is not as clear in all areas. For example, electric power supply and hospital operation are two major activities that are provided by both government agencies and by private organizations. There are conflicting data, however, as to the relative performance of each sector.

One can conclude that contracting for service is generally superior to government-provided service, presumably because competition replaces government monopolies. By now the procedures are well established for creating and maintaining a competitive environment, for writing and enforcing service contracts, and for monitoring the performance of contractors. This is not to say that every government activity that could be contracted out ought to be, because the necessary conditions for competition within the private sector may be absent; nevertheless, it seems clear that the American people can save billions of dollars annually if more government services, at all levels of government, are contracted out to the private sector.

While there is growing recognition of the benefits of privatization via prudent contracting, progress is relatively slow, even with all the pressure to reduce government expenditures. Opposition from public employee unions is predictably intense, and political patronage considerations are not entirely absent either. Moreover, regardless of the accumulated evidence and satisfactory experiences elsewhere, the lethargy of long tradition and the appeal of the vague feeling that the public interest requires public agencies and public employees often suffice to stifle change. The very word *privatization* summons opponents to the battlements, and therefore the Reagan administration, for instance, found a less inflammatory banner, "productivity enhancement through competition," under which to encourage consideration of contracting out.

NEW DIRECTIONS

Despite the modest pace of privatization in any given area, a number of new fields are experiencing privatization. It seems that private firms are able to build and operate suitable detention facilities cheaper and better than government correction agencies can! The first customer was the Immigration and Naturalization Service, which contracted for detention of illegal aliens awaiting deportation.

Private firms have begun performing air-traffic control at small airports, in the wake of the strike by government employees in 1981. Private water supply systems have existed for a long time and are common in Europe; in the United States, sales of public water systems to private firms have taken place recently, spurred by a new tax law that made such sales attractive. The result was a transition from government to franchise service. Similarly, private firms have also been purchasing or constructing, and then operating, waste-water treatment plants.

The burgeoning problems of the social security system have attracted advocates of privatization. One proposal envisions a system composed of two separate elements: an actuarially sound retirement system and a means-tested welfare system for the elderly. The retirement portion would depend on tax-sheltered individual retirement accounts and employer-sponsored retirement plans (in other words, self-service and market arrangements), while the welfare portion would remain a tax-based government service.

Space is also being privatized, in the sense that privately owned communications satellites, mapping satellites, and manufacturing facilities in orbiting space stations are moving ahead. A contrary example, however, can be found in the near-nationalization of the Continental Illinois Bank.

The sale of government land, particularly in the West, has been vigorously advocated to promote better stewardship, to encourage conservation, and to depoliticize land-use decisions. This movement hasn't gotten very far, however, because current beneficiaries of government ownership are able to graze, mine, and otherwise use the land at a much lower cost than if they owned it; why buy it if you can get nearly free use of it when "the public" owns it?

Privatization is proceeding apace in Great Britain under Prime Minister Thatcher; it is also called denationalization when it involves selling off the loss leaders in the inventory of previously nationalized companies. One of the areas attracting international attention is the sale of public housing (called "council housing" in the U.K.) at bargain rates to current tenants. Close to 10 percent of such housing has been sold. Of great political interest is the observation that the families who changed from tenants to homeowners often changed their political proclivities as well, from Labor to Conservative. This program was eyed by the Reagan administration for possible emulation in the United States. Its potential here is not nearly as great as in the U.K., however, because of differences in income levels of public-housing tenants in the two countries and because of differences in the physical nature of public housing: In the United States much of it is in multifamily buildings, whereas in the U.K. much of it consists of one-family dwellings; the latter are much easier to sell than the former.

A final international example of successful privatization: Instead of relying on government for financial support, the 1984 Olympics relied on the private sector to pay for the events in Los Angeles, selling advertising rights to commercial sponsors in an imaginative and resourceful way. The success of this novel approach is already having a major impact on the planners of future Olympics. This cannot help but influence leaders all over the world to reevaluate the potential of the private sector vis-à-vis government.

CONCLUSION

Privatization offers more and often better ways to satisfy society's need for goods and services. Most so-called public services can be privatized through one institutional arrangement or another, but each service has to be considered individually to determine which arrangement, if any, is likely to be an improvement. Sensible guidelines are available to help make those decisions.

More often than not, the real issue is monopoly versus competition rather than public versus private, as it is so often posed for rhetorical purposes. The public-private dichotomy is too simplistic a formulation, as all methods of providing services involve some role for government. Even free markets require governments to establish weights and measures, control the value of currency, and enforce contracts. Progress in achieving a better balance between the public and private sectors will be most rapid if ideology is avoided and the focus is instead placed on more efficient, effective, and equitable arrangements for providing the desired services, bearing in mind the great potential of privatization.

Nonprofit Organizations, Government, and the Welfare State

MICHAEL LIPSKY
STEVEN RATHGEB SMITH

Since the early decades of the American republic, nonprofit organizations have played a critical role in helping people in need by providing education, training, residences, counseling, and in-kind and cash support. Moreover, President George Bush has followed Ronald Reagan in calling upon nonprofit agencies to take the leading role in American society in addressing social problems. Their belief in the efficacy of nonprofits (President Bush's "thousand points of light") combined with the current political and financial constraints on government spending, suggests an even larger service role for nonprofit organizations in the future.

Nonprofit organizations invoke the images of community, voluntarism, civic dependability, and neighbor-helping-neighbor that have always exerted a powerful impression on American public consciousness.[1] However, largely as a result of this expanded role in providing services for government, these images are at variance with the contemporary reality of nonprofit service organizations. Rather than depending mostly on private charity and volunteers, most non-profit service organizations depend on government for over half of their revenues; for many small agencies, government support comprises their entire budget. In contrast to the traditional relationship of two independent sectors, the new relationship between government and nonprofits amounts to one of mutual dependence that is financial as well as technical; increasingly, the lines between public and private are blurred. For instance, a recent survey of the Child Welfare League of America concluded that government support comprised, on average, 59 percent of their member agency revenue in 1986.[2] On the other hand, government relies on nonprofits to provide social services. In 1988, fifteen Massachusetts state agencies were budgeted to spend over $750 million, about 7 percent of the state budget, to purchase from over 1,200 contractors such services as alcoholism rehabilitation, family crisis intervention, English-as-a-second-language, and daycare. Overall, the state recognizes 200 distinct types of social services in its purchase-of-service system.[3] Until recently, our understanding of the development of the welfare state in advanced industrial countries assumed that the hallmark of a progressive welfare state was a large public sector that relegated the private sector to a small residual role. In this view, the United States with its smaller public sector and larger private nonprofit sector compared unfavorably. The expansion of government contracting with nonprofit agencies calls the prevailing view into question. In the recent period, government has used nonprofit agencies to expand the boundaries of the welfare state in the United States in a host of service categories—from child abuse to domestic violence to homelessness. The result is a welfare state that is more expansive than would be the case if policy makers relied solely on the public sector.

It is also a welfare state that has compromised some of the values that the private voluntary sector contributes to social welfare provision. These values include the variety, independence, and legitimacy of community-based agencies, and the capacity of such agencies to pursue distribution policies that tolerate responsiveness to clients over equity among clients if the two values conflict.

Broadly speaking, we reach the following conclusions about the effects of government spending in nonprofit organizations and public policy. As government funding of nonprofit organizations grows, the pressures on government officials to maintain accountability over public funds increases as well. Over time, government officials respond to increased reliance on private agencies by instituting new regulations, changing contract requirements, and increasing administrative oversight. The effect is to shift the organizational norms of nonprofit agencies from their historical emphasis on being responsive to the individual to focusing more on treating all clients alike, an orientation that bears resemblance to that of government service agencies. This shift is particularly noticeable in the areas of staffing, client selection and treatment, and physical plant. Thus, government may require nonprofit agencies to hire professional staff as a condition of receiving a contract. Or government may force a contract agency to accept only client referrals from government bureaus, rather than allowing contract agencies to have the flexibility to respond to all clients in need who present themselves to the agency. Government may also require a contract agency to modify its physical plant in order to meet official standards on public safety and health. We will argue that government funding of nonprofit agencies transforms the management of contract agencies and the politics surrounding social service expenditure.

In sum, government spending of nonprofit agencies should not be viewed simply as "privatization," if this term means reducing or minimizing government involvement in policy matters by turning over responsibility to private agencies and providing them with additional funds. Rather, the new public-private funding arrangement means increased government intrusion into the affairs of nonprofit agencies, thereby altering the character of social policy and the American welfare state.

Our views are based upon systematic research on the development and growth of government funding of nonprofit agencies in Massachusetts, supplemented with research in Connecticut, New Hampshire, and Rhode Island. In addition, thirty case studies of nonprofit service agencies were conducted to assay the effects of government funding on these agencies and social policy in general. Our findings are also based upon previous research conducted for other purposes on food banks, shelters for the homeless and battered women, and rape crisis centers.[4] Further, we have drawn on our experiences as members of the boards of directors of several nonprofit service agencies.

THE GROWTH AND SCOPE OF THE NONPROFIT SERVICE SECTOR

Government support of nonprofit service agencies has expanded dramatically in the last twenty years.[5] Over 50 percent of federal social service expenditures is now devoted to nonprofit organizations; virtually none went to such sources in 1960. Advances in daycare, sheltering, counseling, employment training, and protection from child abuse and neglect have all proceeded through government contracting with nonprofit service agencies. Thus, for example, when the problems of homelessness and hunger have arisen, the predominant response of government has been to launch programs through nonprofit agencies. In many states, nonprofit organizations under contract to government deliver the publicly-funded services in categories such as daycare, foster care, protective services for children and adults, and community programs for the mentally ill and developmentally disabled.

Government purchase of social services affects vast numbers of people. A 1986 study of the nonprofit sector in St. Louis indicated that there were over 2,500 nonprofit service organizations in the metropolitan St. Louis area. Eighty-five thousand people, or 7 percent of the local work force, were employed in these agencies.[6] In 1982, over 4 million people worked nationwide for private nonprofit health, social, and legal service organizations.[7] It is undoubtedly fair to say that most of these people worked for agencies whose incomes in part reflected contract revenues. In Massachusetts, service providers to government under contract employed roughly 48,000 persons,[8] a number that compares favorably with the number of state workers involved in human services.[9] Social service agencies funded by government call upon armies of volunteers to supplement the ranks of workers and provide direction through their boards of directors. The survey of St. Louis area residents revealed that almost half of the adult population (45 percent) of the region's 900,000 adults volunteered at least once during the year in support of area organizations.[10]

The clients of nonprofit agencies make up the most important constituency of these organizations from a social services point of view. Every United Way campaign heralds the numbers of needy people its agencies serve. The report of the American Public Welfare Association that 633,000 individuals in twenty-three states received services under the U.S. government's Social Service Block Grant in 1988 undoubtedly understates by a considerable margin the numbers in these states served by all the agencies with some public funding.[11]

Until the 1960s, most nonprofit service organizations relied upon fees, donations, and in some cases endowment income for revenue. Government funding tended to be restricted to a few service categories and was generally small-scale relative to total agency revenues. Only in selected urban areas such as New York City was government funding extensive. Typically, these public funds would be used to purchase services for a child or adult when there was popular support for service provision (for example, residential care for emotionally disturbed children) but no government capacity to provide a particular service. In these cases, government rarely made extensive demands on the private agencies, relying on the judgment of the agencies' administrators on important issues such as treatment and discharge.

The substantial growth of government support of nonprofit agencies has raised the concern of many observers that government funding would have harmful effects on the independence and overall missions of nonprofits and on their viability as autonomous, community-based agencies. The concern is not simply of academic interest. Virtually every American is likely to have contact with a nonprofit service organization during any given year—whether it is a hospital, a community mental health clinic, a family service agency, or a nursing home, to name just a few of the possibilities. These organizations serve as intermediate institutions between the individual and the state, providing a vital link for the citizen and helping to shape citizens' views of themselves and their places in society. To the extent that government extends its influence into the world of nonprofit organizations, it is likely to alter the relationship between the citizenry, nonprofit organizations, and the state—perhaps fundamentally changing the life possibilities of citizens and the role of their community organizations.

THREE TYPES OF NONPROFIT AGENCIES

Before developing our analysis we need to make some important distinctions that recognize the diversity of nonprofit service organizations. Keeping the diversity of organizations in mind should help us avoid analytic difficulties encountered by earlier critics who tried to assess the impact of contracting on the nonprofit sector *in general*, without seeing that some kind of nonprofit organizations might be severely affected, while others might be unaffected.

One type is the traditional social service agency, the old-line service association such as the Massachusetts Society for the Prevention of Cruelty to Children, which was established in 1878. Founded by affluent civic leaders, these agencies typically were established many decades before the New Deal. They usually have endowments (sometimes very substantial ones), and therefore tend to be less dependent on government funds than other agencies. Often they offer many different services and programs and thus are also less dependent than other agencies on demand for any single service.

A second type of nonprofit social service organization is the agency founded within the last twenty years directly in response to the availability of government funds for job training, mental health, and other services. An example is the Key Program, a large youth services agency established in Boston in 1973 to provide community and residential services for delinquent youth. These agencies usually derive most of their revenues from government. Often they were established by social activists who used government funds to create an organization dedicated to addressing their version of social reform.

A third type of organization is the agency founded in response to unmet neighborhood or other community needs. These may be organizations devoted to solving problems experienced as local concerns, such as homelessness, hunger, or runaway youth. Or they may be established to solve problems for communities of people who are less identifiable by geography than by some other characteristic, such as shelters for battered women, respite care for the developmentally disabled, or hospices for victims of AIDS. These organizations tend to be started and staffed by volunteers or underpaid workers out of strong personal commitments to alleviate the suffering their organizations address, or to help other people realize their potential that is otherwise thwarted by social conditions. Particularly at their start, they are typically shoestring operations built on shaky financial grounds.

Seen from the perspective of their relationship to government these three types of organizations form a kind of continuum: At one pole, there are the new community-based organizations that tend to act most like volunteer associations—non-bureaucratic and held together by the freely given commitments of their members. At the other pole, there are the organizations founded in response to the availability of government funds. These tend to be rulebound, concerned with consistency, and highly responsive to the priorities of the government agencies whose grant programs were the occasion for their establishment and development in the first place. These distinctions are important, because they suggest that different types of nonprofits are affected by government funding priorities in different ways. The most pronounced shifts and the greatest conflicts with government occur among those agencies that initially resemble government least. In contrast, where nonprofit agencies arise directly in response to the availability of public funds, the impact of contracting is less pronounced, if only for the reason that such agencies have at their inception conformed to government contracting expectations. For all these agencies, however, some degree of change is virtually inevitable as government contracting increases. As we shall see during the course of this analysis, government contracts eventually create difficult organizational dilemmas for nonprofit organizations. While contracts may allow an agency to expand services, pay their staff better salaries, and move into new service areas, contracts bring administrative and accountability demands that may conflict with an agency's mission.

THE IMPERATIVES OF SERVICE ORGANIZATIONS

Public and private service organizations share many characteristics: the need to process clients through systems of eligibility and treatment, to field a staff, to be effective, and to account for financial expenditures. Also, they are expected to pursue a similar range of objectives. They are expected to be fair (equitable); to accommodate likely and unanticipated complexities (responsive); to protect the interests of sponsors in minimizing costs (efficient); to be true to their mandated purposes (accountable); and to be honest (maintain fiscal integrity).

Simultaneous pursuit of a handful of objectives, however, means that the objectives are likely to come into conflict with one another. Adherence to rules may insure equity, for example, but may be pursued at the expense of responsiveness. A guidance counselor may be fair in allocating to each advisee exactly the same amount of time, for example, but his formula would surely be counterproductive if some students needed little help and others needed special attention.

Modern governments must use universalistic criteria in client selection or develop elaborate rationales for favoring one group over another. In contrast, the different emphases of nonprofit agencies allow some nonprofit organizations to pick and choose their clients on the basis of some group characteristics, such as place of residence or ethnic background. They also allow "creaming" to a greater degree—for example, screening out clients with the lowest educational levels, severe mental illness, or in the case of private schools, children with handicaps who are disruptive or costly to serve. Such screening is rationalized as appropriate to the focused mission of the organization and because these excluded or hardest-to-reach clients are deemed to be the responsibility of the public sector.

However, government service agencies are not free from bias in client selection and treatment either, although such practices are generally unsanctioned. Workers in government agencies often discriminate against the poor through efforts to control the demand for services, despite the official policy of their agencies to serve everyone in need.[12]

In sum, nonprofit and government service organizations should not be analyzed as radically different in their approaches to clients. Rather, they should be understood as sharing the same organizational service norms, although in different measures. To understand the effects of government contracting out to nonprofit organizations, we must start with an appreciation of the different weights that governmental and nonprofit agencies accord to organizational imperatives.

EQUITY AND RESPONSIVENESS IN GOVERNMENT AND NONPROFITS

In the distribution of social policy benefits, government is overwhelmingly driven by concerns of equity. So long as scarcity of resources requires government to make choices among claimants, policy makers will seek to impose norms of equity or at least give the appearance of fairness in resource distribution. Public officials require a rationale for public action that legitimizes the fact that in the use of public resources some will be helped and others not.

Government requires not only unambiguous eligibility criteria, but also unambiguous indicators that people meet those criteria. Even if eligibility categories are clear, proof in meeting those standards must be unambiguous if benefit distributions are to be fair.[13] Unambiguous indicators include age (over 65 in social security, 3 to 21 in special education) and prior government service (for example, veterans status). Slightly more ambiguous, but still able to meet the appearance of fairness, are indicators of income and assets.

Government, to be sure, also pays attention to responsiveness. But even in some concerns over responsiveness, the primacy of equity is illustrated in the ways in which policies designed to be responsive historically have been structured to conform to norms of equity. Consider, for example, public welfare payment rules that attempt to respond to unique family circumstances and differences in work-related expenses, housing costs, and assets. To achieve responsiveness within the strictures of equity, welfare agencies have developed policies that recognize differences but are articulated in increasingly elaborate formal rules.

Nonprofit service agencies weigh equity and responsiveness differently from government. The traditional nonprofit organizations were distinguished from providers of public benefits precisely because they were particular in their choice or clients. We are reminded of this particularism by the names of many of these agencies that have come down through the years: the Catholic Charitable Bureau and the Jewish Family and Children's Bureau in Boston, for example.

Consistent with this particularism, nonprofit agencies are less concerned than government in serving all clients within a specific target group. Instead, nonprofits focus on serving clients compatible with the agency's service mission. For example, shelters for battered women tend to conceptualize their role as offering an important service alternative to traditional health and welfare organizations for some women. Government, in contrast, prefers that all agencies providing counseling service to abused women provide similar service so that a minimum standard of equivalent care should prevail across all agencies. Furthermore, there is much less need for independent verification and much more trust of clients' testimony in private nonprofit agencies than in government. Nonprofit agencies consequently invite criticism from government officials that service is being provided inefficiently or inequitably.

These general tendencies of nonprofit agencies lead to two different responses to clients that sometimes lead to conflicts with government agencies. First, if people say they are hungry, or homeless, or recently assaulted and fearful for their safety, nonprofit organizations are inclined to accept such testimony as sufficient. Government officials upholding the equity requirement cannot tolerate such an accepting attitude.

To be sure, nonprofit organizations recognize potential problems arising out of a generous intake policy. If challenged, nonprofit organizations deal in several ways with the possibility that some people will take advantage or become "freeloaders." First, they may acknowledge that there are costs to increasing the accuracy of program targeting, but calculate that they will accept a small degree of "advantage-taking" because the cost of reducing advantage-taking would be too high in organizational effort and morale. Second, they may defend their policies by pointing to the rationing impact on clients of certain barriers to seeking aid. Entry into the orbit of a homeless shelter, for example, may mean losing privacy, agreeing to accept counseling, taking a make-work job, giving up one's weapon, or exposing oneself to a religious message. Third, they may act to reduce the accessibility of services by raising the eligibility threshold for those who would take unfair advantage, or even by cutting back services if too many untargeted clients begin to appear. Rather than directly confront clients who seemed to be freeloaders, for example, a mobile van feeding the homeless in Boston simply moved to a new location when too many people who did not appear to be homeless (although they may have been hungry) began to line up for a free meal.

A second response of nonprofit agencies to clients is to reject clients deemed incompatible with their service mission or restrict their intake to clients within their primary mission area. The former may lead to creaming, with the very poor or severely disabled referred to other programs. The latter may lead to a focus on a specific community (for example, co-religionists), though citizens in other communities may need service. Either situation can lead to charges by government officials that nonprofit agencies are not providing service to the "neediest" clients, who unambiguously are deemed "deserving."

EXPLAINING THE PRIMACY OF RESPONSIVENESS

The primacy of responsiveness over equity in private, nonprofit agencies follows from their origins, the people who work for them, and their structure of accountability. Many nonprofit social service providers tend to be neighborhood or community based. Workers or volunteers in these agencies are more likely than government workers to know individual clients, their families, and their circumstances. Moreover, it is a strength of such organizations that their workers are presumed to be interested in claimants as individuals, even if they do not actually know them. For example, a shelter for battered women may be staffed by other women who empathize with the victims' plights and want to make them feel safe through personal contacts. Thus they are inclined to know people seeking help in a holistic way. Unlike government administrators of rulebound eligibility standards, providers in private service agencies resist reducing clients to their bureaucratically relevant characteristics.

Supporting these propositions is the voluntary nature of personnel in nonprofit organizations. When workers cannot be presumed to be motivated by bureaucratic incentives, other mechanisms to insure worker conformity to organizational tasks must operate. Such mechanisms include providing workers with a sense of well-being derived from valuing their work and convincing them of its importance, and supporting workers' desire to give expression to altruistic impulses. It also means that if the organization depends upon them for labor, volunteers and workers who are not primarily motivated by income considerations have a certain power in the organization. (It also follows that as agencies "outgrow" their dependence on volunteers, they will not have to cater so much to their implicit demands.)

Voluntarism in nonprofit agencies takes many forms. The newer agencies are often founded by social activists, sometimes based in religious communities, who are committed to solving certain social problems, sometimes at great personal sacrifice. They may receive no pay for their efforts and work unusually long hours. Many shelters for battered women, for example, were founded by volunteer women who had a particular vision of addressing the problem of spouse abuse.

Aside from agency founders, social service agencies are often staffed by volunteers (possibly former clients) whose work is given at least in part in exchange for the feeling of well-being they get from helping in the organization. For some who work in nonprofit organizations the transactions between providers and clients themselves may be the point of their involvement in work that otherwise seems hopeless. People volunteer or work for low pay in drug treatment storefronts, foodbanks, and legal advice centers not because they expect fully to solve the problems these agencies address, but because they find altruistic behavior rewarding.

In the more established agencies, professional staff members often work for low salaries by comparison to what they could earn in government or elsewhere. In Massachusetts, for example, salary disparities between the private and the public sector for direct care positions are said to range from 12 to 29 percent. Thus many workers in nonprofit agencies must be considered at least in part volunteers, who take at least some of their compensation in nonmonetary form.[14]

In addition, emergency services are likely to be governed by volunteer boards consisting of community activists or leaders playing traditional civic roles as supporters of nonprofit agencies. Such people may be relatively single-minded in their willingness to pursue the interest of their organization's clients without regard for competing organizational interests. Board members of traditional agencies, for example, in the past regularly permitted their organizations to make up deficits by spending the endowment, believing that they were trustees for needs that had to be met. They were also surprisingly tolerant of management that incurred annual losses. Board members of younger agencies may have come out of a social movement environment in which they too, perhaps even more aggressively, may be willing to support their agencies in pursuing responsive client policies.

SIGNIFICANCE OF DIFFERENCE BETWEEN GOVERNMENT AND NONPROFITS

Several corollaries that find their way into actual practice follow from these differences in orientations between government and private, nonprofit agencies. First, in contrast to government, nonprofit agencies are more tolerant of client selection procedures that are not based upon rigid standards of equity—both in client selection by staff and client self-selection. Nonprofit organizations are more willing to say that they can help some people and not others. Private agencies are also more comfortable with self-selection. They act as if first-come, first-served is an adequate decision rule when resources are scarce and need is great. If they apply rationing mechanisms to discourage people who perhaps are less needy, the mechanisms tend to be advisory rather than definitive.

Second, nonprofit agencies strive to be responsive to individual clients, even at the expense of other policy objectives. Government agencies, though, try to spread resources evenly over affected populations. For example, many child welfare advocates have complained over the years that the long-term involvement of some nonprofit agencies with their clients led to inappropriate, excessive treatment of many children, both in residential centers and foster care. It also meant that there were fewer resources available to a burgeoning client population. In the 1980s, government control of the purse strings and a reaction against long-term treatment has produced new policies aimed at limiting the length of time children spend in residential centers and foster care.

Third, public and private agencies to a degree are both likely to define agency clients in terms of their ability to be effective with them. But government agencies are more likely to define the scope of the client population primarily to achieve greater consistency with equity, rather than the ability of the agency to be effective. This tendency is noticeable in at least two distinct instances.

In one instance, government will define unrealistically large catchment areas that, while providing formal "coverage" for all, cannot because of distances reasonably serve many of the people in the areas. This situation commonly occurs with homeless shelters, mental health services, and food distribution centers in many rural and other underserved areas.

In another instance, government will seek to narrow eligibility criteria, for example, by lowering income limits or imposing more severe distress requirements in order to be able to serve a greater proportion of those people in the pool. Thus, government will appear to assist a larger proportion of those clients defined as eligible to receive assistance under the policy.

By contrast, nonprofit agencies are more likely than government to prefer a relatively large pool of potential clients, primarily because the pool allows a nonprofit agency to manage its client selection process in a way that is consistent with its sense of mission. Thus, a large pool of potential clients for shelters for battered women means that the shelters will be able to serve women deemed responsive to their particular treatment orientation. And shelters will be in a stronger position to reject individuals who may be perceived as potentially disruptive. This situation is particularly true of various residential programs: group care for children, emergency shelters for adolescents, and shelters for battered women and the homeless. There is also a financial consideration involved in the preference for a large client pool. Since most nonprofit agencies are of modest size and severely undercapitalized, a small pool of potential clients may be insufficient to guarantee a steady stream of clients—and hence revenue—into the agency, producing major financial and organizational strains on the agency.

The differences between government and nonprofit agencies regarding the appropriate size of a nonprofit agency's client pool is evident in the recent political conflict over participation in the Women, Infants and Children Supplemental Nutrition Program (WIC). Federal officials have strived to target aid to the poorest and most distressed women and children; nonprofit WIC distributors have wanted to retain a more expansive definition of eligibility. It is also evident in the assignment of public daycare slots to welfare recipients. In the program to distribute surplus agricultural products to the hungry, federal officials sought to persuade states to restrict eligibility to families with lower incomes so that a higher proportion of eligibles would receive free cheese and butter.

There are important political considerations in conflicts over the size of the client pool. If one's objectives include maintaining pressure on public authorities to act more vigorously with respect to a target population, it makes sense to support an expansive conception of the needy group. The larger the numbers of people who cannot receive help from a program for which they qualify, the more pressing the claim that not enough resources are being applied to a recognized problem, particularly if need cannot strictly be defined by income. This is why it is disingenuous for public officials to maintain that their interest in restricting eligibility to the "truly needy" in any program is based solely on their desire for more effective targeting. To limit program eligibility criteria is simultaneously to reduce political pressures to expand program resources to meet the need.

GROWTH OF GOVERNMENT CONTRACTING
WITH NONPROFIT AGENCIES

Despite the differences in organizational norms between government and the nonprofit sector, government officials are utilizing nonprofit agencies to deliver public services at an unprecedented rate. Let us now take a brief look at the advantages public officials believe accrue to government that may attract them to contracting with nonprofit agencies. These reasons have varied in importance to public officials over the period that contracting has been ascendant.

First, government agencies can respond to emerging service needs more quickly and effectively by contracting than by mounting new efforts utilizing public employees and public agencies. Second, public officials can purchase specialized services that would be difficult to find or develop within government ranks. Third, by using nonprofit agencies, public officials recognize that they can change program direction with relative impunity and can cut back on services more easily than they could if public employees were involved. Fourth, government agencies can take advantage of the legitimacy already won for program initiatives of private organizations while avoiding the political costs that would be associated with attempting to usurp their role. Fifth, in contracting, government shifts the political and financial risks of providing service at least in part onto the nonprofit sector.

Beyond these pragmatic reasons for encouraging contracting, other motives for contracting appear to operate as well. In particular, contracting for services is viewed by some analysts as a way to shift resources and responsibilities to the private sector, thereby reducing the role of government in public policy and halting the postwar rise in government's size and influence. This would be accomplished because of two additional advantages often thought to accompany contracting.

Sixth, government will save money, because competition among agencies bidding for government contracts will result in efficiencies spurred by competition. Finally, government will save money because nonprofit contractors tend to pay lower wages and employ volunteers, allowing government to contract at low prices. As a result of these aspects of contracting, many analysts believe a new dynamic will arise in which public services will be sustained at a high level of quality by competition in the private market.[15]

This view is in error. It is based upon a model of independent buyers and sellers, when in reality the world of government and service providers is one of mutual dependency. It is faulty because it is inherently difficult to hold human service providers accountable for the quality of performance outcomes. Hence, improvements in service quality and increased savings while holding quality constant are unlikely to be achieved in contracting for human services.

Moreover, this view neglects recognition of the political interests that form around government's new way of doing business and the new clients of government (the nonprofits) that are created by contracting activities and are thus in a position to make demands. Contracting is not simply an administrative procedure that changes the mode of service delivery from public to nonprofit (or for profit). Rather, it fundamentally alters the politics of public service delivery. Over time this new politics brings issues of equity and of community autonomy to the fore.

CONSEQUENCES FOR NONPROFIT SERVICE ORGANIZATIONS

Critics of government contracting often express concern that nonprofits may compromise their original service mission in the process of responding to government priorities.[16] However, it should be noted that government contracting requirements may alter nonprofit agencies' approaches to services and clients, even if their goals are entirely compatible with those of government. In essence, they may be forced to conform to standards imposed by contracting policy at the expense of their homegrown notions of what constitutes effective service delivery.

In the following section we discuss the trade-offs between government demands for accountability and nonprofits' conceptions of effective services in terms of three areas: staffing clientele and program, and facilities. Two caveats apply to these generalizations. First, the extent to which nonprofits will find government accountability demands onerous is likely to vary, depending upon whether the agencies had previously been independent of government influence, as suggested above in our discussion of three types of nonprofit agencies. Second, while we focus discussion on conflicts between governmental and private conceptions of service, we do not mean to imply that the contracting parties are invariably in conflict or always troubled by differences in perspectives. Our article is intended to highlight inherent conflicts under contracting difficulties and the places where differences in perspective are most likely to result in compromising requirements for the nonprofit sector.

Staffing

The people who arise to establish and direct community organizations are often not the people government officials regard as most appropriate to lead the organizations with which they contract. For example, shelters for battered women and rape crisis centers, developed and directed by nonprofessional feminist activists, have been encouraged and sometimes required to hire human service professionals as a condition of funding. Public officials have considered the founders of the shelters too ideologically oriented and insufficiently trained to meet what they regard as the therapeutic and coping needs of shelter clients. Emergency housing shelters also have been pressured to add (and have sometimes welcomed) social workers to their staffs.

If these examples illustrate government concerns over accountability, other staffing requirements demonstrate the press of efficiency considerations. In recent years, many mental health centers, job-training programs, and child welfare services have been forced to lay off professional staff as state and federal officials reduced funding support.

At times these reductions were required simply because of insufficient government funds. However, government officials also have forced layoffs because they charge that nonprofit agencies did not need as many staff members to provide quality service. For example, a traditional child welfare agency had obtained a government contract in the 1970s to provide protective services. In the early 1980s, state officials gave the agency the choice of either terminating the contract or reducing the degree of its staff's involvement with clients. The agency decided to give up the contract and has struggled financially ever since. Other agencies subjected to the same pressures accepted the state's conditions and changed their service profiles.

In the requirement to hire social workers or psychologists, staff upgrading results. In the case of staff layoffs, deprofessionalization occurs, as workers are less able to use their own judgment in responding to clients' needs. Both cases illustrate the imposition of governmentally-derived requirements on private nonprofit agencies. They also highlight that government is interested in obtaining minimum standards of care: in the case of new agencies, such as shelters established through nonprofessional auspices, government seeks to establish minimum care standards through professionalization; in traditional agencies with high levels of professional care, government concern with higher productivity leads to a reduction in professional standards.

Clientele and Program

One way in which these pressures for equity and accountability are particularly felt is in government's concern over the apparent open-endedness of enrollment in some community services. Government agencies are likely to pressure emergency service providers to establish or clarify and elaborate eligibility standards; to establish or improve and enforce eligibility verification and enforcement; to restrict the amount of service any single recipient can obtain.

These propositions can be illustrated with reference to the federal surplus-commodity distribution program. In 1982, when the program was just getting started, it emphasized giving away as much food as possible through networks of private agencies, which first had to be located and then persuaded to participate. However, when the program was cut back sharply a year later in response to food retailers' complaints that the program was hurting their sales, the federal Food and Nutrition Service (FNS) began to worry that the mismatch between the number of people eligible to receive food and the amount of food available would become too great. Accordingly, it promulgated regulations that required states to establish more precise and restrictive eligibility guidelines, and it started procedures to insure that those guidelines were being followed. The FNS later proposed regulations that would further tighten the loose verification procedures of the food banks and soup kitchens.

It is evident that in developing policy for nonprofit contractors, governments often see the contract for services as a resource by which it can achieve ancillary service goals. Government seeks not only to provide services in general, but to improve its performance in other aspects of its activities. Thus, the Massachusetts Department of Social Services (DSS) reduced the number of contracts that permitted agencies to take referrals from any source (known as open referral contracts) and instead required the agencies to take referrals only from DSS staff (known as closed referrals contracts). The state did the same with its daycare slots to support its employment and training programs for welfare recipients; and it restricted the use of some of its subsidized housing vouchers to support its policies to reduce homelessness.

In the interest of equity, government standards push nonprofit agencies to broaden their client mix. Thus, battered women's shelters have been required to expand their catchment areas and to take clients from different racial and ethnic communities. A community agency in Boston that was established to serve a predominantly Hispanic community in the early 1970s now serves clients from the entire Boston area.

Increasingly, government also imposes various limitations on the actual treatment provided by a contract agency. Battered women's shelters have been required to limit the amount of time women can stay in the shelters, although the shelters prefer to allow women to stay until they are deemed able to act independently.

Similar pressures are felt by old-line agencies whose traditional policies and practice of family social service encouraged working with the family until it was judged to be stable and well or well-enough adjusted. Government contracts, however, require the agencies to limit (say, to a year) the amount of time any single family receives counseling from a caseworker. While this shift prevents gross disparities in length of treatment, it also constrains treatment discretion by limiting the opportunity for long-term treatment for clients who need it.

Some of the same strain is currently experienced by emergency housing shelters, which must agree to maximum-stay limits when they contract with government. Here, however, there is generally agreement between government and providers that every effort should be made to limit the extent to which guests come to depend upon shelters as permanent refuges.

Finally, government applies the equity standard that the neediest should be served first to a host of nonprofit services including group care for children, emergency shelter programs for adolescents, and counseling. The result is that these agencies are now serving an increasingly disturbed client population that requires intensive service intervention. For emergency youth shelter programs, for example, this shift represents a sharp break from the founding vision of these organizations as vehicles for early treatment and prevention in a non-threatening supportive environment. In the case of counseling for children and their families, many nonprofit agencies that began to provide services under contract in the 1970s served children and families who could be described as experiencing adjustment problems. In recent years, however, these contracts have been restructured to emphasize protective services for abused and neglected children—a high priority for state government and a more profoundly needy group.

In general, government pressures toward accountability in admission to the rolls and equity in distribution will be more evident under some conditions than others. If government is paying on a per capita basis, as is the case, for example, in job training and some emergency services, government is more likely to make demands for careful scrutiny of the rolls than if it is contracting with agencies for blocks of service. Further, if quasi-objective indicators of need are utilized, such as income or participation in other government programs, government can demand accountability from agencies overseeing eligibility standards.

Facilities

Community-based services are often located in unlikely places. Although sometimes they are housed in multiservice neighborhood centers with good facilities, they are also found in church basements, dilapidated storefronts, and even private homes. Government funding is often accompanied by demands to upgrade the quality and extensiveness of the facilities. These demands range from fire code compliance to greater scrutiny over cooking and washing facilities, and more space per client.

In themselves, government demands on facilities often have some validity. But they also skew the allocation of private resources by creating absolute requirements for some concerns (which usually can be articulated quantitatively), while leaving other program components to be satisfied with what is left over. A shelter that is required to remodel its kitchen may not be able to buy the used van it considers critical to help homeless residents search for housing. If a program must hire a clinical psychologist as director at $30,000, it may not be able to hire more night staff.

In some cases, service organizations may be required to invest in facilities that they would not otherwise develop, although they have no promise of reimbursement. Residential treatment programs may remodel facilities only to find themselves stuck with them if the program is closed down or their contracts are not renewed. Small food banks and community action agencies have obligated themselves or used fundraising resources to obtain trucks, freezers, and other food storage facilities in order to serve their constituents. Yet, community action agencies are not otherwise in the emergency feeding business.

THE POLITICS OF CONTRACTING OUT

We have suggested that among their organizational objectives governments will give high priority to norms of equity. They will also emphasize accountability. Government agencies must adhere to legislative and administrative mandates across their jurisdictions. Most straightforwardly, they do so to insure that the public receives the services for which it is paying. They also do so to achieve at least two other objectives. They must provide the same service throughout their jurisdiction to meet equity needs. And they must (in theory, at least) protect the objects of their attention by intervening responsibly (as responsibility is defined in legislation or administrative action). To achieve accountability among contractors, government routinely will seek to set standards to protect citizens from harm delivered through their agents (insuring, for example, that teachers are qualified or that there are adequate sanitary facilities in daycare centers).

However, when contracting with nonprofit agencies began to grow significantly in the late 1960s and 1970s, government officials faced many impediments to imposing norms of equity on nonprofit contract agencies.

- Government contract administrators tended to be inexperienced and lacked adequate financial and personnel resources.

- Many nonprofit agencies, especially the established traditional agencies, possessed monopoly power within their service area; thus government officials were in a weak position to demand that these agencies alter their admission or treatment practices.

- Federal funding for contracted services was rising. Consequently, government officials were not required to address politically difficult choices of client and service priorities.

- In part because of the nature of many of the contracted services, government officials lacked adequate information on their contracted programs.

- Initially, government officials emphasized quick program start-up and tended to place on the back burner issues of program accountability and management.

In addition, at least in some cases, government officials may have wanted deliberately to avoid facing issues of equity and program targeting. In using nonprofit agencies under contract, the fragmented, diffuse character of the network of nonprofit agencies could obscure aggregate client and service trends among public clients served by nonprofit agencies. In a related vein, public officials may have wanted to shift the risk of addressing a particular social problem from government to the nonprofit sector. This has been particularly evident within controversial services such as family planning, day-care, and protective services. In these situations, government officials may be able to avoid facing issues of equity in service delivery.

At some stage the contracting relationship between government and nonprofit agencies usually signals an increase in the salience of an issue on the public agenda, and program support and government expenditures have tended to rise as contracting develops. Consequently, public officials come under greater pressure to impose equity standards on nonprofit contract agencies as program visibility increases. These standards include new regulations and contract requirements on client eligibility. However, government officials encounter agencies' resistance to their efforts to achieve greater accountability due in part to basic differences in ethos and priorities between the two parties in their approaches to issues of accountability. While government agencies are accountable to legislatures and public executives for execution of policy and fiscal responsibility, nonprofit organizations are subject to no such powerful sanctions.

Nonprofit organizations tend to be mission-oriented. They often arise in response to emergent social problems and remain motivated toward solving problems rather than worrying (in the short run) about agency maintenance. It is not uncommon for line workers in nonprofit service agencies to work overtime or long hours without compensation, or to accept cuts in salary if the organization falters financially. It is not unheard of for the agency executives to mingle accounts to sustain underfunded programs or to dip into an endowment to maintain current activities. Such passion for realizing an agency's mission is unlikely and borders on the illegal in the public sector. Moreover, their dependence upon local contributions and voluntarism often requires them to style themselves to attract and maintain the volunteers upon whom they depend. Nonprofit organizations to varying degrees will strive to maintain services even if their objectives conflict with articulated procedures. The mission orientation at times tends to be matched by disregard for organizational control mechanisms. Historically, accountability systems in nonprofit organizations have been crude or nonexistent. Performance indicators were lacking. Executive directors were in relatively weak positions to monitor their organizations' financial status; administrative functions tended to be underfunded. Trustees tended to be intrusive, but not excessively worried about organizational efficiency.

A CHANGED RELATIONSHIP

As contracting with nonprofit agencies has become more prevalent, several developments have occurred that give government added leverage in insisting that nonprofit agencies adhere to equity norms and accountability objectives.

First, the number of nonprofit contract agencies has increased. As a result, government has greater choice in selecting contractors, although the degree of choice still varies with the geographic locale and type of service. More choices mean that government agencies are in better bargaining positions with contractors.

Second, federal budget cuts in social spending have forced nonprofit agencies to compete far more aggressively for the remaining public and private service funds. The cuts have undermined the financial health of some agencies, leaving them vulnerable to government influence.

Third, government administrators have become more experienced in managing contracts. In addition, governments, particularly at the state level, have developed elaborate rules and regulations for the contract process and the actual delivery of service.

Fourth, state governments have improved their information-gathering capacity, notably by implementing sophisticated management information systems. Improved information can give administrators enhanced leverage in contract negotiation and bargaining with contract agencies.

Fifth, overall service demand has increased dramatically in a host of categories, including foster care, home care, child abuse and neglect, homeless shelter, and service to battered women. While increased demand gives contract agencies more bargaining power, government officials are pressured more than ever to ration services equitably in the face of high demand.

The response of government to escalating pressure for greater accountability is complicated by the mutual dependence of government and nonprofit agencies. Because of physical plant requirements and the need for specialized experience and expertise, contract agencies cannot easily be replaced. Shifting contracts from one agency to another may also be disruptive to clients. In addition, new providers cannot easily bid to provide contract services because of providers' high start-up costs.

Although some governments might like to use the threat of changing agencies to gain concessions from nonprofit agencies, the difficulty of switching providers is a major factor in pushing governments to develop more rigorous standards for nonprofit performance. Contracting for services with nonprofit agencies does not follow the competitive market model; instead, government purchase of services from nonprofit agencies is a substantially political process undertaken against a backdrop in which a market model is said, wrongly, to apply.

RESISTANCE AND ACCEPTANCE OF GOVERNMENTAL PRIORITIES

We have indicated three areas—personnel, clients, and facilities—in which nonprofit service agencies are vulnerable to government influence. Regulations in these areas significantly raise the overhead cost of operating a program and reduce the potential contribution of private revenues to operating expenditures. For example, many residential care programs for emotionally disturbed youth have been required to make expensive changes in their physical plants and hire new professionals to cope with the increased severity of illness of the children they serve under government contracts. The result is that per client costs have risen enormously. These agencies face strong disincentives to refuse government referrals or contract demands so as to keep their costs in line with their resources in the event, not uncommon, that government changes policy direction or cuts back on service contracts.[17]

To be sure, some nonprofit agencies refuse to accept the governmental emphasis on equity. The more a nonprofit agency is committed to a specific mission as opposed simply to perpetuating itself on a stable basis, the more it is likely to resist government demands that it screen clients closely for eligibility, obtain independent verification, or otherwise conform to external demands for staffing and facilities. A traditional agency in Rhode Island, for example, decided against reapplying for government contracts rather than accept the accompanying rules and regulations. The agency subsequently struggled financially for several years before it was able to stabilize its operations.

There are other strategies available to nonprofit organizations that wish to resist the impositions of government. For example, food banks have consented to new regulations, but neglected to enforce new procedures in practice. They have questioned clients about eligibility, but nonetheless screened everyone in. They have submitted false compliance reports, particularly when they believed they would not be closely checked. Agencies with little control over their admissions may try to manage their client population by discharging clients who do not fit within the organization's mission. However, such practices are increasingly difficult to pursue. Public and private funders now expect contractors to meet high standards of fiscal and program integrity. And as the era of contracting for services matures, governments have developed improved monitoring capacities. Also, financially vulnerable agencies will be reluctant to discharge clients if this would result in reductions in revenues.

Despite the service compromises nonprofit organizations may have to make, overall they tend to be attracted to government funds in order to expand or sustain their activities. There are severe costs to refusing government money, and it is increasingly difficult to accept government funds while trying to finesse the accompanying obligation. With the option of "exit" from the contractual relationship closed off, most nonprofit agencies find themselves pursuing one of the two other responses that economist Albert Hirschman has suggested are available to people or organizations confronted with unsatisfactory circumstances. They may try to change existing conditions (giving "voice," in Hirschman's terms) or to nestle closer to authorities in hopes of reward.[18]

Nonprofits may exercise their voice to try to minimize the impact of government on their organizations. In our study, nonprofit agencies routinely tried to affect contract requirements or state regulations governing their programs, either through direct action or indirectly through umbrella coalitions and state organizations. Many nonprofit agency personnel, however, are very worried about alienating government officials if they speak out about contracting arrangements. They fear that their outspokenness may lead to loss of a contract, although this is rare. But government officials can make life difficult for executive directors and their staff in many other ways. They can delay or impede nonprofit agency requests for more money or more favorable contract terms. They can request a new audit or site visit. They can make client referrals that they know are unacceptable to the agency. And they can fail to steer new contracts toward the agency. All of these actions can have a major impact on the life of the organization and the success or failure of an executive director. Thus, the effectiveness of an executive director—if defined in terms of organizational growth and stability—is tied more than ever before to good relations with government officials.

Concern over relationships with government officials is related to the other major response of nonprofits to the vagaries of contracting. This is their effort to be "model citizens"—to demonstrate their acceptance of government directives and willingness to help government officials faced with a problem. Thus some nonprofit staff leap to support government officials in legislative hearings and in the press. Some agencies, against their better judgement, accept particularly troubling or controversial referrals from government agencies (called "hot" referrals) to help defuse difficult situations that agencies are facing. They expect government officials in return to be sympathetic to future requests for rate increases or other agency priorities.

This loyalty can exact significant costs. It may corrode the morale of nonprofit staff who feel compelled to cooperate with government despite their own reservations and objections. It may also hide serious problems within agencies, since government may reward a loyal provider despite quality problems and financial difficulties.

Of course, it is often difficult to tell when private agencies support public officials because of the merits of their positions, and when they extend themselves on behalf of public officials to curry favor. No doubt both perspectives at times apply. But whatever the mix, it is difficult to escape the conclusion that the contractual relationship between government and nonprofit agencies cannot be viewed in terms of arms-length buyers and sellers of services. It is clear that the relationship is a fundamentally political one where nonprofits' programmatic and financial outlooks are often linked with the political skills and savvy of their directors.

CONCLUSION

Ultimately, our argument that developments in government contracting with nonprofit organizations vitally affect the future of the welfare state depends upon recognizing that these organizations have traditionally played a role in integrating the individual into community-sponsored activities (as client, donor, or volunteer) and in offering an alternative to public policies derived from governmental power and coercion. It is thus critical whether nonprofit organizations operate according to standards derived from the community of interest from which they arise, or whether they are operated according to standards imposed by law and the values of public agencies. We maintain that a significant change in the balance of effort and responsibility among private firms, government, and the nonprofit sector augurs an important change in the principles governing the delivery of social welfare service.[19] Changes in the capacities of nonprofit organizations affect the diversity and quality of community life.

The broad expansion of government contracting with nonprofit agencies for social welfare services has resulted in a wider role for private agencies in social service provision, and also an enhanced position for government, as public agencies become increasingly dominant in affecting the character of the services nonprofit agencies provide. Thus we see, paradoxically, not only greater dependence on private agencies for social service provision, but a heightened role for government as well, even as these developments are championed in the name of privatization.

Two other, perhaps unexpected, developments deserve comment here. First, despite the enhanced role of government in funding services, the trend toward contracting places nonprofit organizations even more certainly in the role of social welfare innovators. In the last twenty-five years, many nonprofit agencies were established, specifically to respond to the opportunity to contract with government for services in policy areas such as employment training, residential programs for the handicapped, and child welfare services. In these areas and others, government officials have made the decision that policy will be designed for and implemented through nonprofit service agencies, albeit under governmental guidelines.

In other arenas, nonprofit organizations have taken the lead in forcing social problems onto the policy agenda. In emergency service areas, where uncertainty over the size of the problem and ambiguities over eligibility make it difficult to mount entitlement programs, community agencies have forced public officials to recognize the urgency of problems. Governments have accepted the need for public action only after nonprofit groups created a clamor and demonstrated the political visibility of the issue.

Shelter programs for battered women provide a good example. Shelters were established in several cities around the country in the early and mid-1970s as service alternatives for battered women. These organizations also served as focal points for individuals interested in changing the existing laws and regulations on spouse abuse. Since then, government has responded with new funding, albeit in varying amounts in different states, and far-reaching legal changes. Many government agencies, such as the police, have adopted new procedures in dealing with domestic violence incidents.

Second, nonprofit agencies have emerged as buffers between the implacable fairness of government norms and the needs of citizens for policies that reflect responsiveness to their problems. Nonprofits can treat as special those clients who might be overlooked or treated routinely under public program standards. The executives of the nonprofit agencies interviewed for our study were very proud of their commitment to individual cases, often permitting workers to devote special attention and resources to help their clients. It is not uncommon for employees in these agencies to work on their days-off to help a client or to try to circumvent a government regulation to obtain special programmatic or financial help. This type of commitment is much more difficult to sustain in a government agency organized on the principle of treating all deserving clients alike. The need for such responsiveness is particularly evident in emergency services where ambiguities of eligibility make equal treatment norms difficult to enforce, yet the severity of the need calls for responsive treatment.

Despite these salutary developments, it is important to recognize that the ability of nonprofits to serve the role of the responsive agents in the welfare state may be in jeopardy. Cost pressures are forcing nonprofit managers to be more attentive to the bottom line. As nonprofit staff come to be viewed as government workers once removed, it becomes more difficult for nonprofit staff to depart from government expectations. The result is a welfare state with a more limited range of potential responses to any given social problem. This produces a complex social policy trade-off. Specific clients are more assured of a minimum standard of response, since less variation exists between nonprofit agencies. But responsiveness to individual clients that can enrich assistance at the local level is diminished, because nonprofit staff are encouraged or required to respond to specific social problems such as spouse abuse or homelessness in a standardized fashion.

The parents of a developmentally disabled adult living in a community residence know that this residence has to conform to state regulations on public safety, health, and coverage. These regulations reassure parents that their children are living in decent surroundings. But compliance with these regulations makes it less likely that nonprofit agencies will offer unusual service packages, take special interest in particular clients, or develop service innovations; compliance creates higher revenue demands on the agency for the same number of service units. The result is an inexorable shift away from flexibility to greater attention to the efficient utilization of staff and resources.

Government funding of nonprofit agencies enlists them as partners and allies in providing important social welfare services to the clients of government. In many states nonprofit agency staff, board members, and volunteers have played key roles in preserving social welfare services in an era of declining federal assistance. The risk is that political resources of the nonprofit sector are marshalled to support their service programs at the expense of a larger social welfare vision that the nonprofit sector traditionally projected. Among the agencies we surveyed, only a few were engaged in social issues that were not directly related to the agency, although many clients of these agencies might be better served by expanded job opportunities and increased welfare benefits and child support.

Ironically, the federal government cutbacks in spending on nonprofit service programs have actually compromised and diminished the intermediate role of nonprofit agencies as buffers between the state and individual by increasing the vulnerability of nonprofit service agencies to government influence. Moreover, these cutbacks have facilitated or encouraged a wave of regulatory efforts at the federal, state and local level designed to "allocate" scarce service resources using an equity standard and to improve accountability. In the process, the role of the citizenry in the formulation of services for the needy has been constrained. Volunteers and citizen boards are enlisted in pursuing the service agenda of government. Social provision is placed on a more equitable basis, and there may exist a broader political constituency for government social programs. However, as government increasingly penetrates the nonprofit sector it undermines the civic virtues or nonprofit organizations, such as citizen participation in service development, voluntarism, and community definitions of proper support for the needy. Those interested in establishing a balance between governmental and nonprofit organizational priorities must find within the contracting regime a way to secure the legitimate public interest in fairness and accountability, while minimizing the negative impact of government influence on community initiative, motivation, and identity.[20]

Notes

1. Robert N. Bellah et al., *Habits of the Heart* (New York: Harper and Row, 1985).
2. Karin E. Malm and Penelope L. Maza, *Sources of Agency Income* (Washington, D.C.: Child Welfare League of America, 1988).
3. Massachusetts Senate Committee on Ways and Means, *Purchase of Service: Protecting the Promise of Community-Based Care* (Boston: Senate Committee on Ways and Means, 1986), 2–3. Funding for state government contracts with private nonprofit agencies is from both state and federal sources.
4. Steven Rathgeb Smith, *Government, Nonprofit Agencies and the Welfare State*, unpublished doctoral diss., Department of Political Science, Massachusetts Institute of Technology, 1988; Steven Rathgeb Smith and Susan Freinkel, *Adjusting the Balance: Federal Policy and Victim Services* (Westport, Conn.: Greenwood Press, 1988); Michael Lipsky and Marc A. Thibodeau, "Feeding the Hungry with Surplus Commodities," *Political Science Quarterly* 103 (Summer 1988): 223–244.
5. See Pacific Consultants, *Title XX Purchase of Service: A Description of States' Delivery and Management Practices*, vol. 1 (Berkeley, Calif.: Pacific Consultants, 1979); Bill Benton et al., *Social Services Legislation vs. State Implementation* (Washington, D.C.: The Urban Institute, 1978), 110; Ruth Hoogland DeHoog, *Contracting Out for Human Services: Economic, Political, and Organizational Perspectives* (Albany: State University of New York Press, 1984), 43–46; Edward T. Weaver, *Implications of Alternative Choices to Purchase or Direct Delivery Selected Title XX Social Services*, unpublished doctoral diss., School of Public Administration, University of Southern California, May 1985.
6. Metropolitan Association for Philanthropy and United Way of Greater St. Louis, *Philanthropy in Greater St. Louis*, 6.
7. Gabriel Rudney, "The Scope and Dimensions of Nonprofit Activity" in Walter W. Powell, ed., *The Nonprofit Sector: A Research Handbook*, (New Haven: Yale University Press, 1987), 57.
8. Massachusetts Council of Human Service Providers, *Confronting Effectiveness: Social Investment in Massachusetts*, advance report, May 1988, 10.
9. These figures provide a sense of the scope of the contracting phenomenon, but they must be interpreted cautiously, because often there is no equivalence between the scope of nonprofit agencies' activities and those activities for which government purchases services. Consider the hypothetical case of a rehabilitation center of twenty beds employing fifty people for which government pays for half the beds and the rest are supported from other sources. The government contract supports the work of all the staff, and from that point of view fifty people are affected in their work by the contract. Yet, strictly speaking, it is possible that only twenty-five are paid for under the contract.
10. *Philanthropy in Greater St. Louis*, 6.
11. American Public Welfare Association (APWA), *A Statistical Summary of the Voluntary Cooperative Information System (VCIS) Social Services Block Grant (SSBG) Data for FY 1985* (Washington, D.C.: APWA, 1988), 12.
12. See Michael Lipsky, *Street Level Bureaucracy* (New York: Russell Sage, 1980), chap. 8.
13. It is no good to have clearly defined eligibility slots if evidentiary standards are slack. A residency requirement only works to insure equity among service recipients if proof of residency is required, standards of proof elaborated (a lease, an identification card, a postmarked letter), and the requirements enforced.
14. The gaps in salaries between public and private workers is a matter of growing concern within the nonprofit community. In Massachusetts, this concern has led to ongoing political action to gain legislative approval for salary upgrading to correct disparities. See "More Salary Upgrading Issues," *The Provider* 8 (June 1987): 5.

15. Many public choice economists subscribe to this view. Their arguments are reviewed by DeHoog, *Contracting Out*, 7. Also see Peter F. Drucker, *The Age of Discontinuity* (New York: Harper & Row, 1969), chap. 10.
16. See Nathan Glazer, "Towards a Self-Service Society," *The Public Interest* 70 (Winter 1983): 63–90. This view is disputed by, among others, Ralph M. Kramer, "Voluntary Agencies and Personal Social Services" in Powell, ed., *The Nonprofit Sector*, 240–257.
17. See Steven Rathgeb Smith, "The Changing Politics of Child Welfare Services: New Roles for Government and the Nonprofit Sector," *Child Welfare* 68 (May-June 1989): 289–299.
18. Albert O. Hirschman, *Exit, Voice and Loyalty* (Cambridge, Mass.: Harvard University Press, 1970).
19. See Michael Walzer, *Spheres of Justice: A Defense of Pluralism and Equality* (New York: Basic Books, 1983), 84–94; also Michael Walzer, "Toward a Theory of Social Assignments" in Winthrop Knowlton and Richard Zeckhauser, eds., *American Society: Public and Private Responsibilities* (Cambridge, Mass.: Harvard University Press, 1986), chap. 4.
20. This research was funded by the Future of the Welfare State project of The Ford Foundation. We have also drawn upon earlier research on emergency food distribution programs supported by the William H. Donner Foundation and on services for victims of crime supported by the National Institute of Mental Health. We are grateful to Paul Dimaggio, Peter Dobkin Hall, Henry Hansmann, Ira Katznelson, Ralph Kramer, Reid Lifset, Robert Morris, Alice O'Connor, and Edward T. Weaver for helpful comments on earlier drafts of this paper. For administrative and secretarial assistance, we are grateful as well to Tobie Weiner.

10

REFORMING PUBLIC ADMINISTRATION?

No "real world" activity or academic field can stand still even if you want it to. Events—"real world" *and* intellectual—continue, and society changes.

Change is increasingly rapid in American life. If public administration and public administrators are to retain their vitality, they must constantly be in the process of adaptation.

A central theme in this edition of *Current Issues in Public Administration* is to understand and overcome *mal*administration in government. A broader question is whether it is time to reform public administration in the United States. The two articles in this final chapter deal with proposals for reform.

The first article is by David Osborne and Ted Gaebler, and is drawn from their already well-known book, *Reinventing Government*. Osborne and Gaebler seek movement from Weberian, centralized, hierarchical bureaucracies to decentralized, mission-driven, entrepreneurial organizations.

In an extensive assessment of reform trends, Michael Barzelay seeks what he contends is a whole new pattern for public administration, from the bureaucratic paradigm to the post-bureaucratic paradigm. Barzelay seeks public agencies that produce results that citizens value, and he seeks public managers who focus on the citizen, the customer of public services.

For Osborne and Gaebler and for Barzeley, some of this is old wine in new bottles. Some aspects of their reform agenda also seem contradictory and often we are left without a map. Others might say that they build on myths in American political culture that something fundamental in public administration needs correcting and that public administration is somehow less effective than business administration, that government's clients are less satisfied than the customers of business.

Still, the orientation of the proposed reforms is clear enough and—especially in the face of public concern about governmental agencies—merits careful consideration by administrative leaders and scholars of public administration. They ask us to go beyond any parochial interest in a public bureaucracy and consider carefully new approaches to public service, to serving the public interest.

There are two basic questions raised by these reform proposals, in some ways another effort at a "new public administration":

- What are some of the proposals for reforming public administration?

- Given what you have learned here and elsewhere, how would you assess the reform proposals as well as their likelihood for success?

In reviewing the entire collection of articles in this book, you might ask yourself:

- What is public administration?

- How is it different from business administration, and what effects do these differences have?

- What are the most important issues in the field generally as well as in specific areas of concern, like budgeting, personnel management, planning, intergovernmental administration, and accountability?

Reinventing Government

DAVID OSBORNE
TED GAEBLER

Our thesis is simple: The kinds of governments that developed during the industrial era, with their sluggish centralized bureaucracies, their preoccupation with rules and regulations, and their hierarchical chains of command, no longer work very well. They accomplished great things in their time, but somewhere along the line they got away from us. They became bloated, wasteful, ineffective. And when the world began to change, they failed to change with it. Hierarchical, centralized bureaucracies designed in the 1930s or 1940s simply do not function well in the rapidly changing, information-rich, knowledge-intensive society and economy of the 1990s. They are like luxury ocean liners in the age of supersonic jets: big, cumbersome, expensive, and extremely difficult to turn around. Gradually, new kinds of public institutions are taking their place.

Government is hardly leading the parade; similar transformations are taking place throughout American society. American corporations have spent the last decade making revolutionary changes: decentralizing authority, flattening hierarchies, focusing on quality, getting close to their customers—all in an effort to remain competitive in the new global marketplace. Our voluntary, nonprofit institutions are alive with new initiatives. New "partnerships" blossom overnight—between business and education, between for-profits and nonprofits, between public sector and private. It is as if all institutions in American life were struggling to adapt to some massive sea change—striving to become more flexible, more innovative and more entrepreneurial.

Most of our leaders still tell us that there are only two ways out of our repeated public crises: we can raise taxes, or we can cut spending. For almost two decades, we have asked for a third choice. We do not want less education, fewer roads, less health care. Nor do we want higher taxes. We want better education, better roads, and better health care, for the same tax dollar.

Unfortunately, we do not know how to get what we want. Ronald Reagan talked as if we could simply go into the bureaucracy with a scalpel and cut out the pockets of waste, fraud, and abuse.

But waste in government does not come tied up in neat packages. It is marbled throughout our bureaucracies. It is embedded in the very way we do business. It is employees on idle, working at half speed—or barely working at all. It is people working hard at tasks that aren't worth doing, following regulations that should never have been written, filling out forms that should never have been invented.

Waste in government is staggering, but we cannot get at it by wading through budgets cutting line items. As one observer put it, our governments are like fat people who must lose weight. We need to get them eating less and exercising more; instead we cut off a few fingers and toes.

To melt the fat, we must change the basic incentives that drive our governments. Our more entrepreneurial governments have shown us the way; the lessons are there. Yet few of our leaders are listening. Too busy climbing the rungs to their next office, they don't have time to stop and look anew. So they remain trapped in old ways of looking at our problems, blind to solutions that lie right in front of them. As the great economist John Maynard Keynes once noted, the difficulty lies not so much in developing new ideas as escaping from old ones."

(Osborne and Gaebler offer ten principles of entrepreneurial government. What follows is the essence of these principles . . . —Ed.)

1. CATALYTIC GOVERNMENT: STEERING RATHER THAN ROWING

During the mid '80s, mayors and governors and legislators chained themselves to the wagon of taxes and services. This was fine as long as tax revenues were rising 5.3 percent a year, as they did from 1902 through 1970. But when economic growth slowed and fiscal crisis hit, the equation changed. Now when problems appeared and voters demanded solutions, public leaders had only two choices. They could raise taxes, or they could say no. For officials who wanted to be reelected, this was no choice at all.

In Washington, our leaders escaped the dilemma by borrowing money. But in state and local government, where budgets have to balance, they began to look for answers that lay somewhere between the traditional yes and no. They learned how to bring community groups and foundations together to build low-income housing; how to bring business, labor, and academia together to stimulate economic innovation and job creation; how to bring neighborhood groups and police departments together to solve the problems that underlay crime. In other words, they learned how to facilitate problem solving by catalyzing action throughout the community—how to steer rather than row.

Most people have been taught that public and private sectors occupy distinct worlds; that government should not interfere with business, and that business should have no truck with government. This was a central tenet of the bureaucratic model. But as we have seen, governments today—under intense pressure to solve problems without spending new money—look for the best method they can find, regardless of which sector it involves. There are very few services traditionally provided by the public sector that are not today provided somewhere by the private sector—and vice versa. Businesses are running public schools and fire departments. Governments are operating professional sports teams and running venture capital funds. And nonprofits are rehabilitating convicts, running banks, and developing real estate. Those who still believe government and business should be separate tend to oppose these innovations, whether or not they work. But the world has changed too much to allow an outdated mind-set to stifle us in this way. "We would do well" as Harlan Cleveland writes in *The Knowledge Executive*, "to glory in the blurring of public and private and not keep trying to draw a disappearing line in the water."

2. COMMUNITY-OWNED GOVERNMENT: EMPOWERING RATHER THAN SERVING

George Latimer, former mayor of St. Paul, likes to quote Tom Dewar, of the University of Minnesota's Humphrey Institute, about the dangers of "clienthood":

> Clients are people who are dependent upon and controlled by their helpers and leaders. Clients are people who understand themselves in terms of their deficiencies and people who wait for others to act on their behalf. Citizens, on the other hand, are people who understand their own problems in their own terms. Citizens perceive their relationship to one another and they believe in their capacity to act. Good clients make bad citizens. Good citizens make strong communities.

Clienthood is a problem that emerged only as our industrial economy matured. Before 1900, what little control existed over neighborhoods, health, education, and the like lay primarily with local communities, because so many products and services, whether public or private, were produced and sold locally. It was only with the emergence of an industrial economy of mass production that we began to hire professionals and bureaucrats to do what families, neighborhoods, churches, and voluntary associations had done.

We started with the best intentions, to heal the new wounds of an industrial, urban society. We moved ahead rapidly when the economic collapse of the Depression strained the capacities of families and communities to the breaking point. And we continued on after the depression, as prosperity and mobility loosened the old bonds of geographic community, leaving the elderly far from their children, the employed uninvolved in their neighborhoods, and the churches increasingly empty. But along the way we lost something precious. The progressive confidence in "neutral administrators" and "professionalism" blinded us to the consequences of taking control out of the hands of families and communities.

AIDS catalyzed perhaps the most profound shift from the old model to the new. "The San Francisco gay and lesbian community adopted the hospice model," explains David Schulman, who runs the Los Angeles City Attorney AIDS/HIV Discrimination Unit. "They got teams of friends and volunteers together to care for people with AIDS at home—at a fraction of the cost of hospital care. It not only works better, it helped San Francisco cope with a problem that could have bankrupted it."

In a powerful article in the *Washington Monthly*, Katherine Boo described the process. It began when a gay nurse at San Francisco General Hospital, Cliff Morrison, convinced his superiors to let him suspend the normal hierarchical, bureaucratic rules on the AIDS ward. He let patients set visiting rules, recruited hundreds of volunteers to help AIDS patients—often just to sit with them—and set up a special kitchen and other facilities.

But "a comfortable hospital is still a hospital," as Boo put it. So Morrison and his staff "began suturing together a network of local clinics, hospices, welfare offices, and volunteers that would get patients out of the ward and back into the community." For two years Morrison spent much of his time "battling the higher-ups." But when San Francisco's average cost of AIDS treatment dropped to 40 percent the national average, they finally understood.

3. COMPETITIVE GOVERNMENT:
INJECTING COMPETITION INTO SERVICE DELIVERY

Phoenix has used competition not only in garbage collection but in landfill operation, custodial services, parking lot management, golf course management, street sweeping, street repair, food and beverage concessions, printing, and security. Between 1981 and 1984, it moved from 53 major private contracts to 179. The city eventually decided that ambulance service, street sweeping, and maintenance of median strips were better handled by public employees. But overall, the city auditor estimates savings of $20 million over the first decade, just in the difference between the bids the city accepted and the next lowest bid. Since competition has forced all bid levels down, this is but a fraction of the real savings.

City Auditor Jim Flanagan has overseen the process from the beginning. There is no truth to the old saw that business is always more efficient than government, he has learned. The important distinction is not public versus private, it is monopoly versus competition: "Where there's competition you get better results, more cost-consciousness, and superior service delivery."

In government, of course, monopoly is the American way. When the Progressives embraced service delivery by administrative bureaucracies, they embraced monopoly. To this day we deride competition within government as "waste and duplication." We assume that each neighborhood should have one school, each city should have one organization driving its buses and operating its commuter trains. When costs have to be cut, we eliminate anything that smacks of duplication—assuming that consolidation will save money. Yet we know that monopoly in the private sector protects inefficiency and inhibits change. It is one of the enduring paradoxes of American ideology that we attack private monopolies so fervently but embrace public monopolies so warmly.

Competition is here to stay, regardless of what our governments do. In today's fast-moving marketplace, the private sector is rapidly taking market share away from public organizations. Public schools are losing ground to private schools. The Postal Service is losing ground to Federal Express and UPS. Public police forces are losing ground to private security firms, which now employ two out of every three security personnel in the nation.

We can ignore this trend and continue with business as usual, watching fewer and fewer people use public institutions. We can sit idly by as a vicious cycle unwinds in which the less people depend on government the less they are willing to finance it, the less they finance it the worse it gets, and the worse it gets the less they depend on it. Or we can wake up—as entrepreneurial leaders from Phoenix to East Harlem to Minnesota have—and embrace competition as a tool to revitalize our public institutions.

The choice is not quite as stark as it would be in a competitive marketplace: compete or die. But it is stark enough. Our public sector can learn to compete, or it can stagnate and shrink until the only customers who use public services are those who cannot afford an alternative.

4. MISSION-DRIVEN GOVERNMENT: TRANSFORMING RULE DRIVEN ORGANIZATIONS

Missions do not respect turf lines. In his book *Neighborhood Services*, John Mudd, a former New York City official, put it this way: "If a rat is found in an apartment, it is a housing inspection responsibility; if it runs into a restaurant, the health department has jurisdiction; if it goes outside and dies in an alley, public works takes over." Similarly, if a poor woman needs health care, she must sign up with Medicaid; if she needs money, she must visit the welfare department; if she needs a job, she must find her way through a maze of training and placement programs; if she needs housing, she must negotiate a similar maze. Improving the lives of the poor is the core mission of none of these agencies or programs. Each simply provides a discrete service.

Organizations built around turf rather than mission tend to be schizophrenic. Commerce departments that handle matters related to business— rather than to a particular mission—must simultaneously regulate existing businesses and try to recruit new businesses. Welfare departments that handle the welfare turf—rather than a mission of helping the poor—often urge people to get jobs with one hand, while stripping those who succeed of their health coverage with the other.

The solution is to reorganize around mission, not turf. When George Latimer became mayor of St. Paul, five organizations dealt with planning and development: the Port Authority, the Housing and Redevelopment Authority, the Office of City Planning, the Community Development Office, and the Planning Commission. All five charged off in different directions. Latimer pushed through a reorganization that left three agencies, each focused on a specific mission and each extraordinarily effective in pursuing that mission.

5. RESULTS-ORIENTED GOVERNMENT: FUNDING OUTCOMES NOT INPUTS

Rewarding success may be common sense, but that doesn't make it common practice. In education, we normally reward failure. "If you're failing, you qualify for aid," explains East Harlem's Sy Fliegel. "If you're doing well, then you lose the aid." In public safety, we also reward failure: when the crime rate rises, we give the police more money. If they continue to fail, we give them even more. In public housing, we reward failure: Under federal funding formulas, the better a local housing authority performs, the less money it gets from HUD.

Rewarding failure creates bizarre incentives. It encourages school principals to accept the status quo. It encourages police departments to ignore the root causes of crime and simply chase criminals. It discourages housing authorities from working to improve their operations.

Our tendency to reward failure has literally crippled our efforts to help the poor. Most of the money we spend on the poor—welfare, food stamps, Medicaid, public housing, housing vouchers, child care vouchers—rewards failure, because it goes only to those who remain poor.

If a welfare recipient saves enough to buy a car so she can look for work, her grant is reduced. If she finds a job, she not only loses her welfare check, she loses her Medicaid coverage (after a year), her food stamps are reduced, and if she lives in public housing, her rent often triples. One study, done in Louisville, showed that a public housing resident with two preschool children had to earn $9 an hour in 1989 just to break even with the total welfare package. And Louisville is not an expensive place to live; elsewhere the figure would be higher.

Under these circumstances, why would a single mother with two or three children ever leave welfare? This explains why even our most effective efforts to move people into jobs seem never to shrink the welfare rolls.

Not only do we punish those who get off welfare, we require little of those who stay on. In fact, we call programs like welfare "entitlements" precisely because people are "entitled" to them, regardless of how they behave. The combination of rewarding failure and expecting nothing in return for benefits breeds dependency—undermining people's motivation to improve their lives.

Healthy relationships are built on mutual obligations. If we expect nothing from people, we usually get it. But if we expect effort in return for what we give, we usually get that. Louisville Housing Services is extremely strict about mortgage payments from the former public housing tenants who buy its condominiums. "If you raise the expectations," says Director David Fleischaker, "people will jump through the hoops."

Increasingly, governments are beginning to build demands for performance into their poverty programs. The federal Family Support Act in 1988 required many welfare recipients to participate in education, training, or work. Minnesota's Learnfare initiative requires teenage mothers of school age to attend school if they want welfare. Wisconsin's Learnfare program penalizes welfare families when their teenage children miss three days of school without a written excuse. Arkansas requires the social security numbers of both parents when birth certificates are issued, then uses that information to track down absent fathers and demand parental support for welfare children.

6. CUSTOMER-DRIVEN GOVERNMENT: MEETING THE NEEDS OF THE CUSTOMER, NOT THE BUREAUCRACY

As we become a society dominated by knowledge workers, we are also breaking into subcultures—each with its own values and life-style, each watching different things on television, each shopping at different kinds of stores, each driving different kinds of cars. We have been transformed from a mass society with a broad and fairly homogeneous middle class to a mosaic society with great cultural diversity, even within the middle class. We have come to expect products and services customized to our own styles and tastes, from television networks to restaurants to beer.

And yet traditional public institutions still offer one-size-fits-all services. Traditional education systems still deliver a "brand X" education. Traditional housing authorities still offer an identical apartment in a cluster of identical high-rises. Traditional public libraries still offer only books, newspapers, and magazines. When consumers accustomed to choices confront public institutions that offer standardized services, they increasingly go elsewhere.

To cope with these massive changes, entrepreneurial governments have begun to transform themselves. They have begun to listen carefully to their customers, through customer surveys, focus groups, and a wide variety of other methods. They have begun to offer their customers choices—of schools, of recreation facilities, even of police services. And they have begun to put their customers in the driver's seat, by putting resources directly in their hands and letting them choose their service providers.

This takes competition a step further: rather than government managers choosing service providers in a competitive bidding process, it lets each *citizen* choose his or her service provider. It establishes accountability to customers. "I can't think of a better mechanism for accountability than parental choice," says Sy Fliegel, of East Harlem's District 4. "If you begin to see that youngsters are not coming to your school, that is the highest form of evaluation."

To make their public institutions as customer-driven as businesses, in other words, entrepreneurial governments have learned to finance them like businesses. If schools lose money every time a student departs—as in Minnesota—do teachers and administration act differently? Of course. If motor vehicle offices were paid only when they processed driver's licenses or registrations—so the more they processed, the more money they received—would their employees act differently? You bet. With the consequences of attracting customers so clear, the scramble to cut waiting times would be intense. We might even find offices staying open evenings and Saturdays, operating drive-by windows, and advertising the shortest waiting lines in town!

7. ENTERPRISING GOVERNMENT: EARNING RATHER THAN SPENDING

Our budget systems drive people to spend money, not to make it. And our employees oblige. We have 15 million trained spenders in American government, but few people who are trained to make money. In most governments, few people outside of the finance and revenue departments even think about revenues. No one thinks about *profits*. Can you imagine the creativity our public employees would turn loose if they thought as much about how to *make* money as they do about how to *spend* it?

Many readers remember the 1984 Olympics. Eight years before, in Montreal, the Olympics had rolled up a $1 billion public debt—a debt Canadians will still be paying off in the year 2000. But the Los Angeles Olympic Organizing Committee, formed about the time Proposition 13 passed in California, understood that the citizens of Los Angeles were not about to pay $1 billion to subsidize the Olympics. So they spent three years convincing the International Olympic Committee that they could break the pattern of 85 years and finance the Olympics without public money.

The Olympic Committee finally agreed, and the organizers went to work. They recycled old facilities. They drummed up corporate sponsors. They recruited 50,000 volunteers—not just to park cars, but to organize transportation, to feed thousands of people from 118 countries, and to help with a sophisticated antiterrorist system. The organizing committee, led by civic entrepreneur Peter Ueberroth, painted a vision that included not only spending money but making money. And the 1984 Olympics turned a profit of $225 million.

Pressed hard by the tax revolts of the 1970s and the 1980s and the fiscal crisis of the early 1990s, entrepreneurial governments are increasingly following Ueberroth's example. They are searching for nontax revenues. They are measuring their return on investment. They are recycling their money, finding the 15 or 20 percent that can be redirected. Some are even running for-profit enterprises.

8. ANTICIPATORY GOVERNMENT: PREVENTION RATHER THAN CURE

In an age when change comes with frightening rapidity, future-blindness is a deadly flaw. "We've all seen companies that were exceptionally well run or cities that were well run—that did everything just right—and suddenly the environment changed around them and they fell apart," says Bill Donaldson, a city manager renowned for his entrepreneurial leadership in Scottsdale, Arizona; Tacoma, Washington; and Cincinnati, Ohio.

In today's global village, events in Japan or Kuwait can suddenly turn our world upside down. Ask the Rust Belt states, which saw entire industries die in the early 1980s. Or ask the oil states, which saw their tax revenues drop through the floor when the price of oil collapsed. "For a long time, government could be somnolent," says political scientist John Bryson. "But now we're sleeping on waterbeds—and we're not alone in the bed. When anybody moves in the bed, we wake up."

Fortunately, the pendulum appears finally to be swinging the other way. New governors in three of our largest states—California, Florida, and Illinois—have made prevention a central theme of their administrations. States, cities, and counties are increasingly banning the sale of unnecessary pollutants: ozone-depleting chemicals, polystyrene foam cups, nonrecyclable plastic packaging. States are shifting dollars from high-technology medicine designed to prolong life for the already feeble to preventive medicine designed to give newborns a healthy start.

"How much better to provide prenatal care to assure 50 or 60 healthy newborns than to pay for neonatal care for one unhealthy baby," says Governor Pete Wilson of California. "How much better to prevent pregnant women from using drugs, than to suffer an epidemic of drug babies."

Anticipatory governments do two fundamental things: they use an ounce of prevention, rather than a pound of cure; and they do everything possible to build foresight into their decision making.

In a political environment, in which interest groups are constantly pressing public leaders to make short-term decisions, neither is easy. Hence anticipatory governments have been forced to change the incentives that drive their leaders. They have developed budget systems that force politicians to look at the 10-year implications of all spending decisions. They have developed accounting methods that force politicians to maintain the programs and infrastructure they build. And they have begun to attack the electoral process—with its political action committees, campaign contributions, and 30-second sound bites—that produces future-blind politicians.

9. DECENTRALIZED GOVERNMENT: FROM HIERARCHY TO PARTICIPATION AND TEAMWORK

Today information is virtually limitless, communication between remote locations is instantaneous, many public employees are well educated, and conditions change with blinding speed. There is no time to wait for information to go up the chain of command and decisions to come down. Consider the school principal who discovers students wearing beepers to stay in contact with their superiors in the drug trade. In a centralized system, the principal asks the school board to promulgate a regulation about beepers. By the time a decision comes down, six months later, the students are carrying mobile phones—if not guns.

In today's world, things simply work better if those working in public organizations—schools, public housing developments, parks, training programs—have the authority to make their own decisions.

In the information age, "the pressure for accelerated decision-making slams up against the increased complexity and unfamiliarity of the environment about which the decisions must be made," Alvin Toffler wrote in *Anticipatory Democracy*. The result is "crushing political overload—in short, political future shock."

Many public managers believe that unions are the greatest obstacle standing in the way of entrepreneurial government. Certainly unions resist changes that threaten their members' jobs—as any rational organization would. But most entrepreneurial managers tell us that unions have not been their primary obstacle. The real issue, they believe, is the quality of management. "Labor-management problems are simply a symptom of bad management," says John Cleveland, who ran the Michigan Modernization Service. "The issue in all organizations is the quality of top managers. And traditionally, in political environments, the top appointees have no management experience. They don't stay around very long, and they don't pay much attention to management."

When the consulting firm Coopers & Lybrand conducted it's Survey on Public Entrepreneurship, it found that local government executives said "governmental regulations," "institutional opposition," and "political opposition" were the greatest barriers to productivity improvements. "Organized labor opposition" ranked fourth out of six choices.

The rank and file are "anxious to help make changes," says Rob McGarrah of the American Federation of State, County and Municipal Employees (AFSCME). They understand what a poor job many public institutions do. If change means losing pay or giving up collective bargaining, they're not interested. "But if it's a question of new opportunities, our people are hungry for new opportunities."

Public sector unions are in much the same position as their private sector counterparts were when foreign competition decimated so many American industries. They can resist change and watch their industry decline. Or they can work with management to restructure their organizations and regain the trust of their customers—the taxpaying public.

10. MARKET-ORIENTED GOVERNMENT: LEVERAGING CHANGE THROUGH THE MARKET

If you had to set out to buy a home in 1930, you would have saved up 50 percent of the purchase price for a down payment and applied at your local bank for a five-year mortgage. That was how people bought houses in 1930, because that was how banks did business. During the New Deal, Franklin Roosevelt's Federal Housing Administration (FHA) pioneered a new form of mortgage, which required only 20 percent down and let the borrower repay over 30 years. Other government corporations created a secondary market, so banks could resell these new loans. And the banking industry converted. Today we take our 30-year, 20 percent down payment mortgages for granted, because the federal government changed the marketplace. Ask yourself: would we be better off if FDR had created half a dozen low- and moderate-income housing programs?

American governments have always used market mechanisms to achieve their goals to one degree or another. We have long used tax incentives to influence individual and corporate spending. We have long used zoning to shape the growth of our communities. We have always set the rules of the marketplace—and often changed them when we wanted different outcomes.

But when confronted with a problem, most people in government instinctively reach for an administrative program. They believe their job is to "run things"—not to structure a marketplace. They share an unspoken assumption with a deputy mayor of Moscow described to us by E.S. Savas. An old guard Communist, he listened skeptically as Savas discussed the need for a variety of service delivery strategies in America's diverse and complex cities. Finally he announced, with great finality: "You cannot have each station master making up the railroad schedule! It's got to be centralized; somebody's got to control it."

In reality, of course, cities are not much like railroads. They don't have master schedules. They don't operate on one set of rails. They don't have one task. Cities are much more like markets: vast, complex aggregations of people and institutions, each constantly making decisions and each adjusting to the other's behavior based on the incentives and information available to them.

In a city, or state, or nation, managers cannot make up "the schedule" or "control" the decisions. They can manage administrative programs, which control specific activities. They could even manage a railroad. But to manage the entire polity, they must earn how to steer. . . . And perhaps the most powerful method of steering is structuring the marketplace: creating incentives that move people in the direction the community wants to go, while letting them make most of the decisions themselves.

Much of what we have discussed . . . could be summed up under the rubric of market-oriented government: not only systems change, but competition, customer choice, accountability for results, and of course, public enterprise. But market mechanisms are only half the equation. Markets are impersonal. Markets are unforgiving. Even the most carefully structured markets tend to create inequitable outcomes. That is why we have stressed the other half of the equation: the empowerment of communities. To complement the efficiency and effectiveness of market mechanisms, we need the warmth and caring of families and neighborhoods and communities. As entrepreneurial governments move away from administrative bureaucracies, they need to embrace both markets and community. In Washington, this would be called moving right and left at the same time. The political media are quick to label "conservative" those who embrace markets and "liberal" those who empower communities. But these ideas have little to do with traditional notions of liberalism or conservatism. They do not address the goals of government, they address its methods. They can be used to implement any agenda. They can help a community or nation wage war on poverty, if that is its priority, or lower taxes and cut spending, if that is its priority. *Reinventing Government* addresses how governments work, not what governments do. And regardless of what we want them to do, don't we deserve governments that work again?

PUTTING IT ALL TOGETHER

Our map is complete. It is now yours to use. We hope that you find it a helpful guide in the process of changing your governments. Used almost as a check list, the ten principles offer a powerful conceptual tool. One can run any public organization or system—or any of society's problems—through the list, and the process will suggest a radically different approach from that which government would traditionally take. This is the checklist's ultimate value: the power to unleash new ways of thinking—and acting.

The Post-Bureaucratic Paradigm in Historical Perspective

MICHAEL BARZELAY
(with the collaboration of BABAK J. ARMAJANI)

The increasingly common use of such terms as *customers, quality, service, value, incentives, innovation, empowerment,* and *flexibility* by people trying to improve government operations indicates that the bureaucratic paradigm is no longer the only major source of ideas and argumentation about public management in the United States.[1] In the search for better performance, some argue for deregulating government.[2] Others make the case for reinventing government, a concept that encourages Americans to take note of marked changes in operating practices taking place in an array of public activities.[3] As a challenge to conventional thinking, many government agencies are investing millions of dollars in training programs structured by a conceptual system that includes customers, quality, value, process control, and employee involvement.[4] To increase flexibility and financial responsibility, some advocate a vast expansion of exchange and payment relationships in place of general fund financing; many also argue for utilizing competition as a device for holding operating units of government accountable to their customers.[5] Among the programmatic concepts that have arisen from studied criticism of the ways in which the bureaucratic reform vision and bureaucratic paradigm have played out in compliance and service organizations are market-based incentives in environmental regulation,[6] promoting voluntary compliance in tax administration, community policing,[7] social service integration,[8] the one-day or one-trial jury system,[9] school-based management,[10] and school choice.[11]

Is there a single core idea—perhaps reducible to a sound bite—behind this ferment in thinking and practice? Some readers will respond that the core idea is service. Or customer focus. Or quality. Or incentives. Or creating value. Or empowerment. But the major concepts of emerging practice are not organized hierarchically, with one master idea at the top. As an indication, the concept of incentives does not subsume the equally useful idea of empowerment, which can be defined as a state of affairs in which individuals and groups feel psychologically responsible for the outcomes of their work. Since emerging argumentation and practice are structured by a paradigm rather than by any single core idea, those who want to make the most of the new conceptual resources should understand how various components of the system are related to one another.[12]

To understand the structure and workings of the newer paradigm well enough to improve public management requires attention and thoughtfulness but not the honed skills of an analytic philosopher or social linguist. The new paradigm, we suggest, can readily be understood by working with the metaphor of an extended family of ideas. The image of an extended family is helpful because it indicates that each idea is somehow related to every other, and it implies that some concentration is required to identify just how. The same metaphor can be pushed much further.[13] Think of the new paradigm, as well as the bureaucratic one, as a generation within an extended family. Although the members of each generation may not enjoy equal standing, their relationships—like those between concepts in either paradigm—are not hierarchical. All the cousins may be compatible in many situations, but their personalities—much like the entailments of the concepts of incentives and empowerment—are likely to differ markedly. Furthermore, just as siblings and cousins seek to prove that they are individually and collectively different from their parents' generation, self-definitions of the new paradigm emphasize divergences from the bureaucratic paradigm. Generational differences in extended families and paradigms also reflect changes in the social, economic, and political environments in which they have lived. To pursue the metaphor one more step, just as the siblings and cousins are influenced more by the preceding generation than they care to see or admit, concepts in the new paradigm are deeply conditioned by their lineal relationships to concepts in the bureaucratic predecessor.

The most appropriate term for the new generation of the extended family of ideas about how to make government operations productive and accountable is the *post-bureaucratic paradigm*. This term implies that the post-bureaucratic paradigm is as multifaceted as its predecessor. An unrelated name would hide the fact that as a historical matter, the younger generation of ideas has evolved from the bureaucratic paradigm.

Table 10-1 depicts this evolution. This framework guides the effort to identify the post-bureaucratic paradigm and to place it in historical perspective.

SHIFTING PARADIGMS

From the Public Interest to Results Citizens Value

The purpose of the bureaucratic reforms was to enable government to serve the public interest.[14] Government would serve the public interest, reformers argued, if it were honest and efficient. By honest, they meant a government

Table 10-1
Comparing the Paradigms

Bureaucratic Paradigm	Post-Bureaucratic Paradigm
Public interest	Results citizens value
Efficiency	Quality and value
Administration	Production
Control	Winning adherence to norms
Specify functions, authority, and structure	Identify mission, services, customers, and outcomes
Justify costs	Deliver value
Enforce responsibility	Build accountability
	Strengthen working relationships
Follow rules and procedures	Understand and apply norms
	Identify and solve problems
	Continuously improve processes
Operate administrative systems	Separate service from control
	Build support for norms
	Expand customer choice
	Encourage collective action
	Provide incentives
	Measure and analyze results
	Enrich feedback

cleansed of particularism, featherbedding, and outright stealing of public funds. By efficient, they meant a government that improved urban infrastructure, provided education, and promoted public health.[15]

In time, the reformers' strategy for serving the public interest came to define the public interest. A central element of that strategy was to recruit, develop, and retain experts in such fields as accounting, engineering, and social work. This strategy was designed not only to achieve results, but also to use expertise as a way to legitimate the actions of unelected officials in an administrative state. As an unintended but unsurprising consequence, these officials came to presume that the public interest was served whenever they applied their various bodies of knowledge and professional standards to questions within their respective domains of authority.

In the age of bureaucratic reform, when the effective demand for combating disease, building civil works, and accounting for public funds had just become significant, the presumption that decisions made in accord with professional standards were congruent with citizens' collective needs and requirements was reasonably defensible. This presumption is no longer reasonable to make. Government often fails to produce desired results from the standpoint of citizens when each professional community within government is certain that its standards define the public interest.

To stimulate more inquiry and better deliberation about how the work of government actually bears on citizens' volitions, the post-bureaucratic paradigm suggests that the specific rhetorical phrase "the public interest" should be confined to books on the history of American politics and administration. A desirable substitute expression is "results citizens value." Compared with its predecessor, the newer expression can be used to motivate more inquiry, clearer argumentation, and more productive deliberation about what results citizens collectively value. This rhetorical construction also conjures up the network of ideas about customer-focused organizations, emphasizes results over inputs and process, and implies that what citizens value cannot be presumed by professional communities in government.[16]

From Efficiency to Quality and Value

Leaders of the scientific management movement in the early twentieth century crafted and popularized a commonsense theory about the causes, nature, and significance of efficiency.[17] This commonsense theory rang true because it explained the industrial progress that characterized the age and because information about the workings of modern factories was widely known. It is a small step to infer that reformers used their knowledge of efficient industrial administration to inform their conception of efficient public administration.[18]

What did reformers know about factory administration? They knew that an efficient factory system succeeded in producing ever-increasing quantities of goods while reducing the cost of production.[19] They also knew recipes for achieving such success. In factories, managers controlled production in great detail through hierarchical supervisory structures. They knew that production and administrative systems were designed and operated by experts, who staffed offices responsible for personnel, accounting, inspection, power and works, engineering, product design, methods, production efficiency, and orders.[20] Bureaucratic reformers also knew that factory managers and experts applied their authority and expertise to industrial administration without partisan political interference.

Thus, industry was not just a source of rhetoric about efficient government; reformers' understanding of the main ingredients of efficient government—reorganization, accounting systems, expertise, and cost control—was rooted in their knowledge about industry.[21] Reformers elaborated some ingredients into specific processes and techniques, such as careful delineation of roles and responsibilities, centralized scrutiny of budget estimates, centralized purchasing, work programming, reporting systems, and methods analysis. However, one key concept—the product—did not make the journey from industry to government.[22]

Since it excluded the concept of product, reformers' influential conception of efficient government was trouble waiting to happen. It encouraged the notorious bureaucratic focus on inputs to flourish and it permitted specialized functions to become worlds unto themselves. More specifically, an increase in efficiency could be claimed in government whenever spending on inputs was reduced, whereas it was much easier to argue in an industrial setting that cost reduction improved efficiency only when it led to a reduction in the cost per unit of output. Industrial managers may not have had an easy time keeping every specialized member of the organization focused on the product, but in this concept—embodied in the goods moving through the production stream and out the door—they at least had a way to think precisely and meaningfully about how integration of differentiated functions could achieve efficiency. For reasons discussed above, the concept of the public interest did not possess the product concept's powers of integration; indeed, the strategy of sharply delineating roles and responsibilities and exalting specialized expertise cut in the other direction.[23] The bottom line . . . is that the pursuit of efficiency without adequate tendencies toward functional integration was a sham.[24]

Efficiency should be dropped from the lexicon of public administration, as it has from sophisticated practical theories of manufacturing and service enterprise management.[25] Public officials, like their counterparts in nongovernmental organizations, instead should make use of such interrelated concepts as product or service, quality, and value when deliberating about the nature and worth of government activities. The claim is that deliberation in these terms is as useful in the public sector as elsewhere.[26]

The post-bureaucratic paradigm does not try to settle most of the controversies about the general definitions of the concepts of product or service, quality, and value.[27] Legislating the precise definition of such rhetorical and analytical categories is probably futile; in any event, what is important for our purposes here is how well people in practice make use of such concepts in formulating and deliberating over made-to-measure or ad hoc arguments about how the performance of particular organizations should be evaluated and improved.[28]

To make the most of such deliberation efforts, some minimal agreement on terms is necessary. First, the appropriate perspective from which these concepts should be defined is that of the customer. By this rule, the recurring definition of quality as conformance to customer requirements is acceptable. Second, net value should be distinguished from value by taking costs into account. By this rule, the claim that reducing expenditures is desirable needs to be scrutinized in terms of the effect on the cost *and* value of products and services. Third, the nonpecuniary costs borne by customers when coproducing services or complying with norms should be taken into account. By this rule, costs measured by conventional accounting systems should be adjusted in service or compliance contexts.

From Administration to Production

The bureaucratic reformers had a theory of how individual public servants contributed to efficient administration. The theory claimed that the purpose of administration was to solve public problems by implementing laws efficiently. Agencies performed their functions by subdividing responsibilities and assigning them to positions. Public servants, assigned to positions on the basis of merit, performed their responsibilities competently by applying their expertise.[29] This theory promised order and rationality in that new domain of public affairs denominated as administration[30] and nicely combined a political argument about administrative legitimacy with an organizational argument about efficiency. The theory also provided a reason to believe that the work of public servants served the public interest.

To some degree, this theory of work in the administrative branch of government lives on. Ask public servants to describe their work and many will relate facts about their organization's functions and their own responsibilities. In order to communicate what the incumbent of a position does, some agencies compose titles mimicking the chain of command. For example, one senior manager in the Veterans Administration carried the title of Assistant Associate Deputy Chief Medical Director.

This strategy of defining work is failing to satisfy public servants.[31] Younger members of the workforce are less willing to accept close supervision.[32] It is a reasonable inference that specifying organizational positions is an unsatisfactory way to characterize their identity and purpose at work. Another problem with the standard account is that citizens are skeptical about the value of work public servants do—and public servants know it.[33] The bureaucratic paradigm offers late-twentieth-century public servants few tools for explaining to themselves and others why their work counts.

The accumulating evidence that production is a powerful alternative to the idea of administration comes from the total quality management (TQM) movement. TQM provides employees with methods—such as process flow analysis—for identifying and improving production processes.[34] Most government employees whose experience with TQM concepts and methods has been positive are deeply committed to the idea of process analysis and control.[35]

Why is production a powerful idea? One reason is that operating-level employees are typically involved in decision making, another is that formalized methods of reasoning are considered—often for the first time—in deliberations about how the production process should be organized. Both employee involvement and objective analysis mitigate the sense of powerlessness among employees in organizational hierarchies.[36] Furthermore, by using methods of process analysis, employees can develop a shared visual representation of the organization without making any reference to its hierarchical structure or boundaries. What is more important is that through process analysis, individual employees can visualize and describe for others how their work leads to the delivery of a valuable service or product. And coworkers develop an understanding of—and appreciation for—the work each does.[37]

To guard against mistaken analogies between production in government and manufacturing, the post-bureaucratic paradigm suggests that the concept of production be rendered as service delivery.[38] This terminology reminds public servants of the complex and intimate relationship between process and product in service delivery: whereas the production of goods is a separate process from distribution and consumption, many services are produced, delivered, and consumed in the same process, often with customers participating as coproducers.[39]

From Control to Winning Adherence to Norms

Within the bureaucratic reformers' vision of government, control was the lifeblood of efficient administration. Control was considered to be so vital that the intention to strengthen it served as an effective major premise in arguments supporting a wide array of practices that deepened and extended the bureaucratic reforms. These practices included accounting systems, budgetary freezes, reorganizations, reporting requirements, and countless measures to reduce the exercise of discretion by most public servants.

Why did such a cold, mechanical idea become revered by advocates of efficient administration? The answer lies in the fact that control was an important concept in each of the several lines of thought that became interwoven in the bureaucratic reform vision.[40] Control was essential to realize the aim of a unified executive branch. Control needed to be exercised to purge administrative decisions of particularistic influences. Control was the basis for the efficient operation of large-scale organizations.[41] And control assured the public that someone, namely the chief executive, was in charge of administration.

Influenced by ideas of rational-legal bureaucracy and industrial practice, the formulators of the bureaucratic paradigm pursued the aims of order, rationality, impersonal administration, efficiency, and political accountability by instituting centrally controlled systems of rules. The focus on rules, commitment to centralization, and emphasis on enforcement spawned worrisome consequences, which have tended to make bureaucracy a pejorative rather than a descriptive term.

Rules The bureaucratic paradigm encouraged control activities to develop ever-denser networks of rules in response to changing circumstances or new problems.[42] When rule systems became extremely complex, staff operations of substantial size—located in both staff and line agencies—were needed to understand, administer, and update them.

Centralization The bureaucratic paradigm urged overseers to centralize responsibility and authority for making administrative decisions in the hands of staff agencies. Centralized staff operations generally lacked the capacity to process incoming requests quickly, either because their power in the budget process was slight or because they were committed to the idea of saving taxpayers money. As a further consequence, decisions made centrally did not take into account the complexity and variability of the situations confronted by line agencies.

Enforcement Staff agencies focused on enforcement were typically blind to opportunities to correct problems at their source.[43] For instance, agencies were often unable to comply with norms because their employees did not know how to apply them to specific situations. Many such compliance problems could have been solved by providing education and specific advice about how to improve administrative or production processes; however, compliance organizations stressing enforcement tended to underinvest in problem solving. Furthermore, an emphasis on enforcement unnecessarily set up adversarial relationships between control activities and compliers. This kind of relationship discouraged efforts to comply voluntarily with norms.[44]

In our view, after more than a half-century of use, the concept of control is so bound up with the obsolete focus on rules, centralization, and enforcement that continued use of the term is an obstacle to innovative thinking about how to achieve results citizens value. Alternative terms currently in use, such as *delegation, decentralization, streamlining, incentive-based regulation,* and *voluntary compliance* are not wholly adequate as substitutes. Whatever term comes to structure post-bureaucratic thinking, the concept should serve to (1) illuminate means other than rules, such as principles, to frame and communicate the norms to which agencies should adhere; (2) recognize the complexity and ambiguity of the choice situations faced by compliers; and (3) underscore the role that rewards and positive working relationships can play in motivating compliers to make good decisions. The term *winning adherence to norms* is designed to fulfill this function. This concept indicates several lines of post-bureaucratic thinking about organizational strategies of compliance activities—one of which deserves to be highlighted here.

Since achieving adherence to norms requires people to make choices among alternatives under conditions of complexity and ambiguity, compliance strategies should empower compliers to apply norms to their particular circumstances. Compliers become empowered, by definition, when they feel personally responsible for adhering to the norms and are psychologically invested in the task of finding the best way to comply. Taking personal responsibility for results is as crucial to making good compliance decisions as to delivering quality goods and services.

As analysts have discovered in studying the sources of productivity and quality in organizations, taking personal responsibility is substantially influenced by the work setting. In particular, researchers argue that employees are most likely to take personal responsibility at work when they receive clear direction about purposes and desired outcomes, education, coaching, material resources, feedback, and recognition.[45] These findings suggest that taking personal responsibility for adhering to norms is likely to be enhanced when compliers understand the purpose of the norms, obtain education and coaching about how to apply the norms to the situations they face, receive timely and useful information about the extent to which compliance is being achieved, and are recognized for their accomplishments.

The willingness to take personal responsibility for complying with norms also depends on several other factors, including the extent to which the community of compliers supports the norms; whether other members of the community are assuming their obligations; whether compliance organizations seek to streamline the compliance process; and whether the capacity to enforce the norms upon those who fail to live by them is apparent.[46] The post-bureaucratic paradigm recognizes that some people may not respond adequately to efforts to win their compliance. For this reason, enforcement remains an indispensable function even when the focus is on winning adherence to norms.[47] These factors are increasingly recognized by tax administrations and other agencies that rely for their success principally on the willingness and ability of people and organizations to bring themselves into compliance with norms.[48]

Beyond Functions, Authority, and Structure

The bureaucratic paradigm defined organizations in terms of their assigned functions, delegated authority, and formal structure. Functions were abstract categories of work to be performed within the larger organizational machinery of government. Authority was the right to make decisions and demand obedience from subordinates on matters related to the grant of authority. Formal structure referred to the system of superior-subordinate relationships, which matched delegated authority with subdivided functions ultimately to the level of individual positions.

The critiques of this outlook are legendary. The focus on functions made organizations seem like technical instruments rather than institutions whose members are committed to achieving purposes.[49] The focus on authority concealed the power of other methods of social calculation and control, including persuasion and exchange.[50] The focus on formal structure put the cart of organizational means before the horse of organizational purpose and strategy.[51]

From a post-bureaucratic perspective, the central challenge of organizations is to channel human energies into thinking about and doing socially useful work. Public servants need better categories than functions, authority, and structure to meet this challenge. The concepts of mission, services, customers, and outcomes are valuable because they help public servants articulate their purposes and deliberate about how to adapt work to achieve them.[52] Missions are claims about the distinctive contribution an organization makes to the public good.[53] Services are the organization's products.[54] Customers are individuals or collective bodies—whether internal or external to the organization—to whom employees are accountable as parties to customer relationships.[55] Outcomes are precisely defined states of affairs that the organization intends to bring about through its activities.[56]

From Enforcing Responsibility to Building Accountability

According to the bureaucratic paradigm, a key role of administrators was to use their authority to enforce responsibility upon their subordinates.[57] As a mandate for managing people in organizations, this formalistic, hierarchical, and remedial conception of accountability left much to be desired. Formalism neglected the roles that emotions, commitments, and peer group norms play in shaping intrinsic motivation and behavior. The focus on hierarchy steered attention away from managing the network of interdependencies between subordinates and employees reporting to different superiors. And the notion of enforcing responsibility gave accountability a retrospective and defect-finding cast.

From a post-bureaucratic perspective, the most effective way to hold employees accountable is to make them feel accountable.[58] This route to accountability is attractive, in part, because employees want to be accountable. They want to be accountable because it is the only way for them, as for us all, to be important. According to a noted contemporary philosopher:

> Importance has two aspects. The first involves having external impact or effect, being the causal source of external effects, a place from which effects flow so that other people or things are affected by your actions. The second aspect of importance involves having to be taken account of, counting. If the first aspect of importance involves being a causal source from which effects flow, the second involves being a place toward which responses flow, responses to your actions, traits, or presence. In some way they pay attention to you and take you into account. Simply being paid attention to is something we want.[59]

Psychologists specializing in the study of work argue that employees feel accountable when they believe intended work outcomes are consequential for other people, receive information about outcomes, and can attribute outcomes to their own efforts, initiatives, and decisions.[60] Informed by this kind of argument, the post-bureaucratic paradigm values efforts by public managers and their overseers to bring about states of affairs in which public servants feel accountable for achieving desired results.

As a way to overcome the hierarchical and remedial thrust of accountability in the bureaucratic paradigm, attention should focus on the spectrum of working relationships, including the customer relationship, through which public servants create results citizens value. (Table 10-2 shows a classification scheme of working relationships.) From a post-bureaucratic perspective, accountability between the parties engaged in such working relationships should be a two-way street. For example, providers should be accountable to customers for meeting their needs for quality and value, while customers should be accountable to providers for clarifying their own needs and for giving feedback. More generally, in thinking and deliberating about accountability to customers and others, public managers should call to mind all the ingredients of well-functioning relationships: a consistent understanding of the purpose and character of the relationship; a detailed understanding of what behaviors and results the parties believe would be satisfactory; the provision of feedback about how well the parties are performing and how they could make improvements; responsiveness to feedback; and reconsideration of the working relationship in light of changing circumstances and cumulative experience.

From Justifying Costs to Delivering Value

Budgeting, according to the bureaucratic paradigm, was a process of arriving at annual spending plans. As part of the budgeting process, administrators were charged with the task of developing estimates of their organization's needs.[61] In practice, administrators assumed the task of developing convincing arguments that their needs in the upcoming budget year were greater than in the current one. The major categories of acceptable evidence for arguments about needs included current spending, expected increases in the cost of doing business, and the estimated cost of expanding the organization's level of activity. Upon receiving estimates of needs, central budget offices built arguments for the claim that the agency's costs were less than the estimate done as part of an effort to judge whose claims for resources were most justified.[62]

The bureaucratic paradigm of budgeting was congruent with its many other aspects. For example, the rhetoric of need was consistent with reformers' idea that government was supposed to satisfy citizens' wants without wasting taxpayers' dollars. It was also consistent with the belief that the responsibility for making government efficient should be vested primarily in the hands of overseers and their budget staffs. And the task of making government efficient meant scrutinizing costs.

Some advocates of the post-bureaucratic paradigm raise provocative questions about this conception.[63] They speculate that citizens are much more interested in the quality and value of public services than they are in costs; hence, it is mistaken for overseers to scrutinize costs during budget deliberations. They envision a world in which budget deliberations enable overseers to make informed purchases of services from agencies on behalf of the public. They further contend that improving the quality and value of public services can be achieved on a routine basis if agencies are expected to track changes in customer requirements and to improve productivity through better manage-

Table 10-2
Working Relationships

CUSTOMER RELATIONSHIPS
Individual or organizational customers
- within the organization
- within government
- outside government

Collective customers
- within the organization
- within government
- outside government

PRODUCTION RELATIONSHIPS
Coproduction relationships with customers

Complier relationships
- within government
- between government and the public

Relationships with providers
- within government
- vendors

Team relationships
- between individuals
- between task groups
- between functions

Partner relationships
- within government
- between public and private sectors

OVERSIGHT RELATIONSHIPS
Relationships with executive branch leadership and their staffs
Relationships with legislative bodies, legislators, and staff
Relationships with courts

MEMBERSHIP RELATIONSHIPS
Employment relationships
- between employees and their organizational leaders
- between employees and their immediate superiors
- between employees and the employer

Communitywide relationships
- among agencies
- among public servants

Peer group relationships
- among executives
- among members of a professional specialty

ment of production processes; they point out that budget processes under the bureaucratic paradigm instead motivate public managers to spend their limited time justifying costs. From a post-bureaucratic perspective, it is urgent to work out the implications of these claims and speculations in theory and practice.

Beyond Rules and Procedures

The premise of countless arguments made from the bureaucratic paradigm is that the proposed course of action (or inaction) is consistent with existing rules and procedures. The prior discussions of the concepts of efficiency, administration, and control explain why such arguments were generally persuasive.

From a post-bureaucratic angle, arguments premised on existing rules and procedures should be greeted with a reasonable degree of skepticism. Arguments premised on rules should be challenged and the issue reframed in terms of achieving the best possible outcome, taking into account the intention behind the rules, the complexity and ambiguity of the situation, and the ability to secure support from those who would enforce the norms. In this way, problem solving rather than following bureaucratic routines can become the dominant metaphor for work. Similarly, arguments premised on current procedures should be countered by instigating deliberation about how process improvements could enhance service quality and value.

Beyond Operating Administrative Systems

Centralized staff agencies were institutional embodiments of the bureaucratic reform vision. By operating administrative systems, these organizations put into practice the concepts of efficiency, administration, and control. Their cultures and routines spawned many of the constraints and incentives facing line agencies, which from a post-bureaucratic vantage point now detract from government's ability to deliver results citizens value.

If the time has come to break through bureaucracy, centralized staff operations must be part of the process. In serving this purpose, centralized staff operations need to transform their organizational strategies. Just like line agencies, they can benefit from using the concepts of mission, services, customers, quality, value, production, winning adherence to norms, building accountability, and strengthening working relationships. More specifically, central staff operations should separate service from control, build support for norms, expand customer choice, encourage collective action, provide incentives, measure and analyze results, and enrich feedback in the context of all working relationships. What this extended family of concepts means in practice should constantly evolve through deliberation and incremental innovation. . . .

ROLE OF PUBLIC MANAGERS

The bureaucratic paradigm informed public administrators that their responsibilities included planning, organizing, directing, and coordinating. Planning meant looking beyond the day-to-day operations of each function in order to determine how the work of the organization as a whole should evolve. Organizing meant dividing work responsibilities and delegating to each position requisite authority over people and subject matter. Directing meant informing subordinates of their respective roles in implementing plans and ensuring that they carried out their roles in accordance with standards. Coordinating meant harmonizing efforts and relations among subordinates.[64] The deficiencies of this role conception have been amply and ably catalogued by management writers for more than forty years.

The post-bureaucratic paradigm values argumentation and deliberation about how the roles of public managers should be framed. Informed public managers today understand and appreciate such varied role concepts as exercising leadership, creating an uplifting mission and organizational culture, strategic planning, managing without direct authority, pathfinding, problem setting, identifying customers, groping along, reflecting-in-action, coaching, structuring incentives, championing products, instilling a commitment to quality, creating a climate for innovation, building teams, redesigning work, investing in people, negotiating mandates, and managing by walking around.[65] As a contribution to current deliberation, we suggest that breaking through bureaucracy is a useful supplement to this stock of ideas. This concept alerts public managers to the need to take seriously the profound influence of the bureaucratic paradigm on standard practices, modes of argumentation, and the way public servants derive meaning from their work.

Historically aware public managers, committed to breaking through bureaucracy, will help coworkers understand that the bureaucratic paradigm mistakenly tended to define organizational purpose as doing assigned work. They will argue that a crucial challenge facing all organizations is to imbue work effort with purpose while thwarting the tendency to presume that current practices deliver as much value as possible. They will build capacity within and around organizations to deliberate about the relationship between results citizens value and the work done.

Public managers guided by the idea of breaking through bureaucracy should employ not only a combination of historical knowledge and post-bureaucratic ideas as tools to diagnose unsatisfactory situations and to spot inadequacies in arguments rooted in the bureaucratic paradigm, but should also deal creatively with the fact that many public servants are emotionally invested in the bureaucratic paradigm. Public servants, in our experience, are generally willing to move on to a newer way of thinking and practicing public management if they are convinced that the efforts they expended in past years will not become depreciated by the move. An effective way to overcome resistance to change stemming from this source is to make an informed argument that the presuppositions of the bureaucratic paradigm as played out in the organization's particular field of action were reasonable during most of the twentieth century, but that times have changed.[66]

Notes

1. The concepts of program budgeting, program evaluation, and policy analysis broadened and improved the bureaucratic paradigm and provided some of the seeds for the post-bureaucratic paradigm, but they did not challenge the bureau-

cratic paradigm's conception of administration, production, organization, and accountability.

2. James Q. Wilson, *Bureaucracy: What Government Agencies Do and Why They Do It* (New York: Basic Books, 1989), 369–76.

3. David Osborne and Ted Gaebler, *Reinventing Government: How the Entrepreneurial Spirit Is Transforming the Public Sector* (Reading, Mass.: Addison-Wesley, 1992). The term was used in the 1991 inaugural address of Massachusetts Governor William Weld. See "What 'Entrepreneurial Government' Means to Governor Weld," *Boston Globe*, January 8, 1991, 17–18.

4. On the quality movement in government, see Christopher Farrell, "Even Uncle Sam Is Starting to See the Light," *Business Week*, Special 1991 Bonus Issue: "The Quality Imperative," October 25, 1991, 132–37. On the origins of quality management concepts and practices, see David A. Garvin, *Managing Quality: The Strategic and Competitive Edge* (New York: Free Press, 1988). TQM's influence in the defense department can be seen in, e.g., Tom Varian, "Beyond the TQM Mystique: Real-World Perspectives on Total Quality Management" (Arlington, Va.: American Defense Preparedness Association, 1990); Defense Communications Agency, "Vision 21/TQM: Venturing Forth into the 21st Century," 2d ed. (Washington, D.C., March 1989); Navy Personnel Research and Development Center, "A Total Quality Management Process Improvement Model" (San Diego, Calif., December 1988). Any scholarly literature on total quality management in government has yet to appear.

5. Donald B. Shykoff, "Unit Cost Resourcing Guidance" (Washington, D.C.: Department of Defense, n.p., October 1990), cited in Fred Thompson and L. R. Jones, "Management Control and the Pentagon," book manuscript, October 1991, 16.

6. Project 1988, "Round II: Incentives for Action: Designing Market-Based Environmental Strategies" (Washington, D.C., 1991); and Robert N. Stavins, "Clean Profits: Using Economic Incentives to Protect the Environment," *Policy Review* (Spring 1989): 58–63.

7. Malcolm K. Sparrow, Mark H. Moore, and David M. Kennedy, *Beyond 911: A New Era for Policing* (New York: Basic Books, 1990).

8. Beth A. Stroul and Robert M. Friedman, "A System of Care for Severely Emotionally Disturbed Children and Youth" (Washington, D.C.: Georgetown University Child Development Center, July 1986).

9. "Middlesex County Jury System," John F. Kennedy School of Government case C16-86-656.0.

10. Theodore R. Sizer, *Horace's Compromise: The Dilemma of the American High School* (Boston: Houghton Mifflin, 1984); and Paul T. Hill and Josephine Bonan, "Decentralization and Accountability in Public Education" (Santa Monica, Calif.: RAND, 1991).

11. John E. Chubb and Eric A. Hanushek, "Reforming Educational Reform," in *Setting National Priorities*, ed. Henry Aaron (Washington, D.C.: Brookings Institution, 1990), 213–47; and John E. Chubb and Terry M. Moe, *Politics, Markets, and America's Schools* (Washington, D.C.: Brookings Institution, 1990), 185–229. For a critical book review of Chubb and Moe by Richard F. Elmore, see *Journal of Policy Analysis and Management* (Fall 1991): 687–94.

12. A paradigm is an experientially grounded conceptual system. More specifically, a paradigm might be thought of as a system of awarenesses, mental schemes, commonsense theories, and general reasons for action. To see how such a system is structured, consider an important concept in the paradigm of modern society: production. The concept of production heightens awareness of certain kinds of work processes (such as factory work) and downplays others (such as domestic work). The concept entails a complex mental scheme, which includes such other concepts as workers, tasks, machines, specialization, skills, organization, supervision,

throughput, work-in-process inventory, bottlenecks, defects, inspection, rework, costs, and efficiency. This complex mental scheme structures commonsense theories about production. A historically important commonsense theory held that modern prosperity and convenience required efficiency; efficiency required reducing production costs; and costs could be reduced through task specialization, close supervision of workers, and rational organization. Out of this commonsense theory came a general reason for action in industrial society: efficiency.

13. On mappings from source to target domains, see George Lakoff and Mark Turner, *More than Cool Reason* (Chicago: University of Chicago Press, 1989), 57–65.

14. These reforms included introduction of civil service protections, the short ballot, reorganization, the executive budget process, and competitive purchasing.

15. The concept of the public interest has been ably scrutinized by political scientists over the years. See, for example, Charles E. Lindblom, "Bargaining: The Hidden Hand in Government (1955)," chap. 7 in *Democracy and Market System* (Oslo: Norwegian University Press, 1988), 139–70. Historian Richard Hofstadter points out that in general the public interest was what reformers—principally middle-class professionals and elites who had lost power to political machines—thought would make America a better society. See *The Age of Reform: From Bryan to F.D.R.* (New York: Vintage, 1955), 174–214.

16. Some may criticize the use of any concept such as the public interest. Arguments can be found in the literature on public deliberation and public management to support our premise that if the public interest rhetorical category is suppressed, it should be replaced by a functionally similar idea. See Steven Kelman, *Making Public Policy: A Hopeful View of American Government* (New York: Basic Books, 1987), 215. See also Robert B. Reich, ed., *The Power of Public Ideas* (Cambridge, Mass.: Harvard University Press, 1990); Dennis F. Thompson, "Representatives in the Welfare State," in *Democracy and the Welfare State*, ed. Amy Gutmann (Princeton, N.J.: Princeton University Press, 1988), 136–43; and Mark H. Moore, "Creating Value in the Public Sector," book manuscript in progress. Support for the premise that rhetoric contributes to deliberation can be found in such diverse works as Donald N. McCloskey, *The Rhetoric of Economics* (Madison: University of Wisconsin Press, 1985); Warren Bennis and Richard Nanus, *Leaders: Strategies for Taking Charge* (New York: Harper & Row, 1985); David Johnston, *The Rhetoric of* Leviathan (Princeton, N.J.: Princeton University Press, 1986); and Giandomenico Majone, *Evidence, Argument, and Persuasion in the Policy Process* (New Haven, Conn.: Yale University Press, 1989).

17. We simplify here by omitting discussion of the concept of economy. Economy was the watchword of those who wanted to reduce government expenditures and taxes; efficiency was highlighted by those who wanted to improve government performance. We also simplify the discussion of efficiency here by focusing on the scientific management movement and factory administration. For a more complete discussion of the concept of efficiency in early public administration, see Dwight Waldo, *The Administrative State*, 2d ed. (New York: Holmes and Meier, 1984).

18. By knowledge in this context we mean ordinary knowledge as discussed in Charles E. Lindblom and David K. Cohen, *Usable Knowledge: Social Science and Social Problem Solving* (New Haven, Conn.: Yale University Press, 1979), 12–14. On mappings from source to target domains, see Lakoff and Turner, *More Than Cool Reason*, 57–65.

19. Robert B. Reich, *The Next American Frontier* (New York: Times Books, 1983), 22–82.

20. Alfred D. Chandler, Jr., "Mass Production and the Beginnings of Scientific Management," in *The Coming of Managerial Capitalism: A Case Book in the History of American Economic Institutions*, ed. Alfred D. Chandler, Jr., and Richard S. Tedlow (Homewood, Ill.: Richard D. Irwin, 1985), 465.

21. "Systematic bookkeeping was revolutionizing control over industrial production, pointing out the direction not only of efficiency and greater profit but honesty as well." Barry Dean Karl, *Executive Reorganization and Reform in the New Deal* (Cambridge, Mass.: Harvard University Press, 1963), 35. In stressing the role of industry as a source domain of knowledge about efficient government, we do not claim that other sources of knowledge were irrelevant. Indeed, Karl points out that early reformers were influenced by city management in Germany and the British parliamentary system, although the influence of these models was mediated by knowledge of business and industry in the United States. See *Executive Reorganization and Reform*, 95–96. Karl also argues that the power of arguments about industrial practice was enhanced by moral outrage against corruption and waste. See *Executive Reorganization and Reform*, 141–43.

22. What explains this puzzle? One argument might be that the outputs of government are different from the outputs of factories. But that argument fails because the concept of product could have served as a structural metaphor—as it does today—in efforts to conceptualize the relation between organizational goals and organizational work. One might argue, against this view, that reformers did not know how to think metaphorically. But the concept of an efficient government entails the use of the structural metaphor "Government is industry." Whether reformers knew they were speaking metaphorically is largely irrelevant. We conjecture that the concept of product was left out because reformers were committed to rationalism and professionalism and shunned market processes and commercial values in the context of government. The influence of legal conceptions of organization was also felt.

23. See Herbert A. Simon, *Administrative Behavior*, 3d ed. (New York: Free Press, 1976), 134–45. Simon restates arguments for respecting lines of authority irrespective of the merits of the particular decision.

24. On the importance of integrating functions and adapting organizations to the environment, see Kenneth R. Andrews, *The Concept of Corporate Strategy*, rev. ed. (Homewood, Ill.: R. D. Irwin, 1980).

25. The word *efficiency* does not appear in the index of either Michael E. Porter, *Competitive Advantage: Creating and Sustaining Superior Performance* (New York: Free Press, 1985), or of James L. Heskett, W. Earl Sasser, Jr., and Christopher W. L. Hart, *Service Breakthroughs* (New York: Free Press, 1990).

26. The information provided in chapters 3–5 of [my] book [with the collaboration of Babak J. Armajani], *Breaking through Bureaucracy: A New Vision for Managing in Government* (Berkeley: University of California Press, 1992)] is evidence for this claim.

27. On rival definitions of the concept of product, see Derek Abell, *Defining the Business: The Starting Point of Strategic Planning* (Englewood Cliffs, N.J.: Prentice-Hall, 1980). For discussions of the concept of value creation, see Porter, *Competitive Advantage*, 33–61; and David A. Lax and James K. Sebenius, *The Manager as Negotiator* (New York: Free Press, 1986), 63–116. The concept of value creation in both works fits in the broad tradition of welfare consequentialism. See Amartya Sen and Bernard Williams, eds., *Utilitarianism and Beyond* (Cambridge, England: Cambridge University Press, 1982).

28. On the role of ad hoc arguments in practical reason and social science, see, respectively, Joseph Raz, *Practical Reason and Norms* (Princeton, N.J.: Princeton University Press, 1990), 28–35; and Charles E. Lindblom, *Inquiry and Change: The Troubled Attempt to Understand and Shape Society* (New Haven, Conn.: Yale University Press, 1990), 169–70.

29. On classical organization theory, see Gareth Morgan, *Images of Organization* (Newbury Park, Calif.: Sage, 1986), 19–38.

30. For a classic argument that administration is an identifiable domain of governmental activity, see Woodrow Wilson, "The Study of Administration," *Political Science Quarterly* (June 1887): 197–222.

31. National Commission on the Public Service, *Leadership for America: Rebuilding the Public Service* (Washington, D.C., 1989), 173–75.

32. Rosabeth Moss Kanter, *The Change Masters: Innovation and Entrepreneurship in the American Corporation* (New York: Simon & Schuster, 1983), 56–58.

33. National Commission on the Public Service, *Leadership for America: Rebuilding the Public Service*, 21–41.

34. For a discussion of process control, see Robert H. Hayes, Steven C. Wheelwright, and Kim B. Clark, *Dynamic Manufacturing: Creating the Learning Organization* (New York: Free Press, 1988), 185–341; and Heskett, Sasser, and Hart, *Service Breakthroughs*, 112–58.

35. This empirical claim cannot be substantiated on the basis of social scientific research. It rests on anecdotal evidence derived from extensive contact with public sector managers and from conducting field work for "Denise Fleury and the Minnesota Office of State Claims," John F. Kennedy School of Government case C15-87-744.0.

36. Marshall Bailey of the Defense Logistics Agency argues that process analysis is a way to combat the PHOG (Prophecy, Hearsay, Opinion, and Guesswork) that impairs employee commitment and organizational performance.

37. One interviewee for the Denise Fleury case reported that before engaging in process flow analysis, coworkers viewed one another as job categories; afterward, they viewed one another as people.

38. Some activities in government, such as minting currency and making weapons, are more like manufacturing than like service delivery. Most compliance activities are more similar to services than to manufacturing. *Winning compliance to norms* is an appropriate term for production in a compliance context.

39. The typical accounts of total quality management fail to make the vital distinction between industrial production and service delivery. For a discussion of this distinction, see James L. Heskett, *Managing in the Service Economy* (Boston: Harvard Business School Press, 1986). Indeed, the source domains for total quality management practices are industries and utilities. Viewed at close range, the failure to make the service/industry distinction is a significant handicap of TQM.

40. A background reason was the influence of machine metaphors on organizational thought. See Morgan, *Images of Organization*, 19–38.

41. See JoAnne Yates, *Control through Communication: The Rise of System in American Management* (Baltimore, Md.: Johns Hopkins University Press, 1989), 1–20. According to Yates, the notions of control and systems were developed into a management philosophy during the 1890s.

42. For a discussion of frequent mismatches between rules and operational realities, see James Q. Wilson, *Bureaucracy*, 333–345; and Steven Kelman, *Procurement and Public Management: The Fear of Discretion and the Quality of Government Performance* (Washington, D.C.: American Enterprise Institute, 1990) 88–90.

43. As mentioned above, the total quality management movement has not focused on compliance processes. If such a focus were to be developed, it might begin by pointing out the similarities between enforcement approaches to compliance and inspection approaches to quality assurance. In diagnosing problems with the enforcement approach, experience with inspection could serve as a useful source domain. Similarly, as a heuristic device to structure a better approach to compliance, TQM's preferred alternatives to inspection should be used as a source domain. From a post-bureaucratic perspective, TQM should not be the only such source domain. Other source domains include the liberal and civic republican strands of American political theory and recent experience with service management.

44. For a discussion of this consequence of an enforcement orientation in the context of social regulation, see Eugene Bardach and Robert A. Kagan, *Going by the Book:*

The Problem of Regulatory Unreasonableness (Philadelphia: Temple University Press, 1982), 93–119.

45. See J. Richard Hackman and Greg R. Oldham, *Work Redesign* (Reading, Mass.: Addison-Wesley, 1980).

46. See generally, Joseph Raz, "Introduction," *Authority*, ed. Joseph Raz (New York: New York University Press, 1990), 1–19.

47. See the discussion of good and bad apples in Bardach and Kagan, *Going by the Book*, 124.

48. See Jeffrey A. Roth and John T. Scholz, eds., *Taxpayer Compliance: Social Science Perspectives*, vol. 2 (Philadelphia: University of Pennsylvania Press, 1989); Malcolm K. Sparrow, "Informing Enforcement"(Cambridge, Mass.: n.p., December 1991); Mark H. Moore, "On the Office of Taxpayer and the Social Process of Taxpaying," *Income Tax Compliance*, ed. Philip Sawicki (Reston, Va.: American Bar Association, 1983), 275–92; Manuel Ballbé i Mallol, Catherine Moukheibir, Michael Barzelay, and Thomas D. Herman, "The Criminal Investigation and Prosecution of Tax Fraud in Advanced Societies" (Madrid: Ministry of Economy and Finance, Instituto de Estudios Fiscales, September 1991); and State of Minnesota, Department of Revenue, "Strategies for the '90s" (St. Paul, 1990).

49. For the classic statement of the difference between organizations as technical instruments and as committed polities, see Philip Selznick, *Leadership in Administration: A Sociological Interpretation* (New York: Harper & Row, 1957). For a recent argument along similar lines, see Albert O. Hirschman, *Getting Ahead Collectively: Grassroots Experiences in Latin America* (New York: Pergamon, 1984).

50. Robert A. Dahl and Charles E. Lindblom, *Politics, Economics, and Welfare* (New York: Harper Bros., 1953), and Charles E. Lindblom, *Politics and Markets* (New York: Basic Books, 1977).

51. Alfred D. Chandler, Jr., *Strategy and Structure* (Cambridge, Mass.: MIT Press, 1962).

52. Another valuable concept is strategy, especially as defined in Lax and Sebenius, *Manager as Negotiator*, 261–68.

53. This definition is influenced by Mark H. Moore, "What Sort of Ideas Become Public Ideas?" *The Power of Public Ideas*, ed. Robert B. Reich (Cambridge, Mass.: Harvard University Press, 1990), 55–83; and Ronald Jepperson and John W. Meyer, "The Public Order and the Construction of Formal Organizations," in *The New Institutionalism in Organizational Theory*, ed. Walter W. Powell and Paul J. DiMaggio (Chicago: University of Chicago Press, 1991), 183–203.

54. As mentioned above, services and products in the public sector are often defined metaphorically. The role of structural metaphors in public sector management thought and practice deserves substantial attention. For a beginning, see Michael Barzelay and Linda Kaboolian, "Structural Metaphors and Public Management Education," *Journal of Policy Analysis and Management* (Fall 1990): 599–610.

55. See the principles discussed in chapter 7 [of my book, *Breaking through Bureaucracy*].

56. The bureaucratic paradigm focused attention on functions and nonoperational goals rather than producing desired states of affairs. The term *outcome* has a different meaning in this context than in the academic public policy literature, where the concept of outcome generally refers to the ultimate intended consequences of a public policy intervention. As used here, an outcome can be proximate results of an organization's work. For example, desired outcomes of a plant management operation include clean buildings and satisfied customers.

57. Herbert A. Simon, Donald W. Smithburg, and Victor A. Thompson, *Public Administration* (New York: Knopf, 1950), 513.

58. The argument that accountability is a psychological state of affairs that can be influenced by the individual's environment is developed in Hackman and Oldham,

Work Redesign, 71–98. In a similar vein, other social psychologists conclude on the basis of experiments that accountability raises "concerns about social evaluation, so that an individual's interest in appearing thoughtful, logical, and industrious overcomes motivation to loaf." See Elizabeth Weldon and Gina Gargano, "Cognitive Loafing: The Effects of Accountability and Shared Responsibility on Cognitive Effort," *Personality and Social Psychology Bulletin* (1988): 160, cited in Robert E. Lane, *The Market Experience* (Cambridge, England: Cambridge University Press, 1991), 49.

59. Robert Nozick, *The Examined Life: Philosophical Meditations* (New York: Simon & Schuster, 1989), 174. Nozick also argues, in effect, that being accountable in this sense is necessary for a full, moral life. Drawing on Lockean political theory, Rogers M. Smith makes a similar argument. See *Liberalism and American Constitutional Law* (Cambridge, Mass.: Harvard University Press, 1985), 205–6.

60. Hackman and Oldham, *Work Redesign*, 77–81. For a recent summary of the literature on intrinsic and extrinsic motivations at work, see Lane, *Market Experience*, 339–71.

61. Simon, Smithburg, and Thompson, *Public Administration*, 508–9.

62. Allen Schick presents a nuanced statement of this aspect of the bureaucratic paradigm: "Spending agencies usually behave as claimants, but most have procedures to conserve the resources available to them. . . . Similarly, the central budget office has a lead role in conserving resources, but it occasionally serves as a claimant for uses that it favors. It is not uncommon for the budget office to argue that some programs should be given more funds than have been requested." See "An Inquiry into the Possibility of a Budgetary Theory," *New Directions in Budget Theory*, ed. Irene S. Rubin (Albany: State University of New York Press, 1988), 65.

63. See Peter Hutchinson, Babak Armajani, and John James, "Enterprise Management: Designing Public Services as if the Customer Really Mattered (Especially Now that Government Is Broke)" (Minneapolis: Center of the American Experiment, 1991); as well as the fiscal 1992–93 budget instructions for Minnesota state government, reproduced as appendix 3 [of my book, *Breaking through Bureaucracy*].

64. Many readers will recognize these responsibilities as a subset of the classic POSDCORB role frame. The definitions of planning, organizing, directing, and coordinating are informed by Luther Gulick, "Notes toward a Theory of Organization," in *Papers on the Science of Administration*, ed. L. Gulick and L. Urwick (New York: Institute of Public Administration, 1937) 3–45; Joseph L. Massie, "Management Theory," *Handbook of Organizations*, ed. James G. March (Chicago: Rand McNally, 1965), 387–401; and Simon, *Administrative Behavior*, 123–53.

65. Among the many authors who have formulated, elaborated, restated, and/or popularized such concepts are Mary Parker Follett, Peter Drucker, Herbert Simon, Philip Selznick, Warren Bennis, Donald Schön, J. Richard Hackman, Harold Leavitt, James Q. Wilson, Rosabeth Moss Kanter, James Sebenius, James Heskett, Robert Behn, Philip Crosby, Thomas Peters, and Robert H. Waterman, Jr. These conceptual themes continue to be extended in the public management literature by such writers as Jameson Doig, Steven Kelman, Mark Moore, Ronald Heifetz, Philip Heymann, and Robert Reich.

66. The change process in Minnesota, described in chapters 3–5 [of my book, *Breaking through Bureaucracy*] accelerated after such arguments—informed by the results of the research leading to [the] book—were made.

Acknowledgments (continued from p. iv)

"Accountability Battles in State Administration" by William T. Gormley, Jr. From *The State of the States*, Second Edition, Carl E. Van Horn, ed., pp. 171–191. Used by permission of CQ Press.

"Accountability in the Public Sector: Lessons from the Challenger Tragedy" by Barbara S. Romzek and Melvin J. Dubnick. Reprinted with permission from *Public Administration Review*, 1987 © the American Society for Public Administration (ASPA), 1120 G Street, N.W., Suite 700, Washington, D. C., 20005. All rights reserved.

"Public Administration and Ethics" by Dwight Waldo. Reprinted by permission of the publisher from *The Enterprise of Public Administration: A Summary View* by Dwight Waldo. Copyright © 1980 by Chandler & Sharp Publishers, Inc. All rights reserved.

"Organization Theory: The Pivotal Controversies" from *Organization Theory: A Public Perspective* by Harold F. Gortner, Julianne Mahler, and Jeanne Bell Nicholson. Copyright © 1987. Used by permission of Brooks/Cole Publishing Co.

"Reframing Organizational Leadership" by Lee G. Bolman and Terrence E. Deal. Used by permission of author.

"What Really is Public Maladministration?" by Gerald E. Caiden. Reprinted with permission from *Public Administration Review*, 1991 © by the American Society for Public Administration (ASPA), 1120 G Street, N.W., Suite 700, Washington, D. C. 20005. All rights reserved.

"The State of Merit in the Federal Government" by Patricia W. Ingraham and David H. Rosenbloom. From *Agenda for Excellence: Public Service in America*, ed. by Patricia Ingraham and Donald F. Kettl. Copyright © 1992. Used by permission of Chatham House Publishers.

"Public Sector Collective Bargaining in the 1990's" by Joel M. Douglas. Reprinted with permission from *Public Administration Review*, © by the American Society for Public Administration (ASPA), 1120 G Street, N.W., Suite 700, Washington, D. C. 20005. All rights reserved. Some material based on his chapter from *Public Personnel Management: Current Concerns, Future Challenges* edited by Carolyn Ban and Norma M. Riccucci. Copyright © 1991 by Longman Publishing Group.

"Managing Diversity: From Civil Rights to Valuing Differences" by Walter D. Broadnax. From *The Public Manager*, Winter 1991–1992. Used by permission.

"Sexual Harassment in the States" by Rita Mae Kelly and Phoebe Morgan Stambaugh. From *Women and Men of the States* edited by M. E. Guy. Reprinted by permission of M. E. Sharpe, Inc., Armonk, New York 10504.

"The Budget Process and Budget Policy: Resolving the Mismatch" by Dennis S. Ippolito. Reprinted with permission from *Public Administration Review*, 1993 © by the American Society for Public Administration (ASPA), 1120 G Street, N.W., Suite 700, Washington, D. C. 20005. All rights reserved.

"Budget Reform and Political Reform: Conclusions from Six Cities" by Irene S. Rubin. Reprinted with permission from *Public Administration Review*, 1992 © by the American Society for Public Administration (ASPA), 1120 G Street, N.W., Suite 700, Washington, D. C. 20005. All rights reserved.

"The Public's Capital" from *Growing Together: An Alternative Economic Strategy for the 1990's* by Alan S. Blinder. Copyright © 1991 by Alan S. Blinder. This book was first published by Whittle Books as part of The Larger Agenda Series. Reprinted by arrangement with Whittle Communications, L.P.

"Policy Analysis" from *Managing Public Policy* by Laurence E. Lynn, Jr., pp. 170–180 (Exclusive of Fig. 7-1 on p. 179). Copyright © 1987 by Laurence E. Lynn, Jr. Reprinted by permission of HarperCollins Publishers, Inc. Excerpt from "Joan Claybrook and NHTSA (C)," case

ABOUT THE AUTHORS

Students are often curious about the authors of the articles they are reading. For that reason, a brief note about each contributor to this volume is included here.

Graham T. Allison, Jr. is Douglas Dillon Professor of Government and former Dean, John F. Kennedy School of Government, at Harvard University, Cambridge, Massachusetts.

Norman R. Augustine is Chairman and Chief Executive Officer of the Martin Marietta Corporation; he previously served two tours as a governmental executive, including Undersecretary of the Army.

Robert W. Backoff teaches public administration in the School of Public Policy and Management, Ohio State University, Columbus, Ohio.

Michael Barzelay is Associate Professor of Public Policy at the John F. Kennedy School of Government, Harvard University.

Peter M. Blau is Robert Broughton Distinguished Research Professor of Sociology at the University of North Carolina, Chapel Hill.

Alan S. Blinder is a member of the President's Council of Economic Advisers; previously, he was Gordon S. Rentschler Memorial Professor of Economics at Princeton University and a regular columnist for *BusinessWeek* magazine.

Lee G. Bolman is Marion Bloch Professor of Leadership at the Bloch School of Business and Public Administration, University of Missouri, Kansas City, and is the coauthor (with Terrence E. Deal) of *Reframing Organizations: Artistry, Choice, and Leadership*.

Walter D. Broadnax is Deputy Secretary of the U.S. Department of Health and Human Services; previously he was President of the Center for Governmental Research, Inc., in Rochester, New York, and President of the New York State Civil Service Commission.

Jeffrey I. Brudney teaches public administration and political science at the University of Georgia, Athens, Georgia.

Gerald E. Caiden is a Professor in the School of Public Administration, University of Southern California, in Los Angeles.

Terrence E. Deal is Professor of Education at Peabody College of Vanderbilt University in Nashville, Tennessee.

A labor mediator and arbitrator, **Joel M. Douglas** is Professor of Public Administration at Bernard M. Baruch College, City University of New York.

Melvin J. Dubnick teaches public administration and political science at the Rutgers University campus in Newark, New Jersey.

A former City Manager of Visalia, California, and Vandalia, Ohio, **Ted Gaebler** is President of the Gaebler Group, a public sector management consulting firm in San Rafael, California.

William T. Gormley, Jr. is Professor of Political Science at the University of North Carolina, Chapel Hill.

Harold F. Gortner is a Professor and formerly Chairman, Department of Public and International Affairs, George Mason University, Fairfax, Virginia.

Sandra J. Hale is President of Enterprise Management, Int'l., a consulting consortium in Minneapolis, Minnesota; from 1983 until 1990, she was Commissioner of the Department of Administration, State of Minnesota.

F. Ted Hebert is Professor of Political Science and Director of the Center for Public Policy and Administration at the University of Utah.

Patricia W. Ingraham is Professor of Public Administration at the Maxwell School of Citizenship and Public Affairs, Syracuse University, Syracuse, New York.

Dennis S. Ippolito is Eugene McElvaney Professor of Political Science at Southern Methodist University in Dallas, Texas.

Rita Mae Kelly is Professor of Justice Studies, Political Science, and Women's Studies and Director of the School of Justice Studies at Arizona State University, Tempe, Arizona.

Frederick S. Lane is Professor of Public Administration and was Director of the Executive Master of Public Administration Program from 1984 to 1992 at Bernard M. Baruch College, City University of New York.

Michael Lipsky is a Program Officer in Governance and Public Policy at the Ford Foundation in New York City; for much of his career, he has been a Professor of Political Science at the Massachusetts Institute of Technology.

Laurence E. Lynn, Jr. is Professor of Public Policy Studies and of Social Service Administration, and formerly was Dean, School of Social Service Administration, at the University of Chicago; in the federal government, he has also served as Deputy Assistant Secretary of Defense, Assistant Secretary of Health, Education, and Welfare, and Assistant Secretary of the Interior.

Julianne Mahler is an Associate Professor in the Department of Public and International Affairs at Virginia's George Mason University.

A sociologist, **Marshall W. Meyer** teaches at the Wharton School of the University of Pennsylvania in Philadelphia.

Jeanne Bell Nicholson is a consultant in organizational and career development and Director of the Professional Development and Equity Resource Center, University of Maryland, College Park.

A Boston-based consultant to governments, **David Osborne** is the coauthor (with Ted Gaebler) of *Reinventing Government: How the Entrepreneurial Spirit Is Transforming the Public Sector.*

Robert B. Reich is Secretary of Labor in President Clinton's Cabinet; he formerly taught political economy, law, and management at Harvard's John F. Kennedy School of Government, and is the author of *The Work of Nations.*

An economist, **Alice M. Rivlin** is Deputy Director of the U.S. Office of Management and Budget; she previously served as the first Director of the Congressional Budget Office and as a Senior Fellow in the Economic Studies Program at the Brookings Institution, a "think tank" in Washington, D. C.

Barbara S. Romzek is Professor and Chairperson, Department of Public Administration, University of Kansas, Lawrence, Kansas.

David H. Rosenbloom is Distinguished Professor of Public Administration at American University in Washington, D. C.

Francis E. Rourke is Benjamin H. Griswold III Professor of Public Policy Studies at Johns Hopkins University in Baltimore, Maryland.

A specialist in state and local budgeting, **Irene S. Rubin** teaches public administration and political science at Northern Illinois University, DeKalb, Illinois.

E. S. (Steve) Savas is Professor and Chairperson, Department of Management, Bernard M. Baruch College, City University of New York; he was formerly Assistant Secretary for Policy Development and Research, U.S. Department of Housing and Urban Development.

A governmental management consultant, **Joseph Sensenbrenner** was Mayor of Madison, Wisconsin, from 1983 to 1989.

Steven Rathgeb Smith is Assistant Professor of Public Policy and Political Science at Duke University, Durham, North Carolina.

Phoebe Morgan Stambaugh is a doctoral student in the School of Justice Studies at Arizona State University, Tempe.

Dwight Waldo is Professor Emeritus of Public Administration and formerly the holder of the Schweitzer Chair in the Humanities at the Maxwell School of Citizenship and Public Affairs, Syracuse University.

Barton Wechsler teaches public administration at Florida State University, Tallahassee.

An economist, **Murray Weidenbaum** holds the Mallinckrodt Distinguished University Professorship and is Director of the Center for the Study of American Business at Washington University in St. Louis, Missouri; he was previously Chairman of President Reagan's Council of Economic Advisers.

James Q. Wilson is James Collins Professor of Management at the John E. Anderson Graduate School of Management, University of California, Los Angeles, and the author of *Bureaucracy: What Government Agencies Do and Why They Do It*.

Deil S. Wright is Alumni Distinguished Professor of Political Science and Public Administration at the University of North Carolina, Chapel Hill, and author of *Understanding Intergovernmental Relations*.